THE ROUTLEDGE INTERNATIONAL COMPANION TO EDUCATIONAL PSYCHOLOGY

The Routledge International Companion to Educational Psychology brings together expert practitioners, researchers, and teachers from five continents to produce a unique and global guide to the core topics in the field. Each chapter includes coverage of the key thinkers, topic areas, events, and ideas that have shaped the field, but also takes the reader beyond typical textbook material and into engagement with current issues, cutting-edge research, and future directions in the field of educational psychology from an international perspective.

With over 30 chapters, the volume is divided into four themed sections: 'An introduction to educational psychology', 'How children learn and develop', 'Issues concerning the assessment of children', and 'Identifying and meeting the needs of children with learning difficulties'. Covering the key issues and fundamental strands of educational psychology, *The Routledge International Companion to Educational Psychology* aims to provide the reader with knowledge of:

- educational psychology (history, child rights, and practice);
- factors that influence children's learning and development;
- issues to do with assessment (a key aspect of educational psychology);
- special educational needs (identification and how to meet these needs);
- the key thinkers, events, and ideas that have shaped the field;
- the core topics across educational psychology in an accessible manner;
- cutting-edge research including recent research evidence and theory;
- future directions in the field of educational psychology;
- educational psychology from an international perspective.

The book is conceived for both student and researcher use, and considers the implications for educational psychology practice in all sections. It will be highly beneficial for both students and lecturers on Education Studies and Psychology undergraduate courses, as well as combined undergraduate degrees.

Andrew J. Holliman is a researcher of children's learning and development, a chartered psychologist, and a senior lecturer in developmental psychology at the University of Coventry.

THE ROUTLEDGE INTERNATIONAL COMPANION TO EDUCATIONAL PSYCHOLOGY

Edited by Andrew J. Holliman

Routledge
Taylor & Francis Group

LONDON AND NEW YORK

First published 2014
by Routledge
2 Park Square, Milton Park, Abingdon, Oxon OX14 4RN

Simultaneously published in the USA and Canada
by Routledge
711 Third Avenue, New York, NY 10017

Routledge is an imprint of the Taylor & Francis Group, an informa business

British Library Cataloguing in Publication Data
A catalogue record for this book is available from the British Library

Library of Congress Cataloging in Publication Data
Andrew Holliman.
  The Routledge international companion to educational psychology/
  Andrew Holliman.
     pages cm
  1. Educational psychology.   2. Educational psychology—Cross-cultural
  studies.   3. Education—Aims and objectives.   I. Title.
  LB1051.H68 2013
  370.15—dc23   2013004362

ISBN: 978-0-415-67558-1 (hbk)
ISBN: 978-0-415-67560-4 (pbk)
ISBN: 978-0-203-80940-2 (ebk)

Typeset in Bembo
by Keystroke, Station Road, Codsall, Wolverhampton

This book is dedicated to my darling wife Victoria, and our adorable son Alexander; to my mother Dawn, and father John; and to my older brothers David and Steven – *thanks to all for making life so wonderful.*

CONTENTS

List of figures   *xi*
List of tables   *xii*
List of contributors   *xiii*
Acknowledgements   *xxi*
Introduction by Andrew J. Holliman   *xxii*

PART I
An introduction to educational psychology   **1**

1   A history of educational psychology   3
    Malcolm W. H. Hughes

2   The rights of the child   12
    Mary Kellett

3   Introduction to educational psychology practice   21
    Terri Passenger

4   A comparative overview of educational psychology across continents   31
    Christopher Boyle and Fraser Lauchlan

PART II
How children learn and develop   **41**

5   Theories of teaching and learning   43
    Janet I. Vousden, Clare Wood and Andrew J. Holliman

Contents

6 Effective teaching practices and classroom management: the role
   of ecological and inclusive understandings   53
   Ozlem Erten, Robert Savage and Maria Di Stasio

7 Educational dialogues   63
   Karen Littleton

8 Learning to read around the world   73
   Juan Zhang and Catherine McBride-Chang

9 Digital technology as enrichment of young children's
   literacy environment   83
   Maria T. de Jong and Marian J. A. J. Verhallen

10 The development of scientific reasoning   92
    Christine Howe

11 Motivation to learn   104
    Andrew J. Martin

12 Children's relationships and the family   117
    Charlie Lewis, Dorothy Miell and Fleur-Michelle Coiffait

13 Childhood stress and its impact on learning and academic
    performance   127
    Meena Hariharan, Sunyana Swain and Usha Chivukula

PART III
Issues concerning the assessment of children   **141**

14 Classroom assessments: informing teaching and
    supporting learning   143
    Spencer Salend

15 Diagnostic assessment: one of the effective ways of
    assessing learning   154
    Sunday Obi and Marty Sapp

16 Purposes, approaches and tensions in assessment
    policy and practice   162
    Kathy Hall

17 Language use and assessment   172
    Nenagh Kemp

18 Multicultural education: the mismeasured but important phenomenon   181
    Festus E. Obiakor

19 Intelligence and individual differences   191
    Constantine Ngara and Marion Porath

20 New frontiers in education neuroscience   202
    Joanna A. Christodoulou, Patricia K. Saxler and Stephanie N. Del Tufo

21 Labelling in special education: where do the benefits lie?   213
    Christopher Boyle

PART IV
Identifying and meeting the needs of children with learning difficulties   223

22 Education and disability: a space where we belong or is
    history repeating itself?   225
    Nancy Hansen

23 Educational psychology and the development of inclusive education   235
    Kieron Sheehy

24 Education of children with sensory needs: reducing barriers
    to learning for children with visual impairment   246
    Mike McLinden and Graeme Douglas

25 Speech and language disorders   256
    David Messer

26 The autism spectrum   265
    Alexandra Fortuna and Patricia Davis

27 Social, emotional and behavioural difficulties (SEBD):
    the need to look beyond the problem   275
    Paul Cooper

28 Attention deficit hyperactivity disorder: characteristics,
    identification and treatment   286
    Robert Reid and Brenton Prosser

29 Dyslexia   297
    Brian Byrne, Stefan Samuelsson and Richard K. Olson

30 Practical implications of research into dyspraxia   307
    John Everatt and Brigid C. McNeill

31 Dyscalculia: research and practice on identification and
    intervention across languages   317
    John Everatt, Gad Elbeheri and Peter Brooks

32 Meeting the needs of gifted learners   327
    Marion Porath

Index   *337*

FIGURES

10.1	Age differences in trajectories predicted when moving objects fall from moving carriers	95
10.2	Inhelder and Piaget's combination of chemicals task	98
10.3	Schematic representation of one piece of apparatus used to examine children's mastery of experimental control	99
11.1	Central theoretical perspectives and associated motivation constructs	108
11.2	Motivation and Engagement Wheel	109
13.1	The autonomic endocrine reaction to stress and its impact on learning and memory	128
13.2	Sources of stress	131
13.3	The triangle of stress	132
13.4	The levels of stress	133
13.5	The psychosocial process of stress perception	134
14.1	Sample mastery measurement graph	146
14.2	Sample caption statement	151
21.1	Well-meaning but flawed programmes in special education?	219
23.1	Educational psychologists' hypothetical placement preferences	238
27.1	Biopsychosocial interactions	279
31.1	Examples of tasks involving an appreciation of number/value	318
32.1	Reflection Activity 1: designing supportive educational contexts	331
32.2	Reflection Activity 2: cultural perspectives on intelligence and success	333
32.3	Reflection Activity 3: supporting students with dual exceptionality	334

TABLES

2.1   UNCRC articles linked to children's education   13

11.1 Brief look at your motivation (your highest score is a strength; your lowest score is an area where you can improve)   116

20.1 Types of brain-based material prevalent in educational products   209

20.2 Resources for information on brain-based educational products   209

30.1 Features experienced by children with DVD   312

CONTRIBUTORS

Christopher Boyle, PhD, is a Senior Lecturer in Psychology in the Faculty of Education at Monash University, Australia. His main research interests are in the area of teacher perceptions of inclusion and students' attributions for success and failure in learning. He is currently Editor of the *Australian Educational and Developmental Psychologist* and he has published widely in psychology and education. His latest edited book, *What Works in Inclusion*, was published in 2012 by Open University Press.

Peter Brooks, MSc, is an Educational Psychologist practising across much of Western Europe. His research and practice focus on effective learning, particularly related to reading, spelling and mathematics, and over much of the 1990s he was Principal Educational Psychologist of the Helen Arkell Dyslexia Centre. As well as publications in many applied-focused journals, he has presented at academic conferences and practitioner meetings around the world, and published assessments of adults' prose reading and spelling abilities.

Brian Byrne, PhD, is Emeritus Professor of Psychology at the University of New England, Australia, Guest Professor at Linköping University, Sweden, and a Chief Investigator with the Australian Research Council's Centre of Excellence for Cognition and its Disorders. His research has focused on early literacy development. In it he has employed small-scale experiments, field trials of instructional materials and behaviour–genetic studies of individual differences in early literacy. He received the Vice-Chancellor's Award for Research Excellence in 2000 and 2009.

Usha Chivukula, MA, holds a Masters' degree in Clinical Psychology. She is a Lecturer at St Francis College, Hyderabad and is pursuing her PhD in Health Psychology from the University of Hyderabad. Her PhD is in the area of intensive care unit trauma. She is also a consultant counsellor in St Francis College and has experience in school and corporate counselling. Her research interests are mainly in the area of holistic health and well-being.

Joanna A. Christodoulou, EdD, works at the intersection of education and neuroscience. She investigates behavioural and neural correlates of language and literacy in regard to development, difficulty, and intervention. She conducts research at the Gabrieli Lab in the Department of Brain and Cognitive Sciences at the Massachusetts Institute of Technology and is a member of the faculty at Harvard University and MGH Institute of Health Professions.

Fleur-Michelle Coiffait, DClinPsy, is a researcher at the University of Edinburgh and an applied psychologist in a Child and Adolescent Mental Health Service for children with intellectual disability and their families in NHS Lothian. Her doctoral research investigated cognitive factors that promote psychological well-being of parents with a child who has profound and multiple intellectual disabilities. Fleur-Michelle's research interests focus on clinical health psychology and family relationships in the context of children who have complex needs.

Paul Cooper, PhD, CPsychol, is Chair Professor of Special Education at the Hong Kong Institute of Education. He has published extensively on social, emotional and behavioural difficulties. He is also Life Long Honorary President of the Social Emotional and Behavioural Difficulties Association and founding co-chair of the European Network for Social-Emotional Competence.

Patricia Davis, MD, attended Harvard College (BA), University of Massachusetts Medical School (MD) and Sydney University (DPH). Dr Davis works as a medical provider at the Integrated Center for Child Development in Newton, Massachusetts where she addresses the complex medical, developmental, and psychopharmacologic needs of her clients with autism spectrum disorders. Prior to ICCD, Dr Davis worked for ten years at the Massachusetts General Hospital Lurie Center (formerly LADDERS) on a multidisciplinary team to address ASDs.

Maria T. de Jong, PhD, is Assistant Professor at Leiden University, The Netherlands. Her main research interest is emergent academic skills: math and in particular literacy development. She published experimental studies about the effects of electronic books on early literacy of kindergarten children. Currently she is involved in experimental studies testing the effect of electronic books in a group of beginning readers, thereby applying behavioural and psycho-physiological measures such as eye tracking.

Stephanie N. Del Tufo is a PhD candidate at the University of Connecticut & Haskins Laboratories, advised by Dr Ken Pugh. Her research focuses on the typical and atypical neuroanatomical and neurochemical developmental organization of reading, language, and executive function through behaviour and neuroimaging.

Maria Di Stasio is a PhD candidate under the supervision of Professor Robert Savage in the Human Development Program at McGill University, Montreal, Canada. Research interests include language and literacy, classroom processes, and children's academic and socio-emotional development.

Graeme Douglas, PhD, is Senior Research Fellow and co-director of the 'Visual Impairment Centre for Teaching and Research' (VICTAR), the Department of Disability, Inclusion and Special Needs (DISN) at the University of Birmingham. Graeme has carried out social and educational research in the area of visual impairment since 1993. His broad research interests are in relation to the identification and reduction of barriers to learning and participation for visually impaired people.

Gad Elbeheri, PhD, is Director of the Foundation Skills Programme at the Australian College of Kuwait and a director/consultant for the Centre for Child Evaluation and Teaching and the

United Nations Development Programme in Kuwait. A qualified school teacher and applied linguist, his research focuses on developmental learning disabilities and currently involves leading projects to develop tests of dyslexia and dyscalculia in Arabic. He publishes extensively in English and Arabic, and is a Board Member of the International Dyslexia Association.

Ozlem Erten, PhD candidate, is continuing her studies under the supervision of Professor Robert Savage in the Human Development Program of McGill University, Canada. Her research interests include effective teaching, inclusive education, and attitudes to disability.

John Everatt, PhD, is a Professor of Education in the College of Education, University of Canterbury, New Zealand. Before moving to New Zealand, he lectured in psychology at the Universities of Wales and Surrey, UK. He lectures primarily on postgraduate courses in special education and in literacy, and supervises PhD students in research related to learning difficulties, additional language learning and cross-language/orthography comparisons. This work has led to collaborative research projects in many countries around the world.

Alexandra Fortuna, MEd, is an Education Specialist at Children's Hospital Boston. She attended Vanderbilt University (BS) where she studied child development and Harvard Graduate School of Education where she received her Masters of Education. Alexandra has been working directly with individuals on the autism spectrum for 10 years in the school, hospital, and research settings.

Kathy Hall, PhD, is Professor of Education and Head of the School of Education at University College Cork. She has published widely on the themes of assessment, learning and literacy. She is currently PI for an Irish Research Council project on inclusive pedagogies and is completing a book, *Networks of the Mind: A Critical Neurocultural Perspective on Learning* (with Curtin and Rutherford) to be published by Routledge.

Nancy Hansen, PhD, is an Associate Professor and Director of the Interdisciplinary Master's Programme in Disability Studies at the University of Manitoba. She is a human geographer and her research interests in disability studies are varied, including education, literacy social policy, employment and healthcare access. Nancy is a former CIHR Post-Doctoral and DAAD Research Fellow, and Past President of the Canadian Disability Studies Association. She has written numerous book chapters and contributed to various international academic journals.

Meena Hariharan, PhD, is Professor and Director in the Centre for Health Psychology, University of Hyderabad. She has a PhD from the Centre for Advanced Studies in Psychology, Utkal University, Orissa, India. She is the author of three books and numerous papers. Her research focus is stress and coping, invulnerability and psychological aspects of chronic illness. She is on the Guest Faculty in a number of universities and research institutes in India, and has completed more than 25 research projects.

Andrew J. Holliman, PhD, is a Senior Lecturer in Developmental Psychology at Coventry University, UK. He is Director of the Masters Programmes in Psychology and Applied Psychology. His research focus is the development of children's reading and phonological awareness and the role of speech rhythm (or prosodic) sensitivity in this development. He also works in collaboration with the Institute of Education, University of London, on research relating to the Reading Recovery programme.

Christine Howe, PhD, is Professor of Education at the University of Cambridge, and a Fellow of Lucy Cavendish College. She is a psychologist whose main research interests are children's reasoning in science and mathematics, peer interaction and conceptual growth, and communication and social relations among children. She has published seven books and over 150 journal articles and book chapters. Christine has edited three academic journals and served on many editorial boards. She has been elected to the Academy of Social Sciences.

Malcolm W. H. Hughes, MPhil, is Associate Director of International Development at the University of the West of England (UWE), UK. After two decades as a school leader and teacher of physical education and mathematics, he moved to lead postgraduate initial teacher education at UWE and became Senior Research Fellow in Developmental Psychology. He has co-authored influential and widely read higher education core texts for Pearson Education, including *Psychology of Education*; *Child Development, Theory and Practice 0-11*; and *Adolescence and Emerging Adulthood*.

Mary Kellett, PhD, is Professor and Director of Childhood, Youth and Education at the Open University. She has over 35 years' experience in the domain of children and young people and is perhaps best known for her pioneering work to empower children as researchers as Founder Director of the Children's Research Centre. She sits on several national and international advisory panels and has published widely on a range of childhood and education issues.

Nenagh Kemp, PhD, is a Senior Lecturer in Psychology at the University of Tasmania, Australia. Her research interests include the development of spelling skills in children and adults, the use of written language in mobile technologies, and the idiosyncrasies of Australian English. She is an associate editor of the *Journal of Research in Reading* and of *Reading and Writing*, and serves on the editorial board of *Scientific Studies of Reading*.

Fraser Lauchlan, PhD, is currently working as a Visiting Professor at the Università di Cagliari, Italy, where he is researching the cognitive benefits of bilingualism in children who speak minority languages. He is a registered educational psychologist and works as a consultant for many local authorities in the UK (www.fraserlauchlan.com). He also holds a post as an Honorary Lecturer at the University of Strathclyde in Scotland, UK. He has published extensively in many areas of educational psychology.

Charlie Lewis, PhD, is Professor of Family and Developmental Psychology at Lancaster University. His main research interests are in parent–child relationships, especially the role of the father, and children's early socio-emotional and social–cognitive development, particularly how preschoolers come to make sense of social relationships. He has published 15 books and over 150 journal articles and book chapters. He has been elected a Fellow of the Royal Society of Arts.

Karen Littleton, PhD, is Professor of Psychology in Education at the Open University and Director of the Centre for Research in Education and Educational Technology. Her research focuses on the significance of dialogue for children's development, learning, and creativity.

Andrew J. Martin, PhD, is Professorial Research Fellow and Australian Research Council Future Fellow in the Faculty of Education and Social Work at the University of Sydney. Andrew specializes in motivation, engagement, achievement, and quantitative research methods. He is also Honorary Senior Research Fellow in the Department of Education, University of Oxford. He is Associate Editor of *British Journal of Educational Psychology* and serves on the Editorial Boards of *Journal of Educational Psychology*, *American Educational Research Journal*, and *Contemporary Educational Psychology*.

Catherine McBride-Chang, PhD, is a Professor in Developmental Psychology at The Chinese University of Hong Kong. She is particularly interested in reading development and impairment across languages and cultures. She is currently an associate of two journals and one encyclopaedia and is incoming president of the Society for the Scientific Studies of Reading.

Mike McLinden, PhD, is Professor and co-director of the Visual Impairment Centre for Teaching and Research (VICTAR) at the University of Birmingham. Mike has researched and taught in the area of visual impairment for over 20 years and is lead tutor for the visual impairment programmes at the university. His research interests have been primarily concerned with the identification and reduction of barriers to learning and participation for children with sensory needs, including those with complex needs.

Brigid C. McNeill, PhD, is a Senior Lecturer in Literacy Education at the University of Canterbury, New Zealand. A former speech and language therapist, she has written many papers in national and international journals. Her research primarily focuses on understanding the nature and educational consequences of developmental speech disorders (particularly developmental verbal dyspraxia).

David Messer, PhD, is a Professor of Childhood Development and Learning at the Open University. He has been involved in the writing of the Open University postgraduate module about Understanding Children's Development and Learning. His research interests include the reasons for language and literacy impairments, digital literacy in young children, and cognitive processes such as executive functioning and inner speech. He has published a number of textbooks and is a member of the editorial board of First Language.

Dorothy Miell, PhD, is Professor of Social Psychology and Vice Principal at the University of Edinburgh. Her research interests are in how relationships and communication are involved in the process of collaborative working in creative areas, whether between children in schools or professional performers. She is the co-editor of *Musical Identities* (2002), *Musical Communication* (2005) and *Musical Imaginations* (2012, all with Open University Press). She is a Fellow of the British Psychological Society and Chair of its Psychology Education Board.

Constantine Ngara, PhD, is an Assistant Professor in Educational Psychology at the University of Bahrain Teachers College. Constantine has taught from elementary school through high school to community college and university levels. His research focuses on intelligence and giftedness. In his main research, he has proposed the Dynamic Interactive Process Model (DIPM) of talent development. Constantine has published several articles, book chapters and a book on gifted education.

Sunday Obi, EdD, is a Professor of Education at Kentucky State University. He is former Director of the Masters' degree in Special Education; he played a role in planning, designing, and implementing the programme. He is a teacher, researcher and scholar. His specific areas of interest include self-concept, inclusion, assessment, classroom management, effective instructional practices. Sunday serves on the Board of Directors of Bluegrass Regional Mental Health Mental Retardation Board, Inc., and on the editorial board of many scholarly publications.

Festus E. Obiakor, PhD, is Chair and Professor, Department of Leadership and Special Education, The City College of New York, CUNY. His research interests include multicultural psychology and special education. He is the author of more than 150 publications, including books, chapters, and articles, and is a frequently invited speaker to many organizations, institutions, and conferences. He is the co-founding and co-executive editor of *Multicultural Learning and Teaching*, a refereed international journal.

Richard K. Olson, PhD, is Professor of Psychology and Neuroscience and Director of the Colorado Learning Disabilities Research Center at the University of Colorado, Boulder. His research focuses on the genetic and environmental aetiology of deficits and individual differences in reading and related skills. He received the Distinguished Scientific Contribution Award from the Society for the Scientific Study of Reading in 2006, and the Norman Geschwind Memorial Lecture award from the International Dyslexia Association in 2005.

Terri Passenger, PhD, is a Senior Partner in a practice of educational psychologists working in London, Oxford and Cheltenham. A chartered educational psychologist and former senior lecturer in psychology, she also holds a research fellowship at the University of Gloucestershire, UK. She has published widely in the areas of educational psychology and special educational needs and co-authored the British Medical Association's 'Family Doctor' publication on *Understanding ADHD, Autism, Dyslexia and Dyspraxia*.

Marion Porath, PhD, is a Professor of Educational Psychology and Special Education at The University of British Columbia, with a concentration on the development and education of highly able learners. She is the author of numerous articles, chapters, and books and has received grants to study artistic, narrative, and social giftedness; gifted learners' understanding of their own learning; the co-occurrence of operatic giftedness and learning disabilities; and adolescent and adult development of highly gifted learners.

Brenton Prosser, PhD, is a Senior Research Fellow in the Centre for Research and Action in Public Health at the University of Canberra. A former schoolteacher and teacher–educator, his expertise includes middle schooling pedagogy, student inclusion and behaviour management. He has published two books and numerous articles on psychosocial and sociological perspectives on ADHD. Currently, he runs a joint Australian National University/University of Canberra evaluation of Australian aged care policy.

Robert Reid, PhD, is a Professor in the Department of Special Education and Communication Disorders, University of Nebraska-Lincoln. He has done extensive work nationally and internationally on children with attention deficit hyperactivity disorders and cognitive strategy instruction. He also co-developed the *ADHD-IV Rating Scale* (Guilford) that is now used in seven countries. He currently serves on the editorial boards of five journals and actively reviews for a number of others.

Spencer Salend, EdD, is a Professor in the Department of Educational Studies at the State University of New York at New Paltz. The author of *Creating Inclusive Classrooms: Effective and Reflective Practices* (7th edition), and *Classroom Testing and Assessment for ALL Students: Beyond Standardization*, he has published and presented on such topics as educational assessment and effective inclusive education practices.

Stefan Samuelsson, PhD, is Professor of Education and Head of the Department of Behavioural Sciences and Learning at Linköping University, Sweden. His research has focused on literacy development and difficulties, with additional interests in preterm infants and their subsequent development, and many publications in international journals on these topics.

Marty Sapp, EdD, is a Professor of Educational Psychology at the University of Wisconsin-Milwaukee. He is a licenced psychologist and Fellow of the American Psychological Association. He is Past-President of Division 30 (The Society of Psychological Hypnosis) of the American Psychological Association, and his substantive areas of interests are cognitive-behavioural therapies, hypnosis, anxiety disorders, research methods and design, measurement, statistics, and counselling theories and issues.

Robert Savage, PhD, is an Associate Professor at McGill University. He obtained his degrees from Oxford, Cambridge, and the University of London. He has published 75 research articles on children's early reading and spelling, school-based assessment, and preventative early intervention projects.

Patricia K. Saxler, EdM, is an EdD candidate at the Harvard Graduate School of Education, and is conducting her research at the Gabrieli Lab at the Massachusetts Institute of Technology. Her research focus is on the development of executive function capacities in early childhood. In collaboration with researchers from Harvard and MIT, she investigates the development of self-regulation in children in both schooling and neuroimaging contexts.

Kieron Sheehy, PhD, is Programme Leader for the Doctorate in Education at the Open University. He has a background in educational psychology and his research interests include pedagogy and inclusive education.

Sunyana Swain is a doctoral student at the Centre for Health Psychology, University of Hyderabad. Her doctoral research is in the area of health communication and chronic illnesses. She has been awarded a Fellowship from the Indian Council of Medical Research, New Delhi. She holds a postgraduate diploma degree in Counselling Psychology and has worked as a counsellor in clinical settings with a psychiatrist. Her research interests vary from health care behaviour and adolescent behaviour to neuropsychology.

Marian J. A. J. Verhallen, PhD, has 27 years of experience in special and primary education, and is currently working as an Assistant Professor at Leiden University, The Netherlands. Her area of research is the emergent literacy development of young preliterate children. Her research has focused on the role of video additions in digital storybooks on language development of young second language learners from low-SES backgrounds and, using eye tracking methodology, on effects of illustrations in picture storybooks on young children's language development.

Janet I. Vousden, PhD, is a Senior Research Assistant in Reading Development at Coventry University, UK. She is interested in identifying what aspects of the language are important in reading development through the use of computational models, and how these theoretical insights relate to instruction. She has worked on many research projects in the field of reading.

Clare Wood, PhD, is a Professor of Psychology in Education at Coventry University, UK. She is director of the Centre for Applied Research in Psychology at Coventry University. Her research encompasses all aspects of reading development, but especially the relationships between spoken and written language development, and the use of new technology to support literacy tuition. She is Editor-in-Chief for *Journal of Research in Reading*, and an Associate Editor on *British Journal of Educational Psychology*.

Juan Zhang, PhD, gained her Doctorate in Developmental Psychology from The Chinese University of Hong Kong in 2011, with a focus on modelling of auditory/speech perception and reading in Hong Kong Chinese children. She obtained a Dissertation Funding Award from the Society for Research in Child Development. She is a postdoctoral fellow at University of Pittsburgh, focusing on learning Chinese as a second language. Her research interests include auditory/speech perception, language and literacy development, dyslexia, reading comprehension disability, and bilingualism.

ACKNOWLEDGEMENTS

I would like to thank Clare Wood for her guidance, wisdom, and support during this work; Peter Barnes for his helpful and pragmatic advice, especially in some of the more challenging moments during this work; David Messer and Kieron Sheehy, for their useful suggestions on the design of this work; and Diane Rigg, for her tireless efforts on the review of this work. I would like to pay a special thank you to Stuart Ross, for his invaluable direction back in 2004 – thanks for getting this 'whole thing' started and for seeing some potential in me that I could not see myself. I would also like to thank all those educational practitioners, researchers, and teachers who were involved in the review of individual chapters in this work: Peter Barnes, Roy Bhakta, Erica Bowen, Julia Carroll, Hugh Coolican, Richard Cowan, Emily Coyne, Sarah Critten, Joanne Foster, Simon Goodman, Emma Jackson, Rebecca Jenks, Evi Katsapi, Laura Lundy, Dona Matthews, Neil Mercer, Sarah Norgate, Mary Parker, Claire Pillinger, Beverly Plester, Robert Reeve, Diane Rigg, Stuart Ross, Luke Sage, Kieron Sheehy, Anita Soni, Steven Stagg, Colin Terrell, Jennifer Thomson, Robert Vardill, Janet Vousden, Janice Wearmouth, Gareth Williams, Nigel Wilson, and Clare Wood. I am also indebted to all of the students on our undergraduate and postgraduate psychology programmes at Coventry University, UK, who provided 'student reviews' of individual chapters.

The authors and publisher would like to thank the following for granting permission to reproduce material in this work: Lifelong Achievement Group Pty Ltd, for a figure of the 'Central theoretical perspectives and associated motivation constructs' from Martin, A. J. (2010) *Motivation and Engagement Scale – Test User Manual*, Sydney: Lifelong Achievement Group; a figure of the 'Motivation and Engagement Wheel' from Martin, A. J. (2010) *Motivation and Engagement Scale – Test User Manual,* Sydney: Lifelong Achievement Group; and an appendix of a 'Brief Look at Your Motivation' from Martin, A. J. (2000–2011) *Motivation and Engagement Scale – User Manual,* 5th edn, Sydney: Lifelong Achievement Group; *The Review of Disability Studies: An International Journal,* for written material from Hansen, N. (2005) 'Spaces of education: finding a place that fits', *The Review of Disability Studies: An International Journal,* 1: 22–36.

Every effort has been made to contact copyright holders for their permission to reprint material in this book. The publishers would be grateful to hear from any copyright holder who is not here acknowledged and will undertake to rectify any errors or omissions in future editions of this book.

INTRODUCTION

Andrew J. Holliman

COVENTRY UNIVERSITY, UK

Welcome to *The Routledge International Companion to Educational Psychology.*

Since its origins in the late nineteenth century, 'educational psychology' – loosely defined here as the application of psychological theories, research, and techniques to the educational development of young people in the context of the home, school, and community – has advanced by leaps and bounds. In the present day, young people with learning difficulties are no longer regarded as 'ineducable' or 'non-improvable'. Instead, there is a worldwide movement towards 'inclusive education' – the idea that all young people, regardless of physical, intellectual, emotional, social, linguistic, or other difficulty, have the right to be educated together. But how far have we come, and how much further is there to go?

As the contributions in this volume make clear, a great deal of progress has been made, and this is reflected in changes in legislation across the globe. However, as some chapters also illustrate, some problems from the past are still very much alive, with history repeating itself, while other chapters raise new issues that warrant further discussion and psychological investigation. It is clear that a great deal of work remains to be done; this volume, not without controversy, provides a contemporary overview of educational psychology from an international perspective.

In 2013 educational psychology is a globally applied practice. Recent estimates indicate that there are tens of thousands of educational psychologists (also referred to as school psychologists, counsellors, and professionals of educational psychology) in at least 83 countries across the globe (Jimerson et al. 2008, 2009). There is much that can be learned by adopting a more global perspective on educational psychology and, for that reason, this Companion includes contributions from a distinguished cast of authors, many of whom are internationally renowned scholars.

While there is a Western emphasis here, contributions are drawn from all over the world. The 52 authors, who include educational practitioners, researchers, teachers, a clinical psychologist, and a medical doctor, are affiliated to institutions across Europe (the United Kingdom, Ireland, Germany, Italy, The Netherlands, Sweden), the Americas (Canada and the United States of America), Australasia (Australia and New Zealand), and Asia (Bahrain, Hong Kong, SAR of China, India, and Kuwait). Some of the authors are of African descent and have previously worked as education professionals in Africa, so five continents are represented in this work.

The international appeal of the contributions is wide-ranging; some chapters, e.g. Christodoulou, Saxler, and Del Tufo (on new frontiers in education neuroscience), are inherently international, with global implications, while others, e.g. Zhang and McBride-Chang (on learning to read around the world) adopt a cross-cultural perspective to make international comparisons. Some chapters focus largely on specific regions, but are of international importance, e.g. Obiakor (on multicultural education), while others may seem more exclusive to the region concerned, and in these instances caution is offered with respect to applying information across borders and cultures.

The 32 chapters are representative of major themes and issues in educational psychology. All raise questions and provoke inquiry, and many do this implicitly. In some chapters, e.g. Howe (on the development of scientific reasoning), questions are interspersed throughout the text explicitly to assist the reader in consolidation and understanding of the major themes. In other chapters, e.g. Porath (on meeting the needs of gifted learners), more substantial reflective activities and 'provocations for learning' are presented. This Companion consciously embraces a variety of styles in terms of presentation, writing, composition, and tone, which enables the reader to engage with the personality of the authors.

This volume is divided into four themed sections comprising four, nine, eight, and eleven chapters respectively. It has been carefully designed to be read sequentially, both within and across sections, although some readers may prefer to dip in and out of different chapters. The first theme, 'An introduction to educational psychology', sets the scene by examining the historical and philosophical origins of educational psychology and considers how these have had an impact on present-day classroom provision. This is followed by a rare chapter in a book of this kind, on tensions in the shift towards children's rights as conceived in the United Nations Convention on the Rights of the Child and their translation into contemporary educational practice. The changing role of the educational psychologist in the United Kingdom is then considered, before the presentation of a comparative account of the nature and role of the educational psychologist in different parts of the world.

The second theme, 'How children learn and develop', begins with coverage of the key ideas and theoretical perspectives (e.g. behaviourism and social constructivism) that have proved influential in informing contemporary ideas of effective teaching and learning. The ecology and management of inclusive classrooms in Canadian schools is then examined, including an exploration of ways to improve the quality of classroom-based educational dialogues to support children's learning. This is followed by a cross-cultural perspective on arguably the most important educational skill, literacy, with a focus on the development of English and Chinese word reading. The role of new technologies (e.g. digital picture stories with oral text and video) and their capacity to support children's independent reading and comprehension is explored; so, too, are teaching strategies that may prove effective in supporting children's scientific reasoning. The influential theories developed to understand and explain students' motivation to learn are then examined, before consideration of other important factors that may affect areas of educational development, namely family relationships and childhood stress (with the latter focusing on children in developing countries).

The third theme, 'Issues concerning the assessment of children', begins with the different types of classroom assessment and the ways in which assessment systems can be used to inform teaching and support the educational performance of students. After this comes a series of chapters that present issues, challenges, and controversies surrounding assessment. Topics include: diagnostic assessment and its uses and abuses; tensions in assessment policy and practice; and the role of language in assessment and the way in which the level of language used and expected during assessments may disadvantage some students, e.g. bilingual children. Moreover, with increasing migration on a global scale (International Organization for Migration 2011), the worldwide-relevant topic of multicultural education (and the way in which it has been mismeasured) is then presented, and this is followed by a related chapter, in terms of cultural issues, on intelligence and individual differences. Another timely chapter explores the role of the brain in learning, specifically with regard to identification, assessment, and prediction of learning from an education neuroscience perspective, where it is argued that neuroimaging methods complement behavioural measures in exploring learning differences, predicting development outcomes, and designing and assessing interventions. This section closes with a consideration of labelling in special education in terms of whether it is necessary and whom it may benefit (or not) within the school system.

The fourth and final theme, 'Identifying and meeting the needs of children with learning difficulties', begins with two chapters on inclusive education. The first provides narrative reflections of women with physical and sensory impairments, to provide a foundation from which to examine the progress of inclusive education policy. The second outlines the origins of inclusive education as an international movement and the assumptions and values that underpin it. The remaining chapters in this section focus on the identification of, and provision for, a wide range of learning difficulties. Chapter topics include: meeting the educational needs of children with visual impairment; speech disorders and specific language impairment (SLI); autism spectrum disorders (ASDs); social, emotional, and behavioural difficulties (SEBD); attention deficit hyperactivity disorder (ADHD); dyslexia; dyspraxia; dyscalculia; and gifted learners. For all chapters in this section, the associated characteristics, origins, diagnostic criteria, and interventions, among other aspects, are discussed. The reader is also encouraged to read some of the chapters in the third section, especially the one on labelling, in conjunction with the topics in this fourth theme.

The chapters in this Companion include coverage of the key thinkers, topics, and ideas that have shaped the field and are designed to take the reader beyond standard textbook coverage and into engagement with current issues, cutting-edge research, and future directions in the field of educational psychology from an international perspective. This is an ambitious target given the word limits to which authors were required to adhere. It is simply not possible to cover all relevant themes in the depth they deserve, but plenty of references are provided at the end of each chapter should you wish to explore any issues in more detail.

Notes on contributors appear in the front of this volume and email contact addresses can be found at the end of each chapter.

It is hoped that this Companion will be of value to educational practitioners, researchers, teachers, their students, and others who are interested in learning more about the current status of educational psychology from an international perspective.

References

International Organization for Migration (2011) *Facts and figures* [online]. Available at www.iom.int

Jimerson, S. R., Skokut, M., Cardenas, S., Malone, H., and Stewart, K. (2008) 'Where in the world is school psychology? Examining evidence of school psychology around the globe', *School Psychology International*, 29: 131–144.

Jimerson, S. R., Stewart, K., Skokut, M., Cardenas, S., and Malone, H. (2009) 'How many school psychologists are there in each country of the world? International estimates of school psychologists and school psychologist-to-student ratios', *School Psychology International*, 30: 555–567.

PART I

An introduction to educational psychology

1

A HISTORY OF EDUCATIONAL PSYCHOLOGY

Malcolm W. H. Hughes

UNIVERSITY OF THE WEST OF ENGLAND, UK

> If I had to reduce all of educational psychology to just one principle, I would say this: The most important single factor influencing learning is what the learner already knows. Ascertain this and teach him accordingly.
>
> *(Ausubel 1968: vi)*

Introducing a history of educational psychology

The challenge of this chapter is to present a history of educational psychology. You may have noticed that many textbooks begin with a background chapter that provides a historical or theoretical context for the chapters to come. This *Chapter 1: A history of educational psychology* could be no exception to the usual practice; that introductory chapters lay the foundations for the rest of the text. An author might use an opening chapter, being introductory in nature, to briefly present ideas that are more fully explored later by writers with specialist expertise, particularly in this instance those who make the connection between psychology and educational settings.

This chapter is about where ideas and connections between ideas originated, and how such understanding can help you appreciate the importance of educational psychology for what happens in schools and other educational settings. It will help you judge the potential influence of educational psychology on teachers and how a thoroughgoing understanding of educational psychology can improve teaching and therefore the life chances of children and young people throughout the world. The aim of this chapter is to present an origin of educational psychology that traces connections between the development of scientific method, the research methods used by psychologists in educational settings, and the main theories (and theorists) that now inform so much of what happens across the globe in our schools and colleges. In summary, it is the connections – adopting a view of learning that is connectionist – that we are looking for, and aim to reveal.

Finding connections – but between what?

While resisting the temptation to present a kind of 'Who's Who' of educational psychology, it can be helpful to identify at an early stage some of the names that will appear during this chapter and many of those that follow. But which names to choose? It is probably fair to say that for the past century or so, educational psychology has been heavily influenced by research carried out in the USA, and reported in international research journals published in either the USA or the UK (Bridges 2006). This is not in any way to exclude work carried out throughout Europe and in Australia and other parts of the developed or newly developed world – often seminal and innovative work that many authors in this text will call upon to support their arguments or conclusions. Rather, this is a realistic declaration of a widely accepted view that without the pioneering and entrepreneurial climate of higher educational institutions in the USA, much of the work that has contributed to the development of the applied science of educational psychology would not have been carried out (Nelson 2001). Neither would the work have been recorded and reported, to the benefit of children and young people throughout the world (Feldman and Desrochers 2004).

The influence of American scholarship is one reason to turn to the American text *Educational Psychology: A Century of Contributions* (Zimmerman and Schink 2002), which looks at the historic contributions of 18 leading psychologists who influenced the field of educational psychology from its origins in the late nineteenth century to its current status in the second decade of the twenty-first century. Each chapter presents a biography of an eminent scholar whose work has had a significant influence on the field of educational psychology – scholars selected by a committee of eight eminent present-day educational psychologists. The committee selected the following biographical subjects:

- Albert Bandura 1925–
- Alfred Binet 1857–1911
- Benjamin Bloom 1913–1999
- Ann Brown 1943–1999
- Jerome Bruner 1915–
- Lee Cronbach 1916–2001
- John Dewey 1859–1952
- Nathaniel Gage 1917–2008
- Robert Gagné 1916–2002
- William James 1842–1910
- Maria Montessori 1870–1952
- Jean Piaget 1896–1980
- Herbert Simon 1916–2001
- Burrhus Frederic Skinner 1904–1990
- Charles Spearman 1863–1945
- Lewis Terman 1877–1956
- Edward L. Thorndike 1874–1949
- Lev Semenovich Vygotsky 1896–1934

It is worth pausing for a moment to take a longer look at this list of key contributors to the origins of educational psychology. How many different ways could you organize this list? Try writing each name on a separate piece of card and sorting and grouping the cards in as many different ways as you can. You may need to do some surfing of the Internet or use the index of this book to give you some basic information to go on. Date order is a good starting point, and many students who engage with this activity also go straight for names they have and haven't heard of, or the birthplace of the psychologist (European or American). Of course, this list of contributors to the history of educational psychology is a selection from a much longer list of possible contenders.

How was this list constructed? What thought processes were the committee of eight engaged in during the selection process for *Educational Psychology: A Century of Contributions*? Well, there is one obvious process, making selections – *selecting*. Members of the committee also employed other processes such as categorizing, comparing, connecting, discarding, refining, evaluating, and explaining. If you did start to sort the list of contributors as suggested in the preceding paragraph then you may also have engaged in similar processes. The committee of eight were also working together, 'bouncing ideas', bringing new insights or unfamiliar knowledge. They built or constructed the list together; an important idea for the kind of ways you can engage with the main ideas of this chapter and with others who might be studying with you. What else might be important?

Setting the scene or setting the learning agenda

This chapter began with an important and telling quotation from the American psychologist David Ausubel (1918–2008). You may already have spotted that he does not appear on the list of 18 eminent contributors, and after you have further engaged in a study of educational psychology you may think it appropriate to add Ausubel's name to the list. For now it is worth noting that Ausubel believed that people acquire knowledge primarily through reasoning from concepts, principles, and ideas presented by a teacher. They do not necessarily discover the knowledge for themselves, as some others on our list of 18 would suggest. Learners understand new knowledge using deductive reasoning – from general ideas to specific cases, not from specific cases leading to general concepts (inductive reasoning). Ausubel's expository teaching model stresses what is known as meaningful verbal learning – verbal information, ideas, and relationships among ideas, taken together. Therefore, Ausubel would assert that learning by heart by repetition (rote memorization) is not meaningful learning, because material learned by rote is not 'connected' with existing knowledge.

Ausubel's teaching strategy always begins with an advance organizer. An advance organizer is an introductory statement broad enough to encompass all the information that will follow (Hung and Chao 2007). Advance organizers can serve three purposes: they can direct your attention to what is important in the coming material; highlight relationships among ideas that will be presented; and remind you of relevant information you already have (Hung et al. 2010).

In general, advance organizers fall into one of two categories, 'comparative' and 'expository' (Gajria et al. 2007). Comparative organizers activate or reactivate (bring into working memory) already existing schemas. They remind you of what you already know but may not yet realize is connectable or relevant. For example, at the start of a biology lesson pupils could be asked 'How would you transform spiders into insects or an amphibian into a reptile?' In contrast, expository organizers provide *new* knowledge that pupils will need in order to understand the upcoming information. The quote from David Ausubel at the start of this chapter could be considered an expository advance organizer. Finding out what the learner already knows and teaching him or her accordingly is a well-constructed and memorable general principle that could inform the remaining exposition of this chapter. However, Ausubel's principle may not be a good advance organizer for what is to follow. Why not? It might be helpful to review the Ausubel quotation against the three purposes of advance organizers explained earlier. How can Ausubel's principle be considered a helpful advance organizer when it doesn't deal with the origins and history of educational psychology, and no-one can know what you already know before you read this chapter? However, something more appropriate can be constructed.

An advance organizer for this chapter

Here is one idea of how a good advance organizer for this chapter might read:

'The history of educational psychology begins with its philosophical foundations in the late nineteenth century, follows attempts to apply scientific method to educational settings and now celebrates its current status as a fully recognized applied science in the second decade of the twenty first century'

The general conclusion of research on advance organizers (e.g. Langan-Fox et al. 2001) is that they do help pupils learn (especially when the material to be learned is quite unfamiliar or complex) if two conditions are met. First, to be effective the organizer must be understood by the pupils. This was demonstrated dramatically in an early study by Dinnel and Glover (1985). They found that instructing pupils to paraphrase an advance organizer – which, of course, requires them to understand its meaning – significantly increased the effectiveness of the organizer. Second, the organizer must really be an organizer! By its internal organization and logic, it must indicate relations among the basic concepts and terms that will be used. How does the advance organizer above match the two conditions?

We can start by looking at some of the terms used: 'philosophical foundations'; 'scientific method'; 'recognized applied science'. Philosophical foundations are the origins of educational psychology, with the word 'philosophy' deriving from the Greek *philosophia* which means 'love of wisdom'. Philosophy is no mere musings about the meaning of life and the universe but rather the use of rational, critical and systematic logic to establish understandings about language, knowledge, values, and mind (Larvor 2008). Furthermore, although in many modern university departmental structures philosophy inhabits liberal arts faculties and schools, it was a term originally applied to scientists. Natural philosophers were early scientists (before the nineteenth century) who studied nature and the physical universe, precursors of the sciences of biology, botany, physics, chemistry, and astronomy (Kaufman 2006).

It shouldn't come as too much of a surprise, therefore, that William James (1842–1910), firstborn of our list of most eminent scholars and widely considered the 'father' of educational psychology, was among other things a philosopher. James was concerned with beliefs, truths, emotions, and how we know what we know – the 'nuts and bolts' of gaining knowledge and developing cognitive abilities through experience. The branch of philosophy that drew James' attention was epistemology, from *epistēmē* (meaning 'knowledge') and *logos* (meaning 'logic' or 'reasoned discourse'), as it is concerned with the nature of knowledge. Epistemology addresses the questions: 'What is knowledge?' 'How is knowledge acquired?' and 'How do we know what we know?' Therefore, empiricism is a theory of knowledge emphasizing the role of experience, especially based on what we can observe and make sense of (Clough 2009).

Developing a theory – developing a scientific method

Did William James invent empiricism? Hardly, as the history of science – or rather scientific method – is rooted in the philosophy of the famous Greek scholar Aristotle. Aristotle (384–322 BC) established empiricism as a theory of knowledge which asserts that all knowledge arises from experience and observation. Almost 1400 years later, the Persian scholar Ibn al-Haytham Alhazen (965–1039) combined observation and experimentation (scientific methods) and rational argument in his *Book of Optics*, to form a theory of vision. The theory stated that light is emitted or reflected from objects rather than from the eyes (El-Bizri 2005). The development of scientific method by Alhazen and later by the likes of Bacon, Copernicus, Leonardo da Vinci,

Galileo, Newton, Kepler, Darwin, Freud, and Skinner allowed for the development of theories in the physical and social sciences, including educational psychology.

As in other forms of scientific research, educational psychology is based on the observation of the phenomena – the happenings – of teaching and learning. Systematic observations are organized into patterns of behaviour that have causes and consequences. The way in which we make sense of what we observe is to construct meanings from the causes, behaviours and consequences of particular phenomena. If these observations in educational settings are conducted in reliable and valid ways (the scientific method) then the meanings we construct are more likely to apply to more learners than just the individuals or groups the scientist observes (Niaz 2004). Scientific observations are real and factual, yet facts alone do not make a science. What is needed is a way of combining and interpreting facts – reasoned discourse or logic – to create a theory that makes sense of what scientists have observed and recorded.

What do we mean by a theory? A theory is a system of concepts that connect to form a framework of ideas (or schema) which allows for understanding. Burrhus Skinner (usually known as B. F. Skinner), a highly influential American psychologist, author, and inventor, provides a more precise definition of the development of theory using scientific methods. He said: 'It [a theory] is an attempt to discover order, to show that certain events stand in lawful relations to other events. The methods of science are designed to clarify these uniformities and make them explicit' (1953: 35).

Therefore a theory is formed (in the context of educational psychology) by the systematic observation of how teachers and learners behave, and the causes and consequences of the behaviour. The scientific method organizes these observations in order to create a theory about the behaviour being observed. However, systematic observation by itself is not enough. At the same time we are looking for explanations of the changes of behaviour by considering earlier observations, contextual or environmental factors and changes in cognition or learning. Together, and over time, systematic observations can be used to create theories about how and why we think teachers teach as they do and how learners learn.

At the beginning of the twentieth century the development of the new discipline of educational psychology rested on the successful application of the scientific methods of observation and experimentation to educational problems. Even in the earliest years of the discipline, educational psychologists recognized the limitations of this new approach. In his famous series of lectures *Talks to Teachers on Psychology*, published in 1899 and regarded by some as the first educational psychology textbook, William James commented that: 'Psychology is a science, and teaching is an art; and sciences never generate arts directly out of themselves. An intermediate inventive mind must make that application, by using its originality' (1899: 7–8).

Therefore, it wasn't just about creating an applied science of how learners learn to inform how teachers should teach, because even James, the 'father of educational psychology', recognized that education is not a simple set of solutions that always work because they have once been observed to work. Rather, teachers call on a range of strategies based on principles adopted by educationalists, founded on theories of learning, cognitive development, authentic assessment of attainment, and developmentally appropriate provision.

Using a scientific method

The Swiss developmental psychologist Jean Piaget (1896–1980) is arguably the most influential figure in educational psychology, particularly when others apply his theories of stages in cognitive development to educational contexts. You will read a good deal about his theories throughout this book (e.g. Howe, Chapter 10, this volume; Vousden, Wood, and Holliman, Chapter 5, this volume). Learner-centred education – good practice (arguably) around the globe in early childhood and primary school settings today – is deeply rooted in Piaget's theory that people learn best about the world through exploration of it rather than being told. Spend just a few minutes in many early years settings and you can observe the freedom children have to explore ideas, materials, and objects through talking about what they are finding and sharing with others. You will also observe the expert way in which teachers support children's activities and language to draw out meanings from the children's experiences.

Piaget was a biologist who originally studied molluscs. By the time he was 21 he had published 20 scientific papers on them, and gained a PhD about them at the University of Neuchâtel. As a teenager, he published two philosophical papers (Piaget, like William James, was considered a philosopher). After graduating, he moved to Paris to teach at the Grange-Aux-Belles Street School for Boys. When marking some intelligence tests at the school, he noticed that young children consistently made types of mistakes that older children and adults did not. Piaget came to think that age differences in patterns of wrong answers reflected differences in how children of various ages 'thought' about the questions and that older children not only know more, but also think differently to younger children. His curiosity led Piaget into the study of the development of children's understanding, through closely observing them – particularly his own three children – and talking and listening to them while they played or worked on exercises he set.

Jean Piaget used scientific methods of observation and experimentation to explore the differences in how children at different ages thought about a problem. An often-quoted example is the pendulum problem – useful for us as the idea is simple to explain – to test at what age children can engage in formal operations. Essentially, formal operations involve the development of an ability to think scientifically and apply the rigour of the scientific method to cognitive tasks. Piaget used this test to judge whether a child had progressed sufficiently to perform formal operations (Inhelder and Piaget 1958).

Children and adolescents are shown a pendulum (consisting of a weight hanging from a string and then set in motion) and asked to try to figure out what determines the speed at which the pendulum sways from side to side. Is it the heaviness of the weight, the length of the string, the height from which the weight is dropped, or the force with which it is dropped? Participants are given various weights and various lengths of string to use in their deliberations.

Children in concrete operations – the developmental stage that precedes formal operations – tend to approach the problem with random attempts, often changing more than one variable at a time. They may try the heaviest weight on the longest string dropped from medium height with medium force, then a medium weight on the smallest string dropped from medium height with lesser force. When the speed of the pendulum changes, it remains difficult for them to say what caused the change because they had altered more than one variable at a time. If they happen to arrive at the right answer – it's the length of the string (but you knew that already!) – they find it difficult to explain why. This is crucial to understanding how Piagetian theory is constructed and applied; cognitive advances at each stage are reflected not just in the solutions children devise for problems, but in their explanations for how they arrived at the solution.

It is only with formal operations that we can find the right answer to a problem like this and explain why it is the right answer. The formal operational thinker approaches the pendulum problem by utilizing the kind of hypothetical thinking involved in a scientific experiment. The thought process spoken out loud could be something like this:

> Let's see, it could be weight; let me try changing the weight while keeping everything else the same. No, that's not it; same speed. Maybe it's length; if I change the length while keeping everything else the same, that seems to make a difference; it goes faster

with a shorter string. But let me try height, too; no change; then force; no change there, either. So it's length, and only length, that makes the difference.

Thus, the formal operational thinker changes one variable while holding the others constant and tests the different possibilities systematically. Through this process, the formal operational thinker arrives at an answer that is not only correct but can be explained and defended. The capacity for this kind of thinking, which Piaget (1972) termed hypothetico-deductive reasoning, is at the heart of his theory of formal operations.

Not all our 18 leading psychologists engaged in scientific method to formulate theory. Remember that William James, as well as being a medical practitioner, was principally a philosopher, an original thinker, and a linker between the disciplines of physiology, psychology and philosophy. His 1,200 page work, *The Principles of Psychology* (1890), is a complex blend of physiology, philosophy, and personal reflection that has given us such ideas as 'the stream of consciousness' and the baby's impression of the world 'as one great blooming, buzzing confusion' (1890: 462).

In contrast, Piaget not only observed and made sense of what he observed, but applied scientific methods to create and check out his emerging theories of cognitive development and learning. Now would be a good time to retrieve your name cards for the 18 leading psychologists. Put William James and Jean Piaget at the top of two columns and place the remaining cards according to whether you think each psychologist is more a philosopher/author like James or more a scientist/author like Piaget. As suggested earlier, you may need to do some surfing of the Internet or use the index of this book to give you some basic information to go on.

How did you get on? Perhaps you had some cards left over. These were probably the names of leading psychologists who contributed enormously to the origins and history of educational psychology, but fitted the identity of neither a philosopher/author nor a scientist/author. One of the cards that might have been left over was Maria Montessori, although you might also have placed her in the philosopher/author column. She is an inspirational example of somebody who successfully linked child development and issues of social justice (Nawrotzki 2006), and her work is worth a short introduction now.

Applying science for a teaching method

Montessori (1870–1952) was an Italian teacher, philosopher, and physician best known for her method of education for children from birth to adolescence. She was the first woman in Italy to receive a medical degree and went on to work in the fields of psychiatry, education, and anthropology. She believed that each child is born with a unique potential which can be 'revealed' by their early experiences including the type of education they receive. Her early work centred on women's rights and social reform, part of which was establishing children's rights to a high-quality education from an early age. The Montessori method of teaching (as it became known) was a revolutionary method of education characterized by personalized teaching and individual learning, children's self-directed activity, teachers matching children's learning environments to developmental level, and the role of physical activity in forming concepts and gaining mastery in practical skills. The method is in use today in many settings (mainly nursery and primary schools) throughout the world, all named after the founder of the method.

Maria Montessori died in the Netherlands in 1952, after a lifetime devoted to the study of child development. She remains one of the few great theorists, who transformed her ideas into a way of organizing classrooms, schools, curricula, and pedagogy. A rich and important seam of research into the applications, effects, and outcomes of her methods remains and continues to grow (Vettiveloo 2008).

Montessori is a wonderful example of a third category of eminent contributors to educational psychology. She was a scholar, a philosopher, a scientist, a medical practitioner, but principally a reformer and founder. She reformed the learning experiences of countless thousands of children founded on the principles and theories of social and cognitive psychology. Her application of what she believed to be principles of social justice and how children develop and learn best made an enormous contribution to the history of educational psychology.

Retrieve the name cards again and this time make three columns: philosopher/authors, scientist/authors and reformers/founders. Of course any categorization can be a rough-and-ready tool, and students with different perceptions and perspectives will produce different configurations. Do not permanently discard your name cards. As you read this text it would be interesting to review your categories or to group the cards in a different way. You may also wish to discard some names or add names to the list pile, like that of David Ausubel.

Finding connections in the chapter

Finally, we can return to the advance organizer used earlier in the chapter. Do you think, or can you agree, that the history of educational psychology begins with its philosophical foundations in the late nineteenth century, follows attempts to apply scientific method to educational settings, and is now a fully recognized applied science? Can you trace the connections between this advance organizer and the ideas presented in the chapter? The three-part nature of the organizer mirrors the structure of the argument that followed in the rest of the chapter and the three eminent contributors to educational psychology who exemplify each part of the discussion.

By the time you finish this book you may have constructed perspectives on educational psychology that allow you to critique the advance organizer about the history of educational psychology and the original selection of the 18 leading psychologists. However, it is not possible to make the connections 'for' you between the history of educational psychology, Jean Piaget, Maria Montessori, William James, scientific method and the application of theory; but 'you' can make those connections for yourself. Now, it is over to you!

Contact address: Mal.Hughes@uwe.ac.uk

References

Ausubel, D. P. (1968) *Educational psychology: a cognitive view*, New York: Holt, Rinehart and Winston.

Bridges, D. (2006) 'The disciplines and discipline of educational research', *Journal of Philosophy of Education*, 40: 259–272.

Clough, P. T. (2009) 'The new empiricism', *European Journal of Social Theory*, 12: 43–61.

Dinnel, D., and Glover, J. A. (1985). 'Advance organizers: encoding manipulations', *Journal of Educational Psychology*, 77: 514–521.

El-Bizri, N. (2005) 'A philosophical perspective on Alhazen's Optics', *Arabic Sciences and Philosophy*, 15: 189–218.

Feldman, M. P., and Desrochers, P. (2004) 'Truth for its own sake: academic culture and technology transfer at Johns Hopkins University', *Minerva*, 42: 105–126.

Gajria, M., Jitendra, A. K., Sood, S., and Sacks, G. (2007) 'Improving comprehension of expository text in students with LD: a research synthesis', *Journal of Learning Disabilities*, 40: 210–225.

Hung, W.-C., and Chao, C.-A. (2007) 'Integrating advance organizers and multidimensional information display in electronic performance support systems', *Innovations in Education and Teaching International*, 44: 181–198.

Hung, W.-C., Smith, T., Harris, M., and Lockard, J. (2010) 'Development research of a teacher's educational performance support system: the practices of design, development, and evaluation', *Educational Technology Research and Development*, 58: 61–80.

Inhelder, B., and Piaget, J. (1958) *The growth of logical thinking from childhood to adolescence*, New York: Basic Books.

James, W. (1890) *The principles of psychology, Volume 1*, New York: Henry Holt and Company.

James, W. (1899) *Talks to teachers on psychology: and to students on some of life's ideals*, New York: Henry Holt and Company.

Kaufman, D. A. (2006) 'Knowledge, wisdom, and the philosopher', *Philosophy*, 81: 129–151.

Langan-Fox, J., Wirth, A., Code, S., Langfield-Smith, K., and Wirth, A. (2001) 'Analyzing shared and team mental models', *International Journal of Industrial Ergonomics*, 28: 99–112.

Larvor, B. (2008) 'What can the philosophy of mathematics learn from the history of mathematics?', *Erkenntnis*, 68: 393–407.

Nawrotzki, K. (2006) 'Froebel is dead; long live Froebel! The National Froebel Foundation and English Education', *History of Education*, 35: 209–223.

Nelson, R. R. (2001) 'Observations on the post-Bayh-Dole rise of patenting at American universities', *Journal of Technology Transfer*, 26: 13–19.

Niaz, M. (2004) 'Exploring alternative approaches to methodology in educational research', *Interchange*, 35: 155–184.

Piaget, J. (1972) *The child's conception of the world*, Towota, NJ: Littlefield Adams.

Skinner, B. F. (1953) *Science and human behaviour*, New York: Macmillan.

Vettiveloo, R. (2008) 'A critical enquiry into the implementation of the Montessori teaching method as a first step towards inclusive practice in early childhood settings specifically in developing countries', *Contemporary Issues in Early Childhood*, 9: 178–181.

Zimmerman, B. J., and Schink, D. H. (eds.) (2002) *Educational psychology: a century of contributions. A Project of Division 15 (Educational Psychology) of the American Psychological Society*, New York: Routledge.

2

THE RIGHTS OF THE CHILD

Mary Kellett

THE OPEN UNIVERSITY, UK

This chapter explores inherent tensions in the shift towards children's rights, articulated in child participation and voice policies, with power dynamics in schools. It focuses mainly on the English educational sector, although illustrative material is also drawn from other global nations. Fundamental children's rights are depicted alongside some teachers' fears that progressive embracement of those rights risks destabilizing and subverting core educational principles and practice. The chapter begins with a brief exposition of the contemporary status of children's rights and how some of these have evolved in school environments. The body of the chapter discusses those articles of the United Nations Convention on the Rights of the Child (UNCRC) that impact on children's educational experiences and the role of educational professionals. A major focus is the perspectives of children themselves as depicted through child agency and child-led research. It concludes with a reflection on future directions and likely global responses.

The status of children's rights

Discourse around children's rights has grown rapidly in the wake of the UNCRC (United Nations 1989). This international edict acknowledged the status of children in society and accrued human rights directly to minors. There are 41 articles, several of which relate to education. A subset of these are simplified and summarized in Table 2.1.

Adopting a rights-based approach to childhood challenges some traditional child development paradigms and necessitates a rethinking of underlying principles. Pertinent to this is the debate about development as natural versus development as cultural (Woodhead 2006). The cultural context in which children live impacts on the way in which we understand and interpret their development rights and gives rise to some tensions. Competence-dominant theories (see James, Jenks, and Prout 1998; Woodhead and Faulkner 2008) limit the self-agency of children in the exercising of their rights, whereas social-constructivist theories recognize the emancipatory status of the children as social actors with evolving capacities (Lansdown 2005).

These articles of the UNCRC demand a reappraisal of children's role in shaping their development, influencing those with responsibilities for their care and education and being listened to in all matters that affect them. It strikes at the heart of conventional authority relationships between children and the adults who regulate their lives, and

Table 2.1 UNCRC articles linked to children's education

Article	Summary of content
2	Governments should ensure that children are protected against all forms of discrimination or punishment that derives from discrimination.
3	The best interest of the child is paramount. Organizations should ensure practices that support children's wellbeing.
4	Governments should make UNCRC rights available and accessible to children.
12	Children have the right to say what they think should happen, when adults are making decisions that affect them, and to have their opinions taken into account according to their age and maturity.
13	Children have the right to express their views freely and to receive and share information as long as the information is not damaging to them or to others.
14	Children have the right to think and believe what they want, and to practise their religion.
19	Governments should ensure that children are properly cared for, and protect them from all forms of violence, abuse, neglect or exploitation by anyone who has care of them. This should include prevention and support programmes.
28	Children have the right to quality education and to be supported to attend school to the highest level of their abilities.
29	Education should enable children to develop their skills and abilities.
30	Children from ethnic minority groups should be allowed to enjoy their own culture, to practise their own religion, and to use their own language.
31	Children have a right to rest and leisure, to engage in play and recreational activities appropriate to their age.

offers the promise of being a major catalyst for social change towards a more respectful view of children's status as young citizens.

(Woodhead 2005: 91)

The United Nations Committee on the Rights of the Child was set up to monitor how states are implementing the Convention. In the immediate aftermath of UNCRC many countries passed new legislation to embed the 41 articles, but the Government in England and Wales maintained that these were already covered by the 1989 Children's Act. However, at the United Nations Special Summit on Children's Rights (in 2002), the UK Government was criticized for not doing enough, especially in relation to children's participation. In response to this criticism, the *Every Child Matters* (ECM) Green Paper 2003 was fashioned and ultimately adopted into English law via the 2004 Children's Act. In the UK's devolved parliaments similar legislation was adopted: the Welsh Assembly Government (2004) publication *Children and Young People: Rights to Action*; the Scottish Executive (2005) publication *Getting It Right for Every Child: Proposals for Action*; and in Northern Ireland, the Office of the First Minister and Deputy First Minister (2006) publication *Our Children and Young People – Our Pledge*.

The onset of ECM has been a significant factor in the advancement of children's rights in education. The aim of ECM was to place children at the centre of service provision and build support around them based on five outcomes – being healthy; staying safe; enjoying and achieving; making a positive contribution; and economic wellbeing. Schools and educational psychologists were required to incorporate these into their planning processes. This brought about a notable shift towards a more child-centred approach to learning coupled with acknowledgement of the importance of listening to children and of promoting their participation and voice. A new respect for the worth of children's views and the knowledge and understanding of their lived experiences began to emerge, which had a major impact on children's rights in education globally (Fitzgerald et al. 2010; Lansdown 2005).

The right to an education

Although the fundamental right of a child to a minimum of a primary education is not in question, the extent to which children have any rights over the 'nature' of that education is less clear. Considering that a large proportion of a typical childhood is spent in full-time education, children have relatively few rights over how this is managed (Devine 2003). Children in most developed countries do not have any right to determine what school they go to, when and how long they attend, or what curriculum is offered. These decisions are determined in law and choices made through the proxy of their parents. Harris (2009) asserts that English education law needs to catch up with child care law if it is to hold to the spirit of the United Nations Convention. For example, in child care law, children can have their accommodation preferences considered but pupils have to wait until Sixth Form (where students aged 16 to 19 typically study for advanced school-level qualifications) before they have any rights over their choice of school.

Essentially, children have the right 'to' an education but no right to 'decline' an education. This raises some interesting tensions and puts Wyness, Harrison, and Buchanan's (2004) assertion of a child's right to self-determination at variance with educational gatekeepers who deny self-determination with regard to school attendance. There is considerable unease about the social injustices in the school exclusion system and the impact these have on attainment and life aspirations for those children caught in the vortex. Few would argue against the benefits of education for children but some would advocate a strengthening of children's rights to decision-making concerning educational processes (Smyth 2006).

Children's Rights Alliance England (CRAE) commissioned research to provide feedback to the United Nations Committee on the Rights of the Child by exploring children's awareness and understanding of the UNCRC and their rights (see Davey 2010). Children and young people completed an online survey (n = 1,362) and took part in focus groups (n = 346). The research looked at six aspects of children's lives: respect and freedom; family and friends; health and safety; education; play and leisure; and crime and neighbourhood. Children and young people had strong ideas about what is important to them. These included:

- knowing about and being able to exercise their rights
- being part of a family (whatever that construction of family was)
- being respected and listened to
- having the right to live in a good area with a sense of community.

Findings showed that very few children and young people knew about or understood their human rights. Even fewer knew how to seek redress if their rights were violated. The 2008 report of the United Nations Committee on the Rights of the Child highlighted a number of concerns about the implementation of the Convention in the UK, not least the level of awareness of their rights among UK children. The committee singled out unsatisfactory levels of discrimination among minority groups and disabled children, especially with regard to attainment and school exclusion. It judged that the principle of the best interests of the child was still not reflected as a primary consideration in all legislative and policy matters affecting children, notably in the area of juvenile justice.

We can learn much about the contemporary status of children's rights in education and likely future directions by reflecting on how some current rights have evolved. Previous generations grew up with corporal punishment as an everyday occurrence in the classroom. Sweden led the way, banning corporal punishment in 1979. Most European countries followed suit over different time scales, e.g. Finland as early as 1983 and Portugal as late as 2007. In the UK, legislation to ban corporal punishment in state schools was passed in 1987 (more than a decade later for private schools). However, corporal punishment is still allowed in many non-European countries, putting them in direct conflict with Article 19 of the UNCRC (see Table 2.1). This illustrates the uneven employment of quite fundamental children's rights in education and signals the distance yet to be travelled before global parity can be achieved.

Wellbeing

In addition to freedom from abuse, children have a right to wellbeing, leisure, and play. These cornerstones of the UNCRC are of primary concern to educational psychologists who seek optimal ways to ensure they are realized. Bullying is a prominent issue in schools affecting a child's right to wellbeing. Understanding the perspectives of perpetrators and victims continually challenges professionals. The school experiences of children with learning difficulties were vividly depicted in Mencap's *Don't Stick It, Stop it!* research campaign in 2007, which revealed that 80 percent of children with learning difficulties were being bullied at school – 60 percent had been physically hurt by bullies. For 27 percent of children with learning difficulties, the bullying lasted three or more years. Children themselves can be powerful anti-bullying advocates and many schools have peer-run anti-bullying initiatives.

Cyberbullying is on the increase. A recent youth-led research study commissioned by the Diana Award (Tarapdar and Kellett 2011) involving 1,512 young people in England found that 38 percent were affected by cyberbullying, some to the point of being suicidal. Interestingly, the report also found that young people felt safer in school than in their own homes, so educationalists are clearly making progress with intervention strategies. There is more discussion about wellbeing in Erten, Savage, and Di Stasio (Chapter 6, this volume), which considers the positive outcomes that accrue when emotional aspects of a classroom are closely linked to the academic business.

Pupil voice

An important element, in most developed countries, that underlines children's right to optimal education is pupil voice predicated on Article 12 of the Convention (see Table 2.1). In England this has grown out of the ECM agenda, albeit slowly because of entrenched paternalist and protectionist perspectives that have historically pervaded the education sector (Leitch and Mitchell 2007). Participation theorists such as Shier (2001: 110) refer to a continuum that has listening at one end and power sharing at the other: *children are listened to* → *children are supported in expressing their views* → *children's views are taken into account* → *children are involved in decision making processes* → *children share power and responsibility for decision making.* Lundy (2007: 933) conceptualizes children's voice as being constituted in four parts, not one:

- *Space:* Children must be given the opportunity to express a view
- *Voice:* Children must be facilitated to express their views
- *Audience:* The view must be listened to
- *Influence:* The view must be acted upon as appropriate.

This perspective highlights the inefficacy of voice operating in a vacuum. There have to be the right conditions in place before children can exercise voice and mechanisms to carry that voice to an audience in order to be influential. Creating space for children to express their views in a safe space without fear of reprisal is underpinned by the 'assurance' of this cited in Article 12.

A number of initiatives, of interest to educational psychologists, are addressing how this ideology can be applied to promote listening cultures and meaningful participation by pupils on school issues. The UK government strengthened its commitment to pupil consultation in the 2002 Education Act and through the Ofsted inspection framework which gives the inspection body powers to request evidence of how schools are consulting with pupils and how they are considering their views. Since 2005, Ofsted has also included children's views directly via a pupil questionnaire.

At the tokenistic end of the spectrum, pupil voice is passive, a perception of voice as being a gift in the power of adults (in this case, teachers) to bestow rather than a fundamental right. Terms such as 'giving children a voice' perpetuate this (Lodge 2005). Adult control is evident where young people are given a voice through their views being 'allowed' to emerge (Hamill and Boyd 2002), which suggests a dependency on adults to provide any such opportunities. Teacher–pupil power dynamics also has a significant bearing on how children's views are accessed. During the Iraq War, adults were allowed to exercise their democratic right to protest against the invasion but children were threatened with school suspension if they took time out of lessons to join protest marches.

The school environment is one of the most governed childhood arenas outside of youth offending institutions, and a location where children are least able to assert their human rights (Kellett 2009; Mayall 2000). Harris (2009) discusses how education law needs to catch up with child care law if it is to hold to the spirit of the Convention. Despite all the rhetoric around pupil voice, teaching and learning are largely forbidden areas of enquiry (Fielding 2001). Although teachers are aware of the shifting nature of children's status in society, this is rarely welcomed if it challenges their own roles and authority (Devine 2003; Hamill and Boyd 2002). Tensions arise when children aspire to raise issues that conflict with those of their teachers (Alderson 2000). In some settings, teachers regard the voicing of pupil views as potentially subversive and destabilizing (Garner 2010). This is familiar territory to educational psychologists, who have to act in the best interest of the child even if this leads to challenging conflicts with teaching staff.

Nevertheless, there has been considerable progress in facilitating pupil participation and voice in some schools, with more and more examples emerging of pupils contributing to – or in some cases researching – teaching and learning issues (Rudduck 2006). Cultural change is proving slower to achieve (Leitch and Mitchell 2007) and there is still a real danger that lip service will be rendered to pupil voice for reasons of a school's accountability rather than for reasons of children's human rights (Robinson and Taylor 2007). This concurs with Bragg's (2001) contention that when rapid results are needed (and performance league tables spring immediately to mind here) it is easier to listen to those voices that accord with the establishment position rather than those that challenge it.

School councils

The growth of school councils has done much to raise awareness about the potential for pupils to play a part in leadership and management. School councils are forums that enable pupil representatives to take forward views and concerns of their peers into governance structures. The 2002 Education Act recommended the setting up of school councils in maintained schools. The Welsh Assembly went a step further in making school councils compulsory in 2006. Despite a strong rationale for school councils to enhance children's rights, they have attracted criticism for being too adult-centric in their agendas and processes (Rudduck and Fielding 2006) and opportunities for pupils to comment on matters that affect their education can be very limited.

Rudduck and Fielding (2006) were concerned about this tokenism and identified three critical factors that impeded the efficacy of school councils. The first was adult–child power relations and a perception that agency was in the gift of the adult to bestow. The second related to inclusion and a perception that school council pupil representatives were drawn from articulate, middle-class groups. Lastly they highlighted authenticity and a perception that staff did not buy into the purpose or ethos of school councils. Whitty and Wisby (2007) also expressed concern about tokenism where insufficient time is allocated for school council meetings and their ensuing feedback processes. Cotmore (2004) drew attention to the general lack of training for student representatives. On a positive note, when school councils work optimally, correlations can be found between these pupil consultation processes and school improvement (Bergmark and Kostenius 2009; Rudduck and Flutter 2004). For examples of school council good practice see www.speakersschoolcouncil.org.

Special educational needs

Pupils fully understand which forms of communication are most likely to be valued (Rudduck and Fielding 2006) and that initiatives such as pupil voice which are intended to be empowering can perpetuate exclusionary practices if they become over-populated by articulate minorities (Lensmire 1998; Rudduck and Flutter 2004). Bragg (2001: 73) refers to this as an implicit contract requiring pupils to 'speak responsibly, intelligently and usefully'. If not handled carefully, voice can create hierarchical pupil power structures that result in silence and suppression for some pupils (John 1996). This is most evident with children who have special educational needs. They are least able to exercise their rights and are among the most marginalized of pupil groups. This resonates with the discourse in Erten et al. (Chapter 6, this volume) about teachers with pathognomonic beliefs having less effective engagement with students than those with interventionist beliefs, which undermines the rights of marginalized students.

For much of the twentieth century, the medical model of disability prevailed and doctors diagnosed children from four categories: feeble-minded, moral-defective, imbecile, or idiot. Idiots were judged to be 'ineducable'. The 1970 Education Act established the absolute right of all children, irrespective of their disability, to a full education and the 'ineducable' category was finally abolished. However, no provision was made for children with severe learning difficulties and many continued to be educated in specialist schools or hospitals where behaviourist techniques were favoured. Notions that this kind of classical conditioning could lead to effective education were heavily criticized as learning without understanding (McConkey 1981) and the creation of banks of non-transferable skills (Collis and Lacey 1996). So at a very basic level, the right of children with severe special needs to an appropriate education was not being met. Moreover, their right to be treated with dignity and respect was being disregarded in language that described them as 'sub-normal' and 'mentally handicapped'.

The Warnock Report (1978) succeeded in replacing these terms with a less stigmatizing descriptor, 'learning difficulties'. This heralded the onset of a social model of disability in which the disabling factors were regarded not as within-child deficits but as the failure of society to adapt learning environments to accommodate their needs. The closure of many special schools followed as increasing numbers of children with learning difficulties were included in mainstream schools. At one level this was an advancement of the rights through the upholding of the prerogative to attend a school within their own local community. At another level, what first appeared to be a valuing of rights later became an infringement of those rights as some parents bemoaned the loss of special schools with their smaller classes and specialist support. The consideration of rights, therefore, is more about the right of children and families to *choose* the educational provision they consider to be most appropriate.

Pupil-led research

The final section of this chapter is devoted to an exposition of children exercising the right to lead their own research about aspects of their education (Fielding 2004; Kellett 2005). This initiative provides an evidence base for issues of concern and increases the likelihood of transformative action (Bucknall 2009). The Children's Research Centre at the Open University (http://childrens-research-centre.open.ac.uk) trains and supports children and young people to undertake their own research. Two examples of projects that raise educational rights issues follow.

Dandridge's (aged 10) research (2008: 5) concerned gender rights. She reported that 62 percent of Year 5 pupils (nine- and 10-year-olds) considered girls were favoured in their primary school. Eighty-six percent of them also thought that boys were punished more than girls. Eighty percent of Year 6 pupils (10 and 11-year-olds) had the perception that girls were more often chosen for 'special jobs'. Dandridge's research also included some lesson observations. She describes one English lesson where 12 questions were asked by the teacher, of which nine were answered by girls and three by boys. In the same lesson there were 19 occasions of boys being told off compared to four occasions with girls. A similar picture emerged from observations in Art and Maths lessons. Dandridge concluded that most teachers wanted to be fair to all pupils irrespective of gender and there was no deliberate intention to favour girls, but suggested they might be doing this without realising it. She presented her research to a panel of teachers and governors. As a consequence, pupil gender equity was added to the school's planning document as a professional development action point.

Priyasha's (aged 13) research (2010) explored issues around homework for Year 8 students (12- and 13-year-olds). She started from the interesting premise that learning occurs in many places and is not confined to school. Her contention was that young people's time outside of school is precious and there are opportunities to learn from many experiences, and homework had the potential to constrain this. Therefore homework needs to be relevant and meaningful, otherwise it risks infringing those rights. Priyasha analysed her findings in conjunction with her school's homework policy document. She found that a lot of students thought that homework was being given for the sake of being given instead of having a purpose, which was at odds with the school homework policy. The time allocation for Year 8 homework was 30 minutes, but 81 percent of students spent much more than that. Data also revealed that a lot of homework did not get marked.

Future directions

Scandinavian countries are most likely to be the trailblazers of children's rights in education. Sweden banned corporal punishment a quarter of a century ahead of some of its European neighbours. Norway lowered the age of participation from 12 to seven, making it a legal requirement that seven-year-olds be given the opportunity to express themselves and legislating for 15-year-olds to make decisions about their own education, religion, and membership of organizations (Skivenes and Strandbu 2006). In other nation states, rights issues in education are following in the wake of child rights issues in society at large, notably the drive towards meaningful participation and voice in matters that affect their lives. In England, children's rights in education are likely to remain a contested domain for some time to come, with patchy execution varying from enthusiastic adoption in some schools to minimal legislative adherence in others. It will be strongest where pupil participation and voice initiatives are embraced.

A great many children spend the largest part of their childhood in full-time education. It is imperative that their human rights during that period are appropriately considered. Educational psychologists are frontline professionals who can do much to realize this goal.

Contact address: mary.kellett@open.ac.uk

References

Alderson, P. (2000) 'School students' views on school councils and daily life at school', *Children and Society*, 14: 121–134.

Bergmark, U., and Kostenius, C. (2009) 'Listen to me I have something to say: students' participation in research for sustainable school improvement', *Improving Schools*, 12: 249–260.

Bragg, S. (2001) 'Taking a joke: learning from the voices we don't want to hear', *Forum*, 43: 70–73.

Bucknall, S. (2009) *Children as researchers: exploring barriers in English primary schools*. Unpublished PhD thesis. Milton Keynes, UK: Open University.

Children's Act 1989 [Act of Parliament] London: HMSO.

Children's Act 2004 [Act of Parliament] London: HMSO.

Collis, M., and Lacey, P. (1996) *Interactive approaches to teaching*, London: David Fulton.

Cotmore, R. (2004) 'Organisational competence: the study of a school council in action', *Children and Society*, 18: 53–65.

Dandridge, H. (2008) *Are boys and girls treated differently in school?* [online]. Available at http://childrens-research-centre.open.ac.uk (retrieved 16 April 2011).

Davey, C. (2010) *Children's participation in decision-making*. Published by Participation Works for CRAE (Children's Rights Alliance England) and NCB (National Children's Bureau).

Devine, D. (2003) *Children, power and schooling: how childhood is structured in the primary school*, Stoke on Trent, UK: Trentham Books.

Education Act 1970 [Act of Parliament] London: HMSO.

Education Act 2002 [Act of Parliament] London: HMSO.

Every Child Matters 2003 Green Paper [Act of Parliament] London: HMSO.

Fielding, M. (2001) 'Students as radical agents of change', *Journal of Educational Change*, 2: 123–141.

Fielding, M. (2004) 'Transformative approaches to student voice: theoretical underpinnings, recalcitrant realities', *British Educational Research Journal*, 30: 295–311.

Fitzgerald, R., Graham, A., Smith, A., and Taylor, N. (2010) 'Children's participation as a struggle over recognition: exploring the promise of dialogue', in B. Percy-Smith and N. Thomas (eds.) *A handbook of children and young people's participation: perspectives from theory to practice*, London: Routledge (pp. 293–305).

Garner, R. (2010) 'Alarm raised at pupils' power over appointment of teachers', *The Independent* [online]. Available at www.independent.co.uk (retrieved 3 April 2010).

Hamill, P., and Boyd, B. (2002) 'Equality, fairness and rights – the young person's voice', *British Journal of Special Education*, 29: 111–117.

Harris, N. (2009) 'Playing catch-up in the schoolyard? Children and young people's "voice" and education rights in the UK', *International Journal of Law Policy and the Family*, 23: 331–336.

James, A., Jenks, C., and Prout, A. (1998). *Theorizing childhood*, Cambridge: Polity Press.

John, M. (1996) *Children in charge: the child's right to resources*, London: Jessica Kingsley.

Kellett, M. (2005) *How to develop children as researchers: step-by-step guidance to teaching the research process*, London: Sage.

Kellett, M. (2009) 'Children and young people's voices', in H. Montgomery and M. Kellett (eds.) *Children and young people's worlds: developing frameworks for integrated practice*, Bristol: Policy Press (pp. 237–252).

Lansdown, G. (2005) *The evolving capacities of the child*, Florence: Innocenti Research Centre.

Leitch, R., and Mitchell, S. (2007) 'Caged birds and cloning machines: how student imagery "speaks" to us about cultures of schooling and student participation', *Improving Schools*, 10: 53–71.

Lensmire, T. (1998) 'Rewriting student voice', *Journal of Curriculum Studies*, 30: 261–291.

Lodge, C. (2005) 'From hearing voices to engaging in dialogue: problematising student participation in school improvement', *Journal of Educational Change*, 6: 125–46.

Lundy, L. (2007) '"Voice" is not enough: conceptualising Article 12 of the United Nations Convention on the Rights of the Child', *British Educational Research Journal*, 33: 927–942.

Mayall, B. (2000) 'Conversations with children: working with generational issues', in P. Christensen and A. James (eds.) *Research with children: perspectives and practices*, London: Routledge Falmer (pp. 120–35).

McConkey, R. (1981) 'Education without understanding', *Special Education: Forward Trends*, 8: 8–11.

Office of the First Minister and Deputy First Minister (2006) *Our children and young people – our pledge: a ten year strategy for children and young people in Northern Ireland 2006–16*, Belfast: OFMDFM.

Priyasha (2010) *Is homework affecting extra-curricular activities?* [online]. Available at http://childrens-research-centre.open.ac.uk (retrieved 16 April 2011).

Robinson, C., and Taylor, C. (2007) 'Theorizing student voice: values and perspectives', *Improving Schools*, 10: 5–17.

Rudduck, J. (2006) 'The past, the papers and the project', *Educational Review*, 58: 131–143.

Rudduck, J., and Fielding, M. (2006) 'Student voice and the perils of popularity', *Educational Review*, 58: 219–231.

Rudduck, J., and Flutter, J. (2004) *How to improve your school: giving pupils a voice*, London: Continuum.

Scottish Executive (2005) *Getting it right for every child: proposals for action*, Edinburgh: Scottish Executive.

Shier, H. (2001) 'Pathways to participation: openings, opportunities and obligations', *Children and Society*, 15: 107–117.

Skivenes, M., and Strandbu, A. (2006) 'A child's perspective and children's participation', *Children, Youth and Environments*, 16: 10–27.

Smyth, J. (2006) '"When students have power": student engagement, student voice, and the possibilities for school reform around "dropping out" of school', *International Journal of Leadership in Education*, 9: 285–298.

Tarapdar, S., and Kellett, M. (2011) *Young people's voices on cyberbullying: what can age comparisons tell us?*, London: Diana Award publication.

United Nations (1989) *Convention on the Rights of the Child*, Geneva: United Nations.

Warnock, M. (1978) *Special Educational Needs. Report of the Committee of Enquiry into the Education of Handicapped Children and Young People*. London: HMSO.

Welsh Assembly Government (2004) *Children and young people: rights to action*, Cardiff: Welsh Assembly Government.

Whitty, G., and Wisby, E. (2007) *Real decision making? School councils in action*, Research report DCSF RR001, Nottingham: DfES Publications.

Woodhead, M. (2005) 'Early childhood development: a question of rights', *International Journal of Early Childhood*, 37: 79–98.

Woodhead, M. (2006) 'Early childhood development: a question of rights', in *A Guide to General Comment 7: Implementing Child Rights in Early Childhood*, The Hague: Bernard van Leer Foundation (pp. 145–50).

Woodhead, M., and Faulkner, D. (2008) 'Subjects, objects or participants? Dilemmas of psychological research with children', in P. Christiansen and A. James (eds.) *Research with children: perspectives and practices*, London: Falmer Press/Routledge (pp. 10–39).

Wyness, M., Harrison, L., and Buchanan, I. (2004) 'Childhood, politics and ambiguity: towards an agenda for children's political inclusion', *Sociology*, 38: 81–99.

3

INTRODUCTION TO EDUCATIONAL PSYCHOLOGY PRACTICE

Terri Passenger

UNIVERSITY OF GLOUCESTERSHIRE, UK, AND PRIVATE EDUCATIONAL PSYCHOLOGIST, UK

The term 'educational psychology' is in itself something of a 'puzzle' for, as James (2001: 3) once said, 'Psychology is a science and teaching is an art'. So, it is important from the outset to appreciate that any combination of these two will clearly call for a unique blend of scientific knowledge and skilled applied practice. Thus, unlike some of their laboratory-bound colleagues, educational psychologists are 'applied scientists' working across the social contexts of the school, the family, and society. Educational psychology, like education itself, is influenced by both political and societal factors and this becomes particularly evident when looking at the broader, international picture where even the 'prevalence' of educational psychologists is quite diverse: while countries such as the USA, Finland, Denmark, and France report a significant presence of educational psychologists, Jimerson and his colleagues found that in German and Italian schools, educational psychologists are 'almost non-existent' (Jimerson et al. 2008: 22). Boyle and Lauchlan's chapter on *A comparative overview of educational psychology across continents* (Chapter 4, this volume) looks in greater depth at this international perspective while the present chapter focuses primarily on the many changes that have taken place in England in response to government directives, and highlights the current 'shifting sand' nature of the job and the resulting reports of low confidence within the profession (Boyle and Lauchlan 2009).

Despite clear published guidance on occupational standards (British Psychological Society, 2006), there is barely an educational psychology book published, or an in-service training session held, that does not begin by asking the question: 'What do educational psychologists do?' Indeed, educational psychologists themselves could be accused of encouraging this 'professional inquisition' by their seemingly persistent introspection of their own role in a way that would be unheard of in any other professional group – lawyers, for instance. Rather than promulgating such self-critical 'navel-gazing', this chapter looks more positively at the valuable role educational psychologists can play in:

- assessment
- collaborative work
- problem solving
- research
- training.

It concludes by considering the future of the profession, both nationally and internationally, in an ever-shifting socio-political climate.

Assessment

From the earliest days of educational psychology, the profession has been associated with 'testing'. This association, and particularly the association with 'psychometric' testing, has however consistently attracted negative comments which, interestingly, in the main appear to emanate from within the profession itself.

Cyril Burt was, and probably remains, the best known of all British educational psychologists. His early work in the 1920s set a 'template' where formal, individual assessments came to be seen as the cornerstone of educational psychologists' work. Burt's earliest assessments were, however, based on a 'deficit' medical model where psychometric tests were used primarily to identify the 'feeble-minded' who were deemed to be in need of 'care' rather than 'education'. Later, when he turned his attentions to more able children, Burt championed the 11+ examination which 'filtered out' children who, regardless of their social class, would benefit from an academic education. At both stages of his career, Burt's test results were wholly influential in decisions regarding school-placements.

However, in the 1960s, there was growing research into the multiple factors 'external' to the child that can affect learning. Assessment began to move away from testing 'within-child' abilities and educational psychologists no longer arrived in school carrying a 'black bag' with a standardized intelligence test. They began instead to focus on a broader assessment of the child's 'life experience' by undertaking observations, recording notes of classroom behaviour, evaluating teaching/learning styles and conducting interviews with pupils, teachers, and parents. However, despite this reported 'surge' in more 'holistic' assessments, a recent international survey of school psychologists across some 48 countries reported that intelligence testing was still the most frequently used form of assessment worldwide (Jimerson, Oakland, and Yu 2010). Thus, it would seem, the public perception of the role remains largely unchanged: educational psychologists are still seen as 'testers'; and, in particular, 'intelligence testers'. It is therefore no surprise that today's highly trained body of educational psychologists continues to report in dismay that 'all teachers, parents and psychiatrists ever want to know is "What is the child's IQ?"' (Burden 1973: 8).

The role of the educational psychologist in the statutory process was, and indeed still is, to provide an assessment of a child's special educational needs and to make recommendations on how these needs can be addressed. There is recurring evidence that teachers and other professionals greatly value the unique role played by the educational psychologists in these individual assessments. So why, when their work in dealing with often complex individual casework is held in such high esteem by 'other' professionals, do many educational psychologists themselves not share this view? Perhaps it could be that educational psychologists themselves continue to see this form of assessment as identifying 'deficits' (Webster et al. 2003), and are trying to steer away from the 'treadmill of psychometric testing' (Love 2009: 5). Miller and Frederikson (2006) suggest that this 'reluctance' may stem from another 'negative' side-effect of such testing whereby the stereotype of an assessor who uses only psychometric testing has become synonymous with that of a 'resources gatekeeper' with the subtle inference that, when additional resourcing from the local authority is not recommended, educational psychologists may simply be protecting their employers' (i.e. the local authority's) budgets (Love 2009). This may offer some explanation for the almost 'guilty by association' mindset that exists within the profession whereby equating 'individual casework' with 'psychometric tests' results in the inherent supposition that psychometric testing should be seen as 'a bad thing' (Boyle and Lauchlan 2009).

The recent Green Paper (Department for Education, 2011), in proposing 'developmental surveillance' of children under the age of five years, would seem to have an inherent assumption that early, timely intervention will significantly lessen the former need for formal assessments. Any reduction in statutory assessment work then should be heralded as professionally 'liberating' for educational psychologists, allowing them 'to use their psychological skills more effectively' (Farrell et al. 2006: 4). Yet such reduction would seem to imply the question, 'Does denying psychometric or cognitive assessment always prove to be as liberating for the pupil?' It remains to be seen whether removing statutory assessments, which have often resulted in the award of additional local authority funding, is more a reflection of fast-growing budgetary constraints than a genuinely benign move towards identifying and meeting the needs of children at a younger age.

Whether scores on standardized tests of cognitive ability have any validity in 'predicting' subsequent academic attainment is also still hotly debated, but to vilify testing, and psychometric testing in particular, could be throwing the baby out with the bath water. Psychometric testing requires a carefully managed blend of science and art. It demands a keen understanding of the procedures and purposes of the test materials; specific interpersonal and observational skills when working one-to-one with pupils who may be young, disaffected, less able, or non-communicative; a sound knowledge of how to analyse and interpret data; and an ability to present this in a way that will be clear to those who may or may not have a full understanding of a pupils' needs (such as other professionals and parents).

The work of the educational psychologist has without doubt evolved from the early days when, line-managed by a County 'Medical' rather than a County 'Education' Officer, educational psychologists were merely 'IQ providers' (Love 2009) charged only with determining whether a child was 'educable'. In identifying a particular cognitive profile in those with complex needs, the educational psychologist in today's multi-disciplinary team not only can make a unique contribution to the diagnosis of a range of developmental disorders (see Section 4, this volume) and syndromes (e.g. Williams syndrome, foetal alcohol syndrome, and Tourette's syndrome) but can also take an active role in identifying the most effective intervention.

Collaborative work

The death of eight year old Victoria Climbie in 2000 led to a UK government-commissioned inquiry (Laming 2003), which highlighted and criticized the lack of appropriate training and liaison between professionals working with children and young people. The resulting report (Department for Education and Skills, DfES 2003) focused on the holistic needs of children and young people with the specific requirement that support services should be restructured into collaborative, community-based Children's Services.

Although, to the untrained eye, the work undertaken in these new multi-disciplinary teams appears little different from that carried out by the former Educational Psychology Services, educational psychologists now find themselves with a far broader remit: working with fostering and adoption teams, with youth offending services, with Child and Adolescent Mental Health (CAMHS) teams and in residential children's homes. The 'change' then, as Fallon and her colleagues suggest, may simply be that these opportunities for educational psychologists to undertake their customary broad range of work now occur 'systemically rather than opportunistically' (Fallon, Woods, and Rooney 2010: 13).

Internationally, the majority of psychologists are still based within the health-care (rather than the education) sector (Jimerson et al. 2008). So it may be that these newly formed Children's Services teams in England and Wales are bringing British-based psychologists more in line with their international colleagues by enabling them to work with professionals from a broad range of disciplines (e.g. health, social services, and law). In so doing, Fallon and her colleagues suggest, educational psychologists not only develop unique 'pragmatic coherence' skills by 'bridge-building' across these agencies but can often exert significant influence on decision-making in terms of educational, care, and mental health provision and placement because of their valuable knowledge of the resources available within a given local authority (Fallon et al. 2010).

Working in this new way with teams from very different professional backgrounds, however, clearly demands a more flexible, coordinated service delivery and unsurprisingly this new way of working has not been without its problems. Despite efforts to 'pull together' professionals from different disciplines, physically (by combining office accommodation) as well as philosophically, Cameron et al. (2008: 259) believe that the advent of integrated children's services in local authorities has resulted in a 'less distinctive' professional identity for educational psychologists. This viewpoint is supported by concerns that the new breadth of educational psychology work, across different contexts and fulfilling different functions, may cause confusion 'within' the profession itself. Reports that many educational psychologists insist they need to maintain their professionalism through regular contact with other educational psychologists emphasizes the 'challenge of collaborating' when educational psychologists working with colleagues from very different backgrounds need to learn the 'language' of these other professionals and to accommodate different professional cultures, visions, and legislative imperatives: a challenge that has proved to be 'at once stimulating and rewarding and sometimes frustrating and exhausting' (Fallon et al. 2010: 13).

Problem solving

If the demands for statutory assessments following the 1981 and 1983 Education and Science Acts (Department for Education and Science, 1981, 1983) may have 'limited' the educational psychologists' role (Farrell et al. 2006), then it seems the introduction of the new multidisciplinary teams may once again enable educational psychologists to use their professional skill more fully by not only contributing to the identification of problems but also promoting new initiatives to address them.

Traditionally, educational psychologists have worked alongside schools to address problems and implement change. Yet, following the *Every Child Matters* (ECM) initiative (DfES 2004) comes the acknowledgement that children's lives are split between school and home and that events in one environment can impact significantly on events in the other (see Lewis, Miell, and Coiffait, Chapter 12, this volume). In line with the ECM focus on the child, rather than focusing solely on the school system, educational psychologists have now begun to employ a range of 'systemic therapies' working across the broader 'systems' of the school, the home and the community.

Fox (2009), however, notes some confusion (even among educational psychologists themselves) regarding the distinction between 'system work' and 'systemic therapy'. Whereas traditional 'system work' focused on organizational change, the newer 'systemic therapies' set out to identify the roles played by individuals within a given community. For example, structural family therapy (Cottrell and Boston 2002) can identify whether problematic behaviour in school or at home arises as a result of blurred boundaries between parent and child, while narrative therapy (White and Epston 1990) highlights the damaging 'person as a problem' effect of using terminology such as 'she is dyslexic' or 'he is autistic'. Although educational psychologists' use of therapies such as these is still comparatively rare, Pellegrini (2009: 281) found solution-focused brief therapy (SFBT) to be 'a clear favourite of educational psychologists' possibly, he suggests, because

SFBT demands only a comparatively short-term commitment and is, understandably perhaps, a form of intervention that is obviously more 'attractive' to a profession already over-burdened with heavy caseloads.

Research

In England, these changes to the delivery of educational psychology services coincided with the long-awaited, much-debated introduction of a three-year doctoral training route for all new educational psychologists. The titles of several of the programmes, such as the University of East London's *Doctorate in Educational and Child Psychology*, make it clear that educational psychologists are now fully trained, competent 'applied' psychologists who will use their research-based knowledge in a working arena far wider than the former close focus on schooling. Interestingly, in Scotland, although there is currently no requirement for doctoral-level qualification, the choice of the term 'psychological services' rather than 'school' or 'educational psychological services' has for some time identified this broader role of the psychologist both within and beyond the education system. The Currie Report (Scottish Executive Education Department 2002), perhaps pre-empting legislation elsewhere in the UK, had clearly outlined the five functions of work (assessment, intervention, consultation, training, and research) that should be delivered at the level of the individual child or family, at the level of the school or establishment such as a children's home, at a post-school level (i.e. in a young offender unit) and at the level of the local authority (Mackay 2009).

The demand for a doctoral training route in England arose in part from comparisons between the parallel people-centred professions of education and medicine: Webster and Beveridge (1997) noted in particular the differing attitudes to research between the two professions. They found that in medicine there was a constant search by practitioners for better diagnoses, more efficient interventions and more effective treatments. Conversely, educational research was usually carried out by academics and neither disseminated in schools nor valued by teachers. So educational psychologists with their scientific training and their propensity to 'oil the wheels' between pupils and teachers, schools and homes, schools and local fund holders were in an ideal position to 'negotiate and design research briefs, prepare bids and secure funding, implement, administer, commission, evaluate research' (Webster and Beveridge, 1997: 161) and so enhance the quality of teaching and learning in schools. Burden (1994) had earlier taken a similar viewpoint and proposed two types of research that should be endemic in educational psychology work: the first, 'process–product' focuses on linear causality between variables and the second, 'interpretative meaning' focuses on the views and the context of the clients themselves.

However, despite the increasing and seemingly convincing calls for the profession to be research-based (Edwards 2002), there is to date a noticeable dearth of evidence that research has taken any 'priority' in the profession. As Boyle and Lauchlan (2009) ask: why, if educational psychologists are fortunate enough to study their discipline not once, but twice at university (i.e. at graduate 'and' postgraduate level), are they not researching and applying their discipline? It may be that once admitted to the profession many educational psychologists find their aspirations to continue research and apply psychology in educational settings are thwarted by administrative work, statutory assessments, and endless meetings (Webster, Hingley, and Franey 2000). Or it could be, as one study noted, the continuing 'preference' of some local authorities to call upon the services of external academic consultants to carry out school-based research and evaluation work (Eodanable 2005).

Whatever the reason, the increasing demand for accountability in the caring professions, coupled with the requirement since 2009 for educational psychologists in the UK to be legally registered with the Health Professions Council, would suggest that the practice of applied or practitioner psychologists not only can but should emulate that of their medical colleagues, in that research should indicate the evidence on which they base their practice. Educational psychologists' professional practice must reflect the best available research evidence and the interventions they recommend or initiate should be monitored using appropriate outcome measures.

However, as Cameron et al. (2008. 266) suggest, the task of making the link between research and the 'often-messy demands of the real world . . . requires considerable creativity and high level communication skills' and, it could be argued, a high level of appropriate professional training.

Training

The debate concerning educational psychology training was waged for years both within and outside the profession. The final decision that there should be 'only' one, doctoral training route (in England) was in response to widespread demands for a greater depth of training that would bring educational psychologists in line with their clinical psychology and medical colleagues. Yet, particularly at a time when there is clear evidence that as few as 20 percent of other countries demand, or indeed offer, doctoral training for school psychologists (Jimerson et al. 2010), the question must be asked: Has the doctoral training really addressed the former concerns that educational psychologists lacked not only the training but the confidence to emulate the practices of their clinical and medical colleagues (Webster et al. 2003)? The answer would seem to be that for newly qualifying trainees it has: reports indicate they are confident in negotiating and designing research briefs and securing funding to implement, evaluate, and communicate their research. However, Monsen et al. (2009) found that educational psychologists who qualified prior to 2006 were still reluctant to undertake research and tended to pass any applied research work to psychology graduates who are working (prior to joining a doctoral training programme) as Assistant Psychologists in the same Educational Psychology Service (EPS).

This reluctance of some educational psychologists to undertake research, Eodanable and Lauchlan (2009) suggest, emphasizes the need for 'research training' programmes to form a regular part of continuing professional development, and that this training should be monitored by the profession's regulatory body, the Health Professions Council. However, as Cameron and his colleagues (2008) comment, there is little incentive for educational psychologists to undertake research training when many local authorities are now disbanding EPS teams and for the individual educational psychologists there is little hope of promotion or any immediate financial reward.

Conclusion

In a paper aptly named *Educational psychologists: the early search for an identity*, Love (2009: 7) cites three topical questions facing educational psychologists some 60 years ago, namely:

- What can you do that no-one else can do?
- Who is the client?
- Who needs Local Education Authority Psychological Services?

Although this chapter began by suggesting that the questions today are little different, the answers would seem both to reflect and to anticipate some significant changes in the profession of educational psychology as a whole.

What can you do that no-one else can do?

Despite continuing debate, to Fallon et al. (2010: 14) the main role of the educational psychologist is clear: educational psychologists are 'fundamentally scientist-practitioners who utilize psychological skills, through consultation, assessment, intervention, research and training, at different levels (organisational, group or individual) across educational, community and care settings, with a variety of role partners'. This chapter has demonstrated that the 'unique' blend of these high-level skills firmly establishes why educational psychologists are professionally qualified and strategically placed to do what 'no-one else can do'.

Who is the client?

The Lamb Inquiry (Department for Children, Schools and Families, DCSF, 2009) investigated ways in which the Special Educational Needs assessment process might be improved and recommended that parents should have 'direct' access to the multi-agency teams working with children and young people. Historically, the work of the educational psychologist has been primarily school-based, working with children, their parents and their teachers, so educational psychologists have always had a unique and 'strategic vantage point' standing between education and the wider community and so have always been in a prime position to alert the education service 'to the community's needs and in particular to the needs of the underprivileged' (Loxley 1978: 103). Educational psychologists may then already be 'ahead of the game' in that their traditional role in working 'with' parents and teachers 'for' the benefit of children and young people indicates they have always had a clear professional understanding of 'who the client is'.

Who needs LEA psychological services?

With a growing number of educational psychologists undertaking expert witness work in educational tribunals and civil law cases (Ireland 2008), there seems good evidence that educational psychology services are 'needed'; what seems less certain at the present time is whether the majority of these services will, necessarily, remain within the jurisdiction of local authorities. The House of Commons Select Committee report on Special Educational Needs (DCSF, 2009) made strong recommendations that an evaluation of a number of different educational psychology service models should be carried out. In response to this, the Association of Educational Psychologists (AEP, 2010) has outlined a range of models whereby educational psychologists would work as now for local authorities but with a service-level agreement between the EPS and local authority that 'guarantees' the EPS has independence in providing advice: it can only be hoped that this may, perhaps, finally rid the profession of its historic 'gatekeeper to resource' label. Alternatively, educational psychologists may be employed in a 'stand alone' service where a local authority 'buys in' their services, yet this is questioned by Fallon et al. (2010) in their observation that there will be less money held centrally within a local authority to 'buy in' these traditional services. As some practitioners in private practice are already reporting an increase in appointments in maintained schools, it seems that the third option of a 'genuine private company' that is fully independent of the local authority may be a real possibility. However, it remains to be seen if these services will be 'publicly funded' as the AEP advocates. So while there is little doubt as to 'who "needs" psychological services?' perhaps the question should be rephrased to ask 'who will actually be able to "access" psychological services?'

This change in how EPS are commissioned will bring into sharp focus the need for regular evaluation of work in relation to its effectiveness in improving outcomes for children and young people. While there are 'clear parallels' between the range of practices apparent today and that of Burt some 90 years ago (Frederikson and Miller 2008: 7), the arguments for and against individual casework continue and, have contributed in no small way to the eternal frustration within the profession (Leadbetter 2000). Yet such 'casework', so positively valued by other professionals, can bring together every aspect of the educational psychologist's skill as assessor, collaborator, problem solver, trainer, and researcher and, in future, with more emphasis on multi-disciplinary and multi-agency working, it seems plausible there will be more opportunities for such 'unique' casework. It would, then, seem perverse, at a time when 'accountability' is paramount, for educational psychologists to move away from an area of work where they are so highly valued; as Boyle and Lauchlan (2009: 76) suggest, 'EPs [educational psychologists] may seem like "turkeys voting for Christmas" if they dismiss their unique professional value in individual assessment and casework'. So what is the future for educational psychologists, not only in England and Wales, but for the profession as a whole?

The profession of psychology, and particularly educational or school psychology, is relatively young and, in many parts of the world, still emerging and, Hall and Altmaier (2008) warn, there is a pressing need for universally agreed standards in recruitment, training and practice within the profession. However, it would seem that such 'global' standards for educational psychology practice may first require educational psychologists in England and Wales to undertake a more productive form of 'professional navel-gazing'. Relatively recently the American psychologist, Martin Seligman, used the term 'Positive Psychology' to address the seemingly intransient 'deficit' model with the aim of changing the focus of psychology 'from preoccupation only with repairing the worst things in life to also building positive qualities' (Seligman and Csikszentmihalyi 2000: 5). Educational psychologists impact on the lives of the children and young people with whom they work, but if they are to realize their own unique and very specific worth as scientific practitioners in the new era of multi-professional, multi-national working, then perhaps they now need to adopt the mantra of Positive Psychology for themselves.

Contact address: tp@aspirepsychologists.co.uk

References

Association of Educational Psychologists (2010) *Principles for the delivery of Educational Psychology Services, AEP/050/10*, London: AEP.

Boyle, C., and Lauchlan, F. (2009) 'Applied psychology and the case for individual casework: some reflections on the role of the educational psychologist', *Educational Psychology in Practice*, 25: 71–84.

British Psychological Society (BPS) (2006) *National occupational standards*, Leicester: BPS.

Burden, R. (1973) 'If we throw the tests out of the window, what is there left to do?', *AEP Journal*, 3(5): 6–9.

Burden, R. (1994) 'Trends and developments in educational psychology: an international perspective', *School Psychology International*, 15: 293–347.

Cameron, R. J., Frederickson, N., Lunt, I., and Lang, J. (2008) 'Changing professional views of continuing professional development doctorates in educational psychology', *Educational Psychology in Practice*, 24: 251–267.

Cottrell, D., and Boston, P. (2002) 'The effectiveness of systemic family therapy for children and adolescents', *Journal of Child Psychology and Psychiatry*, 43: 573–586.

Department for Children, Schools and Families (2009) *Special educational needs and parental confidence* (The Lamb Inquiry), Nottingham: DCSF Publications.

Department for Education (DfE) (2011) *Support and aspiration: a new approach to special educational needs*, London: DfE.

Department for Education and Science (DES) (1981) *Education Act*, London: HMSO.

Department for Education and Science (DES) (1983) *Education Act*, London: HMSO.

Department for Education and Skills (DfES) (2003) *Every Child Matters (Green Paper)*, London: HMSO.

Department for Education and Skills (DfES) (2004) *Every Child Matters: Change for Children*, London: HMSO.

Edwards, A. (2002) 'Responsible research: ways of being a researcher', *British Educational Research Journal*, 28: 157–168.

Eodanable, M. (2005) *Practitioner-research by educational psychologists*. Unpublished MSc Education thesis. Edinburgh: University of Edinburgh.

Eodanable, M., and Lauchlan, F. (2009) 'The advance of research and evaluation skills by EPs: implications for training and professional development', *Educational Psychology in Practice*, 25: 113–124.

Fallon, K., Woods, K., and Rooney, S. (2010) 'A discussion of the developing role of educational psychologists within Children's Services', *Educational Psychology in Practice*, 26: 1–23.

Farrell, P., Woods, K., Lewis, S., Rooney, S., Squires, G., and O'Connor, M. (2006) *A review of the functions and contribution of educational psychologists in England and Wales in light of 'Every Child Matters: Change for Children'*, Nottingham: DfES Publications.

Fox, M. (2009) 'Working with systems and thinking systemically – disentangling the crossed wires', *Educational Psychology in Practice*, 25: 247–258.

Frederikson, N., and Miller, A. (2008) 'What do educational psychologists do?', in N. Frederikson, A. Miller, and T. Kline (eds.) *Educational psychology*, London: Hodder Education.

Hall, J., and Altmaier, E. (2008) *Global promise: quality assurance and accountability in professional psychology*, New York: Oxford University Press.

Ireland, J. (2008) 'Psychologists as witnesses: background and good practice in the delivery of evidence', *Educational Psychology in Practice*, 24: 115–128.

James, W. (2001) *Talks to teachers on psychology and to students on some of life's ideals*, New York: Dover Publications.

Jimerson, S., Graydon, K., Skokut, M., Alghorani, M., Kanjaradze, A., and Forster, J. (2008) 'The International School Psychology Survey: Data from Georgia, Switzerland and the United Arab Emirates', *School Psychology International*, 29: 3–28.

Jimerson, S., Oakland, T., Renshaw, T., Fraser, S., and Ruderman, M. (2010) 'Prevalence and characteristics of school psychology preparation programs around the world', *Research Brief*, 4.1.2010, International Institute of School Psychology.

Jimerson, S., Oakland, T., and Yu, R. (2010) 'Assessment, interventions, and conceptual foundations used by school psychologists around the world', *Research Brief*, 6.22.2010, International Institute of School Psychology.

Laming, H. (2003) *Report of the inquiry into the death of Victoria Climbie*, London: HMSO.

Leadbetter, J. (2000) 'Patterns of service delivery in educational psychology services: some implications for practice', *Educational Psychology in Practice*, 16: 449–60.

Love, P. (2009) 'Educational psychologists: the early search for an identity', *Educational Psychology in Practice*, 25: 3–8.

Loxley, D. (1978) 'Community psychology', in W. Gillham (ed.) *Restructuring educational psychology*, London: Croom Helm.

Mackay, T. (2009) 'Post-school educational psychology services: international perspectives on a distinctive Scottish development', *Educational and Child Psychology*, 26: 8–21.

Miller, A., and Frederikson, N. (2006) 'Generalizable findings and ideographic problems: struggles and successes for educational psychologists as scientist-practitioners', in D. A. Lane and S. Corrie (eds.) *The modern scientist practitioner: a guide to practice in psychology*, Hove: Routledge.

Monsen, J., Brown, E., Aktha, Z., and Khan, S. (2009) 'An evaluation of a pre-training assistant educational psychologist programme', *Educational Psychology in Practice*, 25: 369–383.

Pellegrini, D. (2009) Applied systemic theory and educational psychology: can the twain ever meet? *Educational Psychology in Practice*, 25: 271–286.

Scottish Executive Education Department (2002) *Review of provision of educational psychology services in Scotland*, Edinburgh: SEED.

Seligman, M., and Csikszentmihalyi, M. (2000) 'Positive psychology: an introduction', *American Psychologist*, 55: 5–14.

Webster, A., and Beveridge, M. (1997) 'The role of educational psychologists in educational research: some implications for professional training', *Educational Psychology in Practice*, 13: 155–164.

Webster, A., Hingley, P., and Franey, J. (2000) 'Professionalization and the reduction of uncertainty: a study of new entrants to educational psychology', *Educational Psychology in Practice*, 16: 431–448.

Webster, A., Maliphant, R., Feiler, A., Hoyle, E., and Franey, J. (2003) 'The development of a profession: reframing the role of educational psychologists within the context of organisational culture', in R. Sutherland, G. Claxton, and A. Pollard (eds.) *Learning and teaching where world views meet*, Stoke-on-Trent: Trentham Books.

White, M., and Epston, D. (1990) *Narrative means to therapeutic ends*, New York: Norton.

4

A COMPARATIVE OVERVIEW OF EDUCATIONAL PSYCHOLOGY ACROSS CONTINENTS

Christopher Boyle and Fraser Lauchlan

MONASH UNIVERSITY, AUSTRALIA; CAGLIARI UNIVERSITY, ITALY; AND THE
UNIVERSITY OF STRATHCLYDE, UK

The profession of educational psychology (also referred to as 'school psychology') is one that has been around in some countries for almost 100 years (e.g. the UK), while in others it is still not yet recognized as a profession at all (e.g. Angola, Bangladesh, and Colombia). While there have been some seminal texts in the past 30 years that have provided interesting data on international comparisons of educational psychology (Burden 1994; Lindsay 1992; Lunt 1991; Oakland and Cunningham 1992) it is really only in the past five to 10 years that one has begun to gain a better understanding of educational psychology across the world. Since 2004, the research by Shane Jimerson and colleagues from the University of California, under the auspices of the International School Psychology Association (ISPA), has played a crucial part in gaining better knowledge of the number of educational psychologists there are across the world, in which countries the profession exists, and the various roles and responsibilities that they have (Jimerson et al. 2004, 2006, 2008a, 2008b, 2009a, 2009b, 2010). This chapter will consider what educational psychology means across the continents and afford the reader an understanding of the role of the educational psychologist in different parts of the world.

Demographics: How many educational psychologists are there in the world?

Previous estimates have put a figure of around 87,000 (Oakland and Cunningham 1992); however, a more recent survey of 51 countries that are known to have educational psychologists has estimated the figure to be around 76,100 (Jimerson et al. 2009b). It is acknowledged that the latter figure is an underestimate since it was taken from just 51 countries included in the study, whereas previous research by the same authors (Jimerson et al. 2008b) reported that, of the 192 Member States of the United Nations, there is evidence of educational psychology in 83 countries across the world.

Oakland and Jimerson (2008) defined the characteristics of those countries where educational psychology is recognized as a profession according to the following five criteria: (i) where there is a highly developed and legally mandated education system, able to provide an education to all children, including those children who have additional support needs, (ii) where there is also an established higher education system, capable of providing suitable training to prospective educational psychologists, (iii) where psychology as a discipline is recognized as an essential part of providing services aimed at helping adults and children, (iv) where there are educational psychology professionals who provide such a service, from preschool through to secondary school and beyond, and who work in mainstream and special schools, (v) where there is a high gross national product that is able to provide the resources necessary to fund such services.

It is perhaps unsurprising, therefore, that less than half of the countries of the world can provide a sustainable educational psychology service led by a burgeoning educational psychology profession. Indeed, of the 1.89 billion population of children across the world, it has been estimated that 379 million children will not have access to any educational psychology service at all, and another 939 million children will have access to a service that has a psychologist–child ratio of less than 1:10,000 (Jimerson et al. 2009b).

Defining the profession of educational psychology

Educational psychologists have long held an obsession with defining their role; one that Gibb (1998: 19) noted anecdotally can sometimes lead to a situation where:

> it is not uncommon for [the educational psychologists] to include a session on 'The Role of the Educational Psychologist'. It is perhaps some kind of psychological phenomenon that the irony of this is seldom remarked upon, even when it is presented year after year by a school's educational psychologist of many years' standing.

It is therefore an almost impossible challenge to provide a definition of the role of the educational psychologist that covers the 83 countries of the world where the profession exists. However, Jimerson et al. (2007: 1), in their research of the identity of the profession the world over, have attempted to do so. They define the role as:

> one that collectively provides individual assessment of children who may display cognitive, emotional, social or behavioural difficulties; develops and implements primary and secondary intervention programmes; consults with teachers, parents and other relevant professionals; engages in programme development and evaluation; conducts research and helps prepare and supervise others.

The current authors endorse this definition, with the possible addition of the specification of the delivery of in-service training, more commonly to teaching staff but also to other professional groups (though it is acknowledged that such training could be covered in the above definition, if not specified as such). Jimerson et al. (2008b: 132) provide an extensive list of the number of different titles that educational psychologists have around the world, the most common being 'school psychologist', but also the following: 'counsellor, professional of educational psychology, psychopedagog, psychologist in education, psychologist in the schools'.

Most of the data-gathering regarding the status of educational psychology across the world has been through the use of the International School Psychology Survey (ISPS) (Jimerson et al. 2008a). It contains 46 items that focus on five key issues: (i) characteristics of educational psychologists, (ii) the training and regulation of the profession, (iii) roles and responsibilities, (iv) challenges, and (v) research. This will now be explored, in some detail, in this chapter.

Characteristics of educational psychologists

Publications by Jimerson and colleagues that have reported the use of the ISPS have involved over 800 educational psychologists in the following 15 countries: Albania, Australia, China, Cyprus, England, Egypt, Estonia, Georgia, Germany, Greece, Italy, New Zealand, Russia, Switzerland, and the United Arab Emirates (UAE) (Jimerson et al. 2004, 2006, 2008a, 2009a, 2010), thus representing the following continents: Europe, Africa, Asia, and Australasia. While some may consider this research to be reasonably representative of the profession of educational psychology across the world, a degree of caution must be exerted in interpreting the results since many countries are not represented. Moreover, there may be sampling issues within the diverse range of countries surveyed and possible implications on the reliability of data for comparative purposes given the necessity to translate the ISPS from English into more than 10 different languages.

Demographics: gender, age, and working hours

The people who make up the profession of educational psychology are predominantly female – up to 90–100 percent in some of the countries surveyed (Albania, Estonia, Georgia, and Russia) – while others were more evenly balanced, around 50 percent (Egypt, Germany, the UAE). However, most countries report a male–female ratio of around 1:2. Indeed, it is predicted that the proportion of females will only increase, as the countries that have an even split have a greater number of older practitioners, more of whom are male, thus distorting the figures somewhat, as more and more females have entered the profession in recent years (Jimerson et al. 2006). The age range of educational psychologists surveyed appears to be related to the number of years the profession has existed, i.e. there are more older psychologists in the countries where the profession has been in existence for more time (e.g. Germany, age range: 33–64, mean = 53 years, compared to the UAE, age range: 20–55, mean = 33 years) (Jimerson et al. 2006, 2008a).

Generally, educational psychologists appear to work similar hours per week, regardless of the country where they are working. The majority of respondents indicated that their average working week was between 36 and 40 hours (Jimerson et al. 2006). There is much more variability in the level of supervision offered for educational psychologists across countries; for example, in Georgia only 3 percent of respondents receive supervision, while in Albania 80 percent of respondents receive such support. In many countries the figure was around 50–60 percent of respondents that receive supervision (Jimerson et al. 2004, 2006, 2008a).

Psychologist–child ratios

Psychologist–child ratios differ widely across countries; a list of ratios for 51 of the 83 countries that practise educational psychology is provided in Jimerson et al. (2009b). In some countries (e.g. the USA) an educational psychologist might be based in only one or two schools, while in others (e.g. England and Wales) educational psychologists might be responsible for 20 or more schools (and possibly other agencies), based in a central office alongside other psychologists who make up the local authority team. Of the 51 countries surveyed in Jimerson et al. (2009b), only 12 were found to have ratios of more than 1:2,000 (Australia, Canada, Denmark, Estonia, Israel, Lithuania, the Netherlands, Scotland, Spain, Switzerland, Turkey, and the USA).

Work preferences of educational psychologists

Respondents were asked about their likes and dislikes about the job, and common responses across countries for what they like about the profession were 'working with students and families, producing positive change', and 'professional autonomy and flexibility'. Common responses regarding least favourite aspects of the job included 'administrative responsibilities', 'overwhelming workload' and 'conflicts', for example between school and parents (Jimerson et al. 2004, 2006, 2008a).

Models of practice

Educational psychology continues to evolve as directions in psychology and education alter and move from more traditional practices. For example, a within-child deficit model that was commonly used by educational psychologists to help inform their assessment and intervention work is now generally considered to be outdated. Instead, more and more practitioners are beginning to involve themselves in a positive psychology paradigm such as that proposed by Seligman (2007), which can be a very effective way for educational psychologists to offer what the authors of this chapter would call 'overt psychological practice' (see studies by Toland and Boyle 2008; Toland and Carrigan 2011, for examples of this type of innovative practice). Overt psychological practice involves psychology that is being practised and can be seen as such by most people, whether they know much about psychology or not. Annan and Priestley (2012: 335) suggest that 'positive psychology appears therefore to have been well integrated into school psychology's story through the recognition of contextualized, systemic models of conceptualization'.

Under the traditional models of practice – that is, based on a deficit model of the child – it is disputable as to whether the level of help afforded to the client was of sufficient quality to change outcomes. However, by moving to a more positive interactionalist model, the relevance of the psychologist's practice to the teachers and students with whom they are working can be more assured.

Training and regulation of the profession

Qualifications

A more detailed discussion on training is provided in Passenger (Chapter 3, this volume) but some complementary material is provided here to give context to the current discussion. In most countries, there is a requirement of at least a Master's degree specialising in educational psychology; indeed in some countries (for example, England and Wales) a doctoral-level degree is required before one can qualify as an educational psychologist. However, in other countries this was found not to be the case, and the majority of respondents to the survey in some countries held a Bachelor's-level degree only (Albania, Estonia, Georgia, Italy, Russia, the UAE) (Jimerson et al. 2004, 2006, 2008a). It should be highlighted that, following the recommendations of the European Union Task Force set up in 1999 to consider training in applied psychology, it is now incumbent on all EU countries to adopt a 'curriculum' for all applied psychologists that includes a three-year undergraduate programme, followed by a three-year professional training programme (Lunt, 2002).

Teaching/School experience

While in England and Wales it is only relatively recently (in 2006) that the requirement for educational psychologists to have previous teaching experience has been annulled, in most other countries this requirement has never been in place, or was abandoned many years ago. The only other country surveyed that had such a requirement was Australia, but due to the federalized system this is not across the whole country and is gradually being phased out (Jimerson et al. 2006). Nevertheless, many of the respondents did report that they had previous teaching experience, as it is common that trainee educational psychologists will require some level of relevant experience prior to their training, including that of teaching, but also related professions (e.g. teaching assistant, researcher working in schools, speech and language therapist, community education worker).

Registration and licensing

In some countries there are regulations, or even laws, that require educational psychologists to be licenced or registered. For example, in the UK, educational psychologists have to be registered by law with the Health Professions Council (HPC), an independent regulatory body that is responsible for setting and maintaining professional standards for all health-related professional groups (e.g. speech and language therapists, physiotherapists) including educational psychologists. Thus, the use of the title 'educational psychologist' is protected by law and can only by used by those registered with the HPC. However, of the 83 countries where educational psychology exists as a profession, only 28 had such a regulatory body or laws that governed the practice of educational psychologists (Jimerson et al. 2008b). In the other 55 countries, there was no such legal requirement. However, in 42 countries there were professional associations of educational psychology (e.g. a division of educational psychology within a national psychology association). Finally, Jimerson et al. (2008b) found that there were specific university training programmes for educational psychologists in 57 of the 83 countries. It is noteworthy that only 11 of the 192 Member States of the UN met all five of the criteria used in the Jimerson et al. (2008b) study – (i) identifiable professionals employed to fulfil duties of an educational psychologist, (ii) regulations or laws requiring educational psychologists, (iii) professional associations of educational psychology, (iv) university training programmes specific to educational psychology (undergraduate or Master's), and (v) university training programmes that provide doctoral level preparation. These were Australia, Brazil, Canada, Cyprus, Greece, New Zealand, Romania, South Africa, South Korea, Scotland, and the USA.

Roles and responsibilities

The ISPS includes questions regarding how much time respondents spend on various educational psychology tasks. Previous research has demonstrated that the two main tasks of educational psychologists are assessment and intervention (Farrell and Kalambouka 2000; Oakland and Cunningham 1992), and the ISPS research indicated similar conclusions. In most countries, the largest proportion of respondents' time was spent on 'psycho-educational evaluations' and 'counselling students individually' (Jimerson et al. 2004, 2006, 2008a); however, there were some exceptions, for example in New Zealand, where educational psychologists spend much less time on psycho-educational evaluations compared to other countries, and more time on providing direct interventions and consultation. In Italy, it was difficult to gauge the number of hours spent on such tasks since Italy does not have the same structure of educational psychology services as most other countries. In Italy, there do not exist local authority educational psychology services, but instead such services are administered on an individual contractual basis; for example, where psychologists will 'bid' for educational psychology work, meaning that educational psychologists in Italy are much less integrated within school settings as compared to other countries (Jimerson et al. 2006).

Educational psychologists clearly benefit from multi-systemic interventions where various participants are involved (e.g. school, student, parents, health services, social workers). This works well because the educational psychologists, working in schools, are usually best positioned to bring together other professionals to formulate an effective plan that will facilitate improvements for the student or group of students requiring assistance (Annan and Priestley 2012).

Generally, across countries, much less time seemed to be spent on the following: 'providing direct interventions', 'providing primary prevention programmes', and 'conducting staff training and in-service programmes' (Jimerson et al. 2004, 2006, 2008a, 2009a, 2010). Respondents were asked about their ideal role as an educational psychologist and, on first inspection of the data, there seemed to be little consensus across the countries surveyed. However, on further examination, it was noticeable that in 11 of the 15 countries (Albania, Australia, China, England, Egypt, Estonia, Georgia, Italy, New Zealand, Switzerland, and the UAE), respondents made reference to 'making a difference, seeing successes or ability to help' as their most liked aspect of the job (Jimerson et al. 2004, 2006, 2008a, 2009a, 2010). As Burden (1996) highlighted, if you were to ask educational psychologists, particularly trainee educational psychologists, why they have chosen to enter the profession, most would probably make reference to helping, or empowering, children as their main motivation.

Aside from this particular aspect of the job, there was a lot of variability in the responses provided. In some countries (e.g. Albania, Germany, Georgia, Switzerland), the educational psychologists surveyed maintained that their ideal role was undertaking psycho-educational assessments; while in others (e.g. England and China) the most popular response was providing consultation to teachers/staff. In yet more countries, other educational psychology tasks were most popular (e.g. counselling students and providing primary prevention programmes). There was much more agreement across countries regarding the least optimal role for educational psychologists: 'administrative responsibilities' (Jimerson et al. 2004, 2006, 2008a).

As has been discussed earlier in this chapter, the role of the educational psychologist has evolved over several decades, and the national differences of the profession are nowhere more prominent than in responses to critical incidents. Rees and Seaton (2011) reported on their study of the various levels of involvement of educational psychologists with these types of events. Whether there are more or fewer major incidents than before that involve school personnel, there has to be preparation for incidents such as, terrorist attacks, suicide, vehicular accidents, and untimely student death, to name but a few.

The authors of this chapter have argued (Boyle and Lauchlan 2009) that the status of educational psychologists is reflected in the type of roles that senior educational personnel expect them to do. If they are seen as only psychometricians then they are not regarded as being a crucial part of the school team. The over-reliance on psychometric work with children can restrict the type of fluid relationships that should exist at the level of family, school, and child (Annan and Priestley 2012). However, it should be noted that in some countries this type of practice is more the norm, as indicated in a comparison between perceptions of what educational psychologists in Thailand and the USA actually do (Archwamety, McFarland, and Tangdhanakanond 2009). In this study, respondents working in Thailand indicated that a large emphasis was placed on the importance of testing when compared to the USA. Archwamety et al. felt that this could be to do with the educational psychology profession being at a fairly early stage in development, thus implying that the expectations are still that educational psychologists are predominantly psychometricians. Rees and Seaton (2011: 91) state that, 'a clear message from the data is that responding to crises is a core aspect of the work of school psychologists'. It is also crucial to note that there may be a lack of confidence on the part of the educational psychologist to move into some of the higher-level consultancy roles, and training for these skills may be required. Many educational systems require an assessment to be provided by the educational psychologist so that a label can be provided so as to access funding, which restricts the services that the educational psychologist can provide (see Boyle, Chapter 21, this volume, and Lauchlan and Boyle 2007, for a wider discussion on labelling in special education).

Challenges

External challenges

The ISPS divides the questions regarding challenges into 'external challenges to the delivery of school psychology services' and 'internal challenges to the delivery of school psychology services'. A common external challenge found in most countries was, perhaps unsurprisingly, 'lack of money to properly fund services', with typically around 60–70 percent of respondents in each country citing this challenge. Other frequently cited threats to the profession across countries included 'low status of school psychology', 'other professional groups taking school psychology jobs', and 'low salaries for school psychologists'. However, it is important to note that while these were general trends, there were some outliers in these responses, e.g. only 1 percent in Switzerland responded that salaries were a challenge, whereas the figure in Georgia and Estonia was 83 percent of respondents (Jimerson et al. 2004, 2006, 2008a, 2009a, 2010).

Internal challenges

Educational psychologists cited many internal challenges to the profession, but there was no overall consensus as found with the external challenges. The lack of research in the profession of educational psychology has frequently been cited as a problem in the UK (Eodanable and Lauchlan 2009; Farrell et al. 2006; Greig 2001) and worldwide (Oakland and Cunningham 1992). It appears from the administration of the ISPS that it continues to be a widespread problem in the 15 countries where the ISPS was administered. The most cited internal challenge across countries was *lack of research and evaluation* (in some countries as many as 84 percent of respondents (China); the mean figure was 42 percent), followed by 'professional burnout' (82 percent in Cyprus, 81 percent in Australia; mean = 41 percent), 'lack of leadership within the profession' (again, particularly in China (75 percent); mean = 32 percent), 'lack of adequate supervision' (mean = 32 percent), and 'lack of professional standards governing professional services' (mean = 29 percent) (Jimerson et al. 2004, 2006, 2008a, 2009a, 2010).

Consultation versus individual casework

As has been discussed earlier in this chapter, the role of educational psychologists should involve an element of consultation in order to be effective as practitioners; i.e. practitioners who are able to advise teachers as well as senior school personnel. It is relatively easy to work at the level of the individual student, and this is perhaps one reason why many educational psychologists prefer not to move to a more consultative model of practice but instead remain attached to the practice of psychometric testing; after all, it is unlikely that a student is going to challenge an educational psychologist about their WISC-IV (Wechsler Intelligence Scale for Children – Fourth Edition) administration. To elucidate this point, Wnek, Klein, and Bracken (2008: 149) in their study looking at current practice in the USA suggest that:

> it appears that consultation, despite its emphasis in training during the past 15 years remains a practice in the US that appears to cause anxiety among practicing psychologists and as such may be an area in which additional training is needed.

However, the authors of this chapter are not advocating a complete move away from individual casework, as there will always be a role for the educational psychologist to work in this way, although it should be noted that individual casework should not equate to the universal practice of psychometric testing, as there are many other ways that an educational psychologist can interact and intervene with a client (see Boyle 2007; Boyle and Lauchlan 2009 for further discussion). As the current authors have argued elsewhere: 'to totally remove oneself from the "bedrock" of the role of the EP [educational psychologist] may be tantamount to folly' (Boyle and Lauchlan 2009: 81).

Research

Perhaps it is unsurprising that alongside the 'lack of research and evaluation' being highlighted as the biggest internal challenge to the profession, it was found that the majority of respondents in 10 of the 15 countries surveyed using the ISPS considered that research was 'very relevant' to the profession of educational psychology, with the majority in the other countries (Albania, Egypt, Germany, Italy, Switzerland) responding that it was 'somewhat relevant'. Only a very small minority in each country, and in some countries no respondents at all, replied that it was 'not relevant' (Jimerson et al. 2004, 2006, 2008a, 2009a, 2010).

Respondents to the ISPS were also asked an open question to suggest topics where research was needed. As one might imagine, a number of different topics were proposed, from motivation and behavioural problems to reading and writing topics to neuropsychology and mental health issues, such as depression and suicide (Jimerson et al. 2004, 2006, 2008b). It is clear from reading the wide range of responses put forward that educational psychologists feel that a dearth of research is being undertaken. It continues to be a considerable challenge to the profession to undertake more research into the diverse number of fields in which educational psychologists work.

Conclusions and future directions

This chapter has attempted to provide an understanding as to the roles that educational psychologists perform in various parts of the world as well as some of the issues that have recently begun to emerge as innovative practice, and perhaps should be considered a more generic part of the role. What about future directions for the profession? Wnek et al. (2008) suggest that educational psychologists need to move more into the health domain or at least be more skilled in that area in order to offer the more holistic set of services that are required in some areas. More knowledge of areas such as depression and posttraumatic stress disorder, which are sometimes viewed as outside the field of practice of educational psychologists, may be needed in order to satisfy the growing concern regarding the mental wellbeing of students. After all, if the services expected of the educational psychologists are not being provided, then it is possible that the school or district will go elsewhere in order to gain the service that is required (Boyle and

Lauchlan 2009). Educational psychology is an expensive business and with many national budgets being reduced, the value of the product has to be delivered or else a less expensive service may be employed.

It is argued here that the main issue to consider is whether educational psychologists across the world are more influenced by the field of education or psychology. Educational psychologists have to decide whether they are educationalists dabbling in a bit of psychology or if they are psychologists involved in the education sphere. If it is the latter then this signifies that they are thinking as psychologists. However, if it is the former then there is the possibility that the psychologist may be under-achieving, and thus in danger of not being able to adapt to the changing environment and the marketplace of educational psychology (Boyle and Lauchlan 2009). This creates the further risk that such professionals may make themselves irrelevant and redundant in the fields of both education and psychology. Instead, if the educational psychology profession is to continue to be widely used in the field of education then continuing to link internationally and understand what is successful elsewhere rather than working in a parochial manner would be useful as a tool of progression. 'Recognising the common ground and variations in the field of school psychology in countries around the world provides perspective on peculiarities and possibilities in the preparation and practices of school psychologists' (Jimerson et al. 2006: 30).

Contact address: christopher.boyle@monash.edu

References

Annan, J., and Priestley, A. (2012) 'A contemporary story of school psychology', *School Psychology International*, 33: 325–344.

Archwamety, T., McFarland, M., and Tangdhanakanond, K. (2009) 'How important are roles/functions of school psychologists and who should substitute for them in their absence? Comparing Thai and American students' perceptions', *School Psychology International*, 30: 255–264.

Boyle, C. (2007) 'The challenge of interviewing adolescents: which psychotherapeutic approaches are useful in educational psychology?', *Educational and Child Psychology*, 24: 36–45.

Boyle, C., and Lauchlan, F. (2009) 'Applied psychology and the case for individual casework: some reflections on the role of the educational psychologist', *Educational Psychology in Practice*, 25: 71–84.

Burden, R. (1994) 'Trends and developments in educational psychology', *School Psychology International*, 15: 293–347.

Burden, R. (1996) 'Meaningful questions or meaningless answers: worthwhile assessment in a changing world', in S. Kriegler and P. Englebrecht (eds.) *Perspectives on learning difficulties*, Hatfield, South Africa: Van Schaik.

Eodanable, M., and Lauchlan, F. (2009) 'The advance of research and evaluation skills by EPs: implications for training and professional development', *Educational Psychology in Practice*, 25: 113–124.

Farrell, P., and Kalambouka, A. (2000) 'Teachers' views of school psychologists in different countries', *International School Psychology Association – World Go Round*, 27: 8–9.

Farrell, P., Woods, K., Lewis, S., Rooney, S., Squires, G., and O'Connor, M. (2006) *A review of the functions and contribution of educational psychologists in England and Wales in light of 'Every Child Matters: Change for Children'*, London: DfES Publications.

Gibb, C. (1998) 'Turkeys voting for Christmas', *Special Children*, 114: 18–21.

Greig, A. (2001) 'The educational psychologist as practitioner–researcher: reality or dream?', *Educational and Child Psychology*, 18: 75–88.

Jimerson, S. R., Alghorani, M. A., Darweish, A. H., and Abdelaziz, M. (2010) 'School psychology in Egypt. Results of the 2008 International School Psychology Survey'. *School Psychology International*, 31: 219–228.

Jimerson, S. R., Annan, J., Skokut, M., and Renshaw, T. L. (2009a) 'Educational psychology in New Zealand. Results of the 2006 International School Psychology Survey', *School Psychology International*, 30: 443–455.

Jimerson, S. R., Graydon, K., Farrell, P., Kikas, E., Hatzichristou, C., Boce, E., Bashi, G., and the ISPA Research Committee (2004) 'The International School Psychology Survey: development and data from Albania, Cyprus, Estonia, Greece and Northern England', *School Psychology International*, 25: 259–286.

Jimerson, S. R., Graydon, K., Skokut, M., Alghorani, M. A., Kanjaradze, A., Forster, J., and the ISPA Research Committee (2008a) 'The International School Psychology Survey: data from Georgia, Switzerland and the United Arab Emirates', *School Psychology International*, 29: 5–28.

Jimerson, S. R., Graydon, K., Yuen, M., Lam, S. F., Thurm, J. G., Klueva, N., Coyne, J., Loprete, L. J., Phillips, J., and the ISPA Research Committee (2006). 'The International School Psychology Survey: data from Australia, China, Germany, Italy and Russia', *School Psychology International*, 27: 5–32.

Jimerson, S. R., Oakland, T. D., and Farrell, P. T. (eds.) (2007) *The handbook of international school psychology*, Thousand Oaks, CA: Sage.

Jimerson, S. R., Skokut, M., Cardenas, S., Malone, H., and Stewart, K. (2008b) 'Where in the world is school psychology? Examining evidence of school psychology around the globe', *School Psychology International*, 29: 131–144.

Jimerson, S. R., Stewart, K., Skokut, M., Cardenas, S., and Malone, H. (2009b) 'How many school psychologists are there in each country of the world? International estimates of school psychologists and school psychologist-to-student ratios', *School Psychology International*, 30: 555–567.

Lauchlan, F., and Boyle C. (2007) 'Is the use of labels in special education helpful?', *Support For Learning*, 22: 36–42.

Lindsay, G. (1992) 'Educational psychologists and Europe', in S. Wolfendale, T. Bryans, M. Fox, A. Labram, and A. Sigston (eds.) *The Profession and Practice of Educational Psychology*, London: Cassell.

Lunt, I. (1991) 'Educational psychology and Europe', *Educational and Child Psychology*, 8: 5–83.

Lunt, I. (2002) 'A common framework for the training of psychologists in Europe', *European Psychologist*, 7: 180–191.

Oakland, T. D., and Cunningham, J. L. (1992) 'A survey of school psychology in developed and developing countries', *School Psychology International*, 13: 99–129.

Oakland, T. D., and Jimerson, S. R. (2008) 'History and current status of school psychology internationally', in A. Thomas and J. Grimes (eds.) *Best Practices in School Psychology*, 5th edn, Bethesda, MD: National Association of School Psychologists.

Rees, P., and Seaton, N. (2011) 'Psychologists' response to crises: international perspectives', *School Psychology International*, 32: 73–94.

Seligman, M. E. P. (2007) *The optimistic child: a proven program to safeguard children against depression and build lifelong resilience*, New York: Houghton Mifflin.

Toland, J., and Boyle C. (2008) 'Applying cognitive behavioural methods to retrain childrens attributions for success and failure in learning', *School Psychology International*, 29: 286–302.

Toland, J., and Carrigan, D. (2011) 'Educational psychology and resilience: new concept, new opportunities', *School Psychology International*, 32: 95–106.

Wnek, A. C., Klein, G., and Bracken, B. A. (2008) 'Professional development issues for school psychologists: what's hot, what's not in the United States', *School Psychology International*, 29: 145–160.

PART II

How children learn and develop

5

THEORIES OF TEACHING AND LEARNING

Janet I. Vousden, Clare Wood and Andrew J. Holliman

COVENTRY UNIVERSITY, UK

The purpose of this chapter is to present a brief overview of the key ideas and theorists that have proved influential in informing contemporary ideas of teaching and learning. By teaching and learning, we mean an understanding of the psychological processes that explain changes in knowledge and behaviour, on the part of both the learner and the teacher. We adopt the view that in order to understand effective teaching and learning we need to understand the psychology of both the student and teacher, and how they interact with and influence each other. As we move through each area, it is worth reflecting on the extent to which it sees the tutor or student as in control of the learning situation, as this is a salient feature that has changed over time.

Behaviourism

Behaviourism, as a learning theory, can be traced back as far as Aristotle (384–322 BC), whose essay entitled 'Memory' focused on the associations made during events such as thunder and lightning. It can be broadly defined as a theory of learning manifested by a relatively permanent change of behaviour as a result of experience with, and feedback from, the environment. The behaviourist approach was driven by attempts to treat psychology as an 'objective science' in which directly observable and measurable events and behaviours, rather than 'mental events', were focused on. Since Aristotle, there have been many key thinkers in behaviourism such as Ivan Pavlov, Edward Thorndike, John Watson, and Burrhus Skinner, whose ideas have had an important and lasting impact on teaching and learning in the education system.

For behaviourism, the process of learning (or behaviour modification) was referred to as 'conditioning'. Classical conditioning – that is, the learnt association between a previously unrelated stimulus and a reflex behaviour – can be traced back to the original works of Ivan Pavlov (1927), who demonstrated that hungry dogs would salivate (unconditioned response) at the mere sound of a bell (neutral stimulus) after simultaneous presentations of the neutral stimulus with the sight of food (unconditioned stimulus). In an education context, the principles of classical conditioning can be used to explain how a previously neutral stimulus (e.g. going to school) can become associated with being bullied to evoke feelings of anxiety, such that the child does not want to attend school. However, a major limitation of this theory (aside from the neglect of cognition) is that it is restricted to retraining 'reflex behaviours' and tells us little about how to evoke behaviours that are not part of a child's involuntary repertoire (e.g., developing knowledge of the 'one-to-one principle' in mathematics).

The form of behaviourism that has had, and continues to have, the greatest impact in the classroom is that of operant conditioning; that is, the learnt association between one's own behaviour and the consequences that will result from it. Burrhus Skinner (1938) derived the word 'operant' from the idea that an individual voluntarily 'operates' on their environment to achieve a desired outcome. The famous 'Skinner Box' experiments demonstrated that non-human animals would perform a behaviour (e.g. press a lever) more frequently if it was 'reinforced' (e.g. with the release of food) and less frequently if it was 'punished' (e.g. with an electric shock). A 'reinforcer' is anything that strengthens the association between the situation and the response and a 'punisher' is anything that decreases this association – the use of reward stickers to commend positive behaviours and the use of corporal punishment to deal with problem behaviours are common examples (respectively), although the latter has been outlawed in UK schools for over two decades. Punishment in schools is seen as less desirable in that it only teaches a child which behaviours not to make and does not emphasise new, positive behaviours, the administrator can be seen (and modelled) in a negative way, and there is also a risk of inappropriate associations and/or generalisations. Contemporary techniques focus more on reinforcement and perhaps the most popular example of this in present-day schools is applied behavioural analysis (ABA).

ABA focuses on three core aspects of the situation: antecedents (environmental features immediately prior to the production of behaviour); behaviour (the behaviour itself, e.g. the production of good work, talking or disruptive attention seeking); and consequences (the consequences for the individual resulting from the production of that behaviour). In a classroom context, this might involve developing an interesting work set in a quiet area (antecedents), working hard or the production of good work (behaviour), and the praise from the teacher (consequences). It follows that both the antecedents and the consequences of the behaviour will determine the likelihood of that behaviour occurring in the future. This systematic approach has been used to improve scholastic abilities and modify problem behaviours, particularly for individuals with learning difficulties (see Cooper, Chapter 27, this volume; Fortuna and Davis, Chapter 26, this volume).

Another operant conditioning technique, which Skinner (1954) argued could be applied in the classroom setting to enhance academic progress and modify problem behaviours, is that of 'programmed instruction'. This typically involves giving a child some new information to learn and then testing their knowledge of it through direct questioning. A correct response would be 'reinforced' with some form of reward (e.g. with praise) and if an incorrect response was given, the question would be repeated or simplified and then 'reinforced' once the correct response was given. Despite some limitations of this approach, such as encouraging 'extrinsic' rather than intrinsic motivation (Long 2000), it has received some support particularly for remediating literacy and numeracy difficulties (Kennedy 1978). Moreover, principles of this approach (e.g. emphasising success, the importance of immediate feedback, and tailoring information to the current level of the learner) are commonly adopted practices in present-day schools (Littleton and Wood 2006).

Despite the rise of other learning theories in the twentieth century (described in this chapter), behaviourism has continued to receive a great deal of research attention. Indeed, Woollard (2010) has identified several current journals that publish articles on some form of behaviourism (e.g. *The Analysis of Verbal Behavior*; *Behavior Analysis in Practice*; *Behavior Modification*; *Journal of Behavioral Education*; *Journal of the Experimental Analysis of Behavior*; *The Behavior Analyst*; *Journal of Applied Behavioral Analysis*; *European Journal of Behavior Analysis*; and *School Psychology Review*).

It is also clear that aspects of behaviourism (e.g. principles of operant conditioning) have continued to feature in classrooms to both support learning and modify and manage problem behaviours (but see Erten, Savage, and Di Stasio, Chapter 6, this volume, for more contemporary approaches).

Social learning theory

Social learning theorists, most notably Albert Bandura, have built on behaviourist principles. Bandura (1977) viewed behaviourism (in its original form) as simplistic in that all behaviours were explained via the environment (neglecting any cognition). Bandura accepted that much learning takes place as a result of 'reinforcement' and 'punishment', thus the consequences of one's actions; however, a key discrepancy in the social learning theory is the view that such 'consequences' do not have to be 'directly experienced'. It was held that merely observing others' behaviour and 'perceiving' the consequences (e.g. reinforcements) through 'observational learning' and 'modelling' can influence learning and behaviour. In essence, this theory holds that children develop behaviours as a result of watching what other people do.

In order for imitation to occur, it was argued that a child must attend to relevant aspects of the 'model' and the 'behaviour', retain what they have seen, be physically able to reproduce the behaviour, and be motivated to do so through the presence of reinforcement or punishment (Oates, Sheehy, and Wood 2005). This was demonstrated in a classic study by Bandura (1965), who found that young children would imitate aggressive behaviour modelled by another person towards a 'Bobo' doll. Indeed, this study lead to a great deal of media coverage spanning decades concerning whether observing television violence has an impact on children's behaviour. Nevertheless, the idea that children learn by observing and imitating the behaviours, emotions, and attitudes of others has been shown to have important applications in the classroom.

Wragg (1984) showed how principles of the social learning theory can reduce (or even prevent) problem behaviours in classrooms. It was argued that children learn from observing the consequences of others' behaviour; thus, they perceive the consequences of their own actions if they were to behave in this way. For example, if a child sees that a 'naughty' pupil misbehaves and goes unpunished, they may be more inclined to behave in this way. However, if the teacher were to punish this behaviour in some way, a child who observed this event might perceive the negative consequences and not misbehave as a result. Aside from classroom management, recent research (e.g. Sheridan et al. 2012) has also shown that social skills programmes (based on social learning theory) can develop children's listening and problem solving skills along with their ability to follow directions, and their prosocial behaviour in a school setting. Therefore observational learning and the modelling of positive behaviours in a classroom context can support the learning process and promote positive behaviour.

Bandura's social learning theory can perhaps be seen as the bridge between the environment and cognition in that attempts were made to consider 'thought processes' in relation to the environment (in terms of perceived consequences). However, the social learning theory does not sufficiently explain (nor is it concerned with explaining) the processes of cognitive change within the child or the complex nature of children's thinking. These issues will be addressed in the following sections.

Constructivism

The central tenet of constructivism is that development is an active constructive process, determined by the child, rather than by external teachings, or even by internal maturation – the child's activities act to progressively build on and develop their own cognitive structures. The work of Jean Piaget (1896–1980) is a prominent example of constructivist theory.

Piaget saw children as active learners, interacting with their environment in an effort to understand how the world works. Piaget thought children's development could be characterized by three processes. 'Assimilation' is the ability to absorb objects, ideas, or information. A young child might try to assimilate a story by relating it to similar experiences or other story schemas, or imagining the characters in the story. 'Accommodation' refers to the ability to change our representations, or cognitive structures to allow new ideas or objects to fit in with our existing cognitive structures. A child may encounter a new object that does not fit in with any existing representations, prompting a change in the way things are represented. Ideas and representations become restructured, or organised, in a logical or coherent manner through the process of 'equilibration', by striking a balance between assimilation and accommodation. It allows the developing child to construct ever more complex structures for dealing with new aspects of their environment (Kohlberg 1968).

Thus according to Piaget, intellectual development depends on actively exploring the environment, through assimilation, accommodation, and organisation, and adjusting one's own cognitive structures according to those interactions to abstract general principles and rules – ultimately in an effort to understand the world in which we live. Constructivism sees the child as the central governing driver in their own intellectual environment, and places much less emphasis on external input in the way of teaching. The main role for external input is to provide an optimal environment in which the child can explore and manipulate their surroundings. Any other external input that hinders this process was even thought to have negative consequences for learning (Newman, Griffin, and Cole 1989).

Teaching through supporting active learning

Piaget's ideas have been central to certain educational approaches that put the child, rather than a teacher, at the centre of the learning process. Piaget's theory has been used to support the ideas of 'readiness' to learn and discovery learning. Piaget stressed the need to match the pedagogical experience of the child to its level of understanding – a child would not be 'ready' to take on the concept of abstract reasoning, for example, if they had not yet reached the appropriate developmental stage where abstract reasoning skills emerge. For teaching to be effective, educators must be mindful of the intellectual growth of children (Sigel 1969), and encourage them to 'discover' rules and principles themselves rather than imitate adult performance.

Building on the idea that cognitive growth is truly constructed from children's own knowledge and active exploration, Constance Kamii focused on Piaget's theory as an application of Piaget's ideas to classroom teaching. Kamii investigated whether children could create their own methods for doing arithmetic, if provided with a conducive environment. Kamii believed that cognitive growth and understanding depends on the child constructing their own knowledge, and will not occur if driven by worksheets and tests – which encourage a misplaced emphasis on 'getting the right answer' rather than promoting the type of problem solving that leads to understanding. Instead, Kamii suggested that children's motivation to problem-solve is stimulated by everyday activities (e.g. is there enough money here to buy everyone an ice-cream?), games (e.g. Old Maid – making 10 with two cards), and discussion of mathematical problems to promote the development of appropriate procedures and understanding.

Kamii tested these ideas with mathematics by comparing the ability of children who had been taught traditional algorithmic procedures for multiplication with children who had instead constructed procedures for themselves. For example, children were asked to solve problems such as 13 'multiplied by' 4, and to explain their answer (Kamii 1996). Both groups were comparable in their accuracy, but only 5 percent of the traditional group were able to explain adequately how they arrived at their answer, whereas 92 percent of the constructivist group could. Similar results have been reported for addition and other problems (Kamii 1989, 1994). Thus, although approximately equal in accuracy, the numerical reasoning skills of the constructivist group were far superior.

Cognitive learning theory

Cognitive learning theory has focused on understanding the cognitive processes involved in learning new information as well as how educational strategies can be shaped to promote student understanding of such material. The role of the teacher in cognitive learning theory is to structure the curriculum in a way that facilitates optimal learning through an understanding of the way the brain represents and processes information.

Cognitive learning theory takes account of the way people represent and process information to develop mental representations that can form the basis for thought. For example, understanding the symbolic representations of language, how concepts are represented, and how different aspects of memory work will facilitate how to best present new material for optimal learning. For example, if we understand how memory works, we may be able to devise teaching strategies to minimise the unwanted effects of poor encoding and forgetting, through techniques such as distributing practice through time. In this case, if the amount of time given to study is spread out over multiple, shorter sessions, then long-term retention of the learned material is better than if the same study time were concentrated in one long session (Kornell and Bjork 2008). This finding has been successfully refined to obtain an optimal spacing schedule, where learned material is regularly revisited at intervals dependent on the time of test (Rohrer and Pashler 2010).

To take advantage of this meta-knowledge, the presentation and structure of material is very important, requiring careful planning by a teacher. Jerome Bruner produced a seminal work in this respect, in his 1977 book *The Process of Education* (Bruner 1977). For Bruner, it was of paramount importance that fundamental principles and structure should be taught, rather than just attempting the basic mastery of facts. Bruner believed that children are able to learn anything as long as the teaching is structured appropriately. Learning structure rather than facts would have the advantage that detail is more likely to be retained if learnt within an appropriate structure, and children are also more likely to be able to transfer their knowledge and skills to new situations.

With this in mind, Bruner believed it was important that teachers worked within the intellectual boundaries of the child to ensure that children grasp the fundamental principles of a subject intuitively, rather than learn facts by rote. He believed that teaching and learning should repeatedly revisit these fundamental principles, each time building on what is known and making connections between them with the goal of fully understanding the concepts involved. This way of repeatedly building on existing knowledge was termed the 'spiral curriculum'. For example, children discover by playing games with dice that rolling a 'six' does not happen very often. Later, they may count the number of times each number appears when everyone in the class rolls, say five times. They may revisit these experiences when they learn about probability and its expression as mathematical formulae.

Thus the child still plays a driving role through learning by discovery, but unlike constructivism, the teacher plays an equally prominent role by ensuring that the materials are structured and presented for optimal learning.

Social constructivism/Sociocultural theory

Social constructivism provides an interesting point of contrast to the ideas of Piaget and constructivism. Piaget saw children's construction of knowledge as essentially a highly personal activity, with adults relegated to a supporting role (of creating a stimulating learning environment for the child to explore), and even portrayed as a potentially problematic influence on children's developing understanding of the world. The only social contribution to learning was seen to arise from socio-cognitive conflict with peers, such as when a child's ideas are challenged as a result of exposure to a different world view during play or problem-solving with a slightly more developmentally advanced friend. However, social constructivism, as its name suggests, sees learning as essentially social in nature.

Lev Vygotsky is seen as the founding father of social constructivism, and contrary to Piaget, he argued that learning first takes place on the social plane, between individuals. This social activity is crucial in developing the learner's capacity for reflection on what is being learned. Once learning has been achieved with the support of a more knowledgeable other, the learner begins to internalize that knowledge and it becomes individualised. We can all think of examples of skills or knowledge that we have acquired from other people, and these are often skills that we would struggle to have achieved on our own. The most obvious examples are practical ones, such as learning how to make something, or learning a skill like driving a car, but this principle of social interaction with others being the basis of effective learning extends to how we come to understand concepts and ideas too.

Assessing learners' potential

This social transmission model of teaching and learning recognizes and reveres the roles that adults can play in supporting children's learning. Related to this, Vygotsky talked about the importance of the 'zone of proximal development' (ZPD), which is defined as the difference between what a learner can achieve unaided and what they can achieve with the support of a more knowledgeable other. Vygotsky argued that children's potential was better assessed by observing what they can achieve with support, rather than focusing on 'snapshots' of their achievements, unaided, at one point in time. If we consider the ways in which children's potential is typically assessed, either in the form of IQ tests or school tests that are intended to be used as the basis for school or classroom allocations, we can see that traditionally the focus is very much on snapshot assessment. However, in recent years there has been more interest in so-called dynamic assessment, which instead looks at potential as children's responsiveness to teaching and intervention, in line with Vygotsky's ideas. What is quantified in these assessments is how much support a child needs to achieve an outcome, rather than their achievement of an outcome per se (e.g. Fuchs et al. 2008; Spector 1992). While these assessments have yet to achieve mainstream recognition as appropriate tools for testing potential either in the classroom or in research contexts, there is now debate and increased interest in the enhanced sensitivity that these measures can offer (e.g. Allal and Ducrey 2000; Barrera 2003; Dwairy 2004).

Understanding effective tuition

In addition to the idea of dynamic assessment, Vygotsky's ideas also stimulated research into how adults go about supporting children through their ZPD. Wood and Middleton (1975) began by observing four-year-old children working with their mothers on a complex three-dimensional jigsaw task; to analyse their interactions, they developed a coding scheme that identified five levels of support offered by the mothers:

- Level 1: General verbal encouragement
- Level 2: Specific verbal instruction
- Level 3: Assisting in choice of material
- Level 4: Preparing material for assembly
- Level 5: Demonstrating an operation.

What emerged from this study was that the most successful children had mothers who varied the amount of support they gave in relation to whether or not their child was succeeding or experiencing difficulty with the task. Wood and Middleton referred to this as 'contingent instruction', and characterised it as the most effective type of adult support: increasing the level of control in direct response to learner difficulty, but equally reducing the level of control when the learner demonstrates competence. This led Wood, Bruner, and Ross (1976) to use the metaphor of 'scaffolding' to describe the need for flexible construction and deconstruction of support during tuition. However, although the principle of contingent instruction is a simple one to grasp, it is extremely difficult to apply in practice even when trained (e.g. Wood, Wood, and Middleton 1978), leading Wood (1998: 164) to comment:

> Monitoring children's activity, remembering what one had said or done to prompt that activity, and responding quickly to their efforts at an appropriate level is a demanding intellectual feat. Effective teaching is as difficult as the learning it seeks to promote.

With this recognition of difficulty comes the need to concede to Piaget that in many instances (especially in the context of classroom tuition) adult support may not be as effective as it could or should be. However, this should not lead us to deny the idea that adults can offer effective support and tuition, or that children can benefit from contact with more knowledgeable adults.

In an extension to the ZPD concept, Tharp and Gallimore (1998) proposed a theory of teaching as assisted performance. They argued that any individual would have multiple ZPDs, one for any given skill or ability being learned. They saw learning as progressing through four stages: in Stage 1, learning is supported by a more able other; in Stage 2, learning is self-regulated; in Stage 3, learning has been internalised and has become automated (unconscious); Stage 4 recognises that sometimes external circumstances (such as stress or fatigue, or even the passing of time), may result in the learning returning to an earlier stage, to re-familiarise or relearn the skill.

Language, learning, and communities of practice

Vygotsky, and the 'sociocultural' researchers who have followed him and developed his ideas, recognized language as one of the most powerful 'cultural tools' that children and their teachers have access to. Vygotsky saw language as important in constructing shared understanding between individuals, and in enabling self-reflection and self-regulation. For example, Vygotsky argued that self-directed speech, far from being immature and egocentric, served an important self-regulatory function when one was confronted with task difficulty. In applying socio-cultural ideas to the classroom, Neil Mercer (2000; Mercer and Littleton 2007) has argued that teachers can enhance the quality of teaching and learning through effective use of classroom dialogue (see Littleton, Chapter 7, this volume) which draws on and elicits students' talk about their own experiences to develop a mutually constructed understanding of what is to be learned. In this way the careful management and fostering of dialogue between peers is offered as a possible solution to the problem of how to ensure effective tuition in a classroom-type environment.

Mercer's observations of children's peer-to-peer discourse in the classroom led him to characterise it under three broad types. 'Disputational talk' indicates disagreement and individual decision making. 'Cumulative talk' is positive but uncritical, and usually characterised by repetition and agreement or elaboration. 'Exploratory talk' offers a constructive critique of others' ideas and then presents explanations and solutions to problems.

Although exploratory talk rarely spontaneously occurs between children, it is seen as the ideal type of talk because the children who talk in this way are making their reasoning transparent for other members of the group. Mercer and colleagues have therefore implemented an approach to training children to talk together in more educationally effective ways, known as 'Thinking Together' (Dawes, Mercer, and Wegerif 2000; Littleton, Chapter 7, this volume). This approach focuses on group talk and the direct tuition of speaking and listening skills, and agreement on a shared set of ground rules for respecting other students' contributions.

The emphasis on group dialogue comes from another sociocultural idea – that of the 'community of practice'. That is, Lave and Wenger (1991) recognised that learning is situated in specific contexts and takes place within a community of learners and practioners. So, for example, as a student of psychology, you participate in a community of other students (some of whom may be more experienced than you are) and experienced tutors, academics, and practitioners. You will be influenced by all members of the community, but community here does not just refer to those you have physical contact with. As a learner, you are effectively an apprentice but one who learns through participation within the community: you learn the 'language' and practices of it and gradually progress from the fringes of the group, to becoming a more central person within it as your competency and experience improve. A community of practice is therefore a system of activity in which learning takes place. A classroom can be seen as a community of practice; an activity system, which has its own culture and practices that necessarily impact on how and what is learned. Mercer (2000) recognised that communities resource shared learning in important ways, including the way that members have a shared history and identity, responsibilities to others in the group, and a continually evolving language and discourse through which participants communicate and demonstrate membership of the group.

Conclusion

The purpose of this chapter was to present a brief overview of the key ideas and theorists that have proved influential in informing contemporary ideas of teaching and learning. Different theories have influenced different approaches to learning, both in the way that they seek to exploit the psychological processes thought to enable optimal learning and in how they conceive of the respective roles played by learner and teacher.

For behaviourists, learning is shaped by the formation of associations between behaviour and some desired outcome. Thus, programmes have been developed that reinforce appropriate behaviour, from behaviour management programmes to those aimed at improving academic performance. The important theme in such programmes is that the desired outcome is always encouraged and praised with the aim of increasing the likelihood of producing it in future. Social learning theory also acknowledges the importance of learning through reinforcement, although it emphasises the role of learning through observation of others' behaviours and consequences. Both approaches place the teacher in an active role in terms of shaping desired behaviour and learning, and modelling desired outcomes so that children will develop the desired associations.

Constructivism contrasts sharply with behavioural approaches in that it seeks to explain the development of the cognitive structures from which abstract rules and principles are then extracted. Thus learning occurs through an ongoing restructuring of cognitive structures driven by a desire to understand how the world works from a child's perspective. Furthermore, constructivists posit that optimal learning occurs when a child constructs their own knowledge rather than trying to imitate adult behaviour. Like constructivism, cognitive learning theory assumes the child learns best through discovery, but unlike constructivism it places the teacher in a more prominent role to structure material to be learned in an optimal way with respect to the cognitive processing involved in learning.

Finally, social constructivism blurs the roles between teacher and learner somewhat by promoting the value of learning as a social process. A strong value is placed on learning from interaction with others, for example by being guided towards a learning goal, or from peer-to-peer discussions. Thus teachers are placed with the task of facilitating the skills necessary for learning from interactions, for example through improving listening and speaking skills or through contingent instruction techniques.

The effectiveness of teaching and learning techniques stands to benefit greatly from the application of a wide range of theories, each offering valuable insight into different aspects of learning. Future directions in this vein should be oriented towards the development of a more integrated framework, taking account of the limitations and applicability of each approach to different stages and areas of development.

Contact address: j.vousden@coventry.ac.uk

References

Allal, L., and Ducrey, G. P. (2000) 'Assessment of-or-in the zone of proximal development', *Learning and Instruction*, 10: 137–152.

Bandura, A. (1965) 'Influence of models' reinforcement contingencies on the acquisition of imitative responses', *Journal of Personality and Social Psychology*, 1: 589–595.

Bandura, A. (1977) *Social learning theory*, New York: General Learning Press.

Barrera, M. (2003) 'Curriculum-based dynamic assessment for new- or second-language learners with learning disabilities in secondary education settings', *Assessment for Effective Intervention*, 29: 69–84.

Bruner, J. S. (1977) *The process of education*, London: Harvard University Press.

Dawes, L., Mercer, N., and Wegerif, R. (2000) *Thinking together*, Birmingham: Questions Publishing.

Dwairy, M. (2004) 'Dynamic approach to learning disability assessment: DLD test', *Dyslexia*, 10: 1–23.

Fuchs, L. S., Compton, D. L., Fuchs, D., Hollenbeck, K. N., Craddock, C. F., and Hamlett, C. L. (2008) 'Dynamic assessment of algebraic learning in predicting third graders' development of mathematical problem solving', *Journal of Educational Psychology*, 100: 829–850.

Kamii, C. (1989) *Double-column addition: a teacher uses Piaget's theory*, New York: Teacher's College Press.

Kamii, C. (1994) *Young children continue to reinvent arithmetic, 3rd grade*, New York: Teacher's College Press.

Kamii, C. (1996) 'Piaget's theory and the teaching of arithmetic', *Prospects*, 26: 99–111.

Kennedy, M. (1978) 'Findings from the follow through planned evaluation study', *Educational Researcher*, 7: 3–11.

Kohlberg, L. (1968) 'Early education: a cognitive-developmental approach', *Child Development*, 39: 1013–1062.

Kornell, N., and Bjork, R. A. (2008) 'Learning concepts and categories: is spacing the "enemy of induction"?', *Psychological Science*, 19: 585–592.

Lave, J., and Wenger, E. (1991) *Situated learning: legitimate peripheral participation*, Cambridge: Cambridge University Press.

Littleton, K., and Wood, C. (2006) 'Education and psychology: understanding teaching and learning', in C. Wood, K. Littleton, and K. Sheehy (eds.) *Development Psychology in Action*, Oxford: Blackwell (pp. 194–229).

Long, M. (2000) *The psychology of education*, London: Routledge.

Mercer, N. (2000) *Words and minds: how we use language to think together*, London: Routledge.

Mercer, N., and Littleton, K. (2007) *Dialogue and the development of children's thinking: a sociocultural approach*, London: Routledge.

Newman, D., Griffin, P., and Cole, M. (1989) *The construction zone: working for cognitive change in schools*, Cambridge: Cambridge University Press.

Oates, J., Sheehy, K., and Wood, C. (2005) 'Theories of development', in J. Oates, C. Wood, and A. Grayson (eds.) *Psychological development and early childhood*, Oxford: Blackwell.

Pavlov, I. (1927) *Conditioned reflexes*, Oxford: Milford.

Rohrer, D., and Pashler, H. (2010) 'Recent research on human learning challenges conventional instructional strategies', *Educational Researcher*, 39: 406–412.

Sheridan, B. A., MacDonald, D. A., Donlon, M., Kuhn, B., McGovern, K., and Friedman, H. (2012) 'Evaluation of a social skills program based on social learning theory, implemented in a school setting', *Psychological Reports*, 108: 420–436.

Sigel, I. E. (1969) 'The Piagetian system and the world of education', in D. Elkind and J. H. Flavell (eds.) *Studies in cognitive development: essays in honor of Jean Piaget*, New York: Oxford University Press (pp. 465–490).

Skinner, B. (1938) *The behavior of organisms*, New York: Appleton Century Crofts.

Skinner, B. (1954) 'The science of learning and the art of teaching', *Harvard Educational Review*, 24: 86–97.

Spector, J. E. (1992) 'Predicting progress in beginning reading: dynamic assessment of phonemic awareness', *Journal of Educational Psychology*, 84: 353–363.

Tharp, R., and Gallimore, R. (1998) 'A theory of teaching as assisted performance', in D. Faulkner, K. Littleton, and M. Woodhead (eds.) *Learning relationships in the classroom*, London: Routledge (pp. 93–109).

Wood, D. (1998) 'Aspects of teaching and learning', in M. Woodhead, D. Faulkner, and K. Littleton (eds.) *Cultural worlds of early childhood*, London: Routledge (pp. 157–177).

Wood, D., Bruner, J., and Ross, G. (1976) 'The role of tutoring in problem solving', *Journal of Child Psychology and Psychiatry*, 17: 89–100.

Wood D., and Middleton, D. (1975) 'A study of assisted problem solving', *British Journal of Developmental Psychology*, 66: 181–191.

Wood, D., Wood, H., and Middleton, D. (1978) 'An experimental evaluation of our face-to-face teaching strategies', *International Journal of Behavioural Development*, 1: 131–147.

Woollard, J. (2010) *Psychology for the classroom: behaviourism*, London: Routledge.

Wragg, E. (1984) *Classroom teaching skills*, London: Croom Helm.

6

EFFECTIVE TEACHING PRACTICES AND CLASSROOM MANAGEMENT

The role of ecological and inclusive understandings

Ozlem Erten, Robert Savage and Maria Di Stasio

MCGILL UNIVERSITY, CANADA

This chapter addresses issues related to effective teaching practices, instructional processes, and classroom management strategies, and is grounded in 'evidence-based practice' (e.g. Rathvon 2008). This research has strongly suggested that teacher behaviours are proximal correlates of student outcomes. Specifically, effective teaching requires practice that is characterized by strong classroom management, clear and 'balanced' skills instruction, and which adapts the curriculum to students' needs through differentiation and feedback in emotionally welcoming but busy classrooms (e.g. Deault and Savage submitted; Louden et al. 2005; Mashburn et al. 2008; Pressley et al. 1998). This chapter reviews recent empirical research identifying the essential characteristics of effective inclusive classrooms, with a particular focus on children's behaviour. We highlight specific steps to reach this goal by examining roles and responsibilities of teachers, learners, and the overall school environment through a holistic contextualized approach to behaviour.

We position our own empirical and theoretical work carried out in the Canadian context. With its multicultural, multilingual, and diverse society, Canada provides a valuable context for examining research on effective teaching for inclusion and diversity, and, it is argued, studies here have made a unique contribution to understanding inclusive practice. The chapter concludes with contextualized implications for effective teaching in diverse and inclusive classrooms.

A historical perspective on effective teaching

Historically, cognitive-behavioural learning theories have been the basis of many behavioural management systems in schools. These theories have focused on the establishment of control over apparently or potentially disruptive students (e.g. Powell and Tod 2004). Behavioural methods such as rewards and reinforcement continue to be implemented in classrooms in public schools throughout the world (e.g. Hoyle, Marshall, and Yell 2011). This model has been updated to fit within tiered response-to-intervention (R*t*I) models of diagnosis of disability (Fletcher and Vaughn 2009; Hoyle et al. 2011).

There is undeniably 'some' value in these models. It seems likely for example that in certain contexts behaviourist approaches can offer teachers a sense of control where previously they felt disempowered. Such models can offer students safe and clear boundaries they may need to regulate their actions better and can sometimes be a platform for more sophisticated engagement in schools. Nonetheless behaviourism may be limiting in capturing the complexity of learning and behaviour, and leave little room for human individuality and the role of expectations, thoughts, emotions, and beliefs that are likely to be central to educational success.

A more fundamental problem for such pupil-based cognitive-behavioural views of children is that contextual features of schools such as 'school ethos' are an extremely important predictor of school success whereas the characteristics of individual students at school entry are often a rather weak predictor of their behaviour outcomes (e.g. Rutter and Maughan 2002; Slee and Weiner 2001). In the anti-bullying literature, for example, both incidence and effective intervention are best understood at the whole school level (e.g. Farrington and Ttofi 2009). Such ecosystemic impacts of social context are problematic for recent strong genetic determinist views of children's behaviour as well. Byrne et al. (2010), for example, have recently argued that most of the variation in children's attainment is explained by genetic factors, not by variation in teaching. However, genetic effects on learning are strong only when teaching is of high quality. Where teaching is of low rated quality, such experiences impede the ability of children to reach their genetic potential (Taylor et al. 2010). These findings show the appropriateness of viewing schools as ecological systems when exploring learning and behaviour.

Effective classrooms

Much recent research suggests that effective teaching practices need to consider both student diversity and the relationship between emotional and social aspects of academic learning (e.g. Louden et al. 2005; Mashburn et al. 2008; Powell and Tod 2004). Building on work by Pressley and colleagues (e.g. Pressley et al. 2001), our own recent research conducted in Canada with diverse students has used 'hierarchical' statistical approaches to identify the effective shared classroom-level features and their relations to student behaviour. Importantly, such hierarchical models first control for pupil-level variance, allowing us to look at classrooms as the 'unit of analysis'.

Our results first suggest that the socio-emotional, academic–instructional, and behavioural–managerial domains of teaching are not distinct but rather are strongly correlated in effective classrooms ($r = .7$ is quite typical) and the socio-emotional construct of classroom atmosphere as well as instructional and behavioural features predicts growth in listening and reading comprehension across 29 Grade 1 (equivalent to UK Year 1) classrooms. Our results also showed that students' perceptions of their involvement in, emotional tone of, and the supportiveness of teachers in diverse regular classroom environments was significantly related to student behaviour in Grade 1 (Deault and Savage submitted; Savage et al. 2011). Specifically, students' rating of the emotional tone of classrooms was strongly related to the same students' observed engagement in classrooms. This is important because observed student engagement has often been identified as a key long-term predictor of academic success, so a possible pathway by which emotionally supportive classrooms aid attainment is suggested. Importantly, data may not suggest a 'one-size-fits–all' approach. Deault and Savage (submitted) found that among the typical ranges of abilities in Grade 1, children who started the year with higher reading skills, classroom management (and specifically, classrooms that encouraged strong behavioural self-regulation among students) predicted growth in reading comprehension. In contrast, for students who started the year with weaker reading skills, student engagement predicted growth in reading comprehension. Finally, for students at risk of attention difficulties (based on a score of 65 or more on the Connors attention questionnaire), those who experienced high-quality teaching made significant gains in listening comprehension compared to students who were in less effectively taught classrooms. These results imply that effective literacy teaching practices are highly tuned to the distinct pedagogical and behaviour supports needs of students with different levels of current attainment and attentional resources. More generally, these findings demonstrate how important classroom practices in elementary schools are for the outcomes of children in them.

High correlations are routinely observed between scales measuring the academic and emotional content of effective classrooms (e.g. Pianta, Le Paro, and Hamre, 2008). In a recent meta-analysis of 223 school-based Social and Emotional Learning (SEL) programmes among over 250,000 students, Durlak et al. (2011) reported that such programmes are associated with significant gains in emotional development, behaviour, and attitudes. Notably, there was also an average 11 standard score point gain in academic terms in such programmes.

Finally, Powell and Tod (2004) carried out a systematic review of research on school behaviour. They found that 'behaviour management' could be improved by promoting 'mastery orientation' rather than 'performance orientation' in the curriculum. From this analysis 'performance' is understood as the demonstration of competence in a domain (e.g. a child demonstrating 'on-task' behaviour when required to do so by an adult), whereas 'mastery' is associated with a child's ability to understand and expertly apply their attention to a task to achieve personally meaningful goals (such as completing a project on a topic of personal significance). Mastery learning produced greater student engagement and motivation than performance learning (see Martin, Chapter 11, this volume, for more information on mastery and performance orientation).

Democratic models of teacher–pupil relationships feature prominently in the Powell and Tod review. Here, promotion of on-task discussion between pupils, the discouragement of competitive classroom contexts, and working in partnership with pupils in setting goals are important features. We also see important links between these concepts and the notions of 'Exploratory Talk' and 'interthinking' discussed by Littleton (Chapter 7, this volume). Powell and Tod encourage 'formative' assessment of social, emotional, and behavioural indicators of learning as well as academic assessment. The expert use of formative models of assessment is also associated with substantial improvements in student learning in other systematic reviews (see Hattie 2009). In addition, the development of partnerships with a shared understanding of learning behaviour issues between teacher and pupil can aid problem resolution. Powell and Tod conclude their review by arguing that increasing the integration of the 'social' and the 'academic' domains *is* effective teaching practice.

So what does this integrated approach look like in practice? Effective teaching begins right from the start of the academic school year. Teachers who establish a classroom atmosphere that is positive, introduce clear expectations, establish consistent procedures and encourage self-regulation are more likely to have students who show enthusiasm for learning and higher academic achievement (Bohn, Roehrig, and Pressley 2004; Roehrig and Christesen 2010). Effective teachers encourage higher student engagement and cooperation through appropriately challenging tasks. Effective teachers offer support consistently, listening carefully to students' thoughts and needs, and demonstrating compassion (Bohn et al. 2004; Mashburn et al. 2008). Quality of relationships as indicated in day-to-day interactions is a central feature of effective teaching (e.g. Hamre and Pianta 2001, 2005). Effective teachers will cover content with enthusiasm and create an interest in the content (Pressley et al. 2001). They consistently express positive expectations for student behaviour and academic achievement; their classrooms are democratic, offering choice and emphasizing students' ownership of the classroom and learning. They help students self-regulate their behaviour and learning. Effective teachers model positive behaviour such as enthusiasm and self-regulation, they offer praise judiciously for students' effort independent of their absolute success in tasks, and point out students who also model positive behaviour, thus further encouraging students to learn from their peers.

Effective teaching incorporates three important components that include holistic, balanced skill instruction, promotion of student emotions and motivation, and good classroom management (Pressley et al. 1998). In this sense, 'behaviour' cannot usefully be decontextualized from the ecosystems in which it operates. We now turn to a yet broader form of ecosystemic influence on children's behaviour: the legal–cultural context of Inclusive Education.

Inclusive education

Inclusive education is the key strategy of the Education for All (EFA) movement of the United Nations which calls for change in current educational practices to ensure equal learning and participation opportunities for all students (Peters 2007; United Nations Educational, Scientific and Cultural Organization (UNESCO) 1994). Inclusive education involves unifying special and general education services and restructuring the whole school system to provide equal access for all (Pather 2007). From a disability-specific perspective, inclusive education, also referred to as inclusion, is defined as providing appropriate educational practices to students with disabilities in regular classrooms of their neighborhoods (Loreman 2007; Porter 2008). Hansen (Chapter 22, this volume) provides a thorough examination of the rationale behind the move towards inclusive education.

Even a modest review of literature reveals differing views between educators regarding the meaning of inclusion (Allan and Slee 2008; Erten and Savage 2012). Classroom teachers are the central agents of all inclusion practices (Howes et al. 2005; Loreman 2007). However, a recent synthesis of international research found no evidence of teachers' acceptance of all students with disabilities in regular classrooms (Avramidis and Norwich 2002). Several studies worldwide reveal that adopting inclusive education policies may not result in teachers' acceptance of inclusive practices (Forlin, Douglas, and Hattie 1996; Sharma, Forlin, and Loreman, 2008). Teachers often report disability-specific factors such as the type and severity of students' disabilities as negatively affecting their inclusive practices (e.g. Anderson, Klassen, and Georgiou 2007; Forlin et al. 1996). Many educators still have difficulty differentiating inclusive education from earlier and traditional forms of special education such as integration (Barth 1996).

Different countries also follow different routes to reach the goal of inclusive education, making it very difficult to reach accurate comparisons across nations (Avramidis and Norwich 2002; Peters 2007; Porter 2008). Thus, given the potentially large literature on inclusion, in this part of the chapter, the focus of evidence on teacher attitudes is narrowed down to the Canadian context. With its multicultural, multilingual, and diverse society, Canada provides a perfect context for examining research on inclusion. Interestingly, Canadian literature on teachers' attitudes to inclusion indicates more positive findings compared to international results (e.g. Brackenreed 2008; Bunch, Lupart, and Brown 1997; Heath et al. 2004; Stanovich and Jordan 1998).

Inclusive education in Canada

Canada was one of the first countries to constitutionally guarantee rights of people with disabilities (Smith et al. 2010). More than two decades of Canadian inclusive education practices have influenced other countries (Peters 2007; Porter 2008; Timmons 2006). In recent decades, Canadian society has witnessed important changes in provincial legislation towards an inclusive model of education. Canada is also a country of great cultural and linguistic diversity and although this diversity may present some challenging societal and political issues, it should perhaps be viewed as the country's greatest strength (Timmons 2006). In this sense, Canada is committed to inclusion not for the purposes of following the international human rights framework, but for the goal of creating an inclusive Canadian society (Hutchinson 2010; Porter 2008). Hence, Canadian schools play a vital role in the quest for becoming a truly inclusive, diverse, and equitable society.

Although Canadian school policies are committed to inclusion, implementation of inclusive practices varies greatly at local levels (Smith et al. 2010). Service delivery models include special education classrooms (self-contained classrooms), resource room pull-out approaches, and full-time inclusive classrooms (Smith et al. 2010). Education is a provincial responsibility and there is no federal office of education (Lupart 1998; Timmons 2006), making national evaluation problematic.

Research evidence on Canadian teachers' inclusive practices

In contrast to research elsewhere documenting teacher resistance to inclusion (e.g. Avramidis and Norwich 2002), Canadian literature presents a more positive picture. Some Canadian studies found that when classroom teachers have resources and support at the whole-school level, implementing inclusive education is not perceived as a stressor (e.g. Brackenreed 2008; Bunch et al. 1997). An often-cited investigation by Bunch et al. (1997) examined attitudes to inclusive education in a nationwide study with 1,492 classroom teachers, administrators, resource teachers, special education teachers, and university students. Participants cited a lack of pro-fessional training and workload as major barriers in implementing inclusion (Bunch et al. 1997). Nevertheless, they were supportive of inclusion as an educational philosophy and reported professional training, guidance, and leadership of school administration and manageable classroom sizes as factors that can aid the implementation of inclusive education. Likewise, in a survey study Brackenreed (2008) examined 269 elementary and secondary school teachers' perceived stressors in inclusive classrooms. The factors that mitigated high levels of stress for teachers were: self-efficacy, professional training, and student behaviour. Results show that inclu-sion is not perceived as a stress factor when teachers receive sufficient support from the school (Brackenreed 2008).

Heath et al. (2004) examined the outcomes of a team-based approach in fostering inclusion of Grade 1–6 students who were identified by their teachers as having emotional and behav-ioural difficulties (EBDs), a student population that is often reported as the most challenging for inclusion (Kauffman 2008). Heath et al. (2004) followed an ecosystemic model and formed a multidisciplinary team of mental health professionals that provided services and support to fami-lies, students, and teachers within the school settings. Teachers reported that working as a team helped them to understand complexities of student behaviour and provided the support they needed in their natural context. Moreover, 93 percent of teachers reported that students with EBDs can be included in regular classrooms. Heath et al. show that teachers' perceptions of even students with EBDs can change through an ecosystemic approach of service delivery model.

Another important series of Canadian research has identified not only teachers' attitudes to students with disabilities but also the relationship between their teaching practices and attitudes to students labelled as 'exceptional' or 'at-risk'. The purpose of the Supporting Effective Teaching Project (SET) was to develop a model of factors that may predict effectiveness of teaching in inclusive classes (Jordan, Glenn, and McGhie-Richmond 2009; Jordan and Stanovich 2001; Stanovich and Jordan 1998). According to the review of SET research studies, there are four indicators of effective teaching practices in inclusive classrooms: (i) teachers' beliefs about disability, their roles and responsibilities for their students with disabilities, (ii) teachers' practices in core subject areas, (iii) teachers' practices in accommodating students with documented disabilities and those at risk, and (iv) collective beliefs of administrators and school staff regarding roles and responsibilities (Jordan et al. 2009). The path model examined in the SET studies proposes that the school norm (operationally defined by the expectations of the school principal), and teachers' beliefs about their roles and responsibilities predict effective classroom teaching practices, which in turn predict student outcomes (Jordan et al. 2009). The SET project shows that effective teachers are also effective in terms of delivering instruction and providing higher quality instruction in inclusive classrooms (Jordan et al. 2009).

Stanovich and Jordan (1998) investigated the relationship between teachers' practices and beliefs in relation to the overall school norm of inclusion. Teacher beliefs about students with disabilities were examined by grouping them on a scale with two polarizations based on interviews: teachers with pathognomonic (PATH) beliefs (those who believe that disability is a pathological condition intrinsic to the leaner), and teachers with interventionist beliefs (INT) (those who believe that all students can profit from learning opportunities irrespective of their individual differences). Multiple sources of data from classroom observations, surveys and interviews revealed significant differences in the way PATH teachers and INT teachers interacted with their students (Stanovich and Jordan 1998). Teachers with PATH beliefs engaged in less effective interaction patterns with all students compared to INT teachers. Similarly, Jordan and Stanovich (2001) found that teachers with INT beliefs, who take responsibility in their students' learning regardless of any diagnosis, interacted more with all of their students compared to teachers with PATH beliefs. Additionally, students with documented exceptionalities or those at risk had lower self-esteem compared to typically developing peers in classes of teachers with PATH beliefs.

The SET project highlighted the complex interrelations in a school context by showing that teachers' and school principals' attitudes to inclusion predict teaching practices and may also influence students' self-concepts (Jordan et al. 2009). Thus the process of change at an attitudinal level requires teachers and principals to investigate and critically examine their own notions of disability and identify their underlying assumptions about learning and teaching, and people 'who are perceived to be on the other side' (Howes et al. 2005: 142).

Supporting the next generation of teachers

A variable often found to influence teachers' attitudes to inclusive education is teacher education. Some studies reveal that the content of courses in colleges and universities has an impact on pre-service teachers' attitudes to inclusion (e.g. Loreman, Forlin, and Sharma, 2007; Sharma et al. 2008). Currently, pre-service teacher education is generally informed by a traditional special education view grounded in the medical model (Loreman et al. 2007), with many university textbooks generally presenting a deficit model of behaviour. Carrington (1999) argues that an emphasis on disability as an abnormality and deviance from the general population may cause teachers to focus on negative characteristics of students' behaviour rather than students' individual strengths in other areas. Teacher education courses that follow a social model aim to focus on the experiences of people with disabilities and create awareness about the role of society in disabling individuals (Loreman et al. 2007; Sharma et al. 2008).

In the USA, Kamens, Loprete, and Slostad (2000) surveyed 71 teachers of kindergarten to Grade 8 classrooms and asked for their opinions about how pre-service training should address inclusion. Participants reported that they would benefit from more information on specific disabilities. Teaching students with behavioural difficulties was reported as their main concern, and the participating teachers stressed the need for knowledge and skills to work with this student population. However, some studies examining the influence of information-based courses on teachers' attitudes to inclusion did not find any significant changes before and after these courses (Tait and Purdie 2000). Kamens et al. (2000) highlight that teachers should also have the opportunity to (i) reflect on their personal philosophies, experiences, and attitudes to people with disabilities, (ii) understand how society may create some barriers and challenges for people with disabilities, and (iii) acknowledge changing roles and responsibilities of all school professionals in an inclusive classroom.

In a cross-cultural survey study on attitudes and sentiments of pre-service teachers in Canada, Hong Kong, Australia, and Singapore, Loreman et al. (2007) found that pre-service teachers gained more confidence and held more positive attitudes by interacting directly with people with disabilities and learning about legislation and policy on inclusive education in their countries. Sharma et al. (2008) also found that teacher education that incorporated direct experiences with people with disabilities and focused on the rationale for a move toward inclusion resulted in more positive attitudes. Pre-service teachers who learn about the experiences of people with disabilities and the rights-based rationale for inclusive education can gain an ethical understanding of disability and engage in critical dialogues on disability and society (Loreman et al. 2007).

Mock and Kauffman (2002) argue that not every teacher can be prepared to teach students with disabilities and that specialized expertise is necessary, arguing that inclusive education draws 'dangerous conclusions' by assuming that every teacher can learn to teach every student (Mock and Kauffman 2002: 206). Loreman et al. (2007) point out that it is highly unlikely that classroom teachers will willingly take on the demanding job of implementing inclusive education since it is a systems-wide approach that should draw on the expertise of different professionals. Several studies have revealed that inclusive education requires collaboration of different school professionals including those with disability-specific expertise such as special education teachers, educational/school psychologists, and mental health professionals (Anderson et al. 2007; Heath et al. 2004; Jordan et al. 2009). Inclusive education invites different school professionals to work together and share their expertise. Teacher education programmes should provide pre-service teachers with opportunities to reflect on their personal experiences with people with disabilities (Carrington 1999; Kamens et al. 2000). Furthermore, we would argue that generating a dialogue on disability and diversity issues across the entire university campus can have powerful long-term educational and societal outcomes (see also Lupart 1998). We could certainly transfer the idea of promoting 'educational dialogues among students', discussed by Littleton (Chapter 7, this volume), to higher education settings and encourage such dialogue on disability among teachers in training.

Conclusions

This chapter has reviewed theory, evidence, and debate on classroom structures and children's behaviour. Pointedly, we have avoided the general class of simple cognitive-behavioural models in this chapter. We do not have anything against such models per se, but chapters on these approaches and practical 'behaviour management' tips from this literature abound. See also Vousden, Wood, and Holliman (Chapter 5, this volume), which also examines how in current times, classroom teachers are required to know and apply various methods from different theories. We also feel that for a number of reasons a richer and more ecosystemic picture is needed to understand and support children's behaviour in schools. Our case for this has been made by drawing out consistent patterns of evidence and best practice across both the effective schools and inclusive education literatures (Erten and Savage 2012).

Specifically we have reviewed a large body of very recent work suggesting that there is a close, even intimate, relationship between the emotional aspects and the academic business of classrooms. These two features are contingencies that teachers can and do influence, and both features influence children's behaviour in a way that is far more synergistic than generally noted. Importantly, some inclusion research in Canada goes a step further in exploring the attitudinal basis of teacher's socially and academically oriented actions. The perception of students as holding immovable within-child disabilities seems to be a major stumbling block to effective action in classrooms. This may be a form of teacher 'learned helplessness' and is particularly prevalent in understanding children's behaviour.

In sum, we feel that this research review suggests three 'take home' conclusions: firstly that children's behaviour relates closely to their engagement in the curriculum and the learning experience more generally; secondly that not only the quality of day-to-day relationships teachers establish with young people but the way (or perhaps the depth to which) teachers view possibilities for change in young people is likely to be central to the enterprise of teaching all effectively; finally, like effective classrooms, one must plan to start supporting teachers at day one: supporting inclusive attitudes in initial teacher education is a central part of a career-long shared approach that the educational community should offer to teachers supporting young children's behaviour in schools.

Contact address: ozlem.erten@mail.mcgill.ca

References

Allan, J., and Slee, R. (2008) 'Doing inclusive education research', in S. L. Gabel and S. Danforth (eds.) *Disability and the politics of education: an international reader*, New York: Peter Lang (pp. 141–59).

Anderson, C. J. K., Klassen, R. M., and Georgiou, G. K. (2007) 'Inclusion in Australia: what teachers say they need and what school psychologists can offer', *School Psychology International*, 28: 131–147.

Avramidis, E., and Norwich, B. (2002) 'Teachers' attitudes toward integration/inclusion: a review of the literature', *European Journal of Special Needs Education*, 17: 129–147.

Barth, F. (1996) 'Integration and inclusion: equal terms?', *British Columbia Journal of Special Education*, 20: 36–42.

Bohn, C. M., Roehrig, A. D., and Pressley, M. (2004) 'The first days of school in the classrooms of two more effective and four less effective primary-grades teachers', *Elementary School Journal*, 104: 269–287.

Brackenreed, D. (2008) 'Inclusive education: identifying teachers' perceived stressors in inclusive classrooms'. *Exceptionality Education Canada*, 18: 131–147.

Bunch, G., Lupart, J., and Brown, M. (1997) *Resistance and acceptance: educator attitudes to inclusion of students with disabilities*, North York, Canada: York University.

Byrne, B., Coventry, W. L., Olson, R. K., Wadsworth, S. J., Samuelsson, S., Petrill, S. A., et al. (2010) '"Teacher effects" in early literacy development: evidence from a study of twins', *Journal of Educational Psychology*, 102: 32–42.

Carrington, S. (1999) 'Inclusion needs a different school culture', *International Journal of Inclusive Education*, 3: 257–268.

Deault, L., and Savage, R. S. (submitted for publication) *Effective classroom contexts to develop literacy and attention skills for typical and atypical children.*

Durlak, J. A., Weissberg, R. P., Dymnicki, A. B., Taylor, R. D., and Schellinger, K. B. (2011) 'The impact of enhancing students' social and emotional learning: a meta-analysis of school-based universal interventions', *Child Development*, 82: 405–432.

Erten, O., and Savage, R. (2012) 'Moving forward in inclusive education research', *International Journal of Inclusive Education*, 16: 221–233.

Farrington, D. P., and Ttofi, M. M. (2009) *School-based programs to reduce bullying and victimization*, Oslo, Norway: Campbell Systematic Reviews [online]. Available at www.ncjrs.gov/pdffiles1/nij/grants/229377.pdf [retrieved 7 November 2012].

Fletcher, J. M., and Vaughn, S. (2009) 'Response to intervention: preventing and remediating academic difficulties', *Child Development Perspectives*, 3: 30–37.

Forlin, C., Douglas, G., and Hattie, J. (1996) 'Inclusive practices: how accepting are teachers?', *International Journal of Disability, Development and Education*, 43: 119–133.

Hamre, B. K., and Pianta, R. C. (2001) 'Early teacher–child relationships and the trajectory of children's school outcomes through eighth grade', *Child Development*, 72, 625–638.

Hamre, B. K., and Pianta, R. C. (2005) 'Can instructional and emotional support in the first grade classroom make a difference for children at risk of school failure?', *Child Development*, 76: 949–967.

Hattie, J. (2009) *Visible learning: a synthesis of over 800 meta-analyses relating to achievement*, London: Routledge.

Heath, N. L., Petrakos, H., Finn, C. A., Karagiannakis, A., McClean-Heywood, D., and Rousseau, C. (2004) 'Inclusion on the final frontier: a model for including children with emotional and behaviour disorders (E/BD) in Canada', *International Journal of Inclusive Education*, 8: 241–259.

Howes, A., Booth, T., Dyson, A., and Frankham, J. (2005) 'Teacher learning and the development of inclusive practices and policies: framing and context', *Research Papers in Education*, 20: 133–148.

Hoyle, C. G., Marshall, K. J., and Yell, M. L. (2011) 'Positive behavior supports: tier 2 interventions in middle schools', *Preventing School Failure: Alternative Education for Children and Youth*, 55: 164–170.

Hutchinson, N. L. (2010) *Inclusion of exceptional learners in Canadian schools: a practical handbook for teachers*, 5th edn, Toronto: Pearson Canada.

Jordan, A., Glenn, C., and McGhie-Richmond, D. (2009) 'The SET project: effective teaching and its relationship to teachers' epistemological beliefs and inclusive teaching practices', *Teaching and Teacher Education*, 26: 259–266.

Jordan, A., and Stanovich, P. (2001) 'Patterns of teacher–student interaction in inclusive elementary classrooms and correlates with student self-concept', *International Journal of Disability, Development and Education*, 48: 43–62.

Kamens, M. W., Loprete, S. J., and Slostad, F. A. (2000) 'Classroom teachers' perceptions about inclusion and preservice teacher education', *Teaching Education*, 11: 147–158.

Kauffman, J. M. (2008) 'Would we recognize progress if we saw it?: A commentary', *Journal of Behavioural Education*, 17: 128–143.

Loreman, T. (2007) 'Seven pillars of support for inclusive education: moving from "Why?" to "How?"', *International Journal of Whole Schooling*, 3: 22–38.

Loreman, T., Forlin, C., and Sharma, U. (2007) 'An international comparison of pre-service teacher attitudes toward inclusive education', *Disability Studies Quarterly*, 27(4).

Louden, W., Rohl, M., Barratt-Pugh, C., Brown, C., Cairney, T., Elderfield, J., et al. (2005) 'In teachers' hands: effective literacy teaching practices in the early years of schooling', *Australian Journal of Language and Literacy*, 28: 175–255.

Lupart, J. L. (1998) 'Setting right the delusion of inclusion: implications for Canadian schools', *Canadian Journal of Education*, 23: 251–264.

Mashburn, A. J., Pianta, R. C., Hamre, B. K., Downer, J. T., Barbarin, O. A., Bryant, D., et al. (2008) 'Measures of classroom quality in prekindergarten and children's development of academic, language, and social skills', *Child Development*, 79: 732–749.

Mock, D. R., and Kauffman, J. M. (2002) 'Preparing teachers for full inclusion: is it possible?', *Teacher Educator*, 37: 202–215.

Pather, S. (2007) 'Demystifying inclusion: implications for sustainable inclusive practice', *International Journal of Inclusive Education*, 11: 627–643.

Peters, S. (2007) 'Inclusion as a strategy for achieving education for all', in L. Florian (ed.) *The Sage handbook of special education*, Thousand Oaks, CA: Sage (pp. 117–130).

Pianta, R. C., La Paro, K. M., and Hamre, B. K. (2008) *Classroom assessment scoring system (CLASS) manual, K-3*, Baltimore, MD: Paul H. Brookes Publishing.

Porter, G. L. (2008) 'Making Canadian schools inclusive: a call to action', *Education Canada*, 48: 62–66.

Powell, S., and Tod, J. (2004) 'A systematic review of how theories explain learning behaviour in school contexts', in *Research Evidence in Education Library*, London: EPPI-Centre, Social Science Research Unit, Institute of Education, University of London.

Pressley, M., Wharton-McDonald, R., Mistretta-Hampston, J., and Echevarria, M. (1998) 'Literacy instruction in 10 fourth- and fifth-grade classrooms in upstate New York', *Scientific Studies of Reading*, 2: 159–194.

Pressley, M., Wharton-McDonald, R., Allington, R. L., Block, C. C., Morrow, L., Tracey, D., et al. (2001) 'A study of effective first-grade literacy instruction', *Scientific Studies of Reading*, 5: 35–58.

Rathvon, N. (2008) *Effective school interventions: evidence-based strategies for improving student outcomes*, New York: Guilford Press.

Roehrig, A. D., and Christesen, E. (2010) 'Development and use of a tool for evaluating teacher effectiveness in grades K–12', in V. J. Shute and B. J. Becker (eds.) *Innovative assessment for the 21st century*, New York: Springer (pp. 207–228).

Rutter, M., and Maughan, B. (2002) 'School effectiveness findings 1979–2002', *Journal of School Psychology*, 40: 451–475.

Savage, R. S., Deault, L., Burgos, G., and Di Stasio, M. (2011) 'The relationship between classroom environment and attainment in grade 1: converging evidence from teacher, observer, and pupil perceptions', Paper presented at the 18th Annual Conference of the Society for the Scientific Study of Reading, St Pete Beach, FL, 14 July.

Sharma, U., Forlin, C., and Loreman, T. (2008) 'Impact of training on preservice teachers' attitude and concerns about inclusive education and sentiments about persons with disabilities', *Disability and Society*, 23: 773–785.

Slee, R., and Weiner, G. (2001) 'Education reform and reconstruction as a challenge to research genres: reconsidering school effectiveness research and inclusive schooling', *School Effectiveness and School Improvement*, 12: 83–98.

Smith, T. E. C., Polloway, E. A., Patton, J. R., Dowdy, C. A., McIntyre, L. J., and Francis, G. C. (2010) *Teaching students with special needs in inclusive settings*, 3rd edn, Toronto: Pearson Allyn and Bacon.

Stanovich, P. J., and Jordan, A. (1998) 'Canadian teachers' and principals' beliefs about inclusive education as predictors of effective teaching in heterogeneous classrooms', *Elementary School Journal*, 98: 221–238.

Tait, K., and Purdie, N. (2000) 'Attitudes toward disability: teacher education for inclusive environments in an Australian university', *International Journal of Disability, Development and Education*, 47: 25–38.

Taylor, J., Roehrig, A. D., Hensler, S. B., Connor, C. M., and Schatschneider, C. (2010) 'Teacher quality moderates the genetic effects on early reading', *Science*, 328: 512–514.

Timmons, V. (2006) 'Impact of a multipronged approach to inclusion: having all partners on side', *International Journal of Inclusive Education*, 10: 469–480.

United Nations Educational, Scientific and Cultural Organization (UNESCO) (1994) *The Salamanca Statement and framework for action on special needs education*, Paris: UNESCO.

7

EDUCATIONAL DIALOGUES

Karen Littleton

THE OPEN UNIVERSITY, UK

Language is a powerful tool for exploring and creating ideas and common knowledge together. Given this, a substantial body of educational research work is concerned with understanding the nature and fostering the efficacy of classroom-based educational dialogues. Classroom talk is not simply a conduit for the sharing of information. Rather, it is the most important educational tool for guiding the development of understanding and for jointly constructing knowledge (Hodgkinson and Mercer 2008; Mercer and Littleton 2007). It is thus vital that educationalists pay careful attention to the quality of classroom talk and induct children and young people into effective 'ways with words' such that they become able to use language as a tool to build and explore ideas together. Harnessing the power of talk for reasoning and learning holds the key to children being able to engage sociably and effectively with others, to benefit from reasoned dialogue with their teacher and peers, and ultimately to be empowered as learners with the reasoning capabilities necessary to learn and rise creatively to the challenges posed by an uncertain future (Mercer and Littleton 2007). This emphasis on the significance of social interaction for learning, and language as one of the principal tools for constructing knowledge and understanding, derives from sociocultural theory and has its roots in the seminal work of Lev Vygotsky (see also Vousden, Wood, and Holliman, Chapter 5, this volume).

Vygotsky (1962, 1978) argued that the acquisition and use of language transformed children's thinking. He described language as both a cultural tool (for the development and sharing of knowledge among members of a community or society) and a psychological tool (for structuring the processes and content of individual thought). He also proposed that there is a close relationship between these two kinds of use, which can be encapsulated in the claim that 'intermental' (social, interactional) activity forges some of the most important 'intramental' (individual, cognitive) capabilities, with children's involvement in joint activities generating new personal understandings and ways of thinking. From a sociocultural perspective, then, language acquisition and use are seen as having a profound effect on the development of thinking (Mercer 2000, 2008; Wells 1999). This gives the study of talk in educational settings a special significance, and implies that its effective use in classrooms is important. It also suggests that knowledge not only is possessed individually, but is created by and shared among members of communities and the ways that knowledge is created are seen to be shaped by cultural and historical factors.

Detailed explanations of the sociocultural approach to education can be found in Wells and Claxton (2000) and Daniels (2001) but, in summary, from this perspective education is seen as a 'dialogic' process, with intellectual development being shaped to a significant extent through interaction. In educational settings it is not only the interactions between students and teachers that are regarded as being of significance and consequence, but also those among students. An important implication of this perspective is that we are encouraged to look for the basis of educational success, and failure, in the nature and quality of the social and communicative processes of education rather than in the intrinsic capability of individual students, the didactic presentational skills of individual teachers, or the quality of the educational methods, materials, and technologies that have been used.

In this chapter we will explore what educational research can tell us about what constitutes effective educational dialogue. The focus will be on: (i) how teachers can use dialogue to help children learn and (ii) the processes through which knowledge and understanding can develop when learners talk and work together relatively autonomously in classroom settings. This dual emphasis recognizes that any 'efficacious pedagogy should be a judicious mix of "immersion" in a community of practice and "overt focusing" and scaffolding from "masters" or "more advanced peers" who focus learners on the most fruitful sorts of patterns in their experience' (Gee 2000: 201–202).

The imperative to understand and promote educationally productive dialogue in classroom settings arises from findings from observational research which indicates that the typical environment for talk in most classrooms is not compatible with children's active and extended engagement in using language to construct knowledge (Wells 1986). This is because teachers often dominate the interaction in the classroom and may offer children limited opportunities for making brief responses to their questions (Alexander 2004) and there is also the paradox of children being seen to be working everywhere in groups but rarely 'as' groups (Blatchford et al. 2003; Littleton and Howe 2010). This is not to deny that teachers want to create a more inclusive and participatory environment for talk in their classrooms. Rather it is to acknowledge that many teachers may not have been trained in how to use the educational tool of language effectively and that some pupils may not have much confidence when it comes to expressing their ideas in words.

The section that follows draws on an encyclopedia on the theme of 'Social Interaction and Learning' (Littleton 2010) and the book *Dialogue and the Development of Children's Thinking* (Mercer and Littleton 2007) to explain how teachers can use dialogue to help children learn and develop.

How teachers can use dialogue to help children learn and develop

Over the past 30 or so years much research has sought to understand how teachers use talk to guide learning and construct a shared version of educational knowledge – common knowledge (Edwards and Mercer 1987) – with their students. Drawing on this body of work, Mercer (1995: 25–26) suggested that teachers use talk to do three things:

> a) 'elicit knowledge from students', so that they can see what students already know and understand and so that the knowledge is seen to be 'owned' by students as well as teachers; b) 'respond to things that students say', not only so that students get feedback on their attempts but also that the teacher can incorporate what students say into the flow of discourse and gather students' contributions together to construct more generalized meanings; and c) 'describe the classroom experiences that they share with the students', in such a way that the educational significance of those joint experiences is revealed and emphasized.

Knowledge elicitation and questioning

When attempting to elicit knowledge from their students, in addition to using direct elicitations, teachers very commonly use a strategy that Edwards and Mercer (1987) have termed 'cued elicitation'. Cued elicitation is a way of gradually drawing out from students the information that is being sought, by providing verbal hints and strong visual cues to the answer that is required.

Cued elicitation is often accomplished through asking questions, and there has been considerable controversy in educational research concerning the use of questions more generally as a strategy for guiding the construction of knowledge. Specifically, there has been disagreement concerning the functions and value of this characteristic form of classroom interaction (see for example Norman 1992; Wells 1999).

At one time researchers were critical of teachers' reliance on the use of questions. This is because researchers were suggesting that most questions asked by teachers are designed to elicit just one brief 'right answer' (see for example Dillon 1988; Wood 1992). Such questioning was also said to constitute a reiteration of information provided earlier by the teacher, with the consequence that students' contributions to the dialogic process of teaching-and-learning become limited and constrained. There was criticism too of the characteristic three-part IRF (initiation–response–feedback) structure of classroom discourse. IRF exchanges open with an initiation, usually in the form of a question, from the teacher. This in turn elicits a response from a student, to which the teacher typically provides an evaluative follow-up or feedback. An example is given below.

- *Teacher:* So how many wives did Henry VIII have?
- *Student:* I know, I know, was it six?
- *Teacher:* Good, good, yes six.

The suggestion was, as Skidmore (2006: 507) explains, that the IRF sequence results in a: 'quiz which requires students to do little more than display their recall of knowledge got by rote' and produces 'a pattern of teacher-led recitation which tends to reinforce the teacher's authority as the "transmitter" of received wisdom and severely restricts the possibilities open to students to contribute thoughtfully to classroom talk'.

However, most classroom researchers would probably now agree that such judgments were premature and simplistic. Such criticisms seemed to be premised on the assumption that all question-and-answer exchanges were performing exactly the same function. Yet, as Mercer and Littleton (2007) have noted, the forms of a language do not have a simple and direct relationship to their functions. In the classroom, teachers' questions can thus have a range of different communicative functions. They can, for example, be used to test children's factual knowledge or understanding, for managing classroom activity, and as a way of finding out more about what pupils are thinking. Of course, even this account is an oversimplification, because any single question can have more than one function. Also, a question takes on a special meaning in the context of ongoing events. Compare, for example, the function of asking for the name of the capital of Finland before beginning a scheme of work with asking the same question after it is completed.

The key point is that there is a need to distinguish between 'form' and 'function' when analysing and evaluating questions in teacher–pupil dialogue: and one can only judge the function of questions, and any other forms of language, in dialogic context. With respect to the IRF it can result in the learners' display of recalled knowledge – something Barnes (2008) has called 'presentational talk'. It can, however, also be used creatively by the teacher to 'help students plan ahead for a task they are about to carry out, or to review and generalize lessons learnt from the tasks they have already performed' (Skidmore 2006: 507). The teacher's follow-up, for instance, can be put to multiple uses – including clarification, exemplification, explanation, expansion, or justification of a student's response. It could also invite a student to do any of those things (Wells 1999).

Rojas-Drummond and Mercer (2004) have pointed to the ways in which the cumulative development of students' understanding can be carefully resourced and supported by the teacher's purposeful use of spiral IRFs. So while teachers' questioning certainly can require children to guess what answer is in the teacher's mind, that is merely one possible function. Teachers' questions can also serve other very important functions in the development of children's learning and their own use of language as a tool for reasoning. They can: encourage children to make explicit their thoughts, reasons, and knowledge and share them with the class; 'model' useful ways of using language that children can appropriate for use themselves, in peer group discussions and other settings (such as asking for relevant information possessed only by others, or asking 'why' questions to elicit reasons); and provide opportunities for children to make longer contributions in which they express their current state of understanding, articulate ideas and reveal problems they are encountering.

Responding to what students say and describing shared classroom experience

While wholly inappropriate or unsuitable contributions to a classroom-based discussion may be rejected or ignored, one of the ways teachers engage with their students is to incorporate their ideas and suggestions into the ongoing teaching–learning process. This is accomplished through confirmation or repetition of things of educational significance (to underscore their salience to the whole class) and the elaboration of contributions to further explain or highlight their significance (Edwards and Mercer 1987; Mercer 1995). This means that the resultant interaction can be construed as an 'improvisational' accomplishment (Sawyer 2004), whereby the instructional dialogue emerges from the interdependent, contingent, and reciprocal interplay of both the students' and the teachers' contributions.

From a student's perspective, school-work should ideally have a cohesive, cumulative quality in which specific activities and their goals can be seen to form part of a greater whole, as part of a purposeful educational journey (Alexander 2004; Mercer and Littleton 2007). Research has identified a number of ways in which teachers try to create continuities in the experience of learners; for example, by referring to past events and implicating these in the joint construction of knowledge with their students. Teachers commonly use 'recaps' to summarize what they consider to be the most salient features of a past event for the current activity (Edwards and Mercer 1987; Mercer 1995). Recaps can be 'literal', when a teacher simply sums up what happens ('Last week, we began reading *The Gruffalo*') or 'reconstructive', where the teacher 'rewrites history', presenting a modified version of events that fits their current pedagogic concerns. Teachers also frequently use 'elicitations' to help students' recall of past events (for example, 'Who can tell me what they found out about magnets in the last lesson?'). It is common too for them to mark past shared experiences as significant and relevant by using 'we statements' (as in 'Remember when we looked at the map of Finland?'). In these ways teachers invoke common knowledge and highlight the continuities of educational experience, trying to draw students into a shared, cumulative and progressive understanding of the activities in which they are engaged.

Alexander (2000), Crook (1999), Mercer and Littleton (2007) and other educational researchers have argued that coherent knowledge and purposeful understanding will not naturally emerge for students from their continuous immersion in classroom life: it has to be pursued actively as a goal, through the use of appropriate teaching strategies. In order to understand how classroom education succeeds and fails as a process for developing students' knowledge and understanding, research is now beginning to focus on exploring the temporal relationship between the organization of teaching-and-learning as a series of lessons and activities and how it is enacted through talk and joint activity (see for example, Littleton, Twiner, and Gillen 2010; Mercer 2008; Mercer and Littleton 2007; Rasmussen 2005; Scott, Mortimer, and Aguiar 2006). The importance of cumulative, rather than simply extended, dialogue is central to the notion of 'dialogic teaching' (Alexander 2004).

Dialogic teaching

Dialogic teaching is a concept that enables us to focus more precisely on the role of the teacher in classroom talk. The concept has emerged from the cross-cultural research of Alexander (2000) and is premised on reciprocity – in the sense that both teachers and pupils make substantial and significant contributions to classroom talk. It highlights the ways that teachers can encourage students to participate actively in dialogues that enable the students to articulate, reflect upon, and modify their own understanding – and, conversely, how they may avoid doing so. Alexander suggests that dialogic teaching is indicated by certain features of classroom interaction: questions are structured so as to provoke thoughtful answers; answers provoke further questions and are seen as the building blocks of dialogue rather than its terminal point, and individual teacher–pupil and pupil–pupil exchanges are chained into cumulative, coherent lines of enquiry rather than left stranded and disconnected (Alexander 2004: 32).

In terms of what the teacher actually does in classroom interaction, dialogic teaching can be characterized as that in which students are given opportunities and encouragement to question, state points of view, and comment on ideas and issues that arise in lessons; the teacher engages in discussions with students that explore and support the development of their understanding of content; the teacher takes students' contributions into account in developing the subject theme of the lesson and in devising activities that enable students to pursue their understanding themselves, through talk and other activity; and the teacher uses talk to provide a cumulative, continuing, contextual frame to enable students' involvement with the new knowledge they are encountering.

Dialogic teaching is essentially a specification of good practice, derived from both theory of the nature of dialogue (drawn from the work of Vygotsky, Bakhtin, and others) and observations of practice across a range of cultural settings. It has clear links, in both its origins and its nature, with some other concepts devised by educational researchers such as 'reciprocal teaching' (Brown and Palincsar 1989), 'contingent tutoring' (Wood and Wood 1999), 'dialogic enquiry' (Wells 1999) and 'dialogic spells' (Nystrand et al. 2003). As an educational concept, dialogic teaching is both descriptive and prescriptive. It represents an approach to classroom teaching that 'aims to be more consistently searching and more genuinely reciprocal and cumulative' (Alexander 2004: 1) than is typically observed in classrooms, anywhere in the world.

Dialogic teaching is that which is collective, reciprocal, supportive, purposeful, and cumulative. It requires a teacher to orient to the state of understanding of students, engage them in exchanges that will reveal the changing limits and possibilities of their developing interests and understandings, and adjust their communication strategies accordingly as classroom interaction progresses. It involves students taking an active, engaged role in both their own learning and that of their classmates; becoming explicitly part of a collective endeavour. It also requires that a teacher uses both authoritative talk (teacher-as-expert: closed questions, instructing, informing) and dialogue (teacher-as-learner: open questions, eliciting students' initial ideas, hearing what groups have achieved, discussing problems and misunderstandings to best effect) (Mortimer and Scott 2008; Scott et al. 2010).

Some key indicators of dialogic teaching also concern the ways in which children are seen to talk and work together in collaborative group settings, and Alexander particularly identifies the following as being important: children listen carefully to each other; they encourage each other to participate and share ideas; they build on their own and each other's contributions; they strive to reach common understanding and agreed conclusions, yet they respect minority viewpoints (Alexander 2004: 33). This characterization of children engaged with each other and each other's ideas clearly contrasts with the paradox, mentioned earlier, of children being seen to work everywhere in groups, but rarely as groups. So it is to an exploration of the processes through which knowledge and understanding can develop when learners talk and work together relatively autonomously in classroom settings that we now turn.

Talking and working together

In the 1970s Barnes and Todd undertook one of the most important early studies of the talk of children working together in school. It involved secondary-age children (Barnes and Todd 1977; Barnes 2008), but the insights that the research provided have informed much other research since, including that focused on the primary years. Barnes and Todd suggested that pupils are more likely to engage in open, extended discussion and argument when they are talking with their peers outside the visible control of their teacher, and that this kind of talk enabled them to take a more active and independent ownership of knowledge.

Based on their detailed observations, Barnes and Todd suggest that classroom discussion has to meet certain requirements for explicitness that would not normally be required in everyday conversation. One of their key ideas was the concept of Exploratory Talk, in which a speaker articulates half-formed thoughts so that they can be tested out in the telling, and so that others can hear them, and comment. In this kind of talk, knowledge is made publicly accountable, relevant information is shared effectively, opinions are clearly explained and explanations examined critically. They also argued that the successful pursuit of educational activity depends on learners (a) sharing the same ideas about what is relevant to the discussion and (b) having a joint conception of what it is intended to achieve. These points have been supported by other research based in primary schools (e.g. Bennett and Dunne 1992; Galton and Williamson 1992; Mercer and Littleton 2007).

The significance of exploratory talk

In the early 1990s, researchers working as part of the Spoken Language and New Technology project (SLANT) observed the talk of children aged eight to 11 years when they worked together in small groups at the computer in classroom settings (as described in Wegerif and Scrimshaw 1997). Classroom talk was recorded in 10 primary school classrooms across five counties in the south east of England. Detailed analysis of the children's joint sessions of work suggested that most of the interactions recorded were not task-focused, productive, or equitable. Some groups' talk involved them in unproductive, often highly competitive, disagreements. On the other hand, much group talk was relatively brief, somewhat cursory, and bland. These observations resonated with those of the other research projects, detailed earlier, that indicated that although grouping children was a common organizational strategy, talk of any educational value was rarely to be heard. That said, very occasionally there was evidence of a distinctive kind of interaction that was qualitatively different and more educationally productive. Here the children engaged in discussions in which they shared relevant ideas and helped each other to understand problems. They were mutually supportive and were constructively critical of each other's ideas, with challenges and counterchallenges being justified and alternative ideas and hypotheses being offered. There was more of the kind of interaction that Barnes and Todd called Exploratory Talk.

On the basis of the patterns of talk observed in the SLANT talk data (as described above), the researchers devised a three-part typology of talk designed to characterize the different ways in which children in the project classrooms talked together (Mercer 1995). The three types of talk characterized within the typology (Disputational, Cumulative, and Exploratory Talk) were defined as follows (Mercer and Littleton 2007).

- *Disputational Talk*, characterized by disagreement and individualized decision making;
- *Cumulative Talk*, in which speakers build positively but uncritically on what the others have said;
- *Exploratory Talk*, in which partners engage critically but constructively with each other's ideas. Compared with the other two types, in Exploratory Talk knowledge is made more publicly accountable and reasoning is more visible in the talk.

In this typology, the concept of Exploratory Talk differs from the original usage by Barnes and Todd by being less focused on individuals sorting out their thoughts and more on collaborating partners thinking together – or 'interthinking' (Mercer 2000).

The purpose of this three-part analytic typology is quite circumscribed: to focus attention on the extent to which talk partners use language to think together when pursuing joint problem-solving and other learning activities. The typology offers a way of exploring the functional variation of talk as a means for pursuing collaborative activity. It also has an evaluative dimension, reflecting a concern with educational effectiveness. In particular the value of Exploratory Talk is emphasized because this type of talk represents a joint, co-ordinated form of co-reasoning in language, with speakers sharing knowledge, challenging ideas, evaluating evidence and considering options in a reasoned and equitable way. By incorporating both constructive conflict and the open sharing of ideas, Exploratory Talk thus constitutes the more visible pursuit of rational consensus through conversation (see also Vousden et al., Chapter 5, this volume). Such talk also foregrounds reasoning. Its ground rules require that the views of all participants be sought and considered, that proposals be explicitly stated and evaluated, and that explicit agreement precede decisions and actions. Other educational researchers have independently come up with very similar characterizations of intellectually stimulating, collaborative, and productive classroom talk. For example, there are strong links between the concept of Exploratory Talk and what some educational researchers have called 'accountable talk' (Michaels and O'Connor 2002; Resnick 1999) and others have called 'collaborative reasoning' (Anderson et al. 1998) or 'argumentation' (Schwarz and Asterhan 2010).

While Exploratory Talk is of educational value, much collaborative activity in classrooms (as the SLANT project confirmed) is 'disputational' or 'cumulative' rather than 'exploratory'. One reason may be that many children do not have much experience or skill in generating talk of an 'exploratory' kind. It has been found, for example, that the amount and quality of talk between parents and young children at home varies considerably (for example, Wells 1986). In some homes, rational debates, logical deductions, extended narrative accounts, and detailed explanations may seldom be heard. The implication of this is that without guidance, instruction, and encouragement from a teacher, many children may not gain access to some very useful ways of using language for reasoning and working collaboratively, because those 'ways with words' are simply not a common feature of the language of their out-of-school communities. Children and young people are undoubtedly capable of using language effectively as a tool for thinking together, but many may not know how to, or at least do not recognize that this is what is expected of them.

Learning to use language as an educational tool clearly does not happen 'naturally', through participation and immersion in ongoing classroom life. Children need to be explicitly inducted into ways of talking and working together – such that the 'ways with words' and 'ground rules' implicated in educationally effective Exploratory Talk become familiar and accessible to them. The 'Thinking Together' classroom-based intervention programme is an example of a programme designed to induct children into using Exploratory Talk (see Mercer and Littleton 2007). Children aged between six and 13 years have been involved, together with their teachers, but research with the age group eight to 11 has been the most substantial. The intervention focuses on the use of talk that integrates teacher-led whole-class dialogue and group activity. Its main aim is to ensure that children enter collaborative activities with a shared conception of how they can talk and think together effectively. Evaluation work evidences the positive effects of the programme in respect of enhancing the quality of children's talk and their collective and individual performance on non-verbal reasoning tests (see Mercer and Littleton 2007). Although the 'Thinking Together' evaluation work was initially focused on examining whether there were changes in children's talk and reasoning as a consequence of involvement in the programme, this research has also demonstrated how teachers make a powerful contribution to the creation of contexts for learning in their classrooms. The ways in which they talk, act, and structure classroom activities convey strong messages regarding how learning and talking are to be done in such contexts. Where 'Thinking Together' was most efficacious the teacher modelled and exemplified exploratory ways of talking during whole-class sessions. By using and modelling exploratory ways of talking the teacher is acting as the children's discourse guide, showing them how to use talk to address problems and solve them.

Concluding remarks

It is an uncontroversial claim that through social interaction, children learn how language can be used to describe the world, to make sense of life's experience and to get things done. However, what children learn from talk in the classroom, and how significant it is for their psychological development and educational progress, will depend a great deal on the range and quality of the dialogues in which they engage. Without guidance, instruction, and encouragement from a teacher, many children may not gain access to some very useful ways of using language for reasoning and working collaboratively. It is vital that education provides children with opportunities for learning new and useful language-based ways of thinking. To do otherwise upholds an inequitable 'status quo' and undermines the empowering potential of school-based education.

Contact address: karen.littleton@open.ac.uk

References

Alexander, R. (2000) *Culture and pedagogy: international comparisons in primary education*, Oxford: Blackwell.
Alexander, R. (2004) *Towards dialogic teaching: rethinking classroom talk*, Cambridge: Dialogos.
Anderson, R. C., Chinn, C., Waggoner, M., and Nguyen, K. (1998) 'Intellectually-stimulating story discussions', in J. Osborn and F. Lehr (eds.) *Literacy for all: issues in teaching and learning*, New York: Guilford Press (pp. 170–188).

Barnes, D. (2008) 'Exploratory talk for learning', in N. Mercer and S. Hodgkinson (eds.) *Exploring talk in school*, London: Sage (pp. 1–15).

Barnes, D., and Todd, F. (1977) *Communication and learning in small groups*, London: Routledge and Kegan Paul.

Bennett, N., and Dunne, E. (1992) *Managing classroom groups*, London: Simon and Schuster.

Blatchford, P., Kutnick, P., Baines, E., and Galton, M. (2003) 'Towards a social pedagogy of classroom groupwork', *International Journal of Educational Research*, 39: 153–172.

Brown, A. L., and Palincsar, A. S. (1989) 'Guided, co-operative learning and individual knowledge acquisition', in L. B. Resnick (ed.) *Knowing, learning and instruction*, Hillsdale, NJ: Lawrence Erlbaum Associates (pp. 393–452).

Crook, C. (1999) 'Computers in the community of classrooms', in K. Littleton and P. Light (eds.) *Learning with computers: analysing productive interaction*, London: Routledge (pp. 102–117).

Daniels, H. (2001) *Vygotsky and pedagogy*, London: Routledge/Falmer.

Dillon, J. J. (ed.) (1988) *Questioning and discussion: a multidisciplinary study*, London: Croom Helm.

Edwards, D., and Mercer, N. (1987) *Common knowledge: the development of understanding in the classroom*, London: Methuen/Routledge.

Galton, M., and Williamson, J. (1992) *Group work in the primary classroom*, London: Routledge.

Gee, J. (2000) 'Discourse and socio-cultural studies in reading', in M. Kamil, B. Mosenthal, P. Pearson, and R. Barr (eds.) *Handbook of reading research, Volume III*, London: Lawrence Erlbaum Associates (pp. 195–208).

Hodgkinson, S., and Mercer, N. (2008) 'Exploratory talk for learning', in N. Mercer and S. Hodgkinson (eds.) *Exploring talk in school*, London: Sage (pp. xi–xviii).

Littleton, K. (2010) 'Learning through interaction', in P. Peterson, E. Baker, and B. McGaw (eds.) *International encyclopedia of education*, Oxford: Elsevier (pp. 698–704).

Littleton, K., and Howe, C. (2010) *Educational dialogues: understanding and promoting productive interaction*, London: Routledge.

Littleton, K., Twiner, A., and Gillen, J. (2010) 'Instruction as orchestration: multimodal connection building with the interactive whiteboard', *Pedagogies*, 5: 130–141.

Mercer, N. (1995) *The guided construction of knowledge: talk amongst teachers and learners*, Clevedon: Multilingual Matters.

Mercer, N. (2000) *Words and minds: how we use language to think together*, London: Routledge.

Mercer, N. (2008) 'The seeds of time: why classroom dialogue needs a temporal analysis', *Journal of the Learning Sciences*, 16: 33–59.

Mercer, N., and Littleton, K. (2007) *Dialogue and the development of children's thinking*, London: Routledge.

Michaels, S., and O'Connor, M. C. (2002) *Accountable talk: classroom conversation that works*, CD-ROM, Pittsburgh: University of Pittsburgh.

Mortimer, E., and Scott, P. (2008) *Meaning making in science classrooms*, London: McGraw-Hill.

Norman, K. (ed.) (1992) *Thinking voices: the work of the national oracy project*, London: Hodder and Stoughton.

Nystrand, M., Wu, L., Gamorgan, A., Zeiser, S., and Long, D. (2003) 'Questions in time: investigating the structure and dynamics of unfolding classroom discourse', *Discourse Processes*, 35: 135–198.

Rasmussen, I. (2005) *Project work and ICT: studying learning participation trajectories*. PhD thesis. Oslo, Norway: University of Oslo.

Resnick, L. B. (1999) 'Making America smarter', *Education Week Century Series*, 18: 38–40.

Rojas-Drummond, S., and Mercer, N. (2004) 'Scaffolding the development of effective collaboration and learning', *International Journal of Educational Research*, 39: 99–111.

Sawyer, R. K. (2004) 'Creative teaching: collaborative discussion as disciplined improvisation', *Educational Researcher*, 33: 12–20.

Schwarz, B., and Asterhan, C. (2010) 'Argumentation and reasoning', in K. Littleton, C. Wood, and J. Kleine Staarman (eds.) *International handbook of psychology in education*, Leeds: Emerald.

Scott, P., Ametller, J., Mortimer, E., and Emberton, J. (2010) 'Teaching and learning disciplinary knowledge: developing the dialogic space for an answer when there isn't even a question', in K. Littleton and C. Howe (eds.) *Educational dialogues: understanding and promoting productive interaction*, London: Routledge (pp. 289–303).

Scott, P., Mortimer, E., and Aguiar, O. (2006) 'The tension between authoritative and dialogic discourse: a fundamental characteristic of meaning making interactions in high school science lessons', *Science Education* 90: 605–631

Skidmore, D. (2006) 'Pedagogy and dialogue', *Cambridge Journal of Education*, 36: 503–514.

Vygotsky, L. S. (1962) *Thought and language*, Cambridge, MA: MIT Press.

Vygotsky, L. S. (1978) *Mind in society*, Cambridge, MA: Harvard University Press.

Wegerif, R., and Scrimshaw, P. (eds.) (1997) *Computers and talk in the primary classroom*, Clevedon: Multilingual Matters.

Wells, G. (1986) *The meaning makers*, London: Hodder and Stoughton.

Wells, G. (1999) *Dialogic enquiry: toward a sociocultural practice and theory of education*, Cambridge: Cambridge University Press.

Wells, G., and Claxton, G. (2000) *Learning for life in the 21st century: socio-cultural perspectives on the future of education*, London: Wiley Blackwell.

Wood, D. (1992) 'Teaching talk', in K. Norman (ed.) *Thinking voices: the work of the national oracy project*, London: Hodder and Stoughton.

Wood, H., and Wood, D. (1999) 'Help seeking, learning and contingent tutoring', *Computers and Education*, 33: 153–169.

8

LEARNING TO READ AROUND THE WORLD

Juan Zhang and Catherine McBride-Chang

UNIVERSITY OF PITTSBURGH, USA; CHINESE UNIVERSITY OF
HONG KONG, HONG KONG, SAR OF CHINA

Around the world, formal literacy education begins when children are between the ages of 3.5 (Hong Kong) and seven (e.g. Sweden) years. Whereas Chinese reading and writing education often begins with holistic rote memorization of characters, learning to read an alphabet typically begins with instruction on letter names and sounds. Most teachers worldwide adopt a mixture of skills-based learning, focused on the mechanics of the script to be learned, and whole-language learning, focused on oral language skills and how print and oral language interact, a way of emphasizing the usefulness and fun of learning to read and write. A mixture of these approaches seems optimal for promoting lasting skills and interest in literacy (for a review, see McBride-Chang 2004).

Literacy development is defined here as learning to read and write individual words; this chapter restricts this focus to young children (zero to seven years). The five topics included in this chapter are of interest in relation to both developmental processes and teaching and training of young children: the more research reveals about the correlates of literacy development across cultures, the more teachers (and parents) can apply this knowledge to their early instructional practices. The first four sections of this chapter focus on children's cognitive skills development for literacy, i.e. alphabet and phonological awareness, writing, morphological awareness, and bilingual reading, respectively. The final (fifth) section is devoted to parent–child interactions in reading and writing.

Letter knowledge, phonological awareness, and early reading development

An important building block of word recognition for the majority of the world's languages is alphabet knowledge. Letter knowledge gives children a way in which to decode print phonologically. The term 'phonological' refers to anything related broadly to speech sounds. Thus, knowing that the letter B makes the /b/ sound most of the time in English helps children to read words such as 'bad', 'tub', or 'blast'. Letters clearly represent phonological units.

Evidence for the importance of letter knowledge for learning to read is broad. The acquisition of an alphabetic principle is crucial for children's reading development (Adams 1990). Researchers across cultures have demonstrated that children's letter knowledge tends to be associated with word reading (e.g. McBride-Chang 2004). Once children learn to associate given symbols with given sounds, they can apply these to sounding out unfamiliar print. This decoding is typically boosted by children's vocabulary knowledge, allowing them to make connections between what they see on a page and what words they know from their language learning.

Letter knowledge includes both letter-name knowledge and letter–sound (or grapheme–phoneme) mapping. Both skills are good longitudinal predictors of beginning reading (e.g. Burgess and Lonigan 1998; McBride-Chang 1999). Some researchers have treated these as representing a single underlying unit because they tend to be highly correlated with one another (e.g. Worden and Boettcher 1990), while others have argued that these skills represent two different abilities because they may develop at different rates and have different developmental trajectories (e.g. Levin and Aram 2004; McBride-Chang 1999; Share 2004; Treiman et al. 1998; Worden and Boettcher 1990).

Apart from letter knowledge, phonological awareness is a core correlate of reading development in young children (Goswami and Bryant 1990). Phonological awareness is awareness of and access to speech sounds within a language. For example, knowing that 'banana' without the final syllable is pronounced 'bana' demonstrates phonological awareness. Awareness of single speech sounds is referred to as phonemic awareness. Single speech sounds include those indicated by letters or letter combinations such as 'b', 't', 'sh', or 'ch' in English. Impaired phonemic awareness can hinder the acquisition of the alphabetic principle – the idea that letters of the alphabet typically represent one or only a few speech sounds. Moreover, the ability to synthesize letter sounds constitutes a large part of the decoding processing in beginning reading. Numerous studies thus far have shown that impaired phonological awareness is the core deficit of dyslexia (for a review, see Bishop and Snowling 2004). Byrne, Samuelsson, and Olson (Chapter 29, this volume) elaborate on this finding.

Chinese is a morphosyllabic language, in which the mapping of orthography–phonology correspondences occurs at the syllable level (McBride-Chang et al. 2003). That is, each Chinese character is mapped onto a single syllable. Character pronunciations are not broken down into smaller phonological units. Syllable awareness is a consistent correlate of early Chinese reading acquisition (e.g. Chow, McBride-Chang, and Burgess 2005; McBride-Chang and Ho 2005), though sensitivity to other aspects of phonological awareness is also sometimes associated with Chinese word reading (e.g. Lin et al. 2010; Newman et al. 2011). According to the 'Grain Size Theory' (Ziegler and Goswami 2005), phonological information is represented by print at different levels with variable grain sizes across languages. Compared to English, Chinese is of a large grain size (i.e. at the syllable, rather than the phoneme, level), and, thus, syllable awareness is particularly important for early reading development in Chinese. The association between phonological awareness and reading ability is likely bidirectional (e.g. Chow et al. 2005; Perfetti et al. 1987; Wagner, Torgesen, and Rashotte 1994).

Apart from phonological awareness, suprasegmental sensitivity may also be important for reading development (e.g. Wood, Wade-Woolley, and Holliman 2009; Zhang and McBride-Chang 2010). Whereas phonological awareness focuses on segmenting words into smaller units such as phonemes, suprasegmental sensitivity focuses on perceptions that extend beyond a single speech sound, such as stress in English or lexical tone in Chinese. In a typical task of stress sensitivity, children are asked to distinguish words that have been mispronounced based on their original metric stress pattern (e.g. MONkey is pronounced instead as monKEY, i.e. with the vowel in the first syllable reduced but that of the second syllable fully articulated) (Holliman, Wood, and Sheehy 2008). Metric stress awareness is significantly associated with word reading (Holliman et al. 2008; Holliman, Wood, and Sheehy 2010), reading fluency (Holliman et al. 2010), and spelling ability, even with phonological awareness statistically controlled (Wood 2006) in English-speaking children. Children at risk for dyslexia (i.e. those with a parent or older sibling with reading difficulties) also manifest relative difficulty in repeating irregularly stressed words in Dutch (DeBree, Wijnen, and Zonneveld 2006). Different from English, Chinese is a tonal language, which means that the same syllable can represent different meanings when combined with different tones acoustically realized through different fundamental frequencies of speech. For example, there are four tones in Mandarin Chinese and the syllable /chi/ means *eat* 吃, *pond* 池, *ruler* 尺 and *naked* 赤 when combined with tones 1, 2, 3, and 4 respectively. Studies have additionally found that lexical tone sensitivity is uniquely associated with children's word reading in Chinese (e.g. McBride-Chang et al. 2008b; Shu, Peng, and McBride-Chang 2008).

Writing

Because phonological skills are crucial for learning to read, some researchers have pursued the idea of children's early writing as a window into their literacy skills (Chomsky 1971; Read 1975). The limited number of letters in an alphabet gives children an opportunity to express themselves fairly early. This opportunity has prompted an exploration of children's early 'invented' spelling.

Invented spelling refers to the process by which children make use of their own knowledge about letters and speech sounds to write words in ways that are sensible to them based on letter–sound correspondences. Although these often deviate from conventional spellings, many are relatively easy to understand. For example, children might spell 'like' as 'lik' or 'enough' as 'enuf'. Some speech sounds are close enough in oral language, though not in print, such that adults who are used to conventional spellings may not recognize them as sensible when in fact they are. For example, the 'tr' in 'train' might be written by children as 'jr' or 'chr'. Both of these are sensible options, as you will note if you try to make your mouth conform to the shape of the beginning of the word 'train' (Tangel and Blachman 1992). Children's early invented spelling in both Hebrew (Shatil, Share, and Levin 2000) and English (McBride-Chang 1998; Morris and Perney 1984) predicts children's early word reading. Furthermore, Ouellette and Sénéchal (2008) showed that those children who experienced a four-week small group intervention focused on invented spelling exhibited significantly better word recognition than did a group focused solely on phonological awareness or a control group following training.

Interestingly, letter–sound knowledge as indicated through early writing may even ultimately be helpful for learning to read Chinese characters. Invented spelling of Pinyin, a phonological coding system comprising both the Roman letters of the alphabet (marking segmental aspects) and lexical tone markers (indicating suprasegmental features) of a given word, is longitudinally independently associated with Chinese character learning (Lin et al. 2010; Pan et al. 2011). The following sentence (meaning 'This apple is delicious') (这个苹果很好吃) written in Pinyin looks like this: Zhè gè píng guǒ hěn hǎo chī. In this example, both the phonemes and the tones of the sentence are marked. In this research, the Pinyin–character recognition connection is presumably indirect. Learning letter sounds and tones explicitly allows these children to pair Pinyin, which is relatively easy to decode, with Chinese characters, which are more challenging to learn.

Invented spelling is an important aspect of literacy development in a second language as well. For example, McBride-Chang and Ho (2005) showed that early invented spelling of English was uniquely associated with Hong Kong Chinese children's word reading in English, though not Chinese. Yu (2006) described a case study of a child followed from ages seven to nine years on invented spelling of Chinese. This Chinese child attended an English-speaking school in Taiwan; thus, his Chinese was not as strong as his English. He made many errors in writing Chinese that parallel those in alphabetic orthographies, including writing homophones, phonological substitutions, and even print that had the global look of word writing but was nonsensical. Overall, children's early independent writing can reflect their understanding not only in terms of phonological sensitivity but also in relation to the form and structure of print more generally.

Morphological awareness

The role of morphological awareness in learning to read is also important. A morpheme is the smallest unit of meaning within a word. In English, morphemes can be represented as individual letters, as when 's' indicates a plural, or as whole words, as in 'lettuce', which also represents a single morpheme. Importantly, one individual Chinese character almost always represents a single morpheme. In English, morphological awareness is particularly obvious in spelling conventions. Without morphological rules, for example, 'bags' might be spelled as 'bagz' or 'walked' as 'walkt'. The 's' in 'bags' and the 'ed' in 'walked' are both inflections of the base words, indicating plural and past tense, respectively.

Researchers identify two other aspects of morphological awareness as important in learning to read across cultures. These are derivational morphology, involving prefixes and suffixes, and lexical compounding. For derivations, endings such as 'sion' or 'tion' typically mark words as nouns (e.g., extension, ascension, explosion; vacation, deprivation, complication). Learning these endings as holistic entities can facilitate their easy recognition, preventing incorrect spellings such as 'shen' or 'shun' or pronunciations such as 'sigh-on' or 'tie-on'. Researchers (e.g. Deacon and Kirby 2004; for a review, see Berninger et al. 2010) have demonstrated that morphological awareness tends to be linked to better reading in children. For example, Rispens, McBride-Chang, and Reitsma (2008) demonstrated that inflectional morphology was uniquely associated with word reading in Grade 1 and with word spelling in Grade 6. Derivational morphological skill was also uniquely associated with both word reading and word spelling at Grade 6.

In Chinese and Korean, there has been increasing interest in lexical compounding for reading acquisition (e.g. Cho, McBride-Chang, and Park 2008; Liu and McBride-Chang 2010; McBride-Chang et al. 2005). Most alphabetic languages make use of lexical compounds. For example, 'snowman' and 'pancake' are compound words. However, in Chinese and Korean, the prevalence of compound words in language is higher. Because there are often many words that make use of the same character in Chinese, it is useful to depend on compounding knowledge to facilitate reading. In English, knowing the word 'snow' might help children to recognize longer words containing it, such as 'snowshoe', 'snowflake', or 'snowmobile'. As a beginning reader, having memorized the word 'snow', an English-speaking child from a cold climate encountering the word 'snowflake' might guess its identity. This would likely make use of morphological awareness ('snow' is often compounded with other words) and phonological awareness (e.g., the 'f' following 'snow' in this word sounds like /f/) so that (s)he might identify the word either as the incorrect 'snowfall', representing incomplete knowledge making use of the 'f' and 'l' in the word or the correct 'snowflake'. In Chinese, use of morphological awareness is perhaps more straightforward than this example because characters represent distinguishable individual units that can be combined. For example, the morpheme 爱 (ài – love) can be found in words such as 可爱 (kě ài – lovely), 爱国 (ài guó – patriotism), and 爱人 (ài rén – lover/spouse).

In both Chinese and Korean, there are many more homophones than there are in most alphabetic languages, so lexical compounding is necessary to disambiguate across words. An analogy in English might be that in order to understand the word 'scent', a teacher might refer to 'scent', as in 'lavender scent', but not as in 'fifty-cent stamp'. Sensitivity to both homophone and lexical compounding knowledge tends to be associated with growth in word reading in

Chinese (and sometimes Korean), either directly (e.g. Chow et al. 2008) or indirectly through an association with vocabulary knowledge (McBride-Chang et al. 2008a).

Bilingual reading for beginning readers

The majority of the world's children speak more than one language. Many of these children also learn to read in more than one language, often in more than one orthography, including Hebrew–English, Chinese–English, or Korean–English. There are a number of factors that likely influence this reading development. Relative exposure to the language, including parents' education levels and comfort with the second language for the purpose of scaffolding the child's learning, is one important factor (e.g. McBride-Chang et al. 2012a). Age of exposure to the language is another, with those learning earlier knowing more words (e.g. McBride-Chang and Kail 2002).

One overarching question is the extent to which there is phonological transfer from a first language to a second language. Researchers have fairly consistently found that children's phonological awareness in the first (L1) and second, or foreign (L2) languages tend to be correlated, suggesting a phonological transfer effect (e.g. Bialystok, Luk, and Kwan 2005; Geva, Wade-Woolley, and Shany 1997). For example, Huang and Hanley (1994) found that phonological awareness in both Chinese and English for Cantonese-speaking Hong Kong children and Mandarin-speaking children from Taiwan was correlated for both groups of children.

Evidence is not conclusive on whether bilinguals have an advantage over monolinguals in phonological awareness, however. In one study, bilingual children had better phonological awareness in kindergarten, but this advantage vanished at Grade 1 with the introduction of formal phonological instruction (Bruck and Genesee 1995). However, results from Bialystok et al. (2005) were different: across four groups of first graders – monolingual English children, Cantonese–English bilinguals, Hebrew–English bilinguals, and Spanish–English bilinguals – recruited by the authors, the latter two groups performed significantly better than the first two groups on a phoneme awareness task; the first two groups performed similarly to one another. Thus, whether bilinguals have better phonological awareness than monolinguals might at least partly depend on whether or not the two languages being learned share a similar writing system.

The bilingual age of acquisition, defined as 'the age when a bilingual child first begins receiving intensive, systematic, and maintained exposure to his/her new language' (Kovelman, Baker, and Petitto 2008: 204), may also influence reading acquisition. For example, Kovelman et al. (2008) found that early bilinguals (age of first exposure from birth to three years old) performed better than late bilinguals (whose age of first exposure ranged from three to six years) on reading ability and phonological awareness, suggesting an advantage of early exposure to second language.

Apart from issues of phonological awareness and reading across two languages, there has been some recent work on transfer of morphological awareness (lexical compounding) across Chinese and English. For example, Wang, Cheng, and Chen (2006) found that for Chinese children learning English at school in the USA, English lexical compounding skill was uniquely associated with character reading and reading comprehension, with other Chinese metalinguistic skills statistically controlled. Pasquarella et al. (2011) found similar results and extended such English compounding skills to Chinese vocabulary development as well in Chinese primary school children. Training of fifth graders in Chinese lexical compounding also facilitated their L2 lexical compounding in English (Zhang et al. 2010). Longitudinal evidence for transfer of morphological skills such as use of inflections in English–French bilinguals has also been demonstrated (e.g. Deacon, Wade-Woolley, and Kirby 2007). Thus, morphological awareness transfer in bilingual children appears to be fairly common, particularly provided that the aspect of morphological awareness that is considered is analogous across languages.

Parent–child interactions for early literacy

Apart from children's individual cognitive skills, how parents scaffold their children's early literacy development is also of great interest to researchers and educators (e.g. Mol and Bus 2011; Whitehurst and Lonigan 1998). The bulk of this research comes from studies of how parents read with their children; such studies consistently show at least a moderate effect of such reading on children's early language development across cultures (e.g. Bus, van IJzendoorn, and Pellegrini 1995; Mol and Bus 2011; Sénéchal et al. 2008; Van Steensel et al. 2011). At the same time, however, parent–child reading seems to have no direct discernible effect on children's literacy skills per se. For example, children rarely look at the print of any given book as their parents read to them (e.g. Evans and Saint-Aubin 2005). Instead, it appears that what parents focus on is what children learn in the shared reading experience (e.g. Aram and Levin 2002; Sénéchal 2006). When parents explicitly teach their children literacy skills by pointing out letters or Chinese characters on the page, children will learn these. However, during 'storytime' in the homes of most young children, the focus tends to be much more on storytelling and language comprehension. Thus, the greatest benefit that children derive from shared parent–child reading tends to be enhanced language skills (e.g. Chow et al. 2008; Kim 2009; Reese and Cox 1999).

Parents' scaffolding of their children's writing is relatively strongly associated with children's literacy development, however. Aram and Levin (2001, 2004) designed a paradigm in which mothers of preschoolers were asked to help their children to write words in any way they wished. The Israeli mothers and children were given the task of writing a few words that were supposed to be orally familiar to the children but that the preschool children should not ordinarily have known how to write. Mothers' approaches to this writing task were recorded, and children's own independent word reading and writing were tested separately. Overall, children whose mothers focused particularly on analytic aspects of writing, by highlighting letter names and letter sounds and their links to the spellings of given words, tended to manifest better literacy skills than did those children whose mothers focused more on unanalysed writing, including simply copying the words. A longitudinal study of Pinyin in Chinese (McBride-Chang et al. 2012b) yielded similar results. Likewise, Lin and colleagues (2009, 2010) found that Chinese mothers' analytic focus on Chinese character writing was associated with better literacy skills in their children. However, for Chinese character writing, the analytic focus tended to centre on morphological skills, rather than phonological cues, which were very rare across all mother–child interactions. Interestingly, Lin et al. (2009) found that the greater mothers' focuses were on simply copying Chinese characters, the worse the children's literacy skills were. Overall, then, parents' interactions with children set the stage for literacy development in different aspects, including both early language development and print skill development.

Conclusion

This chapter has highlighted some important components of children's early reading development across cultures. How both segmental and suprasegmental phonological sensitivity, including letter sound knowledge in alphabetic orthographies, are associated with word reading skills in young children, including the idea of phonological skills sensitivity as manifested in children's own writing via invented spelling, was first discussed. The role of morphological awareness in learning to read was then considered cross-culturally. One crucial point about children's literacy development is the fact that the majority of the world's children are learning to read in at least two languages simultaneously. Some research on phonological and morphological awareness across languages was, therefore, reviewed in the section on bilingual reading development. The review ended with a consideration of parent–child scaffolding of early literacy activities, given that both joint book reading and joint writing activities can influence children's reading development.

Apart from these factors, perhaps the most obvious one may be formal instruction at school. The topic of teaching techniques for literacy learning is beyond the scope of this chapter. However, perhaps one good example of the effects of teaching is reflected in diversities in teaching and learning of Chinese. Children in Mainland China are taught to learn Chinese with the assistance of Pinyin, a phonological system; however, Hong Kong Chinese children learn characters through rote memory only. As a result, mastery of phonological awareness seemed to be more difficult for Hong Kong children as compared to their Mainland counterparts (Zhang and McBride-Chang 2011).

To conclude, worldwide, phonological sensitivity, morphological awareness, and scaffolding by parents and teachers in a context that allows for some experimentation with and an analytic focus on print are all essential ingredients for children's early success in literacy development.

Contact address: cmcbride@psy.cuhk.edu.hk

References

Adams, M. J. (1990) *Beginning to read: thinking and learning about print,* Cambridge, MA: MIT Press.

Aram, D., and Levin, I. (2001) 'Mother–child joint writing in low SES: sociocultural factors, maternal mediation, and emergent literacy', *Cognitive Development*, 16: 831–852.

Aram, D., and Levin, I. (2002) 'Mother–child joint writing and storybook reading: relations with literacy among low SES kindergartners', *Merrill-Palmer Quarterly*, 48: 202–224.

Aram, D., and Levin, I. (2004) 'The role of maternal mediation of writing to kindergartners in promoting literacy in school: a longitudinal perspective', *Reading and Writing*, 17: 387–409.

Berninger, V. W., Abbott, R. D., Nagy, W., and Carlisle, J. (2010) 'Growth in phonological, orthographic, and morphological awareness in grades 1 to 6', *Journal of Psycholinguistic Research*, 39: 141–163.

Bialystok, E., Luk, G., and Kwan, E. (2005) 'Bilingualism, biliteracy, and learning to read: interactions among languages and writing systems', *Scientific Studies of Reading*, 9: 43–61.

Bishop, D. V. M., and Snowling, M. J. (2004) 'Developmental dyslexia and specific language impairment: same or different?', *Psychological Bulletin*, 6: 858–886.

Bruck, M., and Genesee, F. (1995) 'Phonological awareness in young second language learners', *Journal of Child Language*, 22: 307–324.

Burgess, S. R., and Lonigan, C. J. (1998) 'Bidirectional relations of phonological sensitivity and prereading abilities: evidence from a preschool sample', *Journal of Experimental Child Psychology*, 70: 117–141.

Bus, A. G., van IJzendoorn, M. H., and Pellegrini, A. D. (1995) 'Joint book reading makes for success in learning to read: a meta-analysis on intergenerational transmission of literacy', *Review of Educational Research*, 65: 1–21.

Cho, J.-R., McBride-Chang, C., and Park, S.-G. (2008) 'Phonological awareness and morphological awareness: differential associations to regular and irregular word recognition in early Korean Hangul readers', *Reading and Writing*, 21: 255–274.

Chomsky, C. (1971) 'Write first, read later', *Childhood Education*, 47: 296–299.

Chow, B. W.-Y., McBride-Chang, C., and Burgess, S. (2005) 'Phonological processing skills and early reading abilities in Hong Kong Chinese kindergarteners learning to read English as a second language', *Journal of Educational Psychology*, 97: 81–87.

Chow, B. W.-Y., McBride-Chang, C., Cheuk, C., and Cheung, H. (2008) 'Dialogic reading and morphology training in Chinese children: effects on language and literacy. *Developmental Psychology*, 44: 233–244.

Deacon, S. H., and Kirby, J. R. (2004) 'Morphological awareness: just "more phonological"? The roles of morphological and phonological awareness in reading development', *Applied Psycholinguistics*, 25: 223–238.

Deacon, S. H., Wade-Woolley, L., and Kirby, J. R. (2007) 'Crossover: the role of morphological awareness in French immersion children's reading', *Developmental Psychology*, 43: 732–746.

DeBree, E., Wijnen, F., and Zonneveld, W. (2006) 'Word stress production in three-year-old children at risk of dyslexia', *Journal of Research in Reading*, 29: 304–317.

Evans, M. A., and Saint-Aubin, J. (2005) 'What children are looking at during shared storybook reading: evidence from eye movement monitoring', *Psychological Science*, 16: 913–920.

Geva, E., Wade-Woolley, L., and Shany, M. (1997) 'Development of reading efficiency in first and second language', *Scientific Studies of Reading*, 1: 119–144.

Goswami, U., and Bryant, P. (1990) *Phonological skills and learning to read,* Hove, UK: Lawrence Erlbaum Associates.

Huang, H. S., and Hanley, J. R. (1994) 'Phonological awareness and visual skills in learning to read Chinese and English', *Cognition,* 54: 73–98.

Holliman, A. J., Wood, C., and Sheehy, K. (2008) 'Sensitivity to speech rhythm explains individual differences in reading ability independently of phonological awareness', *British Journal of Developmental Psychology*, 26: 357–367.

Holliman, A. J., Wood, C., and Sheehy, K. (2010) 'Does speech rhythm sensitivity predict children's reading ability 1 year later?' *Journal of Educational Psychology*, 102: 356–366.

Kim, Y.-S. (2009) 'The relationship between home literacy practices and developmental trajectories of emergent literacy and conventional literacy skills for Korean children', *Reading and Writing*, 22: 57–84.

Kovelman, I., Baker, S. A., and Petitto, L.-A. (2008) 'Age of first bilingual language exposure as a new window into bilingual reading development', *Bilingualism: Language and Cognition*, 11: 203–223.

Levin, I., and Aram, D. (2004) 'Children's letter names contribute to early literacy', in D. Ravid and H. Bat-Zeev Shyldkrot (eds.) *Perspectives on language and language development,* Dordrecht: Kluwer (pp. 223–241).

Lin, D., McBride-Chang, C., Aram, D., Levin, I., Cheung, Y. M., Chow, Y. Y., and Tolchinsky, L. (2009) 'Maternal mediation of writing in Chinese children', *Language and Cognitive Processes*, 24: 1286–1311.

Lin, D., McBride-Chang, C., Shu, H., Zhang, Y., Li, H., Zhang, J., Aram, D., and Levin, I. (2010) 'Small wins big: analytic Pinyin skills promote Chinese word reading', *Psychological Science*, 21: 1117–1122.

Liu, P. D., and McBride-Chang, C. (2010) 'What is morphological awareness? Tapping lexical compounding awareness in Chinese third graders', *Journal of Educational Psychology*, 102, 62–73.

McBride-Chang, C. (1998) 'The development of invented spelling', *Early Education and Development*, 9: 147–160.

McBride-Chang, C. (1999) 'The ABC's of the ABC's: the development of letter–name and letter–sound knowledge', *Merrill-Palmer Quarterly*, 45: 285–308.

McBride-Chang, C. (2004) *Children's literacy development,* London: Oxford Press.

McBride-Chang, C., Cho, J.-R., Liu, H., Wagner, R. K., Shu, H., Zhou, A., Cheuk, C. S.-M., and Muse, A. (2005) 'Changing models across cultures: associations of phonological and morphological awareness to reading in Beijing, Hong Kong, Korea, and America', *Journal of Experimental Child Psychology*, 92: 140–160.

McBride-Chang, C., and Ho, C. S.-H. (2005) 'Predictors of beginning reading in Chinese and English: a 2-year longitudinal study of Chinese kindergartners', *Scientific Studies of Reading*, 9: 117–144.

McBride-Chang, C., and Kail, R. (2002) 'Cross-cultural similarities in the predictors of reading acquisition', *Child Development*, 73: 1392–1407.

McBride-Chang, C., Liu, P. D., Wong, T., Wong, A., and Shu, H. (2012a) 'Specific reading difficulties in Chinese, English, or both: longitudinal markers of phonological awareness, morphological awareness, and RAN in Hong Kong Chinese children', *Journal of Learning Disabilities,* 45, 503–514.

McBride-Chang, C., Lin, D., Liu, P. D., Aram, D., Levin, I., Cho, J.-R., Shu, H., and Zhong, Y. (2012b) 'The ABCs of Chinese: maternal mediation of Pinyin for Chinese children's early literacy skills', *Reading and Writing*, 25: 283–300.

McBride-Chang, C., Shu, H., Zhou, A., Wat, C. P., and Wagner, R. K. (2003) 'Morphological awareness uniquely predicts young children's Chinese character recognition', *Journal of Educational Psychology*, 95: 743–751.

McBride-Chang, C., Tardif, T., Cho, J.-R., Shu, H., Fletcher, P., Stokes, S. F., Wong, A., and Leung, K.-W. (2008a) 'What's in a word? Morphological awareness and vocabulary knowledge in three languages', *Applied Psycholinguistics*, 29: 437–462.

McBride-Chang, C., Tong, X., Shu, H., Wong, A. M-Y., Leung, K., Tardif, T. (2008b) 'Syllable, phonemes, and tone: psycholinguistic units in early Chinese and English word recognition', *Scientific Studies of Reading*, 12: 171–194.

Mol, S. E., and Bus, A. G. (2011) 'To read or not to read: a meta-analysis of print exposure from infancy to early adulthood', *Psychological Bulletin*, 13: 267–296.

Morris, D., and Perney, J. (1984) 'Developmental spelling as a predictor of first grade reading achievement', *Elementary School Journal*, 84: 440–457.

Newman, E. H., Tardif, T., Huang, J., and Shu, H. (2011) 'Phonemes matter: the role of phoneme-level awareness in emergent Chinese readers', *Journal of Experimental Child Psychology*, 108: 242–259.

Ouellette, G., and Sénéchal, M. (2008) 'Pathways to literacy: a study of invented spelling and its role in learning to read', *Child Development*, 79: 899–913.

Pan, J., McBride-Chang, C., Shu, H., Liu, H., Zhang, Y., and Li, H. (2011) 'What's in the naming? A 5-year longitudinal study of early rapid naming and phonological sensitivity in relation to subsequent reading skills in both native Chinese and English as a second language', *Journal of Educational Psychology*, 103: 897–908.

Pasquarella, A., Chen, X., Lam, K., Luo, Y. C., and Ramirez, G. (2011) 'Cross language transfer of morphological awareness in Chinese–English bilinguals', *Journal of Research in Reading*, 34: 23–41.

Perfetti, C. A., Beck, I., Bell, L., and Hughes, C. (1987) 'Phonemic knowledge and learning to read are reciprocal: a longitudinal study of first grade children', *Merrill-Palmer Quarterly*, 33: 283–319.

Read, C. (1975) *Children's categorizations of speech sounds in English,* Urbana, IL: National Council of Teachers in English.

Reese, E., and Cox, A. (1999) 'Quality of adult book reading affects children's emergent literacy', *Developmental Psychology*, 35: 20–28.

Rispens, J. E., McBride-Chang, C., and Reitsma, P. (2008) 'Morphological awareness and early and advanced word recognition and spelling in Dutch: a cross-sectional study', *Reading and Writing*, 21: 587–607.

Sénéchal, M. (2006) 'Testing the home literacy model: parent involvement in kindergarten is differentially related to grade 4 reading comprehension, fluency, spelling, and reading for pleasure', *Scientific Studies of Reading*, 10: 59–87.

Sénéchal, M., Pagan, S., Lever, R., and Ouellette, G. P. (2008) 'Relations among the frequency of shared reading and 4-year-old children's vocabulary, morphological and syntax comprehension, and narrative skills', *Early Education and Development*, 19: 27–44.

Share, D. L. (2004) 'Knowing letter names and learning letter sounds: a causal connection', *Journal of Experimental Child Psychology*, 88: 213–233.

Shatil, E., Share, D. L., and Levin, I. (2000) 'On the contribution of kindergarten writing to grade 1 literacy: a longitudinal study in Hebrew', *Applied Psycholinguistics*, 21: 1–21.

Shu, H., Peng, H., and McBride-Chang, C. (2008) 'Phonological awareness in young Chinese children', *Developmental Science*, 11: 171–181.

Tangel, D. M., and Blachman, B. A. (1992) 'Effect of phoneme awareness instruction on kindergarten children's invented spellings', *Journal of Reading Behavior*, 24: 233–258.

Treiman, R., Tincoff, R., Rodriguez, K., Mouzaki, A., and Francis, D. (1998) 'The foundations of literacy: learning the sounds of letters', *Child Development*, 69: 1524–1540.

Van Steensel, R., McElvany, N., Kurvers, J., and Herppich, S. (2011) 'How effective are family literacy programs? Results of a meta-analysis', *Review of Educational Research*, 81, 69–96.

Wagner, R. K., Torgesen, J. K., and Rashotte, C. A. (1994) 'Development of reading related phonological processing abilities: new evidence of bi-directional causality from a latent variable longitudinal study', *Developmental Psychology*, 30: 73–87.

Wang, M., Cheng, C., and Chen, S.-W. (2006) 'Contribution of morphological awareness to Chinese–English biliteracy acquisition', *Journal of Educational Psychology*, 98: 542–553.

Whitehurst, G. J., and Lonigan, C. J. (1998) 'Child development and emergent literacy', *Child Development*, 69: 848–872.

Wood, C. (2006) 'Metrical stress sensitivity in young children and its relationship to phonological awareness and reading', *Journal of Research in Reading*, 29: 270–287.

Wood, C., Wade-Woolley., and Holliman, A. J. (2009) 'Prosodic awareness: beyond phonemes', in C. Wood and V. Connelly (eds.) *Contemporary perspectives on reading and spelling,* London: Routledge (pp. 9–23).

Worden, P. E., and Boettcher, W. (1990) 'Young children's acquisition of alphabetic knowledge', *Journal of Reading Behavior*, 22: 277–295.

Yu, M.-C. (2006) 'Explorations in language and literacy learning: a two-year case study on a nine-year-old Chinese–English bilingual child's Chinese invented spelling', *Journal of Language and Linguistics*, 5: 132–157.

Zhang, J., Anderson, R. C., Li, H., Dong, Q., Wu, X., and Zhang, Y. (2010) 'Cross-language transfer of insight into the structure of compound words', *Reading and Writing*, 23: 311–326.

Zhang, J., and McBride-Chang, C. (2010) 'Auditory sensitivity, speech perception, and reading development and impairment', *Educational Psychology Review*, 22: 323–338.

Zhang, J., and McBride-Chang, C. (2011) 'Diversity in Chinese literacy acquisition', *Reading Systems Research*, 3: 87–102.

Ziegler, J., and Goswami, U. (2005) 'Reading acquisition, developmental dyslexia, and skilled reading across languages: a psycholinguistic grain size theory', *Psychological Bulletin*, 131: 3–29.

9

DIGITAL TECHNOLOGY AS ENRICHMENT OF YOUNG CHILDREN'S LITERACY ENVIRONMENT

Maria T. de Jong and Marian J. A. J. Verhallen

LEIDEN UNIVERSITY, THE NETHERLANDS

Despite the wide use of computers in households and schools, there is a dearth of research about how their unique features contribute to young children's learning (Tamim et al. 2011). This chapter starts with a discussion about the importance of reading picture storybooks for comprehension skills to develop. Next, in order to unravel effects of digital picture storybooks, which are available in ever increasing numbers, nuanced studies are presented that compare how different computer features affect different comprehension skills. First parent-led shared reading is contrasted with children interacting with digital picture storybooks. Effects of different digital features and the number of interactive possibilities and their congruency with the storyline were tested next.

Picture storybooks as impetus for comprehension skills development

Learning to read means learning to crack the code of written language and discovering the meaning of the text. Although there are differences between countries related to the transparency of the language, most children can decode words relatively soon after they have started learning to read (Seymour et al. 2003; Ziegler et al. 2010) whereas reading comprehension skills are harder to master and need much more practice (Ouellette and Beers 2010). Decoding skills are a prerequisite but not a guarantee that comprehension will occur (Aaron, Joshi, and Williams 1999; Kendeou et al. 2009). It is easy to see that comprehension difficulties may have detrimental effects on children's motivation to read outside school but also in school, where reading is the vehicle to learn from textbooks (Anderson et al. 2003; Cunningham and Stanovich 1998). This chapter focuses on how technology can help young children to develop skills for what is the essence of reading: extracting meaning from text.

An important stimulus for comprehension skills to develop is out-of-school (shared) reading. That is, not the fact that reading takes place outside the school setting but the fact that reading is a common daily activity. A meta-analysis by Mol and Bus (2011) showed that more frequent readers had indeed better comprehension skills. The study provided meta-analytic evidence for this relation when children are as young as four years of age but also later, at the age of 21. Apparently, the influence of (shared) reading is not restricted to the years in which children learn to read (Bus, van IJzendoorn, and Pellegrini 1995) but is still noticeable in adolescents when the word decoding process is fast and effortless.

What does it mean to extract meaning from a text? It means that the reader has to distinguish essential from less essential information and needs to understand how information within the text is related and how it is related to relevant background information (van den Broek 2010). Readers have to interpret the information in the text as the meaning is often left implicit, and even more so when the text is complex. The inferences thus generated by the reader fill in the gaps, making the text into a coherent whole.

Readers recognize descriptions of situations or places that they are familiar with and combine this knowledge with the information in the text, resulting in a representation of the events in a story. A young child needs to learn how to make these inferences (Kendeou et al. 2008), a process that starts long before they learn to read themselves (Feirrero and Teberosky 1978). Even simple picture storybooks require cognitive skills to draw conclusions, although the inferences may be relatively simple. That is, similar to texts for adults, stories written for young children can only be comprehended when the child makes assumptions about the events in the story. Young readers can not stick to the story facts but need to search for deeper layers in the story. In *Kikker is bang* [Frog is Frightened], a picture storybook by Max Velthuijs (1994), Frog, Piglet, and Duck are all afraid of ghosts. At night, in the dark, they tell each other that they are afraid of nothing or nobody. Children have to read between the lines to understand that they are actually terrified. Understanding these deeper layers requires not only reflecting on the story, but also abstracting information from the story text. As stories become more complex the interpretation of the information is more ambiguous and there will be a higher demand for reflection and abstraction. In other words, reading requires 'con-text' (Watson 2001), the cognitive environment in which the interpretation takes place, and that is defined by non-text factors.

Sulzby's (1985) descriptions of how young children in the age range of two to six years retell a story show a development from very concrete to more abstract stories including reflective elements. Little by little the retelling develops from labelling story elements ('Frog') or telling unrelated story actions ('he is frightened … he talks') to stories in which specific linguistic utterances are used to specify relations within the story. When children are more experienced they do not say 'he goes away' (while pointing to the picture) but they make explicit that the mouse in *Doedel en het rode gevaar* [Dudley and the Strawberry Shake] (Taylor 1986) fetches his wheelbarrow to go and pick strawberries.

Stories for young children in new formats

All over the world children in literate families are read to (Anderson et al. 2003). Children acquire new cognitive skills through shared book reading and learn to abstract from and reflect on stories (Mol, Bus, and de Jong 2009; Mol et al. 2008; National Center for Family Literacy 2008). Until 20 years ago, printed materials were the basis of literate experiences with narrative picture storybooks, but in recent decades stories became available in other formats as well and the range of possibilities expands further and further (Cunningham et al. 2000; Hagood 2003; Marsh 2005; Sekeres and Watson 2011). These can include stories on TV or DVD (*Bob the Builder, Maisy Stories*) or picture storybooks on the computer or on the Internet (e.g. www.storylineonline.net; www.bereslim.nl). The spectacular growth of the use of tablet computers further expands the digital accessibility of stories for the very young (e.g. see the Random House collection of award-winning picture storybooks for iPad). *Pat the Bunny* (by Dorothy

Kunhardt 2001) for instance, originally published in 1940, is now reissued but as an interactive app and available for iPad, iPhone, and iPod Touch.

Stories presented via new media often include additions not available in the print version of the same books (de Jong and Bus 2003; Korat and Shamir 2004). When for instance in the Dutch television show *Mister Stay* [Meneer Logeer] a story is read, it is richly furnished with animations. Game-like stories on (tablet) computers, also called interactive stories, have numerous additional features such as video and animated hotspots (de Jong and Bus 2003). The Internet provides ample examples of interactive animated stories (e.g. www.funwithspot.com; www.maisyfun. com; www.nijntje.nl; www.raz-kids.com; www.storylineonline.net; http://disneydigitalbooks. go.com). Can these multimedia additions help children to understand the stories, a role an adult normally has in 'traditional' print book shared reading?

The verbal rendering of the story text makes young children independent of an adult to get access to the story. Access, however, does not guarantee understanding. Are special features such as animations suited to bridge the gap between the content of the story and what the child can understand without help (de Jong and Bus 2003)? Many books on the computer stimulate active behaviour by inviting children to interact with text and pictures while at the same time the number of interactions with an adult might decline. Anecdotal evidence gives the impression that there is less opportunity for questions during the shared reading (e.g. 'Why do you think that Sam is crying?') or for explanations ('I think that he is frightened, he is all alone now'). Cynthia Smith (2001), for instance, describes that her son James while interacting with the computer when he is 2.5 to 3.5 years of age is mainly focused on the computer screen. Even if she sits next to him James interacts more with the computer screen than with her. She describes that he is directly responding to what he sees on the computer screen. Reading *The Tortoise and the Hare*, in one of the screens James clicks eight times on the hare, which always results in a verbal response by the computer programme ('Hey, I was supposed to win') to which he immediately reacts ('Well, he already winned') as opposed to questions or comments made by his mother. According to Smith these reactions of James are not just episodic but show that computer sessions proceed differently than sessions in which a printed picture storybook is read (see also Korat and Or 2010). Insofar as mother and son share information in CD-ROM reading sessions they discuss technical aspects of CD-ROMs and not the story. Discussions concern, for instance, artefacts of the medium such as the use of the computer mouse. Or the child makes comments while he is clicking on the screen ('Click on this apple. It doesn't do anything. These crayons . . .').

Whether the extra bells and whistles added to multimedia stories are indeed suited to stimulate early comprehension skills is the central research question in a series of experiments that were carried out in the past decade (de Jong and Bus 2002, 2003, 2004; Verhallen and Bus 2009, 2010; Verhallen, Bus, and de Jong 2006).

Unlike printed storybooks, digital storybooks provide extras that might or might not help children to develop comprehension skills (de Jong and Bus 2003). One option in some computer stories is the possibility for children to interact with parts of the story text or with details in the illustrations. For instance, animations can be activated when the cursor changes into a bear paw or a square, the so-called hotspots. These animations sometimes support the storyline. In *Arthur's Birthday*, for instance, one screen shows Arthur holding invitations in his hand. Clicking on his younger sister results in the spoken text 'Don't forget to hand them out'. The child is being prepared for what will happen next and curiosity about the outcome is aroused ('will he forget to hand out the invitations?'). In most computer stories, however, these hotspots and animations were found to be incongruent with the story text (de Jong and Bus 2003). A towel turns into a dove, or an army of ants marches across the screen. The animations in all these examples are unrelated to the storyline or to any of the events in the story.

Do hotspots help story understanding?

When children are asked to retell these stories, they report on what they successively have seen on the screen. It does not become a coherent story. Labbo and Kuhn (2000) observed a child reading *Arthur's Teacher Trouble*, a story with many incongruent animations. The child told many details but none had anything to do with the main story. He got lost in the distracting details.

Stella Luna, a CD–ROM without incongruent details, led to different results. In this CD–ROM 90 to 95 percent of the animations were in some way related to the main storyline. When children had listened to this story their retellings were more sophisticated and coherent and included a setting, a problem, and solution (Labbo and Kuhn 2000).

Do interactive books on the computer elicit young preliterate children to focus on game-like elements at the expense of attention for the storyline? A large experimental study was executed to answer this question. Participants were 48 kindergarten children in the age range of four to six years, speaking Dutch as a first language (de Jong and Bus 2002). Per screen the children had many choices: (i) watching the animated illustration (story events are dramatized: P. B. Bear yawns and gets out of bed and puts on his bathrobe); (ii) activating short animations by clicking on icons on the 'page' (a locomotive starts to puff and whistle, or a waistband meanders around a bathrobe); (iii) playing a game; (iv) listening to the story; (v) reading of text fragments by clicking on words in the story text, and (vi) clicking to access the next screen. Children played six times with the story *P. B. Beer is Jarig* [P. B. Bear's Birthday Party] and each session lasted long enough to listen to the complete story. However, most children only played with the animations, the games, and the dramatized illustrations. Options such as reading the text or clicking on words to read sentences or text fragments were less often chosen. Kindergartners who had the possibility to choose from many options were seldom focused on the story content. There was only one child who heard the whole story once, whereas children in the same number of sessions but led by an adult had heard the story six times. As a result, the playful interactions with animations and illustrations hampered the process of meaning making. Children in the computer condition could retell only 31 percent of the pages correctly whereas children who listened to the story read by an adult were able to correctly retell about 50 percent of the pages.

A follow-up study with a book that offered fewer choices per screen, *Ik Maak Je Weer Beter, Zei Beer* [I'll Make You Well, Said the Bear], showed that not all books on the computer will elicit a game-like stance (de Jong and Bus 2004). This book was interactive too, but in comparison to *P. B. Beer is Jarig* [P. B. Bear's Birthday Party] there were fewer options to choose from. Each screen (or 'page') automatically starts with a voice that tells the story while at the same time the animated version of the story is shown on the screen. The book offers hotspots, but their number is restricted. Per screen about five hotspots can be activated by clicking on places in the illustrations where the cursor changes into a bear paw. Most animations are unrelated to the story's content. In this study most kindergarten children who spoke Dutch as a first language were involved in the story although they could access incongruent hotspots. All children in the computer condition heard the Dutch story of *Ik Maak Je Weer Beter, Zei the Beer* [I'll Make You Well, Tiger, Said the Bear], several times spread over 12 sessions. That is, they heard the story as often as children who were read to by an adult in 12 sessions. After the intervention, children in the computer condition, who independently accessed the story on the computer, could retell as much as children in the adult-led sessions. These results favour the hypothesis that interactive stories on the computer can significantly add to adult-led shared reading. Similar results were found in an Israeli study with kindergarten children by Korat and Shamir (2007). If the programs do not appeal too strongly to a game-like and plot-independent stance, computers can help provide young children with meaningful experiences with storybooks in addition to what teachers can bring about. Whether this is also true for at-risk children who enter preschool with less well developed language skills was not tested in this experiment. The children had a lot of fun with the animations (they activated about 20 animated hotspots per session) but kept their focus on the storyline at the same time. That they could retell the story irrespective of their attention for the incongruent animations contradicts Labbo and Kuhn's (2000) hypothesis that incongruent animations are always detrimental for story understanding. Our results do not exclude the possibility that incongruent animations indeed interfere with understanding the storyline when they elicit complete attention, but this awaits further research.

The first evidence that congruent hotspots can enhance comprehension skills comes from Smeets and Bus (2012). In their study, interactive behaviour was controlled by the computer, meaning that clicking on objects in the picture was only possible when the story scene froze (four times per reading). After clicking on the object in the frozen scene the definition of the object was provided. Interaction with the story via these hotspots enriched word knowledge of partly familiar words (words already known receptively). Novel words (i.e. words not in children's receptive vocabularies) were learned when a computer pal posed four multiple-choice questions and provided appropriate feedback on children's response (by clicking). This study adds to the existing body of literature on interactive storybook reading (Higgins and Cocks 1999; Higgins and Hess 1999; Korat 2010; Segers and Verhoeven 2002, 2003; Shamir and Korat 2009) in two ways. First, it shows that interaction can be beneficial for word learning as opposed to non-interactive digital book reading. Second, prior knowledge determines what type of interaction with congruent hotspots is most successful.

Games distract children from the story content

Digital stories often offer built-in games; however, these games appear to be highly distractive. When children were allowed to play the built-in games they spent about half of the time on these games in *P. B. Beer is Jarig* [P. B. Bear's Birthday Party] (de Jong and Bus 2002). Games were thematically related to the story's content (party) but were not an extra aid for story understanding. Children needed to match the shapes of presents for instance, or were asked to prick the balloons before they flew off the screen. When they were allowed to play games each child, after six sessions of 15 minutes, had read only one third of the story. The children in this group had barely learned more than the children in the no-intervention control condition who were only pre- and post-tested. These meagre effects may have been caused by the game-playing disposition that is the result of too many options from which to choose. Compared to print books the options are less constrained in stories on the computer. In *P. B. Beer is jarig* [P. B. Bear's Birthday Party] children can listen to the story, click on the illustrations, watch the animations or play games (puncture balloons before they fly off the screen). The many different functions often built into digital storybooks act as 'junk food' and evoke 'snacking' behaviour. They are attractive but do not facilitate literacy development.

Video stories

The research presented so far tested effects of interactive digital stories in children who are first language speakers and within the normal range of language development. Children with less well developed language skills, especially second language learners, may have difficulty understanding the story text as the language used in books is complex. Interactive features might divert children's attention at the expense of attention for the storyline. They may benefit more from the use of animation to direct their attention to relevant visual information while listening to the accompanying text. The animated story might thus scaffold these children's emergent story comprehension.

Most kindergarten children of Turkish or Moroccan origin in the Netherlands start learning Dutch as a second language when they enter preschool at the age of 3.5 years. Not surprisingly, they experience difficulties in understanding stories because they do not grasp much of the language in which these stories are read to them. Are animated stories on the computer, television, or the Internet an incentive for language development skills in this group of children with very weak language skills? As long as children have difficulty understanding the linguistic information in stories they might profit from video, where animations, music, and sound effects are added to the spoken story text (Lewalter 2003). Besides the verbal information, children can extract meaning from the video presentation of the story as it visualizes the story events. Perhaps children can overcome their problems with understanding the verbal text and succeed in constructing a complete representation of the story with the support of non-verbal sources of information. Paivio's (2007) model of dual coding acknowledges two different systems to code and store information – one that is specialized in non-verbal information and the other in verbal information – whereby connections can be formed between the two systems of information representation. Paivio postulated that the two forms of representation are controlled by different systems but that they are able to support and supplement each other structurally and functionally (Mayer and Anderson 1992).

Another possibility is that video attracts all attention at the cost of attention for the verbal story text – the so-called 'visual superiority hypothesis' (Hayes and Birnbaum 1980). According to this hypothesis the multimedia additions, such as animations and sound effects, hinder the verbal information processing system. Children watch but forget to listen to the story text because they are absorbed by the non-verbal additions to the story.

These two hypotheses were tested in an experimental study with 60 kindergarten children from inner-city schools in the Netherlands who learned Dutch as a second language (Verhallen et al., 2006). Children in this study scored in the 25th percentile on a Dutch standardized language test, meaning that they belonged to the 25 percent of children who scored lowest compared to their peers. The results of the study showed that children understood the story better when video was added to the verbal text compared to children who listened to the same story with only static pictures as an additional source of information next to the spoken story text. A remarkable result was that the added video was especially helpful in understanding the more complex story elements (such as internal responses). The retellings of children in the video condition not only included the story actions, but also the reasons for actions, such as goals of main characters and emotions (e.g. in *Hekenspul met Hennie de heks en de kat Helmer* [Winnie the witch], 'Winnie is furious when she trips over the cat for the umpteenth time'). Children's retellings, after listening to a video storybook, were still incomplete but they no longer consisted of a series of unrelated actions. They included reasons for actions such as internal responses of main characters that connect the actions to a logical whole. To put it differently, multimedia helps children understand how actions within a story are related.

The results of the study are remarkable considering the fact that story elements that form causes for actions, thus creating a coherent story, are more explicitly presented in the verbal part of the story than in the non-verbal visualizations. The verbal story text explains that 'Winnie decided something had to be done' or that 'Winnie was worried.' Only a good observer will discern these elements in the video. For instance, tripping over her black cat on the stairs because she could not see him in her black house elicited Winnie's decision that something had to be done. The static illustration shows Winnie lying at the bottom of the stairs in a hallway full of witches' paraphernalia. Her face shows a slight frown, indicating her discontent. The video version of the story shows Winnie tripping over her cat Wilbur on the stairs. She is seen falling down the stairs and at the end the camera zooms in on Winnie lying on the floor at the foot of the stairs while the text is spoken, thus increasing the chance that children are able to connect these two sources of information. This allows young children to build a mental representation of the story's meaning. Seeing the cause of Winnie's feeling may alert children to her state of mind and increases the chance that children will interpret Winnie's facial impression correctly. The same processes will also be elicited by the static picture, but here these processes may be less well aligned. Children need to find the right visual details amid a large number of irrelevant details and thus may find it difficult to connect the verbal and visual representations. Whether congruent hotspots may have similar positive effects with children at risk might be a logical next step in this line of research.

Future

Until recently research in the field of emergent literacy has mainly focused on shared book reading as scaffolds for language and literacy development (e.g. Biemiller 2006; Feitelson et al. 1993). This chapter reported studies testing the learning effects of a different kind of stories to which multimedia such as animation and sounds are added. The results showed that, if well designed, these stories can add to common practices of shared print book reading. However, these evidence-based materials do not seem to find their way into school curricula. The programs are not part of the curriculum and to watch the programs at home is hardly encouraged by schools. In this way, many opportunities to stimulate emergent literacy development are lost (see also van Dijken, Bus, and de Jong 2011). Digital stories, on TV or (tablet) computers, are a powerful means not only to increase the number of book encounters for young children, but also to stimulate story comprehension and language learning.

Contact address: jongtm@FSW.leidenuniv.nl

References

Aaron, P. G., Joshi, M., and Williams, K. A. (1999) 'Not all reading disabilities are alike', *Journal of Learning Disabilities*, 32: 120–137.

Anderson, J., Anderson, A., Lynch, J., and Shapiro, J. (2003) 'Storybook reading in a multicultural society: critical perspectives', in A. van Kleeck, A. Stahl, and E. B. Bauer (eds.) *On reading books to children, parents and teachers*, London: Lawrence Erlbaum Associates (pp. 203–230).

Arthur's birthday [CD-ROM]. 1997. Brøderbound.

Arthur's teacher trouble [CD-ROM]. 1994. Brown.

Biemiller, A. (2006) 'Vocabulary development and instruction: a prerequisite for school learning', in S. Neuman and D. Dickinson (eds.) *Handbook of early literacy research, Volume 2*, New York: Guilford Press (pp. 41–51).

Bus, A. G., van IJzendoorn, M. H., and Pellegrini, A. D. (1995) 'Joint book reading makes for success in learning to read: a meta-analysis on intergenerational transmission of literacy', *Review of Educational Research*, 65: 1–21.

Cunningham, J. W., Many, J. E., Carver, R. P., Gunderson, L., and Mostenthal, P. B. (2000) 'How will literacy be defined in the new millennium?', *Reading Research Quarterly*, 35: 64–71.

Cunningham, A. E., and Stanovich, K. E. (1998) 'What reading does for the mind', *American Educator*, 22: 8–15.

de Jong, M.T., and Bus, A. G. (2002) 'Quality of book-reading matters for emergent readers: an experiment with the same book in a regular or electronic format', *Journal of Educational Psychology*, 94: 145–155.

de Jong, M.T., and Bus, A. G. (2003) 'How well suited are electronic books to supporting literacy?', *Journal of Early Childhood Literacy*, 3: 147–164.

de Jong, M.T., and Bus, A. G. (2004) 'The efficacy of electronic books in fostering kindergarten children's emergent story understanding', *Reading Research Quarterly*, 39: 378–393.

Feirrero, E., and Teberosky, A. (1978) *Literacy before schooling*, Exeter, NH: Heinemann.

Feitelson, D., Goldstein, Z., Iraqi, J., and Share, D. L. (1993) 'Effects of listening to story reading on aspects of literacy acquisition in a diglossic situation', *Reading Research Quarterly*, 28: 70–79.

Hagood, M. C. (2003) 'New media and online literacies: no age left behind', *Reading Research Quarterly*, 38: 387–391.

Hayes, D. S., and Birnbaum, D. W. (1980) 'Preschoolers retention of televised events: is a picture worth a thousand words?', *Developmental Psychology*, 16: 410–416.

Heksenspul met Hennie de heks en de kat Helmer [Winnie the witch] [CD-ROM]. 1996. Bombilla/VNU Interactive Media.

Higgins, N. C., & Cocks, P. (1999) The effects of animation cues on vocabulary development. *Journal of Reading Psychology*, 20: 1–10.

Higgins, N., and Hess, L. (1999) 'Using electronic books to promote vocabulary', *Journal of Research on Computing in Education*, 31: 425–430.

Ik maak je weer beter, zei beer [I'll make you well again, said the bear] [CD-ROM]. 1998. Het Spectrum Electronic Publishing.

Kendeou, P., Bohn-Gettler, C., White, M. J., and van den Broek, P. (2008) 'Children's inference generation across different media', *Journal of Research in Reading*, 31: 259–272.

Kendeou, P., White, M. J., van den Broek, P., and Lynch, J. S. (2009) Predicting reading comprehension in early elementary school: the independent contributions of oral language and decoding skills', *Journal of Educational Psychology*, 101: 765–778.

Korat, O. (2010) 'Reading electronic books as a support for vocabulary, story comprehension and word reading in kindergarten and first grade', *Computers and Education*, 55: 24–31.

Korat, O., and Or, T. (2010) 'How new technology influences parent–child interaction: the case of e-book reading', *First Language*, 30: 139–154.

Korat, O., and Shamir, A. (2004) 'Do Hebrew electronic books differ from Dutch electronic books? A replication of a Dutch content analysis', *Journal of Computer Assisted Learning*, 20: 257–268.

Korat, O., and Shamir, A. (2007) 'Electronic books versus adult readers: effects on children's emergent literacy as a function of social class', *Journal of Computer Assisted Learning*, 23: 248–259.

Kunhardt, D. (2001) *Pat the bunny*, New York: Random House.

Labbo, L. D., and Kuhn, M. R. (2000) 'Weaving chains of affect and cognition: a young child's understanding of CD-ROM talking books', *Journal of Literacy Research*, 32: 187–210.

Lewalter, D. (2003) 'Cognitive strategies for learning from static and dynamic visuals', *Learning and Instruction*, 13: 177–189.

Marsh, J. (2005) 'Digikids: young children, popular culture and media', in N. Yelland (ed.) *Contemporary issues in early childhood*, Maidenhead: Open University Press (pp. 181–96).

Mayer, R. E., and Anderson, R. B. (1992) 'The instructive animation: helping students build connections between words and pictures in multimedia learning', *Journal of Educational Psychology*, 84: 444–452.

Mol, S. E., and Bus, A. G. (2011) 'To read or not to read: a meta-analysis of print exposure from infancy to early adulthood', *Psychological Bulletin*, 137: 267–296.

Mol, S. E., Bus, A. G., and de Jong, M. T. (2009) 'Interactive book reading in early education: a tool to stimulate print knowledge as well as oral language', *Review of Educational Research*, 79: 979–1007.

Mol, S. E., Bus, A. G., de Jong, M.T., and Smeets, D. J. H. (2008) 'Added value of dialogic parent–child book readings: a meta-analysis', *Early Education and Development*, 19: 7–26.

National Center for Family Literacy (2008) *Developing early literacy: report of the national early literacy panel: a scientific synthesis of early literacy development and implications for intervention*, Washington, DC: National Institute for Literacy.

Ouellette, G., and Beers, A. (2010) 'A not-so-simple view of reading: how oral vocabulary and visual-word recognition complicate the story', *Reading and Writing*, 23: 189–208.

Paivio, A. (2007) *Mind and its evolution: a dual coding theoretical approach*, Mahwah, NJ: Laurence Erlbaum Associates.

P. B. Beer is jarig [P. B. Bear's Birthday Party] [CD-ROM]. 1996. Bombilla/VNU Interactieve Media.

Segers, E., and Verhoeven, L. (2002) 'Multimedia support of early literacy learning', *Computers and Education*, 39: 207–221.

Segers, E., and Verhoeven, L. (2003) 'Effects of vocabulary training by computer in kindergarten', *Journal of Computer Assisted Learning*, 19: 557–566.

Sekeres, D. C., and Watson, C. (2011) 'New literacies and multimediacy: the immersive universe of the 39 clues', *Children's Literature in Education*, 42: 256–273.

Seymour, P. H. K., Aro, M., Erskine, J. M., Wimmer, H., Leybaert, J., Elbro, C., et al. (2003) 'Foundation literacy acquisition in European orthographies', *British Journal of Psychology*, 94: 143–174.

Shamir, A., and Korat, O. (2009) 'The educational electronic book as a tool for supporting children's emergent literacy', in A. G. Bus and S. B. Neuman (eds.) *Multimedia and literacy development*, New York: Taylor and Francis (pp. 168–181).

Smeets, D. J. H., and Bus, A. G. (2012) 'Interactive electronic storybooks for kindergartners to promote vocabulary growth', *Journal of Experimental Child Psychology*, 112: 36–55.

Smith, C. R. (2001) 'Click and turn the page: an exploration of multiple storybook literacy', *Reading Research Quarterly*, 36: 152–183.

Stella Luna [CD-ROM]. 1996. Cannon.

Sulzby, E. (1985) 'Children's emergent reading of favorite storybooks: a developmental study', *Reading Research Quarterly*, 20: 458–481.

Tamim, R. M., Bernard, R. M., Borokhovski, E., Abrami, P. C., and Schmid, R. F. (2011) 'What forty years of research says about the impact of technology on learning: a second-order meta-analysis and validation study', *Review of Educational Research*, 81: 4–28.

Taylor, J. (1986) *Doedel en het rode gevaar* [Dudley and the strawberry shake], Utrecht, The Netherlands: De Blauwe Olifant.

The tortoise and the hare [CD-ROM]. 1994. Brøderbund.

van den Broek, P. (2010) 'Using texts in science education: cognitive processes and knowledge representation', *Science*, 328: 453–456.

van Dijken, M. J., Bus, A. G., and de Jong, M. T. (2011) 'Open access to living books on the internet: a new chance to bridge the linguistic gap for at-risk preschoolers?', *European Journal of Special Needs Education*, 26: 307–318.

Velthuijs, M. (1994). *Kikker is bang* [Frog is frightened]. Amsterdam: Leopold.

Verhallen, M. J. A. J., and Bus, A. G. (2009) 'Video storybook reading as a remedy for vocabulary deficits: outcomes and processes', *Journal for Educational Research Online*, 1: 172–196.

Verhallen, M. J. A. J., and Bus, A. G. (2010) 'Low-income immigrant pupils learning vocabulary through digital picture storybooks', *Journal of Educational Psychology*, 102: 54–61.

Verhallen, M., Bus, A. G., and de Jong, M. T. (2006) 'The promise of multimedia stories for kindergarten children at risk', *Journal of Educational Psychology*, 98: 410–419.

Watson, R. (2001) 'Literacy and oral language: implications for early literacy acquisition', in S. B. Neuman and D. Dickinson (eds.) *Handbook of early literacy research*, New York: Guilford Press (pp. 43–53).

Ziegler, J. C., Bertrand, D., Toth, D., Csepe, V., Reis, A., Faisca, L., et al. (2010) 'Orthographic depth and its impact on universal predictors of reading: a cross-language investigation', *Psychological Science*, 21: 551–559.

10

THE DEVELOPMENT OF SCIENTIFIC REASONING

Christine Howe

UNIVERSITY OF CAMBRIDGE, UK

As Dunbar and Fugelsang (2005) note, scientific reasoning can be characterized in two ways. It can be regarded as referring to the established body of scientific knowledge when drawing inferences, e.g. when planning, predicting, explaining, and arguing. Reference can be made in informal contexts as well as scientific ones, e.g. 'How can anyone talk about global warming after two terrible winters?', 'Well, scientists say that as the Greenland Ice Cap melts …' Alternatively, scientific reasoning can be viewed as applying scientific methods of enquiry, e.g. observing and experimenting in accordance with established principles. Again, this is not restricted to formal science: many social researchers employ the methods while not regarding themselves as scientists. Promoting the two forms of reasoning constitutes the substance of science education at primary, secondary, and tertiary levels, and therefore practitioners and policy makers have a profound interest in how they develop. Accordingly, the present chapter outlines key messages from contemporary research, initially treating the two forms separately but gradually integrating and, in doing this, highlighting implications for practice. Five 'reflective questions' are interspersed throughout the text: consideration may assist in consolidation and understanding of the major themes.

Reasoning with scientific knowledge

The impetus for much research into reasoning with scientific knowledge has been Piaget's studies relating to physical events (e.g. Inhelder and Piaget 1958; Piaget 1930, 1974 – see also Vousden, Wood, and Holliman, Chapter 5, this volume, for the theoretical perspective that informed these studies). The studies covered numerous topics, e.g. object flotation, pendulum oscillation, and rolling down slopes, but employed a common methodology. Semi-structured interviews (termed 'clinical interviews') were held in one-to-one sessions with four- to 15-year-olds. Interviewees were asked to explain familiar events, e.g. why boats float on nearby lakes, or to predict outcomes and justify predictions, e.g. what happens to oscillation when pendulum mass increases. Regardless of method, reference to scientific accounts was rare before mid-adolescence, a limitation that was attributed to structural complexity. Flotation, for example, is complex because it depends on object density relative to fluid, with each density depending on mass relative to volume.

While Piaget emphasized structure, it was soon recognized that his data provided rich information about content. It was noted that when Piaget's interviewees lacked scientific knowledge, they did not respond with puzzlement. Rather they reasoned with alternative conceptions that appeared to change with age. Since content is arguably more revealing than structure from an educational perspective, alternative conceptions were quickly identified as potentially significant (Driver and Easley 1983), resulting in extensive subsequent research. A constantly updated bibliography suggests that by the mid-2000s there had been over 8,000 descriptive studies of children's conceptions (Duit 2007). Interestingly, the studies perpetuate many aspects of their Piagetian ancestry. For instance, they focus on physics: White and Gunstone (2008) report that about two-thirds of the bibliography's entries address reasoning in physics, with biology and chemistry less prominent (for examples in these areas, see Driver 1985; Inagaki and Hatano 2002). Moreover, the clinical interview remains the modal technique. Indeed, when written tests are employed for convenience, their validity is usually justified via previous work using interviews.

Question 1: Why did Piagetian research focus on physics?

Cosmology

One of the best-known examples of research into alternative conceptions relates to cosmology, particularly the earth's shape. The initial work was conducted with eight- to 14-year-olds in Israel and the USA, and summarizing its results Nussbaum (1985) reported changes with age from believing that: (a) the earth is flat with sky above to appreciating that it is spherical and surrounded by space; (b) people live at the top to avoid falling off to appreciating that they can live anywhere. Confirming these findings with American children aged six to 11 years, Vosniadou and Brewer (1992) argue that age profiles suggest progression from 'initial models' (flat-earth) through 'partial models' (flattened spheres with people on top, dual earths that are flat but have a planetary sphere in the sky) to 'scientific models'. They indicate that by 11 years most children employ scientific models, a finding that has been widely replicated (Brewer 2008).

Vosniadou and Brewer suggest that initial models may be derived from direct observation, while partial models are 'synthetic', resulting from attempts to reconcile initial models with the correct message that culture provides (teachers, parents, artefacts, etc). One implication is cross-cultural universality at the beginning and end of the developmental process, but possible variation when synthetic models are ascendant due to culture-specific emphases (and, as a consequence, possible variation in the ages at which scientific models are acquired). In essence, this is what emerges from cross-cultural comparisons. For instance, Indian children often envisage ball-like earths floating in water (Samarapungavan, Vosniadou, and Brewer 1996), while this particular synthetic structure has not been reported among other samples. Nepali children are reported to display a four-year lag relative to American children (Mali and Howe 1979).

Despite the cross-cultural support, the above research has been criticized (Nobes, Martin, and Panagiotaki 2005; Panagiotaki, Nobes, and Banerjee 2006). One concern is that conceptions are often explored through drawings, when children are typically poor at drawing, and even adults produce flat scenes when drawing the earth. However, the initial research reported in Nussbaum (1985) did not rely on drawings yet the results are equivalent to other studies. A second criticism is that drawings are often contextualized via clinical interviews, when modern psychology has challenged Piagetian methods as confusing and likely to underestimate understanding. The recommended alternative is typically forced-choice between competing options, but as Brewer (2008) points out, many forced-choice studies omit cosmologies that interview-based research has identified. While Panagiotaki et al. (2006) and Vosniadou, Skopeliti, and Ikospentaki (2004) appear to achieve comparability across methods and indicate superior (albeit imperfect) performance with forced-choice, interview data are surely also significant. Adults would consistently deny that the earth is flat, so children's use of primitive conceptions when interviewed signals insecure understanding. A third criticism is that by referring to pre-scientific and scientific conceptions as 'models', Vosniadou and Brewer imply greater consistency within the former than is actually the case. At the synthetic level, the evidence for inconsistency in children's thinking seems compelling, but it is hard to see why consistency at this level was ever contemplated. The transitional, culturally imbued nature of synthetic constructs implies variation – between cultures, between individuals, and within individuals with different tasks.

> *Question 2:* What conclusions can be drawn from research into children's conceptions about the Earth's shape?

Force and motion

Whatever the verdict on the specific concerns, it would be unwise to extrapolate from the above research to physical events in general, for there are areas where age-related changes differ markedly. One such area is force and motion, for here: (a) eventual acquisition of scientific models is exceptional; (b) conceptions used in reasoning do not necessarily improve with age; (c) initial conceptions are not straightforwardly derived from direct observation. As regards the former, adult reasoning about force and motion is known to employ misconceptions (e.g. McDermott 1984), even after extensive experience with science. For instance, when university undergraduates (some studying physics) predict the direction in which objects fall when dropped from moving carriers (e.g. when litter is dropped from moving vehicles), they typically anticipate vertical fall, backward descent, forward fall along a diagonal, or horizontal continuation in space followed with vertical descent. They seldom identify the parabolic paths in a forward direction that objects actually follow (McCloskey 1983). Undergraduates also frequently expect heavy balls to fall faster than light balls rather than travelling at speeds that are actually almost identical. Furthermore, they often expect balls to reach maximum velocity quickly, and then fall with constant velocity (Champagne, Klopfer, and Anderson 1980; Gunstone and White 1981).

Thus, conceptions of force and motion are often pre-scientific even in adulthood, and it is perhaps for this reason that they are typically as inconsistent and unstable as the pre-scientific cosmologies discussed above (diSessa 1993; diSessa, Gillespie and Esterly 2004). For instance, Howe (1998) reports eight- to 12-year-olds using 250 distinct factors to interpret scenarios involving object flotation. These factors covered weight, temperature, shape (round, log-shaped), orientation (tilted, balanced), surface (muddy, peeled), constitution (wood, alcoholic), contents (air, germs) as well as non-physical characteristics (bravery, effort). Nearly 80 percent of the children mentioned at least 10 factors each, with some mentioning as many as 40. Yet no child used more than three factors with any single scenario.

Nevertheless, despite such variability, research into force and motion has also identified conceptions that are used with high frequency, and the nature of these conceptions appears to change with age. In some cases, the changes can be interpreted as improvement. For example, young children often believe that propelled objects continue with constant (even accelerating) speed until they run out of 'impetus' or hit a barrier, whereupon stopping is instantaneous (Gunstone and Watts 1985; Howe 1998). Older children typically recognize deceleration and realize that surface friction is involved (Twigger et al. 1994). This is progress, but it is none the less limited as friction is characteristically restricted to rough surfaces (Howe 1998; Stead and

Osborne 1981). In one study for instance, speed had to be predicted as billiard balls rolled across baize and glass surfaces (Howe, Taylor Tavares, and Devine 2009). While six-year-olds invariably predicted constant speed, eight- and 10-year-olds sometimes anticipated deceleration, but only with the rough baize surface.

By contrast, research into force and motion has also identified age-related changes that are non-progressive or even regressive. As regards non-progressive change, mass makes virtually no difference to the speed with which balls roll down slopes. However, studies with physical slopes (Howe 1998) and computer-simulated slopes (Hast 2010) have identified shifts in middle childhood from expecting light balls to roll faster to expecting heavy balls to do this. Likewise, while research cited above indicates that adults often expect objects to fall through air with constant velocity, Howe, Taylor Tavares, and Devine (2012) found that deceleration accounted for over 90 percent of errors from a six- to 10-year-old sample. Howe et al. also questioned their sample about direction of fall, including from moving carriers where, as noted, adults typically make errors. Consistent with other research with children (e.g. Kaiser, Proffitt, and McCloskey 1985), correct forward parabolas were predicted on only 2.5 percent of trials, and accuracy did not change with age. However, among errors, forward (but non-parabolic) trajectories decreased with age, while backward trajectories increased (see Figure 10.1). Since forward trajectories are correctly oriented even if the path is wrong while backward trajectories are incorrect on both counts, the implication is age-related regression.

Finally, no matter whether change is progressive, regressive, or neutral, reasoning about force and motion cannot, in contrast to what has been proposed for cosmology, move from observationally to culturally based conceptions. The reason is that whatever children glean from observation must be reasonably accurate, for they can discriminate between natural and non-natural displays. For instance, differential patterns of gaze show that six-month-olds recognize that: (a) acceleration when rolling down slopes is natural while deceleration is non-natural (Kim and Spelke 1992); (b) falling when support is removed is natural but hovering is non-natural (Needham and Baillargeon 1993); (c) direct proportionality between force and distance rolled is natural while inverse proportionality is non-natural (Kotovsky and Baillargeon 1998). In Howe et al.'s (2009, 2012) studies, prediction tasks were supplemented with computer simulations of natural and non-natural motion, with the children pressing on-screen buttons to indicate

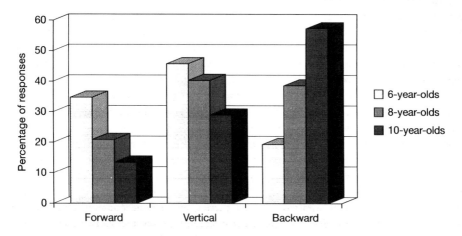

Figure 10.1   Age differences in trajectories predicted when moving objects fall from moving carriers (adapted from Howe et al. 2012)

whether displays were correct or not. Regardless of age, the children recognized that: (a) deceleration across glass and baize surfaces is natural and acceleration is non-natural; (b) acceleration during fall through air is natural and deceleration is non-natural; (c) fall after horizontal motion naturally follows a forward parabola, while other paths are non-natural.

It is unsurprising that children develop good observational understanding of force and motion and poor observational understanding of cosmology. Experiences of force and motion abound in everyday life, whereas celestial bodies are less salient and in any event viewed from perspectives that endorse typical errors. Nevertheless, the fact that observational understanding of force and motion is good when reasoning in this domain is poor argues against developmental models that, as in Vosniadou and Brewer (1992), regard initial reasoning as purely observational. Consistent with Carey (2009), it is more likely that when cultural practices (such as schooling) require reasoning in science, they trigger 'selective' elevation of observational constructs. This implies that the conceptions children call upon when reasoning are culturally imbued from the outset, and as a consequence denies discontinuities between early processes and later ones. Indeed, this interplay between cultural practices and observation readily accounts for the contrasting developmental outcomes documented above. With cosmology, practices typically concur with science: flat-earthers are rare in contemporary society. Therefore, eventual acquisition of scientific models can be anticipated. With force and motion, subscription to scientific models is exceptional among adults, so there is nothing surprising about shifting patchworks of alternative conceptions where age-related changes are as often non-progressive as 'developmental'.

Question 3: Which cultural practices are relevant to children's conceptions? Is everyday language important?

Reasoning through scientific methods

The studies summarized above used tasks that rely on prediction or explanation. Children are asked to predict the earth's shape or explain why objects float. It is clear from the studies that very young children can comply; the problems identified so far lie with the conceptions on which responses are based, not with predicting or explaining per se. However, in addition to providing tasks for probing conceptions, prediction and explanation are part-and-parcel of science's methodology: scientific methods revolve around formulating and testing predictions, and observing and explaining outcomes. Therefore, it can be assumed from material presented already that by the time they start school, children understand something about scientific methods. What is unclear is how far their understanding goes, because while prediction and explanation are central, there is a lot more involved than these two skills. Predictions in science are hypotheses, i.e. expectations about what should happen if theories are correct and if they are false. Testing is a technical skill, which often involves controlled experimentation. Explanation means relating test results to hypotheses and, through this, to theories. Accordingly, the section to follow presumes that children can predict and explain, and examines their ability to hypothesize, experiment, and relate evidence to theory.

Hypothesizing

In pioneering research, Kuhn, Amsel, and O'Loughlin (1988) report studies where balls that varied in size, colour, texture, and flat or ridged surfaces were used to establish what nine- to 15-year-olds and young adults believed to be the factors that influence serving in tennis. Taking one factor that the individual identified as influential plus one that was identified as irrelevant, each participant was asked to envisage evidence that would support and confound their theories. Kuhn (1991) reports parallel exercises relating to social theories, i.e. ideas about unemployment, recidivism, and school failure, this time with teenagers and adults up to 60 years of age. Success rates were very low in both investigations, and responses were strongly suggestive of failure to hypothesize. Many participants (termed 'absolutists') implicitly called on existing theories to generate evidence, but because the process was implicit there was no contemplation of theories being false and therefore no possibility of generating counter-evidence. Other participants (termed 'multiplists') recognized the possibility of alternative theories, but could not relate alternatives to evidence. With age, absolutism decreased and multiplism increased.

While suggestive, this early research confounds: (a) adopting the epistemological perspective that underpins hypothesizing; (b) generating relevant evidence. Recognition of this may be why recent work has examined epistemology more directly. For instance, Kuhn et al. (2008) presented 12-year-olds and adults with contemporary and historical events, and asked whether certainty is ever possible about their causes. Once more they found predominant use of absolutist and multiplist perspectives, with age-related variation in frequency. Driver et al. (1996) identify 'phenomenon-based reasoning' among nine-, 12- and 16-year-olds. Phenomenon-based reasoning treats perceptual evidence as the warrant for theories, and is therefore relatable to absolutism. It was the modal form of reasoning at all age levels, while decreasing with age. Bullock, Sodian, and Koerber (2009) report that many 11-, 18- and 23-year-olds construe science as concerned with establishing 'facts'. All in all, then, studies point to enduring difficulties with articulating theory and knowing what is supportive and unsupportive, and therefore with hypothesizing.

Question 4: What methods would you use to differentiate children's ability to hypothesize from their ability to predict?

Experimentation

Skill with experimentation has been extensively explored, starting perhaps with Inhelder and Piaget (1958). Employing tasks such as that shown in Figure 10.2 with five- to 15-year olds, Inhelder and Piaget found that very few participants proceeded systematically, laying out all possibilities (A + X, B + X, A + B + X, etc.) and testing these in turn. Rather, combinations were identified erratically and repetitively, and it was a matter of luck whether the correct combination was examined. Equivalent results have been reported subsequently in: (a) Dunbar and Klahr (1989), where nine- to 12-year-olds and adults tried to discover the operation of a control key; (b) Kuhn et al. (2008), where 12-year-olds explored predictors of avalanche risk; (c) Schauble (1990), where nine- to 12-year-olds examined factors that dictate speed around computerized micro-worlds. In general, these studies indicate older participants performing better than younger ones, and choosing strategies from presented options proving easier than planning afresh (Bullock and Ziegler 1999; Bullock et al. 2009). Nevertheless, as with Inhelder and Piaget, haphazard approaches to experimental design and limited success with identifying relationships appear to be the norm.

Most studies report undue focus on factors that are expected to influence outcomes. To Kuhn et al. (1988), this suggested confusion between 'finding out' and 'making things happen'. However, Driver et al. (1996) asked their nine- to 16-year-old sample to classify events according to whether or not they constitute experiments, e.g. following a recipe, deciding which towel dries best. A clear distinction was made between finding out (the main criterion for experiments) and causing to happen. Likewise, Sodian, Zaitchik, and Carey (1991) found that over half of a

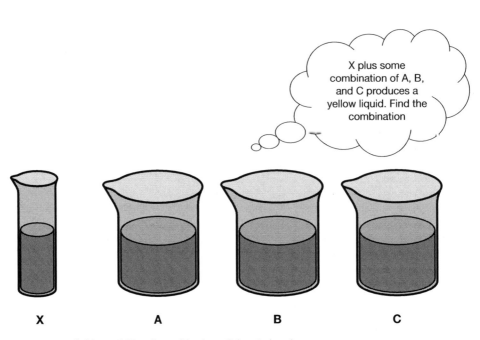

Figure 10.2 Inhelder and Piaget's combination of chemicals task

six- to seven-year-old sample appreciated that cage-door size needs to be varied differently when determining an unseen mouse's size (finding out) than when ensuring access to food (creating effects). Nowadays, it is generally accepted that children differentiate between finding out and making things happen, but prefer to invest energy with factors that matter. As one child claimed when exploring the factors relevant to motion down an incline (Howe, Tolmie, and Sofroniou 1999): 'You don't have to do a test about colour. It's the weight. It's just the weight, starting position and slope. Colour's got nothing to do with it.'

Inhelder and Piaget (1958) focused on research designs and conclusions after design implementation. The implementation process was not studied in depth. By contrast, much subsequent work emphasizes what happens when children actually 'find out' (see Zimmerman 2007, for details). For instance, in Howe et al.'s (1999) research, nine- to 14-year-olds tested how specified factors affect shadows, flotation, pressure, or motion, using apparatus that permitted manipulation of multiple factors (illustrated in Figure 10.3). Tschirgi (1980) asked adults and eight- to 12-year-olds to examine how baking ingredients (e.g. butter vs. margarine, sugar vs. honey) affect cake quality. Zimmerman and Glaser (2001) asked 12-year-olds to indicate how they would test whether water is bad for plants and coffee is good. Task specifics influence performance, e.g. whether good or poor outcomes are appraised, whether the focus is on correct or incorrect beliefs. Nevertheless, no study demonstrates error-free experimentation, and while performance typically improves with age, ceiling levels are seldom reached. The factor being explored is usually manipulated, e.g. when ascertaining whether object size affects shadow size, object size is varied. However, other factors are seldom controlled.

Relating evidence to theories

Flawed design and experimentation preclude identification of valid relations from empirical research. If such relations are detected, this must be in spite of rather than because of observed

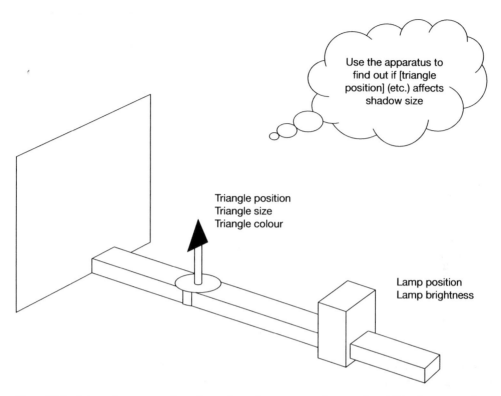

Figure 10.3 Schematic representation of one piece of apparatus used to examine children's mastery of experimental control (adapted from Howe et al. 2000)

results. This creates a confusing situation for scholars who wish to address the conclusions that are drawn from evidence, and one way in which they have sidestepped the problem is by presenting pristine datasets and requesting interpretations. In effect, this is the strategy adopted by Ruffman et al. (1993) in research with four- to seven-year-olds. The research involved pictures where food colour co-varied with healthy or rotten teeth. Most children could reliably identify which colour was associated with which type of teeth. However, Ruffman et al.'s paradigm is not equivalent to concluding in science. Test results are not related to hypotheses or theories, and a single-factor relation is examined when multi-factor relations are typical in science. Reviewing studies that more closely approximate science, Chinn and Brewer (1993) identify seven characteristic responses to data: (a) ignoring and using prior beliefs to draw conclusions; (b) rejecting as flawed or fraudulent, e.g. claiming that faulty thermometers are responsible for different rates of cooling from otherwise identical black and white containers (Howe and Tolmie 2003); (c) defining as beyond theoretical analysis, e.g. admitting to bewilderment about why heavy ships float (Howe 1998); (d) withholding judgment; (e) reinterpreting to accord with prior beliefs; (f) making peripheral theoretical changes, perhaps Vosniadou and Brewer's (1992) dual earths; (g) (rarely) accepting and making appropriate theoretical changes.

Chinn and Brewer suggest that the likelihood of the final option depends on the plausibility of alternative theories, a suggestion that concurs with studies outlined in Koslowski (1996). Here, the probability of 12- to 15-year-olds and adults interpreting perfectly co-varying relations as causal rested on plausible mechanisms. For instance, even when mileage per litre was said to co-vary perfectly with type of fuel additive, associations between additives and plausible mechanisms were required for causal attribution (e.g. additives differ in their burning efficiency). More recently, Fugelsang and Dunbar (2005) presented young adults with plausible and implausible theories relating to the alleviation of depression. In one plausible theory, a drug was claimed to elevate serotonin, which was said to be positively associated with feelings of happiness. In an implausible theory, a drug was described as inhibiting staphylococcus, which was presented as having no known relation to feelings. Datasets were then presented, such that each participant saw data that strongly co-varied or weakly co-varied with one plausible and one implausible theory. fMRI scanning indicated that brain areas associated with learning and memory were only activated by strongly co-varying data when theories were plausible. The implication is that even if adequate evidence is obtained (in itself a significant challenge from material presented earlier), its consequences will be resisted unless these concur with existing frameworks.

Question 5: Would the study of scientific reasoning benefit from more extensive use of neuroscience?

Conclusions

The chapter's aim has been to document how scientific reasoning develops. However, although age-related changes have been identified, they do not signal reliable progress towards mastery of science. Development turns out to be highly constrained as regards reasoning with scientific knowledge and through scientific methods. Yet just about everything considered in the chapter is taught in schools, so one implication is that current methods of instruction are insufficient to overcome the constraints. While it is beyond the chapter's scope to analyze instruction in depth, it may be helpful to highlight incompatibilities between the above claims about plausibility and the popular classroom technique of using experimentation to challenge alternative conceptions (Scott, Asoko, and Leach 2007). The idea has been that if children subject their ideas to controlled investigation, they will appreciate the inadequacies and be receptive to scientific conceptions. We now know that children not only have great difficulties with experimental control, but they are also unlikely to change their conceptions unless target constructs seem plausible. The implications are, first, that children need to be well on their way towards curriculum targets before experimentation will nudge them, and second that techniques for effecting conceptual change should, initially at least, by-pass the scientific method.

One technique that could contribute is collaborative group work. As noted, the prescientific conceptions that children hold constitute loosely connected ideas. Based on physical and cultural experiences, each child's ideas will overlap but differ from ideas held by classmates. Therefore, if children work in small groups on suitable tasks, the need to reconcile differences might trigger growth. While reconciliation is unlikely to result in scientific knowledge per se, there might be sufficient progress to ensure that target conceptions seem plausible. This, in essence, was the reasoning behind the c. 20 studies conducted with eight- to 15-year-olds that are summarized in Howe (2010). The studies used tasks that required groups to agree predictions, e.g. whether an empty aluminium box floats in water, whether the water in a thin metal container cools quickly. Groups were invited to test predictions using provided apparatus, and formulate joint interpretations of outcomes. Without exception, the tasks proved effective so long as differences were articulated and discussed. Then significant progress was made from individual pre-tests prior to group work to individual post-tests a few weeks later. Moreover, in two studies where testing during group work was guided towards controlled experimentation (Howe and Tolmie 2003; Howe et al. 2000), the consequences were: (a) receptiveness to teaching about experimental procedures; (b) use of experimental results to inform conceptual understanding; (c) significant progress with methods as well as concepts.

Collaborative group work is not a panacea for reasoning difficulties identified in this chapter. In any event, significant issues remain about how to embed the approach in classrooms, so that its potential can be optimized. Nevertheless, group work is an example of how, through co-ordination of developmental psychology with curriculum goals, challenges can begin to be addressed. It is hoped that the chapter stimulates further co-ordinations of this kind, so that teaching becomes more successful and, in the fullness of time, the troubling picture that the chapter has painted is superseded through positive results.

References

Brewer, W. F. (2008) 'Naïve theories of observational astronomy: review, analysis, and theoretical implications', in S. Vosniadou (ed.) *International handbook of research on conceptual change*, New York: Routledge (pp. 155–204).

Bullock, M., Sodian, B., and Koerber, S. (2009) 'Doing experiments and understanding science: development of scientific reasoning from childhood to adulthood', in W. Schneider and M. Bullock (eds.) *Human development from early childhood to early adolescence: findings from a 20 year longitudinal study*, New York: Psychology Press (pp. 173–197).

Bullock, M., and Ziegler, A. (1999) 'Scientific reasoning: developmental and individual differences', in F. E. Weinert and W. Schneider (eds.) *Individual development from 3–12: findings from the Munich longitudinal study*, Cambridge: Cambridge University Press (pp. 38–54).

Carey, S. (2009) *The origin of concepts*, Oxford: Oxford University Press.

Champagne, A. B., Klopfer, L. E., and Anderson, J. H. (1980) 'Factors influencing the learning of classical mechanics', *American Journal of Physics*, 48: 1074–1079.

Chinn, C. A., and Brewer, W. F. (1993) 'The role of anomalous data in knowledge acquisition: a theoretical framework and implications for science instruction', *Review of Educational Research*, 63: 1–49.

diSessa, A. A. (1993) 'Toward an epistemology of physics', *Cognition and Instruction*, 10: 105–225.

diSessa, A. A., Gillespie, N. M., and Esterly, J. B. (2004) 'Coherence versus fragmentation in the development of the concept of force', *Cognitive Science*, 28: 843–900.

Driver, R. (1985) 'Beyond appearances: the conservation of matter under physical and chemical transformations', in R. Driver, E. Guesne, and A. Tiberghien (eds.) *Children's ideas in science*, Milton Keynes: Open University Press (pp. 145–169).

Driver, R., and Easley, G. (1983) 'Pupils and paradigms: a review of literature related to concept development in adolescent science students', *Studies in Science Education*, 5: 61–84.

Driver, R., Leach, J., Millar, R., and Scott, P. (1996) *Young people's images of science*, Milton Keynes: Open University Press.

Duit, R. (2007) *Bibliography STCSE (students' and teachers' conceptions and science education)*, www.ipn.uni-kiel.de/aktuell/stcse/stcse.html

Dunbar, K., and Fugelsang, J. (2005) 'Scientific reasoning and thinking', in K. J. Holyoak and R. G. Morrison (eds.) *The Cambridge handbook of thinking and reasoning*, Cambridge: Cambridge University Press (pp. 705–725).

Dunbar, K., and Klahr, D. (1989) 'Developmental differences in scientific discovery processes', in G. M. Green (ed.) *Complex information processing*, Hillsdale, NJ: Lawrence Erlbaum Associates (pp. 107–143).

Fugelsang, J. A., and Dunbar, K. N. (2005) 'Brain-based mechanisms underlying complex causal thinking', *Neuropsychologia*, 43: 1204–1213.

Gunstone, R., and Watts, M. (1985) 'Force and motion' in R. Driver, E. Guesne, and A. Tiberghien (eds.) *Children's ideas in science*, Milton Keynes: Open University Press (pp. 85–104).

Gunstone, R. F., and White, R. T. (1981) 'Understanding gravity', *Science Education*, 65: 291–299.

Hast, M. (2010) *Explicit versus tacit knowledge in early science education: the case of primary school children's understanding of object speed and acceleration*. Unpublished PhD thesis. Cambridge: University of Cambridge.

Howe, C. J. (1998) *Conceptual structure in childhood and adolescence: the case of everyday physics*, London: Routledge.

Howe, C. (2010) 'Peer dialogue and cognitive development: a two-way relationship?', in K. Littleton and C. Howe (eds.) *Educational dialogues: understanding and promoting productive interaction*, London: Routledge.

Howe, C., Taylor Tavares, J., and Devine, A. (2009) 'Beliefs and children's tacit understanding of horizontal motion: a challenge for theories of consciousness', Paper presented at 12th Annual Conference of the BPS Consciousness and Experiential Psychology Section, Oxford, 11–13 September.

Howe, C., Taylor Tavares, J., and Devine, A. (2012) 'Everyday conceptions of object fall: explicit and tacit understanding during middle childhood', *Journal of Experimental Child Psychology*, 111: 351–366.

Howe, C. J., and Tolmie, A. (2003) 'Group work in primary school science: discussion, consensus and guidance from experts', *International Journal of Educational Research*, 39: 51–72.

Howe, C., Tolmie, A., Duchak Tanner, V., and Rattray, C. (2000) 'Hypothesis testing in science: group consensus and the acquisition of conceptual and procedural knowledge', *Learning and Instruction*, 10: 361–391.

Howe, C., Tolmie, A., and Sofroniou, N. (1999) 'Experimental appraisal of personal beliefs in science: constraints on performance in the 9 to 14 age group', *British Journal of Educational Psychology*, 69: 243–274.

Inagaki, K., and Hatano, G. (2002) *Young children's naïve thinking about the biological world*, New York: Psychology Press.

Inhelder, B., and Piaget, J. (1958) *The growth of logical thinking*, New York: Basic Books.

Kaiser, M. K., Proffitt, D. R., and McCloskey, M. (1985) 'The development of beliefs about falling objects', *Perception and Psychophysics*, 38: 533–539.

Kim, I. K., and Spelke, E. S. (1992) 'Infants' sensitivity to effects of gravity on visible object motion', *Journal of Experimental Psychology: Human Perception and Performance*, 18: 385–393.

Koslowski, B. (1996) *Theory and evidence: the development of scientific reasoning*, Cambridge, MA: MIT Press.

Kotovsky, L., and Baillargeon, R. (1998) 'The development of calibration-based reasoning about collision events in young infants', *Cognition*, 67: 311–351.

Kuhn, D. (1991) *The skills of argument*, Cambridge: Cambridge University Press.

Kuhn, D., Amsel, E., and O'Loughlin, M. (1988) *The development of scientific thinking skills*, San Diego: Academic Press.

Kuhn, D., Iordanou, K., Pease, M., and Wirkala, C. (2008) 'Beyond control of variables: what needs to develop to achieve skilled scientific thinking', *Cognitive Development*, 23: 435–451.

Mali, G. B., and Howe, A. (1979) 'Development of earth and gravity concepts among Nepali children', *Science Education*, 63: 685–691.

McCloskey, M. (1983) 'Naïve theories of motion', in D. Gentner and A. L. Stevens (eds.) *Mental models*, Hillsdale, NJ: Lawrence Erlbaum Associates (pp. 299–324).

McDermott, L. C. (1984) 'Research on conceptual understanding in mechanics', *Physics Today*, 37: 24–32.

Needham, A., and Baillargeon, R. (1993) 'Intuitions about support in 4.5-month-old infants', *Cognition*, 47: 121–148.

Nobes, G., Martin, A. E., and Panagiotaki, G. (2005) 'The development of scientific knowledge of the Earth', *British Journal of Developmental Psychology*, 23: 47–64.

Nussbaum, J. (1985) 'The earth as a cosmic body', in R. Driver, E. Guesne, and A. Tiberghien (eds.) *Children's ideas in science*, Milton Keynes: Open University Press (pp. 170–192).

Panagiotaki, G., Nobes, G., and Banerjee, R. (2006) 'Children's representations of the earth: a methodological comparison', *British Journal of Developmental Psychology*, 24: 353–372.

Piaget, J. (1930) *The child's conception of physical causality*, London: Routledge and Kegan Paul.

Piaget, J. (1974) *Understanding causality*, New York: Norton.

Ruffman, T., Perner, J., Olson, D. R., and Doherty, M. (1993) 'Reflecting on scientific thinking: children's understanding of the hypothesis–evidence relation', *Child Development*, 64: 1617–1636.

Samarapungavan, A., Vosniadou, S., and Brewer, W. F. (1996) 'Mental models of the earth, sun, and moon: Indian children's cosmologies', *Cognitive Development*, 11: 491–521.

Schauble, L. (1990) 'Belief revision in children: the role of prior knowledge and strategies for generating evidence', *Journal of Experimental Child Psychology*, 49: 31–57.

Scott, P., Asoko, H., and Leach, J. (2007) 'Student conceptions and conceptual learning in science', in S. K. Abell and N. G. Ledermann (eds.) *Handbook of research on science education*, Mahwah, NJ: Lawrence Erlbaum Associates (pp. 31–56).

Sodian, B., Zaitchik, D., and Carey, S. (1991) 'Young children's differentiation of hypothetical beliefs from evidence', *Child Development*, 62: 753–766.

Stead, K., and Osborne, R. (1981) 'What is friction? Some children's ideas', *Australian Science Teachers' Journal*, 27: 51–57.

Tschirgi, J. E. (1980) 'Sensible reasoning: a hypothesis about hypotheses', *Child Development*, 51: 1–10.

Twigger, D., Byard, M., Driver, R., Draper, S., Hartley, R., Hennessy, S., Mohamed, R., O'Malley, C., O'Shea, T., and Scanlon, E. (1994) 'The conception of force and motion of students aged between 10 and 15 years: an interview study designed to guide instruction', *International Journal of Science Education*, 16: 215–229.

Vosniadou, S., and Brewer, W. F. (1992) 'Mental models of the earth: a study of conceptual change in childhood', *Cognitive Psychology*, 24: 535–585.

Vosniadou, S., Skopeliti, I., and Ikospentaki, K. (2004) 'Mode of knowing and ways of reasoning in elementary astronomy', *Cognitive Development*, 19: 203–222.

White, R. T., and Gunstone, R. F. (2008) 'The conceptual change approach to the teaching of science', in S. Vosniadou (ed.) *International handbook of research on conceptual change*, New York: Routledge (pp. 619–628).

Zimmerman, C. (2007) 'The development of scientific thinking skills in elementary and middle school', *Developmental Review*, 27: 172–223.

Zimmerman, C., and Glaser, R. (2001) 'Testing positive versus negative claims: a preliminary investigation of the role of cover story in the assessment of experimental design skills', Technical Report No. 554, UCLA National Center for Research on Evaluation, Standards, and Student Testing, Los Angeles.

11

MOTIVATION TO LEARN

Andrew J. Martin

UNIVERSITY OF SYDNEY, AUSTRALIA

Theory, concepts, and constructs

Academic motivation

Motivation is defined here as students' inclination, energy, and drive to learn, work effectively, and achieve to potential (Martin 2007, 2009). Motivation is relevant to students' interest in study, enjoyment of study, participation in class, and academic achievement (Martin, Marsh, and Debus 2001a, 2001b, 2003; Pintrich 2000, 2003; Schunk and Miller 2002). It is therefore not surprising that a major rationale for the study of motivation is prompted by declines in academic achievement and participation. For example, international tests have identified a decline in the mathematics achievement of middle-school students (Thomson et al. 2010). There are declining numbers enrolling in advanced and intermediate mathematics and science courses at school (Barrington 2006). Other research has identified significant differences in motivation and engagement and literacy between boys and girls, with girls often outperforming boys (Martin 2007; Thomson et al. 2010). There are gaps in problem solving and achievement for immigrant youth (Organisation for Economic Cooperation and Development (OECD), 2006) and significantly lower achievement for indigenous students (Thomson et al. 2010). Even among high-performing nations in international testing (e.g. Australia), there is significant intra-nation variability in achievement and engagement, with some states scoring significantly higher than OECD averages and other states performing below OECD averages (Thomson et al. 2010). Taken together, there is a national and international context for the role and presence of student motivation.

Theories of motivation

There are numerous theoretical contributions to our understanding of motivation. In this chapter, some of the salient and influential perspectives are summarized, including self-efficacy theory, expectancy-value theory, need achievement theory, self-worth motivation theory, attribution theory, control theory, goal theory, self-regulation theory, and self-determination theory.

Perceived competence: self-efficacy and expectancy-value theory

One aspect of motivation theorizing involves appraisals of one's competence – here discussed by way of self-efficacy and expectancies. One major line of theory and research concerns the appraisals students make about their task-related academic capacity. Much of this thinking and research has centred on 'self-efficacy'. According to Bandura (1997), students who are self-efficacious are more likely to generate and test alternative courses of action, tend to function better in the classroom through greater effort and persistence, and respond to problems more effectively through enabling cognitive and emotional processes. In contrast, students low in self-efficacy are more likely to dwell on their deficiencies and view situations as particularly difficult (Bandura 1997). The educational evidence supports these theoretical and operational claims: self-efficacy is significantly associated with self-regulation, effort, persistence, and achievement (e.g. Martin 2009; Schunk and Miller 2002).

Furthermore, in 'additive' self-system models such as expectancy-value theory (Wigfield and Eccles 2000), alongside student expectations/efficacy is the issue of 'valuing': students with high task-related expectations and who value the task are more motivated to do it. Thus, when students see the utility and importance of what they are taught, they tend to be more motivated in their learning and also achieve at a higher level (Martin 2007, 2009).

Need achievement and self-worth motivation theory

From the perspective of need achievement and self-worth motivation theories, it is possible to characterize students in terms of their motive to approach success and avoid failure (Covington 1998). Based on these perspectives, three student typologies are evident: success-oriented, failure-avoidant, and failure-accepting (see also Martin and Marsh 2003). Success-oriented students tend to be optimistic, adopt proactive orientations to their studies, and respond to setback and adversity with optimism and energy (Covington and Omelich 1991; Martin et al. 2001a). Failure-avoidant students tend to be motivated by a fear of failure and tend to be uncertain about their ability to avoid failure or achieve success (Covington and Omelich 1991; Martin and Marsh 2003). Sometimes in response to this fear of failure, students may actively handicap their chances of success (e.g. procrastinate or not study at all) so that they have an excuse if they do not succeed (Covington 1998; Martin and Marsh 2003). Finally, failure-accepting students (sometimes referred to as disengaged or learned helpless) have given up or are disengaged and display a helpless pattern of motivation (Covington 1998). From need achievement and self-worth motivation perspectives, then, a number of factors emerge that have become salient in the motivation domain. In terms of the success-oriented student, there is evidence of high 'self-efficacy' and 'control'. In terms of the failure-avoidant student, 'anxiety' and 'failure avoidance' (or 'performance avoidance orientation') are salient. In terms of failure-avoidant and failure-accepting students, 'self-handicapping' and 'disengagement' are evident (see Martin 2007, 2010a for further discussion).

Attribution theory and control

Attribution theory describes how the causes individuals attribute to events impact their behaviour, cognition, and affect (Weiner 2010). For example, in the educational domain, attributions impact students' persistence, optimism, emotion, and performance (e.g. Craven, Marsh, and Debus 1991; Weiner 2010). Causes are hypothesized to vary along three main dimensions: stability, locus, and controllability (Weiner 2010). Stability refers to the extent to which the cause is temporary, variable, or relatively situational – or, whether it is present in most (or all) situations and across time. Examples of stable causes may include ability or intelligence. Effort is an example of an unstable cause. Locus refers to whether the cause is internal to the individual or external to the individual. An example of internal locus is effort and an example of external locus is good luck or bad luck. Of particular focus here is the 'control' dimension, as this very much influences students' responses to academic outcomes and motivation (Martin et al. 2001b, 2003). While recognizing various perspectives on control (see Skinner 1996 for a review of numerous control dimensions), in the context of the present discussion, control refers to students' belief that they have major determination in attaining success and avoiding failure. Students believing they have little or no control are uncertain about their capacity to avoid failure or attain success. Indeed, Patrick, Skinner, and Connell (1993) found that perceived control predicts students' persistence, attention, effort, and participation. Similarly, Harter and Connell (1984) found that uncertain control is negatively correlated with achievement, mastery motivation, competence evaluation, and competence affect.

Goal and self-regulation theories

Goal theory sheds explanatory light on the reasons students have for striving and achieving (or not). The 'classic' goal perspective emphasizes mastery and performance goals. More recent work has suggested a 'revised' perspective incorporating avoidance and approach dimensions (Elliot 2005). Mastery orientation is focused on factors and processes such as effort, self-improvement, skill development, and learning. Performance orientation is focused more on demonstrating relative ability, social comparisons, and outperforming others (Elliot 2005). When integrated with approach–avoidance dimensions, performance avoidance is focused on avoiding appearing incompetent (Elliot 2005). The links between these goals and academic outcomes tend to be clearest for mastery orientation and performance avoidance: mastery is positively related to persistence, interest, choice, effort, self-regulation, and deep processing whereas performance avoidance tends to be negatively associated with these academic factors and processes (Elliot 2005). Thus, in highlighting factors clearly salient in motivational modelling, 'mastery orientation' is emphasized – as is 'performance avoidance'.

It is also important to understand the means by which mastery is operationalized in students' academic lives. Thinking around self-regulation has been influential here with researchers identifying the important role of factors and processes such as 'planning', 'task management', and 'persistence' (e.g. Zimmerman 2002). In studies of motivation and self-regulation, these constructs have been found to predict achievement and positive behaviours important for completion of academic tasks (Martin et al. 2001b, 2003). Thus, in line with self-regulatory approaches to academic motivation and engagement in learning, factors such as planning, task management, and persistence are useful.

Self-determination theory

Mastery orientation is also identified because of its interface with self-determination theory (SDT; Ryan and Deci 2000). SDT distinguishes between intrinsic motivation (motivation based on inherent interest in or satisfaction with an activity) and extrinsic motivation (motivation based on external attributes of a task such as reward, approval, or grades). Of relevance to this discussion, mastery orientation is conceptually and empirically aligned with intrinsic motivation. For example, as with intrinsic motivation, mastery is associated with interest, autonomy, and desire for learning and challenge among students (La Guardia and Ryan 2002) – further supporting the centrality of mastery in motivational theorizing and practice. Another important element of SDT involves individuals' psychological needs – in particular, the need for autonomy, competence and relatedness. These needs provide 'essential nutriments for growth' (Ryan and Deci 2010: 174). The former two are relevant to this chapter. According to Ryan and Deci (2010: 174), 'intrinsic motivation flourishes under conditions supporting autonomy and competence and wanes when these needs are thwarted'. The need for competence relates directly to 'self-efficacy' and the need for autonomy is relevant to the 'control' factor in theorizing. The third need, relatedness, has often been identified as a predictor of student motivation. For example, teacher–student, peer, and parent relationships have been found to impact academic motivation (Liem and Martin 2011; Martin and Dowson 2009). Whereas relatedness also involves aspects of the environment (e.g. teachers, peers), competence and autonomy are more internal to the individual and thus represented here as part of an individual's motivation profile.

Key factors in salient motivation theories

There have been calls for more integrative approaches to motivational research and theorizing (Murphy and Alexander 2000; Pintrich 2003). This has led to the recent development of a model of motivation that is built in two steps. First, theory and component concepts are distilled into a manageable set of constructs that is readily identifiable by educators and students alike. Second, these constructs are organized into a structure that is relatively simple to articulate and represent. In terms of the first step, Figure 11.1 shows the key theories discussed above and a proposed set of constructs that reflects these theories. This figure comprises each of the central constructs described above (self-efficacy, valuing, mastery orientation, persistence, task management, planning, failure avoidance, anxiety, uncertain control, self-handicapping, and disengagement) connected to related theory. Figure 11.2 represents the second step in this process: the Motivation and Engagement Wheel (Martin 2007, 2009, 2010a).

The Motivation and Engagement Wheel

The Motivation and Engagement Wheel is aligned with thinking proposed by Pintrich (2003), who identified numerous conceptual areas for integrative motivational science, as follows: self-efficacy, attributions, valuing, control, self-determination, goal orientation, need achievement, self-regulation, and self-worth. Hence, as described previously (e.g. Martin 2007, 2009, 2010a) – and in line with the factors and processes described under each motivational theory above – (a) self-efficacy theory (e.g. Bandura 1997) is reflected in the self-efficacy dimension of the Wheel, (b) attributions and control are reflected in the uncertain control dimension (tapping the controllability element of attributions – see Connell 1985; Weiner 2010), (c) valuing (e.g. Wigfield and Eccles 2000) is reflected in a valuing dimension, (d) self-determination (in terms of intrinsic motivation – see Ryan and Deci 2000) and goal orientation (see Elliot 2005) are reflected in a mastery orientation dimension, (e) self-regulation (e.g. Zimmerman 2002) is reflected in planning, task management, and persistence dimensions, and (f) need achievement and self-worth (see Covington 1998) are reflected in failure avoidance, anxiety, self-handicapping, and disengagement dimensions. Hence, the Wheel comprises 11 factors that Martin (2007, 2009, 2010a) has grouped under four overarching clusters: (i) adaptive cognition (self-efficacy, valuing, mastery orientation), (ii) adaptive behaviour (planning, task management, persistence), (iii) maladaptive cognition (anxiety, failure avoidance, uncertain control), and (iv) maladaptive behaviour (disengagement, self-handicapping) – see Figure 11.2.

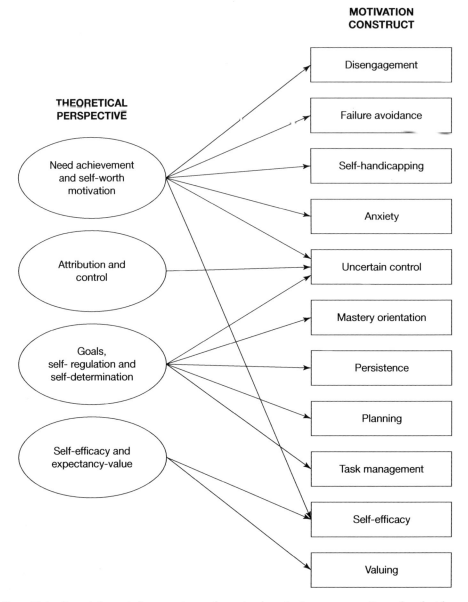

Figure 11.1 Central theoretical perspectives and associated motivation constructs. Reproduced with permission from Martin, A. J. (2010b) *Motivation and Engagement Scale – Test User Manual*, Sydney: Lifelong Achievement Group

Measurement

Most motivational theories can be empirically assessed using instrumentation that in one way or another quantifies students on the various factors or dimensions residing within them. Understandably, given that each theory focuses on a relatively small set of factors, accompanying instrumentation is also rather narrowly developed along these lines. However, there are some notable examples of instrumentation reflecting diverse motivation-related dimensions such as

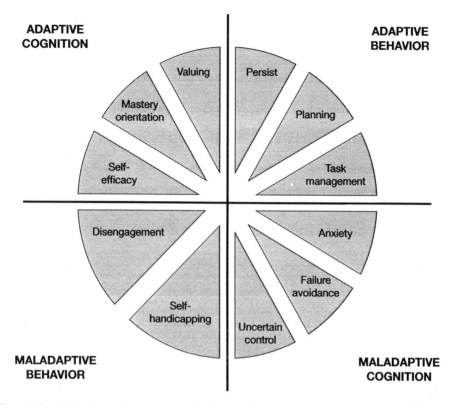

ADAPTIVE COGNITION

ADAPTIVE BEHAVIOR

MALADAPTIVE BEHAVIOR

MALADAPTIVE COGNITION

Valuing
Mastery orientation
Self-efficacy
Persist
Planning
Task management
Disengagement
Anxiety
Self-handicapping
Failure avoidance
Uncertain control

Figure 11.2 Motivation and Engagement Wheel. Reproduced with permission from Martin, A. J. (2010b) *Motivation and Engagement Scale – Test User Manual*, Sydney: Lifelong Achievement Group

Patterns of Adaptive Learning Survey (PALS) by Midgley et al. (1997) and the Motivated Strategies for Learning Questionnaire (MSLQ), by Pintrich et al. (1991).

In a similar vein, the Motivation and Engagement Scale (MES; Martin 2011) seeks to represent a wide range of motivation factors – namely, those represented in the Motivation and Engagement Wheel (Figure 11.2). The MES is a 44-item self-report instrument comprising four items for each of the 11 factors. To each item, students rate themselves on a scale of 1 (strongly disagree) to 7 (strongly agree). Originally administered to high school students, the Motivation and Engagement Scale – High School (MES-HS; Martin 2011) factors are reliable, normally distributed, and reflect a strong factor structure that is invariant across gender and age (however, there are mean-level differences where girls typically score higher on motivation than boys and middle high school students score lower than junior and senior high students) (Martin 2007). In terms of predictive validity, factors in the MES-HS have predicted educational processes and outcomes such as enjoyment of school, classroom participation, educational aspirations, and achievement (Martin 2007). The MES-HS has also been empirically useful in specific school subjects such as mathematics, science, and English (Green, Martin, and Marsh 2007). Now, a suite of three academic forms has been developed and validated (Martin 2009, 2011): the MES-HS, the Motivation and Engagement Scale – Junior School (MES-JS, for elementary/primary school students), and the Motivation and Engagement Scale – University/College (MES-UC). As a brief exercise for training teachers, psychologists and counsellors, there are motivation items in the Appendix to consider. These are brief and indicative items for each factor in the Wheel (but note that motivation and engagement are formally assessed using the complete and validated MES; Martin 2011).

International and cross-cultural research

A major focus on international and cross-cultural motivation research has involved students from the East and West. Cross-cultural motivation research among Asian students has been popular because of their strong performance in large-scale international academic testing projects (e.g. Leung 2002). These results have prompted a number of motivational studies seeking to explain why Asian students often outperform students in the West. Here, two constructs central to motivation (Pintrich 2003) are selected for cross-cultural review: attributions and achievement goals.

Attributions and achievement goals: East and West

Attribution theory traverses factors such as effort, ability, task, and chance (Weiner 2010). Effort has been proposed as an important factor behind Chinese students' high achievement (e.g. Lau and Chan 2001). However, other research has identified nuances relevant to such findings. For example, in the Trends in International Mathematics and Science Study (TIMSS) there is a shared view across all countries (not just among Asian nations) that hard work is important for doing well in mathematics. Similarly, students from the four high-achieving East Asian countries (Hong Kong, Japan, South Korea, and Singapore) did not differ from many Western countries in their beliefs about the importance of ability (Leung 2002).

Students' achievement goals (mastery, avoidance, performance, and social goals) have also been a focus for cross-cultural research. As described by Martin and Hau (2010), it has been suggested that in collectivist Asian societies, socially oriented goals are an important dimension that has not been well developed in Western goal theory (Yu and Yang 1994). In relation to mastery and performance goals, studies conducted in contexts such as Hong Kong and Singapore have provided evidence for a positive rather than a negative correlation between these, with both types of goal yielding positive academic effects (e.g. Ho, Hau, and Salili 2007). Further, Sagie, Elizur, and Yamauchi (1996) found that mean goal levels were quite different between East and West, with collectivistic (e.g. Japanese) participants reporting lower personal achievement tendencies than individualistic (e.g. US) participants.

Culture and the Motivation and Engagement Wheel

Factors in the Motivation and Engagement Wheel have also been studied in different international and national cultural contexts. For example, Martin and Hau (2010) administered a Chinese translation of the MES-HS to Hong Kong students. Like its English counterpart, the MES-HS was invariant across gender and age groups in Hong Kong. Further, there was invariance in factor loadings, correlations/variances, and residuals between the Chinese and English samples, suggesting that there are no fundamental cross-cultural structural differences on core motivation factors. Interestingly, however, Martin and Hau found that although there were no structural differences between Hong Kong and Australian students, there were some mean-level differences such that Hong Kong students reported lower motivation. They concluded that although there were no differences 'of kind' between Hong Kong and Australian students, there were differences 'of degree'. In another cultural context, Bodkin-Andrews, Craven, and Martin (2006) have demonstrated the psychometric properties of the MES-HS among Australian

Indigenous/Aboriginal students. Similarly, Munns, Martin, and Craven (2008) employed the Motivation and Engagement Wheel to better conceptualize and support the motivation of Indigenous students in the classroom.

Practice

Can motivation change?

In response to calls for a more integrative approach to the study of motivation (see Murphy and Alexander 2000; Pintrich 2003), recent studies have employed intervention programmes that are shaped by multidimensional motivation. For example, Martin (2005) tested the effects of a series of workshops targeting students' motivation. The workshops were focused on each facet of the Wheel and measurement involved the MES-HS at the outset of the programme, towards the end of the programme, and again six to eight weeks later. Data showed there were gains on key facets of students' motivation by the end of the programme, which were sustained six to eight weeks later. A second intervention study implemented a motivation workbook intervention using a pre/post and treatment/control group design (Martin 2008). Analyses comparing pre- and post-intervention scores on the MES-HS revealed significant improvements in the treatment group's motivation and no such significant changes for the control group. Encouragingly, results of these two studies suggest that motivation can change through intervention targeting clearly and specifically defined motivation factors.

Strategies for enhancing motivation to learn

Importantly, many researchers have provided helpful guidance on strategies targeting specific facets of motivation. The following is advice from Martin (2007, 2009, 2010a) targeting key dimensions of the Motivation and Engagement Wheel (also see Covington 1998; Hattie 2009; Marzano 2003 for further practical advice). Effectively developing students' self-efficacy will rely on their access to and opportunities for competence – for example, through individualizing schoolwork, promoting more positive self-beliefs, successfully challenging negative thinking, and developing students' goal-setting skills (Bandura 1997; Locke and Latham 2002). Valuing is developed through communicating to students the ways and reasons that school and schoolwork are relevant and important to their lives now and their lives in the future. It is also important that educators are positive role models for valuing what they teach (Covington 1998; Martin 2007, 2009). Mastery orientation, planning, task management, and persistence are addressed through applications of goal theory and self-regulation. Consistent with goal theory, mastery orientation is developed through reducing an emphasis on comparisons with others and evaluative concerns and encouraging an emphasis on the task at hand and the effort needed to attain mastery (Elliot 2005). Developing students' self-regulatory skills is an important means of enhancing planning, task management, and persistence. For example, teaching students how to use time effectively, prioritize, and develop strategies for doing and checking schoolwork can be useful ways to promote self-regulation (Zimmerman 2002).

Researchers have also identified strategies for addressing maladaptive dimensions of motivation. In terms of uncertain control, it can be helpful for students to see the link between their efforts and their achievement (Martin 2010a). Similarly, administering consequences that are directly contingent on what students do enhances the predictability of academic life and promotes control (Thompson 1994). Importantly, fostering a sense of control is a helpful avenue for addressing potential disengagement. Due to chronically low levels of control, students can come to abandon effort (Peterson, Maier, and Seligman 1993). Through a greater sense of control, students are more likely to invest effort and less likely to disengage. Finally, in relation to failure avoidance, anxiety and self-handicapping, research suggests there can be yield in reducing students' fear of failure (Covington 1998). This can be achieved through promoting courageous and constructive views of mistakes and failure – for example, making it clear that mistakes provide diagnostic information about how to improve and do not imply a lack of worth. Through a reduction in fear, there is a reduction in the motivational bases of students' anxiety, avoidance, and self-handicapping (Covington 1998; Martin 2007, 2009, 2010a).

Motivation now – and in the future

It is recognized that alongside motivation itself, there exists a constellation of constructs that can facilitate or hamper the motivational process. Given the limitations of space, this chapter will summarize some of the more recent offerings and future directions that have been proposed. They traverse personal best (growth) goals and interpersonal relationships. Also discussed is the future place of motivation research in the 'Asian Century'.

Personal best goals

A large amount of evidence demonstrates the yields of mastery approaches; however, there is evidence demonstrating some yields for performance approaches. This has led to questions about the most adaptive balancing of performance and mastery approaches (Brophy 2005), and personal best (PB) goals have been proposed as a functional integration of the two (Martin 2006; Martin and Liem 2010). Specifically, PB goals encompass mastery approaches because they are self-improvement-based and comprise performance elements because the student competes with his or her own previous performance or attainment. Research among high school students has shown that PB goals are predictive of motivation in the short term (Martin 2006) and causally predictive of motivation and achievement one year later (Martin and Liem 2010). PB goals, then, appear to have substantive (in addressing theoretical tensions in goal theory) and applied (in predicting enhanced motivation) merit in the motivational literature.

Connective instruction: pedagogy and interpersonal relationships

A consistent theme in the literature concerns the role of interpersonal relationships in shaping students' motivation to learn (Furrer and Skinner 2003; Martin and Dowson 2009). Given this, Martin (2010a; see also Martin and Dowson 2009) offered an instructional approach to position interpersonal connectedness more centrally in the motivation literature. This approach is described as 'connective instruction' – pedagogy that connects the student and teacher on three levels: the level of substance and subject matter, the interpersonal level, and the instructional level. Thus, connective instruction comprises three relationships: the substantive relationship (the connection between the student and the subject matter and substance of what is taught – i.e. connecting to the 'what'), the interpersonal relationship (the connection between the student and the teacher him or herself – i.e. connecting to the 'who'), and the instructional relationship (the connection between the student and the instruction/teaching – i.e. connecting to the 'how'). Connective instruction, then, may be viewed as an approach to learning that centrally recognizes the interpersonal foundations of motivation.

The 'Asian Century'

Over the past 50 years, substantial economic growth in many Asian economies has increased their global economic and strategic impact and influence. These nations are experiencing tremendous internal transformation, with increasing numbers moving out of poverty and into the middle class (Australian Department of Prime Minister and Cabinet 2012). Given the massive transformations occurring in this region of the world and the impact this will have on the existing global order, the term 'Asian Century' has been coined. Education is a major driver of this and also a major sector that must service this transformation. Understanding key educational phenomena in these contexts will be of increasing importance and interest.

Given that many measures and theoretical models of achievement motivation have been developed in Western contexts, they have at times been criticized for being culturally entrenched in the ideology of individualism and inappropriate for application to collectivist cultures (e.g., Yang 1991; see also Ngara and Porath, Chapter 19, this volume, for related discussions on the subject of 'intelligence testing'). Although there has been research exploring motivation among Chinese and Western students, there continues to be a lack of clarity about the applicability of Western-developed achievement motivation in the East. Future motivation research will be needed to address this.

Conclusion

A number of influential perspectives and theories have been developed to understand and explain students' motivation to learn. Each of these has provided deep insights into the cognition, affect, and behaviours that are relevant to students' inclination, energy, and drive to apply themselves and persist in their academic lives. Taken together, these theories and their component processes and factors hold implications for researchers studying issues relevant to motivation and learning and are also relevant to practitioners seeking to enhance student learning.

Contact address: andrew.martin@sydney.edu.au

References

Australian Department of Prime Minister and Cabinet (2012) *Australia in the Asian Century: White Paper*, Canberra: Australian Government Publishing.

Bandura, A. (1997) *Self-efficacy: the exercise of control*, New York: Freeman and Co.

Barrington, F. (2006) *Participation in Year 12 mathematics across Australia 1995–2004*, Melbourne: Australian Mathematical Sciences Institute.

Bodkin-Andrews, G., Craven, R. G., and Martin, A. J. (2006) 'Motivational behaviours and cognitions of Indigenous Australian secondary students', in R. G. Craven, J. S. Eccles, and T. M. Ha (eds.) *Self-concept, motivation, social and personal identity for the 21st century*, Proceedings of the Fourth International Biennial SELF Research Conference, Ann Arbor: University of Michigan.

Brophy, J. (2005) 'Goal theorists should move on from performance goals', *Educational Psychologist*, 40: 167–176.

Connell, J. P. (1985) 'A new multidimensional measure of children's perceptions of control', *Child Development*, 56: 1018–1041.

Covington, M. V. (1998) *The will to learn: a guide for motivating young people*, New York: Cambridge University Press.

Covington, M. V., and Omelich, C. L. (1991) 'Need achievement revisited: verification of Atkinson's original 2 × 2 model', in C. D. Spielberger. I. G. Sarason, Z. Kulcsar, and G. L. Van Heck (eds.) *Stress and emotion*, New York: Hemisphere. (pp. 85–105).

Craven, R. G., Marsh, H. W., and Debus, R. L. (1991) 'Effects of internally focused feedback and attributional feedback on the enhancement of academic self-concept', *Journal of Educational Psychology*, 83: 17–26.

Elliot, A. J. (2005) 'A conceptual history of the achievement goal construct', in A. J. Elliot and C. S. Dweck (eds.) *Handbook of competence and motivation*, New York: Guilford (pp. 52–72).

Furrer, C., and Skinner, E. (2003) 'Sense of relatedness as a factor in children's academic engagement and performance', *Journal of Educational Psychology*, 95: 148–62.

Green, J., Martin, A. J., and Marsh, H. W. (2007) 'Motivation and engagement in English, mathematics and science high school subjects: towards an understanding of multidimensional domain specificity', *Learning and Individual Differences*, 17: 269–279.

Harter, S., and Connell, J. P. (1984) 'A model of children's achievement and related self-perceptions of competence, control, and motivation orientation', in J. Nicholls (ed.) *The development of achievement motivation*, London: JAI Press (pp. 219–50).

Hattie, J. (2009) *Visible learning: a synthesis of over 800 meta-analyses relating to achievement*, London: Routledge.

Ho, I. T., Hau, K.-T., and Salili, F. (2007) 'Expectancy and value as predictors of Chinese students' achievement goals', in F. Salili and R. Hoosain (eds.) *Culture, motivation, and learning: a multicultural perspective*, Greenwich, CT: Information Age Publishing (pp. 69–90).

La Guardia, J. G., and Ryan, R. M. (2002) 'What adolescents need: a self-determination theory perspective on development within families, school, and society', in F. Pajares and T. Urdan (eds.) *Academic motivation of adolescents*, Greenwich, CT: Information Age Publishing (pp. 170–193).

Lau, K. L., and Chan, D. W. (2001) 'Motivational characteristics of under-achievers in Hong Kong', *Educational Psychology*, 22: 417–430.

Leung, F. K. S. (2002) 'Behind the high achievement of East Asian students', *Educational Research and Evaluation*, 8: 87–108.

Liem, G. A., and Martin, A. J. (2011) 'Peer relationships and adolescents' academic and non-academic outcomes: same-sex and opposite-sex peer effects and the mediating role of school engagement', *British Journal of Educational Psychology*, 81: 183–206.

Locke, E. A., and Latham, G. P. (2002) 'Building practically useful theory of goal setting and task motivation', *American Psychologist*, 57: 705–717.

Martin, A. J. (2005) 'Exploring the effects of a youth enrichment program on academic motivation and engagement', *Social Psychology of Education*, 8: 179–206.

Martin, A. J. (2006) 'Personal bests (PBs): a proposed multidimensional model and empirical analysis', *British Journal of Educational Psychology*, 76: 803–825.

Martin, A. J. (2007) 'Examining a multidimensional model of student motivation and engagement using a construct validation approach', *British Journal of Educational Psychology*, 77: 413–440.

Martin, A. J. (2008) 'Enhancing student motivation and engagement: The effects of a multidimensional intervention', *Contemporary Educational Psychology*, 33: 239–269.

Martin, A. J. (2009) 'Motivation and engagement across the academic lifespan: a developmental construct validity study of elementary school, high school, and university/college students', *Educational and Psychological Measurement*, 69: 794–824.

Martin, A. J. (2010a) *Building classroom success: eliminating academic fear and failure*, New York: Continuum.

Martin, A. J. (2010b) *Motivation and Engagement Scale – Test User Manual*, Sydney: Lifelong Achievement Group.

Martin, A. J. (2011) *The Motivation and Engagement Scale*, 5th edn, Sydney, Australia: Lifelong Achievement Group.

Martin, A. J., and Dowson, M. (2009) 'Interpersonal relationships, motivation, engagement, and achievement: yields for theory, current issues, and practice', *Review of Educational Research*, 79: 327–365.

Martin, A. J., and Hau, K.-T. (2010) 'Achievement motivation amongst Chinese and Australian school students: assessing differences of kind and differences of degree', *International Journal of Testing*, 10: 274–294.

Martin, A. J., and Liem, G. A. (2010) 'Academic Personal Bests (PBs), engagement, and achievement: a cross-lagged panel analysis', *Learning and Individual Differences*, 20: 265–270.

Martin, A. J., and Marsh, H. W. (2003) 'Fear of failure: friend or foe?', *Australian Psychologist*, 38: 31–38.

Martin, A. J., Marsh, H. W., and Debus, R. L. (2001a) 'A quadripolar need achievement representation of self-handicapping and defensive pessimism', *American Educational Research Journal*, 38: 583–610.

Martin, A. J., Marsh, H. W., and Debus, R. L. (2001b) 'Self-handicapping and defensive pessimism: exploring a model of predictors and outcomes from a self-protection perspective', *Journal of Educational Psychology*, 93: 87–102.

Martin, A. J., Marsh, H. W., and Debus, R. L. (2003) 'Self-handicapping and defensive pessimism: a model of self-protection from a longitudinal perspective', *Contemporary Educational Psychology*, 28: 1–36.

Marzano, R. (2003) *What works in schools*, Alexandria, Virginia: ASCD.

Midgley, C., Maehr, M., Hicks, L., Roesser, R., Urdan, T., Anderman, E., Kaplan, A., Arunkumar, R., and Middleton, M. (1997) *Patterns of Adaptive Learning (PALS)*, Ann Arbor: University of Michigan.

Munns, G., Martin, A. J., and Craven, R. (2008) 'To free the spirit? Motivation and engagement of Indigenous students', *Australian Journal of Indigenous Education*, 37: 98–107.

Murphy, P. K., and Alexander, P. A. (2000) 'A motivated exploration of motivation terminology', *Contemporary Educational Psychology*, 25: 3–53.

Organisation for Economic Cooperation and Development (OECD) (2006) *Where immigrant students succeed*, Paris: OECD.

Patrick, B. C., Skinner, E. A., and Connell, J. P. (1993) 'What motivates children's behavior and emotion? Joint effects of perceived control and autonomy in the academic domain', *Journal of Personality and Social Psychology*, 65: 781–791.

Peterson, C., Maier, S. F., and Seligman, M. E. P. (1993) *Learned helplessness: a theory for the age of personal control*, New York: Oxford University Press.

Pintrich, P. R. (2000) 'Educational psychology at the millennium: a look back and a look forward', *Educational Psychologist*, 35: 221–226.

Pintrich, P. R. (2003) 'A motivational science perspective on the role of student motivation in learning and teaching contexts', *Journal of Educational Psychology*, 95: 667–686.

Pintrich, P. R., Smith, D. A. F., Garcia, T., and McKeachie, W. J. (1991) *A manual for the use of the Motivated Strategies for Learning Questionnaire (MSLQ)*, Ann Arbor, MI: National Center for Research to Improve Postsecondary Teaching and Learning.

Ryan, R. M., and Deci, E. L. (2000) 'Self-determination theory and the facilitation of intrinsic motivation, social development, and well-being', *American Psychologist*, 55: 68–78.

Ryan, R. M., and Deci, E. L. (2010) 'Promoting self-determined school engagement: motivation, learning, and well-being', in K. R. Wentzel and A. Wigfield (eds.) *Handbook of school motivation*, New York: Routledge (pp. 171–196).

Sagie, A., Elizur, D., and Yamauchi, H. (1996) 'The structure and strength of achievement motivation: a cross-cultural comparison', *Journal of Organizational Behavior*, 17: 431–444.

Schunk, D. H., and Miller, S. D. (2002) 'Self-efficacy and adolescents' motivation', in F. Pajares and T. Urdan (eds.) *Academic motivation of adolescents*, Greenwich, CT: Information Age Publishing (pp. 29–52).

Skinner, E. A. (1996) 'A guide to constructs of control', *Journal of Personality and Social Psychology*, 71: 549–570.

Thomson, S., De Bortoli, L., Nicholas, M., Hillman, K., and Buckley, S. (2010) *PISA in brief: highlights from the full Australian report*, Melbourne, Australia: ACER.

Thompson, T. (1994) 'Self-worth protection: review and implications for the classroom', *Educational Review*, 46: 259–274.

Weiner, B. (2010) 'The development of an attribution-based theory of motivation: a history of ideas', *Educational Psychologist*, 45: 28–36.

Wigfield, A., and Eccles, J. S. (2000) 'Expectancy-value theory of motivation', *Contemporary Educational Psychology*, 25: 68–81.

Yang, C. F. (1991) 'A review of studies on self in Hong Kong and Taiwan', in C. F. Yang and H. S. R. Kao (eds.) *Chinese and Chinese heart* (in Chinese), Taipei, Taiwan: Yuan Liu (pp. 15–92).

Yu, A. B., and Yang, K. S. (1994) 'The nature of achievement motivation in collectivist societies', in U. Kim, H. C. Triandis, C. Kagitcibasi, S. C. Choi, and G. Yoon (eds.) *Individualism and collectivism: theory, method, and applications*, Thousand Oaks, CA: Sage (pp. 239–250).

Zimmerman, B. J. (2002) 'Achieving self-regulation: the trial and triumph of adolescence', in F. Pajares and T. Urdan (eds.) *Academic motivation of adolescents*, Greenwich, CT: Information Age Publishing (pp. 1–27).

Appendix

Table 11.1 Brief look at your motivation (your highest score is a strength; your lowest score is an area where you can improve)

	Disagree strongly	Disagree	Neither agree nor disagree	Agree	Agree strongly	
Adaptive cognition						
I believe in my ability to get on top of my university/school work	1	2	3	4	5	Self-efficacy
I believe that what I do at university/school is important	1	2	3	4	5	Valuing school
I focus on learning and improvement more than competition, being the best, or how I'll be evaluated	1	2	3	4	5	Mastery orientation
Adaptive behaviour						
I think through how I will do my university/school work and check how I'm going as I do it	1	2	3	4	5	Planning
I use my time well and try to study under conditions that bring out my best	1	2	3	4	5	Task management
I persist even when my studies are challenging or difficult	1	2	3	4	5	Persistence
Maladaptive cognition						
I'm quite anxious about my university/school work	1	2	3	4	5	Anxiety
I mainly do my study to avoid failure or disapproval rather than to aim for success	1	2	3	4	5	Failure avoidance
I do not think I have much control over how I perform at university/school	1	2	3	4	5	Uncertain control
Maladaptive behaviour						
I seem to limit my chances of success (e.g. waste time, disrupt others, procrastinate) at university/school	1	2	3	4	5	Self-handicapping
I often feel like giving up or quitting at university/school	1	2	3	4	5	Disengagement

Note: These items are indicative and not validated – motivation and engagement are best assessed using the complete and validated form of the Motivation and Engagement Scale. Reproduced with permission from Martin, A. J. (2011) *Motivation and Engagement Scale – User Manual*, 5th edn, Sydney: Lifelong Achievement Group.

12

CHILDREN'S RELATIONSHIPS AND THE FAMILY

Charlie Lewis, Dorothy Miell and Fleur-Michelle Coiffait

LANCASTER UNIVERSITY, UK; UNIVERSITY OF EDINBURGH, UK;
UNIVERSITY OF EDINBURGH, UK

If there is anything that we wish to change in the child, we should first examine it and see whether it is not something that could better be changed in ourselves.

(Jung 1939: 285).

Children's development is primarily a social process, with the family being the central context of learning and development (Bronfenbrenner 1986). Relationships in other settings such as school, peer groups, and the wider community also significantly influence children's development (Brown 1990; Rubin, Bukowski, and Parker 1998). The composition of family, education, and community systems varies widely throughout the world, as do the experiences and values that children and their families are exposed to both within and across cultures (Tudge et al. 2006). Furthermore, families exist as fluid and changing systems. Therefore it is useful to think about 'the family' in two complementary ways. First, it is a network of significant others in the child's immediate psychosocial world (Walsh 2003). Second, and as a result, it is a continually changing enactment of everyday experiences for each member. The sociologist David Morgan (1998) captured this fluidity by coining the term 'doing the family' – development occurs within families but each individual is active in making this process happen.

This chapter will explore the universal elements of relationships that promote children's social, emotional, cognitive, and behavioural development across different cultures, with the aim of encouraging consideration of wider systemic factors that may affect a child's learning and education. We suggest that it is the quality of children's relationships with others that is of huge importance, rather than the form they take. Furthermore, we urge consideration of the importance of children's relationships to all areas of their development, especially their learning. O'Connor (2002) pointed out there is no 'unifying theory' of parenting, because family relationships are multidimensional and in constant flux. However, there are patterns and themes in families that can be shown to have a clear influence on children's social, emotional, and cognitive development.

We explore the interface between family relationships and children's educational engagement. To do this we describe how analyses of family processes have attempted to capture individual change within a complex and ever-changing network of social processes. We start with an analysis of the theory that has dominated the field of family relationships, the construct of attachments. This theory, *par excellence*, captures the dynamic of developmental change within a social context. Secondly, we show that different relationships appear to influence children's development in complementary ways. We use the comparison between mothers and fathers in studies in which longitudinal processes are teased apart. Thirdly, we consider means by which home–school (or other educational process) links have to be understood at different levels, described very elegantly by the Russian-American theoretician, Urie Bronfenbrenner. If human development is a dynamic and changing process we need to take account of the variety of life experiences that might influence an individual's experiences of education. The fourth and final section considers the diversity of types of these experiences and their interactive effect on development.

Development within the family context: early relationships as foundations of learning

Recent research studies and meta-analyses indicate that it is important to take a relationship approach to understanding how children's social, emotional, cognitive, and behavioural development is influenced by those around them and how they in turn influence others, rather than an approach that focuses on individual factors (e.g. parenting skills) alone (Lamb and Lewis 2010). Individual factors identified as important include the child's temperament and personality, but it is crucial to note that a child's temperament influences parental behaviours as much as the reverse. This point was first made by R. Q. Bell (1968) as the major blow against behaviourism – the belief that parents simply shape the course of their children's development. For example, it has long been shown that toddlers who are less skilled in controlling their actions to attain a goal, such as following a command in the game 'Simon says', are more likely to develop early behaviour problems in primary school (e.g. Kochanska and Knaack 2003). Recent research shows that these longitudinal connections are mediated by whether parents support or undermine each other's 'co-parenting'. So when parents are highly supportive to each other, not only does this have a reciprocal influence on their toddlers' ability to suppress impulsive actions, but these children who show poor 'effortful control' do not necessarily show later behaviour problems (Schoppe-Sullivan et al. 2009).

How can we theorize the complexity of family relationships and their influence on each individual? Sameroff and Chandler (1975) coined the term 'transactional influences' to accentuate how family members influence each other continuously over time. Such influences require longitudinal research to make them visible. These transactional models show the development of children's (and parents') understandings of relationships, and changes to these over time. Following the main tradition in this area of research, attachment theory, these understandings are known as 'internal working models' as the inferences drawn are about relationships from the patterns of social interaction that we are exposed to early in life.

Family relationships begin with the initial bond between a baby and their main caregiver(s). This bond is essential for the child to survive (van IJzendoorn and Kroonenberg 1998), as infants depend entirely on adults to have their physical and emotional needs met (e.g. nutrition, warmth, shelter, security, comfort). We write 'adults' here as in most settings siblings, while close to one another, do not serve as close attachment figures to one another (Kier and Lewis 1993). However, in exceptional circumstances such as the death of one's parents (as in the current sub-Saharan HIV/AIDS epidemic), siblings can step into this role (Yanagisawa, Poudel, and Jimba 2010). It has long been suggested that the first six years of childhood, especially the initial 36 months, are crucial to a child's development and that the main development task of infancy is to bond with and trust other people (Bowlby 1969). The process of learning through experience that the world is a safe and satisfying place to live (or an unsafe, frightening, painful, and uncertain place to live) is considered by some to be essential before a child can even begin to learn in other ways (Erikson 1965).

In Bowlby's (1969) attachment theory, adults are thought to be biologically predisposed to respond to infants' spontaneous signals of pleasure, fear and, particularly, distress. Adults' reactions promote infants' survival in the months when they are completely dependent on others for care. At the same time as they influence their caregivers' attentiveness, infants pick up on key signals in the ways in which they are cared for. From about two months babies start to distinguish significant individuals and from about six months show a clear and robust fear of others, especially strangers. Bowlby suggested that adults' sensitivity determines the child's grasp of relationships and of themselves. These are termed 'internal working models'. Central to attachment theory is the part played by infant–caregiver interactions in shaping these models, which determine the child's later interactions and understandings.

Bowlby's ideas have maintained their prominence over the past 50 years in large part because his disciple, Mary Ainsworth developed a procedure – the Strange Situation – for measuring the strength of infant–adult attachment (Ainsworth et al. 1978). In seven brief episodes, infants are exposed to increasingly stressful experiences involving being in an unfamiliar environment, the entrance of an unfamiliar adult, and two separations from the parent. The key measure is the infants' attachment behaviours with their parents when reunited. The theory predicts that a caregiver's return should lead infants to seek comfort but soon to re-engage in play and exploration. In scores of studies, 60–70 percent of infants show this pattern (Thompson 1998). These are termed securely attached, or Type B, because their behaviour conforms to theoretical predictions about how babies should behave towards their 'attachment figures'.

The remaining 30–40 percent of infants appear unable to use their parents as secure bases from which to explore, and they are termed insecure. Some show clear ambivalence when the parent returns to the room, demanding contact but showing anger when it is offered and not being placated. These 15 percent of infant–adult interactions are thought to demonstrate insecure–resistant, ambivalent, or Type C, attachments (Thompson 1998). A third group of infants seems less upset by their parents' departure from the room then appears to ignore their parents on reunion. These 20 percent of infants are said to exhibit insecure–avoidant or Type A attachments (Thompson 1998). The fourth category of relationships, termed Type D, shows disorientation or 'disorganized' (i.e. inconsistent) behaviour across two reunion episodes (Main and Solomon 1990). Together, these three types of insecure attachments in infancy predict later psycho-social problems into the school years.

Those who follow Bowlby argue that such continuities show the importance and inflexibility of internal working models in childhood and into adulthood. In samples where families do not change, continuities are shown between attachments at age 1 and early adult adjustment (Waters et al. 2000). Overall there is support for the proposal that sensitive parenting predicts concurrent and future secure infant interactions in the Strange Situation, not only in the USA, where most research has been conducted (Thompson 1998), but also from a diversity of cultures (De Wolff and van IJzendoorn 1997). The general pattern holds that insecure–avoidant attachments are linked with intrusive or rejecting parenting, while insecure–resistant attachments are linked to inconsistent, unresponsive parenting (De Wolff and van IJzendoorn 1997). Disorganized attachments are more frequent following abuse or maltreatment (Baer and Martinez 2006). Training to help parents become more sensitive to their infants increases the probability of a secure attachment (Bakermans-Kranenburg, van IJzendoorn, and Juffer 2003).

In this section we have stressed the importance of parental sensitivity or responsiveness in influencing the nature of adult–infant attachment. However, we must return to the issue that we started the chapter with – that patterns of influence are two-way; they do not simply run from parent to child. This is shown neatly in the very recent research trying to find the genetic influences on developmental psychopathology. A first study suggested that infants with a mutated gene (DRD4) were more likely to fit the disorganized pattern of attachments (Gervai et al. 2005). However, as a series of follow-up studies have examined genetic markers like this, Gervai et al.'s findings have not been fully replicated. A series of recent studies has found that known genetic variations associated with poor attachment, such as a mutation in the mineralocorticoid receptor (MR) genes, leads to insecure attachment if the parent shows low sensitivity to the infant, but a 'greater' likelihood of a secure attachment when the parent is highly sensitive (Luijk et al. 2011). Thus the infant's biological propensities are shaped by their interactions and their relationships with their caregivers.

External influences on family relationships

So far, this chapter has explored relationship factors that influence a child's development. However, relationships are complex and transactional, thus we need to think about their broader context, as this will inevitably impact on the child. It is useful to consider different areas or 'systems' when thinking about different contexts and relationships in a child's life and how these are interconnected. Urie Bronfenbrenner (1986) made it his life's work to theorize about how social processes might operate to influence children and families. His Ecology of Human Development suggests that the individual is immersed in a network of social relationships. Born in Russia, and educated in the USA, he was very aware that families have very different experiences in different countries. He suggested that the individual is like the solid doll in the middle of the many individual Russian dolls depicting different social levels that stack into one another. He depicted these in terms of the 'microsystem' (the child's immediate family relationships), 'mesosystem' (the different settings, such as school, in which a child also lives), 'exosystem' (the network of relationships around the child – for example the parents' experiences in paid employment), and 'macrosystem' (the way in which a culture is organized). He added the dimension of the life course under the banner of the 'chronosystem' (the passage of time or individual's life course).

Examining family influences within wider social processes: home-preschool links

Bronfenbrenner's identification of different levels of influence on the child is well supported by the evidence – how well parents can care for the child depends on their own commitments in the workforce, the support given by local or national government to child care and education, and wider social beliefs and expectations about, and provision for, the care of children. In this section we attempt to show the complexities of these influences, first by looking at relationships between the family (the 'microsystem') and the nearest layers of Bronfenbrenner's model, particularly the 'mesosystem'.

As the child develops beyond infancy, their relationships with caregivers continue to foster early cognitive development and the home becomes a social context of teaching and learning. Tizard and Hughes (1984) investigated the role of the home environment in cognitive development by studying the language of four-year-old children from families with different socio-economic backgrounds at home and at their early years centre. Regardless of socio-economic status, the home was a richer context for learning than the early years centre, providing children with key shared experiences and talking points.

As the child enters more formal schooling, the same influences are in evidence. Pianta, Nimetz, and Bennett (1997) examined how children's relationships with their parents and with teachers contributed to their outcomes at school. Following 55 children from families with very low incomes longitudinally, they found that the mother–child relationship predicted the child's early school adjustment and was a more consistent and significant influence on children's adjustment outcomes than their relationships with preschool teachers. It was suggested that: 'affective sharing and warmth and an age-appropriate balance of control and autonomy in mother–child interaction predicated peer social skills, good work habits, frustration tolerance, lack of behaviour problems and overall competency in children's adjustment to school' (Pianta et al. 1997: 276).

In a large-scale study of the effects of preschool education on over 3,000 children in the UK (Sylva et al. 2003), active parental engagement in activities with their child promoted children's intellectual and social development. The quality of the home learning environment was more strongly related to child outcomes than family socio-economic status and parental level of education. The home learning environment was moderately associated with socio-economic status, suggesting that the extent of the nurturing relationship between children and their parents was more influential than socio-economic status or level of parental education. So, parental influences on the educational process are in evidence, but are relationships between family and wider social processes this straightforward?

Subtle influences of the social system on the family

The research on child development suggests that different family members may have different influences. This may well be because each individual addresses their own life tasks at any stage and each of us has different points of contact with the 'mesosystem' and beyond. We will illustrate this by comparing how mothers and fathers interact with, and influence, their children.

In the main, parents usually have similar styles; however, there are some differences that start early in the child's life. Mothers tend to specialize in smoothly modulated interaction, while fathers show more exciting games (Borke et al. 2007). In play, mothers specialize in pretence, while fathers engage more in physical activity (Lindsey and Mize 2001), particularly with their sons. Indeed there is evidence to suggest that men are more likely to protect their daughters from falling off apparatus (Hagan and Kuebli 2007). Not only do mothers specialize in emotional expressiveness, but such displays towards three-year-olds predict the children's understanding of the nature of emotion, while fathers' more rational and logical language predicts theory of mind understanding over this time period. LaBounty et al. (2008) reported that mothers' emotional expressiveness with three-year-olds was related to the children's grasp of emotions at age five, whereas fathers' use of 'causal explanatory' language in conversation predicted their children's concurrent and later 'theory of mind' understanding.

Children's early educational engagement and success are also related to parental styles. Most research suggests that parenting that is both sensitive and limit-setting relates to the child's achievement, with no advantage of one parent over the other (Scott 2004). Similarly, secure attachments predicted reports of higher academic performance, particularly if children had secure attachments with both parents (Booth-LaForce et al. 2006). However, there is also evidence of unique contributions from both parents. Mothers' and fathers' support for their two-year-olds each provide unique contributions to children's language and arithmetic scores on entry to school (Martin, Ryan, and Brooks-Gunn 2007). Indeed, one study found that support from fathers was a better predictor of children's cognitive and language levels (Cabrera, Shannon, and Tamis-LeMonda 2007).

Similar patterns are discernible in the school years. Men's involvement in school activities seems to contribute unique variance to children's educational performance. Flouri and Buchanan (2004) found that British children with more involved fathers have higher IQs at seven years of age. Belsky et al. (2008) report that, while both parents' academic involvement was related to reading and arithmetic at six to eight years, it was fathers' support for independent thinking that best predicted changes across this period. Such interactions exert demands on their children's concentration on and expertise in these subjects (Tenenbaum and Leaper 2003).

Why is it that fathers' contributions to interactions with and demands on their children seem to correlate with later advantages in educational performance? Two reasons have been given, which are not mutually exclusive. First, fathers may not provide a unique contribution to child development, but their involvement means that all family relationships work smoothly (Lewis, Newson, and Newson 1982). Second, fathers might inadvertently provide an impetus to their children's intellectual development, because they are usually more connected to the outside world. Gleason (1975) argued that men do not know their children as well and they therefore act a bridge between the family and wider social systems. If a man tells his two-year-old that he is being 'aggravating', this has the effect of stretching the child's linguistic and cognitive competence.

Beyond the parent–child relationship?

Throughout this chapter we have stressed that family relationships should be seen as embedded within the larger relational contexts of extended families, friendships, school, work, neighbourhoods, and institutions such as places of worship, nurseries or clubs:

> The story of the study of social development in recent years is thus very much a matter of increasing awareness of the importance of context, that is, the realisation that the behaviour of individual children is given meaning by the relationships in which the child is embedded, that these relationships in turn are embedded in systems such as families, and that these too can only be fully understood within the context of the society of which they form a part.
>
> *(Schaffer 1996: 12)*

Gradually friends, teachers, and many others attain significance in the child's life. The quality of the relationships that parents/caregivers have among their own social networks may influence the quality of their relationships with their children (Belsky 1990; Cochran and Niego 2002). This provides parents with stress relief and psychological support, which in turn enable them to cope with the demands of parenting (Widmer et al. 2006).

There is a dramatic increase in interaction with same-age peers in middle childhood. The extent to which school mates' families are known to each other varies, but children from higher socio-economic backgrounds are more likely to have friendships with children whom their parents know (Rubin et al. 2011). Nevertheless, such differences between families from different backgrounds are less obvious in friendships based on other, non-school contexts. The extent of shared networks of friends and families, and indeed the involvement of families more generally in adolescents' peer relationships, typically becomes much less in teenage years (Brown 1990), when young people manage what their parents know about their activities (Coleman 2011).

Relationships with the wider, extended family such as grandparents, cousins and, in the case of increasing numbers of families, biological parents not living with the child/children also serve important roles for children. In a study of nearly 1,600 young people growing up in the UK,

Julia Griggs and colleagues (2010) uncovered the extensive part that many grandparents play in their grandchildren's lives. In an earlier study, Clarke and Roberts (2004) surveyed nearly 1,000 grandparents and established that only 0.5 percent had custodial care of their grandchildren, but 61 percent looked after them during the day and more than half regularly looked after the children.

Non-normative life experiences: what happens when relationships are adverse or are disrupted?

All the processes we have outlined so far – attachments, social relationships, parental styles, and the ecology of family experiences – describe what life-span developmental psychologists define as 'normative'. By this they mean typical, in that most of us share a range of experiences, such as having families and going to school between the age of entry and the usual time at which they leave. However, we also go through life-changing events that are unique, such as experiencing the death of a parent early in childhood, an economic depression that greatly reduces our life chances, or a host of other experiences. These events may not necessarily be negative. Research has long shown, for example, that having a good relationship with one key teacher (Rutter 1989) or attending a 'good school' (Rutter et al. 1979) can offset previous negative experiences.

One life experience that has received much attention is parental separation. Around 50 percent of the children in the USA and Europe experience the separation of their parents before they reach adulthood (Amato 2010). This experience is linked with a greater susceptibility to behaviour and academic problems at school, lower educational attainment, and poorer employment trajectories (Amato 2010). Nevertheless, only a minority of children in separated families experience such problems and these are usually transient during a period of intense adjustment (Hetherington and Kelly 2002).

Even parental separation cannot be treated in isolation from other social processes. For a start, single parenthood is linked with financial hardship (Crockett, Eggebeen, and Hawkins 1993). Not only do two households cost more to run, but the resident parent(s) must do so on their own. Secondly, separation commonly disrupts one of the child's most important and enduring relationships, usually the father (Lamb and Kelly 2009). Outcomes in children are more positive when non-resident fathers maintain a high level of involvement (Fabricius et al. 2010). Thirdly, residential parents usually have to work longer hours than their married counterparts and thus spend less time caring for their children (McLanahan 1999). Fourthly, and most importantly, conflict between the parents has been found to be the most accurate predictor of the child's adjustment, and this often continues long beyond the separation (Cummings, Merrilees, and George 2010).

Summary

If you started this chapter wondering what relevance 'the family' has to a grasp of children's educational skills and performance, the chapter has attempted to persuade you of three issues that make it not only relevant but also important. First, family relationships are the most lasting in most people's lives, so any analysis of educational processes must take these into account. Secondly, the evidence shows that the quality of children's educational performance is predicted by particular aspects of the parent–child relationship. Finally, studying families forces us to think about the interconnectedness of different aspects of our lives – we have drawn on Bronfenbrenner's theoretical framework to show these processes. So, any analysis of the child's development and learning must take account of the complexity of the interrelation between the 'microsystem' of the family and much wider social processes.

Contact address: c.lewis@lancaster.ac.uk

References

Ainsworth, M. D. S., Blehar, M. C., Waters, E., and Wall, S. (1978) *Patterns of attachment: a psychological study of the strange situation*, Hillsdale, NJ: Lawrence Erlbaum Associates.

Amato, P. R. (2010) 'Research on divorce: continuing trends and new developments', *Journal of Marriage and Family*, 72: 650–666.

Baer, J., and Martinez, C. D. (2006) 'Child maltreatment and insecure attachment: a meta-analysis', *Journal of Reproductive and Infant Psychology*, 24: 187–197.

Bakermans-Kranenburg, M. J., van IJzendoorn, M. H., and Juffer, F. (2003) 'Less is more: meta-analyses of sensitivity and attachment interventions in early childhood', *Psychological Bulletin*, 129: 195–216.

Bell, R. Q. (1968) 'A reinterpretation of the direction of effects in studies of socialization', *Psychological Review*, 75: 81–95.

Belsky, J. (1990) 'Parental and nonmarital child care and children's socioemotional development: a decade in review', *Journal of Marriage and the Family*, 52: 885–903.

Belsky, J., Booth-LaForce, C., Bradley, R., Brownell, C. A., Burchinal, M., Campbell, S. B., et al. (2008) 'Mothers' and fathers' support for child autonomy and early school achievement', *Developmental Psychology*, 44: 895–907.

Booth-LaForce, C., Oh, W., Kim, A. H., Rubin, K. H., Rose-Krasnor, L., and Burgess, K. (2006) 'Attachment, self-worth, and peer-group functioning in middle childhood', *Attachment and Human Development*, 8: 309–325.

Borke, J., Lamm, B., Eickhorst, A., and Keller, H. (2007) 'Father–infant interaction, paternal ideas about early child care, and their consequences for the development of children's self-recognition', *Journal of Genetic Psychology*, 168: 365–379.

Bowlby, J. (1969) *Attachment and loss, Volume 1: Attachment*, Harmondsworth: Penguin.

Bronfenbrenner, U. (1986) 'Ecology of the family as a context for human development: research perspectives', *Developmental Psychology*, 22: 723–742.

Brown, B. B. (1990) 'Peer groups and peer cultures', in S. S. Feldman and G. R. Elliott (eds.) *At the threshold: the developing adolescent*, Cambridge, MA: Harvard University Press (pp. 171–196).

Cabrera, N. J., Shannon, J. D., and Tamis-LeMonda, C. (2007) 'Fathers' influence on their children's cognitive and emotional development: from toddlers to pre-K.' *Applied Developmental Science*, 11: 208–213.

Clarke, L., and Roberts, C. (2004) 'The meaning of grandparenthood and its contribution to the quality of life of older people', in A. Walker and C. H. Hennessy (eds.), *Growing older: quality of life in older age*, Milton Keynes, UK: Open University Press (pp. 188–208).

Cochran, M., and Niego, S. (2002) 'Parenting and social networks', in M. Bornstein (ed.) *Handbook of parenting*, Mahwah, NJ: Lawrence Erlbaum Associates (pp. 393–418).

Coleman, J. C. (2011) *The nature of adolescence*, New York: Routledge.

Crockett, L. J., Eggebeen, D. J., and Hawkins, A. J. (1993) 'Father's presence and young children's behavioral and cognitive adjustment', *Journal of Family Issues*, 14: 355–377.

Cummings, E. M., Merrilees, C. E., and George, M. W. (2010) 'Fathers, marriages, and families: revisiting and updating the framework for fathering in family context', in M. E. Lamb (ed.) *The role of the father in child development*, 5th edn, Hoboken, NJ: Wiley (pp. 154–76).

De Wolff, M. S., and van IJzendoorn, M. H. (1997) 'Sensitivity and attachment: a meta-analysis on parental antecedents of infant attachment', *Child Development*, 68: 571–591.

Erikson, E. (1965) *Childhood and society*, Harmondsworth, UK: Penguin.

Fabricius, W. V., Braver, S. L., Diaz, P., and Velez, C. E. (2010) 'Custody and parenting time: links to family relationships and well-being after divorce', in M. E. Lamb (ed.) *The role of the father in child development*, 5th edn, Hoboken, NJ: Wiley (pp. 201–240).

Flouri, E., and Buchanan, A. (2004) 'Early fathers' and mothers' involvement and child's later educational outcomes', *British Journal of Educational Psychology*, 74: 141–153.

Gervai, J., Nemoda, Z., Lakatos, K., Ronai, Z., Toth, I., Ney, K., et al. (2005) 'Transmission disequilibrium tests confirm the link between DRD4 gene polymorphism and infant attachment', *American Journal of Medical Genetics*, 132B, 126–130.

Gleason, J. B. (1975) 'Fathers and other strangers: men's speech to young children', in D. P. Dato (ed.) *Language and linguistics*, Washington, DC: Georgetown University Press (pp. 289–297).

Griggs, J., Tan, J-P., Buchanan, A., Attar-Shwartz, S., and Flouri, E. (2010) '"They've always been there for me": grandparental involvement and child well-being', *Children and Society*, 24: 204–214.

Hagan, L. K., and Kuebli, J. (2007) 'Mothers' and fathers' socialization of preschoolers' physical risk taking', *Journal of Applied Developmental Psychology*, 28: 2–14.

Hetherington, E. M., and Kelly, J. (2002) *For better or for worse: divorce reconsidered*, New York: W.W. Norton.

Jung, C. G. (1939) *The integration of the personality*, Oxford: Farrar and Rinehart.

Kier, C., and Lewis, C. (1993) 'Sibling attachment: the development of a new infant-based measure', *Early Development and Parenting*, 2: 243–246.

Kochanska, G., and Knaack, A. (2003) 'Effortful control as a personality characteristic of young children: antecendents, correlates and consequences', *Journal of Personality*, 71: 1087–1112.

LaBounty, J., Wellman, H. M., Olson, S., Lagattuta, K., and Liu, D. (2008) 'Mothers' and fathers' use of internal state talk with their young children', *Social Development*, 17: 757–775.

Lamb, M. E., and Kelly, J. B. (2009) 'Improving the quality of parent–child contact in separating families with infants and young children: empirical research foundations', in R. M. Galatzer-Levy, L. Kraus, and J. Galatzer-Levy (eds.) *The scientific basis of child custody decisions*, 2nd edn, Hoboken, NJ: Wiley (pp. 187–214).

Lamb, M. E., and Lewis, C. (2010) 'The role of parent–child relationships in child development', in M. H. Bornstein and M. E. Lamb (eds.) *Developmental science: an advanced textbook*, 6th edn, Mahwah, NJ: Lawrence Erlbaum Associates (pp. 469–517).

Lewis, C., Newson, E., and Newson, J. (1982) 'Father participation through childhood and its relationship with career aspirations and delinquency', in N. Beail and J. McGuire (eds.) *Fathers: psychological perspectives*, London: Junction (pp. 174–193).

Lindsey, E. W., and Mize, J. (2001) 'Contextual differences in parent–child play: implications for children's gender role development', *Sex Roles*, 44, 155–176.

Luijk, M. P. C. M., Tharner, A., Bakermans-Kranenburg, M. J., van IJzendoorn, M. H., Jaddoe, V. W. V., Hofman, A., et al. (2011) 'The association between parenting and attachment security is moderated by a polymorphism in the mineralocorticoid receptor gene: evidence for differential susceptibility biological psychology', 88: 37–40.

Main, M., and Solomon, J. (1990) 'Procedures for identifying infants as disorganized/disoriented during the Ainsworth Strange Situation', in M. T. Greenberg, D. Cicchetti, and E. M. Cummings (eds.) *Attachment during the preschool years: theory, research and intervention*, Chicago: University of Chicago Press (pp. 121–160).

Martin, A., Ryan, R. M., and Brooks-Gunn, J. (2007) 'The joint influence of mother and father parenting on child cognitive outcomes at age 5', *Early Childhood Research Quarterly*, 22: 423–439.

McLanahan, S. S. (1999) 'Father absence and the welfare of children', in E. M. Hetherington (ed.) *Coping with divorce, single parenting, and remarriage: a risk and resiliency perspective*, Mahwah, NJ: Lawrence Erlbaum Associates (pp. 117–145).

Morgan, D. (1998) 'Risk and family practices: accounting for change and fluidity in family life', in E. B. Silva and C. Smart (eds.) *The new family?*, London: Sage (pp. 13–30).

O'Connor, T. G. (2002) 'Annotation: the "effects" of parenting reconsidered: findings, challenges, and applications', *Journal of Child Psychology and Psychiatry*, 43: 555–572.

Pianta, R. C., Nimetz, S. L., and Bennett, E. (1997) 'Mother–child relationships, teacher–child relationships, and school outcomes in preschool and kindergarten', *Early Childhood Research Quarterly*, 12, 263–280.

Rubin, K. H., Bukowski, W., and Parker, J. G. (1998) 'Peer interactions, relationships, and groups', in N. Eisenberg (ed.) *Handbook of child psychology, Volume 3, Social, emotional, and personality development*, New York: Wiley (pp. 619–700).

Rubin, K. H., Coplan, R., Chen, X., Bowker, J. C., McDonald, K., and Menzer, M. (2011) 'Peer relationships in childhood', in M. H. Bornstein and M. E. Lamb (eds.) *Social and emotional development: an advanced textbook*, New York: Psychology Press (pp. 309–360).

Rutter, M. (1989) 'Pathways from childhood to adult life', *Journal of Child Psychology and Psychiatry*, 30: 25–51.

Rutter, M., Maughan, B., Mortimore, P., and Ouston, J. (1979) *Fifteen thousand hours: secondary schools and their effects on children*, London: Open Books.

Sameroff, A. J., and Chandler, M. J. (1975) 'Reproductive risk and the continuum of caretaking casualty', in F. D. Harrowitz, S. Scarr-Salapatek, and G. Siegel (eds.) *Review of child development research, Volume 4*, Chicago: University of Chicago Press (pp. 187–244).

Schaffer, R. (1996) *Social development*, Oxford: Blackwell.

Schoppe-Sullivan, S. J., Weldon, A. H., Cook, J. C., Davis, E. F., and Buckley, C. K. (2009) 'Coparenting behavior moderates longitudinal relations between effortful control and preschool children's externalizing behavior', *Journal of Child Psychology and Psychiatry*, 50: 698–706.

Scott, J. (2004) 'Family, gender and educational attainment in Britain: a longitudinal study', *Journal of Comparative Family Studies*, 35: 565–589.

Sylva, K., Melhuish, E., Sammons, P., Siraj-Blatchford, I., Taggart, B., and Elliot, K. (2003) *The effective provision of pre-school education (EPPE) project: findings from the pre-school period*, London: University of London.

Tenenbaum, H. R. and Leaper, C. (2003) 'Parent–child conversations about science: the socialization of gender inequities?', *Developmental Psychology*, 39: 34–47.

Thompson, R. A. (1998) 'Early sociopersonality development', in W. Damon and N. Eisenberg (eds.) *Handbook of child psychology, Volume 3, Social, emotional, and personality development*, 5th edn, New York: Wiley (pp. 25–104).

Tizard, B., and Hughes, M. (1984) *Young children learning*, London: Fontana.

Tudge, J. R. H., Doucet, F., Odero, D., Sperb, T. M., Piccinini, C. A., and Lopes, R. S. (2006) 'A window into different cultural worlds: young children's everyday activities in the United States, Brazil and Kenya', *Child Development*, 77: 1446–1469.

van IJzendoorn, M. H., and Kroonenberg, P. M. (1998) 'Cross-cultural patterns of attachment: a meta-analysis of the Strange Situation', *Child Development*, 59: 147–156.

Walsh, F. (2003) *Normal family processes*, 3rd edn, New York: Guilford.

Waters, E., Merrick, S., Treboux, D., Crowell, J., and Albersheim, L. (2000) 'Attachment stability in infancy and early adulthood: a 20-year longitudinal study', *Child Development*, 71: 684–689.

Widmer, E., Le Goff, J.-M., Levy, R., Hammer, R., and Kellerhals, J. (2006) 'Embedded parenting? The influence of conjugal networks on parent–child relationships', *Journal of Social and Personal Relationships*, 23: 387–406.

Yanagisawa, S., Poudel, K. C., and Jimba, M. (2010) 'Sibling caregiving among children orphaned by AIDS: synthesis of recent studies for policy implications', *Health Policy*, 98: 121–130.

13

CHILDHOOD STRESS AND ITS IMPACT ON LEARNING AND ACADEMIC PERFORMANCE

Meena Hariharan, Sunyana Swain and Usha Chivukula

UNIVERSITY OF HYDERABAD, INDIA

Stress has become a potential source of threat in the growth and development of children, having both short-term and long-term effects. Unremitting stress in children has an impact on the autonomous and endocrine system, thereby bringing about interference in learning, transfer of learning, and memory. While culture plays a vital role, the triggers of stress can be both external and internal. The child's interaction with their immediate environment and the child's own abilities to counteract the stressful situation also play a vital role. Interventions aimed at changing the way children perceive stress can go a long way towards optimizing their potential in dealing with stressful situations.

Stress arises when the demands of the situation exceed an individual's ability to cope with and resolve the problem, resulting in emotional, behavioural, and cognitive disturbances that can adversely affect their physical and mental wellbeing (McCance, Forshee, and Shelby 2006). Stress is often a product of an interface between a stressor and an individual's perception of the stressor. Lazarus (1999) emphasized the dimensions of an individual's perception in assessing a situation as stressful. According to him, the individual variations in stress perception can be traced to the meaning attributed. The meaning can be explained in terms of 'the degree of relevance of the situation' (stressor) to the individual, which is nothing but subjective evaluation. The effect of stress starts on the foetus during the pre-natal stage and continues through the process of child-birth and thereafter. For example, King and Laplante (2005), in a prospective study of the effects of maternal stress on the foetus, argued that exposure to natural disasters *in utero* can have a negative impact on later language and cognitive development. Early life stress has a negative impact on the development of the brain, and this impact can be short-term or long-term (Middlebrooks and Audage 2008)

Childhood is not a 'stress-free' stage. The trauma starts during the birth process and often continues to every stage in the life span. The growing child continues to develop cognitive abilities and coping skills and yet there is a demand on the child to reach milestones and attain goals at a pace sometimes beyond the natural process of growth and development. Language and expression are significant skills that are not optimally developed in growing children. Hence children are not likely to have the linguistic competence to express with clarity that certain demands and situations are stressful for them.

The complexity of stress experienced by a child will be appreciated from the point of multiple reactions to stress from physiological and psychosocial dimensions. The physiological reactions to stress can be termed universal, while wide individual differences are noticed in cognitive and behavioural responses to stress.

Stress, physiological disturbances, and impact on performance

The experience of stress brings about a chain of physiological reactions initiated by the autonomic nervous system (ANS), with consequences for the digestive, circulatory, respiratory, excretory, reproductive, muscular, and endocrine systems of the body through the sympathetic and parasympathetic nervous system (Baron 2001). The ANS, along with the endocrine system, plays an active role in responding to stress. During a stressful period the hypothalamus–pituitary axis is activated (see Figure 13.1).

When a child encounters stress, the hypothalamus and pituitary gland are stimulated and release the adrenocorticotrophic hormone (ACTH) which, in turn, stimulates the adrenal glands. These signals cause the adrenal glands to release stress hormones such as epinephrine and norepinephrine (catecholamines, also referred to as adrenaline and noradrenaline respectively) and cortisol. These stress hormones can easily travel through the blood into the brain. Catecholamines are water-soluble and are 50 percent bound to plasma proteins, so they circulate in the

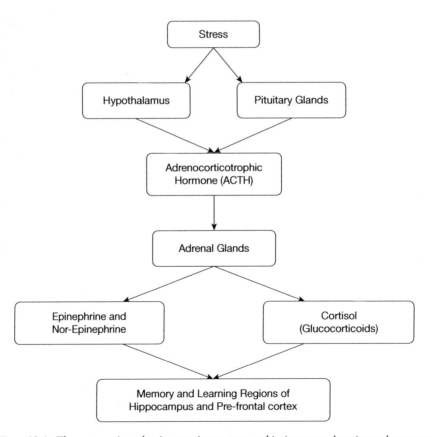

Figure 13.1 The autonomic endocrine reaction to stress and its impact on learning and memory

bloodstream. They bind with receptors located in the various learning and memory regions of the brain and can influence learning (Lupien et al. 2007) and memory (McClelland 1996). The cortisol released during stress is associated with damage to neurons in the hippocampus. Such damage affects the neurons and dendritic branching, resulting in deficits in any new learning (Woolley, Gould, and McEwen 1990). The hippocampus also plays a crucial role in long-term memory (Bunsey and Eichenbaum 1995). It is involved in the transfer of information, sorting out the decoded information (from the cortical regions) and creating associations. Exposure to stress interferes with such transformation of information. The memory areas of the brain, mainly the hippocampus and the pre-frontal cortex, have a number of glucocorticoid (GC) receptors that are sensitive to the levels of corticosteroids in the body, activation of which has an impact on behavioural responses, mood, attention, and cognition (Roozendaal 2002, 2003). The elevation of cortisol levels (which happens due to stress) influences cognition and the formation of new memory (Wolf 2003).

The pre-frontal cortex is the region of the highest order cognitive abilities. It is sensitive to the detrimental effects of stress. While acute stress causes rapid and dramatic loss of cognitive abilities, prolonged exposure to stress leads to architectural damage in the pre-frontal cortex (Arnsten 2009). The prefrontal cortex is also involved in 'working memory', which refers to a brain system that provides temporary storage and manipulation of the information necessary for such complex cognitive tasks as language comprehension, learning, and reasoning. Working memory has been found to require the simultaneous storage and processing of information (Baddeley 1992). Children exposed to acute stress have problems in recall and verbal memory. A neuropsychological evaluation of children who developed posttraumatic stress disorder (PTSD) showed impaired performance on verbal learning tests compared to healthy children without PTSD (Beers and De Bellis 2002). A child's inability to reproduce immediately learned information is often misjudged and criticized as lack of interest, stubbornness, indifference, non-cooperation, or callous attitude. While these reasons cannot be totally ruled out, it could also be because of problems in functioning of the pre-frontal cortex, caused by trauma. The autonomic endocrine response to a perceived stress is uniform in human beings across culture, age, and gender. However, appraisal of an external situation as stressful or otherwise is influenced by a variety of factors such as past experience, culture, age, gender, and personality (Hariharan and Rath 2008).

Given their initial stages of exposure to and experience of culture, any new experience for children constitutes change or demand for adaptation. The demand for change is often positive, invoking a developmental activity and adaptation to a new situation or pressure to perform and achieve. Such demands, when within the limits of the learnt skills or bordering their upper limits, may function as effective motivators, helping the child to reach yet another developmental milestone. However, the demands of schools on children are based on the broad averages of expected abilities based on developmental stages. Not much consideration is given to individual differences in the pace of development. Thus, the demand that is perceived as positive by some children may exert pressure and create stress in others. Stress, in turn, affects their interpersonal relationships, thought processes, performance, achievement, and activities.

Sources of stress

Children are exposed to different kinds of stress stemming from a variety of sources. Typically, stress in children can originate from external or internal sources. A stressor can be an event or situation in life or it can be a condition brought about by certain changes in life.

External sources

The external sources of childhood stress can be classified as major life changes (Holmes and Rahe 1967) and daily hassles (Kanner et al. 1981). DeBord (1996) categorized death, divorce, remarriage of parents, moving places, long illness, abuse, family or community violence, cultural conflict, and natural disaster as some of the major sources of stress in children. When a child comes across any of these life events they may undergo stress.

The other sources of stress in a child's life originate from their immediate environment, both home and school. The significant social agents for the child are parents, teachers, peer group, and neighbours. Academic stress and social pressure are two major causes of childhood stress. High expectations from school, and social pressure such as the pressure to be popular with friends and classmates, are included under major sources of stress (Moksnes et al. 2010). Hesketh et al. (2010) reported school-related factors (examinations, punishment by teachers and parents, and bullying) as major sources of stress, with manifestations in the form of psychosomatic complaints such as headaches (37 percent) and abdominal pain (36 percent). The US-based National Kids Poll (2008) revealed the top three causes of stress in children as grades in school and homework (36 percent), family (32 percent) and peer group (21 percent). Interviews with a sample of Indian children between the ages of five and 15, conducted by the authors for the purpose of this chapter, also revealed that the sources of stress are comparable (in terms of most and least prevalent) to those of American children (school 50 percent, family 46 percent, and peer group 16 percent), wherein the children could identify more than one source of stress.

The social network of an Indian child is typically broader and includes extended families. The child's cognitive limitations in managing the overloaded school curriculum and the guilt feelings generated by an inability to meet parental expectations not only result in low self-esteem but also sometimes turn their aggression towards self, leading to self-harming behaviour to the extent of committing suicide. It is reported that the demand for scholastic achievement on students in the year 2006 resulted in an alarming increase in the rate of suicide to one on every alternate day in the second half of the year (Hariharan and Rath 2008).

While there may be cultural variations in external sources of stress, the internal sources of stress are often an offshoot of external stress and largely linked to the developmental stage of children.

Internal sources

The child experiences an unrest caused by the internal stress. Inferiority, jealousy, and guilt are some of the feelings that originate from the mismatch between external demands and abilities. They are negative and stressful. Other examples of internal stressors include hunger, pain, fatigue, sensitivity, fears, low self-esteem, negative self-talk, and unrealistic self expectations (Jewett 1997). Children suffer from the interaction of multiple stressors which have a cumulative effect on the developmental process (Stansbury and Harris 2000). Figure 13.2 presents a classification of sources of stress. The list is not exhaustive and may vary between cultures.

Though the sources of stress are classified as external and internal, external stress need not necessarily be a distress for every child. For some children the external stress may work as a motivator.

Figure 13.3 illustrates the triangle of stress for a child and shows how appraisal plays a significant role in interpreting a stressful situation as distress or 'eustress' (a positive stress that works as a motivator).

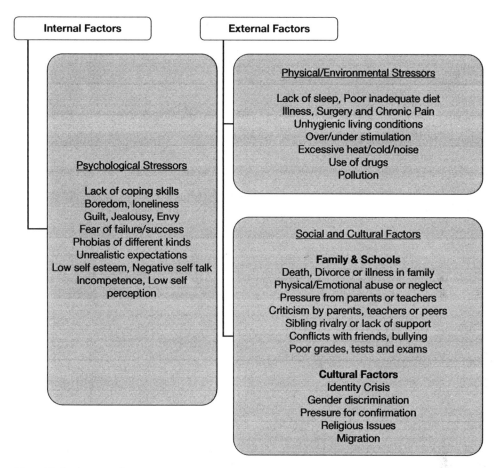

Figure 13.2 Sources of stress

The left side of the triangle presents stress situations: change, ambiguity, timeline, unexpectedness, and discomfort. A child with strong internal resources such as skills and abilities and enriched experiences or external resources such as strong social support may appraise such situations as a challenge or opportunity. As a result, the child receives it as an opportunity for progress, success or achievement. This is explained by Hariharan and Rath (2008) in terms of 'eustress'. On the other hand, if the child assesses an inadequacy in the internal or external resources, they may perceive a threat in the situation. As a consequence, they may experience tension, anxiety, frustration, strain, trauma, and fear, which lead to the triangle of distress. Thus, whether a situation becomes a distress or eustress is largely determined by the child's own appraisal.

Stress and academic performance

When the school curriculum matches the cognitive development of the child, stress functions as a drive to perform and achieve. For these children the curriculum is appraised as a 'challenge' and the stress is positive. They perform efficiently because they function at 'optimum stress level'

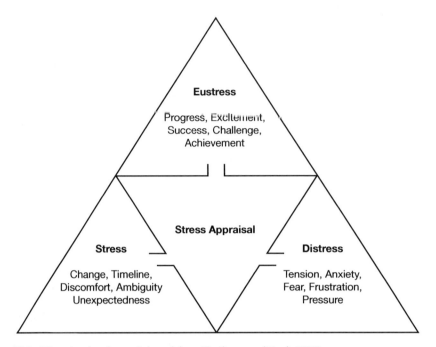

Figure 13.3 The triangle of stress (adapted from Hariharan and Rath 2008)

(OSL). However, those children already suffering a structural or functional cognitive inadequacy, due to either stress or deprivation, may perceive the curriculum as highly demanding and see a 'threat' in it; they perform at arousal level. The stress arising out of threat perception is negative. On the other hand, children who are gifted perceive the curriculum as unchallenging and hence remain at 'relaxed' state. They suffer from what is termed 'boredom stress' (Hariharan and Rath 2008; Sharpe 1995). This phenomenon is illustrated in Figure 13.4.

Figure 13.4 presents three degrees of stress. The OSL is positioned between boredom stress and arousal and distress. OSL is the degree of stress where the child appraises the change, ambiguity, timeline, and demand for performance as challenging, which in turn functions as an effective motivator to enhance performance. Failure, underperformance, and underachievement are the natural consequences of both boredom stress and distress. Based on the outcome of stress determined by its degree and duration, Middlebrooks and Audage (2008) classified childhood stress into positive stress, tolerable stress, and toxic stress. Instances and situations demanding marginal adaptation to changes causing mild physiological responses, such as increased heart rate and hormone level, are termed positive stress. Such stressors are considered normal, function as catalysts for children to attain developmental milestones, and equip them with coping skills.

Tolerable stress refers to a short-lived higher degree of adverse events. With a supportive adult, the child can overcome the negative impact. It results from more intense stressors such as the death of loved ones, separation or divorce in the family, or watching a horrific accident or a disaster. Without adequate support the child may feel distressed and the impact on their health and performance may be long-lasting. What is tolerable stress for one child could well be conceived as positive stress for another, depending on their developmental stage; physical, psychosocial and environmental exposure; and experience.

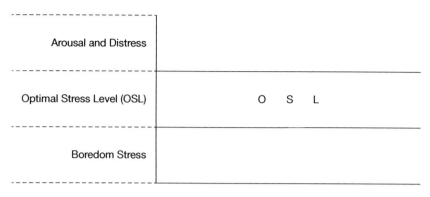

Arousal and Distress

Optimal Stress Level (OSL)   O   S   L

Boredom Stress

Figure 13.4 The levels of stress (adapted from Hariharan and Rath 2008)

Toxic stress is described as experiences that may persist for longer duration. The impact of such experience may be multidimensional and spread over the life span. Neglect, abuse, and ill-treatment are some examples of toxic stress. Research shows that children exposed to toxic stress develop an exaggerated stress response in the long run. For example, Tuakli-Williams and Carrillo (1995) conducted a study on a minority group (African-American and Latino) pre-school children. They found that children exposed to psychosocial stressors of intense severity such as poverty, violence, racism, or environmental pollution coupled with poor physical health tended to exhibit lowered mood, reduced attention span, and stunted emotional development.

Childhood stress: psychosocial factors

The relation between external demands, abilities, and subsequent response constitutes psychosocial factors associated with stress. Figure 13.5 illustrates the perceptual process of stress from a psychosocial perspective.

The environmental demand is appraised against two significant factors, namely personal abilities and external resources. Personal abilities include cognitive, social and physical competence. External resources refer to social support networks and material resources. Children who are adequate in both internal and external resources do not perceive any stress. When there is inadequacy on both fronts, the child perceives stress and threat in the situation. In such instances, the child has the potential danger of taking refuge in learned helplessness syndrome. This has a direct adverse effect on academic performance (Rudolph, Kurlakowsky, and Conley 2001). On the other hand, if the child perceives an inadequacy on one front and adequacy on the other, they may feel a sense of challenge, even though the situation is perceived as complex and stressful. Adequacy in internal resources and inadequacy in external resources are typical of resilient children. Resilient children are those who manifest high academic competence amid a number of environmental adversities. Research has identified several protective factors such as maternal support (Werner and Smith 1982), a constant readiness to confront adversities, organizing priorities on a needs hierarchy (Hariharan 1995), a sense of coherence (Antonovsky 1979), or hardiness (Kobasa 1984). Many factors contributing to resilience are acquired by children during the process of development. Resilience can be developed and trained. Maintaining positive attitude, active coping styles, cognitive flexibility, and a positive school and home environment are some of the factors that can help children acquire resilience (Southwick et al. 1997). Supportive family and friends and the good temperament of significant others

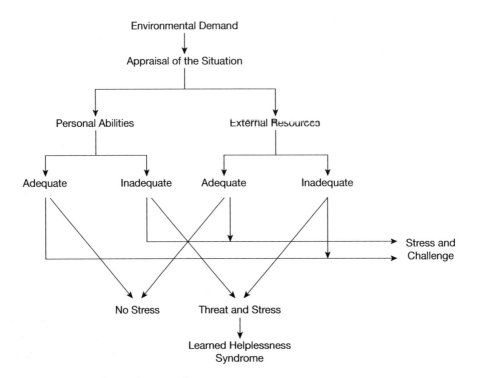

Figure 13.5 The psychosocial process of stress perception

enhance positive adjustment, even in children who are at high risk (Werner 2000). Further information on the impact of family relationships on educational engagement can be found in Lewis, Miell, and Coiffait (Chapter 12, this volume).

Coping with stress is learned along the process of development. Many situations that appear trivial for adults may be stressful for children. Since the child's repertoire of experience is not so large, even situations demanding small changes may have an impact on the child's sense of security. Children manifesting inhibitions and fear in the classroom need to be studied through close interviews, case histories, and psychological testing. This may give an insight into the multiple stressful experiences of their lives (Rath, Dash, and Dash 1979; Sinha, Tripathi, and Misra 1982).

Behavioural indicators of stress

It is observed that the negative impact of stress is more pronounced in those who are below 10 years, shy/introvert, or born prematurely, and also those exposed to pre-natal stress (Monk et al. 2000). This, in turn, is found to limit their cognitive capacity, leading to academic difficulties. McLoyd (1998) found that children who experience impoverished socio-economic conditions, violence in communities, or are victims of bullying in school settings experience higher degrees of external stress than other children. Such children may develop a fear of school and apprehension about leaving home, fearing for the security of their parents. Stress may also manifest in the form of aggressive behaviour and defensive outbursts. When such behaviour is met with punishment in the school, it adds to the existing degree of stress and dislike for school-related activities.

Frequent absence from school owing to illness also needs to be examined from a bio-psychosocial perspective, investigating the possible origins of illness as a consequence of stress. Headaches, stomach aches, sweating palms, toilet accidents, and sleep disturbances may be traced to stressful experience in children (Alfven, Osterberg, and Hjern 2008; Fallin, Wallinga, and Coleman 2001; Hjern, Alfven, and Ostberg 2008; Marion 2003; Stansbury and Harris 2000).

Research also indicates the manifestation of stress in the form of some of the very common nervous fine motor behaviours such as hair twirling or pulling, chewing and sucking, and biting of skin and fingernails. Dacey and Fiore (2000) cited studies suggesting that reactions to stress are observed in children in extreme forms of avoidance behaviour, shyness, brooding, hypervigilance, and 'freezing up' in social situations. The attention and concentration levels of such children may be short, leading to difficulties in comprehending and processing the information, knowledge, and skills taught in the classroom as part of the curriculum. While manifesting stress behaviourally, the child also attempts to cope with the stressful situation.

Coping with childhood stress

Children adopt passive coping strategies such as escape–avoidance, distancing, self-control, which are always not productive. This is because they are still acquiring effective coping strategies (Hariharan and Rath 2008). They are in the process of learning skills and understanding and building support systems. Thus, the internal and external resources with which they have to cope with a stressful situation are limited. Hence the coping style is likely to be uniformly rigid across cultures. Coping style refers to the number of strategies the child has in their repertoire.

A comparison of coping in children in the USA and India offers some insight into the similarities in coping among children. The National Kids Poll (2008) revealed that the majority of American children reported coping strategies of escape–avoidance, which is a strategy where the child engages in activities that keep them at bay from the problem. Children reported coping with stressful situations by indulging in play, music, watching TV, video games, or eating more. The other frequently used method was found to be distancing, which refers to avoidance of acknowledging the stressful experience. The children also reported emotion-focused coping, such a losing their temper, self-injury, crying. A fairly low percentage of the sample reported problem-focused coping (28 percent) or seeking social support (22 percent). In interviews with 30 Indian children, conducted by the authors of this chapter to gain insight into the subject, it was found that 32 percent had recourse to passive and unproductive coping such as distancing and avoidance, 25 percent applied self-control (not expressing the feelings to others but indulging in self-talk) and 25 percent chose social support. Thus it may be observed that children across the two cultures adopted passive, emotion-focused coping, suggesting a rigid style.

This suggests that children need timely support and intervention from significant adults such as parents at home and teachers in the school. The basic principles of intervention have to be empathy, understanding, and avoidance of branding and labelling the child as 'incompetent'. Recent lines of research focus on cultural variations in expression of pain and the way different cultures train children in expression of stress (Hariharan 2010).

Childhood stress: interventions

Research findings discussed in this chapter clearly indicate that childhood stress has a devastating impact on the child, encompassing the structural and functional aspects of brain, and reflected in cognitive function, academic performance, and behaviour. In the light of disproportionately severe consequences of stress and inadequate coping skills, effective intervention strategies involving preventive, diagnostic, and remedial models are the immediate need.

Intervention includes analysing and understanding undesirable and deviant behaviour such as 'sick role behaviour' (that is, a behaviour pattern in which a person adopts the symptoms of a physical or mental disorder to be cared for, sympathized with, and protected from the demands and stresses of life), learning difficulties, sudden drop in school attendance or performance, change in social behaviour manifested in aggressive outbursts or withdrawal, and self-isolation. Persistence in one or more of these manifestations should warrant consulting a professional psychologist for timely diagnosis and intervention. While that takes care of the diagnostic measure, the preventive and remedial measures call for the involvement of school and teachers.

Preventive measures

- Adults can help children to anticipate stressful events, such as the first day at school or the birth of a sibling, so as to reduce the stressful impact (Marion 2003). Parents and teachers play a significant role in discussing with the child forthcoming events such as a change of class or teacher, change of residence, birth of a sibling, imminent divorce and separation of parents, or illness in the family. This not only helps in preparing the child but also opens the opportunity for seeking support from parents or teachers. Seeking social support is considered a 'win–win situation' that addresses both the problem and the emotional disturbance.
- There are instances of emotional displacement in children where anger is expressed in crying, fear in aggression, etc. In this context, appropriate intervention is to help the child identify, accept and regulate their emotions in ways appropriate to the context. Training in identification and endorsement of emotions can start at a very early stage of schooling, and proper regulation of emotional expression may continue until late schooling.

Diagnostic measures

- A child exposed to prolonged stress may suffer from non-performance and underachievement because of a major functional disruption of the hippocampus region. When intensive remedial teaching or other academic interventions fail to achieve the desired results in a child's school performance, a psychological assessment is in order. Research in neuropsychology is currently focusing on the assessment tools (see Christodoulou, Saxler, and Del Tufo, Chapter 20, this volume) and this should include neuropsychological assessment of childhood stress.
- When a child manifests problems with verbal memory that relate to 'working memory' and does not respond to remedial measures, it is essential to investigate the stress levels of the child and attention needs to be focused on the life stress for the child. Remedial measures in such cases have to be directed towards handling the child's stressful environment.
- Children manifesting persistent problems in learning and memory should not be branded as slow learners, as having attention deficit hyperactive disorder (ADHD), or as being stubborn and apathetic. Instead, there is a need for a neurological assessment to rule out deformity or functional limitations in their hippocampus or prefrontal cortex.

Remedial measures

- Introvert children may not give adequate expression to their emotions while under stress. These children are likely to adopt coping strategies such as self-control, which prompts the children not to reveal the stress to anyone and handle it all by themselves. Given the inadequate coping skills, such strategies are not likely to have a desirable outcome. Gross and Clemens (2002) felt that integrating 'play therapy' into school activities may create an appropriate context and platform for the expression of pent-up emotions and also serve as a laboratory for a scientific diagnosis. The teacher or therapist may assume the role of an observer to identify the emotional manifestations of children and use them as an initial screening tool to be reinforced with more intensive techniques of diagnosis and therapeutic intervention.

- It may be a good step to train the children in a variety of coping strategies. To start with, training on hardiness (involving assessment and use of commitment, control, and challenge) may help children to gain a realistic appraisal of the stress situation and application of problem-focused coping strategies to a variety of stressful situations. Children need to be helped in identifying a variety of school-related stressors and trained in effective coping strategies to manage them (Fallin et al. 2001).

- However much one may try, children may still encounter stress where the locus of control is external. Under such circumstances they need to have skills to relax and restore the emotional equilibrium. Training in simple relaxation techniques such as deep breathing and backwards counting can help such children to control and avoid impulsive and aggressive outbursts (O'Neill 1993).

Childhood stress is an inevitable experience. School and the curriculum can be designed to create a platform for the venting of extreme emotions and to absorb and channel childhood stress to productive activities leading to enhanced performance and achievement. Planning and implementing school education in the context of children's developmental stages, their emotional fragility, limitations of language expression, and coping strategies can save them from succumbing to stress and provide them with an opportunity to unfold their potential optimally.

Contact address: meena.healthpsychology@gmail.com

References

Alfven, G., Osterberg, V., and Hjern, A. (2008) 'Stressor, perceived stress and recurrent pain in Swedish school children', *Journal of Psychosomatic Research*, 65: 381–387.

Antonovsky, A. (1979) *Health, stress and coping*, San Francisco: Jossey Bass.

Arnsten, A. F. T. (2009) 'Stress signalling pathways that impair prefrontal cortex structure and function', *Nature Reviews Neuroscience*, 10: 410–422.

Baddeley, A. (1992) 'Working memory', *Science*, 255: 556–559.

Baron, R. A. (2001) *Psychology*, New Delhi: Prentice-Hall of India Pvt.

Beers, S. R., and De Bellis, M. D. (2002) 'Neuropsychological function in children with maltreatment-related posttraumatic stress disorder', *American Psychiatric Association*, 159: 483–486.

Bunsey, M., and Eichenbaum, H. (1995) 'Selective damage to the hippocampal region blocks long-term retention of a natural and nonspatial stimulus–stimulus association', *Hippocampus*, 5: 546–556.

Dacey, J. S., and Fiore, L. B. (2000) *Your anxious child*, San Francisco: Jossey-Bass.

DeBord, K. (1996) *Helping children cope with stress* [online]. Available at http://4h.missouri.edu/programs/military/resources/manual/Helping-Children-Cope-with-Stress.pdf

Fallin, K., Wallinga, C., and Coleman, M. (2001) 'Helping children cope with stress in the classroom setting', *Childhood Education*, 78: 17–24.

Gross, T., and Clemens, S. G. (2002) 'Painting a tragedy: young children process the events of September 11', *Young Children*, 57: 44–51.

Hariharan, M. (1995) 'Invulnerable children: the torchbearers for intervention policies for the disadvantaged', *Trends in Social Science Research*, 2: 33–38.

Hariharan, M. (2010) 'Cultural markers in expression of pain and trauma', in M. Hariharan, G. Padmaja, and M. Padhy (eds.) *Pain and trauma management: a biopsychosocial perspective*, New Delhi: Sage (pp. 71–78).

Hariharan, M., and Rath, R. (2008) *Coping with life stress: the Indian experience*, New Delhi: Sage.

Hesketh, J., Zhen, Y., Lu, L., Dong, Z. X., Jun, Y. X., and Xing, Z. W. (2010) 'Stress and psychosomatic symptoms in Chinese school children: cross sectional survey', *Archives of Disease in Childhood*, 95: 136–140.

Hjern, A., Alfven, G., and Ostberg, V. (2008) 'School stressors, psychological complaints and psychosomatic pain', *Acta Paediatrica*, 97: 112–117.

Holmes, T. H., and Rahe, R. H. (1967) 'Holmes-Rahe Social Readjustment Rating Scale', *Journal of Psychosomatic Research*, 11: 213–218.

Jewett, J. (1997) 'Childhood stress', *Childhood Education*, 73: 172–173.

Kanner, A. P., Coyne, J. C., Schaefer, C., and Lazarus, R. S. (1981) 'Comparison of two modes of stress measurements: daily hassles and uplifts versus major life events', *Journal of Behavioral Medicine*, 4: 1–39.

King, S., and Laplante, D. P. (2005) 'The effects of prenatal maternal stress on children's cognitive development: Project Ice Storm', *Stress*, 8: 35–45.

Kobasa, S. C. (1984) 'Test for "hardiness". How much stress can you survive? The answer depends on your personality', *American Health*, 3: 64–77.

Lazarus, R. S. (1999) *A new synthesis: stress and emotions*, New York: Springer.

Lupien, S., Maheu, F., Tu, M., Fiocco, A., and Schramek, E. (2007) 'The effects of stress and stress hormones on human cognition: implications for the field of brain and cognition', *Brain and Cognition*, 65: 209–237.

Marion, M. (2003) *Guidance of young children*, 6th edn, Upper Saddle River, NJ: Prentice Hall.

McCance, K., Forshee, B., and Shelby, J. (2006) 'Stress and disease', in K. McCance and S. Huether (eds.) *Pathophysiology: the biologic basic for disease in adults and children*, 5th edn, St Louis: Elsevier Mosby (pp. 311–332).

McClelland, J. L. (1996) 'Role of the hippocampus in learning and memory: a computational analysis', in T. Ono, B. L. McNaughton, S. Molotchnikoff, E. T. Rolls, and H. Nishijo (eds.) *Perception, memory and emotion: frontiers in neuroscience*, Oxford: Elsevier Science (pp. 601–613).

McLoyd, V. C. (1998) 'Socioeconomic disadvantage and child development', *American Psychologist*, 53: 185–204.

Middlebrooks, J. S., and Audage, N. C. (2008) *The effects of childhood stress on health across the lifespan*, Center for Disease Control and Prevention, National Center for Injury Prevention and Control, Atlanta, GA [online]. Available at www.cdc.gov/ncipc/pub-res/pdf/childhood_stress.pdf

Moksnes, U. K., Moljord, I. E. O., Espnes, G. A., and Byrne, D. G. (2010) 'The association between stress and emotional states in adolescents: the role of gender and self-esteem', *Personality and Individual Differences*, 49: 430–435.

Monk, C. F., Fifer, W. P., Myers, M. M., Sloan, R. P., Trien, L., and Hurtado, A. (2000) 'Maternal stress responses and anxiety during pregnancy: effects on fetal heart rate', *Developmental Psychology*, 36: 67–77.

National Kids Poll (2008) '*What kids say about handling stress?*' Nemours Foundation, Jacksonville, FL [online]. Available at http://kidshealth.org/parent/emotions/feelings/kids_stress.html

O'Neill, C. (1993) *Relax*, Auburn, ME: Child's Play International.

Rath, R., Dash, A. S., and Dash, U. N. (1979) *Cognitive abilities and school achievements of the socially disadvantaged children in primary school*, New Delhi: Allied Publishers.

Roozendaal, B. (2002) 'Stress and memory: opposing effects of glucocorticoids on memory consolidation and memory retrieval', *Neurobiology of Learning and Memory*, 78: 578–595.

Roozendaal, B. (2003) 'Systems mediating acute glucocorticoid effects on memory consolidation and retrieval', *Progress in Neuropsychopharmacology and Biological Psychiatry*, 27: 1213–1223.

Rudolph, K. D., Kurlakowsky, K. D., and Conley, C. S. (2001) 'Developmental and social-contextual origins of depressive control-related beliefs and behaviour', *Cognitive Therapy and Research*, 25: 447–475.

Sharpe, R. (1995) *Thrive on stress – how to make it work to your advantage*, New Delhi: Rupa Publications.

Sinha, D., Tripathi, R. C., and Misra, G. (1982) *Deprivation: its social roots and psychological consequences*, New Delhi: Concept Publishing.

Southwick, S. M., Krystal, J. H., Bremner, J. D., Morgan, C. A., Nicolaou, A. L., Nagy, L. M., Johnson, D. R., Heninger, G. R., and Charney, D. S. (1997) 'Noradrenergic and serotonergic function in posttraumatic stress disorder', *Archives of General Psychiatry*, 54: 749–758.

Stansbury, K., and Harris, M. L. (2000) 'Individual differences in stress reactions during a peer entry episode: effects of age, temperament, approach behaviour, and self-perceived peer competence', *Journal of Experimental Child Psychology*, 76: 50–63.

Tuakli-Williams, J., and Carrillo, J. (1995) 'The impact of psychosocial stressors on African-American and Latino preschoolers', *Journal of National Medical Association*, 87: 473–478.

Werner, E. E. (2000) 'Protective factors and individual resilience', in J. P. Shonkoff and S. Meisles (Eds.) *Handbook of early childhood intervention*, 2nd edn, New York: Cambridge University Press.

Werner, E. E., and Smith, R. S. (1982) *Vulnerable but invincible*, New York: McGraw-Hill.

Wolf, O. T. (2003) 'HPA axis and memory', *Best Practice and Research. Clinical Endocrinology and Metabolism*, 17: 287–299.

Woolley, C. S., Gould, E., and McEwen, B. S. (1990) 'Exposure to excess glucocorticoids alters dendritic morphology of adult hippocampal pyramidal neurons', *Brain Research*, 531: 225–231.

PART III

Issues concerning the assessment of children

14

CLASSROOM ASSESSMENTS

Informing teaching and supporting learning

Spencer Salend

STATE UNIVERSITY OF NEW YORK AT NEW PALTZ, USA

Ms Lopez was concerned about her students who had struggled to learn fractions. She created an assessment measure to examine their fluency in adding and subtracting fractions and administered it to obtain a baseline measure. Following each instructional session, she administered the assessment measure and graphed the data, which she examined to monitor her students' progress and to make adjustments in her teaching. Periodically, she asked students to make journal entries related to their learning of fractions by asking them to respond to 'I understand . . .', 'It helped me when you . . .', 'I am not sure how to . . .', and 'I would like you to review . . .'.

Ms Lopez noticed that her students' error patterns showed that they sometimes didn't pay attention to the sign and had difficulty with fractions that had different denominators. Therefore, she taught her students to use the mnemonic LAP (Look at the denominator and sign; Ask yourself if the smallest denominator will divide into the largest denominator an even number of times; and Pick your fraction type) (Test and Ellis 2005), and monitored their use of the strategy by asking them periodically to think aloud.

Ms Molfese had been teaching her students about the solar system. Using an interactive whiteboard, she reviewed visuals about the sun, the moon, and the planets they had learned about so far. She then asked her students to use their wireless active responding clickers to rate their levels of understanding on a scale of one to four. After examining her students' ratings, Ms Molfese felt comfortable that the class was ready to start learning about constellations. She introduced some of the constellations and sometimes asked students to use their clickers to identify the specific constellations that were displayed on the whiteboard. Periodically, she asked students to think aloud and explain how they arrived at their answers. Based on a summary of the students' answers provided to her, Ms Molfese quickly assessed student understanding and determined which students were ready to start researching constellations on their own. She also used individualized student response data to identify those students who needed additional instruction before starting their research projects. At the end of class, she had her students complete an exit ticket that asked them to identify the things they learned about constellations and the things that were still puzzling to them. She examined their responses and used the information to plan her next class.

As part of the geography curriculum, Mr Loreman's class worked on an instructional unit related to geographical landforms. To assess their mastery of the material in the unit, Mr Loreman created a menu of technology-based performance assessment activities aligned to his instructional goals. Mr Loreman shared the menu with his students, who then worked in groups to create their projects and share them with their classmates. As the students worked on their assignments, they accessed instructional rubrics posted on the class website, which Mr Loreman and his students had developed from a bank of rubrics available online.

Ms van Alstyne worked with her students to create a digital literacy portfolio. She made recordings of students' reading and used them to track their reading fluency, and made digital observations of students engaged in literature discussion groups. Throughout the school year, her students selected drafts and final products across a range of writing genres to be included in their portfolios. Ms van Alstyne and her students wrote caption statements to describe the items and why they were selected, and included comments reflecting on what the item showed about the students' progress. To assist her students in reflecting on their items, Ms van Alstyne initially asked them to complete the following statements: 'I am proud of this work because _____', and 'The things that helped me were _____'. The items and their corresponding caption statements were stored in a digital portfolio by date and subject.

While the international movements toward teacher accountability mandates and high-stakes testing emphasize the role of standardized testing in education, educators throughout the world such as Ms Lopez, Ms Molfese, Mr Loreman, and Ms van Alstyne are using classroom formative and summative assessments reflecting the outcomes associated with daily instruction (Salend 2009). Formative classroom assessments are particularly helpful in monitoring the learning progress of students and providing educators with data to inform and improve their instructional practices. Conversely, summative classroom assessments aligned with instructional goals are used to document student mastery.

Recognizing the critical importance of classroom assessments, this chapter describes and presents examples of a range of formative and summative classroom assessments that educators throughout the world have employed in inclusive education classrooms to collect data to inform their teaching and support the educational performance of their students, including those with learning disabilities (Salend 2009, 2011). For a more detailed critique of high stakes testing and a discussion of formative and summative assessment, see Hall (Chapter 16, this volume).

Progress monitoring systems

Progress monitoring systems are characterized by educators conducting frequent assessments to monitor student learning as well as the effectiveness of their instructional practices. In these systems, assessment data are continuously collected and analysed over time to identify students who are progressing and ready for new instruction as well as students who have not yet achieved proficiency and need additional or revised instruction (Salend 2009, 2011). Teachers also examine the data collected to inform their teaching and make any necessary adjustments that will foster their students' learning. Examples of progress monitoring systems include the Response-to-Intervention model (RtI) and curriculum-based assessment (CBA).

Response-to Intervention model

To assess the effectiveness of instructional practices and improve the special education identifica-tion process, schools are implementing RtI systems, an emerging practice in North America (McIntosh et al. 2011; Salend 2011). RtI is a multi-tiered instructional and identification model for determining the extent to which students respond to a series of increasingly intensive and individualized research-based interventions (Fuchs and Fuchs 2007). The RtI model involves the following.

- *Universal screening:* All students are assessed several times via the use of norm-referenced tests or norm-based curriculum-based measures.
- *Implementation of research-based interventions:* Teaching programmes, strategies, practices, supports, resources, technologies, and materials based on sound educational theory that research has shown to be effective in promoting student learning are systematically delivered to all students.
- *Identification of students needing more intensive instruction:* Cut-off scores on universal screening measures and aimlines for judging student progress are established and used to identify students who are not benefiting from research-based instruction.
- *Tiered instruction:* A series of more intensive research-based interventions are delivered in tiers based on students' responses to them. Tiers differ in terms of the interventions implemented, the group sizes, the targeted instructional goals and content mastery levels, the length and frequency of instructional sessions, the settings where instruction is delivered, the educators involved in delivering instruction, and the frequency of the assessment for examining student progress.
- *Fidelity in the implementation of interventions:* Data are collected to ensure that research-based interventions are delivered as planned.
- *Collaboration among educators:* General, special, literacy, and bilingual educators and ancillary support personnel work together and share their expertise to plan, deliver, assess, and change instruction.
- *Progress monitoring:* Data are collected and analysed on an ongoing basis to assess students' response to interventions, to make adjustments in the instructional programme, and to move students from tier to tier.
- *Decision rules:* District determined guidelines are established for judging the effectiveness of interventions, and placement in tiers.
- *Identification for special education:* Students who do not respond to a series of effective interventions are evaluated to determine if they would benefit from special education services (Mellard, McKnight, and Jordan 2010).

Curriculum-based assessment

CBA is a progress-monitoring technique that involves repeated assessments of individual student progress in mastering content and skills directly related to the curriculum and classroom instruction (Cheng-Lai and Chan 2008; Kaminitz-Berkooza and Shapiro 2005; Madelaine and Wheldall 2005; McMaster et al. 2011). Educators have a choice between two forms of CBA: curriculum-based measurement (CBM) and mastery measurement (MM) (Salend, Baker, and Gardner 2012). While the systematic use of norm-based CBM is an essential component of the RtI model, teachers like Ms Lopez use MM more informally to assess their students' learning progress and determine the efficacy of their teaching practices. For instance, Ms Lopez employed

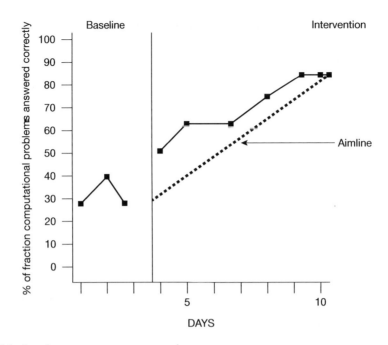

Figure 14.1 Sample mastery measurement graph

MM to document and graph her students' progress in mastering the addition and subtraction of fractions and used the data she collected to document their learning and inform her instruction (see Figure 14.1).

As described by Salend et al. (2012), the steps in implementing MM are as follows.

1. *Identify and define the meaningful school-related tasks to be assessed:* Teachers begin by determining and defining the critical thinking, problem solving, academic, or performance skills to be assessed. For example, Ms Lopez's objective was for her students to be able to add and subtract fractions with like and unlike denominators.

2. *Create an assessment measure:* Teachers develop a measure to assess students' mastery of the identified learning objective. In creating the assessment measure, educators consider: (a) the number and types of items; (b) the length of time and materials available to students; and (c) the criterion employed to score the assessment measure. In the case of Ms Lopez, her assessment measure consisted of five addition and subtraction items with like denominators and five addition and subtraction items with unlike denominators, which students were to complete in three minutes.

3. *Obtain a baseline:* Teachers administer the assessment measure to establish a baseline, an initial level of student performance on the assessment measure prior to initiating instruction. The baseline is used to begin to plan instruction and as a criterion for validating the effectiveness of instruction.

4. *Establish an aimline:* Baseline data also are employed to establish an 'aimline', a dotted line that offers a visual representation of a student's estimated rate of progress (see Figure 14.1). The aimline also serves as a visual to guide teachers in assessing the effectiveness of their instruction.

5. *Design and deliver varied, research-based, motivating, and differentiated instruction:* Teachers examine the data to plan and implement varied, research-based, motivating, and differentiated instructional strategies.
6. *Administer the assessment measure for each instructional session and graph the data:* After each instructional session, teachers administer the assessment measure to collect and graph the data (see Figure 14.1).
7. *Analyse the data to assess student learning progress and inform instruction:* Teachers analyse the data by examining the graph and the aimline to determine if the student is making sufficient learning progress. The data are also used to inform instruction and make necessary changes to teaching strategies.
8. *Perform an error analysis:* As part of the data analysis, teachers also examine students' responses to determine error patterns and to plan instruction to remediate these patterns. For example, Ms Lopez's error analysis showed that her students needed to focus on paying attention to the sign and struggled with adding and subtracting fractions with unlike denominators, which led her to teach them to use the 'LAP' mnemonic device (Test and Ellis 2005).
9. *Reflect on the effectiveness of the instructional strategies:* Teachers engage in a reflective process to examine the efficacy of instructional interventions and make evidence-based decisions about their instructional practices. They reflect on: (a) What did my students learn? (b) What strategies helped my students learn? (c) Were my instructional practices effective? Why? Why not? (d) What are the positive and negative consequences associated with using the intervention(s)? (e) What steps can be taken to improve the effectiveness of my instructional strategies? (f) What instructional practices are likely to be successful with my students in the future? (Salend et al. 2012).
10. *Communicate results and collaborate with students, families, and other educators:* Teachers share their data, graphs, and reflections about students' learning progress with students, families, and other educators and collaboratively plan future instructional goals and strategies.

Real-time assessment systems

Teachers like Ms Molfese are using real-time assessments to monitor their students' understanding during instruction (Salend 2009). The data collected are then employed by teachers to assess student learning and to make adjustments in their teaching practices. Teachers can use a range of motivating and novel ways to collect real-time assessment data including observations, active responding systems, learning logs/journals, and think-alouds.

Observations

Teachers use observational techniques to record their students' academic performance and social behaviours and to improve their instruction (Glynn and McNaughton 2002; Kontu and Pirttimaa 2008). When the academic skill or social behaviour has a clear beginning and end, teachers can employ event recording to maintain a record of the number of times the behaviour or academic skill occurred throughout the instructional period. For example, Ms van Alstyne used event recording to assess her students' reading fluency by counting the number of reading errors students make while reading. When time is an essential component of the skill or behaviour being assessed, teachers can use duration recording to assess the length of time the behaviour occurs.

Observational data also can be collected via an anecdotal record, which is a narrative presentation of the specific academic and social behaviours of students and teachers and the activities that took place in the classroom (Salend 2009). The narrative is then analysed to pinpoint student behaviours that impact learning and the classroom environment. Teachers also can use rating scales or checklists to structure and report their observations.

Active responding systems

Active responding systems provide teachers like Ms Molfese with a way to assess their students' learning by asking them to respond collectively or individually. After teaching content, teachers have their students respond actively by:

- presenting cards to show their levels of understanding (a green card or a plus card can denote good comprehension, a yellow card or question card can suggest a minimal level of comprehension, and a red card or minus card can signify limited or no level of comprehension);
- answering with physical gestures or brief verbal statements of agreement or disagreement to brief statements or examples;
- writing answers to questions or problems on dry erase boards; and
- responding to questions posed at the beginning or end of class related to the content taught that day or the day before, respectively (Salend 2009).

As Ms Molfese and her students demonstrated, teachers also can employ wireless systems that involve students using handheld devices to periodically respond to questions; predict outcomes of readings, word problems, and science experiments; and rate their levels of mastery of content taught. Individual student and class-wide responses are presented to teachers who use the data to inform their instruction.

Learning journals/logs

Real-time data concerning students' learning progress also can be collected via use of learning journals/logs (Salend 2009). After receiving instruction, students compose journal entries related to the things they learned and how they learned them as well as the content that is confusing to them and the additional assistance that could support their learning. Journal entries also can address their educational strengths and challenges, progress in and questions about learning new material, reactions to instructional activities, events or conditions that are affecting their learning, and the learning strategies they use. They also can be asked to comment on the things they did well and the things they can do better. Teachers then examine journals to identify content that needs to be re-taught as well as alternative ways to teach it.

Think-alouds

Teachers like Ms Lopez and Ms Molfese are also using think-alouds to collect real-time data to assess student learning and the ways students approach learning activities (Bannert and Mengelkamp 2008; Janssen, Braaksma, and Rijlaarsdam 2006; Sainsbury 2003; Yu-Fen 2006). Teachers implement think-alouds by prompting their students to identify the processes they are using and describe their thoughts while working on a task, by asking questions such as 'What do you mean by . . .?' and 'How did you arrive at that answer?' (Salend 2011). See Littleton

(Chapter 7, this volume) for additional information and strategies for using dialogues with students to help support teaching and learning.

Performance/authentic assessment systems

Like Mr Loreman, teachers also employ performance assessment, also referred to as authentic assessment, to monitor their students' learning and to examine the efficacy of their instruction (Koh and Luke 2009; Palm 2008). Performance/authentic assessment involves having students complete meaningful, complex, open-ended learning activities that result in authentic products aligned to the curriculum and individualized learning goals (Hume and Coll 2009; Min Kyeong and Sunsook 2010). The authentic products are examined to assess students' ability to apply the knowledge and skills they have learned to contextualized problems and real-life settings (Salend 2011). Because performance/authentic assessments encourage and foster self-regulation, self-reflection and collaborative skills, they are integral aspects of effective teaching in inclusive classrooms (see Erten, Savage, and Di Stasio, Chapter 6, this volume).

Technology-based performance assessments

Educators are finding that technology is an excellent way to implement performance/authentic assessment (Scholtz 2007). As demonstrated by Mr Loreman, several technologies appear to be particularly appropriate for use by students to present the products of their learning, including using presentation software and wikis, creating online and digital learning products such as web pages/websites, blogs, podcasts and digital movies/stories, engaging in computer simulations and virtual learning experiences, and completing webquests and tracks (Salend 2009).

Portfolio assessment

Performance assessment is linked to portfolio assessment, which involves teachers, students, and family members collaborating to create a collection of authentic learning products across a range of content areas (Birgin and Baki 2007; Segers, Gijbels, and Thurlings 2008). These authentic products are periodically reviewed to reflect on and document student learning progress, and the instructional strategies used to help students learn (Shaaban 2000). Teachers and students implement portfolio assessment by implementing the following steps (Salend 2009).

1. *Identifying the goals of the portfolio:* Portfolios usually relate to individualized and broadly stated goals that are linked to the curriculum.
2. *Choosing authentic products aligned to the goals of the portfolio:* Students, teachers, and family members select a range of authentic classroom products that address the goals of the portfolio. To involve students in the selection process, teachers can ask them to choose an assignment that: (a) was their favourite or made them feel particularly proud; (b) was initially difficult for them; (c) demonstrates their understanding or mastery of content; and/or (d) showcases their creative and problem-solving abilities.
3. *Storing and organizing students' products:* Portfolio items are stored in file folders, binders, and boxes with dividers and organized chronologically (e.g. early/intermediate/later works), by academic skills or content-area subjects.
4. *Using a range of technologies:* Like Ms van Alstyne, teachers can use a range of technologies to record items and create digital portfolios (Chi-Cheng 2009). Digital recorders and scanners

can be used to record students performing academic and social activities and portfolio items. Software programs offer ways to: (a) digitize a range of student work samples and observations of students engaged in learning activities; (b) present items by subject, theme, project, date, and title and align them to curricular standards, and instructional rubrics; and (c) share portfolios with others.

5. *Reflecting on the portfolio items:* Selected portfolio items are accompanied by captions statements, which are brief descriptions written by teachers and students addressing: (a) What is the item? (b) Why was it selected? (c) Under what conditions was it produced? Caption statements also include teacher and student reflections related to what each item shows about student learning. A sample caption statement written by Ms van Alstyne and one of her students is presented in Figure 14.2. Like Ms van Alstyne, teachers can foster student reflection in a variety of ways (Salend 2009). Initially, teachers can promote student reflection by providing their students with prompts such as 'I used to _____ but now I _____,' 'The things I liked about working on this were _____,' and 'I still need to work on _____.' As students become more proficient at reflecting on their work, they can be asked to respond to questions related to: their learning (What things did I learn from working on this project?); their successes (What things did I do well on this project?); their goals for improvement (How could I improve this project?); and their learning process (What strategies did I use to complete this project?) (Salend 2011). Students also can be asked to compare their current projects with those that they completed earlier in the school year.

6. *Examining portfolios to assess student learning and teaching effectiveness:* Portfolios are examined throughout the school year by teachers, students, family members, and administrators. At portfolio conferences, participants can discuss the items in terms of what they show about the student's: (a) academic, behavioural, language, functional, and social–emotional performance; (b) learning strengths/challenges; and (c) learning strategies, attitudes, motivation, and interests.

Portfolio items also are examined to identify the teaching strategies that best support student learning. At the end of the conference, participants can compose or dictate a statement to be included in the portfolio that presents their perspective on what the portfolio reveals about the student's progress and the ways to enhance the educational programme.

Instructional rubrics

The use of instructional rubrics, a listing of the specific criteria associated with varying levels of mastery in evaluating student work products, is an integral component of performance/authentic assessment and portfolio assessment (Salend 2009, 2011). Rubrics provide educators like Mr Loreman and Ms van Alstyne with a means of evaluating student products by identifying the distinct categories related to assessment tasks, the varying levels of proficiency, and the specific indicators delineating each level. Because rubrics help teachers delineate and share their expectations, their use can make grading and feedback more objective and consistent, which can aid students in reflecting on their learning.

Rubrics are most effective when they are developed collaboratively by teachers and their students using the following process (Salend 2009, 2011).

- *Step 1. Determine whether to use instructional rubrics:* Identify the learning goals to be assessed by the assignment, and consider whether a rubric is the best strategy for assessing learning.

Emily selected her persuasive essay for her literacy portfolio because she was proud of it and felt that it showed a good example of her writing skills. The essay was written to convince the school's principal to expand the school's recreation areas. Students composed their persuasive essays in stages from draft to final product over a three-week period. Students worked in collaborative writing groups and received feedback from their classmates and teacher using a rubric that the class developed. In her essay, Emily expressed the opinion that the playground area was an important source of socialization and entertainment for students. She also argued that the recess on the playground helped students burn off excess energy, which made them better learners. The essays were sent to the school's principal who spoke to the class about ways to expand the school's recreational areas.

Teacher Reflection:

I was impressed with Emily's persuasive essay, which met all of the criteria outlined in the persuasive essay rubric. Her essay contained a clear position and strong counter-arguments that were supported by facts, statistics, citations, examples, and reason. Additionally, Emily's essay showed that she understands how to use persuasive words and her personal experiences to advocate for her point of view. In addition to demonstrating her mastery of the fundamentals of writing a persuasive essay, Emily learned what it means to be passionate about something and the importance of standing up for what she believes. Her essay was well-organized and well-written as evidenced by her correct grammar, spelling, and punctuation, her appropriate word choice and transitions and her engaging opening, thoughtful and informative middle and concluding summary.

Student Reflection:

I was very proud of this essay and think I did a really good job on it. One thing that really helped me was learning that there are certain words you can use to persuade others. It was very helpful to me when our teacher taught us about words you can use to persuade others and gave us a list of them. From that, I was able to choose the words that I thought sounded good and worked the best to prove my points. I also liked working in groups and my group gave me good feedback, which helped me write my essay and avoid run-on sentences.

Our essays went to the principal, which gave it meaning and showed us the essay had a reason behind it. It taught me that if you stick up for what you believe, you have a chance of succeeding.

Figure 14.2 Sample caption statement

- *Step 2. Delineate the important features and relevant categories:* Identify the critical qualities that characterize excellent, good, mediocre, and inadequate assignments, and use them to determine the relevant categories that the rubric will address.
- *Step 3. Determine the levels of performance:* Develop an age-appropriate scale related to three or four different performance levels such as beginning; developing; accomplished; exemplary. Also, determine whether it is appropriate to assign point values to each level, and whether the different categories should be weighted.
- *Step 4. Compose a set of indicators:* Specify indicators, concise statements that present the specific attributes associated with the rubric's categories and performance levels. Indicators can be number-based (at least four, none), time-based (all of the time, frequent), or descriptive (clearly described, unclear). Review the indicators to eliminate redundancies and irrelevant ones, and to add relevant ones that are not included.
- *Step 5. Examine the instructional rubric:* Assess the extent to which the rubric is positive, understandable, and unbiased. Make sure that it supports student learning and does not stifle student creativity.

- *Step 6. Teach and prompt students to use the rubric:* Prompt students to use the rubric while working on assignments by reminding them and modelling how to use it, and conducting conferences to reflect on ways they can use it.
- *Step 7: Use and revise the instructional rubric:* Use the rubric, reflect on its impact on teaching and learning, and revise it if necessary.

Summary

This chapter has presented classroom-based assessment strategies used by educators to monitor and document their students' learning progress, and to reflect on the impact of their instructional practices (see Salend 2009, for additional information on these assessment strategies). Educators throughout the world are employing a range of assessment strategies (e.g. curriculum-based assessment, observations, think-alouds, portfolio assessment, instructional rubrics), and technology-based assessments are starting to assume a more prominent role in classrooms. While the RtI model is being employed predominantly in North America (e.g. USA and Canada), variations of the RtI model are starting to be implemented in others countries (Worrell and Taber 2009). Since the practices described in this chapter vary in scope (i.e. school-wide, programme, class, group, individual), focus (i.e. academic, socio-emotional, behavioural), and resources (i.e. technology, preparation, materials) and individuals involved (i.e. educators, students, family members), educators should consider these variables as well as socio-cultural factors unique to their countries as they select the assessment strategies they employ.

Contact address: salends@newpaltz.edu

References

Bannert, M., and Mengelkamp, C. (2008) 'Assessment of metacognitive skills by means of instruction to think aloud and reflect when prompted. Does the verbalization method affect learning?', *Metacognition and Learning*, 3: 39–58.

Birgin, O., and Baki, A. (2007) 'The use of portfolio to assess student's performance', *Journal of Turkish Science Education*, 4: 75–90.

Cheng-Lai, A., and Chan, A. L. (2008) 'Parental paired-reading intervention for Chinese dyslexic children: using curriculum-based measurement to assess responsiveness to instruction', *International Journal of Learning*, 15: 235–251.

Chi-Cheng, C. (2009) 'Self-evaluated effects of web-based portfolio assessment system for various student motivation levels', *Journal of Educational Computing Research*, 41: 391–405.

Fuchs, L. S., and Fuchs, D. (2007) 'A model for implementing responsiveness to Intervention', *Teaching Exceptional Children*, 39: 14–23.

Glynn, T., and McNaughton, S. (2002) 'Trust your observations: assessment of reader and tutor behaviour in learning to read in English and Maori', *International Journal of Disability, Development and Education*, 49: 161–173.

Hume, A., and Coll, R. K. (2009) 'Assessment of learning, for learning, as learning: New Zealand case studies', *Assessment in Education: Principles, Policy and Practice*, 16: 269–290.

Janssen, T., Braaksma, M., and Rijlaarsdam, G. (2006) 'Literary reading activities of good and weak students: a think aloud study, *European Journal of Psychology of Education*, 21: 35–52.

Kaminitz-Berkooza, J., and Shapiro, E. S. (2005) 'The applicability of curriculum-based measurement to measure reading in Hebrew', *School Psychology International*, 26: 494–519.

Koh, K., and Luke, A. (2009) 'Authentic and conventional assessment in Singapore schools: an empirical study of teacher assignments and student work', *Assessment in Education: Principles, Policy and Practice*, 16: 291–318.

Kontu, E., and Pirttimaa, R. (2008) 'The assessment of severely intellectually disabled students', *European Journal of Special Needs Education*, 23: 75–80.

Madelaine, A., and Wheldall, K. (2005) 'Identifying low-progress readers: comparing teacher judgment with a curriculum-based measurement procedure', *International Journal of Disability, Development and Education*, 52: 33–42.

McIntosh, K., MacKay, L. D., Andreou, T., Brown, J. A., Mathews, S., Gietz, C., and Bennett, J. L. (2011) 'Response to intervention in Canada: definitions, the evidence base and future directions', *Canadian Journal of School Psychology*, 26: 18–43.

McMaster, K. L., Du, X., Yeo, S., Deno, S. L., Parker, D., and Ellis, T. (2011) 'Curriculum-based measures of beginning writing: technical features of the slope', *Exceptional Children*, 77: 185–206.

Mellard, D., McKnight, M., and Jordan, J. (2010) 'RTI tier structures and instructional intensity', *Learning Disabilities Research and Practice*, 25: 217–225.

Min Kyeong, K., and Sunsook, N. (2010) 'Alternate mathematics assessment: a case study of the development of descriptive problems for elementary school in Korea', *Eurasia Journal of Mathematics, Science and Technology Education*, 6: 177–190.

Palm, T. (2008) 'Performance assessment and authentic assessment: a conceptual analysis of the literature', *Practical Assessment, Research and Evaluation*, 13(4).

Sainsbury, M. (2003) 'Thinking aloud: children's interactions with text', *Reading*, 37: 131–135.

Salend, S. J. (2009) *Classroom testing and assessment for all students: beyond standardization*, Thousand Oaks, CA: Corwin Press.

Salend, S. J. (2011) *Creating inclusive classrooms: effective and reflective practices*, 7th edn, Columbus, OH: Pearson Education.

Salend, S. J., Baker, A., and Gardner, A. (2012) 'Collecting practice-based evidence to support teaching and learning', *Educator's Voice*, 5: 12–19.

Scholtz, A. (2007) 'An analysis of the impact of an authentic assessment strategy on student performance in a technology-mediated constructivist classroom: a study revisted', *International Journal of Education & Development Using Information and Communication Technology*, 3: 42–53.

Segers, M., Gijbels, D., and Thurlings, M. (2008) 'The relationship between students' perceptions of portfolio assessment practice and their approaches to learning', *Educational Studies*, 34: 35–44.

Shaaban, K. (2000) 'Assessment of young learners' achievement in ESL classes in the Lebanon', *Language, Culture and Curriculum*, 13: 306–317.

Test, D. W., and Ellis, M. F. (2005) 'The effects of LAP fractions on addition and subtraction of fractions with students with mild disabilities', *Education and Treatment of Children*, 28: 11–24.

Worrell, J. L., and Taber, M. (2009) 'Special education practices in China and the United States: what is to come next?', *International Journal of Special Education*, 24: 132–142.

Yu-Fen, Y. (2006) 'Reading strategies or comprehension monitoring strategies?', *Reading Psychology*, 27: 313–343.

15

DIAGNOSTIC ASSESSMENT

One of the effective ways of assessing learning

Sunday Obi and Marty Sapp

KENTUCKY STATE UNIVERSITY, USA; UNIVERSITY OF WISCONSIN-MILWAUKEE, USA

Assessment is a process of collecting information about individuals or groups for the purpose of making decisions. In education, assessment ordinarily refers to testing, interviewing, and observing students. Assessment serves various purposes, including screening (quick measures to determine who may need further assessment), diagnosis (measures to identify specific problems), progress monitoring (frequent measures to help guide instruction), and outcomes measures (assessments to determine the effectiveness of educational programming).

More specifically, assessment is a critical component of the educational process. Educational institutions, government agencies, and professional associations are placing increasing emphasis on assessing performance in relevant areas of their domains. Growing emphasis on 'accountability' has become a hallmark of the early twenty-first century. Consequently, a good deal of light has been cast on institutional assessment. We strongly believe that teachers' assessment practices help in determining the level of performance of students as well as the effectiveness of educational programming. Knowing where students are in the curriculum and what they need next is a key focus for assessment. Such knowledge is critical for differentiating instruction to meet the range of needs students bring to the classroom. Some teachers downplay the importance of assessment, believing that time spent assessing would better be spent teaching. If, however, appropriate assessment procedures are conducted, the information obtained can be used to enhance the remediation of the perceptual teaching process. In other words, remediation of perceptual, cognitive, linguistic, social, academic, and behaviour disorders, as well as related disabilities, is an ultimate goal of assessment.

Throughout the history of education, there has always been the concern that classroom evaluations may not be fair (Cooper and TenBrink 2003). Standardized tests are often biased, teacher-made tests are not very reliable, and assessment strategies are often artificial. In other words, the assessment is not an 'authentic' assessment. It is not naturalistic-based assessment or performance-based assessment. Although these concerns are often valid, they do not deter excessive reliance on tests and grades. Teachers will always be involved in making judgements and decisions about student performance. Teachers must teach and assess students using authentic assessment instruments. The primary purpose of this chapter is to provide a review of assessment from a diagnostic approach, focusing on the importance of diagnostic instruments and the utilization of this assessment strategy for the identification of a student's skill level. This chapter will focus on (a) how relevant diagnostic assessment is to the identification of students, (b) the benefits of diagnostic assessment, and (c) some examples of diagnostic assessment instruments along with other forms of assessment.

Diagnostic assessment: how relevant to the identification of students' skills level?

Assessment from a diagnostic approach focuses on the identification of effective instructional strategies for children differing on any number of variables related to academic learning. Assessment from the diagnostic approach includes: (i) the cause of the learning problem for purpose of classification, (ii) diagnostic information about a child's style of learning and psychological processes, and (iii) academic content needs for instructional purposes.

'Diagnosis' is a word we usually associate with the medical field in the negative sense of figuring out what is wrong with a patient. But we use it more broadly in education. For example, when a teacher starts a new academic year, they want to know many things about their students. One of the most important is their current level of academic performance. Accurately understanding what students know and what they are able to do from the beginning of the year is crucial in designing instruction for them that challenges but does not overwhelm them (Earl 2003; Moon 2005). This process is termed 'diagnostic assessment'. In other words, diagnostic assessment is critical to designing instruction that meets the needs of these students. Many educators/teachers have termed this process as 'differentiation' or 'differentiated instruction'.

The basic idea of differentiation is that the teacher finds out student needs and readiness before starting instruction so they can use this information to tailor or differentiate (diversify) instruction for them. These procedures are critical because of the wide range of student cultures, abilities, and needs in every classroom today. Diagnostic assessment must be the first step in differentiating instruction because you use diagnostic assessments to learn what your students' varying needs are (Moon 2005; Tomlinson 2008). Also, at the beginning of each school year, it is important for a teacher to learn about their students' likes and dislikes, from food, games, activities, or music to academic interests. Understanding student preferences about types of assignments can help the teacher work from their strengths to address their needs. Another important time for diagnosis is when a teacher begins a new unit, because students' new learning is usually dependent on their prior knowledge (Pelligrino, Chudowsky, and Glaser, 2001).

Cogent examples of such an assessment process would utilize standardized instruments to identify a child's strengths and weaknesses on subtest items, followed by extrapolation of the information to provide a plan for instruction. This approach stresses the diagnosis of specific constructs, such as form discrimination, auditory sequencing, and anxiety, which are related to learning or affective processes, and the training and instruction in specific abilities, which are assumed to improve academic functioning.

Currently, diagnostic assessment procedures are methods of procedure for assessment of the various disability conditions, such as learning disabilities. Procedures for the development of a diagnostic assessment instrument can be logically broken down for classroom implementation as follows: (i) select a construct (for example, language, perception) on the nature of the learning process for consideration; (ii) divide the construct into sequential, quantifiable, measurable categories; (iii) administer a test (or tests) to evaluate performance in these categories; and (iv) develop a programme to remediate the deficit in the test-related skills.

In the USA, achievement tests are designed to provide the educator with a general view of the student so that they can determine areas of strengths and weaknesses. This information assists the educator in designing an evaluation plan to assess weaknesses diagnostically. The special educator assesses general areas of weakness in greater depth through the use of diagnostic instruments. These instruments aid the teacher in educational planning by revealing the types of errors the student makes as well as strengths that may be used to determine the proper instructional level and possible teaching and learning strategies. The use of diagnostic assessment instruments can also help the teacher in designing informal instruments and probes to assess student progress using direct measurement techniques.

Progress monitoring has, of late, been on the agenda of educational policy decision makers and administrators in the USA. With standard-based reform and school accountability at the forefront of educational policy (e.g. the No Child Left Behind Act in 2001), it has become clear that if all students are to meet rigorous academic standards, assessment tools are needed to track student progress toward those standards and to quickly and accurately identify students at risk for failing to meet them. Moreover, some have suggested the use of progress monitoring as part of a nondiscriminatory, response-to-intervention approach for special education referral and identification (Fuchs and Fuchs 2006; Speece, Case, and Molloy 2003). For students receiving special education services, progress monitoring is viewed as a way to uphold major tenets of the Individuals with Disabilities Education Improvement Act (IDEIA 2004) by aligning goals and objectives on Individualized Education Programmes with performance and progress in the general curriculum (Nolet and McLaughlin 2000).

Diagnostic assessment: the benefits to assessing learning

The importance of diagnostic assessment in designing instruction as well as in determining the placement of students cannot be over-emphasized. As indicated by Engelmann, Granzin, and Severson (1979), assessment must begin with instructional diagnosis, the purpose of which is 'to determine aspects of instruction that are inadequate, to find out precisely how they are inadequate, and imply what must be done to correct their inadequacy' (p. 361). In addition, the special educator assesses general areas of weakness in greater depth through the use of diagnostic instruments. These instruments aid the teacher in educational planning by revealing types of errors the student makes as well as strengths that may be used to determine the proper instructional level and possible teaching and learning strategies. The use of diagnostic instruments can also help the teacher in designing informal instruments and probes to assess student progress using direct measurement techniques.

Even though measurement is seldom addressed specifically with special education, it is important for the assessment process. Within educational psychology, a test is a systematic measure for a sample of behaviour. Measurement is the assignment of numbers to test scores or the qualitative description of behaviour based on rules. These are six steps to test construction. First, a table of specification is developed that explains the purpose of a test. Second, from the table of specification, the forms and content of test items are generated. Third, items are tested with individuals and modified based on feedback from the individuals taking the test and individuals administering the test. Fourth, the procedures for administering and scoring the test are standardized. Fifth, reliability (consistency of test scores) and validity (determining what a test measures) are developed from the test data. Sixth, norms (averages and standards for test performance) are developed for the test.

Measurement, whether it is quantitative or qualitative, involves levels. Traditionally, psychologists have broken down measurement into four levels or hierarchies: naming, ranking, quasi-intervals, and real intervals. The naming of variables is called nominal levels of measurements. For example, the names in a classroom would represent this level of measurement. Ordinal measures assign numbers to correspond to ranks of some attribute. For example, international talent shows use judges to rank distinct characteristics of the contestants. Quasi-intervals are common levels of measurement within educational psychology. This level of measurement includes scores of various tests such as IQ scores, achievement tests, personality tests e.g. the Minnesota Multiphasic Personality Inventory (MMPI), and college entrance examinations.

Quasi-intervals occur when equal differences between measures represent the same amount of difference. For example, the difference between 25 degrees Celsius and 30 degrees Celsius, and 15 degrees Celsius and 20 degrees Celsius is five degrees; hence the difference is equal. One major difficulty with quasi-interval measures such as IQ scores is that the IQ difference between 90 and 100 does not have the same meaning as the difference between scores of 120 and 130. Specifically, quasi-interval scores do not have true zero points. For example, what would the meaning of zero IQ suggest, or do zero degrees suggest the absence of temperature? Apparently, zero is a relative value for quasi-interval test scores. Ratio scales of measurement have real intervals. For example, 6 centimetres is twice the distance of 3 centimetres, and zero centimetres represents that no distance exists. In essence, ratio scales, many of which are used in physics and chemistry, have absolute or real zeros.

Measurement and its results-testing and assessment are based on theories. As previously stated, before students can be diagnosed and assessed, reliable and valid measures must be used. Unlike the general confusion within educational psychology, reliability and validity are based on test theories. Classical test theory, generalizability theory, and item response theory are the three dominant test theories within educational psychology (Allen and Yen 2001).

'Classical test theory' is the model often presented within educational psychology measurement courses, and educational psychologists have used this theory since the early 1900s (Allen and Yen 2001). This model is useful for small research projects, and it states that a student's score received on a test or assessment is the result of that student's true score plus some error. A student's true score and error score are both theoretical constructs. Specifically, a student's true score is the mean or average of the theoretical distribution of a student's scores that would be obtained from an infinite number of repeated testings of the same student with the same test or assessment. Because an infinite number of testings is impossible, a student's true score is a theoretical score. A student's error score takes account of the inconsistency or lack of perfect ability to measure concepts; it is not a mistake, but a theoretical construct.

Several assumptions can be drawn from the classical test theory. First, the observed variance of a group of students' scores equals the students' true score variance on a test plus the students' error variance, and this assumption leads to a theoretical definition of reliability or the consistency of test scores. Basically, reliability is the ratio of a group of students' true score test variance divided by their observed score test variance. Since variances are being divided, reliability is always a squared value or analogous to a square correlation. The Wechsler Adult Intelligence Scale, 4th Edition (WAIS-IV) has an average of 100 and a standard deviation, or the degree to which scores vary from the average, of 15. Also, the standard error of measurement is 5. Even though this test can be criticized for lacking adequate samples of minorities (see Obiakor, Chapter 18, this volume, and Obiakor 2007), another issue in interpretation of a student's score is not using confidence intervals.

Ferguson (2007) and Sapp (2004) defined a confidence interval as an interval among an infinite number of intervals for a parameter such as population mean, population reliability coefficient, population proportion, population correlation coefficient, or population difference, in which one minus the alpha level (level of significance) would capture the population parameter for a certain percentage of the time. For example, for a population mean, 95 percent of these intervals would capture the population mean and 5 percent would not. In contrast to point estimates, which describe sample data, confidence intervals describe population characteristics. In reality, confidence intervals allow researchers to put a lower limit and an upper limit around a population parameter. The 95 percent and 99 percent are the most used intervals, but any interval width can be established. For the 99 percent interval, a researcher is assuming that 99 percent of these intervals capture these population parameters, and 1 percent would not. Clearly, a 99 percent interval is wider than a 95 percent one (Sapp et al. 2007; Thompson 2002).

Confidence intervals can be placed around IQ and other standardized scores. For example, as previously stated, the WAIS-IV, a commonly used measure of intelligence, has a standard error of measurement of 5. Because the standard error of measurement is interpreted in terms of the normal distribution curve, confidence intervals can be formed around IQ scores. For example, if a student had an IQ score of 100 on the WAIS-IV, this IQ score of 100 plus or minus one times the standard error approximates the 68 percent confidence interval. The IQ score of 100 minus the standard error of 5 equals 95, which is the lower limit and the IQ score of 100 plus 5 equals the upper limit. This means for 68 percent of the time we can expect this student's true IQ score to fall between 95 and 105. Similarly, 100 plus or minus 1.96 times the standard error of measurement (5) represents the 95 percent confidence interval. Finally, 100 plus or minus 2.8 times the standard error of measurement forms the 99 percent confidence interval.

'Generalizability theory' broadens and extends classical test score theory by showing that reliability did not have to be restricted to the parts theorized within the classical theory – true scores and error scores. This theory allows a practitioner to determine how many occasions, test forms, and test administrations are needed to get reliable scores. For example, if a group of students were measured on three occasions, on three variables, this could be analysed through a generalizability analysis. Often, such a design is described as 'individuals by occasions by variables'; hence, there are more sources than the two-component design of the classical theory.

Both the classical test theory and generalizability test theory are based on groups of students or participants. In contrast, 'item response theory' is not a group method and it is a form of item analysis that is often used in large-scale testing. In reality, item response theory is an individual method of assessment, while classical test theory and generalizability theory are group methods of assessment. Moreover, classical test theory is based on the number of students or persons who succeed on an item (item difficulty) and the degree to which items discriminate among students or individuals (item discrimination). Both item difficulty and item discrimination are based on norms of a standardization sample. In contrast, item response theory makes no assumptions about the students or individuals involved; instead, a student's or individual's score is the arithmetic product of their ability on an item and item difficulty. The greater a student's or individual's ability, the more likely it is that a student or individual will get an item correct.

Diagnostic tests may be used to measure mastery of specific skills, strengths, and weaknesses whenever the educator wishes to monitor student progress or change the educational programme. These tests may be used as a part of the eligibility testing, for re-evaluation for annual reviews, or for further diagnostic planning within the classroom (Overton 1996). Because these instruments may be used more frequently than general achievement tests, the educator should select the tests or subtests carefully. The special education teacher should select diagnostic assessment tools based on the content area, the method of assessment (oral questions, oral reading, maths paper and pencil items, silently read items, timed or untimed tests, etc.), and the method of response (written responses, oral responses, pointing, etc.) required of the student. The format for presentation and response should be considered when interpreting results and making educational intervention plans.

When deciding what information to examine and use, it is important to draw from several kinds of information to avoid hasty conclusions based on one piece of data. You want to see a pattern emerge across several sources before you draw any firm conclusions (Chapman and King 2005). This process of developing an accurate conclusion based on several sources is often called 'triangulation'. When getting a sense of student skills and knowledge, you must look for convergence from several sources of information. As indicated earlier, assessment can allow teachers to identify students' current strengths and, as a consequence, can help them avoid superfluous and wasteful instruction. Thus, by measuring students' current status, teachers can discern (i) where to put their instructional energies to ameliorate a student's weaknesses and (ii) what already mastered skills or knowledge can be instructionally avoided. Such diagnostic assessment is particularly useful for a teacher's planning if the assessment is carried out at the beginning of an instructional sequence. This kind of early diagnosis is often referred to as 'pre-assessment' because it is assessment that takes place prior to the teacher's initiation of instruction. In other words, diagnostic assessment is a detailed evaluation of a child's strengths and weaknesses in several areas, such as cognitive, academic language, and social functioning. It involves a range of purposes, including diagnosis (determining the classification that best reflects the child's level and type of functioning), assisting in the determination of mental illness or educational disabilities, and making suggestions for placement and intervention.

To design an effective pre-unit diagnostic assessment, a few key steps must be followed. The procedures listed below will help the teacher choose simple and efficient methods for gathering the information needed to design instruction that works for all students.

1. *Prioritize content from the learning goals:* Learning goals and standards are the foundation for every unit. In designing pre-assessment, the teacher must consult these goals and prioritize the content. If a learning goal has several parts, you will probably focus on the most central or important for your pre-assessment.
2. *Design and administer brief measures of top-priority content:* The purpose of the diagnostic assessment is to provide general patterns of gaps and mastery so the teacher can get the unit's instructional sequence started. Therefore, the teacher must decide what methods of assessment capture prioritized learning goals.
3. *Measuring knowledge/understanding:* If the teacher is measuring knowledge and understanding, they can have students answer questions orally or on paper. Usually two or three questions per learning goal are sufficient, especially when one is quite certain that students are not likely to have encountered the content of the unit before.
4. *Measuring skills/strategies/procedures:* If the learning goal requires students to perform skills, strategies, or procedures, before instruction begins, the teacher needs to set up a method for observing them perform the key skills or a representative subset of skills. The teacher rates their level of performance with a scoring guide. Measuring skills is crucial in disciplines where most learning is centred on performing specific skills, such as physical education, art, music, or dance (Green and Johnson 2010).

Unlike screening instruments, which provide an overview of learning problems, diagnostic instruments produce a comprehensive, in-depth evaluation of performance. As indicated earlier, special educators require such diagnostic information to identify students who require special education services, to place students into appropriate special education programming, to develop intervention objectives, and to measure progress. To meet these diverse requirements, professionals may select from a variety of diagnostic scales. It is beyond the scope of this chapter to provide a full list of the different diagnostic assessment instruments that are available; however, some examples of those most commonly used by teachers in the USA (Overton 2012) include the KeyMath3 Diagnostic Assessment (Connolly 2007) and the Woodcock-Johnson III Diagnostic Reading Battery (Schrank, Mather, and Woodcock 2004). In the United Kingdom and wider Europe, other diagnostic assessment instruments such as the British Picture Vocabulary Scales

II (Dunn et al. 1997) and the British Ability Scales II (Elliot, Smith, and McUlloch 1996) are commonly used. Additionally, within the USA and around the globe, the Diagnostic and Statistical Manual of Mental Disorders (DSM) is commonly used to make diagnoses (Sapp 2010), although the International Classification of Diseases (ICD) is also used. An educational psychologist is likely to use a range of diagnostic assessments to arrive at a diagnosis using the criteria outlined in either the DSM or the ICD.

Other types of assessment

'Formative' assessment refers to the ongoing assessment carried out by teachers, both formally and informally, during a unit of work. The results of formative assessments have a direct impact on the teaching materials and strategies employed immediately following the assessment. Results and observations are kept in the teacher's record books, or the children's own books. 'Summative' assessments occur at defined periods of the academic year such as pre-determined SAT tests, PRAXIS I or at the end of a unit of work. Summative tests help teachers in making end-of-key-stage 'best fit' assessments and are also of use in determining the overall subject level for pupil record cards. Further information on formative and summative assessments can be found in Hall (Chapter 16, this volume). Lastly, 'dynamic' assessment is an interactive form of assessment. For example, if a child is given a pre-test or 'before' measure and an intervention or treatment, and then given a post-test or 'after' treatment measure, this allows an assessor to determine if the child is responding to an intervention. Dynamic assessment was influenced by Dame Marie Clay (1929–2007), who transformed the way educators and developmental psychologists viewed reading. In contrast to diagnosing students, she emphasized one-to-one support and early intervention (Clay 2005; McNaughton 2007).

Conclusion

Unlike screening tests, which provide an overview of learning, diagnostic assessment instruments produce a comprehensive, in-depth evaluation of performance – a methodology used to determine the instructional needs of students based on their performances within existing course content. More specifically, diagnostic assessment uses the material to be learned as the basis for assessing the degree to which it has been learned. Diagnostic assessment data provide useful information at three stages in the teaching process: before instruction, immediately following instruction, and periodically throughout the year to assess long-term retention.

Although diagnostic assessment data are useful for planning instruction for all students, the method is especially appropriate for use with students with special needs. Diagnostic assessment results focus attention on classroom-relevant skills students need to learn. As indicated earlier, special educators require such diagnostic information to identify students who require special education services, to place students into appropriate special education programmes, to develop intervention objectives, and to measure progress. To meet these diverse requirements, professionals may select from a variety of diagnostic assessment instruments.

In conclusion, assessment can be used differently throughout the world, and dynamic assessment appears to have greater utility than traditional assessment methods that are commonly used within the USA. Internationally, researchers and scholars understand that assessment must be tied to enhancing education, and assessment that is used just to classify is of little utility.

Contact address: sunday.obi@kysu.edu

References

Allen, M. J., and Yen, W. M. (2001) *Introduction to measurement theory*, 2nd edn, Belmont, CA: Wadsworth/ Thompson Learning.

Chapman, C., and King, R. (2005) *Differentiated assessment strategies*, Thousand Oaks, CA: Corwin Press.

Clay, M. M. (2005) *Literacy lessons designed for individuals: part two: teaching procedures*, Portsmouth, NH: Heinemann.

Connolly, A. J. (2007) *KeyMath 3: Diagnostic Battery*, Minneapolis, MN: NCS Pearson, Inc.

Cooper, J. M., and TenBrink, T. (2003) *An educator's guide to classroom assessment*, New York: Houghton.

Dunn, L. M., Dunn, L. M., Whetton, C., and Burley, J. (1997) *British Picture Vocabulary Scales II*, Windsor: NFER-Nelson.

Earl, L. (2003) *Assessment as learning*, Thousand Oaks, CA: Corwin Press.

Elliot, C. D., Smith, P., and McUlloch, K. (1996) *British Ability Scales II*, Windsor: NFER-Nelson.

Engelmann, W., Granzin, A., and Severson, H. (1979) 'Diagnosing instruction', *Journal of Special Education*, 13: 355–365.

Ferguson, C. J. (2007) 'Evidence for publication bias in video game violence literature: a meta-analytic review', *Aggression and Violent Behavior*, 12: 470–482.

Fuchs, D., and Fuchs, L. S. (2006) 'Introduction to responsiveness-to-intervention: what, why, and how valid is it?', *Reading Research Quarterly*, 41: 92–99.

Green, S. R., and Johnson, D. K. (2010) *Assessment is essential*, New York: McGraw-Hill.

Individuals with Disabilities Education Improvement Act (2004) [online]. Available at http://idea.ed.gov

McNaughton, S. (2007) 'Dame Professor Emerita Marie Clay, DBE, MA (Hons), Dip Ed, PhD, FRSNZ, FNZPSS, FNZEI, 1926–2007', *Journal of Early Childhood Literacy*, 7: 263–266.

Moon, T. (2005) 'The role of assessment in differentiation', *Theory into Practice*, 44: 226–233.

Nolet, V., and McLaughlin, M. J. (2000) *Accessing the general curriculum: including students with disabilities in standards-based reform*, Thousand Oaks, CA: Corwin Press.

Obiakor, F. E. (2007) *Multicultural special education: culturally responsive teaching*, Upper Saddle River, NJ: Pearson.

Overton, T. (1996) *Assessment in special education: an applied approach*, 2nd edn, Upper Saddle River, NJ: Merrill.

Overton, T. (2012) *Assessment in special education: an applied approach*, 7th edn, Upper Saddle, NJ: Pearson.

Pelligrino, J. W., Chudowsky, N., and Glaser, R. (2001) *Knowing what students know: the science and design of education assessment*, Washington, DC: National Academy Press.

Sapp, M. (2004) 'Confidence intervals within hypnosis research', *Sleep and Hypnosis*, 6: 169–171.

Sapp, M. (2010) 'Diagnosis and classification', in E. Baker, P. Peterson, and B. McGaw (eds.) *International encyclopedia of education*, 3rd edn, Oxford: Elsevier (pp. 577–583).

Sapp, M., Obiakor, F. E., Scholze, S., and Gregas, A. J. (2007) 'Confidence intervals and hypnosis in treatment of obesity', *Australian Journal of Clinical Hypnotherapy and Hypnosis*, 28: 125–133.

Schrank, F. A., Mather, N., and Woodcock, R. W. (2004) *Woodcock-Johnson III diagnostic reading battery*, Rolling Meadows IL: Riverside Publishing.

Speece, D. L., Case, L. P., and Molloy, D. E. (2003) 'Responsiveness to general education instruction as the first gate to learning disabilities identification', *Learning Disabilities Research and Practice*, 18: 147–156.

Thompson, B. (2002) '"Statistical," "practical," and "clinical". How many kinds of significance do counselors need to consider?', *Journal of Counseling and Development*, 80: 64–71.

Tomlinson, C. (2008) 'Learning to love assessment', *Educational Leadership*, 65: 8–13.

16

PURPOSES, APPROACHES AND TENSIONS IN ASSESSMENT POLICY AND PRACTICE

Kathy Hall

UNIVERSITY COLLEGE CORK, IRELAND

This chapter examines some current thinking in relation to assessment, noting the disconnect that sometimes obtains between policies and research perspectives. Current research on learning and assessment points to the significance of feedback, the learner's meaning making, understanding of success criteria, and personal involvement in target setting and judging success. However, policies are frequently oriented towards accountability, summative judgements, and normative evaluations, thus setting up a tension between assessment designed to support curriculum, teaching and learning, and assessment designed to support accountability and comparability agendas.

The chapter starts by noting the significance of assessment to school life and by describing what one educationist recommended about the assessment system in England. It goes on to define and explain key concepts in assessment pertaining to curriculum including different assessment purposes and functions, paying particular attention to formative and summative approaches. The chapter highlights the difficulties of designing assessments that address both learning-oriented and accountability purposes. In so doing it draws on the author's research on how England compares with other countries in the status it attributes to different kinds of assessment for primary school learners. It concludes by highlighting the kind of assessment that best fits with lifelong learning and with contemporary thinking about the learning process, and it speculates about the implications of global trends in assessment.

Testing testing

Virtually all of us who have been through the school system will recall many times when we were assessed as individuals, times when we were not allowed to confer with our peers but had to sit silently, possibly in a long hall with few resources other than pencil and paper, and try to remember facts, ideas, reasons, solutions, words, definitions, even formulae, and reproduce them in legible handwriting within a specified time period. Most of us will have long forgotten much of what we reproduced in such circumstances but we will have obtained marks or grades according to a mix of our labours, luck, and ability to remember on the day, as well as according to how we were taught the material in question and how well we learned the game of doing the test.

Test results will have had life consequences for many of us. While we may have forgotten the subject matter of the tests we sat, we will not have forgotten the emotions that went along with being tested: emotions that may still linger and may emerge, for some of us, as nightmares about not having started to write the answers to the test paper questions with the time almost up, and we are truly panicked. Tests, assessments, being judged, being compared with peers, and having our performance measured remain part and parcel of school life. In some respects little has changed on the assessment front over several generations. Yet we now know a great deal about different kinds of assessment and their impact on learning, and we understand much more about the interplay of politics, policies, and assessment practices.

Before discussing different types and purposes of assessment, consider an interesting, perhaps radical, suggestion by one eminent researcher of assessment – Dylan Wiliam (2001:61). Referring to England, he is concerned about the way external testing compromises the notion of a broad and balanced curriculum since teachers inevitably feel forced to concentrate their teaching on the narrow aspects that get tested ('teaching to the test') and to neglect broader aspects of learning that go untested. He asks the following questions.

- Why are students tested as individuals, when the world of work requires people who can work well in a team?
- Why do we test memory, when in the real world engineers and scientists never rely on memory? If they're stuck, they look things up.
- Why do we use timed tests when it is usually far more important to get things done right than to get things done quickly?

Wiliam proposes that all external tests, including those currently taken at the end of compulsory schooling and at the end of post-primary education, should be replaced with teacher assessment. He suggests that good teacher assessments should be extended over several years of a learner's schooling, with built-in procedures for supporting consistency and fairness across schools. He envisages that there would be a large number of assessment tasks available for use but that not all students would undertake the same tasks. These assessment tasks would cover the entire curriculum and would be allocated randomly. This would guard against teaching to the test. As he puts it, 'the only way to teach to the test would be to teach the whole curriculum to every student' (Wiliam 2001: 62). Schools that risked teaching only some of the curriculum, or that concentrated their resources on only some children – say, the most able children – would be shown up as ineffective in this scenario.

It is interesting to note that in Sweden and, to a lesser extent, in Norway, assessments are randomly allocated to students. In other words, one would not have to sit all the assessments though one would study for all of them. One would not know until close to the assessment time whether one would sit, say, mathematics or geography. It is likely that it would be quite difficult to persuade various groups in society in England and the UK in general to shift towards a Scandinavian approach as described here.

What is assessment and what is it for?

Assessing learning is about collecting information or evidence on learners and making judgements about it. The evidence may be based on one or more of the following: what the learner says; what the learner does; what the learner produces. The evidence may come from the learner's response to a set task, a test, classroom activity, a game or a puzzle. It may come from an event that is planned, or it may arise spontaneously from an unplanned happening. It may come from a task where several students work together on the same problem, or from tasks that they do on their own without interacting with other children. All the following settings offer potential opportunities for assessment: the classroom, the school dining room, the playground, the after-school club, the school gym, the assembly hall and many more.

Assessment may serve the following diverse purposes: to establish a level of student knowledge and understanding; to monitor student progress; to diagnose difficulties; to determine student ability to co-operate on a task with others and problem solve; to inform teaching and 'next steps' for the learner; to compare or rank students as groups or as individuals; to provide information to outside agencies such as parents, other teachers/professionals, government; i.e. to hold the class, teacher, school, or education system to account. Some purposes can be addressed simultaneously; for example, monitoring student progress and seeking information to help decide the next steps for a learner.

However, other purposes are usually in tension: assessing learners for the purpose of helping them to improve can't easily be accommodated alongside assessing them for the purpose of comparing schools and holding them to account in a public way. Comparisons are facilitated through the publication of results in the press or school prospectuses where schools are ranked according to their results. When the purpose of assessment is to facilitate school comparisons, the emphasis shifts from the individual learner to individual schools. Also, when the emphasis of assessment is on ranking or comparing individuals to allocate candidates to third level courses that are in limited supply, once again the emphasis shifts from the individual learner's absolute result and progress to the individual learner's results compared to other candidates who took the same assessment.

Assessments that emphasize the relative success of schools or individuals are described as 'high stakes' assessments since their results have very significant consequences. In the case of individuals, the consequences can be life-changing. Such assessment methods need to be designed so that they are comparable across all schools and individuals and across the country as a whole (Black et al. 2003). The main assessment method for such purposes is formal tests (devised externally). Such tests are usually removed from day-to-day teaching and learning, and tend to be carried out at particular times of the year.

In contrast, assessments designed to inform student learning tend to be informal, integrated into day-to-day teaching and learning, and carried out in different ways by teachers and teaching assistants. Assessments used in schools, regardless of purpose, tend to be criterion-referenced and curriculum-related. Teachers tend not to use norm-referenced tests. However, criterion-referenced assessments, such as national curriculum assessments, are used in normative ways when students are compared and ranked against other students and when schools are compared and ranked one with another for the purposes of compiling tables sometimes called 'league tables'.

Broad curriculum-related criteria (or learning outcomes) are specified for various stages of a student's school career in all subject areas and these criteria are intended to inform teachers about what is an age-appropriate level to be achieved. These criteria are specified in terms of level descriptions. Used in all four parts of the UK, level descriptions are summary prose statements that describe the types and range of performance which pupils are expected to demonstrate at various stages in their schooling. Teachers have to judge which level 'best fits' a student's performance for each area of the curriculum. This involves crosschecking against adjacent levels in a scale and considering the balance of strengths and weaknesses for each particular student. The specification of assessment expectations or criteria in terms of curriculum achievement fits with an emphasis on opportunity to learn. In other words, assessment is focused on the curriculum and not on attributes such as potential or on aspects of learning that are not part of the official curriculum. This is an important point and a key merit of the approach to assessment.

The titles and content of two further chapters in this volume – on 'diagnostic' assessment (Obi and Sapp, Chapter 15) and 'classroom' assessment (Salend, Chapter 14) – attest to the wide range of terminology and descriptors of assessment forms, functions, and purposes. Most types of assessment can also be described as either primarily formative or summative in orientation, and the next section considers assessment in relation to these terms.

Formative and summative assessment

The term 'formative assessment' describes any assessment that is used to support learning. Assessment is formative when the learners use information from assessment to bridge the gap between what they can do and what they need to be able to do, or between what they know and what they need to know. It is formative when the learner uses the information to improve.

In formative assessment it is arguable that the most important assessors are the students themselves. This might take the form of individual students reflecting on and assessing themselves against their previous performance or achievement. This is sometimes referred to as 'ipsative assessment'. It could also take the form of peer assessment, where students are encouraged to judge the performance of peers and explain their reasons for their interpretations and judgements. Getting students to reflect on their own learning and to assess themselves is the key to linking assessment and learning. The following list describes some practices that teachers have successfully used to help children use assessment to assess themselves (see Black et al. 2003).

1. Sharing learning intentions with the class or the group at the start of the lesson.
2. Allowing time for individuals or groups to feed back on what they have learnt at the end of the lesson.
3. Allowing 'wait time' after questions to give children thinking time.
4. Abandoning the requirement for children to raise hands for permission to speak.

If one asked young learners (up to about age eight years), especially those who are finding learning difficult, how they produce good work, many would say that 'effort' plays a major role but they would not mention 'skill'. They often assume that 'trying harder' is the solution to their lack of success in a task. This could lead one to conclude that children believe learning is heavily influenced by effort and, as such, is very much within their control. There would seem to be some truth in this; a lot of learning in school does require that children make an effort, especially when adults are setting the tasks. However, young learners are often naïve in their judgements, implicating the need for more effort, even when they have tried very hard. Teachers/assessors frequently comment positively on the amount of effort learners make. But what is crucial is that assessors make explicit 'what' learners need to do to improve. Of course, time and practice play their part, but an emphasis on 'how to improve' is key. If this does not happen, assessors may be contributing to children's somewhat naïve beliefs about the role of effort in correcting learning problems.

If one knows the criteria against which one's work is judged, then one is clearly better placed to produce a good piece of work. Making the rules of learning explicit for students tells them what they must do to improve. Research has shown that so-called 'low achievers' do especially well in classrooms where formative assessment is a strong feature (e.g. Black and Wiliam 1998; Wiliam 2011). One explanation offered by these researchers for this is that such children may have previously suffered from a lack of clear guidance on what counted as success rather than from any lack of ability. This is an interesting and important point, as it shows how schooling practices can be implicated in the production of failure or at least low achievement. It also shows how assessment practices are not neutral – they may have unintended consequences for learners and may disempower as well as empower.

Already mentioned is how external tests or national tests are used as a basis for the compilation of league tables in England. These assessments are described as 'summative', although they are not the only form of summative assessments used in schools. Summative assessment tries to sum up a student's attainment in a given area of the curriculum. The intention is to make an assessment 'of' (as opposed to 'for') learning. These tests usually assess a very limited range of learning, but because of their high profile, they can exert a powerful influence over what is taught in schools and are therefore 'high stakes' assessments. This is especially the case at Key Stage 2 (11-year-olds/end of Year 6 in primary school). In England and Northern Ireland, children are obliged to take national tests at the end of Key Stage 2. In addition, some schools use optional tests before Year 6. In Scotland, national assessments comprise assessment materials designed to confirm teachers' judgements about children's levels of attainment in English language and mathematics (see Learning and Teaching Scotland 2012). England's Department for Education (DfE) recently reported (June 2011) on a review of the primary and secondary National Curriculum assessment (DfE 2011). There is a recognition in this work that teacher assessment merits greater status in England since it is better placed (than external tests) to support and record children's holistic development, to enhance creativity, and to describe progression. This recognition brings assessment policy in England somewhat closer to policies and practices in other countries, a theme that is briefly discussed later in this chapter.

Summative assessment is retrospective in that it looks back at what has been achieved, perhaps over a term, year, or key stage. Formative assessment, in contrast, is prospective: it looks forward to the next steps of learning. However, debate continues over whether and how summative and formative assessment should be distinguished (Threlfall 2005).

The use of a variety of ways of assessing learning allows the production of evidence of learning from diverse contexts, thus avoiding making judgements about learning based on a single source of evidence, e.g. a pencil and paper test. This yields information that is more accurate and trustworthy than results deriving from just one assessment in one situation and enhances validity and dependability. Looking across several instances in which a student uses, say, reading provides valuable, potentially wide-ranging information about a student as a reader. Judgements based on the use of a variety of sources of assessment information are of course more demanding on time and resources. This means that teachers and policy makers have to consider how to get an appropriate balance between validity and trustworthiness of assessment evidence on one hand and manageability and cost on the other. Getting this balance right is a major source of contention, at least in England.

The impact of 'high stakes' assessment

Much has been written about the impact on pupils of different assessment purposes and practices (e.g. Harlen and Deakin-Crick 2002). The research shows that schools feel under considerable pressure to get more of their pupils achieving at higher levels in national tests. This pushes some teachers, especially those who have classes about to take national tests, to spend more time and energy on helping pupils to get good at doing those tests. This 'teaching to the test' means there is less time to develop pupils' skills and understanding in the various areas of the curriculum that are not assessed, and this in turn compromises the notion of a broad and balanced curriculum, the latter being an important principle of primary curriculum across the UK.

There is evidence that external pencil-and-paper tests, which are designed to offer evidence to the government about how schools are raising standards, get enormous attention in the daily life of pupils (e.g. Hall et al. 2004). Such is the perceived pressure in schools to do well in league tables that they sometimes feel unable to place sufficient emphasis on assessment designed to promote learning across the curriculum or on assessing learning through a variety of modes. The research shows that 'high stakes' assessment tends to push teachers to adopt transmission styles of teaching and to promote acquisition of knowledge at the expense of problem solving, skills, and more creative approaches to learning.

Assessment in England compared to other countries worldwide

An international comparative study of England's primary curriculum and assessment policies (Hall and Özerk 2010) showed that England is broadly in line with international trends in its curricular emphasis on language and literacy, mathematics, science, environmental studies, information technology, history, geography, social studies/civics, creative arts, music and dance, health and physical education, and religious education. Some time ago this state of affairs led Benavot et al. (1991: 98) to proclaim: 'We may speak with some confidence about a relatively standard world curriculum'. It would seem that as countries have reformed their curricula over the past two decades, greater convergence in curriculum provision is the result, not only in Anglo-American democracies and in Europe but in developing countries as well (Davies and Guppy 1997; Le Metais 2003).

Also there has been a strong trend in recent times in most countries towards external assessment, both statutory and voluntary. However, England stands out from other countries in relation to its emphasis on published league tables where individual schools are listed in relation to the aggregated attainments of their pupils, thus holding schools to account in a very public way (Hall and Özerk 2010). The USA and Norway are increasingly following this trend, but most other countries disseminate the results back to schools along with national aggregated results or they publish national trends only – the aim being to enable schools to compare their own performance with national trends and to alert schools to their relative weaknesses and strengths.

Individual school results are not typically published in the form of league tables in the national press in other countries. Some countries, specifically South Korea, Japan, and New Zealand, limit external assessments by requiring that only samples of pupils rather than a full population be assessed (Andrews, Brown, and Sargent 2007; Le Metais 2003). However, there is an increasing trend towards assessing all learners at some stage in their primary schooling – Spain for instance recently introduced external testing for all pupils. The USA and Australia operate external testing at the level of all and most states respectively, and several provinces in Canada implement provincial assessment programmes in the primary phase. England introduced its standard assessments earlier than many other European countries (Hall and Özerk 2010).

A more in-depth comparison of England with three other countries, namely, France, Norway, and Japan, and with the three other parts of the UK found that the scale of assessment for the purpose of monitoring and accountability is of quite a different order in England. Assessment for accountability purposes is significantly more stressed in England than in other parts of the UK, or in France, Norway, and Japan. England appears to be unique in subjecting its students to more external testing in more subjects and doing so more frequently. The comparative study conducted for the Cambridge Primary Review concluded that assessment in England is pervasive, highly consequential, and more generally assumed by the public to portray objectively the actual quality of primary education in schools (Hall and Özerk 2010).

As a result of the foregrounding of assessment for accountability in England there is a complex assessment industry and machinery within and without schools that is not paralleled in most other countries. Within schools, teachers administer and mark the externally designed tests (with some external moderation and monitoring) within specified time frames, while externally there are various national and local agencies that design, monitor, collect, check, record, and publish the results. Many researchers (e.g. Hall et al. 2004; Harlen 2010) have demonstrated the negative impact on pupil learning of the priority accorded to assessment for accountability over assessment that is designed to support learning directly. This has been found to impact in terms not only of motivation and self-esteem but also of the principle of the broad and balanced curriculum as noted earlier.

Since the conduct and publication of the Research Surveys associated with the Cambridge Primary Review (Alexander et al. 2010), it is noteworthy that England has tempered its emphasis on assessment for accountability by dropping its insistence on external testing for seven-year-olds; the latter are now only required to be assessed through teacher assessment.

How might one explain England's divergence from other countries in relation to the prominence of assessment for accountability purposes? A key explanation is that governments in England since the 1980s were preoccupied with 'standards' and with providing evaluative information about the country's education system. There was a significant breakdown in trust in the education system, and indeed in other parts of the public sector as well. Governments of all hues, but especially conservative governments, were eager to hold the education system to account. Part of this involved providing information about how effective schools are and to facilitate school choice on the part of parents. All of this is highly contentious and has been analysed and researched extensively (e.g. Wilkins 2011). The perceived link between educational achievement and international economic competitiveness is another explanation, although in itself this couldn't account for the emphasis England placed on assessment for accountability purposes in schools, since it would apply to other countries as well.

The status of assessment to support learning

This aspect has been emphasized earlier in the chapter and the use of formative assessment attests to a view of the learner as active, a chaser after meaning, and an agent with ideas, views, and feelings about how and why they are being assessed. There is considerable stress in England, as in other parts of the UK, on this kind of assessment: the kind that involves negotiation with learners, and involvement of pupils as self and peer assessors, and is integrated into teaching and learning in the classroom. Assessment policy right across the UK explicitly recognizes the role of the learner in the assessment enterprise and gives much attention in its guidance material to what is commonly called 'assessment for learning'.

Self-assessment and peer assessment are recommended for helping learners to understand, and sometimes frame, the criteria against which their work is judged. Qualitative accounts and prose descriptions of performance, as opposed to marks or grades, are encouraged, the intention being to focus learner attention on descriptions of quality and understanding of success criteria rather than merely obtaining 'high marks'. Having learners assess themselves in relation to their own previous performance, rather than normative evaluations involving ranking with peers, is also encouraged. This approach to assessment invites learners to negotiate and discuss their learning, to set targets for themselves, to monitor and describe their own progress and to consider their achievements in relation to evidence. It privileges talk and discussion about learning and links very well the idea of learning how to learn (James et al. 2007).

However, while policy in England promotes formative assessment and assessment for learning purposes, the high stakes nature of the assessments overall compromises its potential benefits for learners. This is a major flaw in assessment policy in England, and one that seriously undermines the potential that is there for formative assessment. The recent shift towards teacher assessment only for the youngest learners is a move towards obtaining a better balance between those two priorities of holding the education system to account on one hand and supporting the learning process itself on the other.

Conclusion: restoring the balance in assessment purposes

A sensible approach to tests and assessment tasks is to see them as indicators and partial snapshots of achievement, and not as a true representation of ability. There is serious danger in viewing test results as indicative of a fixed ability, and this is especially problematic in the case of similar ability teaching, streaming, and setting, where students are grouped for long periods based on test results. Such practices can and do have significant negative consequences, since similar ability grouping can limit what can be achieved by students. In this regard it is noteworthy that a recent large-scale study conducted at London's Institute of Education (Lucey 2012) shows that in the UK the practice of teaching primary pupils in ability 'streams' is much more common than might have been expected, with one in six UK children being taught in ability groups by age seven.

The point to note from the perspective of this chapter is that attention to the consequences of assessments is vital. That assessment data are at best a snapshot of a learner's achievement and that assessment evidence is always partial and context-dependent are principles that, if adopted, are likely to guard against the use of assessment information in ways that put boundaries around what learners can achieve.

Formative assessment aligns well with a contemporary (if not dominant) research-informed perspective on learning that recognizes the situatedness of all learning, the significance of the network of relations among co-participants in any learning setting, the influence of peers and co-participants, including the teacher, and the histories and identities that all participants bring to the task of learning. Central to this sociocultural view of learning (Hall, Murphy, and Soler 2008) is the idea that meanings are multiple, that all learners do not necessarily share the same view of a given task (including an assessment task or test) and that, therefore, dialogue, negotiation and sharing are necessary dimensions that have to be facilitated. In recognizing the importance of context on assessment, educators, assessors, and designers of assessment need to take account, for instance, of how the learner understands the assessment task and how the setting itself (peers, relationships, classroom, culture etc.) may influence the learners' take on the assessment task set for them. This is extremely important for day-to-day classroom assessment which is most likely to be formative in orientation, but it is also important in relation to summative assessments since the latter have the power to impact learners' sense of themselves, depending on how the results are used (Reay and Wiliam 1999).

There is still considerable scope for reducing the current emphasis on high stakes assessment in England in the interests of foregrounding assessment designed to promote learning. This seems to be better recognized now than in the 1990s and early 2000s, as evidenced by the reduction overall in the statutory external assessment that is required in the early years of school and by the greater dependence on teacher assessment. However, the introduction of a phonics screening check remains controversial (Rosen 2012). Formative assessment incorporating feedback and self and peer assessment has tremendous potential to advance student learning and motivation to learn, because it recognizes the need for negotiation with learners, for exploring meanings, and for discussing what the learner needs to do in precise terms in order to bridge the gap between where the learner is and where the learner needs to get to.

Learners also need to be able to establish their own goals for learning, which in turn suggests that they need to have the opportunity to negotiate with their teacher their own learning targets. This is vital if students are to become lifelong learners. It is also worth noting that educationists and researchers in England (e.g. Gipps 1994) did much pioneering work on formative assessment and along with other key researchers outside the UK (e.g. Shepard 2001) contributed hugely to theory building on assessment for learning. The political influence over the past three decades in England, however, with its emphasis on accountability, school choice, and comparisons, meant that policy didn't always capitalize on the pioneering work done on formative assessment.

In line with the international convergence evident in curriculum matters, it is likely that globalization means that we can expect increasing convergence in assessment matters as well. Yet it is also likely that individual countries will interpret and apply policies in locally specific ways, taking account of their particular histories, traditions, and needs.

Contact address: k.hall@ucc.ie

References

Alexander, R., Doddington, C., Gray, J., Hargreaves, L., and Kersher, R. (eds.) (2010) *The Cambridge primary review research surveys*, London: Routledge.

Andrews, C., Brown, R., and Sargent, C. (2007) *INCA Comparative Tables, Primary Education* [online]. Available at www.inca.org.uk/comparative_tables.html

Benavot, A., Cha, Y. K., Kamens, D., Meyer, J. W., and Wong, S. W. (1991) 'Knowledge for the masses: world models and national curricula, 1920–1986', *American Sociological Review*, 56: 85–100.

Black, P., Harrison, C., Lee, C., Marshall, B., and Wiliam, D. (2003) *Assessment for learning: putting it into practice*, Buckingham, UK: Open University Press.

Black, P., and Wiliam, D. (1998) 'Assessment and classroom learning', *Assessment in Education*, 5: 7–74.

Davies, S., and Guppy, N. (1997) 'Globalization and educational reforms in Anglo-American democracies', *Comparative Education Review*, 41: 435–459.

DfE (2011) *Independent Review of Key Stage 2 testing, assessment and accountability: Final Report*, Lord Bew, London: Stationery Office.

Gipps, C. (1994) *Beyond testing*, London: Falmer Press.

Hall, K., Collins, J., Benjamin, S., Sheehy, K., and Nind, M. (2004) 'SATurated models of pupildom: assessment and inclusion/exclusion', *British Educational Research Journal*, 30: 801–817.

Hall, K., Murphy, P., and Soler, J. (eds.) (2008) *Pedagogy and practice: culture and identities*, London: Sage.

Hall, K., and Özerk, K. (2010) 'Primary curriculum and assessment: England and other countries', in R. J. Alexander, C. Doddington, J. Gray, L. Hargreaves, and R. Kersher (eds.) *The Cambridge primary review research surveys*, London: Routledge (pp. 375–414).

Harlen, W. (2010) 'The quality of learning: assessment alternatives for the primary school', in R. J. Alexander, C. Doddington, J. Gray, L. Hargreaves, and R. Kersher (eds.) *The Cambridge primary review research surveys*, London: Routledge (pp. 435–460).

Harlen, W., and Deakin-Crick, R. (2002) 'A systematic review of the impact of summative assessment and tests on students' motivation for learning (EPPI-Centre Review, version 1.1)', in *Research Evidence in Education Library*, London: EPPI-Centre, Social Science Research Unit, Institute of Education.

James, M., McCormick, R., Black, P., Carmichael, P., Drummond, M. J., Fox, A., MacBeath, J., Marshall, B., Pedder, D., Procter, R., Swaffield, S., Swann, J., and Wiliam, D. (2007) *Improving learning how to learn: classrooms, schools and networks*, London: Routledge.

Learning and Teaching Scotland (LTS) (2012) *Assessment* [online]. Available at www.ltscotland.org.uk/learningteachingandassessment/assessment/index.asp

Le Metais, J. (2003) International trends in primary education (INCA/QCA thematic study No. 9) [online]. Available at www.mpn.gov.rs/resursi/dokumenti/dok24-eng-INCA_international_trends.pdf

Lucey, C. (2012, 13 January) 'To set or not to set? You decide', *Times Educational Supplement*.

Reay, D., and Wiliam, D. (1999) '"I'll be a nothing": structure, agency and the construction of identity through assessment', *British Educational Research Journal*, 25: 343–354.

Rosen, M. (2012) *Phonics in the nursery?* [online]. Available at http://michaelrosenblog.blogspot.ie/2012/08/phonics-in-nursery-practitioner-writes.html

Shepard, L. A. (2001) 'The role of classroom assessment in teaching and learning', in V. Richardson (ed.) *The handbook of research on teaching*, 4th edn, Washington, DC: American Educational Research Association (pp. 1066–1101).

Threlfall, J. (2005) 'The formative use of assessment information in planning – the notion of contingent planning', *British Journal of Educational Studies*, 53: 54–65.

Wiliam, D. (2001) 'What is wrong with our educational assessment and what can be done about it?', *Education Review*, 15: 57–62.

Wiliam, D. (2011) 'What is assessment for learning?', *Studies in Educational Evaluation*, 37: 2–14.

Wilkins, A. (2011) 'Community and school choice: geographies of care and responsibility', *Journal of Community and Applied Social Psychology*, 21: 1–13.

17

LANGUAGE USE AND ASSESSMENT

Nenagh Kemp

UNIVERSITY OF TASMANIA, AUSTRALIA

Children are assessed regularly during their years at school. From early on, teachers ask children informal questions, give weekly quizzes, or set more formal tests. In many countries, children participate in regional or national tests of educational attainment. Educational psychologists administer standardised tests to individual children, and researchers sometimes invite children to complete specific experimental tasks. In all of these types of assessment, there is an important role for language, whether written or spoken. Children's performance depends not only on the extent to which they understand the task instructions, but also on the extent to which their expressive language abilities match the level required by the task.

This chapter considers the role of language in child assessment. The research presented comes largely from English-speaking countries, but the issues, and their potential solutions, are broad ones that extend across national, cultural, and linguistic borders. In some cases, a child's language skills might be poorer than expected because of a learning or language disability, or because the child is bilingual and still learning the language used at school. It is important to consider individual children's language skills when administering assessment tasks and interpreting their results, as general ability can be underestimated in tasks that rely heavily on language. The wording of the task itself can also be complex or misleading, and lead to underestimation of the assessed ability even in children with age-typical language skills.

Researchers and educators have devised various ways to overcome some of the difficulties associated with language-based testing. These 'accommodations' can be made to assessment materials or administration procedures, to allow students to demonstrate the full extent of their knowledge and skills. The chapter reviews some of the accommodations that have been used, with varying success, for various types of assessments. A child's performance on an assessment task can have important implications. The score or diagnosis can affect the opinion and expectations of the child and of parents and teachers; it can determine the extent of any academic support that might be required, and more generally, it can influence the conclusions drawn about children's skills at a given age. The role of language in assessment is thus relevant to anyone involved in testing children, including teachers, educational psychologists, and researchers.

Language difficulties experienced by children being assessed

In most school-based assessments, a child's level of language or literacy skill is the most important determinant of his or her ability to respond to the questions asked (Welsh and Bierman 2003). Children who have problems understanding or producing spoken, and especially written, language will find their school experience affected in numerous ways (Borgers, de Leeuw, and Hox 2000; Calhoon, Fuchs, and Hamlett 2000). Although the early emphasis is on 'learning to read', as students progress through the school grades, they need to 'read to learn'. This is the case not only for subjects that rely heavily on reading, such as English or geography, but also for science and maths, which depend on language skills to solve word problems, and to recall and use steps and rules (Calhoon et al. 2000). As noted in Littleton (Chapter 7, this volume), having effective educational dialogues can help children to make the most of the language skills they do have, to interact and learn in the classroom. However, language problems can have consequences for assessment throughout the school years.

Language-dependent assessment in children with learning or language disorders

Children diagnosed with a language disorder can struggle with the receptive and expressive language demands of many tests, even if their disorder is mild, or has been largely overcome. Children with a current or previous language impairment may experience specific difficulties with verbal learning and verbal memory (Baird et al. 2009; Bishop and McDonald 2009). This can mean they have difficulty remembering and understanding complex language; the very type of language often used in classrooms (Baird et al. 2009) and in some assessments.

Accommodations for children with learning or language disorders

It is important to minimise the potential barriers in assessments, and allow children with a disability to demonstrate their knowledge (Fuchs et al. 2000). Although the use of various forms of language-related accommodations is generally associated with improved performance, the evidence is inconsistent in places (as discussed below), and is the topic of continued research.

The 'read-aloud' accommodation seems to be one of the most effective for children with a reading or learning disability (for reviews see Cormier et al. 2010; Thompson, Blount, and Thurlow 2002). For example, children with a learning disability have been shown to perform significantly better on a maths test when a teacher reads the items aloud than when students read the text themselves (Calhoon et al. 2000; Tindal et al. 1998). This accommodation seems most beneficial when the questions require problem-solving (and thus a reasonable level of reading and writing skill), rather than more conventional mathematical concepts and computations (Fuchs et al. 2000). Oral presentation, at least in a group format, has the potential disadvantage of forcing all children to work at the same pace, which could lead to boredom for some students and distress for others. However, this accommodation is easily implemented, and does not require modifications to the test itself (Thompson et al. 2002). Individual oral administration is less time-efficient, but has the added advantage of giving each child the opportunity to work at his or her own pace (Thompson et al. 2002).

Instead of hand-writing, students can type their responses, or dictate them to a scribe or a computer programme. Students with a learning disability have been shown to produce longer and more complex responses when allowed to word-process rather than hand-write test answers (MacArthur and Graham 1987; Russell and Plati 2000), especially when the answers require more extended writing skills (Fuchs et al. 2000). Another simple and cost-effective accommodation is to allow more time for students to complete a task. Some studies have shown that children with a learning disability do better, and attempt more items, on standardised tasks when given extra time (e.g. Lewandoski, Lovett, and Rogers 2008), although other studies have not (e.g. Munger and Loyd 1991). The potential benefits may depend on a number of factors, including the literacy demands of the task (Fuchs et al. 2000). Allowing extra time is one of the most common accommodations offered to students with disabilities (Cormier et al. 2010), but it remains controversial, in terms of the extent to which it really benefits students and to which it allows scores to be compared with those of others.

Language-dependent assessment in children still learning the language of assessment

As outlined in Obiakor (Chapter 18, this volume), language difficulties are just one of the many challenges that may affect the school experience of children from immigrant or minority backgrounds, in classrooms around the world. With increasing migration worldwide (International Organization for Migration 2011), there are increasing numbers of children who are disadvantaged in academic assessments not because of a language disability, but because their home language is not the one used at school. A discrepancy between children's underlying knowledge and their ability to express that knowledge in the language of assessment can have serious consequences for academic opportunities (Robinson 2007).

There is ample evidence that students who are not proficient in the language of a test consistently receive lower scores than their peers in all subject areas (Abedi, Hofstetter, and Lord 2004). The vocabulary used in reading comprehension tests, for example, can be especially difficult for language learners, because they do not always know the synonyms often employed to prevent test takers from simply recognizing a previously used word (e.g. 'dog' vs. 'canine', 'mongrel'; García 1991). The use of overly complex sentence structures can also make understanding difficult, as can reading demands. In these cases, the challenges of the test language can reduce the validity and reliability of the test itself, and lead to unrealistically low estimates of ability assessed (Abedi 2002; Haladyna, Downing, and Rodriguez 2002).

Making a test appropriate for later learners of the test language is not a straightforward exercise. Sometimes it might be desirable to present a test in a child's first language instead, especially if the child is young, and/or has limited competency in the test language (Robinson 2007). However, assessors would be ill-advised simply to translate a test word-for-word into a second language. A word or phrase in one language often differs from the same word or phrase in another language, in terms of frequency, exact meaning, or typical word associations (Mueller Gathercole 2010). Further, some languages have multiple dialects, and so providing a translation into, for example, standard Urdu or Mandarin might not be helpful for children who are fluent in a dialect of this main language (Olson and Goldstein 1997).

If children are judged to have sufficient proficiency to be tested in the language of assessment, care must still be taken to ensure that gaps in linguistic skill are not interpreted as gaps in knowledge or ability. A child who does not know a word in one language is not necessarily ignorant of the concept it represents, and a child who cannot understand a question's wording will find it difficult to answer that question, no matter how deep his or her understanding of the underlying ideas. Assessors should therefore exercise caution in using monolingual norms to interpret the test performance of bilingual or multilingual children (Abedi et al. 2004), and consider finding tests with norms for both monolingual and bilingual test-takers (e.g. Verhoeven and Vermeer 1993).

Assessments of bilingual children's second language proficiency should also be made carefully. Many children's oral skills in their second language far outstrip their literacy skills (Cummins 1980). Thus, if a teacher uses a child's oral skills in a social context to estimate her second language level, the child may be allocated to a class whose written language requirements are too high, which can lead to reductions in performance, self-confidence, and motivation (Robinson 2007). Of course, there are some children learning a second or later language who also have a language or learning disorder. It is equally important that these children's difficulties be identified, so that they are not denied the opportunity to receive the support that they might need. If a bilingual child is to be diagnosed as having a learning or language disorder, it is clear that he should be diagnosed in both languages, not just one (Håkansson, Salameh, and Nettelbladt 2003).

Accommodations for children still learning the language of assessment

The use of test accommodations can reduce some of the gap between native speakers and learners of the language of assessment. As mentioned, the test can be translated into a child's native language. However, it is important to ensure that construct validity is maintained. As noted earlier, individual words and concepts do not always have a direct equivalent in another language. Another issue is that bilingual or multilingual children will be more familiar with the vocabulary of some academic subjects in the language of their school, rather than their home language. Thus, doing a test translated into the home language can be confusing and lead to lower scores (Butler and Stevens 1997). Abedi et al. (2004) therefore recommend that tasks translated back into students' home language should only be used with students who have had instruction in that language.

To avoid the potential problems of translation, a test can be kept in its original language, and students given access to a dictionary during the test, although dictionaries sometimes provide some of the very information being tested (Abedi et al. 2004). Even so, dictionary access does not necessarily lead to improved performance. Its efficacy seems to depend on students having the second-language proficiency, and the time, to make use of this accommodation (e.g. Abedi et al. 2000; Albus et al. 2001). Another possibility is to simplify the test's construct-irrelevant sentence structure and/or vocabulary. However, this accommodation appears to have mixed success, with some researchers reporting clear benefits (e.g. Abedi and Lord 2001) and others reporting no significant effects (e.g. Brown 1999; Floyd and Carrell 1987).

Many bilingual students find it impossible to complete tasks whose time limits are based on mainly monolingual samples (García and Pearson 1994), and thus bilingual students are often allowed extra time to complete assessments. Again, the evidence seems to be mixed, with some researchers reporting improvements (e.g. Abedi et al. 2000), and others reporting poorer performance on some tasks (e.g. Miller et al. 1999). Finally, children who do not yet have a high level of literacy in the language of the assessment may benefit from having the test administered orally, rather than in writing. As noted earlier, children may attain oral proficiency in their second language much earlier than written proficiency. Thus, this accommodation can allow children to demonstrate their knowledge without being hampered by their still-developing second language skills.

Issues in providing accommodations to help with language difficulties

In providing any of these extra supports, educators and researchers must take care that the accommodations give a realistic view of children's abilities, and do not reduce test validity or the comparability of scores with those of other children (Thompson et al. 2002). As Thompson et al. point out, the aim of providing accommodations should be to achieve valid measurement of children's abilities, rather than optimal scores. However, issues of time and resources mean that teachers tend to prefer test accommodations that do not require extensive or individualised modifications (Gajria, Salend, and Hemrick 1994).

In any case, it can be difficult for individual teachers to decide on the appropriate accommodations to allow. Fuchs et al. (2000) reported that children with a learning disability were sometimes denied accommodations that would have been helpful, but sometimes awarded more accommodations than were required. Both of these situations raise important issues. Denying valid accommodations may prevent children from demonstrating their competence to its full extent, which can have long-term effects on such children's educational trajectories, as well as their self-confidence (Robinson 2007). On the other hand, overly permissive accommodations can lead to spuriously inflated scores, which can in turn mean less incentive for children to improve, or for schools to provide the continued support that these children might need (McDonnell, McLaughlin, and Morison 1997). For these reasons, careful consideration should be given to the type and extent of accommodations offered to children to help them overcome language-based obstacles in assessment.

Language difficulties caused by the wording of the test

The language difficulties discussed so far have been those that result from children having atypically low levels of proficiency in the test language, which may limit their ability to demonstrate their knowledge. However, if the wording used in an assessment task has not been carefully crafted, problems can arise even for children with typical language skills. This issue is probably greater in smaller-scale assessments and in tasks designed by experimental researchers than in large-scale, standardised assessments. Nevertheless, the type of language used in smaller and experimental studies remains imperative to consider, as their results can still have implications for individual children, or for conclusions about children's abilities. Even for typically developing, monolingual children, the knowledge being measured by a task can be affected by the reading and vocabulary demands (Haladyna et al. 2002) and syntactic complexity (Welsh and Bierman 2003) of its questions.

The format of the test should be appropriate for the age and abilities of the intended respondents. For example, before about Grade 3, children's reading vocabulary and reading comprehension are usually too limited for them to respond reliably to written questionnaires (Stone and Lemanek 1990). The test items should also be constructed at a level that is appropriate for the age group being assessed. If questions or demands are too difficult to understand, children tend to respond idiosyncratically, or not at all (e.g. Crosby 1976; Kaler and Kopp 1990; Tyack and Ingram 1977). The exact wording of test questions also deserves some thought. Welsh and Bierman (2003) note that preschool children respond best to short, simple, concrete questions, using 'who', 'what', and 'where' (e.g. 'Who is your best friend?'), rather than open-ended or abstract questions, or questions using 'when' and 'why' (e.g. 'Why do you like that friend?'). Young children also tend to be very literal, and so questions should be worded carefully to avoid misunderstanding (Holoday and Turner-Henson 1989). Research reviewed by Borgers et al. (2000) confirms that question writers should avoid ambiguous wording and negatively worded questions, as well as depersonalised or indirect questions, which even older teenagers can find confusing. Finally, test designers should consider the demands on working memory, which is associated with children's reading comprehension (Higuchi et al. 2003).

Sometimes children are too shy to respond verbally to test questions. Building rapport before assessment can help improve response rates, but tests for younger children, especially, can also be designed to allow more minimal responses. For example, children can point to the correct answer (as in the Peabody Picture Vocabulary Test) or respond simply with 'yes' or 'no'. However, scoring should take account of children's bias to answer 'yes' (e.g. Moriguchi, Okanda, and Itakura 2008), or to select the final choice each time (e.g. Crandall, Crandall, and Katovsky 1965). Another possibility is to present children with an adapted Likert scale, using an unhappy, neutral, and happy face, or a picture of a gradated thermometer (Welsh and Bierman 2003). In these cases, it is important to check that children understand the measure before formal assessment begins.

The pragmatics of the questions asked can also influence children's ability to demonstrate their understanding. One striking example is the way that young children's performance on classic Piagetian tests of cognitive development (e.g. Piaget 1972) can vary with alterations to the way that questions are asked. For example, in one version of a task of conservation of number, a child is shown two equal rows of buttons, and asked 'Are there the same number of buttons in this row as there are in this row, or are there more here, or more here?'. Once the child has confirmed that the rows contain the same number, the experimenter moves the buttons in one row further apart, so that they form a longer row. The child is then asked the same question again. Up until the age of six or seven years, children who initially agreed that both rows contain the same number of buttons tend to reply that the spread-out row now contains more buttons. Piaget interpreted this robust finding as showing that children answering in this way could not 'conserve' number.

However, later research suggests that children's understanding of the task might be underestimated by the pragmatics of asking the same question twice, a practice which in everyday life suggests that the first answer needs to be amended. Children show greater apparent conservation in a range of Piagetian conservation tasks when the first question is simply omitted (e.g. Rose and Blank 1974; Samuel and Bryant 1984), when a different person asks the second question (e.g. Perner, Leekam, and Wimmer 1984), or when the child is distracted by an annoying or exciting disruption (Light, Buckingham, and Robbins 1979; McGarrigle and Donaldson 1975). These classic tasks, and their well-known variations, underscore the importance of considering pragmatic factors in the wording of questions in experimental tasks, if children's abilities are to be accurately assessed.

Even the words with which a task is presented can affect children's performance. Strang, Bridgeman, and Carrico (1974) found that when told that they would be 'playing a game', Grade 3 children did significantly better on three non-verbal subtests of the Wechsler Intelligence Scales for Children (WISC) than when told that they would be 'doing a test'. However, in a similar study with two WISC verbal subtests, children in Grade 6, but not in Grade 3, performed significantly better when told that they would be doing a test, rather than playing a game (Bridgeman, Strang, and Buttram 1974). Using a different task, Nguyen, Kemp, and Want (2011) found no difference in the ability of children in Grades 1 and 5 to learn novel words for novel concepts when they were told that the task was a 'fun game' than when it was an 'important test'. In contrast, Grade 2 children, who were given a difficult task and told that it was 'important', did better than when told it was 'fun', or given no instructions. Grade 5 children remained unaffected by task instructions (Kemp, Nguyen, and Walton 2008). Researchers should thus consider the verbal instructions that they use to present tasks to children, as the expectations created by the wording can affect performance.

The research discussed above highlights the importance of paying close attention to the language used to introduce and administer assessment tasks to children, whether these tasks are standardized or experimental. The individual words, the sentence structure, and memory load of the task instructions and content should all be appropriate for the age and abilities of the children being assessed. Test designers and administrators should also be aware that the pragmatics and the presentation of a task can, in some circumstances, influence performance.

Conclusions: language matters in assessment

Across languages and cultures, children are assessed informally and formally throughout their schooling. The nature of the language used in assessment, and the linguistic ability of the children being assessed, can both play an important role in determining the short- and long-term consequences of the assessment. As discussed in Littleton (Chapter 7, this volume), the 'classroom talk' that a teacher fosters can also influence children's ability, and willingness, to use language as a tool for learning and explaining concepts. Further, the opinions that teachers form about students from in-class assessment can influence their expectations about students. Teacher expectations can in turn influence the expectations that students have about themselves, and lead to self-fulfilling prophecies in terms of eventual school achievement (see Jussim and Harber 2005 for a review).

If a child receives a test score that is depressed by poor language ability, or by the confusing language of a test, he may lose interest or confidence and fail to put in as much effort in future. Further, the score that a child achieves in a regional or national testing programme may determine which class she enters, or whether she is eligible to receive extra support at school. In the experimental arena, if a test's wording is confusing or misleading, researchers may underestimate or overestimate children's abilities. While this may not affect individual study participants, it has important implications for the overall conclusions that are drawn about the abilities that children possess at a given age or educational level. Thus, teachers, assessors, and researchers should pay close attention to the role of language in assessment, and bear in mind the potentially important consequences it can have in making decisions about children's abilities, and the possible implications of such decisions for schools, for scientific understanding, and for individual students.

Acknowledgement

Thanks to Abbie Grace for help with the literature search.

Contact address: nenagh.kemp@utas.edu.au

References

Abedi, J. (2002) 'Standardized achievement tests and English language learners: psychometric issues', *Educational Assessment*, 8: 231–257.

Abedi, J., Hofstetter, C. H., and Lord, C. (2004) 'Assessment accommodations for English language learners: implications for policy-based empirical research', *Review of Educational Research*, 74: 1–18.

Abedi, J., Hofstetter, C. H., Lord, C., and Baker, E. (2000) 'Impact of accommodation strategies on English language learners' test performance', *Educational Measurement: Issues and Practice*, 19: 16–26.

Abedi, J., and Lord, C. (2001) 'The language factor in mathematics tests', *Applied Measurement in Education*, 14: 219–234.

Albus, D., Bielinski, J., Thurlow, M., and Liu, K. (2001) *The effect of a simplified English language dictionary on a reading test (LEP Projects Rep. 1)*, Minneapolis, MN: University of Minnesota, National Center on Educational Outcomes.

Baird, G., Dworzynski, K., Slonims, V., and Simonoff, E. (2009) 'Memory impairment in children with language impairment', *Developmental Medicine and Child Neurology*, 52: 535–540.

Bishop, D. V. M., and McDonald, D. (2009) 'Identifying language impairment in children: combining language test scores with parental report', *International Journal of Language and Communication Disorders*, 44: 600–615.

Borgers, N., de Leeuw, E., and Hox, J. (2000) 'Children as respondents in survey research: cognitive development and response quality', *Bullétin de Métholodogie Sociologique*, 66: 60–75.

Bridgeman, B., Strang, H. R., and Buttram, J. (1974) '"Game" versus "test" instructions for the WISC', *Journal of Educational Measurement*, 11: 285–288.

Brown, P. B. (1999) *Findings of the 1999 Plain Language Field Test (Publication T-99-013.1)*, Newark, DE: Delaware Education Research and Development Center, Inclusive Comprehensive Assessment Systems Project.

Butler, F. A., and Stevens, R. (1997) *Accommodation strategies for English language learners on large-scale assessments: student characteristics and other considerations (CSE Technical Report 448)*, University of California, Los Angeles: National Center for Research on Evaluation, Standards, and Student Testing.

Calhoon, M. B., Fuchs, L. S., and Hamlett, C. L. (2000) 'Effects of computer-based test accommodations on mathematics performance assessments for secondary students with learning disabilities', *Learning Disability Quarterly*, 23: 271–282.

Cormier, D. C., Altman, J. R., Shyyan, V., and Thurlow, M. L. (2010) *A summary of the research on the effects of test accommodations: 2007–2008 (Technical Report 56)*, Minneapolis, MN: University of Minnesota, National Center on Educational Outcomes.

Crandall, V. C., Crandall, V. J., and Katovsky, W. (1965) 'A children's social desirability questionnaire', *Journal of Consulting Psychology*, 29: 27–36.

Crosby, F. (1976) 'Early discourse agreement', *Journal of Child Language*, 3: 125–126.

Cummins, J. (1980) 'Psychological assessment of immigrant children: logic or intuition?' *Journal of Multilingual and Multicultural Development*, 1: 97–111.

Floyd, P., and Carrell, P. (1987) 'Effects on ESL reading of teaching cultural content schemata', *Language Learning*, 37: 89–108.

Fuchs, L. S., Fuchs, D., Eaton, S. B., Hamlett, C. L., and Karns, K. M. (2000) 'Supplemental teacher judgements of mathematics test accommodations with objective data sources', *School Psychology Review*, 29: 65–85.

Gajria, M., Salend, S. J., and Hemrick, M. (1994) 'Teacher acceptability of testing modifications for mainstreamed students', *Learning Disabilities Research and Practice*, 9: 236–243.

García, G. E. (1991) 'Factors influencing the English reading test performance of Spanish-speaking Hispanic students', *Reading Research Quarterly*, 26: 371–392.

García, G. E., and Pearson, P. D. (1994) 'Assessment and diversity', *Review of Research in Education*, 20: 337–391.

Håkansson, G., Salameh, E.-K., and Nettelbladt, U. (2003) 'Measuring language development in bilingual children: Swedish-Arabic children with and without language impairment', *Linguistics*, 41: 255–288.

Haladyna, T. M., Downing, S. M., and Rodriguez, M. (2002) 'A review of multiple-choice item-writing guidelines for classroom assessment', *Applied Measurement in Education*, 15: 309–334.

Higuchi, K., Takahashi, T., Komatsu, S., and Imada, R. (2003) 'Children's ability to comprehend language: assessment tests for children with difficulties in reading and listening comprehension', *Japanese Journal of Special Education*, 41: 227–234.

Holoday, B., and Turner-Henson, A. (1989) 'Response effects in surveys with school-age children', *Nursing Research*, 38: 248–250.

International Organization for Migration (2011) *Facts and figures* [online]. Available at www.iom.int/cms/en/sites/iom/home/about-migration/facts—figures-1.html

Jussim, L., and Harber, K. D. (2005) 'Teacher expectations and self-fulfilling prophecies: knowns and unknowns, resolved and unresolved controversies', *Personality and Social Psychology Review*, 9: 131–155.

Kaler, S., and Kopp, C. (1990) 'Compliance and comprehension in very young toddlers', *Child Development*, 61: 1997–2003.

Kemp, N., Nguyen, D., and Walton, J. (2008) 'Fun or important? The effects of task content and instructions on children's performance', Poster presented at the 20th Annual Meeting of the International Society for the Study of Behavioural Development, Würzburg, Germany, 14–17 July.

Lewandoski, L. J., Lovett, B. J., and Rogers, C. (2008) 'Extended time as a testing accommodation for students with reading disabilities: does a rising tide lift all ships?' *Journal of Psychoeducational Assessment*, 26: 315–324.

Light, P. H., Buckingham, N., and Robbins, A. H. (1979) 'The conservation task as an interactional setting', *British Journal of Educational Psychology*, 49: 304–310.

MacArthur, C. A., and Graham, S. (1987) 'Learning disabled students' composing under three methods of text production: handwriting, word processing, and dictation', *Journal of Special Education*, 21: 22–42.

McDonnell, L. M., McLaughlin, M. W., and Morison, P. (1997) *Educating one and all: students with disabilities and standards-based reform*, Washington, DC: National Academic Press.

McGarrigle, J., and Donaldson, M. (1975) 'Conservation accidents', *Cognition*, 3: 341–350.

Miller, E. R., Okum, J., Sinai, R., and Miller, K. S. (1999) 'A study of the English language readiness of limited English proficient students to participate in New Jersey's statewide assessment system', Paper presented at the Annual Meeting of the National Council on Measurement in Education, Montreal, 20–22 April.

Moriguchi, Y., Okanda, M., and Itakura, S. (2008) 'Young children's yes bias: how does it relate to verbal ability, inhibitory control, and theory of mind?' *First Language*, 28: 431–442.

Mueller Gathercole, V. C. (2010) 'Bilingual children: language and assessment issues for educators', in K. Littleton, C. Wood, and J. K. Staarman (eds.) *International handbook of psychology of education*, Bingley, UK: Emerald (pp. 713–47).

Munger, G. F., and Loyd, B. H. (1991) 'Effect of speededness on test performance of handicapped and nonhandicapped examinees', *Journal of Educational Research*, 85: 53–57.

Nguyen, D., Kemp, N., and Want, S. C. (2011) 'The effects of funny and serious task content and expectations of fun versus importance on children's cognitive performance', *Australian Journal of Psychology*, 11: 27–38.

Olson, J. F., and Goldstein, A. A. (1997) *The inclusion of students with disabilities and limited English proficiency students in large-scale assessments: a summary of recent progress. NCES Publication No. 97-482*, Washington, DC: National Center for Education Statistics.

Perner, J., Leekam, S., and Wimmer, H. (1984) 'The insincerity of conservation questions', Paper presented at British Psychological Society Developmental Section Conference, Lancaster, UK, September.

Piaget, J. (1972) 'Development and learning', in C. S. Lavatelli and F. Stendler (eds.) *Readings in child behaviour and development*, New York: Harcourt Brace Jovanovich (pp. 38–46).

Robinson, J. P. (2007) 'The effects of test translation on young English learners' mathematics performance', *Educational Researcher*, 39: 582–590.

Rose, S. A., and Blank, M. (1974) 'The potency of context in children's cognition: an illustration through conservation', *Child Development*, 45: 499–502.

Russell, M., and Plati, T. (2000) *Mode of administration effects on MCAS composition performance for Grades 4, 8, and 10. A report of findings submitted to the Massachusetts Department of Education (Report ED456142.)*, Chestnut Hill, MA: National Board on Educational Testing and Public Policy.

Samuel, J., and Bryant, P. E. (1984) 'Asking only one question in the conservation experiment', *Journal of Child Psychology and Psychiatry*, 25: 315–318.

Stone, W. L., and Lemanek, K. L. (1990) 'Parental report of social behaviours in autistic preschoolers', *Journal of Autism and Developmental Disorders*, 20: 513–522.

Strang, H. R., Bridgeman, B., and Carrico, M. F. (1974) 'Effects of "game" versus "test" task definition for third grade children on three subtests of the Weschler Intelligence Scale for Children', *Journal of Educational Measurement*, 11: 125–128.

Thompson, S., Blount, A., and Thurlow, M. (2002) *A summary of research on the effects of test accommodations: 1999 through 2001 (Technical Report 34)*, Minneapolis, MN: University of Minnesota, National Center on Educational Outcomes.

Tindal, G., Heath, B., Hollenbeck, K., Almond, P., and Harniss, M. (1998) 'Accommodating students with disabilities on large-scale tests: an empirical study of student response and test administration demands', *Exceptional Children*, 64: 439–450.

Tyack, D., and Ingram, D. (1977) 'Children's production and comprehension of questions', *Journal of Child Language*, 4: 221–224.

Verhoeven, L., and Vermeer, A. (1993) *Taaltoets Allochtone Kinderen-bovenbouw (Language Test for Immigrant Children)*, Tilburg, The Netherlands: Zwijsen.

Welsh, J. A., and Bierman, K. L. (2003) 'Using the clinical interview to assess children's interpersonal reasoning and emotional understanding', in C. R. Reynolds and R. W. Kamphaus (eds.) *Handbook of psychological and educational assessment of children*, New York: Guilford Press (pp. 204–222).

18

MULTICULTURAL EDUCATION

The mismeasured but important phenomenon

Festus E. Obiakor

THE CITY COLLEGE OF NEW YORK, CITY UNIVERSITY OF NEW YORK, USA

More than half a century ago, Dewey (1958) argued that 'education must have the tendency, if it is education, to form attitudes' (p. 56). From his perspective, these attitudes should 'express themselves in intelligent social action' (p. 56). Dewey's views appear to be very relevant today, especially as they relate to fulfilling the goals of multicultural education in different institutions, communities, nations, and the world. In many parts of the world, the dream of achieving multicultural communities where people's voices are treated with parity appears elusive. Even within nations, the voices of minorities (i.e. religious and tribal minorities) are silenced by the dominant majority (Obiakor 2004a; Ogbu 1978). In developed nations (e.g. the USA, France, and the UK) and developing nations (e.g. Nigeria, Egypt, Libya, Syria, Sudan, Haiti, and Iraq), there are apparent similarities on how minority voices are dominated. For instance, dominations are visible in economic, political, cultural, linguistic, educational, and societal policies that specifically result from inequity, tribalism, nepotism, favouritism, oppression, xenophobia, sexism, homophobia, terrorism, and war. Is there any wonder that dominated minorities all over the world are looking for ways to have their voices heard, as heretical as they may seem?

In the USA, the UK, and other parts of the world, there are cravings for human valuing and equitable treatment of minorities. For instance, in many countries of Africa, South America, the Middle East, and Asia, there are real mistrusts and tensions that sometimes result in wars. Going back to Dewey's introductory premise, it is unclear today whether multiculturalism, as important as it is, has been measurably successful in forming attitudes that express themselves in intelligent social actions. While the world continues to enjoy some fragile harmony in some areas, there are visible signs of turmoil in many areas. In fact, many continue to complain about disenfranchisement and dehumanization in different quarters of the world.

Consider the multicultural reputation of the USA, a country that elected the first African American President, Barack Obama, the son of an immigrant father from Kenya. Yet it is a country that frequently has outbursts of racism, police brutality, xenophobia, and so on. Using the USA as a model, this chapter exposes how multicultural education has been systemically mismeasured and mistargeted. In addition, it addresses how educators, service providers and communities all over the world can move beyond the multicultural rhetoric to improve multicultural education that can finally advance human valuing and equitable treatment.

Conflicting multicultural values on the world stage

It appears that current socio-educational actions have not matched current world-wide proclamations at world stages. For example, every 'global' body (e.g. the United Nations, United Nations International Children's Educational Fund, United Nations Educational and Scientific and Cultural Organization, World Bank, and World Health Organization) has made multicultural pleas geared towards attacking global inequities. Yet, at worldwide levels, perceptions of others, whether right or wrong, continue to affect how economic, political, educational, cultural, and social relationships and/or policies are formed and advanced. Put another way, these perceptions affect how people (a) psychologically relate to each other, (b) learn from each other, (c) teach each other, and (d) work with each other (Brooks 2004; Cortes 2000; Obiakor 2001a, 2001b). Interestingly, like most constructs, perceptions are imprecise scientific concepts that cannot be rigorously and thoroughly defined (Dember 1961); and they are loaded with unwarranted assumptions and illusory conclusions that affect how people teach, learn, and interact with others (Loury 2002; Obiakor 2001a; Obiakor and Algozzine 2009).

Because of the influence of perceptions on how knowledge is framed and constructed all over the world, it is difficult to use perceptions to either make correct judgments about situations and events or improve teaching, learning, human valuing, and human interactions, the very essence of multicultural education or multiculturalism (Banks 2002; Banks and Banks 2007; Obiakor, 2007, 2008, 2009; Utley and Obiakor 2001). Again, going back to Dewey's introductory premise, it has become increasingly clear that the current knowledge of multicultural education in today's world at least has not improved attitudes and interactions between different people. Even if it has, it is unclear if today's multicultural attitudes and interactions have expressed themselves in intelligent and measurable political, educational, economic, and social actions at school, community, national, and global levels.

Mismeasurement of multicultural education in the USA

As indicated earlier in this chapter, the USA has been used as a model in exposing the intricacies of multicultural education. The rationale for using it is two-fold: (a) its stature as a world leader and great democracy, and (b) the power of its foundational motto, *E Pluribus Unum* – one out of many. By all measurable standards, the USA has prided itself as a multicultural nation; and it continues to be inclusive through myriad advocacy, litigation, and legislation. Additionally, it has continuously and heavily invested financially through development or military aids to (a) resolve conflicts that may have global impacts, (b) advance countries that are less developed, and (c) build a world where silenced voices are heard. On the other hand, it continues to struggle to respond to demographical changes in its economics, politics, education, and society (Gould 1981). For example, it continues to struggle with how to incorporate the voices, cultures, and languages of culturally and linguistically diverse (CLD) individuals in its political, economic, societal, and educational programmes. In fact, many of these CLD children and youth continue to be misidentified, misassessed, miscategorized, misplaced, and misinstructed (Obiakor 2001a, 2007, 2008). In this book, these issues are addressed by other authors in the following chapters: Ngara and Porath, Chapter 19; Kemp, Chapter 17; Obi and Sapp, Chapter 15; Hall, Chapter 16; Salend, Chapter 14; and Boyle, Chapter 21. These issues have worldwide implications. If the USA can struggle with CLD-related issues, what will be the plight of homogeneous societies that have not stretched their imaginations to reach out to the 'different others?' For example, there are countries that continue to treat their 'different others' as 'outcasts' and 'untouchables' to the extent that when they report their levels of educational attainment, they fail to include these human beings in their overall activities and data (see Ogbu 1978).

It is common knowledge that multiculturalism, in theory and practice, seeks inclusive avenues that equalize opportunities for all individuals (Sue 2004). To a large measure, it incorporates multiple voices, including those of CLD persons and communities, in solving local, national, and global problems. For instance, in the USA, CLD learners are the majority in some of the largest school districts (Grossman 1998; Ladson-Billings 1994; Obiakor 2004b; Obiakor and Beachum 2005). Ladson-Billings noted that these learners 'represent 30 percent of the public school population. In the twenty largest school districts, they make up over 70 percent of total school enrollment' (p. x). This revelation is particularly important today, especially since the composition of educational and psychological professionals and service providers still does not reflect the changing cultural and linguistic compositions of children in schools and societies in the USA (Obiakor and Green 2011; Utley and Obiakor 2001). It appears that the progressive goals of the 1954 Brown versus the School Board of Education in Topeka, Kansas, USA case have somehow failed (Obiakor and Utley 2004). The Brown case was against discrimination and exclusion in educational processes – it was to buttress inclusion at all educational levels in the USA. However, in today's educational and psychological programmes, there seems to be a failure to ask and answer the right questions. As a result, wrong and simplistic answers are used to tackle serious educational and psychological problems confronting children and youth. With legislative, technological, and multicultural advances in the USA, there is a plethora of evidence to suggest that ethnic divisions and savage inequalities have continued to exist in schools and communities across the nation (Kozol 1991; Obiakor 2001a, 2001b, 2007, 2008, 2009; Obiakor, Grant, and Dooley 2002; Obiakor, Grant, and Obi 2010).

In the USA, there appears to be some interest in equalizing opportunities and choices. While some knowledge of multicultural education has been a good thing; it has become increasingly evident that 'having the knowledge is not enough anymore – knowledge must be followed by measurable commitment and action' (Obiakor and Algozzine 2009: ii). Additionally, there is no denying that far too many devastating games have been played with multicultural education in schools, institutions, communities, and governments all over the world (Cortes 2000; Loury 2002; Obiakor 2004a). As indicated elsewhere (see Obiakor and Algozzine 2009), in the USA, individuals and institutions have falsely responded to multiculturalism by:

1. 'practicing paternalistic patronization' (i.e. when a CLD person is treated in a child-like manner as if he/she does not have a brain to think or fend for himself/herself)
2. 'encouraging tokenism' (i.e. when a CLD faculty or staff is hired as a figurehead to appease requests for inclusion and equanimity)
3. 'engaging in suicide mission' (i.e. when a culturally sensitive faculty or staff, especially White (or member of a dominant group), is intentionally made irrelevant, destroyed, or victimized because he/she dared to support equity)
4. 'playing the divide-and-conquer game' (i.e. when CLD faculty or staff are set up to fight against each other based on the White supremacist idea of 'goodness')
5. 'encouraging the crab-bucket syndrome' (i.e. when proactive efforts are made to pull down or devalue a high-performing CLD faculty or staff)
6. 'favouring quota' (i.e. when an incompetent and mediocre CLD faculty or staff, or administrator is hired in place of qualified ones)
7. 'engaging in fraudulent multiculturalism' (i.e. when multiculturalism is discussed in a half-hearted fashion to appease the masses or accreditation bodies and create a phony sense of community)

8. 'silencing of voices' (i.e. when the White supremacist strategy of one-person-one-vote is adopted to impose majority views on a situation)
9. 'playing the revolving door game' (i.e. when a CLD faculty or staff is hired to serve a major purpose and let go after that purpose is achieved)
10. 'making visible talents invisible' (i.e. when talented CLD faculty and/or staff are made invisible by under-utilizing them or pretending that they do not exist)
11. 'rationalizing race-related issues' (i.e. when racism against a CLD person is simplistically explained and justified as differences in personality or perception).

The future beyond multicultural rhetoric

The world can learn a lot from the USA, especially for its perceived efforts to be inclusive. As indicated, it continues to struggle with multiculturalism. But the future is not that bleak! For multicultural education to be truly 'multicultural' in the USA and the world over, it must involve knowledge, analysis, commitment, action, and risk-taking. Current demographic changes in respective schools and communities must be clearly valued. This is the 'season' for positive change and risk-taking in the world! In her book, *There Is a Season,* Chittister (1999: 53) argued that:

> The thought of constant change colors our sense of the future. We wear it like a logo as we race from place to place, and now, in our time, from idea to idea, from concept to concept, from social revolution to social revolution ... change, after all, is not a given. Change follows in the wake of something that preceded it, quiet as a shift in the wind. It does not just happen; it is not a timed process. 'If we're just patient; if we just wait long enough it has to come,' we say when we do not want to be responsible ourselves for the change. But change does not just come; change is brought somehow.

It is apparent that change agents for multicultural education are needed. In many countries of the world, especially in the African continent, change has not been coming as expected, members of minority tribes are yet to find their footing and multiculturalism seems to be far from reach (Obiakor 2004a). For example, even though President Goodluck Johnson (from a minority tribe) was elected President of Nigeria (the most populated Black nation in the world), recent unrests and killings have exposed the lack of multicultural valuing in the country. Going back to the USA, there have been court cases to fight for individual rights; laws have been passed to give the citizenry more rights; and programmes have been designed to see that everyone's rights are protected; but the society seems to flounder in mediocrity when it comes to producing measurable positive results. In frustration, some scholars (e.g. Bell 1985, 1992) have posited that racism and discrimination in education will never end. However, while race and tribalization matter (see Loury 2002), change is an inevitable force in life. This is not in consonance with the 'what will be, will be' natural law. This is the kind of change that comes with human efforts and risk-taking. It truly behooves educators, psychologists, and leaders to think outside the box and challenge the status quo, especially when it comes to instituting change (Chomsky 2000). To challenge the status quo in the present and future, it is critical that educators and psychologists (a) take altruistic risks, (b) match knowledge with positive actions, and (c) value the 'enemy within' and 'enemy without'.

Taking altruistic risks in education

Generally, positive change results from positive risk-taking and some risky actions. For example, where would the Socratic question-and-answer method be today without the risk taken by Socrates to challenge the wealthy Greek Sophists who were more interested in maintaining the status quo than in challenging the Athenian youth to maximize their fullest potential? Though his ideas seemed innovative and far-reaching, he was accused of impiety to the gods and of corrupting the Athenian youth. In the end, he became a great equalizer who wanted the masses to be involved in the socio-educational discourse of his time (Sagal 1983). Proponents of multicultural education seem to have a similar equalizing effect; and they challenge the status quo to educate all disenfranchised persons from different cultural, linguistic, and racial backgrounds. Like the Sophists, opponents of multicultural education, whether they are from the 'left' or 'right', appear to be more interested in assimilating all persons in spite of cultural differences and personal idiosyncrasies (Caesar 1998; Chavez 1998; D'Souza 1991; Melzer, Weinberger, and Zinman 1998; Schlesinger 1992; Sowell 1993). For instance, D'Souza (1991: 214–215) argued that multiculturalism creates a 'monolithic ideological focus that places minority sentiments on a pedestal while putting majority ones on trial.' Similarly, Caesar (1998: 155) concluded that multicultural education perpetuates a perverse psychology whereby 'people of different groups thus vie in unseemly process to claim that they have been oppressed – even in cases when they manifestly have not been.'

In the face of the above conflicting views, many of today's children with atypical manifestations are improperly identified, unfairly assessed, inadequately labeled, disproportionately placed, and frequently misinstructed (Obiakor 2007, 2008, 2009). The critical question is – with these kinds of thinking, how can inclusive multicultural communities be built, formed, and advanced in the USA, or anywhere for that matter?

Clearly, for multicultural education to work in the USA and the world, it must involve novel thinking that goes beyond modern-day liberal or conservative rhetoric. To a large measure, it must involve altruistic risk-taking that leads to positive change. For instance, any robber from any CLD background who knows that there is a camera in the bank and still goes there to rob is a risk-taker; but his/her risk-taking behaviour will not lead to positive change. It will land him/her in jail! On the other hand, a young African man who protects an elderly White woman from being robbed by some armed marauders has taken some risk; and his risk is a positive altruistic one. Not only do such risks reduce negative stereotypes and generalizations, they also make long-term positive psychological impressions on people. Using a biblical allusion, one is reminded of the 'Parable of the Good Samaritan,' in which the supposedly 'good' people left a man stranded and the unsuspected stranger saved him (Obiakor 2011). This allusion presents a wonderful lesson to educators and psychologists all over the world. In a truly multicultural programme or environment, people will take risks that lead to positive decisions and actions.

Matching knowledge with positive actions

As indicated, when infused properly, multicultural education has the power to change attitude and enhance quality education, especially when it (a) exposes individuals to maximum learning and new dimensions of problem-solving; (b) acquaints individuals with divergent view-points and multiple voices to societal discourse; (c) removes limits set on how people are defined, understood, and valued; and (d) increases how people collaborate, consult, and cooperate with each other. To a larger measure, multicultural education capitalizes on the resources and endowments of all individuals and fosters pragmatic efforts in discovering the greatness of the world's peoples. More than two decades ago, Gollnick and Chinn (1990: iii) explained that:

> An overall goal of multicultural education is to help all students develop their potential for academic, social, and vocational success. Educational and vocational options should not be limited by sex, age, ethnicity, native language, religion, class, or exceptionality. Educators are given the responsibility to help students contribute to, and benefit from, our democratic society. Within our pluralistic society, multicultural education values the existing diversity, positively portrays that diversity and uses that diversity in the development of effective instructional categories for students in the classroom. In addition, multicultural education should help students think critically about institutionalized racism, classism, and sexism.

To properly infuse multicultural education, we must go beyond rhetoric to let positive actions to speak. In his book *Let Your Life Speak*, Parker (2000) challenged educators and service providers to be more dedicated than ever to achieve their life mission even when confronted by predictable and unforeseen drawbacks. He urged them to find their 'sacred center' in their journey of life, and concluded that:

> Most of us arrive at a sense of self and vocation only after a long journey through alien lands. But this journey bears no resemblance to the trouble-free 'travel packages' sold by the tourism industry. It is more akin to the ancient tradition of 'pilgrimage' – 'a transformative journey to a sacred center' of hardships, darkness, and peril . . . In the tradition of a pilgrimage, those hardships are seen not as accidentals but as integral to the journey itself. Treacherous terrain, bad weather, taking a fall, getting lost – challenges of that sort, largely beyond our control, can strip the ego of the illusion that it is in charge and make space for true self to emerge. If that happens, the pilgrim has a better chance to find the sacred center he or she seeks. Disabused of our illusions by much travel and travail, we awaken one day to find that the sacred center is here and now – in every moment of the journey, everywhere in the world around us, and deep within our own hearts.
>
> *(Parker 2000: 17–18)*

Parker's statement was reiterated by Ford (2002) in her final comments as the first editor of *Multiple Voices*, the journal of the Division for Ethnically Diverse Exceptional Learners (DDEL), the Council for Exceptional Children. In her comments, she recounted the story of four people named everybody, somebody, anybody, and nobody. As the story goes:

> An important job needed to be done, everybody was sure that somebody would do it. Anybody could have done it, but nobody did. Somebody became angry because it was everybody's job and everybody thought that anybody could do it. It ended up that everybody blamed somebody when nobody did what anybody could have done!
>
> *(Ford 2002: vii)*

Clearly, everyone must 'let our work speak' as he/she works collaboratively and consultatively with others for the common good (Obiakor and Utley 2007). The society cannot afford to fake it in education and psychology! The critical question is – did educators and leaders do all they needed to do as professionals to solve problems of others different from them, or did they betray their souls to achieve a phony sense of satisfaction? Yes, some have tried to solve cultural and racial problems in their respective organizations; however, for one reason or another, some have tried to create these problems even when they did not exist. The fact remains, as Parker (2000: 16) put it, that:

> Our deepest calling is to grow into our own authentic selfhood, whether or not it conforms to some image of who we ought to be. As we do so, we will not only find the joy that every human being seeks – we will also find our path of authentic service in the world.

It is not too late to wonder how posterity will remember us in our chosen profession, and this should be our motivation to do right by others. Our personal and professional multicultural question should be – did I barely survive to boost my ego envenomed by the 'me, myself, and I' syndrome or did I make some positive contributions to the lives of others different from me? Following are endemic reflective questions that will increase current discourse in multicultural education and psychology (see Obiakor and Utley 2003).

- Do race and culture influence the identification of individuals?
- Do assessment tools measure the construct that they purport to measure for individuals?
- Do categorical labels of individuals reflect their capability?
- Do placement options used for individuals restrict their abilities to maximize their fullest potential?
- Do instructional/intervention techniques take into consideration the rich cultural backgrounds of individuals?

Valuing the 'enemy within' and the 'enemy without'

In any human action, there is an 'enemy within' or an 'enemy without.' To advance our professions, educators and psychologists must be interested in challenging ourselves just as we challenge others. Individual changes must flourish to make collective positive changes possible. Though the world has more goodness than evil, educational and psychological professionals have not been personally proactive as they should have been, especially in dealing with mistrusts, misrepresentations, and other critical problems such as tribalism, oppression, pogrom, xenophobia, sexism, homophobia, terrorism, and war. As a matter of urgency, concerted and proactive efforts must reduce or eliminate (a) the silencing of invisible voices (Ellison 1972), (b) self-hating or 'player-hating' behaviours (Obiakor 2001a), and (c) the mismeasurement, mistargeting, and bastardization of multicultural education (Obiakor 2011). Indeed, measurable self-reflections will buttress the understanding that race, balkanization, and tribalization truly matter. And, as a consequence, we must personally stabilize our sacred existence not just as multicultural educators and psychologists but also as positive human beings (Chomsky 2000; Duvall 1994; Gould 1981; James 1958; Loury 2002). Put another way, we must look at the 'enemy within' (i.e. engage in personal reflections that lead to positive actions as educators and psychologists) and the 'enemy without' (i.e. gain knowledge of external commitments and forces that impinge on education and psychology) to inspire the spirits of hard-working individuals dedicated to making a difference in their profession.

In the end, nagging global questions about multicultural education and psychology will be answered when measurable efforts and positive actions are made to think outside the box on issues related to:

- taking altruistic risk
- acknowledging our personal pride and prejudice
- valuing integrity, loyalty, and commitment
- being open-minded in spite of our trials and tribulations
- respecting all voices even if they seem heretical
- reanalyzing definitions of what is 'good' or 'bad'
- being pragmatic as we challenge old ideas and create new ones
- becoming realistic mentors/role models to help our growing scholars, educators, and students
- valuing 'quality with a heart'
- continuing to learn, our experiences notwithstanding
- becoming the change that we want.

Conclusion

In this chapter, multicultural education has been presented as a powerful force in our lives, schools, communities, nations, and world. One axiom is clear: multiculturalism is here to stay even though it continues to conjure scepticism because of its mismeasurement in education and psychology. While the author of this chapter believes multicultural education complements other theories of learning, and to a large extent needs to be studied, learned, taught, and practiced, the author also believes it can create divisions, balkanization, tribalization, and disunity when improperly infused in schools, communities, and societies. Some people and institutions have played games with multicultural education, and have tried to masquerade their bigotry as they dealt with it. This does not however mean that multicultural education is meaningless to our lives, schools, communities, nation, and world. Going back to Dewey's (1958) introductory premise, we must make multicultural education more frantic, relevant, meaningful, and productive than ever before in our teaching, learning, and human interactions in our societies.

To a large measure, educators, psychologists, and service providers must strive for measurable change and go beyond the rhetoric of multiculturalism to improve the quality of our humanity. To foster measurable multicultural changes in education and psychology, we must reduce our blindness on human differences without defining our relationships based on our narrow differences. Not long ago, President Obama (2009: 1) reiterated that:

> So long as our relationship is defined by our differences, we will empower those who sow hatred rather than peace, and who promote conflict rather than the cooperation that can help all of our people achieve justice and prosperity. This cycle of suspicion and discord must end.

He concluded (2009: 3):

> Recognizing our common humanity is only the beginning of our task. Words alone cannot meet the needs of our people. These needs will be met only if we act boldly in the years ahead; and if we understand that the challenges we face are shared, and our failure to meet them will hurt us all.

Contact address: fobiakor@ccny.cuny.edu

References

Banks, J. A. (2002) 'Race, knowledge construction, and education in the USA: lessons from history', *Race, Ethnicity and Education*, 5: 8–27.

Banks, J. A., and Banks, C. A. M. (2007) *Multicultural education: issues and perspectives*, 6th edn, Hoboken, NJ: Wiley.

Bell, D. (1985) *And we are not saved: the elusive quest for racial justice*, New York: Basic Books.

Bell, D. (1992) *Faces at the bottom of the well: the permanence of racism*, New York: Basic Books.

Brooks, R. B. (2004) 'To touch the hearts and minds of students with learning disabilities: the power of mindsets and expectations', *Learning Disabilities*, 2: 1–8.

Caesar, J. (1998) 'Multiculturalism and American liberal democracy', in A. M. Melzer, J. Weinberger, and M. R. Zinman (eds) *Multiculturalism and the American democracy*, Lawrence, KS: University Press of Kansas (pp. 139–156).

Chavez, L. (1998) 'Civic education in a changing society', in A. M. Melzer, J. Weinberger, and M. R. Zinman (eds.) *Multiculturalism and the American democracy*, Lawrence, KS: University Press of Kansas (pp. 165–172).

Chittister, J. (1999) *There is a season*, Maryknoll, NY: Orbis Books.

Chomsky, N. (2000) *Chomsky on miseducation*, Lanham, MD: Rowman and Littlefield.

Cortes, C. E. (2000) *The children are watching: how the media teach about diversity*, New York: Teachers College Press.

Dember, W. (1961) *Psychology of perception*, New York: Holt, Rinehart and Winston.

Dewey, J. (1958) *Philosophy of education*, Ames, IA: Littlefield, Adams and Co.

D'Souza, D. (1991) *Illiberal education: the politics of race and sex on the campus*, New York: Free Press.

Duvall, L. (1994) *Respecting our differences: a guide to getting along in a changing world*, Minneapolis, MN: Free Spirit.

Ellison, R. (1972) *Invisible man*, New York: Vintage.

Ford, B. A. (2002) 'Final remarks', *Multiple Voices*, 5: vii.

Gollnick, D. M., and Chinn, P. C. (1990) *Multicultural education in a pluralistic society*, 3rd edn, New York: Merrill.

Gould, S. J. (1981) *The mismeasure of man*, New York: Norton.

Grossman, H. (1998) *Ending discrimination in special education*, Springfield, IL: Charles C. Thomas.

James, W. (1958) *Talk to teachers on psychology, and to students on some life's ideas*, New York: W. W. Norton.

Kozol, J. (1991) *Savage inequalities: children in American schools*, New York: Harper Perennial.

Ladson-Billings, G. (1994) *The dream keepers: successful teachers of African American children*, San Francisco: Jossey-Bass.

Loury, G. C. (2002) *The anatomy of racial inequality*, Cambridge, MA: Harvard University Press.

Melzer, A. M., Weinberger, J., and Zinman, M. R. (1998) *Multiculturalism and the American democracy*, Lawrence, KS: University Press of Kansas.

Obama, B. (2009) President Barack Obama's speech at Cairo University, Egypt, North Africa [online]. Available at www.nytimes.com/2009/06/04/us/politics/04obama.text.html

Obiakor, F. E. (2001a) *It even happens in 'good' schools: responding to cultural diversity in today's classrooms*, Thousand Oaks, CA: Corwin Press.

Obiakor, F. E. (2001b) 'Multicultural education: powerful tool for preparing future general and special educators', *Teacher Education and Special Education*, 24: 241–255.

Obiakor, F. E. (2004a) 'Building patriotic African leadership through African-centered education', *Journal of Black Studies*, 28: 399–406.

Obiakor, F. E. (2004b) 'Impacts of changing demographics in public education for culturally diverse learners with behavior problems: implications for teacher preparation', in L. M. Bullock and R. A. Gable (eds.) *Quality personnel preparation in emotional/behavioral disorders: current perspectives and future directions*, Denton, TX: Institute for Behavioral and Learning Differences, University of North Texas (pp. 51–63).

Obiakor, F. E. (2007) *Multicultural special education: culturally responsive teaching*, Upper Saddle River, NJ: Pearson/Merrill Prentice Hall.

Obiakor, F. E. (2008) *The eight-step approach to multicultural learning and teaching*, 3rd edn, Dubuque, IA: Kendall/Hunt.

Obiakor, F. E. (2009) 'Demographic changes in public education for culturally diverse exceptional learners: making teacher preparation programs accountable', *Multicultural Learning and Teaching*, 4: 90–110.

Obiakor, F. E. (2011) 'Beware of false prophets of multicultural education', *Multicultural Learning and Teaching*, 6: 1–6.

Obiakor, F. E., and Algozzine, B. (2009) 'Executive editors' comments: the mismeasure of multiculturalism in teacher preparation programs', *Multicultural Learning and Teaching*, 4: i–iv.

Obiakor, F. E., and Beachum, F. D. (2005) *Urban education for the 21st century: research, issues, and perspectives*, Springfield, IL: Charles C. Thomas.

Obiakor, F. E., Grant, P. A., and Dooley, E. A. (2002) *Educating all learners: refocusing the comprehensive support model*, Springfield, IL: Charles C. Thomas.

Obiakor, F. E., Grant, P. A., and Obi, S. O. (2010) *Voices of foreign-born teacher educators in the United States*, New York: Nova Science Publishers.

Obiakor, F. E., and Green, S. L. (2011) 'Racial identity and teacher preparation: how they matter to culturally and linguistically diverse urban learners', *Myriad*, 18–22.

Obiakor, F. E., and Utley, C. A. (2003) 'Preview: fraudulent multiculturalism reduces the goodness of general and special education', *Multiple Voices*, 6: v–vi.

Obiakor, F. E., and Utley, C. A. (2004) 'Educating culturally diverse learners with exceptionalities: a critical analysis of the Brown case', *Peabody Journal of Education*, 79: 141–156.

Obiakor, F. E., and Utley, C. A. (2007) 'Preview: let your work speak: challenge to multicultural general and special educators', *Multiple Voices*, 10: v–vii.

Ogbu, J. U. (1978) *Minority education and caste*, San Francisco: Academic Press.

Parker, P. J. (2000) *Let your life speak: listening for the voice of vocation*, San Francisco: Jossey–Bass.

Sagal, P. T. (1983) *Introducing philosophy: a Socratic dialogue*, Las Cruces, NM: Dialogue Press.

Schlesinger, A. M. (1992) *The disuniting of America: reflection on a multicultural society*, New York: Norton.

Sowell, T. (1993) *Inside American education: the decline, the deception, the dogmas*, New York: Free Press.

Sue, D. W. (2004) 'Whiteness and ethnocentric monoculturalism: making the "invisible" visible', *American Psychology*, 761–769.

Utley, C. A., and Obiakor, F. E. (2001) *Special education, multicultural education, and school reform: components of quality education for learners with mild disabilities*, Springfield, IL: Charles C. Thomas.

19

INTELLIGENCE AND INDIVIDUAL DIFFERENCES

Constantine Ngara and Marion Porath

UNIVERSITY OF BAHRAIN TEACHERS COLLEGE, BAHRAIN; THE UNIVERSITY OF
BRITISH COLUMBIA, CANADA

Intelligence is something in which everyone is interested. All cultures recognize certain abilities as outstanding and encourage and support the individuals they consider highly intelligent; they also strive to support those who are considered less intelligent. In this chapter we present an overview of theories of intelligence, discuss the role of culture in defining intelligence, and consider the implications of intelligence tests. To begin, we present some questions to help you reflect on your own ideas about intelligence. Each of us has beliefs about what intelligence is that are important to acknowledge.

*   How do you define intelligence?
*   Think about your family, friends, colleagues, and classmates. Do any of them stand out because of their intelligence? Why do you think so?
*   What is considered intelligent in your culture and community? What is considered intelligent in school? Are the two conceptions of intelligence different? Are there a number of different ideas about intelligence related to cultural background?

You might also want to consider the second set of questions at the beginning of a later chapter in this text on 'Meeting the needs of gifted learners' (Porath, Chapter 32, this volume). These highlight potential influences on intelligence and its development.

Intelligence and intelligence testing

Defining and measuring intelligence has a long history. A civil service testing programme was developed in China several thousand years ago; knowledge of ceremonies and horsemanship – skills pertinent to life then – were among the skills tested (Thorndike 1997). In the Western world, the nineteenth and early twentieth centuries were dominated by hereditarian (belief in genetic factors as predominant in determining one's intelligence) views of intelligence (Gould 1996) and the conception of intelligence as a single measurable entity that captured one's capacity to reason. Titles such as *Hereditary Genius* (Galton 1884) and *Genetic Studies of Genius* (Terman 1926) reflected the view that genes were what mattered in intelligence, and intelligence was conceived of as a unitary capacity.

Spearman (1904) argued for general intelligence or 'g' based on his statistical analyses of mental tests. Spearman noted that performance on tasks measuring different aspects of reasoning were positively correlated and concluded that a general ('g') capacity to reason must underlie how well we perform on different sorts of tasks. At about the same time, Alfred Binet and his colleague, Theodore Simon, working in France, were asked by the minister of education to develop a test to identify children who needed extra help in school (Gould 1996). Binet and Simon focused on what they believed to be basic reasoning capabilities – ordering, comprehension, invention, and correction (Gould 1996), assigned an age level to each task, and derived a single score of 'potential' from the tests. This score was the forerunner of the intelligence quotient (IQ), a statistic developed by Stern, a German psychologist, and brought into widespread use by Lewis Terman, an American psychologist (Ziegler and Stoeger 2007).

- What do you think IQ means?
- Have you ever taken an intelligence test? What are your memories of the experience?

See Porath (Chapter 32, this volume) for an overview of how intelligence test scores are interpreted.

Binet cautioned against the use of a single score to represent a child's intelligence, believing that intelligence is too complex to be subsumed in one number. His aim 'was to identify in order to help and improve, not to label in order to limit' (Gould 1996: 182). He suggested that intelligence is influenced by a number of factors and changes over time (Siegler 1992). Binet's work, though, was taken up by others in ways that often did lead to labelling without considering other factors and time in the development of intelligence.

Working at Stanford University, Terman (1916) adapted Binet's test and published the first standardized intelligence test, the Stanford computed tomography Binet Intelligence Scale. A standardized test is administered in the same way to each individual, following rigorous procedures. Graduate-level training is necessary to administer, score, and interpret standardized intelligence tests. The tests are 'normed' on thousands of individuals to ascertain the average performance of each age group who took the test. These tests are considered reliable and valid. That is, an individual will achieve similar scores when they retake the test (reliability); the test items correlate with each other (reliability); and the tests measure what they claim to measure, as determined by correlations with other tests (validity). The Stanford-Binet Intelligence Scale has undergone several revisions, the latest in 2003 (SB5; Roid 2003). Revisions are done to ensure that test items are current (e.g. a test item using a picture of a rotary phone would be unfair for today's population) and to reflect current thinking about the processes that constitute general intelligence.

The Stanford-Binet Intelligence Scale 5th edition includes a nonverbal subtest requiring identification of geometric shapes and completion of patterns and verbal subtests requiring descriptions of what is occurring in a picture, identification of absurdities in statements, and completion of verbal analogies. It also includes computation skills, mathematical reasoning, working memory subtests (working memory is the ability to keep the results of information processing in memory while continuing to process information; for example, counting multiple arrays of dots and remembering the totals), and completion of visual–spatial tasks that involve seeing patterns and relationships (Salvia, Ysseldyke, and Bolt 2007). These subtests are believed to measure 'fluid reasoning' (Salvia et al. 2007). Cattell (1963) and Horn and Cattell (1967) identified two types of intelligence: 'fluid intelligence' (Gf), flexible reasoning ability that can be applied across different tasks, and 'crystallized intelligence' (Gc), mental ability that is culture-specific and influenced by school learning experiences. Subtests that measure 'Gc' include general knowledge of the world and vocabulary.

The other widely used standardized tests are the different versions of the Wechsler Scales of Intelligence (preschool through adult). Wechsler began work on intelligence tests in the USA in the 1940s (see Wechsler 1944). Like the Stanford-Binet, the Wechsler scales are revised regularly (e.g. Wechsler 2003). The Wechsler scales measure similar aspects of intelligence to the Stanford-Binet – that is, verbal and mathematical ability, visual–spatial processing, working memory capacity, knowledge, and overall reasoning ability – and the two tests correlate highly. The Wechsler scales include more timed items than the Stanford-Binet, with bonus points assigned for completing tasks quickly. But is solving problems quickly necessarily intelligent behaviour? Some argue that reflective thinking is more intelligent than speed of thinking (e.g. Sternberg 1985).

The nature vs. nurture question

Is intelligence inherited (the 'nature' argument), as early intelligence theorists believed, or can it be developed (the 'nurture' argument)? It is now recognized that this is not an 'either/or' argument; there is an interactive relationship between innate capacity and environment. Environment affects the realization of inherited potential either positively or negatively (Sternberg and Grigorenko 1997). The context and culture in which one is raised and the sex-role expectations to which one is exposed influence intelligent behaviour (Ceci 1996), as does the degree of support one receives (Bloom 1985; Fischer and Pipp 1984). Personal characteristics such as motivation, ability to delay gratification, belief in the power of effort in achievement, and strong sense of identity are believed to be more important than IQ in life success (Ceci 1996; Dweck 2006; Goleman 2005).

Intelligence and culture

Western intelligence tests have been criticized for their failure to measure intelligence in other cultures (Ceci 1996; Gardner 1983; Suizzo 2000). Consider the following examples of intelligence.

- Australian Aboriginal peoples believe all children to be clever; to stand out from the group is unacceptable. Thus, the ability to belong to the group and related characteristics such as interdependence, helpfulness, responsibility, and reliability are considered intelligent (Gibson and Vialle 2007).
- In Shona society (of Zimbabwe), intelligence is considered as ability to solve problems in one's community; high intelligence is believed to be inborn (Mpofu, Ngara, and Gudyanga 2007; Ngara and Porath 2004).

While the abilities measured by intelligence tests may be valued in other cultures, they do not universally dominate conceptions of intelligence across cultures. Furthermore, even if, for example, the comprehension of verbal information is valued, the items may not be appropriate in some contexts, e.g. 'why is it important to wear boots after a large snowfall?' (Salvia et al. 2007: 303). Also, if Western intelligence tests are administered to individuals of diverse culture, the individuals' culture can influence their perceptions of what is being tested.

It is always questionable whether the item types used in the Western intelligence tests measure the same underlying traits in the Chinese world. A Chinese child may see the same things as a Western child but may respond and perceive differently because experience and background play an important role in the interpretation of the same information or stimulus (Chan 2007: 39).

A study of intelligence among the Luo of Kenya (Sternberg et al. 2001) established that the Luo community understood intelligence in terms of community adaptation. Children considered intelligent by community standards were not considered bright at school by the teachers, illustrating the multi-level understanding of intelligence that may be present in some societies. For example, Mpofu et al. (2007: 225–226) noted that intelligence is understood at the 'modern-industrial, traditionalist-rural, and transitional (in between traditionalist and modern)' levels in Central–Southern Africa.

Culture cannot be ignored in our quest to understand human intelligence and human abilities in general (Sternberg and Grigorenko 2004; Vygotsky 1978). Intelligence and individual differences cannot be fully understood outside their cultural contexts, as intelligence is a social construct. Culture not only describes people's ways of life and customs and folklore, it encompasses a people's world views and their ways of knowing, including how they perceive and construct reality from their experiences in their environments.

Determining intelligence in different cultures

Despite the recognized shortcomings of Western intelligence tests for cross-cultural use, they continue to be used internationally (Phillipson 2007). As an alternative, some advocate the use of tests that are believed to be 'culture-fair' such as Raven's Progressive Matrices (Raven, Raven, and Court 2000, updated 2004) and the Naglieri Nonverbal Ability Test (Naglieri 2007), both of which use perceptual pattern problems to measure nonverbal reasoning and general problem-solving ability. However, the nonverbal reasoning tests discussed do not measure the same cognitive ability as is measured with verbal tests (Lohman, Korb, and Lakin 2008) and, while they may provide helpful information about reasoning ability, 'one cannot assume that nonverbal tests level the playing field for children who come from different cultures or who have had different educational opportunities' (Lohman et al. 2008: 293). These test's norms are outdated or improperly computed, making any comparison between a student's score and the statistics summarizing the performance of those who took the test during its development questionable (Lohman et al. 2008). The tests, despite their use of patterns, do not measure spatial ability, an ability that underlies success in fields such as engineering and architecture (Webb, Lubinski, and Benbow 2007). On the other hand, the tests may favour some cultures. For example, Chan (2007) pointed out that the format of the Raven's test favours readers of Chinese since the diagrams form visual patterns and can be analyzed horizontally, vertically, and diagonally.

The identification of intelligence in authentic ways among students from different cultures is especially important in our increasingly multicultural communities (see the discussion on 'educational implications' below). In addition, some Western theorists have worked on new models of intelligence that favour multiple ways of being intelligent, rather than focusing only on general intelligence.

Beyond the IQ paradigm

Two contemporary psychologists have contributed to thinking about intelligence in different ways than the unitary view of intelligence captured by IQ. Howard Gardner (1983) and Robert Sternberg's (1985) work began during the 'cognitive revolution' of the 1980s when reservations about how intelligence had been conceptualized, interest in how the mind works, and cross-cultural studies of intelligent behaviour led to extensive research on thinking and learning.

Multiple intelligences

Arguing that intelligence tests reflect, and privilege, the verbal and logical–mathematical foci of Western societies, Gardner (1983, 1993, 1999) discounted the notion of general intelligence and proposed relatively distinct modes of intelligence based on neuropsychological and cross-cultural research. In his Multiple Intelligences (MI) theory, Gardner (1993: x) defined intelligence as 'ability to solve problems or to create products that are valued within one or more cultural settings'. Initially, Gardner (1983) identified seven distinct forms of intelligence.

1. *Logical–mathematical:* the ability to use deductive reasoning and logical thinking and use mathematical operations effectively.
2. *Verbal–linguistic:* the ability to use both spoken and written language effectively.
3. *Musical:* the art and skill of performing, composing, and appreciating musical patterns.
4. *Visual–spatial:* the ability to visualize images, recognize and use patterns, spatial orientation, and graphically represent visual and spatial ideas.
5. *Bodily kinaesthetic:* mind and body coordination in artistic performances and sports.
6. *Interpersonal:* the capacity to understand others and their intentions, motivations, and desires.
7. *Intrapersonal:* the capacity to understand oneself including knowledge of one's own strengths, weaknesses, feelings, and motivations.

More recently, Gardner (1999) added 'naturalistic intelligence' (the ability to identify patterns in nature) and speculated on the existence of 'existential intelligence' (sensitivity to questions about human existence). Gardner also emphasized that intelligence is often demonstrated through a combination of intelligences (e.g. lawyers combine logical and verbal intelligences).

MI theory is popular with educators, possibly because it reflects teachers' experiences with the different ways their students think and learn (Kornhaber 2001). MI supports a broader vision of education than schooling based on an IQ model (Kornhaber 2001) (see the discussion on rethinking IQ in Porath, Chapter 32, this volume). The MI teaching approach fosters deep approaches to learning by providing appropriate motivational context, activity-based learning, opportunities for interacting with peers and teachers, and a structured knowledge base (Biggs and Telfer 1987). Further, MI theory has informed an instructional approach in which different abilities are developed in a single lesson. A teacher might, for example, use a story, artistic representations, and a hands-on activity to introduce a new concept. Educators accept MI but theorists criticize it for its lack of specific criteria for measuring each type of intelligence (Smith 2008).

Goleman (2005) further expanded the notion of multiple intelligences, hypothesizing 'emotional intelligence' (EQ) as an identifiable intelligence in its own right. EQ is a close equivalent of Gardner's 'interpersonal' (socially oriented) and 'intrapersonal' (self-knowledge-oriented) ways of knowing. EQ involves self-awareness, motivation, altruism, and empathy (Goleman 2005). EQ is believed to be even more critical for an individual's success in life than IQ. EQ is critical in successful social relations and in understanding ourselves and fulfilling our own goals (Smith 2008). Goleman's contribution shows how fluid and complex the notion of intelligence is (Smith 2008).

Triarchic theory of intelligence

Robert Sternberg is an American psychologist rated among the top 100 psychologists of the twentieth century by the American Psychological Association (Haggbloom et al. 2002) for his contributions to understanding intelligence. Of significance is the fact that Sternberg did not fare well on an IQ test in elementary school. However, he later became inspired by his fourth grade teacher, who believed in his potential and challenged him to greater heights. 'I define [intelligence] as your skill in achieving whatever it is you want to attain in your life within your sociocultural context by capitalizing on your strengths and compensating for, or correcting, your weaknesses' (Plucker 2003: para. 1). In Sternberg's view, intelligence is not a unitary trait but involves a number of cognitive and other skills that educators need to learn how best to assess and educate in students.

Sternberg's (1985, 1988) triarchic theory of intelligence comprises three subtheories. The abilities described in the subtheories can be developed; they are not considered fixed characteristics of an individual (Sternberg 1988).

1. *The componential subtheory (analytic intelligence)* refers to cognitive components of information processing, especially analytical and abstract reasoning. Analytical abilities include analysing, judging, comparing and contrasting ideas, situations and possible solutions. The componential subtheory specifies the cognitive structures and processes that underlie intelligent behaviour. It involves the planning, execution, and evaluation of intelligent behaviour. Individuals excelling in componential intelligence are likely to score highly on intelligence tests.

2. *The experiential subtheory (creative intelligence)* proposes that intelligent behaviour depends on the amount of experience an individual has on a particular task. More experience facilitates adjustment to novel situations and allows information to be processed automatically. Experientially oriented individuals tend to show high capacity for novelty and creativity; that is, generation of new ideas, invention, discovery, imagination, and other divergent thinking endeavours. Experientially oriented individuals may not score high on IQ tests.

3. *The contextual subtheory (practical intelligence)* specifies what is considered intelligent behaviour in a given cultural context. It involves 'purposive adaptation to, shaping of, and selection of real-world environments relevant to one's life' (Sternberg 1984: 271). Intelligence is thus goal-directed in three practical ways: environmental adaptation, selection, and shaping. Contextually oriented individuals may not fare well on intelligence tests since these tests contain few items relevant to functioning optimally in one's environment.

The three subtheories of the triarchic theory of intelligence provide the basis for characterizing the nature of intelligent behaviour through specifying tasks that are more appropriate for assessing 'real world' intelligence, although Gottfredson (2003) criticized the triarchic theory for its unempirical nature. According to Gottfredson, Sternberg's theoretical claims are speculative and not easily supported by researchers.

Analytical, creative, and practical abilities operate collectively to enable individuals to achieve success in their sociocultural contexts. Collectively, these abilities constitute 'successful intelligence'. Successful intelligence is the ability to capitalize on one's strengths and make up for one's weaknesses through a balance between, and integration of, the three abilities (Sternberg 1985, 1988, 1997, 1999). Noting that schools focus on analytical intelligence, Sternberg and Grigorenko (2000), in collaboration with classroom teachers, developed a series of lessons to develop successful intelligence. Skills in problem solving target analytical thinking; strategies such as the generation of ideas, toleration of ambiguity, and uncovering true interests teach creative thinking; and learning how to motivate oneself, translating thought into action, and developing self-confidence teach practical thinking. Sternberg and Grigorenko also offer suggestions for how to integrate these thinking skills and subject-specific suggestions for implementation of teaching for successful intelligence.

Individual differences in intelligence

Theories of multiple intelligences have dominated debate in educational psychology for some time. Gardner's (1983, 1993) theory is criticized because it does not address the question of 'why' individuals differ in intelligence. Gardner (1983) believes there may be a general processing capacity that 'drives' intelligence in different domains, but he resists calling it general intelligence. Those who adhere to the construct of general intelligence ('g') note its corroboration by a number of researchers (e.g. Johnson et al. 2004; Williams, Myerson, and Hale 2008). These studies suggest that the difference in intelligence among individuals can be explained by differences in individuals' general intelligence. Williams et al. noted that the resumption of interest in the existence of general intelligence arises from assumptions based on the correlations between different subtests on intelligence tests. For example, on the Wechsler Adult Intelligence Scale individuals who achieve an above-average IQ consistently score above average in most subtests, and individuals with below-average IQ consistently score below average in most subtests. The consistency in individuals' performance is taken as support for general intelligence (Williams et al. 2008).

Consistent performance has also been demonstrated in individuals' processing speed across diverse tasks (e.g. Hale and Jensen 1994; Myerson et al. 2003), with some individuals being consistently fast and others consistently slow. Individual differences therefore could be explained by differences in cognitive processing speed (Salthouse 1996; Vernon 1983). If an individual is slow in processing information, their working memory capacity is likely to be impaired as well (Salthouse 1996). Other researchers (e.g. Kane et al. 2007; Williams et al. 2008) suggested that the differences in individuals' working memory and associative learning explain the variance in general intelligence. Associative learning is the acquisition of knowledge and skills that underlie performance on tests of crystallized intelligence such as vocabulary and general information. Fluid intelligence is an individual's natural ability to think quickly and solve problems; it is not based on acquired knowledge and past experiences. However, according to Knox (1977), it is difficult to comprehend how the ability to think and solve problems can be regarded as separate from individuals' acquired knowledge and skills. Knox argued that both fluid and crystallized intelligences 'constitute the global capacity to learn, reason and solve problems that most people refer to as intelligence. Fluid and crystallized intelligence are complementary in that some learning tasks can be mastered mainly by exercising either fluid or crystallized intelligence' (Knox 1977: 420).

Intelligence and intelligence testing: educational implications

Psychologists use intelligence tests in combination with other assessment tools such as academic achievement tests, observations of students, and reports from teachers and parents to try to understand how children learn. It is best practice to have multiple sources of data on a student; in no case should an educational decision be made on the basis of one test score (Salvia et al. 2007). As you have seen, there is not universal agreement on what intelligence is. Salvia et al. (2007: 331) note important considerations:

> Intelligence is not a fixed thing that we measure. Rather, it is an inferred entity, one that is understood best by evaluating the ways in which individuals who have different

kinds of acculturation perform several different kinds of tasks. Intelligence tests differ markedly; individuals differ markedly.

Lohman et al. (2008) also note that identification of ability level is best done by measures that are related to the ability of interest. For example, if a teacher is interested in a student's ability to write, opportunities to learn writing skills and engage in writing are good indicators of talents and/or weaknesses. If standardized tests are given, they should also be well matched to the aptitude of interest and compared to scores of 'other children who have had roughly similar opportunities to develop the abilities that are measured' (p. 293). See Porath (Chapter 32, this volume) for specific capabilities to observe; the 'mastery model' (Matthews and Foster 2009) applies across all levels of intelligence.

Future directions

Internationally, there is a movement away from reliance on IQ in making educational decisions (Phillipson and McCann 2007), although 'intellectual ability' is often alluded to in both the definition and the diagnosis of some learning difficulties (see Part IV of this volume). It is an exciting time to be thinking about intelligence as research looks more carefully at the roles of culture and language in intelligent behaviour (Phillipson and McCann 2007), the important role of educational opportunities and support in 'creating' intelligence (Hymer 2009; Porath, Chapter 32, this volume), and neuroscientific research. These new directions have the potential to uncover the richness of human potential.

Neuroscience and intelligence

In the past two decades, the study of intelligence and individual differences has advanced to include neuroimaging technology (e.g. Haier et al. 2004; Jung and Haier 2007; McDaniel 2005). Neuroimaging involves computed tomography (CT) scan techniques to study the neural basis of intelligence through imaging the structure and function of the brain. While it is commonly believed that a bigger brain suggests higher intelligence, Haier et al.'s (2004) study revealed that brain volume explains only about 16 percent of differences in general intelligence (measured in IQ scores). Meanwhile, McDaniel's (2005) neuroimaging studies established a small but consistent correlation between whole-brain volume and IQ ($r = .33$). Intelligence can still be measured by psychometric tools despite the controversy surrounding IQ (Jung and Haier 2007); however, the cautions noted in this chapter regarding intelligent use of intelligence tests still apply. Jung and Haier noted that neuroimaging studies are still in their infancy and, as yet, there are no conclusive results. Such studies seem to suggest that individual differences in intelligence may be explained by studying varying patterns of brain activity.

Concluding thoughts

'Intelligence is not a static structure, but an open, dynamic system that can continue to develop throughout life' (Feuerstein, as cited in Malone 2003: 211). In addition, Jonsson and Beach (2008: 31) assert, 'according to research on motivation, learning goals and feedback, it is better to encourage beliefs that intelligence is dynamic and malleable rather than fixed and inborn' (see also Dweck 2006).

Think back to your definition of intelligence and consider circumstances, opportunities, and teaching approaches that you think fostered or inhibited expression of intelligence. Think also about personal characteristics that may have affected your achievement and potential.Would you like to change your definition in any way, and why? What would you like to see as a future direction in thinking about intelligence? We hope this chapter has provoked your thinking about intelligence and how our understanding of intelligence is relevant to education.

Contact address: cngara@btc.uob.bh

References

Biggs, J., and Telfer, R. (1987) *The process of learning*, Sydney: Prentice Hall.

Bloom, B. S. (ed.) (1985) *Developing talent in young people*, New York: Ballantine Books.

Cattell, R. B. (1963) 'Theory of fluid and crystallized intelligence: a critical experiment', *Journal of Educational Psychology*, 54: 1–22.

Ceci, S. J. (1996) *On intelligence: a bioecological treatise on intellectual development*, Cambridge, MA: Harvard University Press.

Chan, J. (2007) 'Giftedness and China's Confucian heritage', in S. N. Phillipson and M. McCann (eds.) *Conceptions of giftedness: sociocultural perspectives*, Mahwah, NJ: Lawrence Erlbaum Associates (pp. 35–64).

Dweck, C. S. (2006) *Mindset: the new psychology of success*, New York: Random House.

Fischer, K. W., and Pipp, S. L. (1984) 'Process of cognitive development: optimal level and skill acquisition', in R. J. Sternberg (ed.) *Mechanisms of cognitive development*, New York: Freeman (pp. 45–80).

Galton, F. (1884) *Hereditary genius*, New York: Appleton.

Gardner, H. (1983) *Frames of mind: theory of multiple intelligences*, New York: Basic Books.

Gardner, H. (1993) *Frames of mind: the theory of multiple intelligences*, 2nd edn, London: Fontana.

Gardner, H. (1999) *Intelligence reframed: multiple intelligences for the 21st century*, New York: Basic Books.

Gibson, K., and Vialle, W. (2007) 'The Australian aboriginal view of giftedness', in S. N. Phillipson and M. McCann (eds.) *Conceptions of giftedness: sociocultural perspectives*, Mahwah, NJ: Lawrence Erlbaum Associates (pp. 197–224).

Goleman, D. (2005) *Emotional intelligence*, 10th anniversary edn, New York: Bantam Dell.

Gottfredson, L. (2003) 'Dissecting practical intelligence theory: its claims and its evidence', *Intelligence*, 31: 343–397.

Gould, S. J. (1996) *The mismeasure of man: revised and expanded edition*, New York: W. W. Norton.

Haggbloom, S. J., Warnick, R., Warnick, J. E., Jones, V. K., Yarbrough, G. L., Russell, T. M., Borecky, C. M., McGahhey, R., Powell, J. L., III, Beavers, J., and Monte, E. (2002) 'The 100 most eminent psychologists of the 20th century', *Review of General Psychology*, 6: 139–152.

Haier, R. J., Jung, R. E., Yeo, R. A., Head, K., and Alkire, M. T. (2004) 'Structural brain variation and general intelligence', *NeuroImage*, 23: 425–433.

Hale, S., and Jensen, J. (1994) 'Global processing-time coefficients characterize individual and group differences in cognitive speed', *Psychological Science*, 5: 384–389.

Horn, J. L., and Cattell, R. B. (1967) 'Age differences in fluid and crystallized intelligence', *Acta Psychologica*, 26: 107–129.

Hymer, B. J. (2009) 'Beyond compare? Thoughts towards an inclusional, fluid and non-normative understanding of giftedness', in T. Balchin, B. Hymer, and D. J. Mathews (eds.) *The Routledge international companion to gifted education*, London: Routledge (pp. 299–307).

Johnson, W., Bouchard, T. J., Krueger, R. F., McGue, M., and Gottesman, I. I. (2004) 'Just one "g": consistent results from three test batteries', *Intelligence*, 32: 95–107.

Jonsson, A. C., and Beach, D. (2008) 'Reproduction of social class in teacher education: the influence of scientific theories on future teachers' implicit beliefs', *Journal for Critical Education Policy Studies*, 8: 1–46.

Jung, R. E., and Haier, R. J. (2007) 'The parieto-frontal integration theory (P-FIT) of intelligence: converging neuroimaging evidence', *Behavioural and Brain Sciences*, 30: 135–187.

Kane, M. J., Conway, A. R. A., Hambrick, D. Z., and Engle, R. W. (2007) 'Variation in working memory capacity as variation in executive attention and control', in A. R. A. Conway, C. Jarrold, M. J. Kane, A. Miyake, and J. Towse (eds.) *Variation in working memory*, New York: Oxford University Press (pp. 21–48).

Knox, A. B. (1977) *Adult development and learning*, San Francisco: Jossey-Bass.

Kornhaber, M. L. (2001) 'Howard Gardner', in J. A. Palmer (ed.) *Fifty modern thinkers on education: from Piaget to the present*, London: Routledge.

Lohman, D. F., Korb, K. A., and Lakin, J. M. (2008) 'Identifying academically gifted English-language learners using nonverbal tests: a comparison of the Raven, NNAT, and CogAT', *Gifted Child Quarterly*, 52: 275–296.

Malone, S. A. (2003) *Learning about learning: an A–Z of training and development tools*, Trowbridge, UK: The Cromwell Press.

Matthews, D. J., and Foster, J. F. (2009) *Being smart about gifted education. a guidebook for educators and parents*, Scottsdale, AZ: Great Potential Press.

McDaniel, M. A. (2005) 'Big-brained people are smarter: a meta-analysis of the relationship between in vivo brain volume and intelligence', *Intelligence*, 33: 37–46.

Mpofu, E., Ngara, C., and Gudyanga, E. (2007) 'Constructions of giftedness among the Shona of Central–Southern Africa', in S. N. Phillipson and M. McCann (eds.) *Conceptions of giftedness: sociocultural perspectives*, Mahwah, NJ: Lawrence Erlbaum Associates (pp. 225–251).

Myerson, J., Hale, S., Zheng, Y., Jenkins, L., and Widaman, K. F. (2003) 'The difference engine: a model of diversity in speeded cognition', *Psychonomic Bulletin and Review*, 10: 262–288.

Naglieri, J. A. (2007) *Naglieri Nonverbal Ability Test – 2nd Edition (NNAT2)*, Boston: Pearson Education.

Ngara, C., and Porath, M. (2004) 'Shona culture of Zimbabwe's views of giftedness', *High Ability Studies*, 15: 189–209.

Phillipson, S. N. (2007) 'A framework for the study of sociocultural perspectives of giftedness', in S. N. Phillipson and M. McCann (eds.) *Conceptions of giftedness: sociocultural perspectives*, Mahwah, NJ: Lawrence Erlbaum Associates (pp. 1–33).

Phillipson, S. N., and McCann, M. (eds.) (2007) *Conceptions of giftedness: sociocultural perspectives*, Mahwah, NJ: Lawrence Erlbaum Associates.

Plucker, J. A. (ed) (2003) *Human intelligence: historical influences, current controversies, teaching resources* [online]. Available at www.intelltheory.com

Raven, J., Raven, J. C., and Court, J. H. (2000, updated 2004), *Manual for Raven's Progressive Matrices and Vocabulary Scales, Section 3: the Standard Progressive Matrices*, San Antonio, TX: Harcourt Assessment.

Roid, G. (2003) *Stanford-Binet Intelligence Scale – 5th edition (SB5)*, Itasca, IL: Riverside Publishing.

Salthouse, T. A. (1996) 'The processing-speed theory of adult age differences in cognition', *Psychological Review*, 103: 4003–4028.

Salvia, J., Ysseldyke, J. E., and Bolt, S. (2007) *Assessment in special and inclusive education*, Boston: Houghton Mifflin.

Siegler, R. S. (1992) 'The other Alfred Binet', *Developmental Psychology*, 28: 179–190.

Smith, M. K. (2008) 'Howard Gardner and multiple intelligences', *The Encyclopedia of Informal Education* [online]. Available at www.infed.org/thinkers/gardner.htm

Spearman, C. (1904) '"General intelligence," objectively determined and measured', *American Journal of Psychology*, 15: 201–293.

Sternberg, R. J. (1984) 'Toward a triarchic theory of human intelligence', *Behavioral and Brain Sciences*, 7: 269–287.

Sternberg, R. J. (1985) *Beyond IQ: a triarchic theory of human intelligence*, New York: Cambridge University Press.

Sternberg, R. J. (1988) *Conceptions of intelligence of intelligence*, New York: Cambridge University Press.

Sternberg, R. J. (1997) *Successful intelligence: how practical and creative intelligence determine success in life*, New York: Simon and Schuster.

Sternberg, R. J. (1999) 'Looking back and looking forward on intelligence: toward a theory of successful intelligence', in M. Bennett (ed.) *Developmental psychology: achievements and prospects*, Philadelphia: Psychology Press (pp. 289–308).

Sternberg, R. J., and Grigorenko, E. L. (eds.) (1997) *Intelligence, heredity, and environment*, New York: Cambridge University Press.

Sternberg R. J., and Grigorenko, E. L. (2000) *Teaching for successful intelligence: to increase student learning and achievement*, Arlington Heights, IL: SkyLight Professional Development.

Sternberg, R. J., and Grigorenko, E. L. (2004) 'Why cultural psychology is necessary and not just nice: the example of the study of intelligence', in R. J. Sternberg and E. L. Grigorenko (eds.) *Culture and competence: contexts of life success*, Washington, DC: American Psychological Association (pp. 207–23).

Sternberg, R. J., Nokes, C., Geissler, W., Prince, P., Okatcha, F., Bundy, D. A., and Grigorenko, E. L. (2001) 'The relationship between academic and practical intelligence: a case study in Kenya', *Intelligence*, 29: 401–418.

Suizzo, M. (2000) 'The social–emotional and cultural context of cognitive development: neo-Piagetian perspectives', *Child Development*, 71: 846–849.

Terman, L. M. (1916) *The measurement of intelligence: an explanation of and a complete guide for the use of the Stanford revision and extension of the Binet-Simon Intelligence Scale*, Boston: Houghton Mifflin.

Terman, L. M. (1926) *Genetic studies of genius*, Stanford, CA: Stanford University Press.

Thorndike, R. M. (1997) 'The early history of intelligence testing', in D. P. Flanagan, J. L. Genshaft, and P. L. Harrison (eds.) *Contemporary intellectual assessment: theories, tests, and issues*, New York: Guilford (pp. 92–104).

Vernon, P. A. (1983) 'Speed of information processing and general intelligence', *Intelligence*, 7: 53–70.

Vygotsky, L. S. (1978) 'Interaction between learning and development' (M. Lopez-Morillas, Trans.), in M. Cole, V. John-Steiner, S. Scribner, and E. Souberman (eds.) *Mind in society: the development of higher psychological processes*, Cambridge, MA: Harvard University Press (pp. 79–91).

Webb, R. M., Lubinski, D., and Benbow, C. P. (2007) 'Spatial ability: a neglected dimension in talent searches for intellectually precocious youth', *Journal of Educational Psychology*, 99: 397–420.

Wechsler, D. (1944) *The measurement of adult intelligence*, Baltimore, MD: Williams and Wilkins.

Wechsler, D. (2003) *Wechsler Intelligence Scale for Children – 4th edition (WISC-IV)*, San Antonio, TX: Harcourt Assessment.

Williams, B. A., Myerson, J., and Hale, S. (2008) 'Individual differences, intelligence, and behaviour analysis', *Journal of Experimental Analysis of Behaviour*, 90: 219–231.

Ziegler, A., and Stoeger, H. (2007) 'The Germanic view of giftedness', in S. N. Phillipson and M. McCann (eds.) *Conceptions of giftedness: sociocultural perspectives*, Mahwah, NJ: Lawrence Erlbaum Associates (pp. 65–98).

20

NEW FRONTIERS IN EDUCATION NEUROSCIENCE

Joanna A. Christodoulou, Patricia K. Saxler and Stephanie N. Del Tufo

MASSACHUSETTS INSTITUTE OF TECHNOLOGY, USA; HARVARD GRADUATE SCHOOL OF
EDUCATION, USA; UNIVERSITY OF CONNECTICUT & HASKINS LABORATORIES, USA

Introduction and overview: What does the brain have to do with learning?

Education neuroscience harnesses tools and concepts from development, psychology, and neuroscience to investigate educationally relevant questions. While earlier tools for understanding the brain–behaviour relationship relied on observations following brain injury, surgery, or autopsies, modern technologies permit non-invasive recording of brain structure and function in learners who vary on dimensions of performance. Education neuroscience has an emphasis on the complex, bidirectional, and developmental relationship between brain and behaviour (Pennington 2009). Education neuroscience folds together the fields of cognitive neuroscience, affective neuroscience, and education to study the multiple layers of performance, process, and outcome across development as it relates to the enterprise of education.

Perspectives on the brain's role in education have ranged between two extremes. On one hand, some argue that teachers work with bodies and minds, and the brain is beyond the scope of relevance and observation. It would follow that because the goal of teaching is ultimately to effect change in learning behaviour, focusing on behavioural interventions and outcomes is relevant, whereas changes in brain structure or function do not clearly relate to behavioural performance. While the roots of this argument are understandable, it is based on an outdated model of the brain as a static, isolated system. In an extreme and opposite view, others argue for a role for the brain that is exaggerated or extended beyond evidence. From such perspectives have emerged brain-based products for education that may have little to do with either education or brain science.

Learning about the brain's role and relevance in education, through a wide range of investigations, will expand the scope and depth of the knowledge and understanding we have regarding the complexities involved in learning. Basic research into the mechanisms of behaviour or the neural basis of behaviours has allowed higher-level inquiries to explore educationally relevant questions. This chapter is structured to address the role of the brain in learning – specifically, to explore identification, assessment, and prediction of learning from an education neuroscience perspective. We discuss the relationship between neuroimaging techniques and behavioural assessments, as well as their strengths, weaknesses, and potential for collaboration in the pursuit of understanding learning and behaviour. Though the brain is neither visible nor measurable in a typical learning setting, learners are the reflection of the strengths and limitations of their neurobiological systems in the context of their development and learning environments.

Tools of neuroscience

Education is ultimately the enterprise of skill development across multiple domains, though outcomes have largely been based on observable behaviour. What has been elusively unobservable to educators is the change brought about in and by neural systems. Neuroimaging tools provide access to the structure and function of the brain, with increasingly precise measurements. The two broad dimensions that neuroimaging tools can index are 'spatial' and 'temporal' resolution. Spatial resolution refers to the degree to which a neuroimaging tool can map the architecture of the brain's structures with precision. Temporal resolution refers to the degree to which a neuroimaging tool can index the timing and sequence of activation in the brain. The time scale of neuronal communication is very fast (on the scale of a few milliseconds), so capturing activity requires highly sensitive measurements.

Magnetic resonance imaging (MRI), commonly used in both research and medical settings, offers excellent spatial resolution. When the term MRI is used to describe brain imaging, it refers to the device used to acquire images (an MRI machine or scanner) or informally to a structural image acquired using the scanner – 'I got an MRI today'. Functional MRI, or fMRI, refers to brain imaging data acquired following explicit task directions to participants. The MRI scanner can produce exquisitely refined images of the brain's architecture on cortical (surface) and subcortical (under the surface) levels. The quality and type of images acquired using MRI can depend on factors such as the type of scanner used (i.e. company/maker) and its strength (the unit of measurement is the tesla (T)). Many other factors dictate the quality of the images as well, including the type of head coil used to acquire the brain image, the acquisition parameters, and the processing of the raw data image information. Being aware of the complexity of data acquisition is important for thinking about these tools in service of education neuroscience research. However, the responsibility falls not only on consumers, but on researchers who could maximize the responsible use of MRI as a tool and advocate for effective communication of study findings (Aue, Lavelle, and Cacioppo 2009).

The data from fMRI yields an indirect index of brain activity and is based on the heamodynamic response. Specifically, when the brain is taxed by task demands, the oxygenated blood in the most active regions is depleted. A rush of oxygenated blood then floods these previously depleted regions, and the MRI scanner detects this influx of blood. Remember that temporal resolution refers to the degree to which a neuroimaging tool can index the timing and sequence of brain activation. In fMRI, the temporal resolution is decreased due to the 4–6 second delay in blood reaching regions of interest (our previously depleted regions). Note that no radiation is used with an MRI scanner, as detection of brain activity is based on characteristics of blood flow and blood oxygenation that are indirectly associated with neuronal communication.

Functional MRI studies yield dynamic information about the brain's activity over time for specific tasks. The most common fMRI study design requires the comparison of two tasks. Researchers first decide what the construct of interest is (i.e. aspect of the mind), which must be narrowly defined. For example, if researchers wanted to know how the brain is being used when rhyming words, then they would create a primary task of interest (i.e. experimental task) and a control task. They could create one task for which the participant decides if two words rhyme (experimental task), and one for which the participant decides whether two words match (control task). For both tasks, participants look at words, but only in the rhyming task do they need to analyze the sounds in the words. Conceptually, the functional brain images acquired during the rhyming condition are subtracted from those acquired during the matching condition to reveal activity specific to the processing of the sounds in words. The resulting data are not an image of an actual brain, as is commonly perceived when images are shown in articles or the media, but rather a statistical map, colour-coded to show where blood flow was relatively greater for one task (rhyming) than for another (matching), based on a statistical threshold. This information is particularly important and debunks a commonly held belief that fMRI data shows the location of activity or absolute amount of blood flow in the brain.

In viewing brain images commonly used in scientific publications as well as in media outlets, several pieces of information are important to consider. First, fMRI images are almost always the data from a group of individuals averaged together, which means that individual variability is not captured. Second, the images shown are often one snapshot from a particular orientation or perspective in the brain, which means that other areas that show activation cannot all be represented easily and the relationships between areas are not always readily apparent. Critical consumers of fMRI research should consider these factors when learning about updates from the field, specifically in regard to the brain regions recruited, the dynamic among and between brain regions, and possible variability.

Electroencephalography (EEG) is a tool that provides excellent temporal resolution and poor spatial resolution. EEG refers to both the technology and the acquisition of brain activity while the participant is not being asked to do a particular task. Event-related potential (ERP) is the use of EEG technologies that acquires data regarding the brain's activity relative to a specific task. The signal is based on electrical activity between communicating neurons. The output of this technology is a series of brain waves detected by electrodes placed on the scalp; an actual image of the brain is not produced. The brain waves are evaluated in regard to valence (positive or negative signal), amplitude (or height), and duration.

Other technologies that have been used for research include tools that measure or manipulate electromagnetic processes (magnetoencephalography (MEG) and transcranial magnetic stimulation (TMS), respectively). Technologies that involve radioactive materials, such as computerized axial tomography (CAT or CT scan) and positron emission tomography (PET), are not favoured for research purposes because they involve radioactive materials and can be replaced with alternatives for greater safety.

In addition to understanding strengths and limitations of neuroimaging tools in isolation, evaluating whether research questions are well matched to the imaging technology used is particularly important. Critical consumers must also evaluate how research is designed or carried out (i.e. methodological dimensions: see Schleim and Roiser 2009). In addition, consumers should be aware of the generalizability of study findings based on the characteristics of participants (Henrich, Heine, and Norenzayan 2010 discuss the dominance of participants who are Western, educated, industrialized, rich, and democratic – WEIRD).

Categories of influence

Below, we focus on definition and etiology, identification and assessment, prediction and intervention. Note that the level of influence in terms of relevant research is not at the basic science level, but rather in applied contexts. Applications described below are only possible because of previous work that established foundational knowledge. The focus across these areas is skewed toward atypical development in childhood but is equally relevant in considering typical development and ages across the lifespan.

Definition and etiology

Education neuroscience offers a unique perspective on our understanding of education. One area of focus and impact has been that of developmental disabilities, which involve learning difficulties or differences. In addition to contributing to the definitions of disabilities and the identification of associated etiologies, modern neuroscience methods have the potential to improve understanding of the essence of individual differences in learning trajectories.

Here, we consider three dimensions: cause, mechanism, and outcome. Regarding the cause, or etiology, of developmental disabilities, neuropsychological profiles that may be driving behavioural manifestations of learning difficulties have been posited and researched well before the tools were available to test the proposed associations between brain and behaviour. For example, Joseph Jules Dejerine, Samuel Orton, and Norman Geschwind, luminaries in the nineteenth and twentieth centuries, among many others, posited brain structure and function associated with behavioural profiles of dyslexia. Byrne, Samuelsson, and Olson (Chapter 29, this volume) offer an overview of current signatures of typical and atypical reading brain systems.

Currently, developmental disabilities are defined almost exclusively by behavioural characteristics as indicated by observations, standardized assessments, or questionnaires. However, definitions of developmental disabilities have integrated the role of the brain in a more formal manner based on replicated research indicating a consistent relationship between behaviour patterns (i.e. deficits) and brain activation patterns. For example, the definition of dyslexia shifted from a working definition proposed in 1994 that described it as being 'constitutional in origin' to the definition still favoured, as proposed in 2003, that explicitly points to the reading difficulty as being 'neurobiological in origin' following converging evidence of a disrupted reading brain system (Lyon, Shaywitz, and Shaywitz 2003). Shifting from a constitutional to a neurobiological explanation of dyslexia narrowed the focus of attribution and offered a specific way to understand that reading difficulties were not the result of laziness, oppositional tendencies, lack of motivation/ability, or lifestyle choices such as diet.

Future directions in education neuroscience have the potential to continue affecting the definition and etiology of education disabilities by informing the boundaries of what defines a disorder and suggesting whether disorders include distinct subtypes. Furthermore, the concept of 'equifinality' (Cicchetti and Rogosch 1996) – different pathways can lead to the same outcome – has yet to be explored at the level of the brain systems in education neuroscience. Research that adopts a 'neuroconstructivist' approach, a process which considers developmental progression in regards to brain systems, assumes three basic premises: (i) interactivity among brain regions, not localization; (ii) dynamic, not static, mapping of structure and function; and (iii) bidirectionality of influence between brain development and environmental impact (Johnson et al. 2002).

Identification and assessment

Two types of identification are the focus of this section. One type refers to the identification of young children who may be 'at risk' for difficulties that affect learning. The other refers to students who are currently presenting with behavioural profiles consistent with diagnoses of learning difficulties. Of note is that a diagnostic label often brings benefits of services or supportive communities, but in other contexts a label primarily confers stigmatization or other negative associations (see Boyle, Chapter 21, this volume).

Identifying at-risk students

Much research has indicated that investments in early education are the most powerful in yielding high returns (Heckman, 2006; Knudsen et al. 2006). Part of what benefits young children is early interventions to offset factors that could compromise development, particularly in those skill domains traditionally focused on in early education, including language/literacy and numeracy/maths

To date, the typical early identification approach has relied on a battery of standardized behavioural measures. For example, to identify preliterate children who may become struggling readers, a typical assessment battery might include measures of phonological awareness (e.g. rhyming activities, removing portions of words), rapid naming speed, vocabulary, letter identification, short-term memory, pseudoword repetition, sentence imitation, and nonword repetition (e.g. Catts et al. 2001; Puolakanaho et al. 2007). However, these clinical measures typically require that children are at least five years old. Furthermore, children don't typically receive diagnostic labels of dyslexia and attention deficit hyperactivity disorder (ADHD), for example, until around age seven or later. Many risk factors associated with each label are evident much sooner, as is reflected in the pending changes (4th to 5th editions) to the age of onset for diagnoses such as ADHD in one of the main manuals used by clinicians internationally, the *Diagnostic and Statistical Manual of Mental Disorders* (DSM; American Psychiatric Association, 2000).

In fact, neural signatures of risk for learning difficulties have been identified in newborns, infants, and children younger than school age (see below). These findings inspire opportunities to create remediation programmes for a younger generation of already identified at-risk students. Thus, for the case of identification, there is a resounding 'yes' to the question of whether understanding the brain adds anything to behavioural research for identification of students at high risk of learning challenges. In the field, the next steps will require a formalization of the process to determine which at-risk children do turn out to have challenges, which do not, and what factors push learners toward successful outcomes.

To date, neuroimaging studies have investigated whether young children with risk factors for learning challenges show distinct brain activity well before school age. Studies indicated that infants designated as at risk due to family history of reading disability show atypical auditory and language processing as measured with neuroimaging tools from the newborn period and beyond (e.g. Guttorm et al. 2001, 2003, 2010; Lyytinen et al. 2003; Pihko et al. 1999). Continued studies have begun to characterize the neural networks associated with different levels of reader competencies using neuroimaging, providing evidence for a developmental shift in engagement from a more diffuse to a more focused recruitment of brain regions in typical readers and early atypicalities in struggling learners as early as age five (Yamada et al. 2011).

Struggling students

Currently, educational labels such as dyslexia, ADHD, and autism are defined based on observations and behavioural performance on tests. These approaches have been successful in identifying struggling learners, but are limited. First, there is a tendency toward reliance on the scores of assessment measures from standardized tests, to the exclusion of considering the process by which the student achieved that score (which is not typically captured outside of clinical settings). Second, there is the risk of relying on a single score or snapshot of performance that is taken as reflective of typical performance by the student.

However, the value of clinical assessments and evaluations should not be underrated. In the hands of skilled users, these tools provide valuable insights into the constellation of strengths and weaknesses for an individual. The goal of assessment is to determine a person's profile, whether from a neuropsychological, psychological, academic, neurological, or other perspective. Clinicians are the professionals who focus on assessment and evaluation regularly. Educators, however, are often in the position of doing informal, or even formal, assessment of students in the classroom. Of primary importance for educators is to understand how to improve the educational outcomes for a particular student, a goal that clinical reports can be highly supportive in achieving.

Neuroscience research has traversed a range of psychoeducational domains to determine the relationship between brain activation patterns and behavioural performance. For example, executive function skills in children (ages six to eight) correspond to brain activity measured with ERP (Molfese et al. 2010). In the domain of reading, brain activations as indexed by fMRI correlate with reading ability (e.g. Hoeft et al. 2007a; Specht et al. 2009). For individual cases, the brain–behaviour dynamic has been especially salient in helping to understand how children with hemispherectomies can recover language and learning capacities (Immordino-Yang 2007), or how rare seizure disorders tied to brain structure and function abnormalities can be linked to reading fluency deficits (Chang et al. 2007; Christodoulou et al. 2012).

Knowing the brain structure or function may aid in clarifying the extent of individual variability and relation to educational constructs. Behavioural assessment remains crucial, however, for educators to learn about the psychoeducational profile of individual students. The intention of assessments, from either a neuropsychological or a psychoeducational framework, is to glean a narrative of how the mind works and how the educational setting should be adapted to better suit the profile of the learner.

Prediction and intervention

'Neuroprognosis' refers to the use of indices of brain function or structure to predict future performance or status as a learner. This area is an emerging research direction in education neuroscience that holds promise (Gabrieli 2009). Neuroimaging studies have revealed activation patterns in the brain that are related to later performance in academic domains. To be used functionally as clinical tools, neuroimaging approaches would require substantial advances in detecting, at an individual level, degrees of risk as a basis for making predictions or for judging the potential for making progress following intervention. However, the incentive to pursue this line of research is great, especially given that the current practices for predicting at-risk status can be imprecise in terms of both overestimation (Gabrieli 2009) and underestimation (Torgesen 2000). Furthermore, without appropriate and targeted reading instruction the odds are no better than chance (50:50) of struggling readers in first grade improving enough to become typical readers later in elementary school (Simmons et al. 2008). Estimates vary widely in the degree to which students benefit from specific interventions (2–6 percent, Torgesen 2000; 30–60 percent, Snow, Burns, and Griffin 1998). Identification and intervention practices are limited, and there is still much to be understood with regard to who may go on to become a struggling learner, and who may benefit to what degree from specific interventions.

In considering autism, behavioural indices have not been effective in characterizing individuals under one year of age (Ozonoff et al. 2010) and more typically autism diagnoses are offered around age three or later (see Fortuna and Davis, Chapter 26, this volume, for related discussion). In an effort to explore whether neuromarkers could facilitate identification of features consistent with autism, infants between six and 24 months of age were grouped by family history of autism (present or absent), and EEG data showed group differences as early as nine months of age (Bosl et al. 2011). While the research advances our understanding of neural risk markers in the emergence and development of disorders such as autism, critics maintain that the application to clinical practice for single individuals is quite distant (Griffin and Westbury 2011).

To date, group analysis has demonstrated that brain activity patterns predict reading, language, and cognitive ability status years later (Choudhury and Benasich 2011). Activity from the first three years of life predicted both language and cognition at ages four and five (Gou et al. 2011). In typically developing children, patterns of brain activity predict word level reading performance at age eight (Espy et al. 2004). Prediction studies with older students have also demonstrated that neuroimaging data can predict which students will benefit from intervention in the long term (e.g. Hoeft et al. 2010; Rezaie et al. 2011).

Performance on neurophysiological measures can 'improve' the predictive power of behavioural assessments alone. For example, neurophysiological indices measured with ERP in pre-reading children with a family history of reading difficulties added to the predictive power of behavioural assessments in the short term, but five years later only the ERP measures predicted reading ability (Maurer et al. 2009). Similarly, combining brain and behaviour measures in poor readers predicted reading gains better than either independently (Hoeft et al. 2007b). Related neuroimaging research has revealed brain activation differences between students who have 'not' benefited from intervention in reading as compared to those who did, further advancing the potential to anticipate for whom treatment effects can be expected (Odegard et al. 2008). Overall, both functional (e.g. reading training: Shaywitz et al. 2004; Simos et al. 2002; Temple et al. 2003) and structural (e.g. ADHD training: Hoekzema et al. 2011) brain changes can follow intervention, and be characterized by degree of intervention efficacy.

Education neuroscience advances can also impact the development of interventions themselves. For example, Butterworth, Varma, and Laurillard (2011) describe the influence of neuroscience findings on dyscalculia (i.e. maths disability) interventions. The authors describe not only the interventions, but also their efficacy with children who were identified as struggling math learners.

Finally, we must make reference more generally to plasticity because it is the basis for change in the brain. When brain systems are modified, there are trade-offs in neurocognitive systems, where particular skills can be enhanced in one condition and compromised in other conditions (Stevens and Neville 2006). This latter point remains an active area of research.

Critical consumerism in education neuroscience

As the field of education neuroscience proceeds, there is a responsibility for those invested to foster critical consumerism. Given that there is no formal oversight of interventions, practices, or recommendations, the onus for monitoring effective science and responsible practice falls on those invested in the future of education neuroscience. Critical consumerism necessitates becoming knowledgeable about the conventions of the field and being aware of the benefits and limitations of the current capabilities.

An initial barrier to engagement in education neuroscience is terminology. One of the most salient terms that is a challenge to interpret is 'brain-based'. A collection of principles, products, and theories abound with the brain-based label assigned to them, without a clear reference for what constitutes or warrants the association with the brain (Sylvan and Christodoulou 2010). In Table 20.1, we offer one framework from which to differentiate the types of material and interpretations of the label with possible intended meanings or associations (see also Table 20.2 for consumer resources). Byrne et al. (Chapter 29, this volume) offer several research-based recommendations for evaluating interventions offered for students with dyslexia. Research is a critical component of this forward movement, but equally important is communicating findings effectively and accurately (e.g. Groetzer 2011; Sylvan and Christodoulou 2010).

Table 20.1 Types of brain-based material prevalent in educational products

- *Brain-based educational theories:* Theories, based partially or entirely on neuroscience work, that propose a framework for understanding how students learn and/or how schools should be organized to facilitate learning.
- *Brain-based principles and corresponding instructional techniques:* Principles that are meant to guide educators in thinking about practice as opposed to specifying what the practice should be.
- *Brain-based neurofeedback training:* Tools that are designed to manipulate brain activity directly as a mechanism for changing behaviour.
- *Brain-based educational products:* Products that are generally available for purchase and marketed toward educators with claims of explicit connections between the programme and neuroscience work.

Adapted from Sylvan and Christodoulou 2010.

Table 20.2 Resources for information on brain-based educational products

- American Academy of Pediatrics (AAP) policy statements: pediatrics.aappublications.org/site/aappolicy
- American Educator
- Ask the Cognitive Scientist Series by Daniel Willingham
- www.aft.org
- American Speech–Language–Hearing Association (ASHA): www.asha.org
- Best Evidence Encyclopedia: www.bestevidence.org
- Campbell Collaboration: www.campbellcollaboration.org
- Florida Center for Reading Research (FCRR): www.fcrr.org
- The International Dyslexia Association (IDA): www.interdys.org
- What Works Clearinghouse: www.ies.ed.gov/ncee/wwc

Adapted from Sylvan and Christodoulou 2010.

Conclusion and future directions

In addressing the role of neuroscience in education, this chapter has reviewed the applicability of neuroscience tools to education issues; neuroprognosis potential for at risk status or likelihood of benefiting from available interventions; and the connection between brain and behaviour profiles. Existing neuroscience discoveries can take on new relevance when re-evaluated with an education neuroscience lens. As invested stakeholders, consumers of information in the field of education neuroscience are obliged to be critical and discerning, which will require reliance on both collaborating colleagues and professional development.

Acknowledgments

The authors wish to thank Alden Blodgett, John Gabrieli, Gigi Luk, and Jeannette Mancilla-Martinez for feedback on concepts and text in this chapter.

Contact address: jchristo@mit.edu

References

American Psychiatric Association (2000) *Diagnostic and Statistical Manual of Mental Disorders,* 4th edn, text revision, Washington, DC: APA.
Aue, T., Lavelle, L. A., and Cacioppo, J. T. (2009) 'Great expectations: what can fMRI research tell us about psychological phenomena?', *International Journal of Psychophysiology*, 73: 10–16.

Bosl, W., Tierney, A., Tager-Flusberg, H., and Nelson, C. (2011) 'EEG complexity as a biomarker for autism spectrum disorder risk', *BMC Medicine*, 9.

Butterworth, B., Varma, S., and Laurillard, D. (2011) 'Dyscalculia: from brain to education', *Science*, 332: 1049–1053.

Catts, H. W., Fey, M. E., Zhang, X. Y., and Tomblin, J. B. (2001) 'Estimating the risk of future reading difficulties in kindergarten children: a research-based model and its clinical implementation', *Language Speech and Hearing Services in Schools*, 32: 38–50.

Chang, D. S., Katzir, T., Liu, T., Corriveau, K., Barzillai, M., Apse, K. A., Bodell, A., Hackney, D., Alsop, D., Wong., S., and Walsh, C. A. (2007) 'A structural basis for reading fluency: white matter defects in a genetic brain malformation', *Neurology*, 69: 2146–2154.

Choudhury, N., and Benasich, A. A. (2011) 'Maturation of auditory evoked potentials from 6 to 48 months: prediction to 3 and 4 year language and cognitive abilities', *Clinical Neurophysiology*, 122: 320–338.

Christodoulou, J. A., Walker, L. M., Del Tufo, S. N., Katzir, T., Whitfield-Gabrieli, S., Gabrieli, J. D. E., and Chang. B. S. (2012) 'Structural and functional connectivity of periventricular nodular heterotopia', *Epilepsia*, 53: 1024–1032.

Cicchetti, D., and Rogosch, F. A. (1996) 'Equifinality and multifinality in developmental psychopathology', *Development and Psychopathology*, 8: 597–600.

Espy, K. A., Molfese, D. L., Molfese, V. I., and Modglin, A. (2004) 'Development of auditory event-related potentials in young children and relations to word-level reading abilities at age 8 years', *Annals of Dyslexia*, 54: 9–38.

Gabrieli, J. D. E. (2009) 'Dyslexia: a new synergy between education and cognitive neuroscience', *Science*, 325: 280–283.

Gou, Z., Choudhury, N., and Benasich, A. A. (2011) 'Resting frontal gamma power at 16, 24 and 36 months predicts individual differences in language and cognition at 4 and 5 years', *Behavioral Brain Research*, 220: 263–270.

Griffin, R., and Westbury, C. (2011) 'Infant EEG activity as a biomarker for autism: a promising approach or a false promise?', *BMC Medicine*, 9.

Groetzer, T. (2011) 'Public understanding of cognitive neuroscience research findings: trying to peer beyond enchanted glass', *Mind, Brain, and Education*, 5: 108–114.

Guttorm, T. K., Leppänen, P. H. T., Richardson, U., and Lyytinen, H. (2001) 'Event-related potentials and consonant differentiation in newborns with familial risk for dyslexia', *Journal of Learning Disabilities*, 34: 534–544.

Guttorm, T. K., Leppänen, P. H. T., Tolvanen, A., and Lyytinen, H. (2003) 'Event-related potentials in newborns with and without familial risk for dyslexia: principal component analysis reveals differences between the groups', *Journal of Neural Transmission*, 110: 1059–1074.

Guttorm, T. K., Leppänen, P. H., Hämäläinen, J. A., Eklund, K. M., and Lyytinen, H. J. (2010) 'Newborn event-related potentials predict poorer pre-reading skills in children at risk for dyslexia', *Journal of Learning Disabilities*, 43: 391–401.

Heckman, J. J. (2006) 'Skill formation and the economics of investing in disadvantaged children', *Science*, 312: 1900–1902.

Henrich, J., Heine, S. J., and Norenzayan, A. (2010) 'Most people are not WEIRD', *Nature*, 466: 29.

Hoeft, F., McCandliss, B. D., Black, J. M., Gantman, A., Zakerani, N., Hulme, C., Lyytinen, H., Whitfield-Gabrieli, S., Glover, G. H., Reiss, A. L., and Gabrieli, J. D. E. (2010) 'Neural systems predicting long-term outcome in dyslexia', *Proceedings of the National Academy of Sciences of the United States of America*, 108: 361–366.

Hoeft, F., Meyler, A., Hernandez, A., Juel, C., Taylor-Hill, H., Martindale, J. L., et al. (2007a) 'Functional and morphometric brain dissociation between dyslexia and reading ability', *Proceedings of the National Academy of Sciences of the United States of America*, 104: 4234–4239.

Hoeft, F., Ueno, T., Reiss, A. L., Meyler, A., Whitfield-Gabrieli, S., Glover, G. H., et al. (2007b) 'Prediction of children's reading skills using behavioral, functional, and structural neuroimaging measures', *Behavioral Neuroscience*, 121: 602–613.

Hoekzema, E., Carmona, S., Ramos-Quiroga, J. A., Barba, E., Bielsa, A., Tremols, V., et al. (2011) 'Training-induced neuroanatomical plasticity in ADHD: a tensor-based morphometric study', *Human Brain Mapping*, 32: 1741–1749.

Immordino-Yang, M. H. (2007) 'A tale of two cases: lessons for education from the study of two boys living with half their brains', *Mind, Brain and Education*, 1: 66–83.

Johnson, M. H., Halit, H., Grice, S. J., and Karmiloff-Smith, A. (2002) 'Neuroimaging of typical and atypical development: a perspective from multiple levels of analysis', *Development and Psychopathology*, 14: 521–536.

Knudsen, E. I., Heckman, J. J., Cameron, J. L., and Shonkoff, J. P. (2006) 'Economic, neurobiological, and behavioral perspectives on building America's future workforce', *Proceedings of the National Academy of Sciences of the United States of America*, 103: 10155–10162.

Lyon, G. R., Shaywitz, S. E., and Shaywitz, B. A. (2003) 'A definition of dyslexia', *Annals of Dyslexia*, 53: 1–14.

Lyytinen, H., Leppänen, P., Richardson, U., and Guttorm, T. (2003) 'Brain functions and speech perception in infants at risk for dyslexia', in V. Csepe (ed.) *Dyslexia: different brain, different behavior*, New York: Kluwer Academic/Plenum Publishers (pp. 113–152).

Maurer, U., Bucher, K., Brem, S., Benz, R., Kranz, F., Schulz, E., et al. (2009) 'Neurophysiology in preschool improves behavioral prediction of reading ability throughout primary school', *Biological Psychiatry*, 66: 341–348.

Molfese, V. J., Molfese, P. J., Molfese, D. L., Rudasill, K. M., Armstrong, N., Starkey, G. (2010) 'Executive function skills of 6 to 8 year olds: brain and behavioral evidence and implications for school achievement', *Contemporary Educational Psychology*, 35: 116–125.

Odegard, T. N., Ring, J., Smith, S., Biggan, J., and Black, J. (2008) 'Differentiating the neural response to intervention in children with developmental dyslexia', *Annals of Dyslexia*, 58: 1–14.

Ozonoff, S., Iosif, A. M., Baguio, F., Cook, I. C., Hill, M. M., Hutman, T., et al. (2010) 'A prospective study of the emergence of early behavioral signs of autism', *Journal of the American Academy of Child and Adolescent Psychiatry*, 49: 256–266.

Pennington, B. F. (2009) 'How neuropsychology informs our understanding of developmental disorders', *Journal of Child Psychology and Psychiatry*, 50: 72–78.

Pihko, E., Leppänen, P. H. T., Eklund, K. M., Cheour, M., Guttorm, T. K., and Lyytinen, H. (1999) 'Cortical responses of infants with and without a genetic risk for dyslexia: I. age effects', *NeuroReport*, 10: 901–905.

Puolakanaho, A., Ahonen, T., Aro, M., Eklund, K., Leppänen, P. H. T., Poikkeus, A. M., et al. (2007) 'Very early phonological and language skills: estimating individual risk of reading disability', *Journal of Child Psychology and Psychiatry*, 48: 923–931.

Rezaie, R., Simos, P. G., Fletcher, J. M., Cirino, P. T., Vaughn, S., and Papanicolaou, A. C. (2011) 'Temporo-parietal brain activity as a longitudinal predictor of response to educational interventions among middle school struggling readers', *Journal of the International Neuropsychological Society*, 17: 875–885.

Schleim, S., and Roiser, J. P. (2009) 'fMRI in translation: the challenges facing real-world applications', *Frontiers in Human Neuroscience*, 3.

Shaywitz, B. A., Shaywitz, S. E., Blachman, B. A., Pugh, K. R., Fulbright, R. K., Skudlarski, P., et al. (2004) 'Development of left occipitotemporal systems for skilled reading in children after a phonologically-based intervention', *Biological Psychiatry*, 55: 926–933.

Simmons, D. C., Coyne, M. D., Kwok, O., McDonagh, S., Harn, B. A., and Kame'enui, E. J. (2008) 'Indexing response to intervention: a longitudinal study of reading risk from kindergarten through third grade', *Journal of Learning Disabilities*, 41: 158–173.

Simos, P. G., Fletcher, J. M., Bergman, E., Breier, J. I., Foorman, B. R., Castillo, E. M., et al. (2002) 'Dyslexia-specific brain activation profile becomes normal following successful remedial training', *Neurology*, 58: 1203–1213.

Snow, C., Burns, M. S., and Griffin, P. (eds.) (1998) *Preventing reading difficulties in young children*, Committee on the Prevention of Reading Difficulties in Young Children, Commission on Behavioural and Social Sciences and Education, Washington, DC: National Research Council, National Academy Press.

Specht, K., Lie, C. H., Shah, N. J., and Fink, G. R. (2009) 'Disentangling the prefrontal network for rule selection by means of a non-verbal variant of the Wisconsin card sorting test', *Human Brain Mapping*, 30: 1734–1743.

Stevens, C., and Neville, H. (2006) 'Neuroplasticity as a double-edged sword: deaf enhancements and dyslexic deficits in motion processing', *Journal of Cognitive Neuroscience*, 18: 701–714.

Sylvan, L. J., and Christodoulou, J. A. (2010) 'Understanding the role of neuroscience in brain based products: a guide for educators and consumers', *Mind, Brain, and Education*, 4: 1–7.

Temple, E., Deutsch, G. K., Poldrack, R. A., Miller, S. L., Tallal, P., Merzenich, M. M., et al. (2003) 'Neural deficits in children with dyslexia ameliorated by behavioral remediation: evidence from fMRI', *Proceedings of the National Academy of Sciences of the United States of America*, 100: 2860–2865.

Torgesen, J. K. (2000) 'Individual differences in response to early interventions in reading: the lingering problem of treatment resistors', *Learning Disabilities Research and Practice*, 15: 55–64.

Yamada, Y., Stevens, C., Dow, M., Harn, B. A., Chard, D. J., and Neville, H. J. (2011) 'Emergence of the neural network for reading in five-year-old beginning readers of different levels of pre-literacy abilities: an fMRI study', *NeuroImage*, 57. 704 713.

21

LABELLING IN SPECIAL EDUCATION

Where do the benefits lie?

Christopher Boyle

MONASH UNIVERSITY, AUSTRALIA

Labelling in special education is not new and identification (or diagnosis) is usually sought by various parties – the school, parent, or even the proposed recipient. Professor Leo Kanner, a child psychiatrist in the USA, writing in 1967, provides an interesting historical account of the beginnings of special schooling around the world. In the USA there was 'The Institution for the Feebleminded Youth' in Ohio (1857); in Belgium there was an asylum created for 270 children deemed to be 'idiots' and 'epileptics' and who were divided into 'improvables' and 'nonimprovables' (1892). In Italy the first school was created for 'mental defectives' (1889) and in 1898 there was the creation of the 'National League for the Protection of Backward Children', which indicates an interest in child welfare (Kanner 1964). Nowadays the language may not be seen to be as severe, but the question of labelling in special education is ever present. Hansen (Chapter 22, this volume) argues that disability is rarely referred to or described in positive terms, thus highlighting the disparity in the reasoning for labelling.

A name can say much about the personality of a person associated with a group or the supposed meaning of the said group. Take, for instance, 'The Lunatics' Friend Society' (Hervey 1986): it would not now be taken seriously as a legitimate advocate for the rights of psychiatric patients due to its name, but in the 1850s this name was not as ridiculous as it would seem today, and the society gained valuable concessions from the UK parliament with regard to voluntary admittance to psychiatric institutions. Terms become softer, but they are still labels and they will develop their own positive or negative persona and take the labelled person on a lifelong journey.

Labelling is the 'old chestnut' of human taxonomy. The need to slot people, events, and things into categories seems to have been around since time immemorial. Heretic, heathen, charlatan, joker, left-wing, right-wing, homosexual, lesbian, and disabled are all evocative terms depending on your particular slant. The concept of labelling has occupied the minds of many influential people including that of the Canadian sociologist Erving Goffman, who in various influential studies in the 1950s and 1960s (see Goffman 1959, 1963) demonstrated that how people perceive you is crucially important to how you outwardly present yourself in 'everyday life', thereby suggesting that even low-level labelling has an influence on how one interacts in any given situation. According to Goffman (1963), having a mental illness meant that you were stigmatized, invariably for life, and this had a bearing on how you were treated in or by 'the system' and, possibly just as crucially, when you were in public and thus out of 'the system'.

Anti-psychiatry and anti-labelling in the 1960s

This could be similar for people in the special education sphere, who are given a label and are treated in a certain way by peers and/or support staff. Does this label allow focus on the ability of the individual or do they become categorized and thus de-individualized? Söder (1989) takes a sociological perspective and discusses the social constructionist approach to labelling, suggesting that 'theories of labeling have become common, emphasizing how categorization through diagnoses and labels underlines the handicap and diminishes opportunities for personal development' (p. 117). The influential Scottish psychiatrist R. D. Laing proposed the notion of allowing psychiatric patients to be involved in their own treatment, despite what the label would normally dictate (Laing and Esterson 1963). This was revolutionary in the 1960s and was part of what was called the 'anti-psychiatry movement' (although Laing did not consider himself to be part of this), which put forward a policy of moving towards less medication of labelled patients, and more focus on an individual's healing journey. The issue, as it relates to labelling in special education, is that for several decades the movement highlighted the folly of relating to people as a labelled category, and inevitably ignoring the important characteristics of their personality. The word 'person' is technically a label, but with only neutral connotations but each person must be understood differently. Overuse of labels denies the individuality of each person who receives a label. There is no negative label for individuality. However, a cautionary word comes from Söder (1989), who states that 'it is suggested that policies intended to be non-labelling are actually attaching a new meaning to disability, a meaning that tends to render disability invisible' (p. 117).

Usefulness of labelling – demands of 'the system'

The argument about whether or not labels are necessary seems always to be a poor second to the somewhat ingrained human obsession of categorization. Since most bureaucratic systems operate in this way, the labelling of people, whether helpful or unhelpful, is inevitable. Individualistic differences do not sit very well in a large system, hence the grouping of various individuals into developed and generally fixed terms. Large systems are not built to work in any other way, so we should not be surprised that labelling in special education is an essential aspect of many governmental systems, which categorize need. However, this does not mean that it is correct and effective in the education sphere (Blum and Bakken 2010; Huang and Diamond 2009), which usually sets out to value individual differences through the aspirational policy of inclusion in schools (Boyle et al. 2011).

Within a public education system there is usually the consideration as to who is involved with the labelling and the categorization of children in schools. It is likely that the educational/school psychologist (who normally would be the main referral point) is part of the system, and when cognitive profiles are produced it is usually, according to Mandell et al. (2008), the same people that make recommendations for a specific service or school placement. This looks to be inherently biased in that decisions of placement or provision are made on reports that may not be independent and may in fact perpetuate a system where 'need may drive the label that children receive' (Mandell et al. 2008: 42). Furthermore, from a social constructivist perspective there is always the consideration that the need to have service providers such as educational psychologists and/or special education teachers and/or specialist provisions thrives on 'keeping others in a dependent position' (Söder 1989: 120). Sheehy (Chapter 23, this volume) discusses the psychologists' role as being the 'gatekeepers of the system' and how some psychologists refer students to specialist provisions far more than others. However, Norwich (1999) suggests that if a label is not applied then some children with special needs will not be provided with the necessary support, thus being disadvantaged by being missed by the 'system'.

So the question that needs to be considered is whether having a system of categorization and labelling actually supports the systems that have been created and is, as indeed was intended, supporting vulnerable people accessing various government services – in this case, access to reasonable educational opportunities. This point is discussed in more detail in the following paragraphs.

In the USA the term 'mental retardation' is still widely used and is a classification in the *Diagnostic and Statistical Manual of Mental Disorders, 4th Edition* (DSM-IV; American Psychiatric Association, 2000); however, many practitioners and the general public may find this term somewhat pejorative and maybe even abhorrent. This term has remained in the psychological nomenclature to label certain characteristics of a person's personality over a number of years, whereas in other countries, such as the UK, labels have tended to shift or be phased out in order to prevent them gaining certain connotations – e.g. 'ineducable' is no longer in usage and 'dyslexia' has quite often been replaced by the somewhat softer label of 'specific learning difficulties' (SLD). However, the dyslexia label has never really found its way out of the special education vocabulary and is easily recognized and understood by most people as a difficulty of reading, whereas the meaning of 'SLD' is not immediately clear and using this label may lead to confusion outside the realm of the education official (see a related discussion in Taylor, Hume, and Welsh 2010). Many labels can be described as derogatory or debilitating, but changing them to a 'new' label usually has no measurable effect. In the UK, in the 1980s, changing 'disability' to 'special educational needs' in essence created a new label – the very object that it was intended to avoid. Many current examples in the playground of peers referring to each other as 'special' in order to put someone down indicate that 'the ball eventually finds the goalposts, no matter how far they are moved'.

Labelling in special education

The notion of labelling in special education has two main purposes: (i) to provide reasonable access to extra support within the standard school system for those that are deemed to require it; (ii) to indicate a cohort of needs and/or learning styles that can inform and strengthen teaching practice. It is necessary for the system to provide schools with a mechanism in order to acquire additional funding so that they are able to follow the principles of supporting the range of needs in the education establishment. However, there is a potential negativity attached to labelling in the school system in that the focus may be on what the student is having difficulty with in school and elsewhere and does not recognize the strengths and individuality of that person (Blum and Bakken 2010). None the less, many teachers can and do understand the limitations of negative labelling and will already be aware of students' strengths due to the intensive nature of classroom teaching. Teachers are best placed to focus on the strengths of their students and thus develop individual programmes that accentuate their individual strengths, irrespective of a label.

The ideal of providing specialist provision to children who require additional support is laudable, but the notion of who should be labelled as opposed to who requires additional support in school is worthy of a brief discussion. An interesting paper by Duhaney and Salend (2010) suggested that we have gone backwards throughout the last two centuries *vis-à-vis* special education. They state that 'the progress in educating individuals with disabilities was thwarted by the advent of intelligence testing in the early twentieth century as it led to an emphasis on more rigid notions of normality' (p. 716). Of course this is debatable, but it emphasizes the erroneous nature of an over-reliance on IQ testing to provide extra support to students. An interesting discussion is contained within Part IV of this volume – 'Identifying and meeting the needs of children with learning difficulties' – where 'intellectual ability' often forms part of the definition and diagnosis of specific learning difficulties. A counter-argument to that of Duhaney and Salend is that gaining a label can be considered helpful and that the results of a cognitive test (usually given as an IQ score) contribute to identification of the difficulty, access to resources, and possibly treatment (Lauchlan and Boyle 2007). Therefore, the label may be necessary, depending on the system that is in place in that country. It would be senseless not to label a child to make a sociological point if that meant that there could be no access to services for the person and family that required it.

In the USA fiscal monies are only provided to schools if an actual disability is identified, suggesting that if a label were not applied it would not be possible to gain access to funding, meaning that the child would not gain the required level of recommended support (Blum and Bakken 2010). On this notion of the need to label for a needs-driven funding system to operate, Norwich (1999) regards labels that are used to describe various syndromes such as attention deficit hyperactivity disorder (ADHD) or autistic spectrum disorder (ASD) as an acceptable practice to give some general context to areas of difficulty. However, Norwich advocates that these types of labels should be used to describe children who receive different levels of support, in addition to that available to all children in the class. In this argument the individuality of the child is lost in the system's demand for a categorization of the child's needs and thus a particular label. Norwich highlights the dilemma that if children are identified and thus labelled then there is the probability of social stigmatization. However, if they are not identified in the abovementioned way then they do not get access to resources, i.e. 'no label' equals 'no money' therefore 'no support'.

Lauchlan and Boyle (2007), who at the time of their study were prominent British educational psychologists, questioned whether the use of labels in special education was useful or not and made a fairly damning assertion that the overall effectiveness of such titles was very limited. As noted above, this point was also made by Söder (1989), who suggested that the very notion of attaching a label meant that others socially constructed the character of that person based on a label that was provided by a professional at some point in time. As Söder puts it, 'characteristics become interpreted in light of his disability. The personality freezes, so to speak, in the format of the disability' (p. 120).

The 'how' of labelling is equally controversial and seems to depend on what 'the system' requires in order to allocate funds. Lauchlan and Boyle (2007) suggested that it was only recently that many Local Education Authorities (LEAs) in the UK were moving away from the psychometric practice (cognitive testing) of providing labels according to scores from those tests. Allocating resources based on this method is inherently flawed, and has been known to be for some time to be so (e.g. Klassan, Neufield, and Monro 2005). Over 30 years ago the questions about IQ testing in schools were being asked, as they are now, and Resnick (1979) suggested that 'IQ tests are likely to be functionally necessary in schools as long as the present form of special education for the mentally handicapped remains with us – or until we are prepared to spend substantially more' (p. 252). Resnick perceived that the labelling of children based on psychometric scoring principles would only continue if the same type of special education set-up was in place. At that time in the USA this referred to the separated (special and mainstream) school system and the fact that there was a finite amount of resources.

Labouring the usefulness or otherwise of psychometric testing is not within the bounds of this chapter, but David Wechsler, who developed many tests based on the notion of general intelligence, was always very clear in his early manuals on the limits of using these types of tests in isolation and that scores are not fixed through a person's life, even though many people in education still believe this (see Ngara and Porath, Chapter 19, this volume, for more information on general intelligence – 'g'). Wechsler opened his 1944 book on adult intelligence on a controversial note as follows: 'some time ago when interest in intelligence tests was at its height, a prominent psychologist is reported to have answered an inquiry as to what he meant by intelligence by saying that it is what intelligence tests measure' (Wechsler 1944: 3). The point is that this statement was made almost 70 years ago and referred to some time before then, thus indicating what one of the pioneers of intelligence testing thought of an over-reliance on scores based on these measures.

'What's in a name?' can be an important question regarding categories in special education, especially when resources are provided based on these labels. However, labels have connotations and can have fairly diverse meanings in different contexts, e.g. in industry being described as having a 'special' qualification is hardly likely to engender any negative descriptions, as it is presumed that the holder has a useful and in-demand qualification. However, if we use the same term to describe a student (whether in mainstream or specialist provision) as having a 'special' qualification or sitting 'special' exams then the emphasis is on the fact that the student has done something alternative that does not 'really' have value in the outside world. The dreaded quotation marks say it all. Norwich (1999) surveyed three groups – pre-service teachers, experienced teachers, and trainee educational/school psychologists – in order to find out if there were negative or positive reactions to certain terms used in special education. He found that more medicalized terms such as 'abnormality' and 'deficit' came out very negatively and were therefore regarded by education staff as being unhelpful and inappropriate in the field. Conversely, terms such as 'special educational needs' and 'learning difficulties' came out positively thus indicating that some DSM labels, for example, are inappropriate and poorly related to the educational environment.

Continuing the 'what's in a name?' theme, in a 2004 High Court Case in the UK (reported in Lauchlan and Boyle 2007) a former student sued the LEA because it had not identified the student as being dyslexic. It was found that the school had taken several steps to ameliorate the reading difficulty and had put in place several strategies that were regarded as effective in helping improve reading and generally supporting the student in school. Even though the term 'dyslexia' was not recorded or specifically used, the support that was provided was proved to be completely in keeping with the level of difficulty irrespective of whether a label was used or not. The Court found in favour of the LEA because the school had put in place an appropriate level of intervention in order to support the student. Lauchlan and Boyle suggest that, 'If the use of the label does not lead to improved, or more appropriate and targeted educational intervention, then one may legitimately question its value' (p. 37). However, despite this particular legal ruling it should not be forgotten that the use of labels can also be of benefit at various levels, official or unofficial (Riddock 2000), and the argument would be about how exactly the labels are applied depending on the requirements of the system and thus the jurisdiction. A basic argument, which simply asks whether labels are good or bad, clearly does not address the complicated nature of why they are applied (or not).

The reliance on labels in special education also affects parents and their belief in the access to resources that comes with a particular label, and judging by the previous evidence in this chapter, this may be an appropriate avenue to pursue in some areas. An article in a UK newspaper highlighted the relevance of labelling in a case in London where a 13-year-old student had been identified six years previously as having 'dyslexic-type difficulties' and 'below average intelligence' after assessment. The mother fought this, with the implication that her daughter was offered a special school placement although this was not explicitly stated in the article, and after reassessment the student was found to have 'severe dyslexia', a speech and language disorder, and to be of 'average intelligence'. As a result a mainstream school placement was offered (Morris 2011). The point is not so much about whether the psychologist originally erred or not, but that so much emphasis was placed on a six-year-old assessment coupled with the label of 'below average intelligence' and that this was going to be the supporting evidence for placing a student outwith a mainstream school. The potentially negative social ramifications for these students are quite often given less credence than they warrant when considering labels in special education, and this is specifically discussed in the next section.

The importance of social factors

'Don't discount them' – this should be one of the major factors in making decisions about including children with special educational needs in mainstream schools. The question that is being asked in this section is whether this aspect is taken into consideration enough. Just how much awareness do children have *vis-à-vis* the labels that are used by professionals? Consider Figure 21.1, which exaggerates a poster showing support groups for children with particular needs in a mainstream school. The names of these groups highlight deficiencies and within-child problems and are, thus, not particularly conducive to change. The author of this chapter remembers, when working as an educational psychologist in the UK, groups of this type being run in schools. They are well meaning, but if one is labelled 'special' in a mainstream school then has to participate in these groups, which usually means being removed from regular classes, this may not sit well with some students trying to maintain a strong social presence. Educational psychologists are becoming more prominent in facilitating these groups (Boyle and Lauchlan 2009), but cognizance needs to be taken in order to appreciate the social aspects of being associated with special needs in this way.

Kelly and Norwich (2004) considered the perception of pupils with special needs and how they responded to certain labels. They found that there was a difference between students who were in specialist provision and those in mainstream school, in that the latter were more aware of negative labels such as 'learning difficulties' than the former group. It should be noted that studies have demonstrated that students in special schools can still have high self-esteem despite the nature of their educational segregation (e.g. Boyle 2007), but it is not clear whether this will detrimentally affect them when they leave school and 'protection' from society is somewhat limited. However, any negative labels that were attached to them outside of school, of which they were acutely aware, affected the students in specialist provision and arguably could instil, from an early age, a feeling of exclusion and not being a full partner in society. Kelly and Norwich (2004) suggest that this 'indicates ... special school pupils' views (boys and girls) on how others saw their educational abilities as mainly positive. This was consistent with their mainly positive self-perceptions' (p. 427). It seems that the context of the students' inclusion in a peer group or not seems to have a bearing on how they perceive themselves and whether labels are noticed or are indeed relevant. Of course, the success or otherwise of any person's school experience must be related to various variables, such as the quality of the country's education system, the individual school, and teachers. Many factors contribute to the schooling experience for all students whether they have additional support needs or not.

From the perspective of a student the information that can be taken from a label will vary with personality and also the type of label so attributed. Connor (2000) considered the differences

---

St Kilda Inclusive High – Social Development Programs for our 'Special' Children

Mental Retardation Group
4pm – Room A435

Combined Mental Retardation and Low Self-Esteem Group
4.30pm – Room B321

Dysfunctional Background Group
3.30pm – Room A143

Soon to be Excluded Group (PLEASE NOTE: Suspended until further notice)
3pm – A356

Angry Boys Group
4.30pm – A12

Assertiveness Group*
4.30pm – A13

(*PLEASE NOTE: Room changed from A12 due to clash with Angry Boys Group)

Figure 21.1 Well-meaning but flawed programmes in special education?

between students in the same school identified as having Asperger syndrome and those who were not but who exhibited similar attributes. There was a difference in self-esteem from being given the label of 'Asperger's' compared to a non-specific general difficulties label. The results indicated that having the former label seemed not to negatively impact on self-esteem compared to the latter, and the author hypothesized that this was due to there being much more information of value attached to the 'Asperger's' label (cf. a similar discussion of dyslexia in Taylor et al. 2010). As was mentioned earlier, it is the opinion of this chapter author that the social ramifications of certain labelling can have a detrimental effect on the self-esteem of some students.

The social stigma of being labelled as having below-average intelligence, for example, seems to be a valid concern for many students and subsequently adults in society. We, as special education, general education, psychology, etc. professionals have to be aware of how far labels travel and how damaging they become as a person goes through life. Bernberg, Krohn, and Rivera (2006) conducted a study on labelling and subsequent delinquency and found that being labelled as a 'delinquent' earlier in one's life meant that there was more chance that subsequently they would behave 'to' the label, and the more they did this, the more they came to believe that this was an acceptable and valid persona. This may also be the case in special education when a student has a label attached, whether erroneously or not: they may fill and then become that label. Their original characteristics are suppressed by the label they have been given and their new social persona takes over accordingly.

Conclusion

This chapter set out to discuss some of the issues around labelling in special education and the concerns that there can be with regard to using labels for students. There is evidence that labels can be detrimental to a student's personal development, as they can be overpowering and can swallow the natural persona of the person so named. However, Kelly and Norwich (2004) indicate that there can be different levels of negativity depending on the label that is used. A theme that came through in this chapter is the notion of 'the system', and it seems that it is necessary for this to exist as a form of 'resource issuer' centred on the judgements based on educational/school psychologist assessments and recommendations, for example. A concern was raised about a conflict of interest in the same person doing an assessment and then making a recommendation. It is the nature of 'the system' that professionals have to provide labels (assessments), therefore not feeding the machine with the necessary information would result in the redundancy of the job and thus system redundancy.

The current situation, which is international in dimension, is that access to funds is difficult to achieve without labelling, therefore labelling is necessary but in some cases may be harmful to the human recipients of such categorization. However, as has also been discussed in this chapter, having a label can provide access to resources that may not have been possible otherwise, and in some cases being given a label can provide the recipient with knowledge and a feeling of 'ah! Now I understand why I behaved in this way.'

There are no straightforward answers to the benefits or otherwise of labelling, as this chapter has demonstrated. For some, having a label has really helped them understand their own characteristics, but for others it has meant a difficult life of stigma and judgement. The British philosopher Hebert Spencer once said, 'education has for its object the formation of character' (1850, republished 1995: 180). Let us hope that labels, if deemed necessary, are applied appropriately and always to the benefit of any recipient.

Contact address: christopher.boyle@monash.edu

References

American Psychiatric Association (2000) *Diagnostic and Statistical Manual of Mental Disorders,* 4th edn, text revision, Washington, DC: APA.

Bernberg, J. G., Krohn, M. D., and Rivera, C. J. (2006) 'Official labeling, criminal embeddedness, and subsequent delinquency: a longitudinal test of labeling theory', *Journal of Research in Crime and Delinquency*, 43: 67–88.

Blum, C., and Bakken, J. P. (2010) 'Labeling of students with disabilities: unwanted and not needed', in F. E. Obiakor, J. P. Bakken, and A. F. Rotatori (eds.) *Current issues and trends in special education: identification, assessment and instruction*, Bingley, UK: Emerald Group Publishing (pp. 115–125).

Boyle, C. M. (2007) 'An analysis of the efficacy of a motor skills training programme for young people with moderate learning difficulties', *International Journal of Special Education*, 22: 11–24.

Boyle, C., and Lauchlan, F. (2009) 'Applied psychology and the case for individual casework: some reflections on the role of the educational psychologist', *Educational Psychology in Practice*, 25: 71–84.

Boyle, C., Scriven, B., Durning, S., and Downes, C. (2011) 'Facilitating the learning of all students: "the professional positive" of inclusive practice in Australian primary schools', *Support for Learning*, 26: 72–78.

Connor, M. (2000) 'Asperger syndrome (Autistic Spectrum Disorder) and the self-reports of comprehensive school students', *Educational Psychology in Practice*, 16: 285–296.

Duhaney, L. M., and Salend, S. J. (2010) 'History of special education', in P. Peterson, E. Baker, and B. McGaw (eds.) *International encyclopedia of education*, 3rd edn, Oxford: Elsevier (pp. 714–720).

Goffman, E. (1959) *The presentation of the self in everyday life*, London: Penguin Books.

Goffman, E. (1963) *Stigma: notes on the management of spoiled identity*, Englewood Cliffs, NJ: Prentice Hall.

Hervey, N. (1986) 'Advocacy or folly: the Alleged Lunatics' Friend Society, 1845–63', *Medical History*, 30: 245–275.

Huang, H.-H., and Diamond, K. E. (2009) 'Early childhood teachers' ideas about including children with disabilities in programmes designed for typically developing children', *International Journal of Disability, Development and Education*, 56: 169–182.

Kanner, L. (1964) *A history of the care and study of the mentally retarded*, Springfield, IL: Charles C. Thomas.

Kelly, N., and Norwich, B. (2004) 'Pupils' perceptions of self and of labels: moderate learning difficulties in mainstream and special schools', *British Journal of Educational Psychology*, 74: 411–435.

Klassan, R. M., Neufield, P., and Munro, F. (2005) 'When IQ is irrelevant to the definition of learning disabilities: Australian school psychologists' beliefs and practices', *School Psychology International*, 26: 297–316.

Laing, R. D., and Esterson, A. (1963) *Sanity, madness, and the family: families of schizophrenics*, London: Tavistock Publications.

Lauchlan, F., and Boyle, C. (2007) 'Is the use of labels in special education helpful?', *Support for Learning*, 22: 36–42.

Mandell, D. S., Davis, J. K., Bevans, K., and Guevara, J. P. (2008) 'Ethnic disparities in special education labeling among children with attention-deficit/hyperactivity disorder', *Journal of Emotional and Behavioral Disorders*, 16: 42–51.

Morris, N. (2011, June 29) 'Legal aid reforms will hit the most vulnerable, hardest, warns top judge. Case Study', *The Independent*, UK, p. 18.

Norwich, B. (1999) 'The connotations of education labels for professionals in the field', *British Journal of Special Education*, 26: 179–183.

Resnick, L. B. (1979) 'The future of IQ testing in education', *Intelligence*, 3: 241–253.

Riddock, B. (2000) 'An examination of the relationship between labelling and stigmatisation with special reference to dyslexia', *Disability and Society*, 15: 653–667.

Söder, M. (1989) 'Disability as a social construct: the labelling approach revisited', *European Journal of Special Needs Education*, 4: 117–129.

Spencer, H. (1850, republished 1995) *Social statics*, New York: Robert Schalkenbach Foundation.

Taylor, L. M., Hume, I. R., and Welsh, N. (2010) 'Labelling and self-esteem: the impact of using specific vs. generic labels', *Educational Psychology*, 30: 191–202.

Wechsler, D. (1944) *The measurement of adult intelligence*, 3rd edn, Baltimore: Williams and Wilkins.

PART IV

Identifying and meeting the needs of children with learning difficulties

22

EDUCATION AND DISABILITY

A space where we belong or is history repeating itself?

Nancy Hansen

UNIVERSITY OF MANITOBA, CANADA

The philosophies of mainstream and inclusive education for disabled students have been in place for over 40 years. They are hardly novel concepts, yet how far have we really come? If recent UK Government Green Paper publications are any indication, it appears that there is some distance to go – 'we will remove the bias towards inclusion' (Department for Education (DfE) 2011: 5). Furthermore, many newly designated educational academies are hesitant to accept disabled students as they are free from Local Authority control (BBC Radio 4 2011).

Why has there been such a reluctance to adopt inclusive education measures? It would seem that a complex intersection of history, culture, politics, and social policy impacts on current educational practice (Barton 1995; Goodley 2011; Sewell 2009). Until very recently in Western culture the exclusion of disabled people in daily social life was quite acceptable (Titchkosky 2011). Movement toward human rights and social citizenship human rights with regard to disability has been slow (Goodley 2011; Sewell 2009). Biological foundations of disability as the individual's impairment or weakness remain widely accepted (Lalvani 2012). As a result, historical understandings remain largely intact and traditional practices unchanged (Byrne 2012).

More often than not, disabled people who are most directly impacted by educational policy have had little if any input on its development and/or implementation. In many ways disabled people are often absent from discussions and the policy development process (Corbett 1996; Goodley 2007). 'Insider knowledge' or lived experiences of disabled persons' education has slowly begun to emerge.

What follows is the narrative reflections on primary education from 40 disabled women from Scotland and Canada with various physical and sensory impairments, ranging in age from mid-twenties to mid-fifties (Hansen 2002, 2005). The dignity and candor with which they relate their experiences is greatly appreciated and provides much-needed depth, dimension, and context to the process and impact of education on disabled people. Although their experiences reach back over several decades, in light of current proposals for educational reforms, we must ask ourselves how far have we come and, more importantly, how far have we yet to go?

Primitive beginnings and privileged bodies

Disability in all its forms has always been a naturally occurring part of human diversity (Hansen, Janz, and Sobsey 2008). Historically, there has been a tendency to fear difference. As a society, we have yet to develop a comfort level with bodies identified as 'different', however that difference is manifested (Holt 2010). In the process, one is not only reduced to one's physicality, but also defined by it. Non-disabled people, women, and members of racial minorities have all experienced this displacement at various points in history (Goodley 2011; Obiakor, Chapter 18, this volume). This may also be reflected in the high number of minorities that found their way to special educational settings (Connor and Ferri 2007).

Those individuals lacking socially valued essential elements of physicality are thereby viewed as lacking in humanity, in effect as sub-human, although this outcome is rarely discussed or acknowledged (Corbett 1996). Impairment and disability are not commonly understood as natural variants in human biology but rather as biology 'gone wrong' (Hansen et al. 2008: 104).

Less familiar forms of the body often assume a pathological nature, being viewed with suspicion, fear and at times disdain (Sewell 2009). Terms such as cripples, invalids, and morons lend credence to this view (Corbett 1996). Similarly, Omansky (2011) cites historical references to blind people as among other things, 'immodest' and 'inhuman' (p. 70). Disability is rarely referred to or described in positive terms, and as such its arbitrary nature has acquired the comfort of convention and rationality (Sewell 2009). Victorian and subsequent eugenicists imported the fundamental notion of associating bodily 'perfection' with intellectual capacity, supporting their claims by the safety and security provided by 'natural' science, supposedly unfettered by cultural tenets (Gleeson 1999; Holt 2010). This subjective framework has been in place for over a century. For this reason, the elements of the frame have rarely been questioned or examined, merely seen as 'the way things are' (Wrigley 1997: 75). Essentialist understandings of the body have not served disabled people well (Goodley 2011). One might argue that although the semantics may have been updated, the underlying tenets remain unchanged (Byrne 2012; Corbett 1996; Hansen et al. 2008).

Primary encounters in educational space

Whereas early education for non-disabled children nurtures creativity, where expectation develops potential, the situation for disabled children has been somewhat different. Currently in many parts of the world and until comparatively recently in North America and Europe, education for disabled people was not compulsory (Omansky 2011). Responsibility for disabled children rested with medical and social service authorities outside the realm of education (Barton 1995, 2003). Consequently, disabled people are often caught up in a series of mixed expectations: care, control, correction, and education (Barton 1995; Corbett 1996).

The social–cultural elements of education process have rarely been critically examined particularly, as it relates to disabled people (Goodley 2011; Holt 2010). How disability is dealt with in an educational setting often reflects how disability is understood by the majority culture (Goodley 2011).

Historically, education authorities have assumed a primary gate-keeping facility, incorporating the mechanistic philosophies of the larger social order by protecting the status and spaces of common physicality (Holt 2010). Thus, entry of the individual into the education process is perhaps the earliest exposure to the effects of this embodied materialism; that is, recognizing the dominant form of physicality as social capital (Gleeson 1999; Goodley 2011). This is arguably further reflected today with the increased 'marketing of educational spaces' (Goodley n.d.: 5).

Schools have not always been welcoming spaces for disabled people and they (disabled students) can be seen as disruptive to established school policies and practices. As a result, the acceptance of these students may be somewhat guarded (Omansky 2011). Often, education for disabled people is not viewed as a usual element, but rather as a privilege granted to these individuals on a highly contingent basis, and only those who 'keep up' belong (Lalvani 2012: 5). Lalvani (2012) also found that a significant number of educators believed that inclusion was unsuitable for many students. Indeed, the very presence of disabled people in educational space is often perceived as unnatural and disruptive (Connor and Ferri 2007). Despite recent legal advances mandating accommodation, access points to education remain limited, strictly regulated, tentative, peripheral, often medicalized, always on approval and subject to withdrawal (Goodley 2011; Holt 2010). What is meant by accommodation or inclusion is unclear, varying from region to region and subject to interpretation (Byrne 2012; Lalvani 2012). Different understandings of legislative and policy terminology may create confusion and thereby can result in traditional approaches remaining intact (Byrne 2012). Access may be required under the law, but the legislation does not mandate that all schools be accessible (Eudaly 2009). As a result, a limited number of schools are accessible and the customary practice is in effect maintained by educating disabled people separately from their non-disabled counterparts (Boyle and Topping 2012).

The medicalization of disability appears to supersede the usual educational considerations when disabled children enter school. Audrey provides a telling account of what was common practice over 50 years ago in the early 1960s:

> When it came time for me to go to [mainstream] school, I was just about to go to school, and the education authorities at home said 'don't let her go': I wasn't educable ... Hadn't done any tests or anything, they just looked at my medical condition and said 'people like that are not educable'.
>
> *(Audrey, Scotland)*

Babette's experience in Canada over 15 years later in the 1970s and 1980s underscores the impact of the medicalized approach to school admission:

> I was misdiagnosed as 'mentally retarded' because of the condition, it was quite a severe condition, it was diagnosed at the age of nine months and my vision problems, although they are congenital as well, they weren't diagnosed until I was five and went to school, where a very attentive teacher said 'this child isn't mentally retarded, she's blind'!
>
> *(Babette, Canada)*

Today's disabled children continue to be viewed through a diagnostic filter which frequently appears to influence the options provided (Holt 2010). The primary focus remains narrow, limited to the impairment with little consideration given to systemic factors that may have a much greater impact on the student (Boyle and Topping 2012).

Educating disabled students in segregated settings appears to remain common practice (Byrne 2012). What has been the purpose of this segregated or 'special' education to which many disabled people have been consigned? Traditional, established practices remain intact and undisturbed (Byrne 2012; Lalvani 2012). Disabled students seem to be subject to hyper-supervision (Holt 2010). In much the same manner as colonial administrators 'managed' the cultural indoctrination of indigenous peoples, similarly trained educationalists have supervised and controlled the disabled education process, channeling disabled children into appropriate disabled spaces (Goodley 2007, 2011; Sewell 2009). It appears as though the focus of 'special' education is geared to obtaining an arbitrary standard commonly known as 'normalcy', thus firmly attaching to these individuals the label of 'different'. Traditionally, achievement in this arena has been limited (Connor and Ferri 2007). Furthermore, educational choice expectation and advancement may be reduced (Goodley 2007).

This is perhaps directed at addressing the projected discomfort of the social majority in schools and beyond around physical, sensory, or intellectual difference, rather than improving the quality of life for disabled individuals. The aim may be to develop a socially acceptable appearance rather than to improve and develop socially. Similarly, Omansky (2011) relates how educators would often sacrifice blindness competencies (e.g. mobility training) of those with vision impairment in favour of a more 'acceptable', more normalized social appearance.

Stacey speaks of the fixation on 'normalization' (note that her education was over 25 years later than Audrey's, in the mid-1980s):

> I used to go to boarding school special school in Edinburgh . . . physical activity was the focus and you had to walk better, talk better and sit right. I remember once I missed my English class because they made me walk to class unaided [Stacey uses a metal walking frame], so by the time I got there it was finished! . . . I just thought the English was more important. Who cares if you can walk unaided, but I needed to write.
>
> *(Stacey, Scotland)*

Elise, reflecting on her experience in the 1980s, elaborates:

> A school for people with cerebral palsy but at the time there wasn't many people as young, that young, with a spinal cord injury . . . at that time there wasn't a lot of special schools, special schools were really . . . if you had a disability you got shoved into a special school . . . Very poor when I was young [laughter], it was very much emphasis on physiotherapy, speech therapy or occupational therapy, which is good, but there was practically no emphasis on education . . . they gave me a book to read, and that's what I did for the whole day, more or less, you know, I was given a kind of workbook, an English workbook, and if I had any problems I would ask the teacher, but basically that's mostly what I did. . . . . I was more self-taught than anything.

Elise, reflecting on the same time period, also explains the difficulties her parents faced trying to get her into the local mainstream school:

> My parents did try and fight for me to go to the normal local school but they [education authority] wouldn't have it at that time, we moved house and outwith the district so I had to go to another school which was even worse, it was everybody mixed in, it was such a big school to start with and then there was actually only four people in wheelchairs, but it was such a big school and there was so many different types of disability there . . . It was very poor, it was sitting doing jigsaws, sitting with Lego . . . if you could read a book that was a bonus, so quite often if I didn't read a book I was sitting playing with some kind of toy, by this time I was about eight, and it was really abysmal, it was like in the dark ages the school . . . I did eventually get out of that school and I went to another school, I went back to the school I was at, because it was the best, although it wasn't really.
>
> *(Elise, Scotland)*

Segregated education did have a positive impact on the lives of some of the women that were interviewed (note: this was a study of disabled women only), particularly in circumstances where medical treatment was required in conjunction with educational requirements, and some women felt that the special school environment may have provided the support – formal and also more informal (through friendship networks) – that was non-existent in mainstream spaces. This underscores the lack of accommodation provided to disabled people in public mainstream spaces. Often, one may be faced with choosing between two extremes, neither of which is really acceptable; segregated environment, which has some support but little stimulation, or an integrated mainstream environment with no support. Effective accommodation does not adopt an 'all or nothing' or 'this or that' approach (Goodley 2007). Established systemic practices remain largely unquestioned (Byrne 2012; Goodley 2004). The following quotes capture something of this ambivalent attitude toward special schools in the 1970s, indicating a few positive assessments, but even here the key message seems to be that the women found the schools ultimately limiting in academic terms in decades past:

> I went to a special school until I was 11, and it was a wonderful experience in terms of the range of subjects, it was like primary school, we got a different teacher for every subject at primary level and we had languages and all sorts, I was totally challenged by the curriculum, but then I don't know what happened, by the age of 11 I was in hospital on and off for a year and so, the school sent me in stuff, and shortly after that I became very unsettled, I think it was because my sisters had gone to the local grammar, and so their mates were around in the community and I wanted to be part of that as well and also I felt that academically I had been challenged and stretched to the age of 11/12 and then the pace was slowing and I was very unhappy.
>
> *(Kim, Scotland)*

Vicki, reflecting on the period 10 years later, explains:

> I went to a special school, didn't feel particularly special! I hated it, just found it like lack of stimulation, over-protective, just like really out of it in terms of holidays and stuff, I didn't have friends that stayed local, like local area, all my friends were from all over Scotland basically, yes I've got good friends from it, I'm still friends with a lot of people I went to school with but I just found it limiting academically [,] there was just no drive in it at all.
>
> *(Vicki, Scotland)*

Interestingly, a few women (reflecting on their time during the 1970s), when asked 'did you ever go to a special school?', did wonder if experiences might actually have been better for them had they attended special school:

> No, never. When I went to primary school I was fine, five to eleven that was fine I got on great but when I went to high school, because I have got like my processing of stuff is not as good because there has been some light brain damage, I am a bit slower. I am better now, but I just felt that in high school I could have been doing with extra help, I think that some of these special schools, there is one in Glasgow, which is great. I think I would have benefited from that.
>
> *(Brenda, Scotland)*

The overwhelming impression is nonetheless that segregated education served its purpose. Although the Disability Discrimination legislation will have some impact on access to education in the future, for many of the women whom the author interviewed, amendments to education legislation have come too late. Despite legislative changes in recent decades, significant numbers of disabled students remain in segregated educational space (Connor and Ferri 2007). Legislative changes have been in place for several decades, and the impacts on access to education have been hit and miss as types of accommodation vary across jurisdictions and the accessible education infrastructure remains underdeveloped (Byrne 2012). The measure of success depends on how the legislation is interpreted and applied. Disability and impairment inequality is sometimes not readily identified as a social inequality concern (Goodley 2007). Funding constraints and perceived inflexibility may negatively impact interpretations of inclusion (Byrne 2012).

Stacey, reflecting on her experience in the 1980s, explains:

> When I left special school they didn't really stretch your mind as to what you would like to do, it was all about what you could do. It was mainly guiding you into office work and office technology. At that time I just thought I'll do this because that's what I can do but I find it so boring!
>
> *(Stacey, Scotland)*

The arrival of disabled children in 'public' education space is seen as an anomaly. Making space for them in the mainstream places of learning is not expected or welcomed, and is perceived as disruptive to the 'natural' social order (Goodley 2011; Hansen and Philo 2007). Those individuals entering into this environment are usually championed by a non-disabled advocate, often a parent demonstrating exceptional personal fortitude to fight against the barriers of fear, ignorance, and simple lack of imagination that have preceded this outcry. Ariel's story of the 1980s in this respect is telling:

> My mother had to fight like hell to get me in, though, into regular school. When I started grade school the nuns that were looking after the school that I went to told my mum that they really weren't able to accept somebody with a disability because it required too much attention and that they thought that I should be placed in a special school. So the very next day my mother pulled my sister out of school and when the principal called to find out why my sister hadn't attended school that day ... my mother said 'well if you're not equipped to take care of one of my daughters, then you're not equipped to take care of either of my daughters', so they called back and said that 'OK we'll pay for an attendant, we've got an attendant to come in and she can start school', but they wouldn't have done that if my mother hadn't pushed the envelope.
>
> *(Ariel, Canada)*

At times, perceived curriculum rigidity and lack of creativity on the part of the school personnel may act as a barrier to inclusion of disabled students (Goodley n.d.; Lalvani 2012)

Today, parents of disabled children may find themselves in the position of having to 'fight their corner' for their children to attend and be 'present' in school (Eudaly 2009). Traditional understandings of educating disabled children (Eudaly 2009) repeatedly relate the need to continually stress the value of classroom inclusion over 'life skills training' for the child (p. 64).

The interviewees repeatedly mentioned the physical difficulties of accessing and moving around in the mainstream school environment, were often stressed, and the teachers clearly worried about the different ways in which disabled children had to move, but the following two quotes demonstrate how, with a little open-mindedness and readiness to accept 'unusual' practices, successful integration can be achieved:

> Didn't help the fact that I didn't have a wheelchair until I was 7! ... They didn't give out wheelchairs to children in those days, and that was another fight! ... I know they didn't give them out because I used to be pushed in a pram or I would crawl around everywhere. I only lived around the corner, and they eventually got agreement that I could go for a trial period, by this time I was eight and they put me in with the seven-year-olds, and that lasted a day, and the teacher of the seven-year-olds said 'ah ah, she's far too fast for this' ... So I went in with the eight-year-olds, and one of the pleasures I had in my life in that year was, I'm bragging about this, there were 36 pupils in the class and ... there was another girl I was friendly with, the Director of Education's daughter and I knew her too in class [laughs], touché ... but then I stayed on at that primary school until I was 11 or 12. If it hadn't been for my mother fighting the cause I would probably have never got into a convent school.
>
> *(Audrey, Scotland)*

> Our house, there's never been a modification in it, three storey terraced, so you stretch yourself, you just do it your own way, that's always been the gist of it, so they had to, I think they had to fight quite a bit to get me in the local school ... but really I was going to be happier in the local school, I was lucky it was a small community, it was a small convent, I had two sisters at the school and there was loads of stairs to classrooms, there wasn't going to be a problem with lifting me up the steps or anything.
>
> *(Kim, Scotland)*

One should note that it is down to creativity of the disabled student to 'fit' as far as possible within the existing academic environment with limited accommodation or disruption of established practice. However, once in mainstream education things are certainly not always straightforward for disabled children. Candi's and Joyce's reflecting on their experience in the 1980s reveals much about the everyday problems of bullying and trying to fit in:

> I was in a regular school all of my academic life ... When I went to school, I was very clumsy and so I got teased a lot because I didn't know that things were that close and I would trip over them or I would run into somebody and I'd get smacked, or ... somebody would hit me or whatever because they just thought I was doing it on purpose. I always sat at the back of the class, I didn't sit at the front of the class and they would force me by the end of the year to go back to the front of the class which would single me out all of the time, because I wasn't seeing so therefore I wasn't learning, but I didn't want to be singled out but I also wanted to be part of the group, so I tried to sit at the back like everybody else. So it wasn't until, I guess I was nine, when my mother and father decided that there was something really wrong with me and they wanted to do something about it, so they took me to an eye specialist and they got me glasses and the glasses were broke within three days because I didn't want to wear glasses and, because of the weak points and the strong, my eyes would get strained and so I would get motion sickness and so it was better for me not to wear glasses than it was to wear them. My teachers would always say 'she could do better, she could always

231

do better', but I was doing the best that I could in the times that they were giving me to do it.

(Candi, Canada)

I always remember the teacher saying 'look at your sister, she can't see and she's streets ahead of you, how come you can't do this?' and sort of making out to Sara that she was really bad and here I was, I couldn't see, and I was doing better than her, you know it was just like a slap in the face.

(Joyce, Scotland)

The difficulties in mainstream education of adapting to the needs of disabled children is evident in many ways, often in the creation of well-meaning regimes that nonetheless set the disabled child apart or seek to be overly helpful (Holt 2003):

They were very understanding, I think perhaps too much, I think what would happen a lot of the time was if I was having difficulty in a particular area they would just take my hand and walk me along and give me a passing grade . . . sometimes I did really well like English grammar and social studies, but it was the maths, geography, those areas, so I never learned how to think for myself like other people do, I had help all the time, I learned helplessness.

(Dolly, Canada)

My first year at school kindergarten was not a happy time for me. My teacher didn't know how to treat me; she didn't know how to treat any of the students! She pretty much made a big thing that I was not co-ordinated and she tried everything in the book to get me out of school . . . Finally, in Grade 1 . . . they basically put me in the library on my own with a teacher's aid [non-professional helper] . . . I was not integrated with the rest of the students and the teacher's aid taught me! . . . When a six-year-old comes home and tells her parents that I'm alone in the library . . . my parents didn't believe me . . . so then one day my mother's friend came to pick her son up and saw me in the library and then she went and told my mother . . . My mom went to see the principal [head teacher]. The principal didn't even know this was happening . . . I was out of that school faster than you can say your name! So then I went to [primary school]. I had a pretty good experience there . . . All through elementary school I was the only disabled student . . . I had one-to-one teachers' aid, which I found very, very tough. The teachers' aid made me feel like they owned me. In grade school I was judged by my braces [callipers] and crutches. They didn't judge my potential, which I now feel I was robbed of.

(Patsy, Canada)

Often the space itself is residual, and devoid of intellectual stimulation, reflecting a lack of expectation. Eudaly (2009) refers to such space accorded her son as 'exile'. Students are frequently shunted from space to space as funding and programme cuts are realized (Eudaly 2009). Repeatedly, the disabled student is expected to accommodate the seemingly inflexible system. Holt (2010) documents how even in integrated settings disabled students are taught in remote areas of the school and the sense of otherness remains unquestioned.

Conclusion

The mainstream primary education experience of these women can best be described as an interesting dichotomy. Although they felt fortunate to have avoided or limited their exposure to segregated school, at the same time they were often painfully aware that their presence in the regular school environment was perceived as a source of tension and conflict. Indeed, the necessity to provide adaptation is frequently perceived as disruptive, and seemingly compromises the education standards of non-disabled students. Difference is often emphasized by education authorities in a negative fashion, a sign of intellectual limitation rather than a failure on their part to provide effective accommodation. Consequently, most of the women rarely felt welcome in these spaces, although they believed that they had the right to be there. Disabled students today face similar issues. The women also identified the need to struggle against 'common knowledge' or negative social perceptions of difference in disability. In their efforts to gain approval, many of the women identified an internalized feeling of personal inadequacy taking root during this period in school at the primary level. Omansky (2011) maintains that such practices continue to foster minimal inclusion for disabled people.

Educational systems reflect those elements most valued by the majority culture (Goodley 2011). We remain haunted to our detriment by the ghosts of what has gone before. A new approach is needed in order to move beyond outdated essentialist ideology and normative practice (Holt 2010). Serious difficult reflection is required, examining the education system envisioned at its very core. Dignity, worth, and respect are not secured or imparted by superficial tinkering with a flawed foundation lacking imagination or creativity (Goodley 2011). Real change and true inclusion will require hard work over an extended period of time, without which the promise of inclusive education risks becoming hollow rhetoric (Byrne 2012; Goodley 2011).

Contact address: hansenn@cc.umanitoba.ca

References

Barton, L. (1995) 'Segregated special education: some critical observations', in G. Zarb (ed.) *Removing barriers*, London: PSI (pp. 27–36).

Barton, L. (2003) 'Inclusive education and teacher education: a basis of hope or a discourse of delusion?', Lecture delivered at the Institute of Education, University of London, 3 July.

BBC Radio 4 (2011) *You and Yours*, Educational Academies Reluctant to Admit Students with Special Educational Needs, 20 June.

Boyle, C., and Topping, K. (2012) *What works in inclusion?*, New York: Open University Press.

Byrne, B. (2012) 'Hidden contradictions and conditionality: conceptualizations of inclusive education in international law, disability and society', published on iFirst, 18 July (pp. 1–14).

Connor, D. J., and Ferri, B. A. (2007) 'The conflict within: resistance to inclusion and other paradoxes in special education', *Disability and Society*, 22: 63–77.

Corbett, J. (1996) *Bad-mouthing: the language of special needs*, London: Falmer Press.

Department for Education (DfE) (2011) *Support and aspiration: a new approach to special educational needs*, London: DfE.

Eudaly. C. (2009) 'Exile to Bridlemile or where the@#%&! is my village?!', in Y. Bertelli, Y. Silverman, and S. Talbot (eds.) *My baby rides the short bus: the unabashedly human experience of raising kids with disabilties*, Winnipeg: Fernwood (pp. 59–71).

Gleeson, B. (1999) *Geographies of disability*, London: Routledge.

Goodley, D. (2004) 'De/constructing learning difficulties in educational contexts: the life story of Gerry O'Toole', in C. Barnes and G. Mercer (eds.) *Disability policy and practice: applying the social model*, Leeds: The Disability Press (pp. 175–190).

Goodley D. (2007) 'Towards socially just pedagogies: Deleuzoguattarian critical disability studies', *International Journal of Inclusive Education*, 11: 317–334.

Goodley, D. (2011) *Disability studies: an interdisciplinary introduction*, London: Sage.

Goodley, D. (n.d.) 'For inclusion: towards a critical pedagogy with marginalised learners', pp. 1–12 [online]. Available at www.leeds.ac.uk/disability-studies/archiveuk/goodley/inclusive%20pedagogy.pdf

Hansen, N. (2002) *'Passing' through other people's spaces: disabled women, geography, and work*. Unpublished PhD thesis. Glasgow: University of Glasgow.

Hansen, N. (2005) 'Spaces of education. finding a place that fits', *Review of Disability Studies*, 1: 22–36.

Hansen, N., Janz, H., and Sobsey, D. (2008) '21st century eugenics?', *The Lancet*, 372: 104–107.

Hansen, N., and Philo, C. (2007) 'The normality of doing things differently: bodies, spaces and disability geography', *Tijdschrift voor Economische en Sociale Geografie*, 98: 493.

Holt, L. (2003) '(Dis)abling children in primary school micro-spaces: geographies of inclusion and exclusion', *Health and Place*, 9: 119–128.

Holt, L. (2010) 'Young people with socio-emotional differences: theorizing disability and destabilizing socio-emotional norms', in V. Chouinard, E. Hall, and R. Willton (eds.) *Towards enabling geographies: 'disabled' bodies and minds in society and space*, Ashgate: Farnham (pp. 145–164).

Lalvani, P. (2012) 'Privilege, compromise, or social justice: teachers' conceptualizations of inclusive education', *Disability and Society*, 28: 14–27.

Omansky, B. (2011) *Borderlands of blindness*, Boulder: Lynne Rienner.

Sewell, D. (2009) *The political gene: how Darwin's ideas changed politics*, London: Picador.

Titchkosky, T. (2011) *The question of access: disability, space, meaning*, Toronto: University of Toronto Press.

Wrigley, O. (1997) *The politics of deafness*, Washington, DC: Gallaudet University Press.

23

EDUCATIONAL PSYCHOLOGY AND THE DEVELOPMENT OF INCLUSIVE EDUCATION

Kieron Sheehy

THE OPEN UNIVERSITY, UK

This chapter outlines the origins of inclusive education as an international movement and the assumptions and values that underpin it. It draws upon international research and presents a framework for understanding the different types of research evidence that contribute to the area. The nature of an inclusive pedagogy is considered and the implications for psychologists are highlighted.

The development of inclusive education

Inclusive education is a worldwide movement (Lindsay 2007) whose origins lie outside of the formal education system. The 'Salamanca Statement' (United Nations Educational, Scientific and Cultural Organization (UNESCO) 1994) adopted a strongly rights-based perspective on education:

> Reaffirming the right to education of every individual, as enshrined in the 1948 Universal Declaration of Human Rights, and renewing the pledge made by the world community at the 1990 World Conference on Education for All to ensure that right for all regardless of individual differences.
>
> *(p. vii)*

Five years later there was a growing international consensus that 'all children have the right to be educated together, regardless of their physical, intellectual, emotional, social, linguistic or other condition, and that inclusion makes good educational and social sense' (UNESCO 1999: 9).

Across the world policies have been introduced to remove barriers to learning experienced by young people, including those with special educational needs. For example, in the USA this is reflected in The Education for All Handicapped Pupils Act (PL-94-142) and Individuals with Disabilities Education Act (PL-99-457) (Lindsay 2007). In England, all schools were required to 'provide effective learning opportunities for "all" pupils' (Long et al. 2010) and a child's 'default' educational placement became the mainstream 'unless parents do not wish this or it is incompatible with the provision of efficient education for other children' (Special Educational Needs and Disability Act in 2001). More recently the 'Convention on Rights of People with Disabilities' (United Nations 2006) re-emphasised this commitment and specified that 'Parties shall ensure an inclusive education system at all levels' (Article 24). Most European countries signed up to this (Department of Economic and Social Affairs (DESA) 2011) and the convention was explicit that professionals, such as psychologists, are required to be sufficiently aware and skilled to support the provision of 'the assistance and services guaranteed by those rights' (United Nations 2006: Article 4 (i)).

The challenge of inclusive education

Inclusive education presents a more profound challenge than simply 'integrating' children, i.e. putting them in a mainstream setting and providing support so they can 'fit in' (Long et al. 2010). This challenge is reflected by the British Psychological Society (BPS 2005) in its commitment to the values underpinning inclusive education:

> Rejecting segregation or exclusion of learners for whatever reason – ability, gender, language, care status, family income, disability, sexuality, colour, religion or ethnic origin; maximising the participation of all learners in the community schools of their choice; making learning more meaningful and relevant for all, particularly those learners most vulnerable to exclusionary pressure; rethinking and restructuring policies, curricula, culture and practices in schools and learning environments so that diverse learning needs can be met, whatever the origin or nature of those needs.
>
> *(p. 2)*

How psychologists support children with a range of special educational needs within schools and classrooms is described in other chapters in this section. Psychologists can play a key role in working with schools and educational providers to support their development as inclusive organisations (BPS 2005). Achieving this has been described as 'the biggest challenge facing school systems throughout the world' (Ainscow and Sandhill 2010: 401). This may explain why after years of inclusive policies and statutory guidance, supported by value statements of professional psychological bodies, the 'health' of the movement towards inclusive education remains uncertain (Long et al. 2010). There may be several factors influencing this situation.

Definition and redefinition

Inclusion has been defined in different ways (Ainscow, Booth, and Dyson 2006). This is a longstanding issue because although the word 'inclusion' appears regularly in government documents:

> no 'official' definition of it exists and, as in the USA, 'inclusion', along with 'inclusive education', 'integration' or 'mainstreaming', appears nowhere in primary legislation. Consequently, when government documents, academics, parents and activists speak of 'inclusion' or 'inclusive education' they may appear to be using the same term while what they mean may not be the same at all.
>
> *(Open University 2005: 14)*

In some countries the term is synonymous with integration or special education, terms that can result in segregation and exclusion for some young people. It is common to talk of a continuum of provision, with inclusion existing under a wide umbrella of options. This continuum can be seen as having 'most separate' and 'most included' extremes, represented by placements in full-time residential schools and full-time in ordinary schools respectively (Norwich 2008). Between lie a variety of full- and part-time placements in various units, schools, and special classes. Reconstructing inclusion to fit within an existing continuum of provision may partly explain why a plethora of inclusive policies within the UK had not dramatically altered the proportion of pupils within segregated special schools (Hick 2009). Inclusive education could be (re) constructed as being 'included' in segregated schools (Keegan 2011). While a similar continuum exists in many countries, there are others where the continuum is constructed differently and mainstream placement is the option for all, or nearly all, pupils (Curcic 2009). This suggests that there are alternative ways of thinking about children's learning other than using a diagnostic category or psychological assessment to identify distinct, mutually exclusive school placements.

Gatekeepers in the system

Internationally, educational psychologists often act as 'gatekeepers' between special and mainstream settings (Rubie-Davis 2011), as part of their role is to provide advice on the appropriate placement and support of children. There are however significant variations in placement recommendations between educational psychologists. For example in a large education authority within the UK 'half the educational psychologists were responsible for referring 91 percent of the children who attend special schools for children with EBD [emotional and behavioural difficulties] and MLD [moderate learning difficulties]' (Farrell and Venables 2009: 118). Psychologists trained more recently were less likely to recommend segregated provision. This draws attention to the importance of psychologists' beliefs when responding to children's needs and ambitions (Farrell and Venables 2009). Figure 23.1 illustrates differences in psychologists' placement preferences for categories of need. These differences may reflect the psychologists' geographical location, experience of particular schools, training, and beliefs.

In terms of actual placements, a survey of all English education authorities also found significant disparities. For example, a disabled child in one location was 24 times more likely to attend a special school than if they lived in a London authority (Centre for Studies on Inclusive Education (CSIE) 2005). These variations in practice highlight different perspectives on what inclusive education, and inclusive legislation, means in practice. This suggests that for some pupils education with peers is not seen as the most appropriate choice, perhaps signalling a belief in 'limits to inclusion' in terms of school placement. For example, only 2 percent of psychologists in Hardman and Worthington's (2000) study saw a mainstream placement for children with profound and multiple learning difficulties as possible, with support. However, such limits are not universal. Such children might routinely be part of mainstream classes in Italy, but excluded from education elsewhere (Rix et al. 2012).

Models of difference

A key factor influencing how children's needs are responded to is the way that 'difference' is perceived. An issue for psychologists operating within a continuum of educational provision is the extent to which a 'medical model' is used to identify and respond to difference. The medical model's discourse constructs a way of thinking about disability and learning difficulties as a

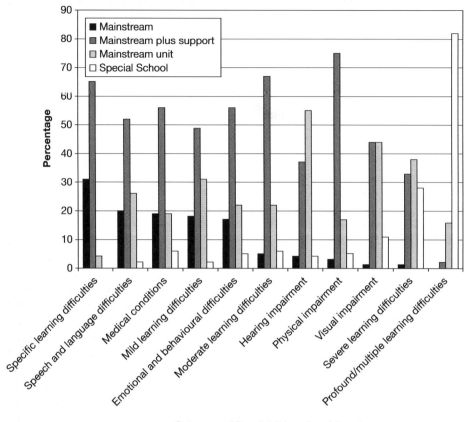

Figure 23.1 Educational psychologists' hypothetical placement preferences (adapted from Hardman and Worthington 2000)

'within-child' deficit in need of individual assessment, diagnosis, labelling/categorization, and treatment or remediation. Copeland (1999) considered the language of special educational needs to be a medicalized one.

> The whole essence of this discourse diverts attention from contextual and pedagogical considerations, to lay the blame upon the personal characteristics and symptoms of the child. Thus, the excluded pupil is pathologised. It also constitutes the rediscovery of the medical model of pupil deficiency to explain an educational phenomenon.
>
> *(p. 109)*

By contrast, the 'social model' of disability highlights external social factors as 'disabling', and barriers to learning (Oliver 1996). These barriers might include: 'attitudes, design of the teaching environment and the structure of pedagogical activities' (Sheehy 2010: 161). The social model contains within it a perspective that difference, such as a physical impairment, can result in oppression from societal views of normality, creating a greater disadvantage than a loss of function alone (Llewellyn and Hogan 2000). By defining disability in terms of disabling environments, the social model leads to a view that through collaboration and cooperation at a societal level, disabled young people can be included in education.

Researching and developing inclusive education

Although the social model has been challenged (Shakespeare 2008), it has carried forward the imperative to remove disabling barriers and underpinned the development of inclusive practices (Open University 2005), and informed new ways in which research proceeds (Slee 1998). The latter perspective is that the 'process' of educational research itself can positively facilitate, or oppose, the development of inclusive education. One example of this is the recent move for psychologists to consult, and seek to empower, young people through educational research.

Children's voice and inclusive research

The United Nations Convention on the Rights of the Child in 1989 established children's rights in relation to educational decisions and is reflected in national initiatives designed to support pupils' participation and 'voice' in their educational lives (Children's Rights Alliance for England (CRAE) 2008). At a basic level, 'It cannot tenably be claimed that schooling is primarily intended to benefit pupils if pupils' own views about what is beneficial to them are not actively sought and attended to' (McIntyre, Pedder, and Rudduck 2005: 150). Consequently, as part of developing inclusive schools, educational psychologists have researched pupils' school experiences. The methods they use can include empowering pupil-researchers, traditional interviews, focus groups (Sheehy and Bucknall 2008) and approaches designed for young children (Ravet 2007). Yet this is not common practice and psychologists require a sensitivity to issues such as power relationships, tokenism, and the potential for 'dressing up' essentialist (i.e. deficit) views of diversity (Sheehy et al. 2004). One promising approach is 'participatory action research' (PAR) (Prilleltensky 2010), in which young people reflect on and articulate their needs and wishes. This allows children to participate meaningfully in research and support their engagement in society. Other radical approaches include young people, including those with learning disabilities, becoming researchers themselves (Kellett, Chapter 2, this volume). What all of these examples do to some extent is to challenge the 'social relations of research production' (Oliver 1992: 106).

However, children with profound and multiple learning disabilities (PMLD) remain vulnerable to exclusion from such consultations. Communication difficulties are an often cited reason for not consulting disabled children, and those with PMLD typically need their communications to be interpreted and mediated by people who know them well. Pupils with PMLD will increasingly be using assistive technologies and the United Nations Convention on the Rights of People with Disabilities (CPRD; United Nations 2006) stresses the importance of such technologies in removing barriers to independence and participation in decision making. Psychologists working with disabled children should therefore consider the affordances of assistance technology both in seeking their voice and in supporting their informed engagement with research (Wright et al. 2011).

Young people's experiences of different types of provision can give insights into inclusive practices. For example, resourced schools cater for children with low-incidence disabilities, by focusing appropriate resources into a single location, to which children travel rather than attending local schools. Pupils in this type of provision have 'access to friends with similar needs and whose levels of maturity and interests may be more evenly matched to their own' (Cuckle and Wilson 2002: 70), but describe difficulties in maintaining social contacts and being able to 'go out' with friends (Keegan 2011). This is important, and deaf pupils, asked about their experiences, make a direct link between friendships and educational success (Jarvis, Iantaffi, and Sinkra 2010). Emerging from such research is an understanding of the impact of geographical and social restrictions on the development of pupils' lives, for example how a higher degree of adult surveillance distorts their peer relationships (Watson et al. 2000). Talking to disabled young people in a resourced school, Keegan (2011) found that nearly all those she consulted would have preferred to have transferred to their local schools with their peers (also see Hansen, Chapter 22, this volume, for testimonies relating to this). However, disabled young people describe an absence of consultation about such placements or discussions concerning their mainstream options (Cook, Swain, and French 2001).

Children typically do not see themselves as disabled in every context, and are ambivalent about the term 'disabled', foregrounding similarities with their peers, whereas adults' reactions and school policies have been seen by children as presenting a much more 'rigid version' of disability and identity (Connors and Stalker 2007). This can produce 'rigid' in-class support which is not always helpful, rather than listening to what pupils say about the level and type of support that they need.

Bullying is a significant factor raised by children in discussions of inclusion, and they attribute this to issues of difference (CRAE 2008). Accounts from children with Asperger's syndrome suggest that their lack of social awareness is associated with being verbally and physically bullied significantly more than their peers (Sofronoff, Dark, and Stone 2011) and resourced and special placements are positively perceived by young people who value their 'safeness' (Cuckle and Wilson 2002). While this fits with data that children with special education needs are more likely to be bullied, comparative studies of mainstream and special placement do not produce clear evidence of either being better in this respect (Rose, Espelage, and Monda-Amaya 2009). Perhaps not surprisingly, research finds that in general terms young people are more likely to develop positive and non-discriminatory attitudes to their disabled peers through direct shared school experiences (Wilson 2004).

Psychologists researching inclusive education

Psychologists are not a homogeneous group and, as indicated previously, bring into their work different discourses and beliefs. It has been suggested that there are two common discourses within inclusive education, which are often combined (Dyson 1999): a 'rationale' discourse that looks for underpinning reasons for inclusion and a 'realization' discourse that attempts to establish inclusion in practice. Within each of these discourses one can identify two sub-themes. Within the 'rationale' discourse are (a) the rights and ethics discourse, which contains arguments that segregated education can never be equitable and sees inclusive education as a way of delivering social justice, and (b) the efficacy discourse that inclusive education is effective education, which produces significant social benefits. Within the 'realization' discourse lie (a) a political discourse that identifies and challenges power relationships, for example the role of vested interests in maintaining exclusionary practices, and (b) the pragmatic discourse that seeks to describe what inclusive practice and pedagogy might look like and the practical steps needed to achieve these ends (Dyson 1999; Open University 2005). The discourses through which psychologists think about inclusive education can shape the types of evidence that they see as being necessary in their research.

A question that is often asked is 'does inclusive education work?' Consequently psychologists can find themselves researching efficacy and pragmatic questions.

Efficacy: does inclusive education work?

An international comparison of the effect sizes of educational outcomes across mainstream and special placements concluded that inclusive settings did not disadvantage children with special educational needs, and in many cases produced better academic outcomes (Canadian Council for Learning 2009). The caveat to this was that such advantages were small and there were variations between individual children and schools, with instructional quality being more significant than 'placement'. Other international reviews, including those drawing on longitudinal research, find positive correlations between mainstream placement and a variety of outcome measures for disabled pupils, such as engagement in class activities, psychosocial measurements, and vocational and academic skills (Curcic 2009).

The results tend to be more mixed regarding specific categories of need. A review of 30 years of studies into the education of children with speech and language problems concluded that in-class support could be as effective as 'pull out' models, but again acknowledged the wide variations between individual settings and pedagogies (Cirrin et al. 2010). A special educational placement does not guarantee better teaching for pupils (McLesky and Waldron 2011), and in general outcome reviews do not find advantages for specialist settings (Buckley et al. 2006; President's Commission on Excellence in Special Education 2002). Again the caveat is that the differences in such studies are small (Lindsay 2007).

Within this area is the discussion of whether specific groups of children require a special pedagogy, as mainstream teachers can feel that a special way of teaching is needed for which they lack the requisite skills and resources (Florian and Black-Hawkins 2010). As discussed in Hansen (Chapter 22, this volume), there are curriculum areas that are obviously specialized, for example mobility training for children with little or no sight. Furthermore, knowledge of a range of options (such as Braille) is essential in teaching literacy skills to children whose visual impairment has been acquired at different times or has different prognoses. However, there is little or no evidence to support a distinctive pedagogy for children with visual impairment at a general 'macro' level (Douglas and McLinden 2004).

Deaf and hard-of-hearing pupils in mainstream settings, assessed across many years, have performed poorly in comparison with their hearing peers (Qi and Mitchell 2012). However, they may fare a little better in special settings (Stinson and Kluwin 2011). Research suggests that pedagogy is the key factor and strategies such as visual concept mapping, mnemonic aides, and scaffolding by teachers in a mainstream classroom not only allow students who are deaf or hard-of-hearing to learn as much as their peers (Marschark et al. 2008), but supports their peers also (Marschark et al. 2011). Perhaps a greater challenge for educators working with deaf students relates to valuing deaf culture and language within inclusive schools, rather than just meeting educational outcomes, reflected in the personnel within the school and the materials and activities that help learners to develop their sense of identity.

In a situation where there is no clear, albeit generally positive, 'efficacy conclusion', psychologists' values will guide decisions regarding school placement and support. Hence psychologists need to be aware of their own ethical position and how this informs their professional recommendations and practice.

Pragmatics: what does inclusive education look like?

While efficacy studies control and compare the outcomes of different settings, pragmatic approaches find examples of 'what works' and build a model of inclusion from this knowledge. Beginning from a premise that an inclusive classroom should be able to deliver curriculum subjects to all pupils within it, an international systematic review identified several factors that were associated with successful outcomes. According to Sheehy et al. (2009), these could be seen as the pedagogic features of an inclusive classroom:

1. Social engagement being intrinsic to the pedagogy.
2. Flexible modes of representing activities.
3. Progressive scaffolding of classroom activities
4. Authenticity of classroom activities.
5. Pedagogic community.

In summary, this refers to the teacher facilitating cooperative group work, using a variety of representations of problems to present and discuss issues. The activities are planned sequentially and supported (for example with mnemonic aids) to allow pupils to engage gradually with concepts and develop the skills they need. Authentic activities are those that the teacher judges as authentic in terms of the curriculum topic and also the learner's own experiences. A key part of delivering an 'inclusive pedagogy' is that the teacher is part of pedagogic community. They are supported by, and contribute to, a group who have a shared view of what they are teaching and why they are teaching it in a particular way. As these features emerged from published research, the pedagogic community typically involved teachers and researchers. This suggests that psychologists could play an important role in the development of inclusive education by contributing to these communities.

Using a more immersive research methodology, Florian and Black-Hawkins (2010) carried out an in-depth study of 'teacher craft' in two Scottish schools. One barrier that emerged resulted from 'bell curve thinking' concerning ability, an issue with which educational psychologists have a long association (Gillard 2009, cited in Florian and Black-Hawkins 2010). In England, for example, the Cognitive Ability Test is taken by over a million 11-year-olds (Deary et al. 2007) and used to: stream children into ability groups; grade their school performance; and predict their results in exams that occur many years later (Open University 2010). Once a child is streamed they are unlikely to move groups (Ireson, Clark, and Hallam 2002), and children with special educational needs are the group most vulnerable to the negative effects of such deterministic thinking (Hart et al. 2004). In creating an alternative approach, Florian and Black-Hawkins (2010) conceptualized an inclusive pedagogy as extending what was usually available in the classroom in ways that did not stigmatize some learners and allowed all to participate in classroom life. This way of approaching inclusion develops pupil choice and collaboration in the classroom. It reflects the innovative work of Hart et al. (2004), who argued that educationalists need to focus on the context of the child's experience and set aside the language of special educational needs.

Other research has taken a different pragmatic route. McLesky and Waldron (2011) examined research evidence that identified teaching components that were effective in delivering 'intensive instruction' across a range of settings and considered the extent to which these could be delivered in inclusive mainstream classes. These components included: grouping; instructional design; delivery of instruction; and independent practice. They concluded that while children with learning difficulties could make significant progress with mainstream classes, part-time separate settings or resourced rooms might potentially offer a more intensive approach. There is an interesting tension between the first two approaches and this one. Inclusive classroom research supports a group-based social constructivist approach to learning. The 'intensive teaching' research makes recommendations that are more in tune with direct instruction models, with grouping by 'instructional needs', which could be operationalized in several ways including individualized teaching. One might suggest that each of these studies is actually describing facets of 'good teaching' for all, and it has been argued that an inclusive pedagogy is just that.

Conclusion

Inclusive education has developed from a belief that all children have the right to be educated with their peers and that their voice should carry weight in decisions that affect their lives. The extent to which this has developed is influenced by how difference and disability are constructed. Inclusive education has influenced psychologists' practice and research, giving an impetus to seeking and empowering young people's voice within the education system, and a need to reflect on their own values and ethics. Pragmatic approaches to research have identified the features of inclusive practice and given an evidence base that is useful in developing future educational approaches. An important part of this will be psychologists working collaboratively with schools, teachers, and young people to develop an understanding of how inclusion can work for all the school community.

Contact address: kieron.sheehy@open.ac.uk

References

Ainscow, M., Booth, T., and Dyson, A. (2006) 'Inclusion and the standards agenda: negotiating policy pressures in England', *International Journal of Inclusive Education*, 10: 295–308.

Ainscow, M., and Sandhill, A. (2010) 'Developing inclusive education systems: the role of organisational cultures and leadership', *International Journal of Inclusive Education*, 14: 401–416.

BPS (2005) British Psychological Society: Inclusive Education Position Paper [online]. Available at http://decp.bps.org.uk/decp/position_statements/position_statements_home.cfm

Buckley, S., Bird, G., Sacks, B., and Archer, T. A. (2006) 'Comparison of mainstream and special education for teenagers with Down syndrome: implications for parents and teachers', *Down Syndrome Research and Practice*, 9: 54–67.

Canadian Council for Learning (2009) 'Does placement matter? Comparing the academic performance of students with special needs in inclusive and separate settings' [online]. Available at www.ccl-cca.ca/pdfs/LessonsInLearning/03_18_09E.pdf

Cirrin, F. M., Schooling, T. L., Nelson, N. W., Diehl, S. F., Flynn, P. F., Staskowski, M., et al. (2010) 'Evidence-based systematic review: effects of different service delivery models on communication outcomes for elementary school-age children', *Language, Speech, and Hearing Services in Schools*, 41: 233–264.

Connors, C., and Stalker, K. (2007) 'Children's experiences of disability: pointers to a social model of childhood disability', *Disability and Society*, 22: 19–33.

Cook, T., Swain, J., and French, S. (2001) 'Voices from segregated schooling: towards an inclusive education system', *Disability and Society*, 16: 293–310.

Copeland, I. (1999) 'Normalisation: an analysis of aspects of special educational needs', *Educational Studies*, 25: 99–111.

CRAE (2008) *Schools must consider the views of students* [online]. Available at www.crae.org.uk/news-and-events/press/schools-must-consider-views-of-students.html

CSIE (2005) Segregation trends – LEAs in England 2002–2004. Centre for Studies on Inclusive Education [online]. Available at www.csie.org.uk/resources/segregation-trends.shtml

Cuckle, P., and Wilson, J. (2002) 'Social relationship and friendship among young people with Down's syndrome in secondary school', *British Journal of Special Education*, 29: 66–71.

Curcic, S. (2009) 'Inclusion in PK-12: an international perspective', *International Journal of Inclusive Education*, 13: 517–538.

Deary, I. J., Strand, S., Smith, P., and Fernandes, C. (2007) 'Intelligence and educational achievement', *Intelligence*, 35: 13–21.

DESA (2011) Disability convention gets 100th ratification [online]. Available at www.un.org/en/development/desa/news/social/disability-ratification.html

Douglas, G. G. A., and McLinden, M. T. (2004) 'Visual impairment', in B. Norwich (ed.) *Special teaching for special children*, Milton Keynes: Open University Press (pp. 26–40).

Dyson, A. (1999) 'Inclusion and inclusion: theories and discourses in inclusive education', in H. Daniels and P. Garner (eds.) *Inclusive education, world yearbook of education*, London: Kogan Page (pp. 36–53).

Farrell, P., and Venables, K. (2009) 'Can educational psychologists be inclusive?', in P. Hick, R. Kershner, and P. Farrell (eds.) *A psychology for inclusion*, London: Routledge (pp. 117–126).

Florian, L., and Black Hawkins, K. (2010) 'Exploring inclusive pedagogy', *British Educational Research Journal*, 37: 813–828.

Hardman, M., and Worthington, J. (2000) 'Educational psychologists' orientation to inclusion and assumptions about children's learning', *Educational Psychology in Practice*, 16: 349–360.

Hart, S., Dixon, A., Drummond, M., and McIntyre, D. (eds.) (2004) *Learning without limits*, Maidenhead: Open University Press.

Hick, P. (2009) 'Reframing psychology for inclusive learning within social justice agendas', in P. Hick, R. Kershner, and P. Farrell (eds.) *Psychology for inclusive education: new directions in theory and practice*, Abingdon: Routledge (pp. 165–176).

Ireson, J., Clark, H., and Hallam, S. (2002) 'Constructing ability groups in secondary schools', *School Leadership and Management*, 22: 163–176.

Jarvis, J., Iantaffi, A., and Sinkra, I. (2010) 'Inclusion in mainstream classrooms: deaf pupils' perspectives', in J. Rix, M. Nind, K. Sheehy, and K. Simmons (eds.) *Equality, participation and inclusion: diverse perspectives*, 2nd edn, London: Routledge (pp. 225–239).

Keegan, G. (2011) *The academic experience of key stage 3 pupils with physical disabilities in mainstream secondary school settings: pupil perspectives*. Unpublished PhD thesis. Milton Keynes: Open University.

Lindsay, G (2007) 'Educational psychology and the effectiveness of inclusive education/mainstreaming', *British Journal of Educational Psychology*, 77: 1–24.

Llewellyn, A., and Hogan, K. (2000) 'The use and abuse of models of disability', *Disability and Society*, 15: 157–165.

Long, M., Wood, C., Littleton, K., Passenger, T., and Sheehy, K. (2010) *The psychology of education: the evidence base for teaching and learning*, 2nd edn, London: Routledge.

Marschark, M., Sapere, P., Convertino, C., and Pelz, J. (2008) 'Learning via direct and mediated instruction by deaf students', *Journal of Deaf Studies and Deaf Education*, 13: 446–461.

Marschark, M., Spencer, P. E., Adams, J., and Sapere, P. (2011) 'Evidence-based practice in educating deaf and hard-of-hearing children: teaching to their cognitive strengths and needs, *European Journal of Special Needs Education*, 26: 3–16.

McIntyre, D., Pedder, D., and Rudduck, J. (2005) 'Pupil voice: comfortable and uncomfortable learnings for teachers', *Research Papers in Education*, 20: 149–168.

McLesky, J., and Waldron, N. L. (2011) 'Educational programs for elementary students with learning disabilities: can they be both effective and inclusive?', *Learning Disabilities Research and Practice*, 26: 48–57.

Norwich, B. (2008) 'What future for special schools and inclusion? Conceptual and professional perspectives', *British Journal of Special Education*, 35: 136–143.

Oliver, M. (1992) 'Changing the social relations of research production', *Disability, Handicap and Society*, 7: 101–114.

Oliver, M. (1996) *Understanding disability: from theory to practice*, Basingstoke: Macmillan.

Open University (2005) *E848 Researching inclusive education: values into practice*, Milton Keynes: The Open University.

Open University (2010) 'The dividing practices', in *Equality, participation and inclusion: learning from each other*, Milton Keynes: The Open University.

President's Commission on Excellence in Special Education (2002) *A new era: revitalizing special education for children and their families* [online]. Available at http://csef.air.org/publications/related/pcesefinalreport_finance.pdf

Prilleltensky, I. (2010) 'Child wellness and social inclusion: values for action', *American Journal of Community Psychology*, 46: 238–249.

Qi, S., and Mitchell, R. E. (2012) 'Large-scale academic achievement testing of deaf and hard-of-hearing students: past, present, and future', *Journal of Deaf Studies and Deaf Education*, 17: 1–18.

Ravet, J. (2007) 'Enabling pupil participation in a study of perceptions of disengagement: methodological matters', *British Journal of Special Education*, 34: 234–242.

Rix, J., Sheehy, K., Fletcher-Campbell, F., Crisp, M., and Harper, A. (2012) *Continuum of education provision for children with special educational needs: review of international policies and practices*, Dublin: National Council for Special Education.

Rose, C. A., Espelage, D. L., and Monda-Amaya, L. E. (2009) 'Bullying and victimization rates among students in general and special education: a comparative analysis', *Educational Psychology*, 29: 761–776.

Rubie-Davis, C. (2011) *Educational psychology: concepts, research and challenges*, Abingdon: Routledge.

Shakespeare, T. (2008) 'Disability: suffering, social oppression, or complex predicament?' *International Library of Ethics, Law, and the New Medicine*, 39: 235–246.

Sheehy, K. (2010) 'Inclusive education and virtual worlds: the teacher embodiment and learning affordance framework (TEALEAF)', in K. Sheehy, R. Ferguson, and G. Clough (eds.) *Virtual worlds: controversies at the frontier of education*, New York: Nova Science Publishers (pp. 186–195).

Sheehy, K., and Bucknall, S. (2008) 'Young people's visions of future educational systems', *Learning, Media and Technology*, 33: 101–114.

Sheehy, K., Nind, M., Rix, R., and Simmons, K. (2004) *Ethics and research in inclusive education: values into practice*, Abingdon: RoutledgeFalmer.

Sheehy, K., and Rix J. R. M., with Collins, K., Hall, K., Nind, M., and Wearmouth, J. (2009) 'A systematic review of whole class, subject based, pedagogies with reported outcomes for the academic and social inclusion of pupils with special educational needs in mainstream classrooms', in *Research evidence in education library*, London: EPPI-Centre, Social Science Research Unit, Institute of Education.

Slee, R. (1998) 'Inclusive education? This must signify "new times" in educational research', *British Journal of Educational Studies*, 46: 440–454.

Sofronoff, K., Dark, E., and Stone, V. (2011) 'Social vulnerability and bullying in children with Asperger syndrome', *Autism*, 15: 355–372.

Stinson, M., and Kluwin, T. (2011) 'Educational consequences of alternative school placements', in M. Marschark and P. E. Spencer (eds.) *Oxford handbook of deaf studies, language, and education*, 2nd edn, New York: Oxford University Press (pp. 47–62).

United Nations (2006) *Convention on Rights of People with Disabilities* [online]. Available at www.un.org/disabilities/convention/conventionfull.shtml

United Nations Convention on the Rights of the Child (1989) [online]. Available at www.unicef.org/crc

United Nations Educational, Scientific and Cultural Organization (UNESCO) (1994) The Salamanca Statement and Framework for Action on Special Needs Education, Paris: UNESCO [online]. Available at http://unesdoc.unesco.org/images/0009/000984/098427eo.pdf

United Nations Educational, Scientific and Cultural Organization (UNESCO) (1999) Salamanca Five Years On: a Review of UNESCO Activities in the Light of the Salamanca Statement and Framework for Action, Paris: UNESCO [online]. Available at http://unesdoc.unesco.org/images/0011/001181/118118eo.pdf

Watson, N., Shakespeare, T., Cunningham-Burley, S., and Barnes, C. (2000) *Life as a disabled child: a qualitative study of young people's experiences and perspectives*, Edinburgh: University of Edinburgh, Department of Nursing Studies.

Wilson, L. (2004) 'Towards equality: the voices of young disabled people in Disability Rights Commission research', *Support for Learning*, 19: 162–168.

Wright, J., Sheehy, K., Parsons, S., and Abbott, C. (2011) *Guidelines for research into the effectiveness of Assistive Technologies (AT)* [online]. Available at www.kcl.ac.uk/sspp/departments/education/research/crestem/steg/recentproj/RGAT2011Wrightetal.pdf

24

EDUCATION OF CHILDREN WITH SENSORY NEEDS

Reducing barriers to learning for children with visual impairment

Mike McLinden and Graeme Douglas

UNIVERSITY OF BIRMINGHAM, UK

Children with sensory needs constitute a heterogeneous group within which there is a wide spectrum of need and ability. This group includes children who are deaf or have a hearing impairment, children who are blind or have a visual impairment, or a combination of the two (i.e. children who are dual sensory impaired, sometimes referred to as 'deafblind' or 'multisensory impaired'). The ways in which individual needs are identified and met will depend on a number of factors including the nature and type of the sensory condition and the nature of additional conditions as well as the available support structures. This chapter provides an overview of these needs with a focus on children who have a visual impairment, and considers ways in which potential barriers to learning and development can be reduced. Introductory resources relating to the needs of children with hearing impairment/deafness (Gregory et al. 1998; Power and Leigh 2004) and deaf blindness (Aitken et al. 2000; Riggio and Miles 1999) are provided in the references at the end of the chapter. A key theme running through the chapter is one of how a child with a visual impairment can be provided with opportunities to access information. This includes how the child's learning environment can be structured to promote learning ('access to learning'), as well as how the child can learn skills in order to independently access the world ('learning to access').

Population of children with visual impairment

Definition of visual impairment

There is no universally adopted definition of visual impairment in relation to children and young people, with the term describing a wide continuum of 'loss in visual function' (Douglas and McLinden 2005). Depending on the context, a number of terms are used in the literature to describe the degree of visual loss in children, including the following.

- *Severely sight impaired/blind:* a designation of visual impairment in the UK that involves a medical diagnosis by an ophthalmologist (i.e. to certify that the individual is eligible to be registered as 'severely sight impaired'/'blind'). Although the term means that a child is likely to function mainly through touch and hearing, it does not necessarily mean that the child has no 'useful' vision at all.

- *Sight impaired/partially sighted:* a designation of visual impairment in the UK that involves a medical diagnosis by an ophthalmologist (i.e. to certify that the individual is eligible to be registered as 'sight impaired'/'partially sighted'). A child will have sufficient vision to manage some tasks but may require the help of specialist teaching methods and materials in school to account for his or her visual difficulties.
- *Low vision:* a commonly used term to describe a broad continuum of loss in visual function. Children described as having 'low vision' have restricted vision but can make use of this for learning with appropriate modification. They may be able to see work or in close-up, with the aid of good lighting, careful positioning and low vision aids such as magnifiers.

A broad distinction is often made in the literature between visual conditions that are 'ocular' or 'cortical' in nature. Ocular conditions affect parts of the eye itself and commonly include refractive errors such as astigmatism and severe myopia (or short-sightedness). The loss arising from a given ocular visual condition can include a number of areas of function such as visual acuity (the ability to resolve detail), accommodation (the ability to focus), field of vision (the area that can be seen), colour vision, and adaptability to light. Cortical visual impairment (CVI) is also known as cerebral visual impairment/dysfunction and affects the child's 'processing' of visual information. CVI is particularly prevalent in children who have more complex needs and may be diagnosed by itself, or 'may coexist with ocular forms of visual impairment' (Roman-Lantzy 2007: 3).

The definition used by the World Health Organisation (WHO) describes the 'degree' of blindness and visual impairment, and is based on a 'clinical' assessment of the individual's ability to resolve fine detail (i.e. visual acuity) using standardized methods (e.g. the Snellen chart) as well as visual field (e.g. WHO 2010). Even so, Tate et al. (2006) note that while relatively mild 'visual impairment' (e.g. acuity of <6/12) is not used internationally to define visual impairment it is reported in some studies as it represents a reduction in visual acuity sufficient to affect lifestyle (e.g. it corresponds to the requirements for sight for the UK driving licence).

It is important to note however that the majority of children with a visual impairment, including those classified as 'blind', do have some residual vision that can potentially be optimized and utilized in daily tasks and activities such as reading and mobility. For those children, it is widely acknowledged that medical descriptions of visual impairment (based on a clinical assessment of visual function) do not provide an accurate indication of how the child is able to use their vision for functional activities – or 'functional vision'. For this reason educational services for visually impaired children will usually make decisions about services they offer to children based on 'need', which draws on 'functional implications' of visual impairment as well as clinical assessments (Douglas et al. 2009).

Numbers and prevalence

The lack of a single definition of visual impairment means it is not possible to provide precise comparative figures on the number of children in a given national context. Indeed, a review of literature by Tate et al. (2006) revealed that terms such as 'visual impairment' and 'visual disability' are often used to mean different things in different studies and contexts. Most of the available data in the UK about visual loss in children comes from surveys of providers of health care, social care, or educational services to children with visual loss (Tate et al. 2006). The UK government also collects statistics on different special educational needs groups as part of its Annual Schools Census in England and Wales.

In a review of prevalence studies in the UK, Tate et al. (2006: 5) note that drawing on 'a broad and pragmatic definition of visual loss' (taken to mean a child is identified as being in need of special educational or social services), the data suggests a prevalence of visual impairment in the region of 1–2 children per 1000. This compares with higher estimates based on the number of children receiving 'educational' support in relation to their visual impairment in the UK 2.1 children per 1000 (Keil 2003). A useful way of translating these figures to educational practice, and indeed to highlight the relative 'low-incidence' nature of visual impairment, is to think about these figures as equating to approximately 1–2 children in a secondary school with a pupil roll of approximately 1000 children.

Many countries (e.g. the UK and the USA) categorize special educational needs according to 'primary type' of need. This is a challenge to establishing precise numbers of children because combinations of disability are not accounted for in population estimates. For example, the American Foundation for the Blind (AFB) argues that numbers of children identified with a primary disability of visual impairment significantly underestimate the overall number of children with visual impairment in the USA (AFB 2009).

Linked to the above point, there is a wealth of evidence that a high proportion of children have disabilities in combination with a recognized visual impairment. For example, Ravenscroft et al. (2008) report that 71 percent of children in Scotland with visual impairment have additional disabilities, while a study by Flanagan, Jackson, and Hill (2003) in Northern Ireland noted that 79 percent of their sample had 'additional medical problems' (p. 493). This high proportion of multiple disabilities can also be linked to changing trends in childhood chronic disease and disability that are themselves linked to an increased survival of premature and very low birth weight babies and children with major anomalies, complex neurological and metabolic diseases, and malignant disease. Of significance therefore in terms of identifying educational needs is that children with the most severe visual impairments are found to be more likely to have additional and often complex disabilities, and as noted by Rahi and Cable (2003), the changing nature of the population will not always be captured in studies, particularly those that rely solely on 'ophthalmic sources', thereby under-representing the number of children with additional disabilities. A number of terms are used in the educational literature to describe such children, with perhaps the most commonly reported being 'multiple disabilities and visual impairment' (MDVI) (e.g. Keil 2003; McLinden and McCall 2002). Although this term has no official status in national surveys of children with special educational needs, as McLinden and McCall (2010) note, it serves as a useful 'signpost' to alert practitioners to the potential implications of the child's visual loss for learning and development, and ensure this loss is not neglected when one is seeking to identify a complex spectrum of need.

Precise figures for the number of children in developing countries are difficult to establish given the challenges posed in collating this information. However, of significance is the number of children in developing countries who have preventable eye conditions. For example, a WHO fact sheet (WHO 2011) reports that globally an estimated 19 million children have a visual impairment, of whom 12 million are visually impaired due to 'refractive errors'. In developed countries such errors can usually be diagnosed and corrected through the use of refractive devices such as glasses or low vision aids, but without these the child effectively has significantly reduced opportunities to draw on his or her vision for learning.

Educational provision

Given the continuum of need for children with visual impairment described above, it is not surprising to find a continuum of educational provision. Although an increasing number of countries have introduced legislation that supports the right of children with special educational needs to an education in mainstream settings, many educationalists in the field of visual impairment education advocate for the continuation of a range of options for school placement supported by specialist services such as visiting teachers of children with visual impairment (e.g. McCall 1997). The continuum of provision for children with visual impairment includes the following.

- Early years/pre-school settings.
- Mainstream school.
- Mainstream school with enhanced resource provision.
- Special school (either day or residential school designated for children with VI or MDVI). A number of these schools are purpose-built with the aim of ensuring that the learning environment is appropriate for children with visual impairment and a range of complex needs.
- Special school (either day or residential designated for children with other special educational needs, e.g. severe learning difficulties).

In the UK the majority of visually impaired children with no additional disabilities are now placed in mainstream schools (Keil and Clunies-Ross 2003), although significantly, children with MDVI for the most part continue to receive their education in special schools that are not designated for visually impaired children. As noted by Porter and Lacey (2008), this creates particular challenges for these schools in terms of 'safeguarding' the needs of children who are described as 'being amongst the most vulnerable in having unrecognized learning needs' (p. 59).

Access to assessment

The educational assessment of children with visual impairment is considered to be important in order to collate information that can enable their teachers and other professionals to optimize their development (Tobin and Hill 2011). The absence of vision can however serve to limit access to information that would normally be processed 'in an unstructured, unprepared manner to their fully-sighted peers', resulting in gaps in experience and understanding that put the children at a disadvantage in relation to their peers (Tobin and Hill 2011: 209). Access to appropriate assessments (related to modality of presentation) is considered therefore to be a challenge to both visually impaired children and their educators (Douglas et al. 2009). As Tobin and Hill (2011) argue, it is not 'entirely satisfactory to resort to the available conventional assessment procedures for sighted children, many of which contain test-items which are biased towards visual imagery, visual memories, and visual search'.

One strategy adopted by practitioners (e.g. teachers, educational psychologists) is to 'adapt' existing 'mainstream' assessment procedures. This can be done 'formally', for example by re-standardizing a reading test for children with visual impairment, and 'informally', for example by using and modifying existing assessment procedures cautiously. A second strategy is the development of specialist or dedicated assessment procedures that assess aspects of development that are 'particularly relevant' to visually impaired children (e.g. Braille reading).

A number of educational assessment procedures have been empirically developed for children with visual impairment at pre-school and school age. A recent example in the UK is the *Early Support Developmental Journal*, which has been designed for use with young visually impaired children and babies to provide a structured sequential guide of expected developmental steps in young children with visual impairment aged 0–36 months (Dale and Salt 2007). As Dale and Salt (2007) report, the journal provides 'finely graded steps of key developmental sequences especially in the areas of object relationships and reasoning, communication and social development, language and meaning, play and learning, movement and mobility and self-help skills' (p. 687). At the time of writing it is the most contemporary and empirically based tool of its kind.

Regardless of the assessment procedures adopted, the 'process' of assessment requires training and experience on the part of the administrator, particularly if a sound interpretation of the results is to be made (Douglas et al. 2009), so that professionals can identify the obstacles to learning that blindness and partial sight can impose, and help identify general from these more specific 'visual impairment difficulties' (Tobin and Hill 2011). In many cases assessment will also need to draw on the observations of others. For example, observations of parents and class teachers are particularly important in the assessment of young children and children with more complex needs. Linked to this is an increased understanding that assessments do not stand alone and are best understood when used in conjunction with information from a broad range of stakeholders (Douglas et al. 2009).

Access to early learning experiences

Vision is often described as a 'coordinating' or 'linking' sense that allows children to integrate information received through their other senses (e.g. McLinden and McCall 2002). When function is not impaired, vision provides opportunities for a young child to learn about the world through a complex developmental process that provides the child with information about an increasingly distant world. Indeed, the vision of a newborn baby is very much focused on a world that is in his or her immediate proximity (e.g. the mother or father's face). Distance vision is poorly developed at this early age, as may be the child's ability to make sense of what she or he is processing through the sensory channels (Barraga 1986).

During the first year of development, the sensory and cognitive abilities become progressively differentiated (McLinden and McCall 2002). Of significance in this process is the role of incidental (or unstructured) learning in which the child is able to access visual information in order to 'make links', including for example: independently 'confirming' information received through one or more sense (turning her head to the sound of footsteps behind her), 'anticipating' what is about to happen next (seeing her mother walking towards her with open arms and lifting up her arms to be picked up), 'responding' to a particular action (smiling in response to her father's smile). Further, there is evidence that in combination with increasing physical abilities, vision serves as an important 'motivator' that guides the hand into space and helps to facilitate independent early grasp and manipulation of objects (Pehoski 1995).

As noted by Warren (1994), as vision has been shown to be so important in the integration of early auditory/tactile stimuli in the young sighted child, it is reasonable to assume that restricted vision has implications for development in children who have reduced 'access' to visual information. Indeed, he identifies three major challenges that face children in their efforts to construct their knowledge of the environment when they have reduced visual information:

- a restriction in the extent of the environment that the infant can engage;
- lower stimulus value on the part of the environment that the infant encounters;
- a lack of appreciation of the infant's impact on the objects manipulated.

As interpreted by McLinden and McCall (2002: 55):

> a young child with a visual impairment may not only have access to a relatively limited environment, but the objects that are in their limited environment may not be stimulating enough to motivate the child to explore them. Further, the child may not appreciate the effects of his or her action on any objects that have been manipulated.

Thus, although the child may be able to draw on information through other senses (including for example hearing or touch) in the absence of the integrating function that vision performs, the information that young children receive through these other senses 'may be fragmentary and difficult to assimilate' (McLinden and McCall 2002: 55).

Drawing on the examples above, this may mean reduced access to linking information normally provided by vision resulting in, for example: a child hearing footsteps nearby but not being able to independently confirm where they were coming from, hearing the mother's footsteps walking towards her but not reaching out in anticipation of her picking her up, and not responding to her father's smiling face as she is not aware that he is smiling at her. The effects of additional or multiple disabilities (for example an additional sensory or physical impairment) can serve to compound this reduced access to information such that the child is unable to gather sufficient information from the environment to learn independently (McLinden and McCall 2002).

In the absence of such information there will be a need for a more structured learning environment in which the child's adult partners (and potentially their siblings and peers) will have an important role in serving to guide, or mediate, early actions on the world (i.e. effectively to provide the child with access to different types of sensory information as a way of helping him or her to make links). For children with multiple disabilities, consistency in approach will be particularly important in order that they can learn about establishing control of their environment.

Language will have an important mediating role to play in this developmental process and, as reported by Webster and Roe (1998), with appropriate 'scaffolding' can assume some of the characteristics of vision as a basis for learning (p. 17). This is captured succinctly by Webster and Roe (1998: 117):

> it is within the context of social relationships that adults guide and scaffold young children's development, and this is particularly important for understanding ways in which children are initiated into using language as a tool for learning. Arguably it is through the co-operative use of language as a 'bridge' that some of the most limiting aspects of visual impairment can be overcome.

Similarly, Priesler (1997) highlights the role of structured social routines (e.g. listening to a fairy tale, playing games and meal time) in facilitating the development of early communication, and these opportunities may be less apparent in free play.

Access to the school curriculum

The shift towards more inclusive practice over the past four decades has seen significant changes in curriculum design and delivery for children with visual impairment (see Hansen, Chapter 22, this volume, for some historical testimonies relating to this). The majority of children with visual impairment and no additional disabilities are now educated in mainstream settings and will therefore participate in most subject areas alongside their sighted peers, with individual teaching activities limited to particular 'additional' curriculum areas (e.g. mobility, Braille instruction, technology). Additional support for children with visual impairment educated in mainstream settings may be provided by a number of practitioners including a qualified teacher of children with visual impairment (QTVI), who has a key role in supporting schools to ensure the curriculum is appropriately designed and delivered to meet an individual child's needs. This shift in practice towards greater inclusion in mainstream settings has implications for the pedagogical approaches that are drawn upon to enable children to access the curriculum alongside their sighted peers.

The work of Lewis and Norwich (2005) provides a helpful framework for considering whether children with different disabilities require unique (disability-specific) pedagogies. In applying this framework to the pedagogical needs of learners with a visual impairment, Douglas and McLinden (2005) argue that at a 'micro-strategy' level of teaching there is evidence that particular approaches are necessary when teaching children with a visual impairment 'which has its basis in *access* to the curriculum' (emphasis added, p. 36). In drawing out the implications for practice, Douglas and McLinden draw the following conclusions.

1. The teaching strategies are necessarily sensitive to the modality of the interaction because of the children's impaired vision (i.e. its accessibility).
2. This can be done by either 'enhancing' the visual mode (e.g. enlarged print) or using 'alternative' presentations (e.g. through speech or a tactile code).
3. The use of micro-strategies may take longer than (or have different qualities to) traditional teaching strategies (most obviously, they may be slower).
4. Irrespective of 'how' children with visual impairment are taught (the pedagogy), the distinctive needs of children with visual impairments have given rise to an 'additional curriculum' considered to be either 'over and above' the mainstream curriculum or areas that are outside the mainstream teacher's expertise and require input from professionals with specialist training/knowledge (e.g. specialist teachers, mobility officer).

In translating these points to practical implications for how the learning can be managed in the classroom environment, the authors note the following.

- Without these strategies access to the curriculum by visually impaired children would be compromised or even denied.
- These adapted methods of teaching may require more time than conventional teaching strategies (partly because children with visual impairment generally require more time to process information and to complete tasks).
- Some aspects of the curriculum may require significant modifications to enable access by children who are visually impaired (e.g. Braille literacy).
- Many children who are visually impaired require an 'additional' curriculum that is 'over and above' the mainstream curriculum (e.g. mobility and independence education, Braille tuition, daily living skills).

Precisely how curriculum areas should be divided is open to debate, but a broad distinction between mainstream curriculum (i.e. areas that require 'modifications' in order for a child to access them) and 'additional' curriculum areas (i.e. areas that require particular intervention strategies in order to develop skills) is useful when considering curriculum design and delivery for children with visual impairment. A literature review of best practice models and outcomes in the education of visually impaired children (Douglas et al. 2009) suggested that a key focus of research in this area has been the concept of 'access', particularly with regard to barriers children with visual impairment face in accessing visual information in education. The potential implications of reduced access to information will depend on a number of factors including the age of onset of the visual impairment; whether the child has additional needs; and the specialist support available to the child to ensure inclusive curriculum design and delivery.

As a way of conceptualizing the support needs of children with visual impairment, a dual view of access has been outlined by Douglas et al. (2011):

- providing children with 'accessible' material in their preferred medium (e.g. large print, Braille).
- teaching children 'access skills' (for example, through the use of a low vision aid, assistive technology, which would typically be described as part of the additional curriculum).

As noted earlier, these approaches can be broadly captured as follows.

- *Access to learning:* the child is provided with access to appropriate information in order to learn about a particular curriculum area.
- *Learning to access:* the child is provided with the means by which he or she is able to access information independently.

In practice, these approaches are not mutually exclusive and each will be required at different stages in the child's educational career, depending on the particular curriculum context. An example would be a teacher developing materials and teaching strategies to give the child 'access to learning' (e.g. through producing bespoke print materials in a particular format), but this might build a dependency on the child's educators. Therefore a strategy would be to develop a school programme that seeks to equip the child with the means of accessing text for himself or herself so as to 'learn to access' as independently as possible (e.g. through the use of a magnifier or appropriate technology). While both approaches are important, there are strong arguments that teaching children access skills (i.e. supporting them in 'learning to access') has important longer term benefits for visually impaired children and young people as they become independent adults (e.g. Corn et al. 2003). Nevertheless, it is reported that this approach to teaching can often be neglected (Douglas et al. 2011), with evidence that educators commonly emphasize 'providing accessible material' to a child, in which those responsible for teaching the child provide material in a predetermined format (e.g. a large-print book in font size 20 point). This argument can be applied to other aspects of the additional curriculum; for example, modifications to the environment and offering sighted guides ('access to learn') must be coupled with teaching students mobility skills ('learning to access').

Conclusion

Within the spectrum of need created by visual impairment, a key barrier faced by children is 'access' to information in order to develop their knowledge, understanding and skills. As reported by Douglas et al. (2011), 'access' is a complex and multi-levelled term. In the context of education, an important role of the educator is to find appropriate ways of reducing potential barriers to access through the deployment of appropriate strategies. As noted by Douglas and McLinden (2005), without these strategies access to the curriculum would be compromised or even denied. Crucially, however, each of these strategies can impact on the child's performance in a number of key areas. For example, providing children with access to print through the use of a low vision aid (such as a hand-held magnifier or computer) is designed to ensure that they are able to 'access' the text alongside their sighted peer group. Ensuring such access may however come at a cost to a child's reading performance – for example, reading text through a magnifier not only may be tiring for the child over a long period but could also result in a slower reading speed (in comparison to his or her sighted peers).

Given that access is a key barrier to education for children with a visual impairment, teaching strategies focus on overcoming this barrier. One broad strategy is ensuring 'access to learning' by providing the child with close support that emphasizes making the educational environment accessible in the 'here and now' (e.g. providing accessible curriculum materials and guided support with mobility). Another complementary strategy is to support the child in 'learning to access'. This is particularly characterized in areas of the 'additional curriculum' that emphasize independence skills such as the use of technology, low vision and mobility. Such approaches can be viewed as a 'longer term' approach to meeting a child's future needs, which will enable them to gain access to information and curriculum materials for themselves, and to navigate social and spatial environments independently.

Contact address: m.t.mclinden@bham.ac.uk

References

Aitken, S., Buultjens, M., Clark, C., Eyre, J., and Pease, L. (2000) *Teaching children who are deafblind: contact, communication and learning*, London: David Fulton.

American Foundation for the Blind (2009) *Letter to Sec. of Education: estimates of severely visually impaired children* [online]. Available at www.afb.org

Barraga, N. C. (1986) 'Sensory perceptual development', in G. T. Scholl (ed.) *Foundations of education for blind and visually handicapped children and youth*, New York: American Foundation for the Blind (pp. 83–98).

Corn, A. L., Bell, J. K., Andersen, E., Bachofer, C., Jose, R. T., and Perez, A. (2003) 'Providing access to the visual environment: a model of low vision services for children', *Journal of Visual Impairment and Blindness*, 97: 261–272.

Dale, N., and Salt, A. (2007) 'Early support developmental journal for children with visual impairment: the case for a new developmental framework for early intervention', *Child: Care, Health and Development*, 33: 684–690.

Douglas, G., and McLinden, M. (2005) 'Visual impairment', in A. Lewis and B. Norwich (eds) *Special teaching for special children? Pedagogies for inclusion*, Milton Keynes: Open University Press (pp. 26–40).

Douglas, G., McLinden, M., McCall, S., Pavey, S., Ware, J., and Farrell, A. (2009) *International review of the literature of evidence of best practice models and outcomes in the education of blind and visually impaired children*, Report for National Council for Special Education (NCSE), Ireland [online]. Available at www.ncse.ie/research/researchreports.asp

Douglas, G., McLinden, M., McCall, S., Pavey, S., Ware, J., and Farrell, A. (2011) 'Access to print literacy for children and young people with visual impairment: findings from a review of literature', *European Journal of Special Needs Education*, 26: 25–38.

Flanagan, N. M., Jackson, A. J., and Hill, A. E. (2003) 'Visual impairment in childhood: insights from a community-based survey', *Child: Care, Health and Development* 29: 493–499.

Gregory, S., Knight, P., McCracken, W., Powers, S., and Watson, L. (eds) (1998) *Issues in deaf education*, London: David Fulton.

Keil, S. (2003) 'Survey of educational provision for blind and partially sighted children in England, Scotland and Wales in 2002', *British Journal of Visual Impairment*, 21: 93–97.

Keil, S., and Clunies-Ross, L. (2003) *Educational provision for blind and partially sighted children in Britain in 2002*, London: RNIB.

Lewis, A., and Norwich, B. (eds) (2005) *Special teaching for special children? Pedagogies for inclusion*, Milton Keynes: Open University Press.

McCall, S. (1997) 'Historical perspectives', in H. Mason and S. McCall (eds) *Visual impairment: access to education for children and young people*, London: David Fulton (pp. 3–12).

McLinden, M., and McCall, S. (2002) *Learning through touch: supporting children with visual impairment and additional difficulties*, London: David Fulton.

McLinden, M. T., and McCall, S. (2010) 'The role of touch in the learning experiences of children who have PMLD and visual impairment', *PMLD Link*, 22: 17–21.

Pehoski, C. (1995) 'Cortical control of skilled movements of the hand', in A. Henderson and C. Pehoski (eds) *Hand function in the child: foundations for remediation*, St. Louis: Mosby–Year Book (pp. 3–15).

Porter, J., and Lacey, P. (2008) 'Safeguarding the needs of children with a visual impairment in non-VI special schools', *British Journal of Visual Impairment*, 26: 50–62.

Power, D., and Leigh, G. (eds) (2004) *Educating deaf students: global perspectives*, Washington, DC: Gallaudet University Press.

Priesler, G. (1997) 'Social and emotional development of blind children', in V. Lewis and G. M. Collis (eds) *Blindness and psychological development in young children*, Leicester: British Psychological Society (pp. 69–85).

Rahi, J. S., and Cable, N. (2003) 'Severe sight problems and blindness in children in the UK', *Lancet*, 362: 1359–1365.

Ravenscroft, J., Blaikie, A., Macewen, C., O'Hare, A., Creswell, L., and Dutton, G. (2008) 'A novel method of notification to profile childhood visual impairment in Scotland to meet the needs of children with visual impairment', *British Journal of Visual Impairment* 26: 170–189.

Riggio, M., and Miles, B. (1999) *Remarkable conversations: a guide to developing meaningful communication with children and adults who are deafblind*, Boston: Perkins School for the Blind.

Roman-Lantzy, C. (2007) *Cortical visual impairment: an approach to assessment and intervention*, New York: American Foundation for the Blind.

Tate, R., Smeeth, L., Evans, J., Fletcher, A., Owen, C., and Rudnicka, A. (2006) *The prevalence of sight problems in the UK: a review of the literature*, Peterborough: RNIB.

Tobin, M., and Hill, E. (2011) 'Issues in the educational, psychological assessment of visually impaired children', *British Journal of Visual Impairment*, 29: 208–214.

Warren, D. H. (1994) *Blindness and children: an individual differences approach*, Cambridge: Cambridge University Press.

Webster, A., and Roe, J. (1998) *Children with visual impairments: social interaction, language and learning*, London: Routledge.

WHO (2010) *Action plan for preventing avoidable blindness and visual impairment 2009–2013*, Geneva: World Health Organization [online]. Available at www.who.int/blindness

WHO (2011) *Visual impairment and blindness*, Fact Sheet No. 282, Geneva: World Health Organization [online]. Available at www.who.int/mediacentre/factsheets/fs282/en

25

SPEECH AND LANGUAGE DISORDERS

David Messer

THE OPEN UNIVERSITY, UK

What are we talking about?

Speech and language are central to human functioning. For children and young people, difficulties with speech and language can have a profound effect on social interaction and learning. These difficulties can vary in their form and nature.

A 'speech disorder' is usually considered to be when a person is unable to produce speech sounds appropriately or fluently, at the appropriate speed and intonation, or has problems with his or her voice; difficulties when pronouncing words and stuttering are examples of speech disorders. A 'language disorder' is usually considered to involve difficulties understanding the language of others, or difficulties in using language when communicating with others. It is worth noting that 'speech' usually involves the spoken form of a language; however, some languages involve communication without the use of speech, as in the case of sign languages. As pointed out by Boyle (Chapter 21, this volume), the terms 'disorder' and 'impairment' are not neutral; Boyle's chapter provides a very useful context for thinking about some of the issues concerned with the labelling of children.

Often people regard the terms 'communication', 'speech', and 'language' as interchangeable, but many psycholinguists give language a special status. Unlike most animal communication, language can involve changes in meaning depending on the arrangement of elements (e.g. the man bit the dog versus the dog bit the man) and also 'agreement' between different elements (e.g. I was tired, we were tired; here the use of the verb was/were depends on whether there is one or several people).

Language disorders occur in children with a range of developmental problems; for example, autistic spectrum disorders, hearing loss, and learning disabilities. Recently, the term 'speech, language and communication needs' (SLCN) has begun to be used in the UK to refer to children who are in need of intervention (e.g. Bercow 2008). This quite rightly reflects the needs of the children rather than the cause of the disability; however, understanding the cause of the language disability can often help with identifying appropriate interventions.

This chapter starts with a consideration of speech disorders and this is followed by a more extensive review of specific language impairment (SLI). Much of the chapter considers SLI because it is an import language disability in terms of the number of children affected.

Speech disorders

All children make errors involving speech sounds, and a disorder is usually considered to exist when these errors are much greater than would be expected in a typical child of the same age. The terminology used to refer to speech disorders is complex, and there is not always agreement about the definition of the terms. Speech disorders usually involve problems in creating or forming the speech sounds needed to communicate with others, and the term 'speech sound disorder' (SSD) has become widespread following the work of Bowen (e.g. 2009). Four important descriptive terms are disfluency, articulation disorders, phonological disorders, and voice disorders (quality of voice, hoarseness, etc.) However, these have been used in different ways across historical time and may be used to refer to quite different processes by different researchers and clinicians.

A 'fluency' disorder is characterized by deviations in continuity, flow, smoothness, and rhythm of speech. One of the best known forms of disfluency involves stuttering, where a person repeats a sound, word, or phrase. Stuttering usually involves a period of up to several seconds when the vocal apparatus is positioned to say a sound but none is produced. During this time expressions such as 'uhmm' or the beginning sound of a word may be spoken, and these are often repeated. For some children stuttering occurs whenever they speak, but for other children stuttering is only problematic in certain circumstances such as speaking in class. In childhood, the highest occurrence of stuttering is between two and four years, and around 5 percent of the population is affected, with about 3 times as many boys being affected as girls. In children it is often difficult to work out whether stuttering will continue, which is often the case, or will resolve; risk factors include a family history of stuttering, stuttering continuing for six months or more, and the occurrence of other related disorders.

There are a range of interventions for people who stutter. Many interventions run by speech and language therapists (SLTs) involve changing the way words are spoken (e.g. altering breathing patterns, slowing rate of speech, practising in less stressful conditions) and trying to resolve tensions associated with the production of speech. It is generally considered that it is better to let children who stutter complete an utterance without interrupting; obviously impatience or annoyance is only likely to make the stuttering worse.

An 'articulation disorder' usually is considered to involve a mechanical problem that results in errors when producing speech sounds: these may be left out, added or replaced by another sound. Sometimes the term 'phonetic disorder' is used to refer to this phenomenon. When identifying articulation disorders it is important to take account of dialects, which can contain systematic differences from the speech used in, say, public broadcasting. Everatt and McNeill (Chapter 30, this volume) provide information about children with developmental verbal dyspraxia, which involves impairments to motor planning in speech production.

'Phonological disorders' are usually thought to involve cognitive problems related to children's understanding of the sound system of their language, and these are sometimes referred to as phonemic disorders. In the sound system of all languages one can identify a system of underlying rules which reflect, for example, which sounds are likely to follow another and the types of speech sounds that are used in the language. This is one of the reasons why people can identify a particular foreign language even though they do not understand or know any words that they hear. Thus, a phonological disorder involves a child making systematic errors that reflect their incomplete knowledge of the sound system of their language. This might consist of producing sounds made in the back of the mouth like 'k' and 'g' for those in the front of the mouth like 't' and 'd' (e.g. saying 'tup' for 'cup' or 'das' for 'gas'). Consequently, articulation and phonological disorders can involve similar errors, but the errors are caused by different processes.

Both articulation and phonological disorders result in speech that is atypical and/or delayed. As a result, it can be difficult to work out why a child has a particular difficulty. Furthermore, documentation of the effectiveness of interventions is not very common, so there are uncertainties about the best forms of therapy.

Language disorders and specific language impairment

As discussed in other chapters in this volume, there are debates about whether and how to identify children and young people who have disabilities and disorders. Psychologists usually identify a disorder on the basis of standardized scores that are below 2 standard deviations from the mean (i.e. 70), and often researchers consider those with standardized scores below 1 standard deviation from the mean (i.e. 85) as having below-average abilities. One issue that complicates the identification of language disorders is that language involves several different domains of functioning, phonology (the sound system), semantics (meanings), pragmatics (how to get things done by using language), and morphosyntax (involving word order and word endings – note that in this chapter the term 'grammar' will be used instead of 'morphsyntax', although sometimes 'grammar' is used to refer to any systematic aspect of the organization of language including the sound system). Thus, a language disorder can involve one or more of these domains. In addition, language disorders are often divided according to whether they involve expressive difficulties (i.e. producing language) or receptive difficulties (understanding language). The identification of language disorders such as SLI is more complicated than has been explained here, but this description provides a useful approximation.

The remaining part of the chapter will focus on children who have SLI, which is one of the most common childhood disorders, affecting approximately 7 percent of children (Hulme and Snowling 2009). These children have a range of problems with language in the absence of an obvious cause, but their non-verbal abilities are relatively unaffected. In other words, children with SLI have lower language abilities compared to children of the same age, such as a smaller vocabulary, a less well developed grammar, poorer comprehension, but these difficulties would not be expected considering a child's other cognitive abilities. Usually, SLI is considered to occur if children have difficulties in more than one major aspect of their use of language. It is useful to think of SLI as being similar to dyslexia; children with SLI have a specific difficulty with language in the same way that children with dyslexia have a specific difficulty with reading (see Byrne, Samuelsson, and Olson, Chapter 29, this volume). Another example of a specific learning disability is dyspraxia, and a high proportion of children with SLI are also identified as having dyspraxia (see Everatt and McNeill, Chapter 30, this volume).

It is easy to make the assumption that some individuals 'have' SLI and others do not. This assumption is reinforced by the process of identifying special needs, where a child is assessed and a decision is made about whether the child has a disability and whether he or she should receive additional teaching resources. In practice it is more realistic to recognize that children have a range of language abilities, much as they vary in how quickly they can run, thus the identification of SLI involves a somewhat arbitrary categorization according to whether a child's scores are above or below a certain point. This type of categorization is partly a response to the need to identify which children should have special support using assessments, which are relatively quick to administer and have been designed so that confounds when testing are eliminated (i.e. the use of standardized tests). This issue also is more fully discussed in Boyle (Chapter 21, this volume). Identification of SLI can be even more complex in the case of bilingual children who have delayed language development (Bedore and Peña 2008; Paradis 2010).

The criteria used in the diagnosis of SLI mean that there can be considerable variation in the children's language difficulties, and there is no generally agreed classification system for identifying different subtypes of SLI. Tomblin and Zhang (2006) investigated the statistical relations between different language subtests from standardized assessments (i.e. vocabulary, grammar) at different ages. The sample included more than 500 children, half of whom were identified as having language impairment and half were typical children. Factor analyses showed that performances on the different subtests were related to one another, and this appears to be because of the existence of a single language dimension. Interestingly, in older children there was evidence of two factors related to vocabulary and grammar.

Another general point to make about SLI is that much of the research has focused on the cognitive processes in children younger than 12 years. Recently, research findings have shown that SLI is highly likely to continue into adolescence and adulthood. In addition, many, but not all, adolescents with SLI appear to be affected by socio-emotional issues. The young people are more vulnerable to feelings of depression, feelings of loneliness, are more likely to have fewer friends, and school achievements are likely to be lower (Clegg et al. 2005; Conti-Ramsden 2008).

Explanations about the causes of SLI

There are a range of explanations about the aetiology of SLI, but so far there is no widely accepted theory. It also should be recognized that there are different 'levels' of explanation, so that explanations involving genetic factors can co-exist with explanations that involve, say, the ability involving linguistic or psychological processes. Some explanations follow linguistic perspectives, with the ideas of Noam Chomsky and his colleagues being an important influence. Others take a psychological perspective and locate the difficulties in the way information is processed by children.

Linguistic accounts of SLI

To a greater or lesser extent, the theories described in this section assume that typical language development is possible because children have access to an innately specified set of 'universal' rules about the grammar of every human language. This innate set of information is supposed to enable very young, cognitively immature, children to acquire language. Young children are believed to match the speech they hear to the details provided by universal grammar and in this way to be able to identify the grammar of the language around them. Universal grammar is thought to be an abstract set of grammatical rules; so different spoken languages could have the same underlying set of principles that are present in universal grammar. For example, all languages are thought to contain nouns and verbs. By extrapolation from this position, SLI is believed by some to be caused by children's lack of appropriate information in their inherited, universal grammar and as a result the children will have language difficulties.

Gopnik and Crago (1991) generated considerable interest in their report about several generations of a family who had difficulties with using the appropriate grammatical endings to words involving tense and plurals (e.g. talk −ed). This fitted in nicely with the ideas just outlined. However, subsequent research has challenged the idea that grammatical rules are totally absent from the speech of the family; individuals were found to produce sometimes correct and sometimes incorrect versions of the same grammatical rule. It was also the case that some sentences could be understood, but there was a difficulty producing similar sentences. Furthermore, there could have been effects on language acquisition because children often heard errors in the speech of their families. All this suggested that there was not the total absence of particular grammatical rules.

A related theory that has received considerable attention concerns the difficulties of children with SLI in using the appropriate endings to verbs. In English, verbs can take finite or non-finite forms. A finite form involves the verb being the main verb of a sentence (e.g. I walk). When used in this way, the verbs need to have appropriate ending for tense and number (e.g. he walks, he walked, they walk). In contrast, non-finite verbs usually involve the presence of another verb in a sentence (e.g. the use of 'go' as a non-finite verb as in 'he wants to go to school'), and the non-finite verbs do not have additional endings (e.g. 'he wanted to go to school', 'they want to go to school'). To complicate matters, the same verb can be used in a finite and non-finite form (e.g. 'he walks', 'they are going to walk').

The use of verbs in this way in English is potentially confusing to children (as well as those not familiar with the rules of grammar): sometimes children hear a verb that has the tense marked with an ending (e.g. –ed) and sometimes without an ending. It also is well established that young children do not add additional endings to verbs (e.g. 'I walk yesterday'). Wexler (1994) suggested that this occurs because young children make a mistake and apply the rules from universal grammar about non-finite verbs to all verbs (e.g. 'she love ice cream'). Wexler also suggested that children with SLI do not progress beyond this stage, and he referred to this as an extended optional infinitive stage (EOI). This provides an explanation of SLI which focuses on the difficulties that these children have in acquiring linguistic rules (Rice, Wexler, and Cleave 1995) and explains why these children often do not provide the appropriate endings to verbs and nouns. This claim has been controversial. There has been disagreement about whether there is an optional infinitive stage in typical children, and computer-based connectionist models have shown that the same patterns of grammatical errors can be produced using samples of speech heard by children and a system where there is low attention to the endings of words (Freudenthal, Pine, and Gobet 2006).

Another 'linguistic' explanation for SLI has been put forward by van der Lely and concerns those children with SLI whose main problem involves grammatical difficulties. Van der Lely has suggested that these children have difficulties with what are termed dependent relationships in their grammar: these involve such things as the relation between a pronoun and a noun. So, for example, van der Lely and Stollwerck (1997) showed pictures to children corresponding to the statements 'Baloo Bear says Mowgli is tickling him' and 'Baloo Bear says Mowgli is tickling himself'. Children with what they termed grammatical SLI often responded 'yes' to 'Baloo Bear says Mowgli is tickling him' when Mowgli was in fact depicted tickling himself. With these more complex sentences, the children with SLI tended to rely on other cues such as gender, number, or semantic constraints. These findings illustrate the difficulties that some children with SLI have with linguistic rules, and the research is valuable in demonstrating the problems that children with SLI generally have with components of the language system. However, there are alternative explanations for these difficulties that need to be tested. For example, it is not clear whether the children's grammatical problems are the result of an inability to implement a linguistic rule or can be attributed to basic general cognitive operations such as memory or processing.

Cognitive theories of SLI

Cognitive theories focus on the possibility that children with SLI have a difficulty in processing the information necessary to acquire language. Inevitably, given the characteristics of children with SLI, cognitive theories concern many of the same types of speech errors as the linguistic theories.

One of the early theories about language impairment was that it was caused by difficulties in perceiving the sounds of speech. Tallal and Piercy (1993) and Wright et al. (1997) have suggested that children with SLI have difficulties with processing sounds that are presented briefly and in rapid succession. Tallal and Piercy found that when two sounds were brief and the interval between them was short, children with SLI had more difficulty than typical children in identifying, by pressing a button, which sound came first. Wright et al. (1997) used a second 'masking' sound which was presented very soon after the first sound, making it difficult to identify or repeat it. Wright et al. (1997) reported that children with language impairments had more difficulty with this task than typical children of the same age. However, a number of researchers doubt that auditory processing deficits are the cause of SLI. There are inconsistencies between studies, and some important subsequent investigations, like that of Bishop et al. (1999), failed to find reliable associations between problems in processing auditory information and the presence of SLI.

A slightly different, but related idea put forward by Leonard (1998) is that the difficulties of children with SLI could be because they fail to identify the critical speech sounds that relate to important grammatical elements. As a result, children's difficulties with the past tense (–ed) in English can be explained by the fact that the '–ed' sound is not usually stressed when it is spoken. Consequently, the problems of SLI are believed to be the result of failures to perceive grammatical characteristics that are not emphasized in a language. As one would expect from this hypothesis, it would appear that children's language difficulties vary depending on their mother tongue. There is evidence that difficulties that children with SLI have with, for example, Hebrew are different from the problems children with SLI have with English (Owen, Dromi, and Leonard 2001). Although this theory provides a provocative link between speech environment and language development, it has not produced a significant body of related research or of intervention programmes.

Another topic of discussion has been the well-established finding that many children with SLI have phonological short-term memory (STM) impairments; the STM system is a component of the working memory model of Baddeley (2007). These STM difficulties mean that if a sequence of words or non-words is spoken, the children with SLI remember fewer words than typical children of the same age. These difficulties are present in children with SLI who speak English and who speak Spanish (Girbau and Schwartz 2007).

Another explanation for SLI has been put forward by Ullman and his colleagues (Ullman 2004; Ullman and Pierpont 2005), who draw on a wide range of linguistic and psychological evidence to propose that there are two memory systems: a declarative memory system and a procedural memory system. They suggest that the declarative system contains factual information relevant to the use of words, and is supposed to be located in the temporal lobe, whereas the procedural system is concerned with automatic activities: for example, riding a bike, or, for most people, knowing a sentence is 'incorrect' but being unable to explain why this is so. Working memory is seen as a key part of the system and this involves the ability to remember information while at the same time carrying out other tasks, for example remembering the last word of a set of sentences while having to say whether each sentence is true or false. These suggestions build on those of Pinker (1994), who argued that regular words which follow a common grammatical pattern (e.g. adding '–ed' to form the past tense of a verb) are acquired by identification of general principles/rules and, in Ullman's terms, involve the procedural system. Because most languages also contain a small number of irregular words (e.g. the past tense of 'swim' is 'swam' rather than 'swimmed'), Pinker supposed that these have to be learnt on an individual basis, and in Ullman's terms would be part of the declarative system. Ullman and Pierpont (2005) have suggested that the language difficulties of SLI are caused by impairments to the procedural system so that both the learning of regular grammatical forms and working memory are affected. Some support for these ideas has been reported by Henry, Messer, and Nash (2011).

Summary: 'explanations' about SLI

Our understanding of the complexity and nature of SLI has increased over the past few decades, and a number of important theories have been advanced to explain why some children have difficulties with language. However, there is no widely accepted explanation of SLI. Part of the reason for this, as has already been mentioned, is that SLI by definition covers a range of different aspects of language difficulty. It is highly unlikely that any one explanation will cover the range of difficulties experienced by children with SLI. The way forward is probably to focus on discrete elements of the language system and try to understand why some children have difficulties with a particular element. This strategy already has been attempted (see Messer and Dockrell 2006; van der Lely 2005).

Interventions for children with SLI

To give a flavour of some of the interventions for children with SLI, two will be described. The first was carried out by Leonard et al. (2008), who targeted young children between three and five years who had difficulties with adding –s to a verb when using the third person singular (he eat–s) or had difficulties using what are termed auxillary verbs (is, are, was). The intervention involved 'recasting' the children's grammatical errors by providing a correct version of what they had said. The children took part in 96 sessions which were about half an hour in length with about four sessions per week. The two interventions showed a greater improvement than a third general intervention condition that involved general verbal stimulation, and these effects lasted for at least one month after the end of the programme. Thus, a carefully targeted and intense intervention was shown to provide lasting improvements.

Another intervention which also focuses on grammatical difficulties has been carried out by Ebbels (2007). Ebbels has drawn on previous work to develop an intervention that uses 'shape coding' for children who are able to read. The intervention involves using shapes that are drawn around written sentences to identify the different parts of speech. This means that a therapist can use the shapes to help explain grammar, and this is supplemented with a set of standard questions that help identify which words should go in which shape. So for example in a very simple sentence, the noun phrase is coded by an oval (e.g. 'The boy'), while the verb phrase is coded by a hexagon (e.g. 'is eating'). Much more complex sentences can be coded using a range of shapes with notations to help identify quite complex aspects of grammar. The shape coding system not only helps with the production of sentences, but also appears to be effective in helping children understand why a sentence was grammatically incorrect. This system appears to help children with SLI by giving them explicit visual guidance that will help them construct and use correctly formed sentences.

Although there are interventions such as those described above that are effective, a review by Law, Garrett, and Nye (2004) provides a less optimistic picture. Law et al., on the basis of a meta-analysis, concluded that interventions are most likely to be effective for children who have difficulties with phonology (sounds) or with expressive vocabulary (i.e. providing names). The evidence about effectiveness was not as clear for children who had problems with grammar. Interestingly, there did not seem to be a difference in the effectiveness of therapy, according to whether it was carried out by parents or clinicians.

Chapter overview

Speech and language are very complex systems involving high-level cognitive operations. Given the complexity of these systems it is unsurprising that many children have difficulties with speech and/or language. These difficulties will affect most of the activities of children and make access to the curriculum more difficult. In addition, these difficulties can have a wider impact on self-concepts and socio-emotional development, which are particularly noticeable in adolescence and beyond (Durkin and Conti-Ramsden 2010).

Not surprisingly, trying to understand the reasons for these difficulties and trying to design interventions to help the children is a major enterprise. Considerable advances have been made in our understanding of the range of difficulties, and there is a much greater appreciation of the complexity of the processes. However, it is also true to say that more work is needed to provide a comprehensive and in-depth understanding of the nature of these disabilities and to have reliable and effective interventions. As already mentioned, future research and intervention may need to be more specific in the targeting of speech and language difficulties, by taking account of the range of these difficulties and the need to address different types of disorder in different ways.

Contact address: david.messer@open.ac.uk

References

Baddeley, A. D. (2007) *Working memory, thought, and action,* Oxford: Oxford University Press.

Bedore, L. M., and Peña, E. D. (2008) 'Assessment of bilingual children for identification of language impairment: current findings and implications for practice', *International Journal of Bilingual Education and Bilingualism,* 11: 1–29.

Bercow, J. (2008) *The Bercow report: a review of services for children and young people (0–19) with speech, language and communication needs* [online]. Available at http://dera.ioe.ac.uk/8405/1/7771-dcsf-bercow.pdf

Bishop, D., Carolyn, R., Deeks, J., and Bishop, S. (1999) 'Auditory temporal processing impairment: neither necessary nor sufficient for causing language impairment in children', *Journal of Speech, Language and Hearing Research,* 42: 1295–1310.

Bowen, C. (2009) *Children's speech sound disorder,* Oxford: Wiley-Blackwell.

Clegg, J., Hollis, C., Mawhood, L., and Rutter, M. (2005) 'Development language disorders – a follow-up in later life. Cognitive, language and psychosocial outcomes', *Journal of Child Psychology and Psychiatry,* 46: 128–149.

Conti-Ramsden, G. (2008) 'Heterogeneity of specific language impairment in adolescent outcomes', in C. F. Norbury, J. B. Tomblin, and D. V. M. Bishop (eds.) *Understanding developmental language disorders: from theory to practice,* Hove: Psychology Press (pp. 117–130).

Durkin, K., and Conti-Ramsden, G. (2010) 'Young people with specific language impairment: a review of social and emotional functioning in adolescence', *Child Language Teaching and Therapy,* 26: 105–121.

Ebbels, S. H. (2007) 'Teaching grammar to school-aged children with Specific Language Impairment using shape coding', *Child Language Teaching and Therapy,* 23: 67–93.

Freudenthal, D., Pine, J. M., and Gobet, F. (2006) 'Modelling the development of children's use of optional infinitives in Dutch and English using MOSAIC', *Cognitive Science,* 30: 277–310.

Girbau, and Schwartz, R. (2007) 'Non-word repetition in Spanish-speaking children with Specific Langauge Impairment (SLI)', *International Journal of Language and Communication Disorders,* 42: 59–75.

Gopnik, M., and Crago, M. (1991) 'Familial aggregation of a developmental language disorder', *Cognition,* 39: 1–50.

Henry, L. C., Messer, D., and Nash, G. (2011) 'Executive functioning in children and young people with specific language impairment', *Journal of Child Psychology and Psychiatry,* 53: 37–45.

Hulme, C., and Snowling, M. (2009) *Developmental cognitive disorders,* Oxford: Blackwell.

Law, J., Garrett, Z., and Nye, C. (2004) 'The efficacy of treatment for children with developmental speech and language delay/disorder: a meta-analysis', *Journal of Speech, Language and Hearing Research*, 47: 924–943.

Leonard, L. B. (1998) *Children with specific language impairment*, Boston: MIT Press.

Leonard, L. B., Camarata, S. M., Pawlowska, M., Brown, B., and Camarata, M. N. (2008) 'The acquisition of tense and agreement morphemes by children with specific language impairment during intervention: phase 3', *Journal of Speech, Language and Hearing Research*, 51: 120–125.

Messer, D., and Dockrell, J. (2006) 'Children's word findings difficulties: descriptions and explanations', *Journal of Speech, Hearing and Language Research*, 49: 309–324.

Owen, A. J., Dromi, E., and Leonard, L. B. (2001) 'The phonology–morphology interface in the speech of Hebrew-speaking children with specific language impairment', *Journal of Communication Disorders*, 34: 323–337.

Paradis, J. (2010) 'The interface between bilingual development and specific language impairment', *Applied Psycholinguistics*, 31: 227–252.

Pinker, S. (1994) *The language instinct*, London: Penguin.

Rice, M. L., Wexler, K., and Cleave, P. L. (1995) 'Specific language impairment as a period of extended optional infinitive', *Journal of Speech and Hearing Research*, 38: 850–863.

Tallal, P., and Piercy, M. (1993) 'Developmental aphasia: rate of auditory processing and selective impairment of consonant perception', *Neuropsychologica*, 12: 83–93.

Tomblin, J. B., and Zhang, X. (2006) 'The dimensionality of language ability in school-age children', *Journal of Speech, Hearing and Language Research*, 49: 1193–1208.

Ullman, M. T. (2004) 'Contributions of memory circuits to language: the declarative/procedural model', *Cognition*, 92: 231–270.

Ullman, M. T., and Pierpont, E. I. (2005) 'Specific language impairment is not specific to language: the procedural deficit hypothesis', *Cortex*, 41: 399–433.

van der Lely, H. J. K. (2005) 'Domain-specific cognitive systems: insights from grammatical SLI', *Trends in Cognitive Sciences*, 9: 53–59.

van der Lely, H. J. K., and Stollwerck, L. (1997) 'Binding theory and specifically language impaired children', *Cognition*, 62: 245–290.

Wexler, K. (1994) *Optional infinitives, head movement, and economy of derivations*, Cambridge: Cambridge University Press.

Wright, B. A., Lombardino, L. J., King, W. M., Puranik, C. S., Leonard, C. M., and Merzenich, M. M. (1997) 'Deficits in auditory temporal and spectral resolution in language-impaired children', *Nature*, 387: 176–178.

26

THE AUTISM SPECTRUM

Alexandra Fortuna and Patricia Davis

CHILDREN'S HOSPITAL BOSTON, USA; INTEGRATED CENTER FOR CHILD DEVELOPMENT, USA

Autism spectrum disorders (ASDs) are a class of neurodevelopmental disorders defined by qualitative impairments in social functioning and communication, accompanied by repetitive behaviours and restrictive interests. As early as 30 years ago, autism was considered a rare childhood disorder. Today, autism is considered one of the most common disorders worldwide (Bauman 2010). Current statistics report that ASDs affect as many as 1 in 88 children, with the condition predominantly affecting males, as it is diagnosed approximately four times more often in males than in females (Center for Disease Control (CDC) 2010).

This chapter examines the history of ASDs and details the autism spectrum, identifying the characteristics of autism, Asperger's disorder, and pervasive developmental disorder – not otherwise specified (PDD-NOS). It discusses diagnostic criteria and the evaluations that have been developed in recent years to diagnose an ASD more accurately. The chapter will also discuss the interventions that are best known to support individuals with a spectrum disorder. Upon completion of this chapter the reader will:

- be aware of the history of ASD;
- understand the autism spectrum and the characteristics that are represented in individuals with autism, Asperger's disorder, and PDD-NOS;
- be familiar with the current diagnostic criteria as well as the impending changes to them;
- be familiar with the process of receiving an ASD diagnosis;
- be familiar with interventions and therapies available for treatment of ASDs.

History of autism spectrum disorders

In 1943, American child psychologist Leo Kanner introduced the term 'autism' to the world. Derived from the Greek word *autos* ('self'), the term was used to describe the disordered social responsiveness of the children he studied. The unusual set of characteristics reported by Kanner included extreme rigidity, described as a 'preservation of sameness', the preference for solitude, accompanied by repetitive language, movements, and restricted interests (Kanner 1943).

Independently of Kanner, Austrian child psychologist Hans Asperger published the first definition of Asperger's disorder in 1944 (Asperger 1944). Asperger observed children and adolescents who displayed impairments in social interaction and social reciprocity, had difficulty comprehending social demands, and engaged in restricted interests and repetitive behaviours. While many of the characteristics identified by Asperger were similar to those evident in Kanner's description of autism, Asperger detailed a key difference. The individuals with Asperger's possessed more developed language skills and a generally greater social awareness.

In 1979, Wing and Gould examined the definitions developed by Kanner and Asperger and reported that there were many individuals who did not fit their criteria, but displayed a mixed set of features. Wing and Gould (1979) introduced the term, 'triad of impairments' to describe the children they studied who displayed impairments of social interaction, social communication, and social imagination. Their findings determined that it was difficult to draw clear boundaries separating Kanner's autism from Asperger's, so the concept of a 'spectrum' developed.

While most research has focused on the behavioural components of autism, Bernard Rimland, a scientist and father of a son with autism, was one of the original pioneers advancing autism research and promoting the idea that autism was neurological in nature (Rimland 1964). His hypothesis has influenced the direction of autism research, diagnosis, and treatment. In 1985, Bauman and Kemper expanded the public's knowledge of ASDs when they identified neuroanatomical abnormalities in the limbic system and cerebellum of people with ASDs, securing the disorders' biological origin (Bauman and Kemper 1985).

Since the time of Kanner and Asperger, research has evolved and a more detailed understanding of ASDs is available. It has become more evident that autism is not the narrow classification it once was, but a much broader spectrum that involves a range of symptoms and severity. It is now understood that ASDs are highly heritable, biologically based neurodevelopmental disorders (Bailey, Phillips, and Rutter 1996). However, despite this knowledge, a clear cause is still unknown. Finding an exact cause has been challenging because of the genetic complexity and phenotypic variation across individuals with ASDs (Johnson and Myers 2007).

Current research is seeking to identify the genetic risk factors, environmental factors, and the neurological phenotypes of persons with ASDs.

The autism spectrum

Autism spectrum disorders are a group of neurodevelopmental disorders classified by qualitative impairments in social functioning and communication, accompanied by restrictive interests and repetitive behaviours. The term 'autism spectrum disorders' has been used to reveal the broader spectrum of characteristics that define the disorder. ASDs include autism, PDD-NOS, and Asperger's disorder (Johnson and Myers 2007). ASDs represent three of the five pervasive developmental disorders described in the *Diagnostic and Statistical Manual of Mental Disorders – 4th Edition* (DSM-IV, American Psychiatric Association (APA) 1994), and the International Classification of Disease-10 (ICD-10; WHO 1993). The term 'pervasive' indicates that the condition affects development across a range of domains. The other members of this diagnostic category are Rett's disorder and Childhood disintegrative disorder (CDD) (APA 1994). In this chapter, we restrict our discussions to ASDs, specifically autism, PDD-NOS, and Asperger's disorder.

Autism

Autism is considered to be the most severe form of an ASD and falls at one end of the spectrum. For individuals with autism, social interaction is extremely impaired. Individuals exhibit difficulties initiating, sustaining, and responding to social interactions. This diagnosis is generally associated with an inability to spontaneously seek others to share enjoyment, interest, or achievement. For example, individuals lack the desire to show, bring, or point out objects of interest. Individuals are often described as living in their own world, and seem to view others, even family members, as objects, or tools, to help satiate certain needs and/or wants. A common characteristic of autism is impaired use of non-verbal behaviours, such as eye contact, facial expressions, body postures, and gesturing. Interest in toys is unusual, as objects are often used in non-functional, unimaginative ways (APA 1994).

For individuals with autism, communication is often severely impaired. Many do not develop language at all, but learn to use pictures and symbols to communicate their wants and needs. Programmes such as the Picture Exchange Communication System (PECS, Frost and Bondy 1994), utilize behavioural principles to help children with social-communication deficits develop functional communication. Individuals learn to generate sentences using pictures (e.g. 'I want' and 'eat'), making communication meaningful. This programme allows the child to become more independent, and also provides communication partners (family members, teachers, community members) with a successful form of communication (Duffy and Healy 2011). Advancements in technology, such as the iPad and voice output devices that provide digitized speech output, have made possible the development of augmentative and assistive communication tools to promote and support communication (Duffy and Healy 2011).

For individuals who develop some language skills, expressive language is often impaired and not effectively utilized for communicative purposes. Immediate echolalia (the act of repeating words or phrases immediately after they are heard) is a communicative behaviour that is often observed among individuals with autism. Language may also predominantly consist of 'scripting', the act of repeating words or phrases heard in the past. This can include, but is not limited to, the repetition of dialogue from a TV show, movie, or videogame. Individuals may use words or phrases that only make sense to them, making it challenging to understand their needs and desires. While this communicative behaviour is often associated with autism and is often considered non-functional, some argue that both forms of echolalia can serve as communicative purposes for the speaker (Tager-Flusberg, Paul, and Lord 2005).

Restricted, repetitive, and stereotyped patterns of behaviours, interests, and activities may manifest themselves in a number of ways (APA 1994). Individuals with autism will often have intense interests or preoccupations that are unusual and consume their ability to interact effectively with their environment. Many individuals prefer that their world remain predictable, often resulting in compulsive ritualistic routines and a strong resistance to change. Individuals with autism are more likely to exhibit self-stimulatory behaviour, such as repetitive hand and finger movements (i.e. hand flapping or hand flicking), and whole-body mannerisms (i.e. body rocking).

Asperger's disorder

Asperger's disorder is defined by impairments in two of the three core domains: social interaction and restricted repetitive and stereotyped patterns of behaviour, interest, and activities. Children with Asperger's disorder may present with mild speech delay, and the recognition of a disorder may be absent until early school age when the inability to make social connections becomes a concern (Johnson and Myers 2007). While speech delay may not be apparent in those with Asperger's disorder, the pragmatics of language, i.e. the social aspects of communication, may be disordered and impaired. Conversations are often self-serving, which can result in one-sided conversations. The ability to shift from one topic to another is also a challenge. The mechanics of how a person with Asperger's disorder speaks is often unusual. Speech can be monotone, and volume, tone, and speed of speech are not regulated appropriately, making it difficult for others to understand the intent of a conversation. Lack of eye contact, facial expressions, and gesturing during conversation are other common characteristics of Asperger's disorder.

Social interactions are challenging tasks for individuals with Asperger's disorder. People with Asperger's disorder have difficulty understanding the feelings of others, often resulting in what appears to be inconsiderate and thoughtless behaviours, when that is often not the intent. The ability to interpret non-verbal social cues is a challenge; therefore simple daily gestures that are used to convey meaning are often neglected. Social rules and social interactions are not innately interpreted for individuals with Asperger's disorder; thus challenges in forming peer relationships often arise. While individuals with Asperger's disorder may desire to develop and maintain relationships with others, their lack of social awareness and inability to initiate and maintain social interactions inhibits this development.

The possession of unusual and preoccupying interests across a wide range of topics is common across this population. They may manifest their specific interest with an abnormal level of intensity (APA 1994) in genetics, vacuum cleaners, cartoon characters, geography, game shows, automobiles, etc.

PDD-NOS

A diagnosis of PDD-NOS applies to individuals who do not fulfill criteria for either autism or Asperger's disorder. They represent a diverse group of individuals who display a wide variety of difficulties in reciprocal social interactions, communication, and stereotyped behaviour patterns or interests. Individuals with PDD-NOS may demonstrate more developed language skills than an individual with autism; however, they exhibit impairments in language pragmatics, comprehension, and the use of specific language forms, such as asking questions, making requests, and initiating conversation. PDD-NOS also inhibits reciprocal social interaction and social relatedness. Unusual sensitivities to environmental stimuli are often present. A PDD-NOS diagnosis applies to a group of individuals who are generally less severely affected than those with an autism diagnosis, and do not meet the criteria for an Asperger diagnosis.

Diagnosis

In understanding ASDs, it is important to recognize that autism is not a 'one size fits all' diagnosis. Striking differences can be seen across children with an ASD. Currently, a single, definitive, medical test does not yet exist to diagnose an ASD. ASDs are considered to be highly hereditable; however, a significant minority of cases are associated with known genetic deficits. A diagnosis is based on observable symptoms, family history, the presence of symptoms by age three (APA 1994), and the completion of an extensive evaluation administered by professionals.

Early identification

In toddlerhood, children with ASDs are often referred to speech and language therapists due to their delayed language acquisition, odd communication (e.g. echoing, making up words, difficulty with pronouns), and/or failure to meet certain developmental language milestones such as the absence of babbling and pointing by age one year, single words by 16 months, and two-word phrases by 24 months of age (Johnson and Myers 2007). Young children will also exhibit symptoms such as reduced initiation of joint attention, reduced gesture use, reduced eye contact, reduced social engagement, inappropriate facial expressions, non-social attachments (e.g. to a block or a piece of string), motor rituals (e.g. hand flapping, rocking, spinning), and unusual preoccupations in routines and rituals. As children move into their preschool years, an individual with an ASD tends to demonstrate limited pretend play and cooperative play, and will often prefer solitary or parallel play activities. Fixations with certain toys or interests may begin to develop in this age. Young children with Asperger's disorder will frequently meet all of the expected language milestones and may not be diagnosed until they are older.

An increasing body of research is dedicated to the earlier identification of ASDs (Landa 2008; Wetherby et al. 2007). Studies involving retrospective viewing of home videos have helped researchers identify specific developmental differences among infants and toddlers who were later diagnosed with an ASD (Landa 2008). Research suggests that infants who displayed developmental disruption in social behaviours, such as gaze avoidance, poor social initiative, and absence of emotional expression present before nine months of age, were later diagnosed with an ASD. Twelve-month old children, who were later diagnosed with an ASD, differed from typically developing children by a limited use of pointing to request or share interest (Landa 2008). The American Academy of Pediatrics suggests that screening for an ASD should begin as early as 18 months and should be repeated at 24 and 36 months. Evidence suggests that intervention beginning ideally between 18 months and four years of age is likely to have the greatest positive outcome, supporting the importance of reliable diagnosis in early years (Veness et al. 2012). An early diagnosis of a possible ASD can help secure an enrolment in an intervention programme appropriate for the individual.

The changing diagnostic criteria

When there is a concern in the development of a child, the paediatrician will often use the DSM-IV criteria to determine whether the impairments should undergo further evaluation and receive an autism spectrum diagnosis. The DSM is undergoing a major revision – the first in 17 years – and the diagnostic criteria for autism spectrum disorders are facing some changes. The current version – DSM-IV – distinguishes autism from Asperger's disorder and PDD-NOS, with each diagnosis based on specific criteria.

The proposed changes to the diagnostic criteria of autism would put all three diagnoses under one category, autism spectrum disorder, removing the Asperger's disorder and PDD-NOS diagnoses. Under the proposed definition, an individual must meet the following criteria:

- persistent deficits in social communication and social interaction
- restricted, repetitive patterns of behaviour, interest, or activities
- symptoms must be present in early childhood
- symptoms together limit and impair everyday functioning.

Deficits in social communication and social interaction may manifest themselves in lack of social–emotional reciprocity, deficits in non-verbal communicative behaviours intended for social interaction, or challenges in maintaining social interaction. Definitive symptoms of restricted, repetitive patterns of behaviour, interest, or activity may present as stereotyped and repetitive speech, motor movements, or use of objects, such as motor stereotypies, echolalia, repetitive use of objects, or idiosyncratic phrases; excessive adherence to routines, excessive resistance to change, and ritualized patterns of verbal or non-verbal behaviour; highly restricted interests; and hyper- or hypo-reactivity to sensory input or unusual interest in sensory aspects of the environment.

Some argue that the proposed changes will help to define autism, and perhaps reduce the rate of increased diagnoses. However, many worry that the proposed criteria may hinder individuals from receiving necessary services, supports, and interventions.

Identification and diagnosis of ASDs

The diagnostic criteria for ASDs has guided professionals to develop assessments, interviews, and checklists that aid in identifying and diagnosing individuals with an ASD. A truly competent evaluation should include observations that are made over multiple occasions and across environments. The novelty of the experience and the evaluator may cause children to experience anxiety, attention deficits, or disruptive behaviours, which in turn could affect the results of the evaluation process. Familiarity of the tester and the testing space often makes the results more reliable.

The assessments described below are considered to be the standards in effectively evaluating individuals that may have an ASD.

The Autism Diagnostic Observation Schedule (ADOS)

The ADOS (Lord et al. 1999) is a semi-structured, standardized observation tool that can be used across all ages and verbal abilities to assess those who are suspected to have an ASD. The goal of the ADOS is to provide social and communication opportunities that elicit a range of spontaneous behaviours in a standardized context.

The ADOS evaluation creates planned social situations, referred to as 'presses' (Lord et al. 1989) that are designed to evoke a range of social initiations and responses. For example, in young children, examiners look for ability to respond to a social smile, initiation of joint attention, response to name, and use of pointing to bring attention to a distant object. In older, more verbally competent individuals, social awareness is assessed through the individual's understanding of their own emotions, the emotions of others, perception of social issues, as well as understanding of friendships and other relationships.

Similarly, communication opportunities are created in order to elicit a range of communicative exchange. For example, opportunities to assess appropriate language skills are created in which the individual will tell a story or teach a task to the examiner. Non-verbal communication is also assessed through the individual's gesture use while reporting an event.

Structured play activities are also included in order to observe the individual's range of imaginative play skills and social role-play. Observers look for the individuals' creative and imaginative use of objects and whether their use of toys goes beyond their obvious meanings. Opportunities for spontaneous engagement in symbolic and functional play are elicited through a make-believe birthday party, in which the examiner observes how the individual uses the provided objects to create an imaginary birthday party.

Upon completion of the ADOS, cut off scores help to indicate and identify whether a child has an ASD, and specifically differentiates autism from Asperger's disorder and PDD-NOS (Lord et al. 1999).

Autism Diagnostic Interview-Revised (ADI-R)

The ADI-R (Lord, Rutter, and Le Couteur 1994) is a standardized, semi-structured parent interview that is used to help professionals determine a diagnosis for a child who is suspected to have an ASD. The ADI-R was developed based on DSM-IV and ICD-10 criteria for autism and pervasive developmental disorders. This diagnostic tool is composed of interview questions that evaluate eight content areas: (i) background, including family, education, previous diagnoses, and medications, (ii) overview of the current behaviour, (iii) early development and developmental milestones, (iv) language acquisition and loss of language or other skills, (v) current functioning in regard to language and communication, (vi) social development and play, (vii) interests and behaviours, and (viii) clinically relevant behaviours, such as aggression, self-injury, and possible epileptic features. The ADI-R provides scores for the individuals' current behaviours and their developmental and behavioural history. This results in specific cutoff scores that indicate whether the individual has an ASD. With this particular tool, a classification of classic autism is given when scores in the domains of communication, social interaction, and patterns of behaviour meet or exceed the specified cutoffs, and onset of the disorder is evident by age three.

Social Communication Questionnaire (SCQ)

The SCQ (Rutter, Bailey, and Lord 2003) is a screening tool that evaluates the communication skills and social functioning in children who are suspected to have an ASD. The SCQ provides a quick assessment of ASD symptoms, and provides a cutoff score that can be used to indicate the possibility of an ASD. This tool is meant to help guide professionals in understanding a child and determine whether further evaluation is necessary.

Checklist for Autism in Toddlers (CHAT)

The CHAT (Baron-Cohen, Allen, and Gillberg 1992) is used to help detect early signs of autism, and is administered at 18 months by assessing the developmental milestones of a child. It comprises 14 items, nine of which are asked to a parent by a physician and five of which are completed by a home health visitor observing the child in their home environment. With a 91.7 percent success rate in diagnosis, this tool continues to help families receive information early in their child's development and is a predictive tool for a later ASD diagnosis (Baron-Cohen et al. 1992).

Modified Checklist for Autism in Toddlers (M-CHAT)

The M-CHAT (Robins, Fein, and Barton 1999) is an extension of the CHAT (Baron-Cohen et al. 1992). The format and the initial nine items are identical to those of the CHAT; however, this tool does not rely on observations by a physician, rather it accounts a parent's report of skills and behaviours. The expansion of the tool includes 21 additional test items that were designed to broaden the checklist and to eliminate the need for a home health visitor. The M-CHAT was developed in order to help detect early cases of onset; however, there is a high false positive rate with this tool, meaning that not all children who score at risk for an ASD on the M-CHAT will be diagnosed with an ASD. The purpose of this tool is to provide professionals with a quick checklist to determine whether early signs of an ASD are present and whether further evaluation is warranted (Robins et al. 1999).

Therapies

Currently there are no proven pharmaceutical treatments for the core symptoms of ASDs. Treatments advised for those with an ASD are medical, psychosocial, and behavioural. The most 'successful' treatments are suggested to be psychosocial and behavioural, involving intense intervention, best if begun in the early years. The most effective interventions often include a variety of elements geared towards the child's particular needs and designed by an experienced team. Interventions should include a programme that is focused on the explicit instruction of communication, social, and play skills. The environment should be highly structured, with predictable daily schedules.

A comprehensive approach usually requires a combination of programmes incorporating many disciplines. Upon evaluation of numerous intervention programmes for children with ASDs, researchers have identified several common traits of success. The successful programmes included the following elements: (i) a curriculum focused on social and play skills, communication, attention, and imitation, (ii) a highly structured environment, with low ratios of student to staff, (iii) predictable daily routines, (iv) explicitly taught strategies for generalizing skills to other environments and contexts, (v) a functional approach to addressing problems, (vi) an emphasis on the necessary skills needed for a mainstream classroom, and (vii) family involvement (Dawson and Osterling 1997; National Research Council 2001).

Applied behaviour analysis (ABA)

ABA is a systematic behavioural approach devised by Dr Ole Ivar Lovaas that aims to improve communication skills, encourage social interaction, modify behaviours, and help children become more independent. Interventions using ABA principles have been found to be effective for individuals with an ASD.

ABA focuses on understanding behaviour and how it is affected by the surrounding environment. Goals are individualized for each child, and intensive, one-on-one instruction is provided to achieve these goals. One key principle of ABA is positive reinforcement. For example, when a behaviour is paired with a positive reinforcement (something that is of value to the child), repetition of that behaviour is likely to be replicated. Using this approach, children learn to repeat/master positive behaviours and after time, apply that behaviour in all environments; a technique known as generalization. ABA focuses on increasing useful behaviours and reducing harmful and interrupting behaviours. The goal of ABA is to address problems and to increase meaningful behavioural change.

Discrete trial training

Discrete trial training (DTT) is an instructional strategy that is often used with children on the autism spectrum who are engaged in an ABA programme. It is useful for teaching children new forms of behaviour and in making new discriminations among events. Teaching new forms of behaviour is the act of teaching an action that the child could previously not perform. Teaching a novel speech sound or an unknown motor movement are examples of new behaviour that is taught through discrete trial training. New discriminations represent teaching a response to a different request. For example, if a child is shown a car and is asked what the object is, if the wrong response is provided by the child, through DTT, they might learn the name of the object (Smith 2001). DTT can also be used to manage disruptive behaviours, by reducing the rate of their occurrence and replacing such behaviours with alternative and more adaptive behaviours (Matson et al. 1996).

Social skills training

For older and higher functioning children, particularly those with Asperger's disorder, a main objective of intervention should focus on the instruction of social and pragmatic language skills. Encouraging these skills will help improve an individual's ability to achieve a more independent lifestyle, aiding in the attainment of employment and higher education. Instruction of these skills should take place across a variety of settings, as it is important that the individual is able to generalize the skills across environments. Encouraging the development of these skills can be achieved through a variety of approaches, e.g. individual or group speech and language therapy, social skills training, supervised social outings and experience, and inclusion in the general education classroom with tutoring from typical peers.

Diet

Gastrointestinal disorders are often associated with ASDs; however, the manifestation and best treatments for these issues are often misinterpreted. Within this population of individuals, gastrointestinal dysfunction has often been reported, but evaluation is often a challenge as many individuals face severe deficits in language and are unable to communicate their discomfort and other symptoms. This inability to express discomfort can lead to long periods of pain, paired with increased behaviours as an undetected sign of discomfort. While research is continuing to develop in this area, individuals with an ASD who exhibit any gastrointestinal symptoms (i.e. abdominal pain, constipation, chronic diarrhoea, and gastroesophageal reflux disease) should be thoroughly examined (Buie et al. 2010).

Few studies have supported the implementation of a gluten-free, casein-free diet to change the behaviour of an individual with an ASD, although a restrictive diet may benefit a subset of children. Many individuals with an ASD have reported food allergies, and those are important to treat and manage. However, research has suggested that placing children who are not allergic to gluten on a gluten-free diet does not lead to improvement/benefit (Elder et al. 2006).

Summary

ASDs are neurobiological disorders with a genetic basis that are characterized by marked impairment in social interaction and communication, as well as the presence of repetitive behaviours and restricted interests. No two persons with an ASD are alike, and each individual exhibits unique traits, strengths, and challenges. There is no 'one size fits all' treatment plan or cure for individuals with this diagnosis. Early identification and intervention have been shown to improve the outcome for individuals with ASDs. Autism spectrum disorder is a puzzling yet remarkable diagnosis that awaits advanced research to continue to improve the standard of care for individuals, their families, care providers, and educators.

Contact address: alexfortuna@gmail.com

References

American Psychiatric Association (1994) *Diagnostic and statistical manual of mental disorders*, 4th edn, Washington, DC: American Psychiatric Association.

Asperger, H. (1944) 'Die "autistischen Psychopathen" im Kindesalter', *Archiv fur Psychiatrie und Nervenkrakheiten*, 117: 76–136.

Bailey, A., Phillips, W., and Rutter, M. (1996) 'Autism: towards an integration of clinical, genetic, neuropsychological, and neurobiological perspectives', *Journal of Child Psychology and Psychiatry*, 37: 89–126.

Baron-Cohen, S., Allen, J., and Gillberg, C. (1992) 'Can autism be detected at 18 months? The needle, the haystack, and the CHAT', *British Journal of Psychiatry*, 161: 839–843.

Bauman, M. (2010) 'Autism spectrum disorders: clinical and medical perspectives', *The Neurochemical Basis of Autism*, New York: Springer (pp. 1–11).

Bauman, M., and Kemper, T. L. (1985) 'Histoanatomic observations of the brain in early infantile autism', *Neurology*, 35: 866–874.

Buie, T., Campbell, D. B., Fuchs, G. J., Furuta, G. T., Levy, J., Vande Water, J. et al. (2010) 'Evaluation, diagnosis, and treatment of gastrointestinal disorders in individuals with ASDs: a consensus report', *Pediatrics*, 125: 1–18.

Center for Disease Control (2010) *Autism Spectrum Disorders*, CDC [online]. Available at www.cdc.gov/ncbddd/autism/data.html

Dawson, G., and Osterling, J. (1997) 'Early intervention in autism: effectiveness and common elements of current approaches', in M. J. Guralnick (ed.) *The effectiveness of early intervention; second generation research*, Baltimore: Brookes (pp. 307 26).

Duffy, C., and Healy, O. (2011) 'Spontaneous communication in autism spectrum disorder: a review of topographies and interventions', *Research in autism spectrum disorders*, 5: 977–983.

Elder, J. H., Shankar, M., Shuster, J., Theriaque, D., Burns, S., and Sherrill, L. (2006) 'The gluten-free, casein-free diet in autism: results of a preliminary double blind clinical trial', *Journal or Autism and Developmental Disorders*, 36: 413–420.

Frost, L. A., and Bondy, A. S. (1994) *The picture exchange communication system training manual*, Cherry Hill, NJ: Pyramid Educational Consultants.

Johnson, C. P., and Myers, S. M. (2007) 'Identification and evaluation of children with autism spectrum disorders', *Pediatrics*, 120: 1183–1215.

Kanner, L. (1943) 'Autistic disturbances of affective contact', *Nervous Child*, 2: 217–250.

Landa, R. J. (2008) 'Diagnosis of autism spectrum disorders in the first 3 years of life', *Nature Clinical Practice Neurology*, 4: 138–47.

Lord, C., Rutter, M., and Le Couteur, A. (1994) 'Autism Diagnostic Interview–Revised: a revised version of a diagnostic interview for caregivers of individuals with possible pervasive developmental disorders', *Journal of Autism and Developmental Disorders*, 24: 659–685.

Lord, C., Rutter, M., DiLavore, P. C., and Risi, S. (1999) *Autism Diagnostic Observation Schedule (ADOS)*, Los Angeles: Western Psychological Services.

Lord, C., Rutter, M., Goode, S., Heemsbergen, J., Jordan, H., Mawhood, L., and Schopler, E. (1989) 'Autism diagnostic observation schedule: a standardized observation of communicative and social behavior', *Journal of Autism and Developmental Disorders*, 19: 185–212.

Matson, J., Benavidez, D., Compton, L., Paclawskyj, T., and Baglio, C. (1996) 'Behavioral treatment of autistic persons: a review of research from 1980 to the present', *Research in Developmental Disabilities*, 17: 433–465.

National Research Council (2001) *Educating children with autism*, Washington, DC: National Academy Press.

Rimland, B. (1964) *Infantile autism: the syndrome and its implications for a neural theory of behavior*, East Norwalk, CT: Appleton-Century-Crofts.

Robins, D., Fein, D., and Barton, M. (1999) *The Modified Checklist for Autism in Toddlers (M-CHAT)*, Storrs, CT: University of Connecticut.

Rutter, M., Bailey, A., and Lord, C. (2003) *Social Communication Questionnaire (SCQ)*, Los Angeles: Western Psychological Services.

Smith, T. (2001) 'Discrete trial training in the treatment of autism', *Focus on autism and other developmental disabilities*, 16: 86–92.

Tager-Flusberg, H., Paul, R., and Lord, C. (2005) 'Language and communication in autism', in F. Volkmar, R. Paul, A. Klin, and D. Cohen (eds.) *Handbook of autism and pervasive developmental disorders*, 3rd edn, New York: Wiley.

Veness, C., Prior, M., Bavin, E., Eadie, P., Cini, E., and Reilly, S. (2012) 'Early indicators of autism spectrum disorders at 12 and 24 months of age: a prospective, longitudinal comparative study', *Autism*, 16: 163–77.

Wetherby, A., Watt, N., Morgan, L., and Shumway, S. (2007) 'Social communication profiles of children with autism spectrum disorders late in the second year of life', *Journal of Autism and Developmental Disorders*, 37: 960–975.

Wing, L., and Gould, J. (1979) 'Severe impairments of social interaction and associated abnormalities in children: epidemiology and classification', *Journal of Autism and Developmental Disorders*, 9: 11–29.

World Health Organization. (WHO) (1993) *The ICD-10 classification of mental and behavioural disorders: diagnostic criteria for research*, Geneva: World Health Organization.

27

SOCIAL, EMOTIONAL AND BEHAVIOURAL DIFFICULTIES (SEBD)

The need to look beyond the problem

Paul Cooper

HONG KONG INSTITUTE OF EDUCATION, HONG KONG, SAR OF CHINA

This chapter explores the issue of social, emotional and behavioural difficulties (SEBD), their nature, and the ways in which they can be addressed in schools. Central to the chapter is contention that a biopsychosocial approach provides significant advantages in understanding and dealing with SEBD. Five 'reflective questions' are interspersed throughout the text: consideration may assist in consolidation and understanding of the major themes covered in this chapter.

The nature of SEBD

SEBD can be usefully defined in terms of (i) 'externalizing' forms of presentation, which include extreme withdrawn behaviour, distortions to self-image, and a preoccupation with self-negating thoughts, and (ii) 'internalizing' forms of presentation, which include defiant, aggressive, destructive, and non-compliant behaviours. While it is important to distinguish SEBD from the extremes of severe psychiatric disturbance and routine misbehaviour, it is also important to understand that mild problems can escalate into SEBD, and SEBD can in turn develop into more serious psychiatric problems (Patterson, Reid, and Dishion 1992). SEBD, therefore, is best understood as a dynamic phenomenon characterized by disturbed and disturbing behaviour patterns that are highly sensitive to social and other ecological influences.

SEBD tend to incur strong, sometimes visceral reactions. For example, in the face of severely aggressive behaviour the teacher's understandable concern for his/her personal safety might foster a tendency to focus disproportionately on 'behavioural problems' that need to be controlled. The 'acting-out' student, however, is often externalizing internal conflict and distress, and the failure to appreciate this sometimes leads to an emphasis on control and punishment at the expense of dealing with underlying problems. Such responses tend to exacerbate underlying and surface problems and promote disaffection and alienation (Cooper et al. 2000).

Question 1: In what circumstances, if any, might suspension or exclusion from school be an appropriate response to SEBD? Consider different stakeholder perspectives.

Terminology

In the UK education context the interchangeable terms 'social, emotional and behavioural difficulties' (Scotland and Northern Ireland) and 'behavioural, emotional and social difficulties' (England) are used, the former of which was chosen for this chapter because it is the longest established and most comprehensive term currently in use in the field. They refer to disturbances to social–emotional and/or behavioural functioning that have a significant impact on the educational engagement of students. This loose definition owes much to the UK's generalized definition of 'learning difficulty' (HM Government 1981), which eschews a focus on medical or psychological disorders in favour of an emphasis on educational functioning. Therefore, students may be classified as having a special educational need as a result of SEBD in the absence of a medical diagnosis. Conversely, children with a formally diagnosed behavioural disorder will not necessarily be deemed to have a special educational need if their condition is being managed in a manner that requires no educational resources beyond those routinely available in the student's school. This said, there is likely to be a strong overlap between the population of students with SEBD and those with diagnosed disorders (Department for Children, Schools and Families 2008). An important point about the term 'SEBD' is that it is usually taken to refer to the student within his or her social context and is taken to imply that the problem may reside primarily in the environment rather than the individual, or, at least, in the interaction between the two.

'Challenging behaviour' is a term that is sometimes used in the UK in health and social care circles to refer to students who exhibit disturbing and or threatening behaviour, and is often associated with students who have significant cognitive impairments (e.g. Harris, Cook, and Upton 1996). 'Emotional and behavioural disorders' is a term that has international currency in psychiatry, and is used in the USA and other countries in health and educational legislation. The term refers to specific psychiatric diagnoses, criteria for which are published by bodies such as the American Psychiatric Association (APA; 2007) and the World Health Organization (1991). These conditions include the following.

- *Conduct disorder:* a disruptive behavioural disorder in which the individual shows marked aggression towards other people, as well as violent and destructive behaviour.
- *Oppositional defiant disorder:* a disruptive behavioural disorder characterized by interpersonal oppositionality, uncooperativeness, and verbal aggression.
- *Attention deficit/hyperactivity disorder/Hyperkinetic disorders:* a behavioural and cognitive disorder characterized by difficulties in sustaining attention to tasks, impulsiveness and, in some cases, difficulties in regulating physical movement (i.e. hyperactivity).
- *Anxiety disorders:* emotional disorders in which the individual becomes distressed, fearful, and hyper-aroused.
- *Depressive disorders:* emotional disorders in which the individual becomes withdrawn, unmotivated, and prone to feelings of low self-worth.

> *Question 2:* Consider the pros and cons of categorical vs. non-categorical approaches to SEBD.

The need to move beyond individual versus environmental explanations

Theories of underlying causation vary widely, from those emphasizing 'within-person' (biopsychological) set of causes to those emphasizing primarily environmental (social) causes. Environmental arguments rightly condemn the reductive nature of biological determinism (e.g. Rose 1995), which denies the significance of human agency and its influences on development. The worst excesses of biological determinism challenge the right to life of individuals and groups deemed biologically 'inferior', as in the case of the eugenic theory that was prominent in Europe and America in the early twentieth century and was used to justify forced sterilization and euthanasia, and, ultimately, genocide (Allen 1997). The same deterministic principles underlie certain social and educational arguments, such as those that relate intelligence quotient (IQ) to human potential (e.g. Herrnstein and Murray 1996).

We must never underestimate the seriousness of fallacious determinist arguments, but we must also appreciate the role biological influences have on development and behaviour. Behavioural geneticists, for example, acknowledge the ways in which genetic inheritance and environmental factors interact (Plomin 1990). A biopsychosocial model, which is explored later in this chapter, adopts a systems perspective whereby the interactions between within-person and environmental factors are the main focus of assessment and intervention, thus going beyond the within-person versus environment debate. It follows from this that legitimate concerns about the pathogenic potential of biological 'labels' and diagnoses on individuals (see Boyle, Chapter 21, this volume) must be tempered by an understanding of the ways in which biological and other 'within-person' variables are understood to operate in relation to external, environmental factors (Cooper, Bilton, and Kakos 2013). From educational and therapeutic viewpoints, a key test to be applied is the 'functional' question; for example: to what extent can an understanding of biopsychological theories that accompany specific diagnoses illuminate the nature of a student's learning/behavioural difficulties, in ways that help us to promote his/her social and academic engagement?'

Question 3: What is the difference between a diagnosis and a label?

Difficulties with the SEBD construct

SEBD is a problematic construct that is sometimes used as a label for individuals who are seen as difficult to engage or manage because they are experienced as disruptive, threatening, emotionally vulnerable, and/or socially inept. Too great a readiness to individualize SEBD can, however, mask the possibility that 'problematic' behaviour is sometimes a legitimate response to intolerable circumstances in the school/classroom environment or in other areas of the young person's life (Cooper, Smith, and Upton 1994). Having said this, people may be socialized into ways of behaving that the wider culture construes as deviant, such as using a coercive social style in order to meet personal needs (Patterson et al. 1992). This means that they are, effectively, trained in deviant ways of behaving, often by their carers. Such 'training' is often unwitting, and may be an unconscious replication of the dysfunctional parenting they experienced as children. In other circumstances young people may apply a non-deviant, socialized approach to what might be termed a deviant situation (for example, in resistance to abuse), which may be misconstrued as a deviant response, because the abusive trigger for their response is unknown to the observer. Furthermore, individuals who have been exposed to deviant environments might respond in non-deviant environments in deviant ways, because they misread the situation on the basis of prior experience.

This suggests that SEBD should be seen as an umbrella term covering a range of possibilities. What might be at first construed as a problem emanating from within an individual may turn out to be the symptom of a problem in some area of the individual's environment. On the other hand, repeated patterns of behaviour that are deemed problematic across a wide range of different settings and over an extended time frame may suggest something more deep-seated in the form of a persistent characteristic which may, in turn, be rooted in the individual's socialization, or in a combination of their socialization and a biological predisposition. In any event, where problems are entrenched and pervasive there is likely to be a need for adjustments to be made to the environment, and possibly the individual's way of relating to it.

Social–emotional competence and well-being

SEBD can be 'internalizing', so that the threat is more toward the individual's own well-being rather than that of others. In spite of this, attention is often drawn to the externalizing, disruptive behaviours, to the neglect of the internalized problems (Schoenfeld and Janney 2008). This is despite the fact that both types of problems appear to have increased considerably over time in many parts of the world (Costello et al. 2003), with current US estimates suggesting up to 39 percent of school students experiencing mental health problems at some point in their development (Forness, Kim, and Walker 2012). While this may be in part due to changes in diagnostic criteria, assessment techniques, and service delivery (Fonagy et al. 2002), it is also suggested that widespread cultural changes have created a more SEBD-provocative world. Increased prosperity and materialism coupled with a disintegration of social cohesion since World War II have helped give rise to the growth of a youth culture that is increasingly isolated from the adult world and exposed as a consumer market to be exploited, leaving young people vulnerable to insecurities that accompany competitive individualism (Layard and Dunn 2009).

It is also important to note that delinquency often overlaps with mental health problems, and both of these problems are exacerbated by adverse social circumstances in some communities and schools. Mental health problems and social deviance/delinquency commonly co-occur with educational difficulties. In the absence of effective intervention, as young people move through the adolescent years, there is likely to be a deterioration across these areas (Rutter and Smith 1995).

> *Question 4:* To what extent are children now more or less susceptible to emotional stress and social difficulties than children of earlier generations?

A biopsychosocial approach

The biopsychosocial approach (Engel 1977, 1980), which was originally concerned with the role of psychological and social factors in physical health, has been developed to apply to a wide range of health, social, and psychological issues (Cooper et al. 2013). In the broad area of SEBD the approach can be seen at work as an underpinning to multi-systemic therapy (MST) (Henggeler et al. 1996, 1997), which has been found to be a highly effective multi-agency and multi-modal intervention for problems such as conduct disorder in older adolescents (Kazdin 2002).

Defining the biopsychosocial approach

A 'bio-psycho-social' perspective derives directly from systems theory (e.g. Bronfenbrenner 1979) and is ecological, positing that nature (genetic inheritance and physiology) and nurture (environmental influences) are best understood as being in constant fluid and dynamic interaction (see Plomin 1990). Thus the approach is to be holistic and, therefore, capable of capturing the complexities of SEBD.

A central feature of the model (see Figure 27.1) is recognition of the fact that biological systems, such as neurology, are strongly influenced by genetic inheritance. However, from the earliest stages of life, the development of biological systems is affected by environmental factors, such as nutrition, and experiential factors, including parenting styles, peer influences and other kinds of stimuli to which the developing individual is exposed. For example, most relevant to the sphere of SEBD is the fact that it has been shown that the neurological development of children can be adversely affected by prolonged exposure to abuse, neglect, or lack of stimulation, leading to cognitive and social impairments. Conversely, adjustments to the environment may, in certain circumstances, help to reverse these effects. Furthermore, neuroplasticity sometimes enables the brains of individuals who have experienced serious neurological insult to compensate for the concomitant loss of functioning in one area by transferring the functions to other brain areas (Geake 2009). In addition, a growing list of so-called 'smart drugs' (e.g. methylphenidate and ampekines) are prescribed by physicians to compensate for neurological dysfunction (Rose 1995).

Other, perhaps more powerful forms of compensation and augmentation are of a social and/ or educational nature. These include the provision of compensatory skills for individuals, in the form of behavioural training, through the application of rewards and sanctions and the manipulation of behavioural antecedents; cognitive strategies (e.g. anger management training and mnemonic strategies) and various therapeutic interventions (e.g. counselling). Within the educational arena psycho-educational interventions, including specific pedagogical (Purdie, Hattie, and Carroll 2002) and emotional literacy (Mosley 1993) strategies, and intervention packages such as nurture groups (Cooper and Whitebread 2007), are shown to enhance social/educational engagement of students with a wide range of social–emotional difficulties, some of which have a biological basis. Other educational interventions that have an augmenting/compensatory effect are of an institutional nature, and include school effectiveness/school improvement interventions (Cooper and Jacobs 2011). More socially focused interventions include systemic and multi-systemic interventions, as well as restorative justice and peer mediation strategies. It follows from a bio-psycho-social approach that the search for effective interventions should range widely across disciplines as diverse as education, psychology, sociology, medicine, and psychiatry. For this reason multi-disciplinary and trans-disciplinary approaches are a focus of major interest in the SEBD area.

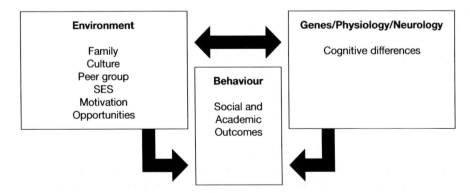

Figure 27.1   Biopsychosocial interactions (based on Frith 1992 and adapted from Cooper and Jacobs 2011)

Applying a biopsychosocial approach to SEBD

The adoption of a biopsychosocial approach to an understanding of SEBD highlights the need to avoid the crude linearity that is sometimes a feature of the field. For example, non-lineal systemic thinking leads us to question the use of the term SEBD as a label to be applied to individuals and to understand the perceived problem ecologically. This often leads to the realization that the apparent 'problem' may not be understood or experienced in the same way by the different actors in the situation. For example, a student may become morose, oppositional, and disruptive in class in response to an emotional trauma in the family situation, or as a consequence of bullying in the school setting. In any event, our assessment of the situation should direct us towards the most promising focus for intervention.

An important insight from the biopsychosocial approach for SEBD is that where biological and/or intrapsychic factors are at work in relation to a manifestation of SEBD, they almost always have implications that must be addressed on the social–environmental level. Therefore, an understanding of biological and/or intrapsychic factors can sometimes help us to target social–environmental interventions with greater accuracy than if we neglect the possibility that such factors 'might' be at work.

By way of illustration, it is useful to consider the value of being able to distinguish between cognitive distortions and cognitive deficits (Barriga et al. 2000). Cognitive distortions are defined as 'inaccurate ways of attending to or conferring meaning on experience' (Barriga et al. 2000: 37). In terms of surface behaviour, cognitive deficits and distortions may be indistinguishable. For example, they may manifest themselves in inattention in class. In seeking a systemic solution to the problem, our first port of call would be to consider what it is that the young person is being expected to attend to, and to make judgements about the appropriateness of this stimulus and to explore ways of making it more accessible. In some cases this does not result in a solution, but leads to a persistent pattern of disengagement/distractibility that seems impervious to the adjustment that the teacher routinely makes and that usually works. In these circumstances it may become appropriate to investigate more closely the characteristics and dispositions of the individual. This will include any possible influences on attitudes that might come from peer interactions. If a cognitive deficit is identified then this will have to be accommodated within the pedagogical approaches that are taken with this young person, and compensatory strategies will need to be developed that will diminish the negative impact of the deficit on the student's social–emotional and educational engagement. In the real world it will sometimes be the case that cognitive deficits and distortions are both present, and that both types of intervention will be necessary.

Question 5: What do teachers need to know (in anything) about biology?

Assessment

This brief section is concerned with the educational assessment of SEBD in the classroom. First, consideration is given to some underlying principles of assessment. This is followed by some examples of assessment tools that can be used in educational settings.

Assessment principles

Effective assessment for SEBD (see Cooper 2006):

1. is reflexive and ongoing
2. is based on rigorous evidence and is free of bias

3. is a holistic process which ensures that the individual's functioning is considered within the developmental, social and interpersonal contexts

4. involves multiple methods for holistic coverage and triangulation

5. identifies influences that help create and maintain difficulties that may reside within the individual, in the social and interpersonal interactions experienced by the individual, or in interactions between individual and social/interpersonal factors

6. privileges and protects the interests of the student and always serves the aim of social inclusion

7. recognizes the value of transdisciplinary perspectives.

Approaching assessment: levels of analysis

It is useful to think of the assessment of SEBD in terms of a systemic hierarchy, whereby we consider the influence of aspects of the educational environment on the generation and maintenance of perceived problems, and seek to address these before considering 'within-person' explanations and interventions.

The levels of analysis are as follows (in order of consideration).

- *The physical environment:* is the physical environment (heat, light, noise level, physical space etc.) appropriate to the demands of the teaching and learning goals?
- *The curriculum:* is the curriculum content appropriate to the child's developmental level, learning preferences and temperament?
- *The instructional environment/pedagogy:* to what extent are the instructional environment and pedagogy facilitative of educational engagement for this and other pupils?
- *The social environment (classroom; school):* what is the point of view of this pupil? Does s/he feel safe, valued and provided with opportunities for acknowledged achievement by his/her peers? What are the consequences of this for the educational engagement of all pupils?
- *The pupil group:* what are the characteristics of the various social grouping in this classroom? Are some children conspicuously disadvantaged? What are the consequences of this for the educational engagement of these pupils? What enables some students to gain social advantage in this class?
- *The individual child:* what is distinctive about this child's manner of engagement (social, emotional, or cognitive) that may create a barrier to achievement?

Some tools

Teachers and teaching assistants can be encouraged to use the following reflective approaches to help them investigate the above issues (see Cooper 2006 for further elaboration of these approaches):

The following tools can be used by teachers to aid reflexivity:

- reflection alone and with colleagues
- reflective diaries
- interviews and consultation with pupils.

Other standardized questionnaires and observational tools that can be used include:

- standardised screening instruments, e.g. *The Goodman Strengths and Difficulties Questionnaire, SDQ* (Goodman et al. 2003)

- behavioural observation, e.g. Goldstein's 'TOAD' schedule (Goldstein and Braswell 1994); the Antecedents Behaviour Consequences protocol
- sociometrics (Moreno 1934/1956).

Intervention

It is impossible to cover the range of psychologically informed SEBD interventions in a short chapter such as this. With this in mind the reader is directed towards lengthier treatments of the topic (e.g. Cooper and Jacobs 2011; Fonagy and Kurtz 2002; Nathan and Gorham 2002). Here a brief overview is given of some key interventions that use empirically supported approaches.

Teachers who demonstrate empathy and emotional warmth have been shown to improve the emotional well-being of students as well as academic achievement (Buyse et al. 2008). There is 'mindfulness training', in which individuals are trained to focus on their immediate situation and thoughts in an accepting and non-judgmental way, and this has recently been shown to be highly effective with both teachers and parents of SEN students, resulting in significant reductions in levels of stress and anxiety, as well as increases in self-compassion, and empathic concern and forgiveness (Benn, Akiva, and Arel 2012).

Behavioural interventions are cost-effective and combine minimal training requirements, ease of implementation, and effectiveness (Walker, Colvin, and Ramsey 1994). One example is The Good Behaviour Game (Barrish, Saunders, and Wolf 1969), which is a team activity designed to promote positive student behaviour through compliance with selected behavioural rules. International (including longitudinal) studies, since the 1960s, have demonstrated its success for a wide range of SEBD with students from four to 18 years (Tingstrom, Sterling-Turner, and Wilczynski 2006).

Researchers have identified and described 52 strongly evidence-based behavioural 'kernels', such as response cost, verbal praise, and 'time out', that are commonly embedded in more elaborate packages and intervention approaches. Evidence shows that competent application of these can produce significant and lasting behavioural change (Embry and Biglan 2008).

Cognitive behavioural (CB) approaches are concerned with mediating and moderating effects of thought processes in relation to behaviour. CB interventions encourage functional ways of thinking by challenging and changing dysfunctional thinking. CB is effective for problems as diverse as self-monitoring difficulties in ADHD (Shapiro and Cole 1995), self-control in oppositional defiance disorder (ODD) and conduct disorder (CD) (Altepeter and Korger 1999; Fonagy and Kurtz 2002), anxiety disorders (Kearney and Wadiak 1999), and depressive disorders (Fonagy et al. 2002).

An important school-based application of CB approaches is in the related area of social problem-solving, which is directed at providing students who exhibit difficulties in engaging in harmonious social relationships with the skills to identify and modify their behaviour (Battistich et al. 1989; De Castro et al. 2003). Another approach is anger management, which involves enabling students to identify triggers to aggressive outbursts and strategies for controlling these (Feindler, Marriott, and Iwata 1984).

Functional behavioural analysis (FBA) combines systematic behavioural analysis with cognitive intervention (Baer, Wolf, and Risley 1968). It involves assessing the individual's relationship to the environment in quantified objective behavioural terms, employing the antecedents, behaviour, consequences protocol. Data is then used to design behavioural and/or CB intervention. The efficacy of FBA is supported by a number of studies (e.g. Kamps, Wendland, and Culpepper 2006). A recent and welcome contribution in this area is the 'Keystone' skills approach (Ducharme and Shecter 2011), which recognizes the challenges classroom practitioners face in relation to FBA and offers instead a highly focused approach that involves the identification of a limited range of target areas for change, which are then the focus for cognitive and behavioural 'compliance' strategies (e.g. reinforcement).

There are also many 'universal' or 'whole-school' approaches to SEBD that draw on behavioural, cognitive behavioural, and humanistic principles and embed these in behaviour management and social–emotional learning systems. These approaches harness the self-regulatory powers of the social system of the school through the fostering of explicit measures designed to promote cooperation, prosocial behaviour and emotional security. School wide positive behaviour support is an example of this, drawing on FBA principles and applying these to whole-school communities. It has been found to produce significant enduring improvements in behaviour and academic performance (Lassen, Steele, and Sailor 2006).

Finally, it is important to refer to other systemic issues. There is a need for schools and other agencies to draw on the wide range of evidence-based strategies available, and to emphasize the central role of school-based teacher competencies (see above) and systems of parent support (Dishion 2011). Crucial here are the relationships between SEBD and other difficulties, especially communication, literacy, and numeracy problems. There is powerful evidence that effective intervention for speech and language problems (Law 2011), literacy (Wills et al. 2010) and maths (Temple-Harvey and Vannest 2011) often have positive knock-on effects for SEBD. This emphasizes the key message of this chapter – that we often have to look beyond the SEBD to find the solution.

Conclusion

The burgeoning literature on SEBD presents a clear consensus that the promotion of well-being, in the widest sense of the term, is a multifactorial issue, involving social, economic, psychological, and physiological factors. This demands a multi-disciplinary and multi-professional effort which follows from a biopsychosocial approach.

Contact address: cooper@ied.edu.hk

References

Allen, G. (1997) 'The social and economic origins of genetic determinism: a case history of the American Eugenics Movement, 1900–1940 and its lessons for today', *Genetica*, 99: 77–88.

Altepeter, T., and Korger, J. (1999) 'Disruptive behaviour: oppositional defiance and conduct disorder', in S. Netherton, D. Holmes, and E. Walker (eds.) *Child and adolescent psychological disorders*, New York: Oxford University Press (pp. 118–138).

APA (2007) *Diagnostic and statistical manual IV-TR*, Washington: APA.

Baer, D., Wolf, M., and Risley, T. (1968) 'Some current dimensions of applied behavioural analysis', *Journal of Applied Behavioural Analysis*, 1: 91–97.

Barriga, A. Q., Landau, J. R., Stinson, B. L., Liau, A. K., and Gibbs, J. C. (2000) 'Cognitive distortion and problem behaviors in adolescents', *Criminal Justice and Behavior*, 27: 36–56.

Barrish, H. H., Saunders, M., and Wolf, M. (1969) 'Good behavior game: effects of individual contingencies for group consequences on disruptive behavior in a classroom', *Journal of Applied Behavior Analysis*, 2: 119–124.

Battistich, V., Solomon, D., Watson, M., Solomon, J., and Schaps, E. (1989) 'Effects of an elementary school program to enhance prosocial behavior on children's cognitive–social problem-solving skills and strategies', *Journal of Applied Developmental Psychology*, 10: 147–169.

Benn, R. T., Akiva, T., and Arel, S. (2012) 'Mindfulness training effects for parents and educators of children with special needs', *Developmental Psychology*, 48: 1476–1487.

Bronfenbrenner, U. (1979) *The ecology of human development*, Cambridge, MA: Harvard University Press.

Buyse, E., Verschueren, K., Doumen, S., Van Damme, J., and Maes, F. (2008) 'Classroom problem behavior and teacher–child relationships in kindergarten: the moderating role of classroom climate', *Journal of School Psychology*, 46: 367–91.

Cooper, P. (2006) *Promoting positive pupil engagement: educating pupils with social, emotional and behavioural difficulties*, Luqa, Malta: Agenda.

Cooper, P., Bilton, K., and Kakos, M. (2013) 'A biopsychosocial approach to SEBD', in H. Daniels, J. Visser, and T. Cole (eds.) *The Routledge international handbook of emotional and behavioural difficulties*, London: Routledge (pp. 89 95).

Cooper, P., Drummond, M. J., Hart, S., Lovey, J., and McLaughlin, C. (2000) *Positive alternatives to exclusion from school*, London: Routledge.

Cooper, P., and Jacobs, B. (2011) *From inclusion to engagement*, Chichester: Wiley.

Cooper, P., Smith, C., and Upton, G. (1994) *Emotional and behavioural difficulties: theory to practice*, London: Routledge.

Cooper, P., and Whitebread, D. (2007) 'The effectiveness of nurture groups on student progress: evidence from a national research study', *Emotional and Behavioural Difficulties*, 12: 171–90.

Costello, E., Mustillo, S., Erkanli, A., Keeler, G., and Angold, A. (2003) 'Prevalence and development of psychiatric disorders in childhood and adolescence', *Archives of General Psychiatry*, 60: 837–844.

De Castro, B., Bosch, J., Veerman, J., and Koops, W. (2003) 'The effects of emotion regulation, attribution and delay prompts on aggressive boys' social problem solving', *Cognitive Therapy and Research*, 27: 153–166.

Department for Children, Schools and Families (2008) *The education of children and young people with behavioural, emotional and social difficulties as a Special Educational Need*, London: DCSF.

Dishion, T. (2011) 'Promoting academic competence and behavioural health in public schools: a strategy of systemic concatenation of empirically based intervention principles', *School Psychology Review*, 40: 590–597.

Ducharme, J. M., and Shecter, C. (2011) 'Bridging the gap between clinical and classroom intervention: keystone approaches for students with challenging behavior', *School Psychology Review*, 40: 257–274.

Embry, D. D., and Biglan, A. (2008) 'Evidence-based kernels: fundamental units of behavioral influence', *Clinical Child and Family Psychology Review*, 11: 75–113.

Engel, G. (1977) 'The need for a new medical model: a challenge for biomedicine', *Science*, 196: 129–136.

Engel, G. (1980) 'The clinical application of the biopsychosocial model', *American Journal of Psychiatry*, 137: 535–544.

Feindler, E. L., Marriott, S. A., and Iwata, M. (1984) 'Group anger control training for junior high school delinquents', *Cognitive Therapy and Research*, 8: 299–311.

Fonagy, P., and Kurtz, A. (2002) 'Disturbance of conduct', in P. Fonagy, M. Target, D. Cottrell, J. Phillips, and Z. Kurtz (eds.) *What works for whom?*, New York: Guilford (pp. 106–114).

Fonagy, P., Target, M., Cottrell, D., Phillips, J., and Kurtz, Z. (2002) *What works for whom? A critical review of treatments for children and adolescents*, New York: Guilford.

Forness, S. R., Kim, J., and Walker, H. M. (2012) 'Prevalence of students with EBD: impact on general education', *Beyond Behaviour*, 21: 3–10.

Frith, U. (1992) 'Cognitive development and cognitive deficit', *The Psychologist*, 5: 13–19.

Geake, J. G. (2009) *The brain at school: educational neuroscience in the classroom*, London: McGraw-Hill.

Goldstein, S., and Braswell, L. (1994) *Understanding and managing children's classroom behavior*, New York: Wiley.

Goodman, R., Ford, T., Simmons, H., Gatward, R., and Meltzer, H. (2003) 'Using the Strengths and Difficulties Questionnaire (SDQ) to screen for child psychiatric disorders in a community sample', *International Review of Psychiatry*, 15: 166–172.

Harris, J., Cook, M., and Upton, G. (1996) *Pupils with severe learning disabilities who present challenging behavior*, Kidderminster: BILD.

Henggeler, S. W., Cunningham, P. B., Pickrel, S. G., Schoenwald, S. K., and Brondino, M. J. (1996) 'Multisystemic therapy: an effective violence prevention approach for serious juvenile offenders', *Journal of Adolescence*, 19: 47–61.

Henggeler, S., Melton, G., Brondino, M., Scherer, D., and Hankey, J. (1997) 'Multi-systemic therapy with violent and chronic juvenile offenders: the role of treatment fidelity in successful dissemination', *Consulting and Clinical Psychology*, 65: 821–833.

HM Government (1981) Education Act, London: HMSO [online]. Available at www.legislation.gov.uk/ukpga

Herrnstein, R., and Murray, C. (1996) *The bell curve*, New York: FPP.

Kamps, D., Wendland, M., and Culpepper, M. (2006) 'Active teacher participation in functional behavior assessment for students with emotional and behavioral disorders risks in general education classrooms', *Behavioral Disorders*, 31: 128–146.

Kazdin, A. (2002) 'Psychosocial treatments for conduct disorder', in P. Nathan and J. Gorham (eds.) *A guide to treatments that work*, 2nd edn, Oxford: Oxford University Press (pp. 57–86).

Kearney, C., and Wadiak, D. (1999) 'Anxiety disorders', in S. Netherton, D. Holmes, and E. Walker (eds.) *Child and adolescent psychological disorders*, Oxford: Oxford University Press (pp. 282–303).

Lassen, S., Steele, M., and Sailor, W. (2006) 'The relationship of school wide positive behavior support to academic achievement in an urban middle school', *Psychology in the Schools*, 43: 701–712.

Law, J. (2011) 'Communication interventions and their impact on behaviour in the young child: a systematic review', *Child Language Teaching and Therapy*, 28: 7–23.

Layard, R., and Dunn, J. (2009) *A good childhood*, London: Penguin.

Macdonald, R. (ed.) (1997) *Youth, the underclass, and social exclusion*, London: Routledge.

Moreno, J. (1934/1956) *Sociometry and the science of man*, New York: Beacon House.

Mosley, J. (1993) *Turn your school round*, Wisbech: LDA.

Nathan, P., and Gorham, J. (2002) *A guide to treatments that work*, 2nd edn, Oxford: Oxford University Press.

Patterson, G., Reid, J., and Dishion, T. (1992) *Anti-social boys, Volume 4*, Eugene, OR: Caselralia.

Plomin, R. (1990) *Nature and nurture: an introduction to human behavioral genetics*, Belmont: Thomson Brooks/Cole.

Purdie, N., Hattie, J., and Carroll, T. (2002) 'A review of the research on interventions for attention deficit hyperactivity disorder: what works best?', *Review of Educational Research*, 72: 61–99.

Rose, S. (1995) 'The rise of neurogenetic determinism', *Nature*, 373: 380–382.

Rutter, M., and Smith, D (eds.) (1995) *Psychosocial disorders in young people*, Chichester: Wiley.

Schoenfeld, N. A., and Janney, D. M. (2008) 'Identification and treatment of anxiety in students with emotional or behavioral disorders: a review of the literature', *Education and Treatment of Children*, 31: 583–610.

Shapiro, E., and Cole, C. (1999) 'Self-monitoring in assessing children's problems', *Psychological Assessment*, 11: 448–457.

Temple-Harvey, K., and Vannest, K. (2011) 'Participation and performance of students with emotional disturbance on a statewide accountability assessment in math', *Remedial and Special Education*, 33: 226–236.

Tingstrom, D., Sterling-Turner, H., and Wilczynski, S. (2006) 'The good behaviour game: 1969–2002', *Behavior Modification*, 30: 225–253.

Walker, H., Colvin, G., and Ramsey, E. (1994) *Antisocial behavior in schools: strategies and best practices*, Pacific Grove, CA: Brooks/Cole.

Wills, H., Kamps, D., Abbott, M., Bannister, H., and Kaufman, J. (2010) 'Classroom observations and effects of reading interventions for students at risk for emotional and behavioral disorders', *Behavioral Disorders*, 35: 103–119.

World Health Organization (1991) *Classification of diseases*, Geneva: WHO.

28

ATTENTION DEFICIT HYPERACTIVITY DISORDER

Characteristics, identification and treatment

Robert Reid and Brenton Prosser

UNIVERSITY OF NEBRASKA-LINCOLN, USA; UNIVERSITY OF CANBERRA, AUSTRALIA

Attention deficit hyperactivity disorder (ADHD) is the most commonly diagnosed psychological disorder of childhood (Barkley 2006). Worldwide, prevalence of ADHD is estimated at 5 percent among school-age children (Polanczyk et al. 2007). The *Diagnostic and Statistical Manual of Mental Disorders* (DSM; American Psychiatric Association (APA) 2000) defines ADHD as a biological dysfunction that results in hyperactive, inattentive, and impulsive behaviour to such an extent that it causes social, educational, or work performance problems. It is a chronic, lifelong disorder and while some symptoms may abate over time, the core problems remain. For children this may result in lower academic achievement and difficulty in social settings. If untreated into adulthood, ADHD can increase the incidence of risk-taking behaviour, dangerous driving, substance misuse, depression, and criminality (Barkley 2006). Given this impact of the disorder, the purpose of this chapter is to provide an overview, particularly in relation to its diagnosis, characteristics, possible causes, and treatment. The chapter also considers explanatory theories and the influence of psychosocial factors.

ADHD diagnostic criteria

The DSM guides the diagnostic criteria for ADHD in North America and Australasia; however, a growing number of other western nations are also adopting these criteria (Bailey 2010). ADHD is characterized by problems with inattention, impulsivity, and hyperactivity (APA 2000). Currently within the DSM-IV (APA 2000), there are three types of ADHD:

- ADHD predominantly inattentive (ADHD-IA)
- ADHD predominantly hyperactive–impulsive (ADHD-HI)
- ADHD combined type (ADHD-C).

Note however, that a fourth type, ADHD inattentive (restrictive; ADHD-IAR), has been proposed for the new DSM-V due out in 2013.

There are nine symptoms of inattention (e.g. difficulty sustaining attention, difficulty following instructions, problems organizing tasks, easily distracted), and 14 symptoms of hyperactivity/

impulsivity (e.g. often fidgets, leaves seat in the classroom, blurts out answers, interrupts or intrudes on others). For children and youth, a diagnosis of ADHD-IA can be made if at least six of the inattention symptoms are present; and diagnosis of ADHD-HI can be made if at least six of the hyperactivity/impulsivity symptoms are present. A diagnosis of ADHD-C requires that a child meets the requirements for both ADHD-IA and ADHD-HI. In the new DSM-V, a diagnosis of ADHD-IAR can be made if the criteria for ADHD-IA are met and no more than two of the symptoms for ADHD-HI are present.

Along with these symptoms, there are other criteria that must be met, as follows.

- Symptoms must have occurred over a span of 'at least six months'.
- Symptoms must occur to an extent that is 'developmentally inconsistent with' age.
- Symptoms must have developed 'before 12 years of age'.
- Impaired functioning should be present in 'two or more settings', and not just in either the home or school context.
- Clear evidence of 'significant impairment' to social, academic, or occupational functioning must be present.

There are exclusionary factors that rule out an ADHD diagnosis (e.g. schizophrenia), and because other disorders (e.g. posttraumatic stress, depression) can result in symptoms of inattention, impulsivity, and/or hyperactivity, symptoms should not be better explained by another problem (e.g. depression).

Characteristics of children with ADHD

Children with ADHD are extremely heterogeneous. Still, there are some broad characteristics associated with ADHD in western nations.

- There is a pronounced gender disparity (Barkley 2006). In research samples, the male to female ratio is around 3 to 1. In community samples it is typically much higher, at around 7 to 1. Why this occurs is a matter of some debate. It may be that social expectations encourage more boys to externalize (i.e. act out) than girls, or there may be a genetic link between ADHD and gender.
- On average, children with ADHD score around one-half standard deviation lower than a non-ADHD group on IQ tests (Frazier, Demaree, and Youngstrom 2004). However, it is possible that this results from a referral bias, as students with lower intelligence may be more likely to be diagnosed or labelled with ADHD.
- Children with ADHD are at high risk of academic failure. The achievement of children with ADHD is significantly lower than that of their peers in reading, maths, and spelling (Frazier et al. 2007). This may include failing courses, grade retention, dropping out of school, or referral for special education services (Barkley 2006).
- Students with ADHD often have deficits in working memory and executive functions (Martinussen et al. 2005). This is significant because both working memory and executive functions are highly correlated with academic outcomes (Alloway, Gathercole, and Elliott 2010; Meltzer and Krishnan, 2007).

Comorbid disorders

ADHD may occur in conjunction with one or more additional disorders: this is termed 'comorbidity'. Comorbid disorders are common with ADHD. Wilens et al. (2002) found that

80 percent of the school-age children referred to a specialized psychiatric clinic in the USA had at least one comorbid disorder. Disorders that are comorbid with ADHD include the following.

- *Oppositional defiant disorder (ODD):* this is by far the most common comorbid disorder (Angold, Costello, and Erkanli 1999). ODD is characterized by defiant, hostile and disobedient behaviour toward authority figures. The behaviours associated with ODD are often aggressive in nature (e.g. losing one's temper, arguing with adults, actively refusing to comply with directions of adults, deliberately doing things that will annoy people). Between 45 percent and 85 percent of children with ADHD will meet the criteria for ODD (Wilens et al. 2002).
- *Conduct disorder (CD):* this consists of behaviours that violate the basic rights of others or age-appropriate societal norms. These may include: (a) aggressive conduct that causes or threatens physical harm to people or animals; (b) behaviours that result in property loss or damage; (c) deceit or theft; and (d) serious violations of rules. Estimates of comorbidity of CD and ADHD range from 15 to 56 percent of children and 44 to 50 percent of adolescents (e.g. Wilens et al. 2002).
- *Depressive disorder:* A child with ADHD is five times more likely to have a depressive disorder than a child without ADHD (Angold et al. 1999). Psychosocial risk factors may contribute to this. Boys who displayed social problems were more likely to have symptoms of depression, as were boys from family environments characterized by frequent conflict (Drabick, Gadow, and Sprafkin 2006).
- *Anxiety-related disorders:* these are common among children with ADHD. The presence of ADHD made it three times more likely that a child would also have an anxiety disorder (Angold et al. 1999). An estimated 25–35 percent of children with ADHD experience anxiety disorders (Tannock 2000).
- *Social, emotional and behavioural difficulties (SEBD):* these are very likely to occur among children with ADHD (see Cooper, Chapter 27, this volume). In the USA, around 60 percent of students diagnosed as having SEBD also have ADHD (Schnoes et al. 2006).

What causes ADHD?

Despite many popular claims and media reports, scientific research into ADHD has not found, replicated, and established a definitive cause for the symptoms; it has, however, provided many fascinating possibilities. Possible causal factors include the neurological and genetic, among others.

Neurological factors

Research suggests that ADHD is related, to some degree, to structural and/or functional differences in the brain. Executive function deficits (e.g. problems with planning, maintaining effort, or monitoring behaviour), which are associated with the frontal–striatal–cerebellar region of the brain, are commonly associated with ADHD symptoms. These include an inability to control behavioural responses, difficulties with working memory and verbal fluency, and difficulties with planning (Barkley 2006). Recent studies suggest that cortical development may be delayed in children with ADHD by several years (Shaw et al. 2007). This study found that the delay was most prominent in prefrontal regions important for control of cognitive processes including attention and motor planning. However, in this research there were no abnormalities in the cortex's structure.

Other research has focused on transmission fibres in the posterior region of the brain. This research found that children with ADHD had fewer transmission fibres, which resulted in less activation in the frontal region of the brain. The posterior region of the brain is responsible for accessing information from previous situations, while the frontal brain applies that knowledge to the situation at hand. Hence, it is possible that fewer transmission fibres may be linked with ADHD (Semrud-Clikeman and Pliszka 2005), especially given the difficulties children with ADHD have in these areas.

Genetic factors

Multiple lines of research provide evidence of a genetic basis for ADHD. Identical twins are commonly used in genetic studies because they share an identical genetic make-up. Numerous studies have demonstrated that if one identical twin has ADHD it is highly likely the other does also; heritability is estimated to around 80 percent (Barkley 2006). This is strong inferential evidence of a genetic basis for ADHD. Familial studies also support a genetic component. If a child has ADHD, between 10 percent and 35 percent of the immediate family is also likely to have the disorder, with the risk to siblings of these children being approximately 30 percent (Levy and Hay 2001). If a parent has ADHD, the likelihood of their children having ADHD is over 50 percent (Biederman et al. 1995). However, it is important to note that while there is sufficient evidence to 'infer' a genetic foundation for ADHD, it is not yet possible to state definitively that ADHD has a genetic cause. It is also critical to interpret 'genetic basis' (Barkley 2006) correctly. ADHD is not analogous to inheriting blue eyes or black hair. It is better understood that an individual can inherit a 'predisposition' to ADHD behaviours, but that other factors influence its development and potential severity.

Other possible causes

A number of other possible environmental causes have been proposed for ADHD. These include the consumption of environmental toxins, prenatal cigarette and alcohol exposure, and maternal smoking during pregnancy (Banerjee, Middleton, and Faraone 2007). Exposure to environmental toxins can result in problems that are similar to ADHD. Lead poisoning can result in distractibility, hyperactivity, restlessness, and lower intellectual functioning (Needleman 1982). Manganese exposure can also result in behavioural characteristics similar to those found in ADHD (Collipp, Chen, and Maitinsky 1983). However, few students diagnosed with ADHD have been shown to be affected by any type of lead contamination (Barkley 2006). It is questionable whether exposure to toxins could account for a significant percentage of ADHD cases. High levels of foetal exposure to alcohol may lead to cognitive impairment of intelligence, learning and memory, language, attention, reaction time, and executive functioning (Huizink and Mulder 2006). Maternal tobacco use during pregnancy can adversely affect cognitive development and behaviour in children and adolescents (Wasserman et al. 1999). However, as with environmental toxins, it is not certain how many cases of ADHD are the result of prenatal cigarette and alcohol exposure.

Explanatory theories of ADHD

At present, there is no generally accepted explanatory theory of ADHD. This is largely due to the failure to establish a definitive cause for the symptoms. However, there are a number of proposed theories to explain the behaviours that are characteristic of ADHD.

- *Behavioural inhibition system (BIS):* this theory posits that our brains have a behavioural inhibition system (BIS) and a behavioural activation system (BAS). The Quay-Gray model theorizes that the BIS is activated by signals of punishment or frustrated non-reward, and the BAS is activated by signals of reward or avoidance and escape. Quay suggested that the impulsivity commonly associated with ADHD resulted from diminished function in the brain's BIS and that those with ADHD did not respond appropriately to signals that they should inhibit a behaviour (Quay 1988).
- *Race model:* this posits that environmental stimuli provide signals for both activation and inhibitory responses in the brain. Signals for activating a response towards the stimuli are in a 'race to the brain' with signals for inhibiting a response towards the stimuli. Whichever signal arrives first is the winner. Children with ADHD have a slower inhibition response and slower ability to adjust their responses when required to do so by circumstances (Schachar, Tannock, and Logan 1993).
- *Delay aversion:* this theory posits that children with ADHD act more quickly than their non-ADHD peers to terminate delays and achieve gratification (Sonuga-Barke 2002). ADHD impulsivity stems from an aversion to delay or waiting.
- *Reward dysfunction:* this suggests that ADHD is a deficit in responding to behavioural consequences and those with ADHD have a 'reward dysfunction' problem in regulating their behaviour (Haenlein and Caul 1987).
- *Optimal stimulation:* this suggests that ADHD is due to difficulty maintaining sufficient arousal. Low-stimulation tasks and settings cause children with ADHD to engage in sensation-seeking behaviour. This behaviour can result in hyperactivity, difficulty in waiting/delaying a response, and a preference for novel situations that result in a failure to attend to tasks at hand (Zentall 2006).

Barkley's theory of ADHD

In terms of impact and practical application within educational psychology, probably the most influential theory has been that of Russell Barkley (2006). In Barkley's theory, difficulty with self-regulation is seen as the primary cause of ADHD. Children with ADHD may be unable to stop their impulsive response to a situation. Their initial reaction comes so quickly that it overwhelms executive functions that would normally help to inhibit behaviour. Children with ADHD fail to monitor situations, assess whether an action is appropriate to the situation, or to plan and consider the consequences of their actions. Hence, ADHD is not the result of a lack of skills or knowledge and neither is it a problem with knowing what to do; it is a problem of doing what one knows (Barkley 2006). Barkley's theory focuses on four processes that are critical to self-regulation of behaviour.

1. *Nonverbal working memory:* this includes self-awareness, sense of time, retrospective function (hindsight) and prospective function (foresight).
2. *Internalization of speech:* this includes self-questioning and problem solving.
3. *Self-regulation of affect/motivation/arousal:* this includes objectivity.
4. *Reconstitution:* this include analysis of behaviour, and planning.

The multi-modal treatment model

ADHD affects academic, behavioural, emotional, and social functioning. Thus, an 'optimal' treatment plan should address all these areas. The multi-modal treatment model (Pfiffner, Barkley, and DuPaul 2006) is accepted in Western countries as a sound foundation for school-based ADHD treatment. The model addresses four areas: medication, behaviour management, instructional accommodations, and ancillary supports (for both child and parent). While each of these areas can be used individually for interventions, approaches that combine all of them are more effective and are more acceptable to both parents and schools (Swanson et al. 2001).

Medication

Psycho-stimulants are the most commonly prescribed medications for children with ADHD (note: antidepressants and anti-hypertensives are less commonly used; for a more comprehensive discussion of medication, see Dulcan 2007). Psycho-stimulants affect the central nervous system and create increased arousal. They are extremely well studied and their effectiveness is well documented (Barkley 2006). Additionally the effects appear rapidly, typically in around 30 minutes. The duration of effects varies greatly among stimulants. The effects of some stimulants such as Ritalin SR® or Adderall® last around four to five hours. With these stimulants multiple doses (i.e. a morning and afternoon dose) may be needed. In contrast, effects of time-release formulations can last eight hours or longer, which would effectively cover the entire school day. Examples of time-release stimulants are Metadate ER®, Focalin XR®, Ritalin LA®, and Concerta®. Around 80 percent of children will respond positively to psycho-stimulants. For these students, medication can have a pronounced effect on their ability to function in the school environment.

If a student responds positively to medication, an educator can expect to see the following (Barkley 2006; DuPaul and Stoner 2003).

- *Significant reductions in ADHD symptoms:* students should be able to better maintain effort and focus on school-related tasks, especially those that are difficult or tedious. The frequency of impulsive behaviours (e.g. calling out) and disruptive physical behaviours associated with hyperactivity (e.g. fidgeting with objects) should also be greatly diminished. Increased compliance with requests and decreases in aggressive behaviours may be evident.
- *Improved academic functioning:* students often show improved cognitive functioning (e.g. better short-term recall, improved retrieval of verbal information). The amount of work completed and overall accuracy often improves. However, it is important to note that there is no evidence of long-term improvement in learning as measured by standardized tests.
- *Improved social functioning:* the frequency of negative social interactions between the student and teacher may decrease. This is likely because of increased compliance. Reductions in impulsive behaviours may help students be more accepted by their peers.

However, there are also distinct limitations to medication, as follows.

1. *Medication is not a cure for ADHD:* children will still have problems with ADHD-related behaviours. Only the intensity or frequency of problems will be reduced.
2. *Students will still need accommodations, behaviour management, and other interventions:* medication alone is seldom sufficient for ADHD treatment. Moreover, the effects of medication are enhanced when combined with other interventions such as behaviour management (DuPaul and Stoner 2003).
3. *The effects of medication are temporary:* when the effects of medication wear off, ADHD-related problems return.

4. *Medication is not a long-term solution for most children:* around 50 percent of children discontinue medication after one to two years (Bussing et al. 2005). Additionally, there is evidence that the effectiveness of medication may decrease markedly after two to three years for some students (Gilchrist and Arnold 2005).

Medication treatment of ADHD has increased dramatically in western nations since 1980; however, there are marked disparities across nations. Until a decade ago, trends within North America, Australia, and New Zealand were much higher than others internationally (Berbatis, Sunderland, and Bulsara 2002). The higher rate of diagnosis and treatment with medication had been attributed to these nations using the DSM diagnostic criteria, while other nations, such as the UK, had used the World Health Organisation's ICD-10 diagnostic criteria (Prosser 2006). However, regional location and socio-economic status have also been identified as psychosocial risk factors in ADHD diagnosis (Counts et al. 2005; Prosser and Reid 2009). What these international and national variations emphasize is the importance of consideration of social factors in the acceptance and efficacy of medical treatment.

Behaviour management

The evidence is clear that behaviour management techniques (systematic reinforcement, response cost, time out) can significantly reduce problem behaviours (e.g. disruptions, noncompliance) and increase appropriate behaviours (e.g. time on-task, assignment completion; Pelham and Fabiano 2008). Note that children with ADHD 'are less sensitive' to reinforcement than their peers (Barkley 2006). These students often will require additional and more powerful reinforcement over and above what is provided through normal classroom management to reinforce the alteration of behaviour sufficiently. Teachers can systematically alter the physical and instructional environment in their classrooms to adapt to the needs of students with ADHD. Prosser (2006) and Reid and Johnson (2011) provide practical instructional adaptations for use by teachers.

Academic support

Academic interventions for children with ADHD are not well researched and as yet there are no validated instructional approaches for children with ADHD (Trout et al. 2007). Recommended instructional accommodations (Prosser 2006; Reid and Johnson 2011) include the following.

*   *Embed curriculum in personally relevant context:* compliance, attention span, and academic productivity are much better when students perform activities they perceive as relevant or meaningful.
*   *Use computer-assisted instruction (CAI):* CAI can provide a highly reinforcing environment with frequent feedback that engages students with ADHD.
*   *Avoid lengthy instructional activities:* break up long activities into smaller chunks and intersperse opportunities to respond actively.
*   *Scaffold instruction to support working memory:* provide prompts and cues to reduce the load on working memory.
*   *Teach students specific strategies to perform task:* strategies provide students with an organizational structure to help them attack a task.
*   *Teach self-regulation strategies:* self-regulation strategies are highly effective for many students with ADHD, and can improve academic productivity and increase time on-task (Reid, Trout, and Schartz 2005).

Other support

Optimal treatment also requires providing support for comorbid and other problems associated with ADHD (Reid and Johnson 2011). This might include counselling for the child to help deal with associated psychological problems (e.g. depression, peer rejection) or social skills training to help the child function more appropriately in the social milieu. Parent training, which includes educating parents about ADHD and instruction in basic behaviour management techniques, is often recommended. Involving parents in a treatment plan that is coordinated across the school and home is also highly recommended.

Psychosocial influences on effective treatment of ADHD

An important aspect of psychosocial approaches is the recognition that ADHD is also a social label. Elsewhere in this book, Cooper (Chapter 27) discusses the purposes, benefits and challenges of labelling for special educators and school psychologists (see also Boyle, Chapter 21, this volume). However, one specific point is worthy of note in our consideration: namely, that ADHD is not just another objective diagnostic category. What is important for special educators and school psychologists to note here is that families, teachers, and significant others may respond in certain (even opinionated) ways to the ADHD label with little real knowledge of it, and that this can potentially create barriers to the success of interventions or learning supports. Further, ADHD and its medical treatment are the subjects of intense media interest. Unlike most diagnostic categories, students also hear about ADHD in popular songs and see characterizations of it on television. Young people are acutely aware of popular culture and this awareness can shape how they behave, see themselves and respond to strategies for intervention.

However, as Cooper (Chapter 27, this volume) points out, the responses of students to labels are anything but uniform. Past research with adolescents labelled 'ADHD' (Prosser 2006) has found that some see the label as stigmatizing, some irrelevant, others redefined it as empowering, while still others refined their use of the label to 'mild ADHD'. Hence, it is important to consider the impact of environmental and socio-cultural influences, as well as the interaction of students with the ADHD label, in and around school contexts (Prosser 2008). In doing so, such considerations align with Cooper's (Chapter 27, this volume) recommendation that the application of labels must always occur with the benefit of the individual recipient as the foremost concern. Hence, a psychosocial perspective focuses on ADHD in relation to the best functioning of individuals, classrooms and schools.

The environmental and instructional support described above is associated with a functional approach (Reid et al. 1998). This approach responds to the challenges emerging from a gap between student capacity and environmental expectations. It tends to focus on the individual; however, functional approaches can equally focus on the roles of teacher and school. In short, educational psychologists seeking the most effective treatment for ADHD might need to look beyond just developing activities and accommodations for the individual student.

For instance, there has been a growing interest in the role of pedagogy in the identification and treatment of ADHD (Cooper 2005). For many years, traditional pedagogy has been the convention within mainstream education. 'Traditional pedagogy' involves teaching practices that rely heavily on the role of the active teacher as source of knowledge, which is transmitted to the passive student. However, this approach can result in a significant gap between teacher expectations and the capacities of (particularly hyperactive) students. The current DSM-IV diagnostic criteria for ADHD can be read as deficits in the student, but can just as easily be read as the result of deficits within traditional pedagogy (Prosser 2008). It is perhaps not surprising, then, that research identifies the classroom as the major site where the identification of ADHD occurs and that the use of alternative pedagogy can be a factor in the success of students diagnosed with ADHD (Prosser 2010). The best interventions for ADHD may not just ask how the student needs to change, but also how the teaching of their teachers needs to adapt.

Meanwhile, a psychosocial approach would point to a growing mismatch between the existing processes of schooling and the needs of today's students (Carrington 2006). Studies in Western nations show that school retention, motivation, and engagement are at record low levels (Martin, Chapter 11, this volume; McInerney 2009). Some have argued that there is a greater generational gap between the practices of schools and the needs of students than ever before, and that schools are facing an increasing crisis of relevance. In recent years, the response of Australian, American, and British has not been to reassess school policy and process, but instead to increase their focus on the management of the behaviour of individuals (Adams 2008; Slee 2006). This has significantly contributed to a growing attention to behavioural disorders in schools. In this view, interventions for ADHD must not stop at the individual, but must extend to interventions that make schools more relevant to, and inclusive of, students.

Concluding remarks

Over the past two decades, ADHD has become an ever more pressing challenge for teachers, counsellors, and educational psychologists. As professionals dedicated to the development and education of all students in our care, we are called to respond appropriately to the needs of children with ADHD. What diagnostic, multi-modal, and psychosocial perspectives on ADHD show is that the successful identification and treatment of ADHD requires a constant sensitivity to both the broad range of environmental factors and the uniqueness of every child.

References

Adams, P. (2008) 'Positioning behaviour: attention deficit/hyperactivity disorder (ADHD) in the post-welfare education era', *International Journal of Inclusive Education*, 12: 113–125.

Alloway, T. P., Gathercole, S. E., and Elliott, J. (2010) 'Examining the link between working memory behaviour and academic attainment in children with ADHD', *Developmental Medicine and Child Neurology*, 5: 632–636.

American Psychiatric Association (2000) *Diagnostic and statistical manual of mental disorders*, 4th edn, text rev., Washington, DC: American Psychiatric Association.

Angold, A., Costello, E. J., and Erkanli, A. (1999) 'Comorbidity', *Journal of Child Psychology and Psychiatry*, 44: 69–76.

Bailey, S. (2010) 'The DSM and the dangerous school child', *International Journal of Inclusive Education*, 14: 581–592.

Banerjee, T. D., Middleton, F., and Faraone, S. V. (2007) 'Environmental risk factors for attention-deficit hyperactivity disorder', *Acta Paediatrica*, 96: 1269–1274.

Barkley, R. A. (2006) *Attention-deficit hyperactivity disorder: a handbook for diagnosis and treatment*, 3rd edn, New York, NY: Guilford Press.

Berbatis, C. G., Sunderland, V. B., and Bulsara, M. (2002) 'Licit psychostimulant consumption in Australia, 1984–2000: international and juristictional comparisons', *Medical Journal of Australia*, 177: 539–543.

Biederman, J., Faraone, S. V., Mick, E., Spencer T., Wilens, T., Kiely, K., Guite, J., Ablon, J. S., Reed, E., and Warburton, R. (1995) 'High risk for attention deficit hyperactivity disorder among children of parents with childhood onset of the disorder: a pilot study', *American Journal of Psychiatry*, 152: 431–435.

Bussing, R., Zima, B. T., Mason, D., Hou, W., Garvan, C. W., and Forness, S. (2005) 'Use and persistence of pharmacotherapy for elementary school students with attention-deficit/hyperactivity disorder', *Journal of Child and Adolescent Psychopharmacology*, 15: 78–87.

Carrington, V. (2006) *Rethinking the middle years: early adolescents, schooling and digital culture*, Crows Nest, Australia: Allen and Unwin.

Collipp, P. J., Chen, S. Y., and Maitinsky, S. (1983) 'Manganese in infant formulas and learning disability', *Annals of Nutrition and Metabolism*, 27: 488–494.

Cooper, P. (2005) 'AD/HD', in A. Lewis and B. Norwich (eds.) *Special teaching for special children*, London, UK: Open University Press (pp. 123–137).

Counts, C., Nigg, G., Stawicki, J., Rappley, M., and von Eye, A. (2005) 'Family adversity in DSM-IV ADHD combined and inattentive subtypes and associated disruptive behavior problems', *Journal of the American Academy of Child Adolescent Psychiatry*, 44: 690–698.

Drabick, D. A. G., Gadow, K. D., and Sprafkin, J. (2006) 'Co-occurrence of conduct disorder and depression in a clinic-based sample of boys with ADHD', *Journal of Child Psychology and Psychiatry*, 47: 766–774.

Dulcan, M. K. (ed.) (2007) *Helping parents, youth, and teachers understand medications for behavioral and emotional problems: a resource book of medication information handouts*, 3rd edn, Washington, DC: American Psychiatric Press.

DuPaul, G. J., and Stoner, G. (2003) *ADHD in the schools: assessment and intervention strategies*, New York, NY: Guilford Press.

Frazier, T. W., Demaree, H. A., and Youngstrom, E. A. (2004) 'Meta-analysis of intellectual and neuropsychological test performance in attention-deficit/hyperactivity disorder', *Neuropsychology*, 18: 543–555.

Frazier, T. W., Youngstrom, E. A., Glutting, J. J., and Watkins, M. W. (2007) 'ADHD and achievement: meta-analysis of the child, adolescent, and adult literatures and a concomitant study with college students', *Journal of Learning Disabilities*, 40: 49–65.

Gilchrist, R., and Arnold, E. (2005) 'Long term efficacy of ADHD pharmacotherapy in children', *Psychiatric Annals*, 38: 52–57.

Haenlein, M., and Caul, W. F. (1987) 'Attention deficit disorder with hyperactivity: a specific hypothesis of reward dysfunction', *Journal of the American Academy of Child and Adolescent Psychiatry*, 26: 356–362.

Huizink, A. C., and Mulder, E. J. (2006) 'Maternal smoking, drinking or cannabis use during pregnancy and neurobehavioral and cognitive functioning in human offspring', *Neuroscience and Behavioral Reviews*, 30: 24–41.

Levy, F., and Hay, D. A. (eds.) (2001) *Attention genes and ADHD*, Philadelphia, PA: Brunner-Routledge.

Martinussen, R., Hayden, J., Hogg-Johnson, S., and Tannock, R. (2005) 'A meta-analysis of working memory impairments in children with attention-deficit/hyperactivity disorder', *Journal of the American Academy of Child and Adolescent Psychiatry*, 44: 377–384.

McInerney, P. (2009) 'Toward a critical pedagogy of engagement for alienated youth: insights from Freire and school-based research', *Critical Studies in Education*, 50, 23–35.

Meltzer, L., and Krishnan, K. (2007) 'Executive function difficulties and learning disabilities: understandings and misunderstandings', in L. Meltzer (ed.) *Executive function in education: from theory to practice*, New York, NY: Guilford (pp. 77–132).

Needleman, H. L. (1982) 'Lead and impaired abilities', *Developing Medicine and Child Neurology*, 24: 196–198.

Pelham, W. E. Jr., and Fabiano, G. A. (2008) 'Evidence-based psychosocial treatment for ADHD: an update', *Journal of Clinical Child and Adolescent Psychology*, 37: 184–214.

Pfiffner, L. J., Barkley, R. A., and DuPaul, G. J. (2006) 'Treatment of ADHD in school settings', in R. A. Barkley (ed.) *Attention deficit hyperactivity disorder: a handbook for diagnosis and treatment*, 3rd edn, New York, NY: Guilford Press (pp. 547–589).

Polanczyk, G., de Lima, M., Horta, B., Biederman, J., and Rohde, L. (2007) 'The worldwide prevalence of ADHD: a systematic review and metaregression analysis', *American Journal of Psychiatry*, 164: 942–948.

Prosser, B. (2006) *ADHD: who's failing who?*, Lane Cove, Australia: Finch Publishing.

Prosser, B. (2008) 'Beyond ADHD: a consideration of attention deficit hyperactivity disorder and pedagogy in Australian schools', *International Journal of Inclusive Education*, 12: 81–97.

Prosser, B. (2010) 'Engaging pedagogies: from psycho-medical deficits to "virtual schoolbags"', in L. Graham (ed.) *(De)Constructing ADHD: critical guidance for teachers and teacher educators*, New York, NY: Peter Lang Publishing (pp. 165–186).

Prosser, B., and Reid, R. (2009) 'Changes in use of ADHD medication in South Australia', *Australian and New Zealand Journal of Psychiatry*, 43: 340–347.

Quay, H. C. (1988) 'The behavioral reward and inhibition systems in childhood behavior disorder', in L. M. Bloomingdale (ed.) *Attention deficit disorder, Vol. 3, New research in treatment, psychopharmacology, and attention*, New York, NY: Pergamon Press (pp. 176–186).

Reid, R., and Johnson, J. (2011) *Teachers guide to ADHD*, New York, NY: Guilford Press.

Reid, R., Reason, R., Maag, J., Prosser, B., and Xu, C. (1998) 'ADHD: A perspective on perspectives', *Educational and Child Psychology*, 15: 56–67.

Reid, R., Trout, A. L., and Schartz, M. (2005) 'Self-regulation interventions for children with attention-deficit/hyperactivity disorder', *Exceptional Children*, 71: 361–377.

Schachar, R. J., Tannock, R., and Logan, G. (1993) 'Inhibitory control, impulsiveness, and attention deficit hyperactivity disorder', *Clinical Psychology Review*, 13: 721–739.

Schnoes, C., Reid, R., Wagner, M., and Marder, C. (2006) 'ADHD among students receiving special education services: a national survey', *Exceptional Children*, 72: 483–496.

Semrud-Clikeman, M., and Pliszka, S. R. (2005) 'Neuroimaging and psychopharmacology', *School Psychology Quarterly*, 20: 172–186.

Shaw, P., Eckstrand, K., Sharp, W., Blumenthal, J., Lerch, J. P., Greenstein, D., et al. (2007) 'Attention deficit/hyperactivity disorder is characterized by a delay in cortical maturation', *Proceedings of the National Academy of Sciences of the United States of America*, 104: 19649–19654.

Slee, R. (2006) 'Limits to and possibilities for educational reform', *International Journal of Inclusive Education*, 10: 109–119.

Sonuga-Barke, E. (2002) 'Psychological heterogeneity in AD/HD-A dual pathway model of behaviour and cognition', *Behavioural Brain Research*, 130: 29–36.

Swanson, J. M., Kraemer, H. C., Hinshaw, S. P., Arnold, L. E., Conners, C. K., and Abikoff, H. B. (2001) 'Clinical relevance of the primary findings of the MTA: success rates based on severity of ADHD and ODD symptoms at the end of treatment', *Journal of the American Academy of Child and Adolescent Psychiatry*, 40: 168–179.

Tannock, R. (2000) 'Attention-deficit/hyperactivity disorders with anxiety disorders', in T. E Brown (ed.) *Attention-deficit disorders and comorbidities in children, adolescents, and adults*, Washington, DC: American Psychiatric Press (pp. 125–170).

Trout, A., Lienemann, T., Reid, R., and Epstein, M. (2007) 'A review of non-medication interventions to improve academic performance of children and youth with ADHD', *Remedial and Special Education*, 28: 207–226.

Wasserman, R. C., Kelleher, K. J., Bocian, A., Baker, A., Childs, G. E., Indacochea, F., Stulp, C., and Gardner, W. P. (1999) 'Identification of attentional and hyperactivity problems in primary care: a report from pediatric research in office settings and the ambulatory sentinel practice network', *Pediatrics* [electronic version], 103: e38.

Wilens, T. E., Biederman, J., Brown, S., Tanguay, S., Monuteaux, M. C., Blake, C., and Spencer, T. J. (2002) 'Psychiatric comorbidity and functioning in clinically-referred preschool children and school-age youth with ADHD', *Journal of the American Academy of Child and Adolescent Psychiatry*, 41: 262–268.

Zentall, S. S. (2006) *ADHD and education*, Columbus, OH: Pearson.

29

DYSLEXIA

Brian Byrne, Stefan Samuelsson and Richard K. Olson

UNIVERSITY OF NEW ENGLAND, AUSTRALIA, AND LINKÖPING UNIVERSITY, SWEDEN;
LINKÖPING UNIVERSITY, SWEDEN; UNIVERSITY OF COLORADO, BOULDER, USA,
AND LINKÖPING UNIVERSITY, SWEDEN

'Dyslexia' refers to marked impairment in reading and spelling. In this chapter you will learn about definitions of this disorder, including popular conceptions, whether there are different types of dyslexia and whether it is different from 'poor reading', and about causes, assessment, and treatment.

There are two main forms, 'acquired dyslexia' and 'developmental dyslexia'. Acquired dyslexia is impairment that results from brain injury or disease, often in adulthood and after literacy skills have been in place. Developmental dyslexia is impairment that emerges during the course of learning to read and for which there appears to be no gross brain damage of the kind seen in the acquired form. Although some researchers have explored the similarities between the two forms (e.g. Coltheart 2005), in this chapter we focus on developmental dyslexia.

Definitions

The fifth edition of the *Diagnostic and Statistical Manual of Mental Disorders* (DSM-5, American Psychiatric Association (APA) 2013), was being planned at the time of writing (please note that at the time of publication of this chapter, the draft definition was no longer available, pending the publication of DSM-5 in May 2013 – see www.dsm5.org/Pages/Default.aspx). The following definition was being proposed:

> Difficulties in accuracy or fluency of reading that are not consistent with the person's chronological age, educational opportunities, or intellectual abilities. Multiple sources of information are to be used to assess reading, one of which must be an individually administered, culturally appropriate, and psychometrically sound standardized measure of reading and reading-related abilities.
>
> *(APA 2013)*

The National Institutes of Child Health and Human Development (NICHHD) and the International Dyslexia Association (IDA) both endorse the following definition:

> Dyslexia is a specific learning disability that is neurological in origin. It is characterized by difficulties with accurate and/or fluent word recognition and by poor spelling and decoding abilities. These difficulties typically result from a deficit in the phonological

component of language that is often unexpected in relation to other cognitive abilities and the provision of effective classroom instruction. Secondary consequences may include problems in reading comprehension and reduced reading experience that can impede growth of vocabulary and background knowledge.

(International Dyslexia Association 2007: para. 1)

These definitions share some common ground. They agree that reading achievement is low compared to what might be expected on the basis of educational opportunities and intelligence (or 'intellectual/cognitive abilities'). Both point to flow-on effects in reading-related activities and broader academic achievements.

The definitions do differ in several respects. One example is the willingness of NICHHD and IDA but not of DSM to characterize dyslexia as neurological in origin and to suggest a cause in 'the phonological component of language'. Others are the addition of fluency (reading speed) to DSM-5 and the exclusion of reading comprehension from it. We will return to some of these differences as we proceed, but we draw attention to them now simply to show that there remain unresolved issues surrounding dyslexia, and to demonstrate that continued analysis and research are needed.

Popular conceptions of dyslexia

The core picture of dyslexia in the definitions as reading achievement that lags behind age, educational opportunities, and intelligence is somewhat at odds with the more dramatic pictures sometimes presented in public. Some of these misconceptions concern the nature of the disorder, for instance that dyslexics read letters and words backwards ('b' for 'd', 'p' for 'q', 'was' for 'saw', 'dog' for 'god', and so on), and that some kind of brain 'reversal' is therefore the cause of dyslexia. Often related to this is the idea that left-handedness is characteristic of dyslexia. Others assert that many geniuses were dyslexic – people such as Albert Einstein, Leonardo Da Vinci, and Thomas Edison – with the implication that dyslexia is not only largely independent of other mental abilities but often a sign of genius.

These ideas are either plain wrong or exaggerated. For instance, Da Vinci was left-handed and his journal writings did contain mirror-reversed text but he did write in normal fashion when he wrote for others, so it was a matter of choice, not necessity. Einstein was said to have spoken late and to have been a poor student at school. He may have 'started' speaking late, but he was producing full sentences between two and three years of age, as is normal, and the claim about school performance appears to be simply false – his mother described his report card at seven as 'brilliant', top of his class, and he had read Kant's *Critique of Pure Reason* by the age of 13 (Pais 1982).

The idea that reversal of letters and words is typical of dyslexics and tells us something about causes was undermined a considerable time ago by a demonstration that such errors are relatively uncommon and no more typical of dyslexics than of younger children at a similar stage of reading: a developmental lag, not a qualitative difference (Fischer, Liberman, and Shankweiler 1978). Finally, some studies have found an association between left-handedness and dyslexia (Tonnessen et al. 1993) whereas others have failed to find one (Pennington et al. 1987). In any case, handedness cannot be a reliable marker for dyslexia even if averaged data suggest a (weak) association because most dyslexics are right-handed and most left-handers are not dyslexic. So popular myths can be misleading even if they contain a grain of truth, and we are better relying on careful investigation to build up a picture of dyslexia, its nature, and its causes.

Issues surrounding definitions

Discrepancy

As is clear from all definitions presented above, dyslexia is only diagnosed when there is some kind of discrepancy between intelligence and reading achievement. But despite apparent broad agreement on this, it is worth considering in more detail. Consider two second-grade children, one with an IQ of 100 and a reading test score of 85, the other with an IQ of 85 and a reading test score of 85. Only Child 1 would be a candidate for a diagnosis of dyslexia because only this child exhibits a discrepancy. This distinction between the two children might matter a great deal because in some educational jurisdictions only the first child would be considered for special education services; a discrepancy is part of the eligibility requirements. The underlying assumptions appear to be that the reasons why Child 1 reads poorly are different from those for Child 2, and that only Child 1 is likely to profit from extra tuition. But neither of these assumptions is borne out by research. The pattern of reading performance and the pattern of associated cognitive deficits (apart from IQ itself) has not been found to differ much between groups of reading-impaired children with and without an IQ discrepancy, and the degree of discrepancy between IQ and reading scores did not predict how well children responded to intensive one-on-one daily tutoring in a large-scale study of remediation (Vellutino and Fletcher 2005). Vellutino and Fletcher say that these 'combined results have led many to conclude that IQ is irrelevant to reading disability' (p. 377).

Note too that even if it were true that dyslexic children with an IQ discrepancy had reading difficulties with a different set of causes than children without a discrepancy, that would hardly be a reason to withhold services from them. Indeed, it would be reasonable to assume that they require 'more' help than higher-IQ children, who might be better all-round learners and therefore have more strategies available to compensate for their difficulties.

Diagnostic implications

We suggest, on the basis of the scientific and ethical considerations just reviewed, that the diagnosis of dyslexia be made simply on the basis of scores on reading and closely related abilities, such as spelling and reading comprehension. This suggestion is bolstered by findings from a large-scale study of children and adolescents defined as dyslexic on the basis of being in the lowest 10 percent of their samples on word-reading tests (Pennington et al. 2012). For these disabled readers, no single cognitive deficit outside reading was a sure sign of a diagnosis of dyslexia.

Is dyslexia a categorical disorder?

Is it better to think of dyslexia as a distinct disability, akin to a disease such as measles that you either have or do not have, or as a graded disability, akin to obesity, that differs from being somewhat overweight only by degree? There is evidence from genetic research with dyslexia, which we will review later, that favours the graded idea, or in the words of Kovas et al. (2007) that 'the abnormal is normal' (p. 60). By this the authors mean that genes that influence reading ability across the normal range are also those that lead to the more severe form that qualifies as dyslexia. Severity will be under the influence of the number of unfavourable alleles one inherits from all the genes that influence reading ability rather than from inheriting a rare specific gene that only manifests itself in the human genome in proportion to the prevalence of dyslexia. Backing up this argument for the 'obesity' rather than 'measles' model is evidence from Snowling,

Gallagher, and Frith (2003) that even among children with a familial risk for dyslexia (parents and/or siblings with dyslexia) the risk liability is a continuous variable, not a categorical one.

Are there different types of dyslexia?

Several researchers contend that dyslexia comes in different forms, defined by different kinds of deficits. One distinction is due largely to Coltheart and his group (Castles and Coltheart 1993). It is between 'phonological' and 'surface' dyslexia, and is manifest in how these readers manage two types of print sequences: 'nonwords' such as 'flub' and 'pontflac', whose pronunciations cannot have been memorized as whole words and need to be computed from individual letter–sound relations, and 'irregular' words, such as 'knight' and 'yacht', whose pronunciations cannot be computed correctly from letter–sound relations and must have been memorized as whole words. Phonological dyslexics are troubled by nonwords but read irregular words (and familiar regular words) adequately, and surface dyslexics show the opposite pattern – adequate 'decoding' ability (reading nonwords) but deficient memorization skills for irregular words.

A second differential diagnosis, originally suggested by Lovett (1984), depends on reading rate versus reading accuracy, with some readers' difficulties characterized by many errors of pronunciation (accuracy-hampered) and others by very slow though more accurate word identification processes (rate-hampered). The former type shows a broad range of language measure deficits, oral and written. The latter, the rate-disabled group, had difficulties that were most apparent in reading connected text and extracting the meaning. A somewhat related typology is due to Wolf and Bowers (1999).

Despite the evidence suggesting different types of dyslexia, it is important to note that most dyslexic individuals show across-the-board impairments. That is, those who have trouble with nonwords also have trouble with irregular (and regular) words; those who read slowly also read inaccurately. Broad impairment is the typical pattern that faces the clinician.

Causes of dyslexia

There is compelling evidence that risk for dyslexia is substantially influenced by the genetic endowment. It has been known for over a hundred years that reading difficulties run in families. Children in families where one or both parents are dyslexic have a much higher than normal likelihood of themselves experiencing reading difficulties (Gilger, Pennington, and DeFries 1991). Families share both genes and environments, but research that can disambiguate genetic from environmental inheritance has confirmed that this familial aggregation is primarily due to shared genes. One way to conduct this research is to take advantage of the 'natural experiment' afforded by the existence of two types of twins: monozygotic ('identical'), or 'MZ', and dizygotic ('fraternal') or 'DZ'. When both members of a pair grow up in the same family and therefore share the family environment, as most do, the degree to which MZ twins are more like each other for a trait than DZ twins represents the degree to which genes are affecting the trait. One way to express this degree of likeness is in terms of 'concordance', the proportion of pairs in which both twins exhibit the trait. In the case of a diagnosis of dyslexia, concordance rates in various studies have been about twice as high for MZ twins as for DZ twins, confirming a substantial role for genes (Pennington and Olson 2005). Other 'behaviour–genetic' methods of analysis have provided converging evidence for the heritability of dyslexia, as well as of normal-range variation in reading ability (Olson, Byrne, and Samuelsson 2009), with estimates of the proportion of variability in dyslexia status and normal-range reading ranging from about 50 percent to as high as 80 percent.

There has been some limited success in identifying actual genes or genomic regions implicated in dyslexia. The search can be done within families by comparing the genomes of family members with and without dyslexia. It can also be done by comparing nonrelated individuals for the presence of candidate genes and determining whether these are more prevalent in individuals with dyslexia than in those without. There are now up to 14 genetic variants that have been associated with severe reading difficulties (Poelmans et al. 2011), though as the authors note not all attempts to replicate the findings for individual loci have been successful. It is also important to note that although some genetic loci have been identified, they do not explain very much of the genetic liability that has been estimated from twin studies. That is, having the suspect alleles of these genes increases the likelihood of exhibiting reading impairment, but not by a great deal – individuals with those alleles may be perfectly fine readers and individuals without them may be dyslexic.

The functions of the genes are not fully understood, though many appear to be implicated in neuronal migration during embryogenesis and/or the directed outgrowth of neurites and axons (Poelmans et al. 2011). Thus they are related to nervous system development and function.

Knowing *that* genes matter for dyslexia does not in itself tell us *why* they matter – what cognitive and other processes they influence. This is a second level of the search for causes of dyslexia. For this one turns to other kinds of research, which seeks to unpack the essential steps on learning to read and to identify what can go wrong. The NICHHD definition ventures the suggestion that dyslexia can 'result from a deficit in the phonological component of language'. Phonology is the study of the sound system of language, the individual sounds that make up words (represented by letters in alphabetic writing systems) and how they combine (rules that allow, for example, 'flub' in English but not 'fbul'), and so on. But the phonological deficit does not manifest itself in problems in speech itself, which is mostly intact in dyslexic readers. Instead, it is said to mainly affect the learner's 'conscious awareness' of those aspects of phonology that are relevant to reading, in particular the fact that spoken words comprise individual units (called phonemes and represented by letters in alphabets). To take an example: most preliterate children do not understand that 'bat' and 'ball' begin with the same phoneme, that 'hat' and 'pot' end with the same phoneme, or cannot say what 'fall' would be if the 'f' was deleted (Byrne 1998). It is this lack of 'phoneme awareness' that undermines learning to read because it undermines a grasp of the 'alphabetic principle', the way letters and letter groups represent the phonemic structure of language. This in turn undermines the ability to 'decode' print, to figure out the pronunciation of words that have not been memorized as wholes.

The evidence for a role for 'phonemic awareness' comes in two main forms. The first is its correlation with reading achievement among children and adults, including as a predictor of subsequent reading growth when assessed in preliterate children (Byrne 1998; Scarborough 1998). For example, the correlation between phonemic awareness assessed just before a child embarks on reading instruction and later reading ability is around .42 (Scarborough 1998). The second form of evidence comes from positive results of studies that train learners, preliterate, and older children experiencing reading problems, to become more aware of the phonemic organization of speech. There are modest but measurable benefits from phonemic awareness training that last for several years (for examples, see Byrne and Fielding-Barnsley 1993; Hindson et al. 2005).

Difficulties in decoding deprive dyslexic learners of many 'self-teaching' experiences enjoyed by better-resourced learners; that is, of the opportunity to commit to memory word forms that they have successfully decoded (Share 1995). Further up the line, failures at the word level to identify written words accurately and/or fluently make extracting meaning from text very difficult (Hoover and Gough 1990).

Even children with adequate levels of phonemic awareness need to actually learn the associations of those sounds with letters, and evidence that early letter knowledge predicts subsequent reading growth and the emergence of dyslexia, independently of phonemic awareness levels (e.g. Scarborough 1998), suggests that variation in this kind of associative learning ability may also play a vital role. Work of a Dutch group headed by Leo Blomert, using elegant, noninvasive measures of brain function, has shown that dyslexics, even in adulthood, fail to develop highly efficient letter–sound integration (Blomert and Froyen 2010). Also relevant are data from Byrne et al. (2012) showing that genes that affect how readily children learn letter names when young are the same genes that affect how well they can read words when they are older. So committing letters and printed words to memory is in part a function of genetic endowment, and is, of course, a vital component of accurate and fluent reading.

Findings from neurosicence

In the past 20 years considerable progress has been made in mapping brain structures involved in skilled reading using brain imaging techniques such as positron emission tomography (PET) and functional magnetic resonance imaging (fMRI). By comparing the brain responses to tasks that differ in some crucial aspect, such as reading a word aloud versus reading it silently, researchers can identify the anatomical location of the additional task demand; in this case, articulating the word as against just identifying it.

Many areas of the left hemisphere are activated during reading tasks, as might be expected from the complex nature of reading, with visual, articulatory, and semantic processes involved. However, a picture of the neurobiology of reading words is emerging, with at least three regions known to be active: a frontal (anterior) region centred in the region of Broca's area, a region at the junction of the parietal and temporal lobes, and a region bordering temporal and occipital lobes. The anterior region appears to be active during phonological recoding of printed words, and may have some functions in the retrieval of meaning. The temperoparietal region appears to be involved in mapping print onto semantic and phonological structures of language, and the occipitotemporal region may be a 'word form' area that stores highly differentiated memories of a large number of words, and operates prior to the activation of phonological and semantic information associated with words (see Frost et al. 2009 for a summary). In addition to this evidence about brain 'centres' involved in the act of reading, recent research has shown that white matter abnormalities are associated with dyslexia (Klingberg et al. 2000). White matter refers to the axonal tracts that link brain regions, such as the corpus callosum, and given the complex nature of reading, with coordination across visual, phonological, semantic, and articulatory components, it should come as no surprise that deficiencies in these structures would undermine fluent and accurate reading. For an extended discussion of the value of neuroimaging techniques for research into developmental disabilities, including issues of definition, aetiology, risk, and remediation, see Christodoulou, Saxler, and Del Tufo (Chapter 20, this volume).

Dyslexia in languges other than English

Among the languages of Europe, all of which employ an alphabet, English is something of an outlier (Share 2008). It is marked by a relatively high degree of inconsistency in the relations between spelling and sound. Even very common words, such as 'the', 'was', 'one', 'once', and 'two', and others such as 'knight' and 'yacht', cannot be pronounced just by decoding from left to right using the most typical sound of each letter. In contrast, many other European languages show a high degree of consistency, where left to right decoding on the basis of individual letters generally yields the correct pronunciation. Finnish, Greek, and Spanish are often cited as prime examples of consistent languages.

One consequence of this difference in regularity of spelling is that children learning to read in consistent languages make quicker progress than English-reading children; they can generally figure out the pronunciations of written words by the end of their first year at school, which is much rarer in English (Seymour, Aro, and Erskine 2003; Share 2008; Ziegler and Goswami 2005). But does this mean that there is no dyslexia among readers of these languages? The answer seems to be a clear 'no'; dyslexia does exist with these languages. But it appears to take a somewhat different form than it does in English, with the major problem being one of fluency because retrieving the pronunciation of printed words is not a highly automatic process, as it is with skilled readers. A dyslexic German can read relatively accurately but generally slowly and hesitatingly, and therefore can have trouble extracting the gist of connected text (Wimmer, Mayringer, and Landerl 2000). It is important to note, however, that poor spelling remains characteristic of dyslexia even in consistent languages, suggesting that similar phonological deficits underlie dyslexia independently of language (Ziegler and Goswami 2005).

Dyslexia exists in nonalphabetic languages, like Chinese, at least when diagnosed in terms of the numbers of characters an individual can recognize and write relative to age norms (that is, a low-end rather than a discrepancy definition – McBride-Chang et al. 2011). Studies indicate that, as for alphabetic languages, awareness of the linguistic units that the writing system is based on, syllables in the case of Chinese, can be a useful predictor of dyslexia (McBride-Chang et al. 2011). The chapter on 'Learning to read around the world' (Zhang and McBride-Chang, Chapter 8, this volume) provides an informative discussion of reading development across many languages, including the interesting case of literacy in bilingual children.

Assessment

Rather than endorse particular tests of reading, we suggest a framework and a sequence for assessment of reading ability (including dyslexia). The framework is supplied by Hoover and Gough's (1990) 'simple view' of reading, which holds that reading comprehension, referred to as R, is the product of processes that support oral language comprehension, L (for language), and D (decoding, or word-level identification processes). $R = L \times D$. This idea has proved robust in a great deal of research (e.g. Keenan et al. 2006).

The purpose of reading is to extract the meaning of the text, and so a good place to start is with assessment of R. If an individual performs below expectation (age or grade norms), the question arises whether the problem lies with L or D, or both. There is a variety of ways to test L, including how well the individual manages spoken sentences and longer stretches of speech, assessment of specific grammatical structures, and tests of vocabulary. If the individual's L outstrips R, then the problem likely lies with D. If performance on L is as deficient as R, the child likely requires remediation in the domain of spoken language, although continued testing for D would be called for in case a dual deficit exists, that is in both L and D. Of course, even identifying L as the primary source of difficulties does not mean that remediation, or even more detailed diagnosis of the nature of the language problems, will be straightforward (see Messer, Chapter 25, this volume).

Dyslexia can be assessed with standardized measures of word reading, and as discussed earlier, low performance for age or grade constitutes the primary criterion for a diagnosis of dyslexia. On the view that there exist differing forms of dyslexia, for example surface versus phonological types, further testing would be called for – specifically, irregular words versus nonwords (or in the case of accuracy- versus rate-hampered children, reading accuracy versus reading speed). A finding of poor word identification skills would invite assessment of phonological awareness to determine if the word-level difficulties stem from underdevelopment in this domain, in which case one of the many programmes to enhance phonemic awareness could be instituted.

Remediation

Myriad schemes are available that promise remediation of dyslexia. Just typing the words 'dyslexia help' into Google generated 4,860,000 results, and a quick scan showed that nutritionists, chiropractors, optometrists, and many other professionals were represented in this parade of cures. So of course it is impossible to review all that is out there, and in any case it is not our role to endorse particular treatments. Instead, we make the following suggestions based on the kind of scientific evidence that we have reviewed.

- Whatever else a treatment does, it should focus on the act of reading. Schemes whose foci are cognitive and behavioural processes distant from the problem, such as balancing on a beam or listening to Mozart, are likely to do little good and at worst to be a distraction that will put the child further behind.
- Enhancing a child's phonemic awareness, when it is shown to lag behind age norms, is likely to afford a good basis for reading development. A child who can think about and manipulate the individual phonemes in spoken words has a good chance of understanding how the alphabet represents speech and of learning to decode.
- Phonemic awareness training by itself may not transfer to actual reading. It is best linked to direct instruction in the role of letters and letter groups.
- Dyslexic children are known to require more exposures to printed words than other children to be able to store them in memory. Thus all programmes should make room for abundant opportunities for actual reading, with texts tuned to the child's level of competence and affording sufficient repetition of words.
- For any child struggling with a task that they find challenging, motivation can be expected to become a significant issue. Thus due attention needs to be paid to keeping children struggling with reading on task, that is, to ensuring that they read a lot. Doing this successfully is by no means easy, and is part of the high art of teaching.

Conclusion

Considerable progress has been made in describing and understanding dyslexia over the past one hundred years. We suggest it is best thought of as the very low end of normal-range reading ability, allowing all the insights into reading that have resulted from voluminous amounts of research to be exploited in the service of individuals whose impoverished reading ability will, if untreated, affect academic and broader life prospects. Despite this progress, much remains unclear, from the detailed biology of the disorder to the cognitive processes that the biology affects to the environmental circumstances that can also contribute. Most importantly, we need to better understand the things we can do to help individuals with dyslexia. We have made a start on all of this, but much needs to be done.

Contact address: bbyrne@une.edu.au

References

American Psychiatric Association (2013) *DSM-5 development* [online]. Available at www.dsm5.org/Pages/Default.aspx

Blomert, L., and Froyen, D. (2010) 'Multi-sensory learning and learning to read', *International Journal of Psychophysiology*, 77: 195–204.

Byrne, B. (1998) *The foundation of literacy: the child's discovery of the alphabetic principle*, Hove, UK: Psychology Press.

Byrne, B., and Fielding-Barnsley, R. (1993) 'Evaluation of a program to teach phonemic awareness to young children: a 1-year follow-up', *Journal of Educational Psychology*, 85: 104–111.

Byrne, B., Wadsworth, S., Boehme, K., Talk, A. C., Coventry, W., Olson, R. K., et al. (2012) 'Multivariate genetic analysis of learning and early reading development', *Scientific Studies of Reading*, DOI: 10.1080/10888438.2011.654298

Castles, A., and Coltheart, M. (1993) 'Varieties of developmental dyslexia', *Cognition*, 47: 149–180.

Coltheart, M. (2005) 'Modeling reading: the dual-route approach', in M. J. Snowling and C. Hulme (eds.) *The science of reading: a handbook*, Oxford, UK: Blackwell (pp. 6–23).

Fischer, F. W., Liberman, I. Y., and Shankweiler, D. (1978) 'Reading reversals and developmental dyslexia: a further study', *Cortex*, 14: 496–510.

Frost, S. J., Sandak, R., Mencl, W. E., Landi, N., Rueckl, J. G., Katz, L., and Pugh, K. R. (2009) 'Mapping the word reading circuitry in skilled and disabled readers', in P. McCardle and K. Pugh (eds.) *How children learn to read: current issues and new directions in the integration of cognition, neurobiology and genetics of reading and dyslexia research and practice*, New York: Psychology Press (pp. 3–19).

Gilger, J. W., Pennington, B. F., and DeFries, J. C. (1991) 'Risk for reading disability as a function of parental history in three family studies', *Reading and Writing*, 3: 205–219.

Hindson, B. A., Byrne, B., Fielding-Barnsley, R., Newman, C., Hine, D., and Shankweiler, D. (2005) 'Assessment and early instruction of preschool children at risk for reading disability', *Journal of Educational Psychology*, 94: 687–704.

Hoover, W. A., and Gough, P. B. (1990) 'The simple view of reading', *Reading and Writing*, 2: 127–160.

International Dyslexia Association (2007) *What is dyslexia?* [online]. Available at www.interdys.org/FAQWhatIs.htm

Keenan, J. M., Betjemann, R., Wadsworth, S. J., DeFries, J. C., and Olson, R. K. (2006) 'Genetic and environmental influences on reading and listening comprehension', *Journal of Research in Reading*, 29: 75–91.

Klingberg, T., Hedehus, M., Temple, E., Salz, T., Gabrieli, J. D., Moseley, M. E., and Poldrack, R. A. (2000) 'Microstructure of temporoparietal white matter as a basis for reading ability: evidence from diffusion tensor magnetic resonance imaging', *Neuron*, 25: 493–500.

Kovas, Y., Haworth, C. M. A., Dale, P. S., and Plomin, R. (2007) 'The genetic and environmental origins of learning abilities and disabilities in the early school years', *Monographs of the Society for Research in Child Development*, 72: 1–144.

Lovett, M. W. (1984) 'A developmental perspective on reading dysfunction: accuracy and rate criteria in the subtyping of dyslexic children', *Brain and Language*, 22: 67–91.

McBride-Chang, C., Lam, F., Lam, C., Chan, B., Fong, C. Y.-C., Wong, T. T.-Y., and Wong, S. T.-Y. (2011) 'Early predictors of dyslexia in Chinese children: familial history of dyslexia, language delay, and cognitive profiles', *Journal of Child Psychology and Psychiatry*, 52: 204–211.

Olson, R. K., Byrne, B., and Samuelsson, S. (2009) 'Reconciling strong genetic and strong environmental influences on individual differences and deficits in reading ability', in K. Pugh and P. McCardle (eds.) *How children learn to read: current issues and new directions in the integration of cognition, neurobiology and genetics of reading and dyslexia research and practice*, New York, NY: Taylor and Francis (pp. 215–233).

Pais, A. (1982) *Subtle is the lord – the science and the life of Albert Einstein*, Oxford, UK: Oxford University Press.

Pennington, B. F., and Olson, R. K. (2005) 'Genetics of dyslexia', in M. J. Snowling and C. Hulme (eds.) *The science of reading: a handbook*, Oxford, UK: Blackwell (pp. 453–472).

Pennington, B. F., Santerre-Lemmon, L., Rosenberg, J., MacDonald, B., Boada, R., Friend, A., et al. (2012) 'Individual prediction of dyslexia by single versus multiple deficit models', *Journal of Abnormal Psychology*, 121: 212–224.

Pennington, B. F., Smith, S. D., Kimberling, W. J., Green, P. A., and Haith, M. (1987) 'Left-handedness and immune disorders in familial dyslexics', *Archives of Neurology*, 44: 634–639.

Poelmans, G., Buitelaar, J. K., Pauls, D. K., and Franke, B. (2011) 'A theoretical molecular network for dyslexia: integrating available genetic findings', *Molecular Psychiatry*, 16: 365–382.

Scarborough, H. S. (1998) 'Early detection of children at risk for reading disabilities: phonological awareness and other promising predictors', in B. K. Shapiro, P. J. Accardo, and A. J. Capute (eds.) *Specific reading disability: a view of the spectrum*, Timonium, MD: York Press (pp. 75–119).

Seymour, P. H. K., Aro, M., and Erskine, J. M. (2003) 'Foundation literacy acquisition in European languages', *British Journal of Psychology*, 94: 143–174.

Share, D. L. (1995) 'Phonological recoding and self teaching: sine qua non of reading acquisition', *Cognition*, 55: 151–218.

Share, D. L. (2008) 'On the Anglocentricities of current reading research and practice: the perils of overreliance on an "outlier" orthography', *Psychological Bulletin*, 134: 584–615.

Snowling, M. J., Gallagher, A., and Frith, U. (2003) 'Family risk of dyslexia is continuous: individual differences in the precursors of reading skill', *Child Development*, 74: 358–373.

Tonnessen, F. E., Løkken, A., Høien, T., and Lundberg, I. (1993) 'Dyslexia, left-handedness, and immune disorders', *Archives of Neurology*, 50: 411–416.

Vellutino, F. R., and Fletcher, J. M. (2005) 'Developmental dyslexia', in M. J. Snowling and C. Hulme (eds.) *The science of reading: a handbook*, Oxford, UK: Blackwell (pp. 362–378).

Wimmer, H., Mayringer, H., and Landerl, K. (2000) 'The double-deficit hypothesis and difficulties learning to read a regular orthography', *Journal of Educational Psychology*, 92: 668–680.

Wolf, M., and Bowers, P. G. (1999) 'The double deficit hypothesis for the developmental dyslexias', *Journal of Educational Psychology*, 91: 415–438.

Ziegler, J. C., and Goswami, U. (2005) 'Reading acquisition, developmental dyslexia, and skilled reading across languages: a psycholinguistic grain size theory', *Psychological Bulletin*, 131: 3–29.

30

PRACTICAL IMPLICATIONS OF RESEARCH INTO DYSPRAXIA

John Everatt and Brigid C. McNeill

UNIVERSITY OF CANTERBURY, NEW ZEALAND

Definitions/Characteristics

Within the literature on educational learning problems, developmental dyspraxia (dyspraxia for short) is a term used to refer to a disorder of motor skill development. Problems can be with fine and/or gross motor movements (e.g. threading a needle versus balancing on a surface), the performance of which is out of line with the individual's age or stage of development. Impairments seem to focus on the organization of movements and suggest that people with dyspraxia can have problems planning and coordinating, as well as completing, motor tasks. Simple motor tasks, such as waving goodbye or touching an object, can be affected, but so also can the coordination of actions in more complex tasks, such as putting on clothes in the right order, brushing teeth, making a bed, learning to drive a car. These examples show how individuals with dyspraxia can have problems with everyday activities (Geuze 2005) – hence dyspraxia is often considered in terms of a disability that requires appropriate intervention.

Although estimates vary (probably due to variations in who to include within the term), it is estimated that dyspraxia affects at least 2 percent of the general population, though there may be around 4 to 6 percent moderately to severely affected and as many as between 6 and 10 percent of a population showing some signs of dyspraxia (Lingam et al. 2009; Wright and Sugden 1995). There is evidence also that problems can be persistent (e.g. Cantell, Smyth, and Ahonen 1994; Cousins and Smyth 2003).

As with much of the field of special education, different terms have been used in the literature to refer to this condition, primarily due to the involvement of different disciplines and/or legislation. The sorts of problems associated with developmental dyspraxia have been referred to as developmental coordination disorder (DCD: see DSM-IV, American Psychiatric Association 2000) – though see also perceptuo-motor dysfunction or motor learning difficulties, or minimal brain damage and clumsy child syndrome (see Ayres 1965; Clemmens 1961; Illingworth 1968; Whiting, Clarke, and Morris 1969). 'DCD' is the term used most often around the world, and is used in much of the research performed in the USA. However, 'dyspraxia' has been the term most often used in the UK education learning difficulties literature and, therefore, it will be the only term used in this chapter.

Although this chapter will consider DCD and dyspraxia as referring to the same condition, this is not always the case in the literature, and indeed some would argue that equating the two adds to the confusion in the field (see Steinman, Mostofsky, and Denckla 2010). The term 'dyspraxia' has come from a background of investigating individuals with acquired movement disorders, typically focusing on deficits in gesture. DCD has a background in developmental disabilities, which more consistently refer to children with atypical development of motor skills.

Differences between typically developing children and children with dyspraxia have been found in accuracy of motor performance, kinaesthesis, speed of reaction, motor timing, and tasks that involve motor planning or the visualization of movements (see review by Geuze 2005). However, dyspraxia has also been associated with a wider range of problems (for example, Colley 2000), including weaknesses in visual skills, and as a non-verbal learning deficit (see Portwood 1999; Rourke 1989). Whether dyspraxia should be considered purely as a motor deficit or related to visual–spatial (perceptual) problems is contested in the literature (contrast Crawford and Dewey 2008 with Wilson and McKenzie 1998).

Older children and adults with dyspraxia have been identified with problems in complex motor skills that involve sequences of movements and, therefore, dyspraxia has been associated with difficulties in learning sequenced information, which may be important in skills such as literacy, numeracy, and organizational skills (Portwood 1999). Poor recall of the correct order of verbal instructions/directions may relate to organizational problems; and poor sequencing in maths calculations, and problems putting written work in the correct order, may explain educational problems over and above those due to poor handwriting. Again, these types of problems have not always been found in the literature (see Gheysen, van Waelvelde, and Fias 2011; Wilson, Maruff, and Lum 2003).

As might be inferred from the above, one of the difficulties with discussions of dyspraxia is the range of problems that have been associated with the disorder. Such variability may be better explained through considering sub-types; for example, separating inabilities to complete simple motor tasks, such as waving goodbye (sometimes referred to as ideomotor dypraxia), from problems with performing and coordinating a series of motor movements, such as tying a shoe-lace (sometimes referred to as ideational dyspraxia). Additional sub-types may focus on deficits in coordinating muscle movements needed to pronounce words (sometimes referred to as oromotor dyspraxia – though see discussion of verbal dyspraxia below) and problems establishing spatial relationships, as in being able to position accurately or move objects from one place to another (constructional dyspraxia). Additionally, overlaps with other childhood learning/ behavioural disabilities (discussed in due course) may mean that some features currently associated with dyspraxia would be better recognized as part of another disability rather than a core specific deficit of dyspraxia.

Another difficulty with work in the area is that the specific cause (or causes) of dyspraxia is/ are unknown. The execution and coordination of planned movements involve a range of different processes from sensory to planning, problems in any one of which may lead to motor weaknesses. Additionally, the perception of dyspraxia as having a constitutional origin, and the existence of acquired forms of motor problems following brain damage, has led researchers to hypothesize a neurological basis. Although dyspraxia is not linked with an obvious gross neurological abnormality, and research is relatively sparse, potential deficits in various areas of the brain have been considered: including parietal regions associated with visual-perceptual processing, and the cerebellum, which has been hypothesized as involved in motor coordin-ation and postural stability (see review in Zwicker, Missiuna, and Boyd 2009). A biological/ neurological cause has a reasonable basis in research evidence given indications of a link between dyspraxia and premature birth (before week 37 of pregnancy) or low birth weight (for example, Roberts et al. 2011). There is also evidence of a genetic predisposition: one of the main predictors of dyspraxia is a family history of the condition, and clinical samples suggest that males are more likely to have the condition than females (Missiuna et al. 2008). However, there may also be environmental influences related to family membership: alcohol consumption, smoking or the taking of illegal drugs during pregnancy have been identified as risk factors. Indeed, a potential range of causes of dyspraxia is not inconsistent with current diagnostic views advocating differentiation between various aspects of motor function in assessment.

Identification of the difficulty

Given that the specific feature of dyspraxia is a problem with motor development, then early signs may be evident (see discussions in Portwood 1999). Infants who avoid crawling or are late in reaching developmental milestones in rolling over, sitting, standing, walking, and speaking may be at risk. Young children who are at risk may be poor at physical games or show difficulty learning how to dress themselves. In school, the child may be slow in learning writing skills and have difficulty copying things from the board. Having such problems does not necessarily mean a person has dyspraxia. Rather, if the problems are severe and persistent, and appear inconsistent with age or stage of development in other areas, then further assessment will be worthwhile.

Formal assessment should be undertaken by a trained professional: in the UK, a paediatrician or occupational therapist, though trained psychologists (including educational psychologists) may be involved. The specific criteria for diagnosis, and methods used, can vary across organizations and practitioners. Typically, there will be an assessment of motor functioning. In the UK, a commonly used standardized test to measure impairment is the Movement Assessment Battery for Children (Henderson, Sugden, and Barnett 2007). This test has been standardized on children between the ages of three and 16 years. The Bruininks-Oseretsky test (Bruininks and Bruininks 2005) is often used in the USA, and is normed up to 21 years. However, further work on test development would seem worthwhile given that the level of agreement between these two tests has been questioned (see Spironello et al. 2010).

Motor functioning has normally not been the only area assessed. Many argue (see Hill 1998) that dyspraxia should be diagnosed only when problems with movement occur in the absence of other difficulties, and DSM-IV criteria argue for the need to assess intellectual functioning. Therefore, many practitioners will use a test of general intelligence (IQ) in order to rule out other areas of difficulty and to consider general level of development. In addition to assessments of motor functioning (and sometimes as an alternative), parents or teachers may be questioned to determine areas of motor deficits; for example, the Developmental Coordination Disorder Questionnaire (Wilson et al. 2000) is a 17-item parent-completed questionnaire that identifies motor coordination problems in individuals aged eight to 18 years. Interviews may also be used to exclude alternative explanations for the problems – DSM-IV criteria require that the problems experienced are not due to general medical conditions or another developmental disorder (though these criteria have been interpreted differently, particularly given recognized levels of comorbidity; that is, conditions that co-occur within individuals at a level higher than expected by the incidence of the condition alone: see discussions in Missiuna et al. 2008). However, there is a great deal of variability in the features presented by children under assessment and there have been arguments that grouping children with motor difficulties together may miss areas of difficulty, such as that of planning or praxis (see Kirby, Sugden, and Edwards 2010).

Consequences and comorbidity

Dyspraxia has been included as a specific learning difficulty (Dighe and Kettles 1996). Many of these learning-related viewpoints also point to how dyspraxia can affect motor movements associated with speech. Such language-related problems can, most clearly, lead to educational difficulties (we will return to this point when discussing developmental verbal dyspraxia in the next section). However, when speech is not affected, there is a dispute as to the educational consequences of dyspraxia.

There has been consensus that dyspraxia affects writing (see Lord and Hulme 1987); probably one of the main features that teachers will notice is poor handwriting development. An inability to write clearly or express oneself through writing (i.e. difficulty expressing thoughts in writing) has been referred to by yet another term: developmental dysgraphia. Therefore, relationships between dyspraxia and dysgraphia may need to be considered. However, even if writing is poor, some researchers argue that reading and spelling can be at normal levels in many children with dyspraxia (Lord and Hulme 1987). Despite this, concentrating on handwriting quality may leave few resources to monitor spelling or the coherence of what is written (see also Everatt, Weeks, and Brooks 2008).

In the UK, literacy learning difficulties, typically, have been associated with the term 'dyslexia', meaning that there is a need to consider the overlap between dyspraxia and dyslexia. Despite the level of comorbidity, there are distinctions in the primary underlying deficits associated with the two conditions. Dyslexia has been most clearly associated with problems with phonological processing (for example, see Byrne, Samuelsson, and Olson, Chapter 29, this volume; Gillon 2004), and evidence indicates that not all dyspraxics have problems with these skills, particularly if those with speech problems are excluded from the sample (see Everatt et al. 2008). Similarly, although a proportion of dyslexic children have been found to have motor-related difficulties (see Nicolson and Fawcett 1995), this is by no means the case with all dyslexics (Everatt et al. 2008; Ramus, Pidgeon, and Frith 2003). Hence, the two conditions are distinguishable and any similarity in literacy learning problems between dyspraxia and dyslexia may be due to different factors. For further discussion of the underlying impairment in dyslexia, please see Byrne et al. (Chapter 29, this volume).

Children who show a lack of motor coordination and competence also have received attention when there is an emphasis on such abilities within the school curriculum (see Dighe and Kettles 1996) and there may be social, emotional, and confidence issues related to such problems (see Engel-Yeger and Hanna-Kasis 2010). Children with dyspraxia will probably compare themselves against their peers and recognize that their writing and other motor skills are not as good as their class-mates'. This can lead to low self-esteem, anxiety, depression, and other emotional and behavioural problems: being clumsy or awkward can be very frustrating and embarrassing. Examinations based on speeded writing can lead to poor assessment results and, without appropriate accommodation of needs, low levels of academic qualifications that can impact on employment options. However, the literature available on the consequences of dyspraxia remains sparse compared to that covering dyslexia, or learning disabilities in general, meaning that the specific consequences on education, employment, and self-development cannot be determined conclusively. One of the problems with deriving conclusions is the level of comorbidity between dyspraxia and other conditions that can lead to the negative consequences. As discussed previously, comorbid dyslexia rather than dyspraxia itself may lead to literacy problems. Similarly, comorbid emotional or behavioural disorders may be responsible for some of the problems outlined above.

Dyspraxia can also exist along with other conditions that impact learning, such as attention deficit hyperactivity disorder (ADHD), emotional-behavioural disorder and autism/Aspergers syndrome (Cairneya, Veldhuizen, and Szatmari 2010; Green et al. 2002; Rasmussen and Gillberg 2000; Visser 2003). Sudgen and Wann (1987) estimated that around 30 percent of children with learning difficulties have coordination difficulties compared with 5 percent of academically able children. One of the problems is that the diagnostic assessments used for dyspraxia include behavioural features associated with one or more of these other conditions. Assessment of the range of difficulties, therefore, may be vital, particularly given the evidence that a combination of disabilities leads to poorer outcomes (Crawford, Kaplan, and Dewey 2006; Rasmussen and Gillberg 2000) and that if a comorbid disorder pattern is not recognized, sub-optimum or ineffective intervention practices may be implemented (Caron and Rutter 1991).

Co-occurrence rates between specific language impairment (SLI) and dyspraxia are also high. For example, Hill (1998) reported that around 60 percent of children with SLI also presented with dyspraxia. The features and causes of SLI are fully discussed in Messer (Chapter 25, this volume). The complex association between motor and linguistic development is perhaps best exemplified by children affected by developmental verbal dyspraxia, who are discussed in detail in the following section.

Developmental verbal dyspraxia

Developmental verbal dyspraxia (DVD), also termed childhood apraxia of speech and developmental apraxia of speech, is a speech disorder caused by a deficit in motor planning for speech production (Royal College of Speech and Language Therapists 2009). DVD is typically reported as a severe speech impairment with symptoms persisting into adolescence, even with ongoing speech therapy support (Lewis et al. 2004a; Stackhouse and Snowling, 1992). The difficulty is generally considered a sub-type of developmental speech disorder (Messer, Chapter 25, this volume). Although formal definitions of DVD tend to focus on the proposed central impairment in motor planning/programming for speech production, those affected exhibit a multitude of difficulties across speech, language and literacy domains (see American Speech-Language-Hearing Association 2007, for review). The broad-ranging symptoms exhibited by children with DVD contribute to the somewhat controversial nature of this disorder, with continued debate over its existence and diagnosis. A recent evaluation of the functional skills of children with DVD (as reported by caregivers) showed difficulties in cognitive and learning problems (including literacy, calculation, and memory deficits), as well as social communication difficulties and behavioural dysregulation (Teverovsky, Bickel, and Feldman 2009). Currently there is consensus in the literature that DVD does exist and is likely to reflect a symptom complex (i.e. a disorder that is identified by a pattern of symptoms reflecting underlying impairment in motor planning for speech production) rather than a unitary disorder (Shriberg, Aram, and Kwiatkowski 1997). However, a valid and reliable set of differentially diagnostic features of DVD has yet to be identified.

As an example, Table 30.1 presents features of DVD that have been reported in the literature along with two case presentations of children (Anna and Eddie) from data obtained in the work of the second author (McNeill, Gillon, and Dodd 2009a). As demonstrated, children with DVD do not present with all the symptoms; rather they show a pattern of features consistent with an underlying impairment in motor speech planning/programming. Characteristics within children will also change over time as their linguistic systems mature and they respond to therapy input (Lewis et al. 2004a).

Epidemiological data for DVD is limited due to the use of clinical rather than population samples in the calculation of figures. Despite such limitations, all reported incident and prevalence data suggests DVD is a rare diagnosis. Broomfield and Dodd (2004) identified two potential cases of DVD out of 936 referrals (including 320 referrals with a primary speech difficulty) to speech language therapy service in the UK, equating to 0.2 percent of referrals. Similarly, Shriberg et al. (1997) estimated DVD to occur in 0.1–0.2 percent of all children. Gender ratio analysis indicates

Table 30.1 Features experienced by children with DVD

Feature	Eddie (6 years, 1 month)	Anna (6 years, 9 months)
Motoric		
• Oral apraxia	+	−
• Limb dyspraxia	+	−
Speech production		
• Inaccurate consonant production	+	+
• Inaccurate vowel production	−	+
• Inconsistent speech error	+	+
• Sound sequencing errors	−	−
Prosody		
• Inappropriate stress within words	−	+
• Inappropriate stress within phrases	+	+
Language		
• Language comprehension impairment	−	+
• Language production impairment	+	+
Literacy		
• Phonological awareness impairment	+	+
• Single-word decoding difficulty	−	+
• Non-word reading difficulty	+	+
• Spelling difficulty	+	+
• Reading comprehension impairment	−	+

+ = performance at least 1 SD below the mean on standardised testing, − = performance within normal limits on standardised testing.

DVD is more prevalent in males than in females. Lewis et al. (2004b) reported a 2:1 ratio of males to females in a sample of 22 children aged three to 10 years. DVD appears to be a heritable condition, with a large percentage of the family members of those affected experiencing speech, language, and/or literacy disorders (Lewis et al. 2004b; Thoonen et al. 1997). Additionally, children with DVD may present comorbidly with other types of coordination difficulties including oromotor dyspraxia (i.e. difficulties with voluntary movements of the tongue, lips, palate, and larynx for non-speech movements), limb dyspraxia, and/or generalized dyspraxia, though there are no firm figures on the rates of comorbidity between DVD and other forms of dyspraxia.

Currently viewpoints on the underlying deficit in DVD are divided into those emphasizing motor and motor plus linguistic causes (American Speech-Language-Hearing Association 2007). Evidence that children with DVD exhibit difficulty using phonological information in the reading and spelling process has led to comparisons between dyslexia and DVD (McCormick 2000; McNeill et al. 2009a). However, children with DVD also exhibit impairment in language comprehension and expression that further contribute to literacy development (Lewis et al. 2004a). The association between these two disorders is best explained by the 'multiple deficit approach' where phonological deficits are proposed to interact with other cognitive factors in literacy development (Pennington 2006). As such, children with DVD have fewer 'protective factors' to support successful literacy acquisition.

Controlled intervention studies including children with DVD are scarce (Morgan and Vogel 2008). There is preliminary support for speech therapy approaches that utilize principles of motor learning in improving speech production for this population (e.g. Iuzzini and Forrest

2010; Martikainen and Korpilahti 2011). Such approaches, however, do not address the literacy difficulties associated with the disorder. An integrated therapy approach that concurrently targets speech accuracy, phonological awareness, and phonics knowledge has lifted the speech, reading, and spelling skills of some children with DVD (McNeill, Gillon, and Dodd 2009b). However, continued intensive support may be necessary to ensure long-term accelerated growth in literacy skills in this population (McNeill, Gillon, and Dodd 2010; Zaretsky, Velleman, and Curro 2010).

Motor interventions

The scarcity of intervention research in DVD is also an issue for those working with children with dyspraxia. Although there is no known cure for dyspraxia, early identification and intervention can support learning/skills development (see Sigmundsson et al. 1998; Sugden and Chambers 1998). Depending on the type and severity of the disability, work with occupational, speech, and physical therapists can improve the individual's ability to function and succeed independently (e.g. Pless and Carlsson 2000). However, there are relatively few clinical programmes designed specifically for individuals with dyspraxia (see Schoemaker, Hijlkema, and Kalverboer 1994). In their review of programmes, Pless and Carlsson (2000) concluded that the types of intervention that seemed most effective were those based on task-specific instruction which involved combinations of correctly performed practice of functional skills, appropriate repetition, and sufficient guidance and time to facilitate skill retention and generalization, and which involved the individual as an active participant in the training process – many of the good pedagogical practices associated with various learning difficulty sub-types. However, in contrast to the work that shows improvements in motor functioning, there has been little conclusive evidence to suggest that improvements in motor behaviours per se will lead to improved academic skills (see Everatt et al. 1999; Kavale and Mattson 1983).

Therefore, probably the best advice is to target intervention at the area of difficulty. If the child is showing difficulties with handwriting, then work to develop handwriting skills specifically is most likely to be successful. As with any area of learning difficulty, alternative forms of presenting or working with information can be useful: learning to type may be easier than learning to write, and can support the use of computers. Computers also can be used to make things fun and support reading and spelling independent of writing, and voice-activated software can be used to circumvent writing/typing problems (see de Jong and Verhallen, Chapter 9, this volume, for more information on how digital technology can support literacy). However, the skills needed to use these alternatives effectively also have to be learnt.

Concluding comments

There is still a need for research to provide clearer direction to inform practice within this field. The lack of specificity of problems associated with dyspraxia argues for the need for very different support procedures, in terms of both reliable identification and appropriate intervention. Variability in dyspraxia is exemplified by DVD. Although DVD can co-occur with other motor problems, its characteristic verbal motor deficits lead to language problems that have been associated with educational difficulties, particularly in literacy learning. Whereas interventions for most types of dyspraxia seem to be best if focused on specific areas of motor skill acquisition problems, the language problems associated with DVD seem to require a concentration on speech and language therapy, and the child with DVD may benefit from educational interventions designed for children with conditions such as dyslexia (e.g. phonological awareness interventions) that may be less appropriate specifically for children with other types of dyspraxia. The lack of systematic research on intervention procedures, particularly methods targeted at different types of dyspraxia, is a cause for concern. However, what the current research literature does tell us is that there are children and adults with motor deficits that impact negatively on day-to-day activities, which also can lead to problems in education, but that, with appropriately targeted support, these negative consequences can be reduced.

Contact address: john.everatt@canterbury.ac.nz

References

American Psychiatric Association (2000) *Diagnostic and statistical manual of mental disorders (DSM-IV-TR)*, Washington, DC: American Psychiatric Association.

American Speech-Language-Hearing Association (2007) *Childhood apraxia of speech* (Technical Report) [online]. Available at www.asha.org/policy

Ayres, A. J. (1965) 'Patterns of perceptual-motor dysfunction in children: a factor analytic study', *Perceptual and Motor Skills*, 20: 335–368.

Broomfield, J., and Dodd, B. (2004) 'The nature of referred subtypes of primary speech disability', *Child Language Teaching and Therapy*, 20: 135–151.

Bruininks, R. H., and Bruininks, B. D. (2005) *Bruininks-Oseretsky Test of Motor Proficiency*, 2nd edn, Windsor: NFER-Nelson.

Cairneya, J., Veldhuizen, S., and Szatmari, P. (2010) 'Motor coordination and emotional–behavioral problems in children', *Current Opinion in Psychiatry*, 23: 324–329.

Cantell, M. H., Smyth, M. M., and Ahonen, T. P. (1994) 'Clumsiness in adolescence: educational, motor and social outcomes of motor delay detected at 5 years', *Adapted Physical Activity Quarterly*, 11: 115–129.

Caron, C., and Rutter, M. (1991) 'Comorbidity in child psychopathology: concepts, issues and research strategies', *Journal of Child Psychology and Psychiatry*, 32: 1063–1080.

Clemmens, R. (1961) 'Minimal brain damage in children', *Children*, 8: 179–188.

Colley, M. (2000) *Living with dyspraxia: a guide for adults with developmental dyspraxia*, Hitchin: Dyspraxia Foundation Adult Support Group.

Cousins, M., and Smyth, M. M. (2003) 'Developmental coordination impairments in adulthood', *Human Movement Science*, 22: 433–459.

Crawford, S. G., and Dewey, D. D. (2008) Co-occurring disorders: a possible key to visual perceptual deficits in children with developmental coordination disorder? *Human Movement Science*, 27: 154–169.

Crawford, S. G., Kaplan, B. J., and Dewey, D. (2006) 'Effects of co-existing disorders on cognition and behavior in children with ADHD', *Journal of Attention Disorders*, 10: 192–199.

Dighe, A., and Kettles, G. (1996) 'Developmental dyspraxia: an overview', in G. Reid (ed.) *Dimensions of dyslexia, Volume 2*, Edinburgh: Moray House Publications. (pp. 231–263).

Engel-Yeger, B. B., and Hanna-Kasis, A. A. (2010) 'The relationship between developmental co-ordination disorders, child's perceived self-efficacy and preference to participate in daily activities', *Child Care, Health and Development*, 36: 670–677.

Everatt, J., McNamara, S., Groeger, J. A., and Bradshaw, M. F. (1999) 'Motor aspects of dyslexia', in J. Everatt (ed.) *Reading and dyslexia: visual and attentional processes*, London: Routledge (pp. 122–136).

Everatt J., Weeks, S., and Brooks, P. (2008) 'Profiles of strengths and weaknesses in dyslexia and other learning difficulties', *Dyslexia*, 14: 16–41.

Geuze, R. H. (2005) 'Motor impairment in DCD and activities of daily living', in D. A. Sugden and M. E. Chambers (eds.) *Children with Developmental Coordination Disorder*, London: Whurr (pp. 19–46).

Gheysen, F., Van Waelvelde, H., and Fias, W. (2011) 'Impaired visuo-motor sequence learning in developmental coordination disorder', *Research in Developmental Disabilities*, 32: 749–756.

Gillon, G. T. (2004) *Phonological awareness: from research to practice*, New York: Guilford Press.

Green, D., Baird, G., Barnett, A. L., Henderson, L., Huber, J., and Henderson, S. E. (2002) 'The severity and nature of motor impairment in Asperger's syndrome: a comparison with specific developmental disorder of motor function', *Journal of Child Psychology and Psychiatry*, 43: 655–668.

Henderson. S. E., Sugden, D. A., and Barnett, A. (2007) *Movement Assessment Battery for Children*, London: Harcourt Assessment.

Hill, E. L. (1998) 'A dyspraxic deficit in specific language impairment and developmental coordination disorder? Evidence from hand and arm movements', *Developmental Medicine and Child Neurology*, 40: 388–396.

Illingworth, R. S. (1968) 'The clumsy child', *Clinical Pediatrics*, 7: 539–543.

Iuzzini, J., and Forrest, K. (2010) 'Evaluation of a combined treatment approach for childhood apraxia of speech', *Clinical Linguistics and Phonetics*, 24: 335–345.

Kavale, K., and Mattson, P. (1983) 'One jumped off the balance beam: metanalysis of perceptual-motor training', *Journal of Learning Disabilities*, 16: 166–173.

Kirby, A., Sugden, D., and Edwards, L. (2010) Developmental co-ordination disorder (DCD): more than just a movement difficulty', *Journal of Research in Special Educational Needs*, 10: 206–215.

Lewis, B. A., Freebairn, L., Hansen, A., Iyengar, S., and Taylor, H. (2004a) 'School-age follow-up of children with childhood apraxia of speech', *Language, Speech, and Hearing Services in Schools*, 35: 122–140.

Lewis, B. A., Freebairn, L., Hansen, A., Taylor, G., Iyengar, S., and Shriberg, L. D. (2004b) 'Family pedigrees of children with suspected childhood apraxia of speech', *Journal of Communication Disorders*, 37: 157–175.

Lingam, R., Hunt, M. L., Golding, J., Jongmans, M., and Emond, A. (2009) 'Prevalence of developmental co-ordination disorder using the DSM-IV at 7 years of age: a UK population-based study', *Pediatrics*, 123: 693–700.

Lord, R., and Hulme, C. (1987) 'Kinaesthetic sensitivity of normal and clumsy children', *Developmental Medicine and Child Neurology*, 29: 720–725.

Martikainen, A., and Korpilahti, P. (2011) 'Intervention for childhood apraxia of speech: a single-case study', *Child Language Teaching and Therapy*, 27: 9–20.

McCormick, M. (2000) 'Dyslexia and developmental verbal dyspraxia', *Dyslexia*, 6: 202–214.

McNeill, B. C., Gillon, G. T., and Dodd, B. (2009a) 'Phonological awareness and early reading development in childhood apraxia of speech', *International Journal of Language and Communication Disorders*, 44: 175–192.

McNeill, B. C., Gillon, G. T., and Dodd, B. (2009b) 'Effectiveness of an integrated phonological awareness approach for children with childhood apraxia of speech', *Child Language Teaching and Therapy*, 25: 341–366.

McNeill, B. C., Gillon, G. T., and Dodd, B. (2010) 'The longer term effects of an integrated phonological awareness intervention for children with childhood apraxia of speech', *Asia Pacific Journal of Speech, Language, and Hearing*, 13: 145–161.

Missiuna, C., Gaines, R., Mclean, J., DeLaat, D., Egan, M., and Soucie, H. (2008) 'Description of children identified by physicians as having developmental coordination disorder', *Developmental Medicine and Child Neurology*, 50: 839–844.

Morgan, A. T., and Vogel, A. P. (2008) 'Intervention for childhood apraxia of speech', *Cochrane Database of Systematic Reviews*, 16, CD006278.

Nicolson, R. J., and Fawcett, A. J. (1995) 'Dyslexia is more than a phonological disability', *Dyslexia*, 1: 19–36.

Pennington, B. F. (2006) 'From single to multiple deficit models of developmental disorders', *Cognition*, 101: 385–413.

Pless, M., and Carlsson, M. (2000) 'Effects of motor skill intervention on developmental coordination disorder: a meta-analysis', *Adapted Physical Activity Quarterly*, 17: 381–401.

Portwood, M. (1999) *Developmental dyspraxia: identification and intervention*, 2nd edn, London: David Fulton.

Ramus, F., Pidgeon, E., and Frith, U. (2003) 'The relationship between motor control and phonology in dyslexic children', *Journal of Child Psychology and Psychiatry*, 44: 712–722.

Rasmussen, P., and Gillberg, C. (2000) 'Natural outcome of ADHD with developmental coordination disorder at age 22 years: a controlled, longitudinal, community-based study', *Journal of the American Academy of Child and Adolescent Psychiatry*, 39: 1424–1431.

Roberts, G., Anderson, P. J., Davis, N., De Luca, C., Cheong, J., and Doyle, L. W. (2011) 'Developmental coordination disorder in geographic cohorts of 8-year-old children born extremely preterm or extremely low birthweight in the 1990s', *Developmental Medicine and Child Neurology*, 53: 55–60.

Rourke, B. P. (1989) *Nonverbal learning disabilities: the syndrome and the model*, New York: Guilford Press.

Royal College of Speech and Language Therapists (2009) *RCSLT resource manual for commissioning and planning services for SLCN*, London: RCSLT.

Schoemaker, M., Hijlkema, M., and Kalverboer, A. (1994) 'Physiotherapy for clumsy children: an evaluation study', *Developmental Medicine and Child Neurology*, 36: 143–155.

Shriberg, L. D., Aram, D., and Kwiatkowski, J. (1997) 'Developmental apraxia of speech I. Descriptive and theoretical perspectives', *Journal of Speech, Language, and Hearing Research*, 40: 273–285.

Sigmundsson, H., Pedersen, A. V., Whiting, H. T. A., and Ingvaldsen, R. (1998) 'We can cure your child's clumsiness! A review of intervention methods', *Scandinavian Journal of Rehabilitation Medicine*, 30: 101–106.

Spironello, C. C., Hay, J. J., Missiuna, C. C., Faught, B. E., and Cairney, J. J. (2010) 'Concurrent and construct validation of the short form of the Bruininks-Oseretsky Test of Motor Proficiency and the Movement-ABC when administered under field conditions: implications for screening', *Child Care, Health and Development*, 36: 499–507.

Stackhouse, J., and Snowling, M. (1992) 'Barriers to literacy development in two cases of developmental verbal dyspraxia', *Cognitive Neuropsychology*, 9: 273–299.

Steinman, K. J., Mostofsky, S. H., and Denckla, M. B. (2010) 'Towards a narrower, more pragmatic view of developmental dyspraxia', *Journal of Child Neurology*, 25: 71–81.

Sugden, D. A., and Chambers, M. E. (1998) 'Intervention approaches and children with developmental coordination disorder', *Pediatric Rehabilitation*, 2: 139–147.

Sudgen, D., and Wann, C. (1987) 'The assessment of motor impairment in children with moderate learning disabilities', *British Journal of Educational Psychology*, 57: 225–236.

Teverovsky, E. G., Bickel, J. O., and Feldman, H. M. (2009) 'Functional characteristics of children diagnosed with childhood apraxia of speech', *Disability and Rehabilitation*, 31: 94–102.

Thoonen, G., Maassen, B., Gabreëls, F., Schreuder, R., and de Swart, B. (1997) 'Towards a standardized assessment procedure for developmental apraxia of speech', *European Journal of Disorders of Communication*, 32: 37–60.

Visser, J. (2003) 'Developmental coordination disorder: a review of research on subtypes and comorbidities', *Human Movement Science*, 22: 479–493.

Whiting, H. T. A., Clarke, T. A., and Morris, P. R. A. (1969) 'A clinical validation of the Stott Test of Motor Impairment', *British Journal of Social and Clinical Psychology*, 8: 270–274.

Wilson, B., Kaplan, B. J., Crawford, S. G., Campbell, A., and Dewey, D. (2000) 'Reliability and validity of a parent questionnaire on childhood motor skills', *American Journal of Occupational Therapy*, 54: 484–493.

Wilson, P. H., Maruff, P., and Lum, J. (2003) 'Procedural learning in children with developmental coordination disorder', *Human Movement Science*, 22: 515–526.

Wilson, P. H., and McKenzie, B. E. (1998) 'Information processing deficits associated with developmental coordination disorder: a meta-analysis of research findings', *Journal of Child Psychology and Psychiatry*, 39: 829–840.

Wright, H. E., and Sugden, D. A. (1995) 'A two step procedure for the identification of children with DCD in Singapore', *Developmental Medicine and Children Neurology*, 38: 1099–1105.

Zaretsky, E., Velleman, S. L., and Curro, K. (2010) 'Through the magnifying glass: underlying literacy deficits and remediation potential in childhood apraxia of speech', *International Journal of Speech–Language Pathology*, 12: 58–68.

Zwicker, J. G., Missiuna, C., and Boyd, L. A. (2009) 'Neural correlates of developmental coordination disorder: a review of hypotheses', *Journal of Clinical Neurology*, 24: 1273–1281.

31

DYSCALCULIA

Research and practice on identification and intervention across languages

John Everatt, Gad Elbeheri and Peter Brooks

UNIVERSITY OF CANTERBURY, NEW ZEALAND; CENTER FOR CHILD EVALUATION AND
TEACHING, KUWAIT; PRIVATE EDUCATIONAL PSYCHOLOGIST, GERMANY/UK

Definition

In this chapter, the term 'dyscalculia' will be used to refer to individuals who have severe and persistent problems with mathematics. The term will be described as synonymous with mathematics learning disability (MLD) and, from this perspective, focuses on children in educational contexts who show difficulties with learning mathematics – in contrast to those who may acquire mathematics difficulties in later life. Such individuals with dyscalculia typically show difficulties understanding simple number concepts, poor intuitive grasp of numbers, problems learning number facts and procedures, and evidence of performing mathematics problems mechanically and without confidence. In the present chapter, dyscalculia will be considered as related to an underlying problem with fully understanding basic concepts in mathematics (such as an understanding of number – examples can be found in Figure 31.1). Although this view is not universal, it is similar to that which has been used in the UK, North America, and elsewhere (e.g. see Butterworth and Yeo 2004; Chinn and Ashcroft 2007; Geary 2004; see also Ramaa 2000, for a discussion of dyscalculia work in India).

Work related to dyscalculia has a reasonably long history (e.g. Cohn 1961 – see also Luria 1980). However, much of the early work focused on adults, and on case-studies following brain damage, rather than on children with learning problems experienced in normal schooling contexts. Work specifically targeted at children with problems consistent with dyscalculia has been less common (see some of the initial work in Kosc 1974), particularly in comparison with that on literacy learning disability or dyslexia (see discussions in Berch and Mazzocco 2007). Dyscalculia as used in this chapter has also been referred to as developmental dyscalculia and has been used alongside terms such as mathematics learning difficulties (Mabbott and Bisanz 2008) and mathematics disorder (or MD, as in the *Diagnostic and Statistical Manual of Mental Disorders* (DSM), American Psychiatric Association (APA) 2000). In the present discussion, 'learning disabilities' (LD) follows the use of the term in the USA; that is, a specific problem with learning that is not necessarily due to low IQ. In 1975, the USA passed public law 94-142 recognizing learning disabilities, including MLD, stating that these required identification and remediation in children. Although both MLD and dyscalculia have been used widely in the literature on

a) The task requires the individual to indicate which circle has the most dots – changes in the number, and spread, of dots will vary the difficulty of the task.

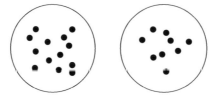

b) A symbolic version of the above task would require the individual to indicate which one of the below is the larger number.

c) The ability to estimate the amount associated with a number can be assessed by asking the individual to indicate a position on a line, as in the example below.

Mark on the
line where 40
should be

0   100

d) A Number-Stroop example in which the task is to state which is the larger written symbol. For the letters, this is not influenced by number-value. In the case of the numbers, saying that the 3 is larger than the 4 should be influenced by number-value and lead to slowed responses.

Which is
bigger?

A B

Which is
bigger?

3 4

e) A second Number-Stroop example: the task is to state the number of items. In this case interference (slowed response when numbers are used compared to when letters are the items) is caused by the sum being incongruent with the number value. (With two longer lists of rows on two sheets of paper – one sheet for letters and a separate one for numbers – the times can be compared with a stop-watch; though make sure that the number-values are only one different from the sum of each row as this seems to increase the level of interference.)

State the
number of
items in
each row?

XXXX
TTTTT
BBB

State the
number of
items in
each row?

3333
222
44444

Figure 31.1   Examples of tasks involving an appreciation of number/value

developmental problems, they have also been used to contrast different conditions: experiential versus congenital problems, or acquired versus developmental disorders (see discussions in Campbell 2005; Geary 2004).

As an LD, dyscalculia is a severe difficulty in mathematics, not explained by general cognitive difficulties or educational opportunities. It runs in families (see Shalev et al. 2001) and although estimates vary, possibly due to the influence of quality of teaching, the most likely prevalence of the condition is around 3 to 6 percent of an educated population (Berch and Mazzocco 2007; Geary 2004; Lewis, Hitch, and Walker 1994; Wilson and Dehaene 2007). An LD also implies that problems should be persistent – though this does not mean that appropriate intervention cannot remediate many problems associated with a disability. Consistent with this, difficulties associated with dyscalculia have been found to continue across grades (Shalev, Manor, and Gross-Tsur 2005). Indeed, facts learnt in earlier classes may be misremembered or misapplied in later grades (Chinn and Ashcroft 2007).

Since an understanding of numbers (or values/amounts) and their relationships (see Wilson and Dehaene 2007) dominates the child's early experiences of mathematics, it seems likely that dyscalculia starts with problems in this area. Consistent with this, relatively early features of problems related to dyscalculia may be a particular slowness in number naming (Bull and Johnston 1997) or difficulties in understanding how numbers work together in patterns, such as recognizing that one number has a larger value than another (Rubinsten and Henik 2006). Additionally, there is likely to be a continued use of basic strategies in calculations (for example, using fingers to support counting – see Geary, Bow-Thomas, and Yao 1992) and evidence of anxiety and poor attitudes to mathematics that are likely to inhibit performance (Beasley, Long, and Natali 2001; Maloney et al. 2010).

Finally, there is also evidence that the impact of dyscalculia can extend to areas outside education, such as when telling the time or counting money, and lead to emotional problems (such as anxiety when dealing with mathematics) that stem from experiences of failure in mathematics (Chinn and Ashcroft 2007; Miles and Miles 1992). Negative emotion can also emanate from feelings of embarrassment, frustration, and anxiety when dealing with mathematical problems. Children may feel stupid and may be teased or stigmatized by classmates, which can lead to low self esteem, anxiety, avoidance, and negative attitude. Adults may be blocked from certain professions, have difficulty managing money and a poor understanding of numbers/values that can influence decision making. Anxiety related to mathematics also may interact with mathematics skills or underlying deficits associated with dyscalculia (Ashcraft and Krause 2007; Maloney et al. 2010). Therefore, even if some problems are overcome, the lack of confidence that failure has produced may remain.

Baroody and Ginsburg (1991) considered dyscalculia as a specific disturbance in learning mathematical concepts and computation which was not due to limited intellectual capacity, a language disorder, emotional problems, or poor teaching. The last of these is important as there is a need to distinguish between dyscalculia as an LD and weak mathematics skills due to poor educational experience: we would not want to say that an individual has dyscalculia when they have not had the opportunity to learn mathematics. Indeed, one of the major problems for those attempting specifically to identify dyscalculia is the large number of individuals who show weaknesses in mathematics. As suggested above, most views of dyscalculia consider it as a condition affecting acquisition irrespective of learning opportunity that benefits most individuals (though experiential background needs to be considered: see Grafman and Boller 1987).

Mathematics skills

Models describing the way in which children develop mathematics skills to adult levels (see Nunes and Bryant 1997) argue for a series of interacting but distinct components. An appreciation of amount (that there is more of one thing than another) may be one of the first mathematics-related skills to develop. Dealing with this concept in non-symbolic forms may support associations with numerical symbols. See examples in Figure 31.1 for tasks in which an appreciation of number/values can be assessed. Learning the names of written digit symbols, as well as their order (in counting), also is an early indicator of acquisition. In addition, learning of the procedural aspects of performing arithmetical calculations, as well as applying basic reasoning skills (Bryant 1985; Geary and Widaman 1992), will support skilled learning. Each of these components of mathematical ability will be influenced by underlying cognitive skills, and some may be influenced by achievement in other academic fields, such as literacy (see the next sub-section of this chapter for a discussion of potential co-occurrence with other LDs such as dyslexia – and Byrne, Samuelsson, and Olson (Chapter 29, this volume) provides a discussion of dyslexia that can be contrasted with the present chapter's description of dyscalculia).

Neurological data also suggest sub-components that may be related to different types of problems (Dehaene, Spelke, and Pinet 1999). For example, an understanding of number seems to be related to activity in the intraparietal sulcus (IPS), an area of the brain that also seems to be involved in thinking about space. Mathematics-based tasks that activate this region involve the comparison of numbers, approximation, and estimation (see Figure 31.1 for examples), as well as non-symbolic tasks (Dehaene et al. 2003). In contrast, the angular gyrus (AG) seems to increase in activation in mathematical tasks that focus on procedural or drill-type learning, such as the use of times-tables in multiplication calculations. This area of the brain also seems to be involved in the more verbal aspects of mathematics, such as in the retrieval of arithmetic facts. This dissociation seems to be consistent with data from patients with acquired mathematics problems. Lemer et al. (2003) discuss one patient (BRI) who was found to have difficulty with counting and fact recall (for example, multiplication problems can be solved through the fact-based recall of times-tables), but was able to approximate well, in contrast to another (LEC) who was poor at approximation but was able to recall addition and multiplication facts.

Specific disability and sub-types

As discussed in the previous sub-section, in order to distinguish it from poor educational opportunity, dyscalculia is considered to be related to abnormal functioning of one or more systems responsible for the development of mathematical skills. In addition, dyscalculia needs to be shown to be specific; i.e. the child can show problems with mathematics but perform normally in areas that are not related to the LD (Baroody and Ginsburg 1991; Jordan and Hanich 2000). If it is shown always to co-occur with specific language impairments (SLI; see Messer, Chapter 25, this volume, for a discussion of SLI), for example, then it may be best to include it as a feature of SLI rather than as a separate condition (see Donlan 1998). One of the problems with identifying the specific nature of dyscalculia is that difficulties with mathematics can co-occur with other LDs. For example, as many as half of those with dyslexia may have weaknesses in mathematics (see Chinn and Ashcroft 2007; Miles and Miles 1992); and there are overlaps between the two conditions (Willburger et al. 2008). However, there are also fundamental differences which mean that the two can be dissociated (see Adams et al. 1999). In particular, dyslexics have been found to show deficits in phonological skills, whereas mathematics weaknesses may be associated with inefficient number comparisons (Landerl et al. 2009; see also Durand et al. 2005; Rubinstein and Henik 2006).

In addition to problems of overlap or co-occurrence with other LDs, research has yet to identify a specific cause of dyscalculia. Indeed, the characteristics associated with mathematics learning problems, as well as both the cognitive processes and brain areas that seem involved in mathematical procedures, argue for several potential causes, and hence sub-types, of dyscalculia. Several such sub-typing theories have been proposed, though none is uniformly accepted. For example, Wilson and Dehaene (2007) discuss the possibility that there may be sub-types focused around problems in: (i) number sense, where conceptual understanding of number will be affected, potentially leading to problems in most elements of mathematics, including in non-symbolic tasks, except simple fact retrieval (as in counting); (ii) verbal aspects of mathematics, leading to difficulty with counting, fact retrieval and word-based problems (this form may be associated with language-related learning problems, including dyslexia); (iii) executive functioning (working memory), which may be associated with difficulties in fact retrieval and strategy/ procedure use (as well as attentional deficits); and (iv) spatial processing, which may lead to specific difficulties in processing patterns, such as in geometry work, and non-symbolic quantities (this form may be most clearly linked with views about non-verbal learning disabilities (NVLD) – see Rourke 1989 for a discussion of NVLD). Although different terminology may eventually be agreed upon to describe these potential sub-types, they may influence the determination of appropriate intervention procedures and, therefore, need to form part of assessment processes that aim to inform education plans.

Assessment

The identification of dyscalculia, typically, has followed the same general principles that guide the assessment of any LD. This would involve the determination of the individual's ability in mathematics, which would be best determined using a standardized test (see next paragraph), although measures that compare performance against a point in a curriculum rather than a standardization sample have also been used in many parts of the world where formally standardized measures do not exist. Some criteria on this mathematics test would be used to determine learning problems: figures such as two years behind expected levels in children in school education or below some percentile score in adults have been most often used, though the exact figures can vary depending on the organization accrediting the assessment. Additionally, a measure of intelligence (IQ) may be used to rule out general learning difficulties or to determine a discrepancy between IQ-determined expected performance and actual performance on a mathematics test (see discussions of the inclusion of IQ in assessments of LD in Brooks and Everatt 2009, and Elbeheri and Everatt 2009a). These may be accompanied by measuring underlying skills related to poor performance in mathematics and/or considered to be the cause of the LD, though again the skills assessed will vary across assessors depending on their theoretical position. Finally, some process of eliminating alternative causes of mathematics weaknesses will be undertaken. For example, interviews may be used to determine the educational history of the individual; information may be sought on birth problems, serious illnesses, or psycho-social disorders in the past; and dyslexia, attention deficit hyperactivity disorder, dyspraxia, or other such developmental learning/behaviour problems may be considered. Given that difficulties related to dyscalculia are developmental, assessments should be related to the expected developmental level.

A comprehensive assessment of mathematics learning should involve a range of tests/tasks. The ability to count has been seen as an important building block for development and, therefore, often forms a part of the assessment of basic skills. Number sense may be tested via symbolic number comparisons, but also non-symbolic comparisons, and estimations (see Figure 31.1). Mathematical knowledge might be tested via basic arithmetic or specific procedures taught at various curriculum levels. For example, KeyMath (Connolly 2007) tests a range of areas (numeration, algebra, geometry, measurement, data analysis, probability), operations (mental computation and estimation, addition and subtraction, multiplication and division), and applications (including the foundations of problem solving, and applied problem solving) – and these are linked to remediation material. The Test of Early Mathematics Ability (TEMA; Ginsburg and Baroody 2003), aimed at children aged three to eight years, focuses on basic numbering, number-comparison facility, numerical literacy, mastery of number facts, calculation, and concept understanding. In contrast, the Comprehensive Mathematical Abilities Test (CMAT; Hresko et al. 2003) is aimed at seven- to 19-year-olds, and focuses on addition, subtraction, multiplication, division, problem solving, and the use of charts, tables, and graphs – and supplemental tests of algebra, geometry, rational numbers, time, money, and measurement. One or more of these tests can be used to provide a profile of the child's skills in mathematics.

Although there are no formal diagnostic tests specifically for dyscalculia, there are English-language dyscalculia screening tools (e.g. Butterworth 2003; Chard et al. 2005; Mazzocco and Thompson 2005). The Butterworth test (Butterworth 2003; Butterworth and Yeo 2004) assesses basic mathematical concepts; such as in Number Stroop tasks (Figure 31.1). As such, it does not depend greatly on skills such as reading, language, or short-term memory, or on a learner's educational experience. It also focuses on the time taken to answer questions in comparison with the average for the child's age group; most children can perform the task, but those with dyscalculia do so less efficiently (or less fluently). The use of such tasks is consistent with most views about the characteristics of dyscalculia, as well as the data in the literature discussed above.

A screener for dyscalculia has also been developed for use within the Arab world (see Elbeheri and Everatt 2009b). The context in which this work was conducted (Kuwait) is an interesting one to study the universality of problems related to dyscalculia (though see also, for example, Ramaa and Gowramma 2002), since as well as differences in language/culture, the teaching of mathematics has differed from that used in those countries where much of the work on dyscalculia has taken place. For example, up to the current time, mathematics has been taught in a very rote-/drill-based way – more so than in many Western schools (used here to refer primarily to schools in the UK, North America, Australia, New Zealand, and Europe). Additionally, number symbols taught in school still are based on a written form that differs from that used in Western schools (i.e., ١, ٢, ٣, ٤ in contrast to 1, 2, 3, 4) – though the Kuwaiti child will experience both forms in everyday life as most phone numbers, road signs, and car licence plates, as well as many prices on goods, are written in numerals used in the West. Writing proceeds from right to left in Arabic texts. However, 10 and above are written as in the West, with the 10 symbol to the left of the unit symbol. Hence, the way numbers are taught and written is different from that found in the West. Despite such differences, and consistent with the view that an understanding of number as related to amount/value is a fundamental aspect of dyscalculia, Arab children with severe and persistent problems with learning mathematics show deficits in conceptual tasks similar to those in Figure 31.1. Also, children with specific problems in number concepts can be distinguished from those with problems with reading and writing, consistent with a dissociation between dyslexia and dyscalculia (Landerl et al. 2009) despite both problems leading to weaknesses with certain aspects of mathematics.

Hence, problems with the concepts underlying mathematics seem a further area where measures can be developed to support the identification of dyscalculia. Indeed, screening before formal learning on non-symbolic and basic symbolic comparisons holds the potential to predict future performance (for example, see Mazzocco and Thompson 2005, for evidence of prediction from behavioural measures in kindergarten) and, if appropriate intervention can be implemented prior to experiences of failure, then negative consequences (including low self-esteem, frustration, and anxiety) should be avoided/reduced.

Intervention/Remediation

Given that an assessment identifies a problem, some process of intervention or support needs to be implemented. Intervention work that can be provided in schools by mainstream teachers can be useful, particularly for those without the more intractable problems that typically require specialist support (see examples see Fuchs and Fuchs 2001; and discussions of response to intervention procedures for MLD in Bryant and Bryant 2008). Many of the techniques used for children with difficulties can be useful with non-LD learners: good pedagogy is good for all (see Gersten et al. 2009). However, for those who are struggling, supportive methods of teaching are often vital for learning to occur and, therefore, special programmes may be required for those with severe difficulties. Given that there are few programmes that focus on remediating the underlying deficits associated with dyscalculia (though see Butterworth and Laurillard 2010; Wilson et al. 2006), only general guidelines, which apply to most intervention procedures used with children with learning difficulties, can be provided (see also Bird 2009; Butterworth and Yeo 2004; Chinn and Ashcroft 2007; Yeo 2003).

Teaching/intervention targeted at children with LD has been considered more effective when taking account of the child's strengths and weaknesses, as well as their interests. The specific support methods used will need to be determined based on both the educational context and the learner (see discussion in Miller and Mercer 1997). However, the current research on dyscalculia suggests that number sense or conceptual understanding may be a common underlying feature of the problems associated with dyscalculia across learning contexts – and this underlying skill/function shows evidence of change/development (see Ansari and Dhital 2006; Lipton and Spelke 2003). Therefore, programmes that focus on teaching this skill, or that provide strategies for learning basic concepts, should be highly useful and might be easily transferred across educational contexts.

The repetition of information/concepts that have been learnt poorly will be required with many LD children, including those with dyscalculia. Repetition also can reduce the focus on memorization and will ensure fact/symbol learning and recall – clearly, this will also increase practice, which is often necessary for LD children. Multisensory learning methods can be useful to reinforce ideas by presenting information in different ways that avoid boredom produced by simple repetition. Multisensory strategies have the defining characteristic of presenting information in different forms so that the child can see, hear, and even feel the ideas presented, in addition to the child producing them by drawing, writing, and speaking. Presenting information in these different ways may also make it easier for the child to remember the information by reinforcing a concept/fact in a way that the child finds accessible and fun (an amusing image can often be recalled to mind more easily than a neutral word).

Particularly for LD students, it is vital to ensure that learning is structured, using logical steps to build on learning and help reinforcement. This can be done by starting at relatively easy levels, which should increase the likelihood of success, and then scaffolding on these learnt skills – but making sure that skills are learnt before moving on. Chinn (see Chinn and Ashcroft 2007) gives the example that most children with dyscalculia-type problems can, with the right support, learn simple multiplication facts for 1, 2, 5 and 10. These facts can then be used to access other facts (e.g. that 9 times is simply 1 times less than 10 times). Therefore, a basic level of skill can be used to teach strategies to deal with additional mathematical problems.

Experience of teaching children with LD suggests that greater benefits will be found when strategies and concepts are taught explicitly, rather than implicitly from rote or simple practice. This will allow the child to form appropriate generalizations, such as from concrete examples to abstract problems, and form links between examples and procedures that need to be learnt. Furthermore, the learning of concepts and procedures needs to be tested appropriately. Non-threatening questions about concepts can get the individual engaged and thinking, and ensure that appropriate generalizations have taken place. Assessments of learning need careful implementation to avoid associations with failure that can lead to negative affect, avoidance, and poor motivation, particularly for children who may experience difficulties in an area. In contrast, concrete examples, or familiar objects/situations, that illustrate ideas will allow the child to relate to the information, thereby supporting understanding and interest. Clearly, making learning active and fun, and using things with which the child is familiar and enjoys, should maintain interest, increase motivation to learn, and provide the basis on which learning is made easier both for the child and the teacher.

Concluding comments

Although much less research has investigated dyscalculia compared to some other developmental learning difficulties, such as dyslexia, tentative conclusions can be derived. The evidence argues strongly for the existence of a specific learning difficulty in mathematics that can lead to problems with day-to-day living both within education and outside. It can be severe (in terms on its impact on learning) and persistent (without appropriate intervention), and there is evidence for a neurological basis and genetic predisposition – though further research is needed to specify these.

Problems with the concept of number, and relationships between numbers, provide the most compelling evidence for an underlying dysfunction that is specific to dyscalculia. This dysfunction shows the potential to be identifiable early (possibly before formal education via non-symbolic tasks) and to be susceptible to change, which affords the possibility of intervention; though further work on early identification and specific interventions is necessary. In addition to this potential specific characteristic of dyscalculia, though, there is evidence for wider deficits in mathematics that may be associated with poor learning opportunity or related to other developmental problems (such as language-related learning difficulties). Whether the latter are better seen as part of support processes for these alternative difficulties or as sub-types of dyscalculia has yet to be resolved. Practical work in educational interventions argues for basic principles common to supporting children with learning problems to be effective in the area of mathematics learning as much as in other areas of education. Therefore, despite the need for more research to better understand the condition, and thereby inform support, there is still a great deal that educators can, and should, do to support individuals with dyscalculia.

Contact address: john.everatt@canterbury.ac.nz

References

Adams, J. W., Snowling, M. J., Hennessy, S. M., and Kind, P. (1999) 'Problems of behaviour, reading and arithmetic', *British Journal of Educational Psychology*, 69: 571–585.

American Psychiatric Association (2000) *Diagnostic and statistical manual of mental disorders (DSM-IV-TR)*, Washington, DC: American Psychiatric Association.

Ansari, D., and Dhital, B. (2006) 'Age-related changes in the activation of the intraparietal sulcus during non-symbolic magnitude processing: an event-related fMRI study', *Journal of Cognitive Neuroscience*, 18: 1820–1828.

Ashcraft, M. H., and Krause, J. A. (2007) 'Working memory, math performance, and math anxiety', *Psychonomic Bulletin and Review*, 14: 243–248.

Baroody, A. J., and Ginsburg, H. P. (1991) 'A cognitive approach to assessing the mathematical difficulties of children labelled "learning disabled"', in H. L. Swanson (ed.) *Handbook on the assessment of learning disabilities: theories, research and practice*, Austin, TX: Pro-Ed (pp. 177–226).

Beasley, T. M., Long, J. D., and Natali, M. (2001) 'A confirmatory factor analysis of the Mathematics Anxiety Scale for Children', *Measurement and Evaluation in Counseling and Development*, 34: 14–26.

Berch, D. B., and Mazzocco, M. M. M. (eds.) (2007) *Why is math so hard for some children? The nature and origins of mathematical learning difficulties and disabilities*, Baltimore: Paul H Brookes Publishing.

Bird, R. (2009) *Overcoming difficulties with number: supporting dyscalculia and students who struggle with maths*, London: Sage.

Brooks, P., and Everatt, J. (2009) 'Phonology, discrepancy, instruction and dyslexia: adversaries or allies?', in J. E. Larson (ed.) *Educational psychology: cognition and learning, individual differences and motivation*, Hauppauge, NY: Nova Science Publishers (pp. 205–22).

Bryant, P. E. (1985) 'The distinction between knowing when to do a sum and knowing how to do it', *Educational Psychology*, 5: 207–215.

Bryant, B. R., and Bryant, D. P. (2008) 'Introduction to the special series: mathematics and learning disabilities', *Learning Disability Quarterly*, 31: 3–8.

Bull, R., and Johnston, R. S. (1997) 'Children's arithmetical difficulties: contributions from processing speed, item identification, and short-term memory', *Journal of Experimental Child Psychology*, 65: 1–24.

Butterworth, B. (2003) *Dyscalculia screener*, London: NFER-Nelson.

Butterworth, B., and Laurillard, D. (2010) 'Low numeracy and dyscalculia: identification and intervention', *ZDM*, 42: 527–539.

Butterworth, B., and Yeo, D. (2004) *Dyscalculia guidance: helping pupils with specific learning difficulties in math*, London: NFER-Nelson.

Campbell, J. I. D. (ed.) (2005) *The handbook of mathematical cognition: developmental dyscalculia series*, Hove: Psychology Press.

Chard, D. J., Clarke, B., Baker, S., Otterstedt, J., Braun, D., and Katz, R. (2005) 'Using measures of number sense to screen for difficulties in mathematics: preliminary findings', *Assessment for Effective Intervention*, 30: 3–14.

Chinn, S. J., and Ashcroft, J. R. (2007) *Mathematics for dyslexia including dyscalculia*, 3rd edn, London: Wiley.

Cohn, R. (1961) 'Dyscalculia', *Archives of Neurology*, 4: 301–307.

Connolly, A. J. (2007) *KeyMath-3*, Minneapolis: Pearson.

Dehaene, S., Piazza, M., Pinel, P., and Cohen, L. (2003) 'Three parietal circuits for number processing', *Cognitive Neuropsychology*, 20: 487–506.

Dehaene, S., Spelke, E., and Pinet, R. (1999) 'Sources of mathematical thinking: behavioural and brain-imaging evidence', *Science*, 284: 970–973.

Donlan, C. (1998) 'Number without language? Studies of children with specific language impairments', in C. Donlan (ed.) *The development of mathematical skills*, Hove: Psychology Press (pp. 255–274).

Durand, M., Hulme, C., Larkin, R., and Snowling, M. (2005) 'The cognitive foundations of reading and arithmetic skills in 7- to 10-year-olds', *Journal of Experimental Child Psychology*, 91: 113–116.

Elbeheri, G., and Everatt, J. (2009a) 'IQ and dyslexia: from research to practice', in G. Reid, G. Elbeheri, J. Everatt, D. Knight, and J. Wearmouth (eds.) *The Routledge companion to dyslexia*. Abingdon: Routledge (pp. 22–32).

Elbeheri, G., and Everatt, J. (2009b) *Developing a computer-based dyscalculia screener to identify monolingual Arabic speaking individuals with dyscalculia in Kuwait*, Report to the Kuwait Foundation for the Advancement of Science.

Fuchs, L. S., and Fuchs, D. (2001) 'Principles for the prevention and intervention of mathematics difficulties', *Learning Disabilities Research and Practice*, 16: 85–95.

Geary, D. C. (2004) 'Mathematics and learning disabilities', *Journal of Learning Disabilities*, 37: 4–15.

Geary, D. C., Bow-Thomas, C. C., and Yao, Y. (1992) 'Counting knowledge and skill in cognitive addition: a comparison of normal and mathematically disabled children', *Journal of Experimental Child Psychology*, 54: 372–391.

Geary, D. C., and Widaman, K. F. (1992) 'Numerical cognition: on the convergence of componential and psychometric models', *Intelligence*, 16: 47–80.

Gersten, R., Chard, D. J., Jayanthi, M., Baker, S. K., Morphy, P., and Flojo, J. (2009) 'Mathematics instruction for students with learning disabilities: a meta-analysis of instructional components', *Review of Educational Research*, 79: 1202–1242.

Ginsburg, H. P., and Baroody, A. J. (2003) *Test of early mathematics ability*, 3rd edn, Austin, TX: Pro-Ed.

Grafman, J., and Boller, F. (1987) 'Cross-cultural approaches to the study of calculation processes', in G. Deloche and X. Seron (eds.) *Mathematical disabilities: a cognitive neuropsychological perspective*, Hillsdale, NJ: Lawrence Erlbaum Associates (pp. 257–272).

Hresko, W., Schlieve, P., Herron, S., Swain, C., and Sherbenau, R. (2003) *Comprehensive Mathematical Abilities Test (CMAT)*, Austin, TX: Pro-Ed.

Jordan, C. N., and Hanich, B. (2000) 'Mathematical thinking in second grade children with different forms of LD', *Journal of Learning Disabilities*, 33: 567–578.

Kosc, L. (1974) 'Developmental dyscalculia', *Journal of Learning Disabilities*, 7: 164–177.

Landerl, K., Fussenegger, B., Moll, K., and Willburger, E. (2009) 'Dyslexia and dyscalculia: two learning disorders with different cognitive profiles', *Journal of Experimental Child Psychology*, 103: 309–324.

Lemer, C., Dehaene, S., Spelke, E., and Cohen, L. (2003) 'Approximate quantities and exact number words: dissociable systems', *Neuropsychologia*, 2003: 1942–1958.

Lewis, C., Hitch, G. J., and Walker, P. (1994) 'The prevalence of specific arithmetic difficulties and specific reading difficulties in 9- to 10-year-old boys and girls', *Journal of Child Psychology*, 35: 283–292.

Lipton, J. S., and Spelke, E. S. (2003) 'Origins of number sense: large number discrimination in human infants', *Psychological Science*, 14: 396–401.

Luria, A. R. (1980) *Higher cortical functions in man*, 2nd edn, New York: Basic Books.

Mabbott, D. J., and Bisanz, J. (2008) 'Computational skills, working memory, and conceptual knowledge in older children with mathematics learning disabilities', *Journal of Learning Disabilities*, 41: 15–28.

Maloney, E., Risko, E. F., Ansari, D., and Fugelsang, J. F. (2010) 'Mathematics anxiety affects counting but not subitizing during visual enumeration', *Cognition*, 114: 721–729.

Mazzocco, M. M. M., and Thompson, R. E. (2005) 'Kindergarten predictors of math learning disability', *Learning Disabilities Research and Practice*, 20: 142–155.

Miles, T. R., and Miles, E. (1992) *Dyslexia and mathematics*, London: Routledge.

Miller, S. P., and Mercer, C. D. (1997) 'Educational aspects of mathematics disabilities', *Journal of Learning Disabilities*, 30: 47–56.

Nunes, T., and Bryant, P. (eds) (1997) *Learning and teaching mathematics: an international perspective*, Hove: Psychology Press.

Ramaa, S. (2000) 'Two decades of research on learning disabilities in India', *Dyslexia*, 6: 268–283.

Ramaa, S., and Gowramma, I. P. (2002) 'A systematic procedure for identifying and classifying children with dyscalculia among primary school children in India', *Dyslexia*, 8, 67–85.

Rourke, B. P. (1989) *Nonverbal learning disabilities: the syndrome and the model*, New York: Guilford Press.

Rubinsten, O., and Henik, A. (2006) 'Double dissociation of functions in developmental dyslexia and dyscalculia', *Journal of Educational Psychology*, 98: 854–867.

Shalev, R. S., Manor, O., and Gross-Tsur, V. (2005) 'Developmental dyscalculia: a prospective six-year follow-up', *Developmental Medicine and Child Neurology*, 47: 121–125.

Shalev, R. S., Manor, O., Kerem, B., Ayali, M., Bidichi, N., Friedlander, Y., and Gross-Tsur, V. (2001) 'Developmental dyscalculia is a familial learning disability', *Journal of Learning Disabilities*, 34: 59–65.

Willburger, E., Fussenegger, B., Moll, K., Wood, G., and Landerl, K. (2008) 'Naming speed in dyslexia and dyscalculia', *Learning and Individual Differences*, 18: 224–236.

Wilson, A. J., and Dehaene, S. (2007) 'Number sense and developmental dyscalculia', in D. Coch, G. Dawson, and K. Fischer (eds.) *Human behavior, learning and the developing brain: atypical development*, New York: Guilford Press (pp. 212–238).

Wilson, A. J., Revkin, S. K., Cohen, D., Cohen, L., and Dehaene, S. (2006) 'An open trial assessment of "The Number Race", an adaptive computer game for remediation of dyscalculia', *Behavioral and Brain Function*, 30: 2–20.

Yeo, D. (2003) *Dyslexia, dyspraxia and mathematics*, London: Whurr.

32

MEETING THE NEEDS OF GIFTED LEARNERS

Marion Porath

THE UNIVERSITY OF BRITISH COLUMBIA, CANADA

This chapter presents research on giftedness and connects it to relevant work in educational psychology. To provide context for current thinking about gifted learners, a short history of the study of giftedness and education of gifted learners is provided. This is followed by contemporary work that recognizes the dynamic and complex nature of giftedness and considers the nature of educational environments that nurture optimal development. The chapter is written from the Canadian perspective, where giftedness is considered a special educational need and the rights of children with special needs to an appropriate education are enshrined in our Charter of Rights and Freedoms. These considerations, however, are not always reflected in practice.

Consistent with contemporary research in educational psychology that emphasizes the importance of the initial understandings people bring to their learning (Bransford, Brown, and Cocking 2000), the chapter begins with a series of questions to stimulate your reflection on what you now know and think about giftedness and intelligence. Before engaging with the chapter it is important that you make explicit your own understandings of what giftedness and intelligence mean and what intelligence means for learning. These reflections will help you to see how your own beliefs and experiences come to play as you learn about giftedness.

- When you hear someone described as 'gifted', what are your first thoughts? What would you expect this person to be like personally, socially, academically, and creatively? Take a moment to jot down your thoughts.
- Now think about what makes a person highly intelligent. Are people intelligent in the same ways? Is intelligence innate, an inherited capability? Is it 'fixed' at birth or can experience, education, and hard work increase intelligence? Do home, community, and educational environments matter?

Questions like these, and other 'provocations for learning' appear throughout the chapter. These provocations take different forms, including several reflection activities to engage you in discussion about meeting the needs of the featured learner. All of the provocations are intended to engage you in thinking about giftedness and to help you ask good questions. Asking good questions is key to advancing and enriching your knowledge.

Historical perspective on intelligence and education of gifted learners

From Plato's discussion, in *The Republic*, of individuals in whom God has mingled gold, silver, or brass and iron and the accompanying roles these individuals took in society, through early attempts to measure intelligence by filling skulls with shot, to more recent efforts to measure intelligence by testing, the Western world has had a fascination with categorizing people by intellectual capacity (Gould 1981). Terman et al (1915) developed the Stanford Binet Scales of Intelligence, scales that are still in use today in a revised form. Terman's conceptualization of the intelligence quotient (IQ) (Shayer 2008) and his subsequent longitudinal study of pupils in California with exceptionally high IQs (Terman 1926) had a long-lasting effect on how we think about intelligence and identify gifted learners. A 'traditional' definition of giftedness is an IQ in the top 2 percent of the intelligence distribution, or >130 (the average IQ is 100). Both identification and education of gifted learners was largely test-driven. Further background on intelligence testing is presented in the chapter on 'Intelligence and individual differences' (Ngara and Porath, Chapter 19, this volume).

Hollingworth (1942) was a child psychologist who studied 12 children with IQs above 180 and was actively involved in ensuring appropriate education for them in the public school system in New York City. Individuals who score this high on intelligence tests are extremely rare and it is challenging to plan educational experiences that meet their needs. Hollingworth gave us a number of educational strategies that are still in use today. Students worked in committees, foreshadowing current work on learning communities and curriculum that builds on students' interests and questions (e.g. Donovan and Bransford 2005). Hollingworth also discussed the social isolation that very bright children experience. We continue to be challenged about how best to meet both the academic and social–emotional needs of gifted learners.

The equating of intelligence with IQ is still prominent in gifted education, despite other theories' potential to inform broader conceptualizations of what it means to be intelligent (Plucker 2001). 'The traditional "find the gifted child" model' (Plucker and Barab 2005: 204) is still a common practice worldwide.

Contemporary perspectives on giftedness and gifted education

Rethinking IQ

At present, there are efforts to move beyond IQ and the implied categorization of individuals as gifted, or not, in our definitions and practice. These efforts hold considerable promise for improving the educational experience of all children. However, while intelligence tests have limitations (e.g. they privilege students who have had opportunities to learn; they are not 'culture-fair'), they can be useful additions to the multiple tools and approaches that help us to understand children's learning profiles (Matthews and Foster 2009). That is, when a test is used as part of an assessment approach to understand a child's abilities and ways of learning, and when the test items tap the abilities about which educators and parents, and perhaps children themselves, are curious, it can be a useful addition to information that helps craft an appropriate educational programme. Today's focus is on using intelligence tests intelligently (Matthews and Foster 2009).

A student's IQ gives a general indication of how they compare to others their age in terms of their general knowledge; short-term memory; and ability to understand language, mathematics, and social norms, reason logically, and process visual information. While this information can help answer questions about how a child compares to his/her peers (e.g. a child whose IQ is 130 is at the 98th percentile, or the top 2 percent of children his/her age), it does little to inform us about their academic achievement. Matthews and Foster (2009) call this the 'mystery model' of giftedness.

Matthews' (1997) work demonstrated that among students defined as gifted by their IQs, there is considerable variability in academic and social developmental profiles. What educators need to know is a student's reading level, including how well he/she decodes text and comprehends what he/she reads; how capable a writer he/she is, both in terms of mechanics and writing cogently; his/her level of mathematical reasoning and computational skills; his/her interests and abilities in science and the arts and humanities; and his/her passions, ambitions, and motivation to achieve. We need to attend to the considerable variability among learners identified as gifted on an intelligence test (Robinson, Zigler, and Gallagher 2000) and discover what their specific academic and non-academic strengths are. This 'mastery model' of giftedness (Matthews and Foster 2009) is most useful for educators since it focuses on the degree of developmental advancement in different curricular areas, providing concrete guidelines for the provision of appropriately matched instruction (see Erten, Savage, and Di Stasio, Chapter 6, this volume, for a broader discussion of how a mastery focus contributes to positive school behaviours and learning).

New directions

Contemporary questions include the following: Is there one intelligence or many (Gardner 1983; Sternberg 1985; Winner 2009)? How does culture influence conceptions of giftedness and the nature of support offered to gifted individuals (Ngara 2009; Ngara and Porath 2004; Ngara and Porath, Chapter 19, this volume; Phillipson and McCann 2007)? Is intelligence a fixed capacity or can it be improved through effort (Dweck 2006)? Is intelligence static or does it develop and change across the lifespan (Horowitz, Subotnik, and Matthews 2009; Jackson 2000)? What other capacities, such as motivation and social–emotional intelligence, influence the achievement of excellence (Goleman 1995; Ziegler 2005)? What is the role of sustained practice in outstanding achievements (Ericsson, Nandagopal, and Roring 2006)? How do educational environments support or constrain intelligent behaviour (Barab and Plucker 2002; Borland 2003; Lai 2009)?

Why do the questions currently being asked about intelligence, giftedness, and gifted education matter? Dweck (2009) emphasized that, when the study of giftedness focused on identification and sorting people into categories, it was an endeavour of limited interest. Now, the enterprise is broader.

> It encompasses many researchers studying many abilities, how they develop, and the factors that can promote them. And, as an enterprise, it takes as its target many people of diverse cultures and backgrounds and ages. It is a field that has become less about 'who' and more about 'how'. What could matter more than understanding how people can fulfill their extraordinary potential?
>
> *(Dweck 2009: xiv)*

Intelligence is only one of the many factors – for example, motivation, effort, mentorship, and supportive home and school environments – that lead to academic and career success (Ziegler 2005). As Ziegler (2005: 431) goes on to argue, our goal 'is not to categorize "persons" as gifted, but rather to identify a "learning path" for an individual that leads to excellence'.

Effort and practice

'Doing one's homework' is essential in outstanding achievement. The '10,000 hour rule' quantifies the amount of practice that is necessary to achieve eminence in one's field (Ericsson et al. 2006). However, it is not simply a matter of putting in the time. One's motivational orientation is important. If you put in the time because you want to build your competence and truly understand your discipline (goal orientation), your practice is much more likely to result in excellence than if you practise to 'look good' and cover up your failures (performance orientation) (Ziegler 2005; see also Erten et al., Chapter 6, this volume, and Martin, Chapter 11, this volume, for further discussion of the role of motivation in learning). Additionally, feedback from teachers/mentors is important. Knowledge of what you are doing that leads to excellence and how you bring that competence 'forward' to the next stage of learning makes the practice meaningful (Ziegler 2005).

Noticing and creating giftedness

Current work in giftedness also emphasizes 'gift creation' (Hymer 2009); that is, noticing clues indicative of intelligence and inventions in learning as interesting and useful (Bamberger 1991) and supporting their development, rather than static identification procedures that focus on labelling learners as gifted (Borland 2003). 'Gift creation' involves being curious about the way students learn and what their learning strengths are, and providing a rich educational environment with a variety of materials that allow gifts and talents to be observed. We need to change our focus from finding 'smart people' to designing 'smart contexts' (Barab and Plucker 2002). This is especially important for children whose talents aren't immediately apparent, who aren't 'skilled-up' (Claxton and Meadows 2009: 7) in the ways of school.

In Reflection Activity 1 (see Figure 32.1), consider how Dylan responds to the classroom environment his teacher, Ben, created. Use the questions at the end of the activity to guide your thinking about other approaches Ben might take to support Dylan.

Student participation in learning

Contemporary work in giftedness and educational psychology highlights the importance of the role of the learner in defining directions for education (Hymer, Whitehead, and Huxtable 2009). What are students' beliefs about learning and teaching? How do they understand their own abilities? Posing questions to students about what learning means to them, how they like to learn different subjects, and how they like to be taught provides fascinating insights into how they view education and their place in it, as well as how these insights change with development and experience with school (Porath and Lupart 2009; Porath et al. 2009, 2010). In addition, understanding what students already know about the curriculum and what questions they have about topics to be studied provides a critical window into how they think about concepts (see also the chapter on 'Educational dialogues', Littleton, Chapter 7, this volume, on the importance of students' perspectives on learning). Using this understanding as a starting point for instruction is critical in facilitating deep conceptual and factual knowledge (Bransford et al. 2000).

What is your 'model of mind' (Bruner 1996); how do you think minds work and what does that mean for teaching? For example, do minds need to be 'filled up' with facts? Should teachers 'stand and deliver' curriculum? How does your mind work? What sort of teaching works best for you? Does one method of instruction work better for some subjects and another method for

Reflection Activity 1

Ben was always looking for ways to make his classroom attractive and enticing to his group of 11- and 12-year-old students. He arranged the students' artwork, with their help and suggestions, in beautiful displays. His science, poetry, and art centres were famous in the school. Students loved the materials he included and the activities that made them think. They also loved that they could suggest ideas for centres and bring in artefacts and that Mr V, as he was fondly known, liked them to ask questions and come up with creative ideas. To Ben, all of this was what made teaching rewarding. He didn't neglect 'the basics' but embedded them, through careful planning, in learning activities.

Dylan's academic history included marginal and failing grades, documented behaviour problems, and several years of support from the school's learning specialist. When he entered Ben's classroom at 11, he was clearly stressed by activities that didn't always have one right answer and by responses to his questions that posed questions back to him. 'How would you find out?' 'What's your opinion?' Slowly, he began to explore and be more comfortable with ideas. By his second year with Ben, certain talents had begun to emerge. Ben was thrilled to read Dylan's sensitive, expressive poetry and see his artistic talents flourish, particularly his ability to understand and use negative spaces in printmaking. Mathematics was still a problem, though. Dylan lacked confidence and Ben knew that his own ability to think creatively in maths wasn't as strong as his ability to come up with creative ideas in other subject areas. He also knew that he had to try to offer Dylan something else in maths.

- What would be a good start? Where would he find out?

Use the following questions as guidelines (Jordan and Porath 2006) to find a way to address Ben's questions. The questions help you to focus on what you see as the 'problem' and what can be done to address it.

- What do you know? (What information is evident in the scenario?)
- What are your preconceptions? For example, do you have a philosophy of education that doesn't align with Ben's approach? How might that affect your interpretation of this scenario?
- What are the issues? What do you need to know and how will you find out? Here, think about relevant research in educational psychology and ideas you glean from internet searches. You can also think about local resources such as a teacher, school principal, or school psychologist.
- Now, come back to identifying the 'problem'. What do you see as the key issue or question to address, and how do you plan to address it?

Our essays went to the principal, which gave them meaning and showed us the essay had a reason behind it. It taught me that if you stick up for what you believe, you have a chance of succeeding.

Figure 32.1 Reflection Activity 1: designing supportive educational contexts

others? Thinking about these questions will give you insight into how you think about the relationship between teaching and learning.

There is a solid research base on learning that highlights critical requirements for deep learning and supports the need to attend carefully to what students already understand about the world (Bransford et al. 2000). These findings apply to all learners.

- Students bring their own understandings about how the world works to school. These initial understandings must be honoured and used in planning instruction. Otherwise, learning becomes an 'overlay' (Jordan and Porath 2006) that students may be able to repeat on a test; however, once the test is over, they go back to their own ways of understanding the world.

This finding is especially important in meeting the needs of gifted learners. They have exceptionally advanced knowledge bases but the conceptual understanding that 'glues' this knowledge to a strong foundation is influenced by maturation and is less advanced in nature, although still precocious (Porath 2006). This mix of developmental levels needs to be considered in instruction, as indicated in the second key finding from research on learning.

- To develop competence, students need a 'deep foundation of factual knowledge' (Bransford et al. 2000: 16) and a conceptual framework within which to understand factual knowledge. This framework enables knowledge to be organized in a way that facilitates its application.
- Students need to be in charge of their own learning, understanding how they learn and their learning progress. In other words, they need to be 'metacognitive' and can be helped in achieving this through instruction that helps them become self-regulated learners (Cartier, Butler, and Bouchard 2010; Perry, Thauberger, and Hutchinson 2010; Porath et al. 2010).

Education of gifted learners: Some additional considerations

Culture and intelligence

Part of the contemporary focus on breadth in conceptualizations of intelligence includes the role of culture in defining intelligence and giftedness (Phillipson and McCann 2007; Sternberg and Grigorenko 2004). As society becomes more and more global, it is increasingly important to consider how ideas about intelligence, giftedness, and the type of education that supports excellence may vary among cultures. In Canada, 200 different ethnic origins were reported in the 2006 Canadian census. Our two largest cities – Toronto and Vancouver – have visible minorities of 43 percent and 42 percent, respectively (Statistics Canada 2011). In Toronto, one of the most multicultural cities in the world, over 150 languages are spoken. There is still much to learn about how different cultural groups in Canada define giftedness; however, in the global community of the twenty-first century, an intercultural perspective is also important, both socially and educationally.

> A great deal can be gained from cross-cultural collaboration in expanding understandings of giftedness, and programming strategies and options. In the educational context, the aim is for Canada to fully embrace its truly multicultural society – to identify, encourage, and support different manifestations of giftedness within cultural groups but also to work toward a broader, intercultural conception of competence.
>
> *(Foster, Porath, and Smyth 2009: 115)*

In Reflection Activity 2 (see Figure 32.2), think about the kind of support needed for Amanda, a student caught between different cultural views of intelligence and career.

Gifted learners who are 'twice exceptional'

Giftedness can co-occur with a number of other special needs; for example, autism spectrum disorder, physical and/or sensory disabilities, and learning disabilities. Learners who are highly able and have additional special needs are often referred to as 'twice exceptional' (sometimes '2E') or as having a 'dual exceptionality', although they can sometimes have multiple special needs. This discussion focuses on giftedness that co-occurs with learning disabilities.

Acknowledgement of the co-occurrence of giftedness and learning disabilities happened relatively recently, about 30 years ago (Brody and Mills 1997). Recognition of this dual

---

Reflection Activity 2

Amanda was exhausted. It was midnight and she still had some maths problems to finish, not to mention studying for the chemistry test tomorrow. OK, she had been texting her friends off and on all evening but still . . . Amanda, at 15, was very close to finishing high school. She was completing a rigorous accelerated programme and would start university in several months. She was happy in the programme. School hadn't challenged her at all when she was in elementary school so she was glad to be offered material that was at her level of understanding. But now she felt overwhelmed. University soon. What would that be like, really? She had a full scholarship to the Faculty of Science and had already checked out the best medical schools. For her to be a doctor – a specialist, preferably – had been her parents' dream ever since they immigrated to Canada from China when she was a baby. They were so proud of Amanda's academic success.

Of course, Amanda could fulfil her parents' dream but the thing was, she didn't really want to. What she really wanted, more and more, was to pursue her interest in art. She loved painting. Her parents opposed this plan. Artists are poor and certainly don't have the status that doctors enjoy. Amanda felt trapped. Her friends were making their own career decisions. She understood the traditions and beliefs that her parents held and didn't want to hurt them or let them down but a future of doing something she didn't have a passion for was beginning to scare her. Maybe she should take up her chemistry teacher's offer to talk. But then what?

- What do you know? (What information is evident in the scenario?)
- What are your preconceptions? For example, what ideas did your family convey to you about intelligence and education?
- What are the issues?
- What do you need to know and how will you find out?

Now, come back to identifying the 'problem'. What do you see as the key issue or question to address, and how do you plan to address it?

Figure 32.2 Reflection Activity 2: cultural perspectives on intelligence and success

exceptionality brought much-needed awareness to research and special education practice in both giftedness and learning disabilities, and highlighted the extent of the issue. In British Columbia, Canada, the number of postsecondary students formally diagnosed with a learning disability (usually during primary or secondary school) increased by 74 percent from 1996 to 2000 (Pacheva 2007); about a third of these students may be gifted (Baum, cited in Brody and Mills 1997). Research is still sparse and many educators in primary, secondary, and tertiary education struggle to understand why otherwise intelligent students are challenged in some areas of their learning. At best, educators try to follow the strategies recommended in the literature of teaching to strengths and using complex material (Brody and Mills 1997; Coleman 2005) but there is little research on best practices to guide them. At worst, these students are assumed to be lazy, unmotivated, and/or obstructive (Brody and Mills 1997) and consequently receive little or no support. The problem is complicated by the many ways in which one's learning can be considered disabled (e.g. dyslexia, written output problems, language processing) (Swanson 1991). However, we can learn a lot from the students themselves about the complexity of their learning. Students who are both gifted and learning disabled can effectively monitor and evaluate their own learning (Hannah and Shore 1995, 2008) and articulate highly perceptive observations about how they learn best (Porath and Lupart 2009).

In Reflection Activity 3 (see Figure 32.3), you meet Nolan, a child with a complex learning profile. Think about how Nolan's learning and well-being can be supported at school.

Reflection Activity 3

Ashley Talbot struggled to control her emotions. For the last month, ever since the new school year started, her son Nolan had come home in tears.

'I can't do it, Mom. I can't read! And there's so much to read. I'm stupid.'

Whereas previously Nolan had always been willing to sit with her in the evenings, reading storybooks and trying to learn rules that would help him read, he now refused. He retreated to his bedroom and spent hours gazing at stars through his telescope.

Ashley had heard so many things – slow to start reading but don't worry, he'll catch up; maybe it's dyslexia; just needs to try harder. Working with his teachers over the past three years, she had managed to keep Nolan's confidence up by reading out loud to him to help with projects, answering his many questions, and encouraging his exceptional drawing ability. That ability and his phenomenal knowledge of astronomy convinced her that Nolan was a gifted child who also happened to have a reading problem. Nolan's father agreed. He and Nolan often went out to gaze at the night sky and talk about constellations, planets, and orbits. Nolan's father was afraid he had reached the limits of his knowledge of astronomy and would soon be unable to answer Nolan's questions.

'He's tapped me out, Ashley. I think we have an astronomer here.'

Ashley arranged an appointment with Nolan's teacher. She described what he was capable of and asked if there were some way they could work together to allow Nolan to use visual presentations of information in place of some of the required reading and perhaps use his interests and strengths to help him with reading. Ms Davis was hesitant. She wasn't convinced that giftedness and reading problems could coexist and she already felt overwhelmed by the special learning needs in her class.

'But he's struggling so much', Ashley said. 'I'm very worried about him. He's so unhappy. I'm offering to help with this. Where can I turn?'

- What do you know?
- What are your preconceptions?
- What are the issues?
- What do you need to know and how will you find out?

Now, come back to identifying the 'problem'. What do you see as the key issue or question to address, and how do you plan to address it?

Figure 32.3 Reflection Activity 3: supporting students with dual exceptionality

In working with the scenarios in this chapter, you have engaged in problem-based learning (PBL) (Jordan and Porath 2006; Plucker and Barab 2005). This is one of the educational strategies believed to contribute to 'smart contexts' (Barab and Plucker 2002) that facilitate learners' interactions with educational environments in ways that allow them to demonstrate their interests and abilities, and that replicate what happens in the 'real world'. It is also important that educational environments include learning activities that start with students' questions and interests, uniting these questions and interests with the formal knowledge of the culture (Bruner 1996). Educators need to be passionately curious about how students learn and what their questions are. This leads to the design of educational environments that, in turn, foster students' curiosity and lead to learning pathways that optimize gifted learners' potential.

Contact address: marion.porath@ubc.ca

References

Bamberger, J. (1991) *The mind behind the musical ear: how children develop musical intelligence*, Cambridge, MA: Harvard University Press.

Barab, S. A., and Plucker, J. (2002) 'Smart people or smart contexts? Talent development in an age of situated approaches to learning and thinking', *Educational Psychologist*, 37: 165–182.

Borland, J. H. (2003) *Rethinking gifted education*, New York: Teachers College Press.

Bransford, J. D., Brown, A. L., and Cocking, R. R. (eds.) (2000) *How people learn: brain, mind, experience, and school*, Washington, DC: National Academy Press.

Brody, L., and Mills, C. (1997) 'Gifted children with learning disabilities: a review of the issues', *Journal of Learning Disabilities*, 30: 282–296.

Bruner, J. (1996) *The culture of education*, Cambridge, MA: Harvard University Press.

Cartier, S. C., Butler, D. L., and Bouchard, N. (2010) 'Teachers working together to foster self-regulated learning through reading by students in an elementary school in a disadvantaged area', *Psychological Test and Assessment Modeling*, 52: 382–418.

Claxton, G., and Meadows, S. (2009) 'Brightening up: how children learn to be gifted', in T. Balchin, B. Hymer, and D. J. Matthews (eds.) *The Routledge international companion to gifted education*, New York: Routledge (pp. 3–9).

Coleman, M. R. (2005) 'Academic strategies that work for gifted students with learning disabilities', *Teaching Exceptional Children*, 38: 28–32.

Donovan, M. S., and Bransford, J. D. (eds.) (2005) *How students learn: history, mathematics, and science in the classroom*, Washington, DC: National Academies Press.

Dweck, C. S. (2006) *Mindset: the new psychology of success*, New York: Random House.

Dweck, C. S. (2009) 'Foreword', in F. D. Horowitz, R. F. Subotnik, and D. J. Matthews (eds.) *The development of giftedness and talent across the life span*, Washington, DC: American Psychological Association. (pp. xi–xiv).

Ericsson, K. A., Nandagopal, K., and Roring, R. W. (2006) 'Giftedness viewed from the expert-performance perspective', *Journal for the Education of the Gifted*, 28: 287–311.

Foster, J., Porath, M., and Smyth, E. (2009) 'Canada: gifted education', in B. Kerr (ed.) *Encyclopedia of giftedness, creativity, and talent*, Thousand Oaks, CA: Sage (pp. 113–116).

Gardner, H. (1983) *Frames of mind: the theory of multiple intelligence*, New York: Basic Books.

Goleman, D. (1995) *Emotional intelligence*, New York: Bantam Books.

Gould, S. J. (1981) *The mismeasure of man*, New York: W. W. Norton.

Hannah, C. L., and Shore, B. M. (1995) 'Metacognition and high intellectual ability: insights from the study of learning-disabled gifted students', *Gifted Child Quarterly*, 39: 95–109.

Hannah, C. L., and Shore, B. M. (2008) 'Twice-exceptional students' use of metacognitive skills on a comprehension monitoring task', *Gifted Child Quarterly*, 52: 3–18.

Hollingworth, L. S. (1942) *Children above 180 IQ Stanford-Binet: origin and development*, Ann Arbor, MI: World Book.

Horowitz, F. D., Subotnik, R. F., and Matthews, D. J. (eds.) (2009) *The development of giftedness and talent across the life span*, Washington, DC: American Psychological Association.

Hymer, B. J. (2009) 'Beyond compare? Thoughts towards an inclusional, fluid and non-normative understanding of giftedness', in T. Balchin, B. Hymer, and D. J. Matthews (eds.) *The Routledge international companion to gifted education*, London: Routledge (pp. 299–307).

Hymer, B., Whitehead, J., and Huxtable, M. (2009) *Gifts, talents and education: a living theory approach*, Chichester, UK: Wiley-Blackwell.

Jackson, N. E. (2000) 'Strategies for modeling the development of giftedness in children', in R. C. Friedman and B. M. Shore (eds.) *Talents unfolding: cognition and development*, Washington, DC: American Psychological Association. (pp. 27–54).

Jordan, E. A., and Porath, M. J. (2006) *Educational psychology: a problem-based approach*, Boston, MA: Pearson Education.

Lai, Y. (2009) 'Reconsidering the education of gifted young children with the Reggio Emilia approach', *Exceptionality Education International*, 19: 96–110.

Matthews, D. J. (1997) 'Diversity in domains of development: research findings and their implications for gifted identification and programming', *Roeper Review*, 19: 172–177.

Matthews, D. J., and Foster, J. F. (2009) *Being smart about gifted education: a guidebook for educators and parents*, Scottsdale, AZ: Great Potential Press.

Ngara, C. (2009) 'The mbira metaphor: inspiring creative thinking through folktale', *Exceptionality Education International*, 19: 128–135.

Ngara, C., and Porath, M. (2004) 'Shona culture of Zimbabwe's views of giftedness', *High Ability Studies*, 15: 189–209.

Pacheva, D. (2007) *College students with learning disabilities: a developmental perspective on conceptions of learning, learning disability, and others in learning.* Unpublished PhD thesis, University of British Columbia, Canada.

Perry, N. E., Thauberger, C., and Hutchinson, L. (2010) 'gStudy traces of children's self-regulated learning in the Lifecycles Learning Kit', *Psychological Test and Assessment Modeling*, 52: 432–453.

Phillipson, S. N., and McCann, M. (eds.) (2007) *Conceptions of giftedness: sociocultural perspectives*, Mahwah, NJ: Lawrence Erlbaum Associates.

Plucker, J. A. (2001) 'Looking back, looking around, looking forward: the impact of intelligence theories on gifted education', *Roeper Review*, 23: 124–125.

Plucker, J. A., and Barab, S. A. (2005) 'The importance of contexts in theories of giftedness: learning to enhance the messy joys of subjectivity', in R. J. Sternberg and J. E. Davidson (eds.) *Conceptions of giftedness*, 2nd edn, New York: Cambridge University Press (pp. 201–216).

Porath, M. (2006) 'The conceptual underpinnings of giftedness: developmental and educational implications', *High Ability Studies*, 17: 145–157.

Porath, M., and Lupart, J. (2009) 'Gifted children's representations of learner identities', *Exceptionality Education International*, 19: 80–95.

Porath, M., Lupart, J., Katz, J., Ngara, C., and Richardson, P. (2009) 'Gifted learners' epistemological beliefs', *Talent Development and Excellence*, 1: 57–66.

Porath, M., Ngara, C., Lai, Y., Fogel, K., and Lupart, J. (2010) 'Children's understanding of teaching: a component of self-regulation?', *Psychological Test and Assessment Modeling*, 52: 454–471.

Robinson, N. M., Zigler, E., and Gallagher, J. J. (2000) 'Two tails of the normal curve: similarities and differences in the study of mental retardation and giftedness', *American Psychologist*, 55: 1413–1424.

Shayer, M. (2008) 'Intelligence for education: as described by Piaget and measured by psychometrics', *British Journal of Educational Psychology*, 78: 1–29.

Statistics Canada (2011) [online]. Available at www.statcan.gc.ca/tables-tableaux/sum-som/z01/cs0007-eng.htm

Sternberg, R. J. (1985) *Beyond IQ: a triarchic theory of human intelligence*, New York: Cambridge University Press.

Sternberg, R. J., and Grigorenko, E. L. (2004) 'Why cultural psychology is necessary and not just nice: the example of the study of intelligence', in R. J. Sternberg and E. L. Grigorenko (eds.) *Culture and competence: contexts of life success*, Washington, DC: American Psychological Association (pp. 207–223).

Swanson, H. L. (1991) 'Operational definitions and learning disabilities: an overview', *Learning Disabilities Quarterly*, 14: 242–254.

Terman, L. M. (1926) *Genetic studies of genius, Volume 1*, Stanford, CA: Stanford University Press.

Terman, L. M., Lyman, G., Ordahl, G., Ordahl, L., Galbreath, N., and Talbert, W. (1915) 'The Stanford revision of the Binet-Simon scale and some results from its application to 1000 non-selected children', *Journal of Educational Psychology*, 6: 551–562.

Winner, E. (2009) 'Toward broadening our understanding of giftedness: the spatial domain', in F. D. Horowitz, R. F. Subotnik, and D. J. Matthews (eds.) *The development of giftedness and talent across the life span*, Washington, DC: American Psychological Association (pp. 75–85).

Ziegler, A. (2005) 'The actiotope model of giftedness', in R. J. Sternberg and J. E. Davidson (eds.) *Conceptions of giftedness*, 2nd edn, New York: Cambridge University Press (pp. 411–436).

INDEX

Locators to figures and tables are in *italics*

ability groups 242
'abnormality' 217
aboriginal peoples 110–11, 193
absolutism 97
abstract reasoning 46
academic performance: ADHD 287, 292;
   psychometric testing 23; resilient children 133;
   stress 130, 131–2, 133 *see also* assessments; IQ
   tests
access 32, 249, 253, 254
accommodations 46, 172–8, 227, 229, 231, 233 *see
   also* inclusive education
accountability 25–6, 28, 154
'accountable talk' 69
achievement motivation 113
achievement tests 155–6, 158, 169
acquired dyslexia 297
active learning 46–7
active responding systems 148
acute stress 129
adaptive behaviour *109, 116*
adaptive cognition *109, 116*
'additive' self-system models 105
ADHD (attention deficit hyperactivity disorder)
   136, 206, 282, 286–94, 310
adults: acquisition of scientific models 94–5; as
   attachment figures 118–19; and children
   relations 17; child support 49; reading to
   children 86–7
advance organizers 5–6
Africa 184
aggressive behaviour 45, 136
Ainsworth, Mary 119
Albania 33
Alexander, R. 66, 67, 68

Alhazen, Ibn al-Haytham 6
alphabetic languages 73, 76, 302–3
Altmaier, E. 28
Amanda (student) *333*
America *see* USA
American Academy of Pediatrics (AAP) 269
American Foundation for the Blind (AFB) 248
American Psychiatric Association (APA): DSM-IV
   160, 206, 215, 269, 286, 309, 317; DSM-5 297,
   298
American Psychological Association 195–6
Amsel, E. 96
analytical intelligence 196
angular gyrus (AG) 320
animations 85–6, 88
Annan, J. 34
Annual Schools Census (England and Wales) 248
'anti-psychiatry movement' 214
anxiety disorders 112, 276, 288
applied behavioural analysis (ABA) 44, 272
applied psychologists 25, 26, 34
Arabic dyscalculia 322
Aram, D. 78
Archwamety, T. 36
'argumentation' 69
Ariel (Canada) 230
Aristotle 6, 43
Arthur's Birthday (Brown) 85
Arthur's Teacher Trouble (Brown) 86
articulation disorders 257–8
ASDs (Autism spectrum disorders) 265–73, 332
Asia 110–11, 113
Asperger, Hans 265–6
Asperger's disorder 219, 240, 267–8, 272–3,
   310

assessments: classroom 143–52; diagnostic 154–61; dyslexia 303–4; educational 35, 36, 249–50, 280–2; and educational psychologists 22–3; external 163, 166, 167–8; language 172–8; learner's potential 48–9; policy and practice 162–70; SEBD 280–2; training 250 *see also* academic performance; IQ tests; tests

'assimilation' 46

assisted performance, teaching as 49

Association of Educational Psychologists (AEP) 27

associative learning 44, 45, 197, 302

astigmatism 247

at-risk children 57, 87, 206

attachment theory 118–19, 120

attention deficit hyperactivity disorder (ADHD) 136, 206, 282, 286–94, 310

attention levels 88, 135, 276

attribution theory 105–6, 110

Audage, N. C. 132

auditory processing deficits 261

auditory stimuli 250–1

Audrey (Scotland) 227, 231

Australia 35, 59, 110–11, 167, 193, 294

Ausubel, David P. 3, 5

authentic assessments 7, 149, 154

Autism 207–8, 310

Autism Diagnostic Interview-Revised (ADI-R) 270–1

Autism Diagnostic Observation Schedule (ADOS) 270

Autism spectrum disorders (ASDs) 265–73, 332

autonomic endocrine system *128*

autonomic nervous system (ANS) 128

Babette (Canada) 227

Baddeley, A. D. 261

Bandura, Albert 45, 105

Barkley, Russell 290

Barnes, D. 65, 68, 69

Baroody, A. J. 319

Bauman, M. 266

Beach, D. 198

behaviour: aggressive 45, 136; and brain activity 205; classrooms 45, 60; deviant 277; learnt associations 7, 43–4; social skills programmes 45; and stress 134–5

behavioural characteristics: Asperger's disorder 267–8; autism 207, 266–7; developmental disabilities 205; SEBD 275

behavioural difficulties, students with 59

behavioural disorders 308, 310–11, 321

behavioural functioning 276

behavioural genetics 277, 300

behavioural inhibition system (BIS) 290

behavioural interventions 282

behavioural performance 207

behavioural training 279

behaviourism 43–5, 50, 54, 118

behaviour management 53–4, 55, 292, 294

Bell, R. Q. 118

'below average intelligence' 218, 219

Belsky, J. 122

Benavot, A. 167

Bennett, E. 121

Ben (teacher) 331

Bernberg, J. G. 219

'best fit' assessments 160

Beveridge, M. 25

Bialystok, E. 77

Bierman, K. L. 176

bilingual children 75, 77–8, 87–8, 174–5 *see also* language acquisition; monolingual children; multilingual children

Binet, Alfred 192

Binet Intelligence Scale 192

biological determinism 277

biopsychosocial approaches, to SEBD 277, 278–80, *279*

births, premature 134

Bishop, D. 261

Black-Hawkins, K. 242

blindness *see* sensory impairments; visual impairments

Blomert, Leo 302

bodily kinaesthetic intelligence 195

Bodkin-Andrews, G. 110–11

Book of Optics (Alhazen) 6

boredom stress 132, *133*

Borgers. N. 176

Bowen, C. 257

Bowers, P. G. 300

Bowlby, J. 119

Boyle, C. 25, 28, 216, 217, 256

Bracken, B. A. 38

Brackenreed, D. 57

Bragg, S. 16, 17

brain activity: ADHD 289; and behaviour 205; mathematics-based tasks 320; prediction studies 207–8; and stress 127, 128–9; task performance 203–4 *see also* neuroimaging

brain-based educational products *209*

brain volume 198

Brenda (Scotland) 229

Brewer, W. F. 93–4, 96, 99

Bridgeman, B. 177

British Ability Scales II 160

British Columbia 333

British Picture Vocabulary Scales II 160

British Psychological Society (BPS) 236

Bronfenbrenner, Urie 118

Brown, Marc Tolon 85, 86

Brown v. School Board of Education (USA) 183

Bruininks-Oseretsky test 309

Bruner, Jerome 47, 49

Buchanan, A. 122
Buchanan, I. 14
Bullock, M. 97
bullying 15, 54, 134, 240
Bunch, G. 57
Burden, R. 25
Burt, Cyril 22, 28
Bus, A. G. 83, 87
Butterworth, B. 208
Butterworth test 322
Byrne, B. 54

Cable, N. 248
Cambridge Primary Review 167, 168
Cameron, R. J. 24, 26
Canada 54, 56–7, 59, 167, 225–33, 332
Candi (Canada) 231–2
caption statement *151*
Carey, S. 96, 97
Carrico, M. F. 177
Carrillo, J. 133
casework 28, 37–8, 38
catecholamines 128–9
categorical disorders 299–300
categorization 214, 328
Cattell, R. B. 192
'causal explanatory' language 121
CD-ROM reading sessions 85
cerebral palsy 228
cerebral visual impairment/dysfunction 247
'challenging behaviour' 276
Chandler, M. J. 118
Chan, J. 194
Checklist for Autism in Toddlers (CHAT) 271
Cheng, C. 77
Chen, S.-W. 77
Child and Adolescent Mental Health teams
    (CAMHS) 23–4
child development 12, 118–20, 122–3
childhood apraxia of speech 311
children 239; acquisition of scientific models 94–5;
    as active learners 46; and computers 84–5;
    consulting 16, 239–40; family relationships
    117–24; as gifted learners 328; labelling 206,
    214; multiple disabilities 248; perception of
    disability 240; psychologist ratios 33; resilient
    133; response to teaching 48–9; stress 127–37;
    visually impaired 247–8 *see also* parents
Children's Act 1989 (England and Wales) 13
Children's Act 2004 (England and Wales) 13
Children's Research Centre (OU) 18
children's rights 12–19, *13*, 239
Children's Rights Alliance England (CRAE) 14
Chinese language 74, 75, 76–7, 78
Chinese students 110, 191, 193, 194, 303
Chinn, C. A. 99
Chinn, P. C. 186

Chinn, S. J. 323
Chittister, J. 184
Chomsky, Noam 259
'chronosystem' 120
classical conditioning 43
classical test theory 157, 158
classroom assessments 143–52, 154, 178, 294
classroom dialogues 49–50, 64, 66, 68–9
classrooms 45, 54–6, 230, 241–2, 252
Claxton, G. 63
Clay, Marie 160
Clemens, S. G. 137
Climbie, Victoria 23
clinical interviews 92–3
clumsy child syndrome 307
cognitive abilities 23, 129, 194–5, 208, 250
Cognitive Ability Test (England) 242
cognitive behavioural approaches (CB) 53, 282
cognitive deficits 280
cognitive development 46–7, 120–1, 131, 134, 257,
    259
cognitive disorders 276
cognitive profiles 214
cognitive theories 260–2
coherent knowledge 66
collaborative activities 59, 100–1
'collaborative reasoning' 69
collaborative support services 23–4
collectivist cultures 110, 113
Coltheart, M. 300
common knowledge 66
communication disorders *see* language disorders;
    speech disorders
communities of practice 49–50
comorbidity disorders 287–8, 309–11, 312
comparative organizers 5
compensatory skills 279
competence 12, 105, 111, 332
compound words 76
comprehension skills 83–4, 85, 87, 88–9, 303 *see
    also* reasoning capabilities
Comprehensive Mathematical Abilities Test
    (CMAT) 322
compulsive ritualistic routines 267
computed tomography scans (CT) 198
computer-assisted instruction (CAI) 292
computerized axial tomography scan (CAT) 204
computers 84–6, 267
concentration 135
conceptual frameworks 323, 332
concrete operations 8
conduct disorders (CD) 276, 282, 288
connective instruction 112
Connell, J. P. 106
Connor, M. 218
consistent languages 302–3
constructivism 45–6, 48, 51

'contingent instruction' 49, 67
Cooper, P. 293
Copeland, I. 238
coping strategies 135, 137
cortical development 288
cortical visual impairment (CVI) 247
cosmology 93–4, 96
Crago, M. 259
Craven, R. G. 110–11
creative intelligence 196
criterion-referenced assessments 164
Crook, C. 66
cross-cultural motivation 110–11
crystallized intelligence (Gc) 192, 197
cued-elicitation 65
culturally and linguistically diverse individuals
    (CLD) 182, 183
cultures: cosmology 93–4; and dyscalculia 322; and
    intelligence 193–4, 332, *333*; motivation
    110–11; and stress *131*, 135
cumulative talk 50, 69
curricula 131, 167, 241, 252–4
curriculum-based assessment (CBA) 145–7, 164
curriculum-based measurement (CBM) 145
cyberbullying 15 *see also* bullying

Dacey, J. S. 135
Dale, N. 250
Dandridge, H. 18
Daniels, H. 63
Da Vinci, Leonardo 298
deaf pupils 240, 241
Deault, L. 54
debates 69–70
DeBord, K. 130
declarative memory system 261
deductive reasoning 5
deep learning 331–2
'deficit' models 22, 28, 34
'deficits,' labelling 217
Dehaene, S. 321
Dejerine, Joseph Jules 205
delay aversion 290
delinquency 219, 278
demographics 33
Denmark 21
depersonalised test questions 176
depressive disorders 276, 282, 288
deprive dyslexic learners 301
determinism 242, 276–7
developed countries 14, 181
developing countries 181, 248
developmental advancement 329
developmental coordination disorder (DCD)
    307–8, 309
developmental disabilities 23, 205
developmental dyscalculia 317

developmental dyslexia 297
developmental dyspraxia *see* dyspraxia
developmental psychopathology 120
'developmental surveillance' 23
developmental verbal dyspraxia (DVD) 257,
    311–13, *312 see also* speech disorders
deviant behaviour 277
Devine, A. 95
Dewey, J. 181, 182, 188
*Diagnostic and Statistical Manual of Mental Disorders,
    4th Edition* (DSM-IV): ADHD 206, 286; Autism
    spectrum disorders (ASDs) 269; dyscalculia 317;
    dyspraxia 309; labels 217; 'mental retardation'
    215
*Diagnostic and Statistical Manual of Mental Disorders
    draft 5th Edition* (DSM-5), dyslexia 297, 298
diagnostic assessments 154–61; ASDs 207, 269–70;
    dyscalculia 322; dyslexia 299; dyspraxia 311;
    stress 136
diagnostic labels 206, 227–8
dialogic teaching 64, 67–8
Dialogue and the Development of Children's Thinking
    (Mercer and Littleton) 64
Diana Award 15
diet 273
digital technology 83–9, 144
Dinnel, D. 6
disability, social model 17, 238–9
disability-specific pedagogies 55, 252, 279, 293–4
disabled education 56, 59, 225–33, 227–8, 238–9
    see also education; inclusive education; special
    education
disabled women, study of 229–32
discovery, learning by 47
discrete trial training (DTT) 272
discrimination 14, 183, 230
discussions *see* group dialogue
disordered social responsiveness *see* autism
disputational talk 50, 69
distancing strategy 135
distress 132, *132, 133*
Doctorate in Educational and Child Psychology
    (University of East London) 25
Doedel en het rode gevaar (Taylor) 84
Dolly (Canada) 232
Don't Stick It, Stop it! (Mencap) 15
Douglas, G. 252, 254
Driver, R. 97
drug treatments 279, 291–2
D'Souza, D. 185
dual coding model 88
dual exceptionality 332–3, *334*
Dudley and the Strawberry Shake (Taylor) 84
Duhaney, L. M., 215–16
Dunbar, K. 92, 97, 100
Dutch language 88
Dweck, C. S. 329

Dylan (student) *331*
dynamic assessments 48–9, 160
dyscalculia 317–24 *see also* learning disabilities (LD); mathematics
dyslexia 74, 205, 215, 217–18, 297–314 *see also* reading abilities
dyspraxia 257, 258, 307–14 *see also* learning disabilities (LD)

early life stress 127
early reading development 73–5, 83–9, 206 *see also* literacy
Early Support Developmental Journal 250
Earth, the, perceptions of 93–4
Ebbels, S. H. 262
'Ecology of the family as a context for human development: research perspectives' (Bronfenbrenner) 120
ecosystemic model 54, 57, 59–60
Edison, Thomas 298
education: access to 56, 254; and brain development 203; continuum of 237, 249; parental influences 121–2; rights to *13*, 14, 17; student participation 330, 332 *see also* disabled education; inclusive education; learning; mainstream education; schools
Education Act 1970 (England & Wales) 17
Education Act 2002 (England & Wales) 16
educational assessments 35, 36, 249–50, 280–2
educational contexts *331*
educational dialogues 59, 63–70
educational labels 206–7
educational outcomes 54, 241
educational psychologists 4–5; as expert witnesses 27; global coverage 21, 31–9; and intelligence tests 22, 23, 197–8; licensing 35; role 27, 36, 38–9, 237; training 26 *see also* 'gatekeepers'; psychologists
Educational psychologists: the early search for an identity (Love) 26
educational psychology 3–10, 21–8, 31–9
Educational Psychology: A Century of Contributions (Zimmerman and Schink) 4–5
Educational Psychology Service (EPS) 23, 25, 26, 27, 35
educational research 25–6, 239–41
Education and Science Acts (UK) 24
education authorities (England) 237
Education for All (EFA) 56
Education for All Handicapped Pupils Act (USA) 235
education neuroscience 202–9
Edwards, D. 65
effective classrooms 54–6
effective educational dialogue 64
effective teaching practices 48–9, 53–60
efficacy studies 241–2

Einstein, Albert 298
electroencephalography (EEG) 204
electromagnetic processes 204
Elise (Scotland) 228
Elizur, D. 110
emergent literacy *see* early reading development
emotional and behavioural difficulties (EBDs) 57, 237, *238*
emotional development 133, 136–7
emotional expression 121, 269
emotional intelligence (EQ) 195
emotional literacy 279
emotion-focused coping 135
endocrine system 128, *128*
Engelmann, W. 156
England: Annual Schools Census 248; assessments 163, 167–9; children's rights 18–19; Children's Services teams 23–4; Cognitive Ability Test 242; Department for Children, Schools and Families (DCSF) 27; Department for Education and Skills (DfES) 23; Department for Education (DfE) 23, 166; league tables 166, 167; legislation 13, 14, 235–6; Ofsted 16; political influence 170; qualifications 25, 26, 34–5; right to education 14; terminology 276
English language: Chinese learning 77–8; dyscalculia screening tools 322; French bilinguals 78; and SLI 260, 261; spellings 75–6, 302–3
environmental demand 133, *134*
environmental factors 193, 277–8, 279, 289, 293
environmental stressors *131*
Eodanable, M. 26
epistemology 6
'equifinality' 205
'equilibration' 46
Erten, O. 17
escape–avoidance strategies 135
essentialism 239
ethnic divisions 183
Eudaly, C. 232
eugenic theory 277
European Union (EU) 34
eustress 130–1, *132*
event-related potential (ERP) 204, 207, 208
Every Child Matters (ECM) (DfES) 13–14, 15, 23, 24
'exceptional' students 57, 327–34
exclusion 14, 17, 183, 225
executive functions 207, 287, 288
'existential intelligence' 195
'exosystem,' of child relationships 120
expectancy-value theory 105
experimentation 97–8, *99*
expert witnesses 27
Exploratory Talk 50, 55, 68–70
expository organizers 5

extended optional infinitive stage (EOI) 260
external assessments 163, 166, 167–8 *see also* assessments
external resources 133, *134*, 135
external stressors 129, 130
extrinsic motivation 106–7
eye contact 267, 268, 269

facial expressions 268
failure, responses to 105, 112
Fallon, K. 23, 24, 27
families 130, 133–4, 206, 300, 319 *see also* genetic influences; out-of-school learning
family relationships 117–24
fathers 121–2, 123
Ferguson, C. J. 157
Fielding, M. 17
fine motor behaviours 135
Finland 21, 303
Fiore, L. B. 135
first language learners 87, 174
Flanagan, N. M. 248
flat-earth cosmology 96
flexible reasoning 192
Florian, L. 242
Flouri, E. 122
'fluency' disorders 257, 288
'fluid intelligence' (Gf) 192
force, and motion 94–6
Ford, B. A. 186
formal operations 8–9
formative assessments 55, 144, 160, 165, 166, 169–70
Foster, J. F. 329, 332
Fox, M. 24
fractions, learning progress 143, 146
France 21
friends 133–4
Frith, U. 299–300
Frog is Frightened (Velthuijs) 84
Fugelsang, J. 92, 100
functional behavioural analysis (FBA) 282–3
functional magnetic resonance imaging (fMRI) 203–4, 207, 302
'functional vision' *see* visual impairment
funding 37, 216

Gallagher, A. 299–300
Gallimore, R. 49
Galton, F. 191
games 85, 86, 87, 121
Gardner, Howard 194–5, 197
Garrett, Z. 262
gastrointestinal disorders 273
'gatekeepers' 14, 22, 27, 215, 237 *see also* educational psychologists
gaze avoidance 267, 268, 269

gender 18, 33, 287
general education services 56
general intelligence ('g') 192, 197, 217
generalizability theory 157, 158
genetic determinism 54
genetic influences: ADHD 289; biological systems 279; developmental psychopathology 120; dyscalculia 319, dyslexia 299–300, 301; dyspraxia 308–9 *see also* families; heritability
Genetic Studies of Genius (Terman) 191
Georgia 33
Germany 21, 303
Gervai, J. 120
Geschwind, Norman 205
Getting It Right for Every Child: Proposals for Action (Scottish Executive) 13
Gibb, C. 32
gifted learners 57, 327–34
Ginsburg, H. P. 319
Glaser, R. 98
Gleason, J. B. 122
globalisation 332
Glover, J. A. 6
glucocorticoid receptors (GC) 129
goal theory 55, 106, 110, 111
Goffman, Erving 213
Goleman, D. 195
Gollnick, D. M. 186
Good Behaviour Game 282
Gopnik, M. 259
Goswami, U. 74
Gottfredson, L. 196–7
Gough, P. B. 303
Gould, J. 266
'Grain Size Theory' (Ziegler and Goswami) 74
grammar 259–62
grandparents 122–3
Granzin, A. 156
Greek 303
Griggs, Julia 123
Gross, T. 137
group dialogues 50, 64, 68–9
group work 68–9, 242
guidance 165–6
guilt, as stressor 130
Gunstone, R. F. 93

Haier, R. J. 198
Hall, J. 28
handwriting 173–4, 313
Hanley, J. R. 77
Hardman, M. 237
hard work, and achievement 110
Hariharan, M. 131
Harris, N. 14, 16
Harrison, L. 14
Harter, S. 106

Hau, K.-T. 110
health-care sector 23
Health Professions Council (HPC) 26, 35
hearing impairments 240, 241, 261
Heath, N. L. 57
Hebrew 75, 261
hemispherectomies 207
Henry, L. C. 262
Hereditary Genius (Galton) 191
heritability 191, 299–300 *see also* genetic influences
Hesketh, J. 130
Het Spectrum Electronic Publishing 86
hierarchical pupil power structures 17
high stakes assessments 166–7, 169
Hill, A. E. 248
Hill, E. L. 311
hippocampus 129
Ho, C. S.-H. 75
Hollingworth, L. S. 328
home 69–70, 120–1, 130, 134, 174
homework 18, 130, 330
homophones 76–7
Hong Kong 59, 75, 110
Hoover, W. A. 303
hormones, reaction to stress 128
Horn, J. L. 192
hotspots, and digital stories 85–7
House of Commons Select Committee, report on Special Educational Needs (2009) 27
Howe, C. J. 94, 95, 98
Huang, H. S. 77
Hughes, M. 120
human rights 14, 187, 225
hyperactivity disorder 276
hyperkinetic disorders 276
hypothalamus 128, *128*
hypothetico-deductive reasoning 9

Ibn al-Haytham Alhazen 6
identification approach, at-risk students 206
identity, and disability 240, 241
Ik Maak Je Weer Beter, Zei the Beer (I'll Make You Well, Tiger, Said the Bear) 86
Ikospentaki, K. 94
illness, and stress 135
immersive research methodology 242
immigrant children 174
impaired phonemic awareness 74
'impairment,' labelling 256
implausible theories 99–100
improvement, guidance to 165–6
'improvisational' accomplishments 66
incidental learning 250
in-class assessments 143–52, 154, 178, 294
inclusive education 56–9, 225, 227, 235–43 *see also* accommodations; disabled education; education; mainstream education; special education

inconsistent languages 302–3
Independent Review of Key Stage 2 testing, assessment and accountability: Final Report (DfE) 166
independent thinking 122
Indian children 93, 130, 135
indigenous peoples 110–11, 193
individual assessments 238
individuality 54, 110
Individuals with Disabilities Education Act 1975 (IDEA) (USA) 235, 317
Individuals with Disabilities Education Improvement Act 2004 (IDEIA) (USA) 156
inductive reasoning 5
'ineducable' children 17
inequalities 183
infants 119, 206
inferiority 130, 277
information 84, 251, 308
Inhelder, B. 97, *98*
initiation-response-feedback exchanges (IRF) 65–6
insecure infant interactions 119–20
Institute of Education (London) 169
instructional diagnosis 156
instructional dialogue 66
instructional rubrics 150–2
integrated approaches, to teaching 55
integrated children's services 24
intellectual capacity 216, 226, 319, 328
intellectual development 46
intellectual functioning 289, 309
intelligence 191–9, 299, 329, 332 *see also* IQ tests
intelligent students *see* gifted learners
'intensive instruction' 242–3
interactive stories 84–9
'intermental' activities 63
internalized problems 278
internal stress 130
International Classification of Diseases (ICD) 160
International Dyslexia Association (IDA) 297–8
International School Psychology Survey (ISPS) 31–9
Internet, the 84
interpersonal intelligence 195
interpersonal relationships 112, 129
'interpretative-meaning' research 25
'interthinking' 55, 69
interventionist beliefs (INT) 17, 58
interventions: dyscalculia 323–4; dyspraxia 313; SEBD 282–3; SLI 262; stress 135–6
'intramental' capabilities 63
intraparietal sulcus (IPS) 320
intrapersonal intelligence 195
intrinsic motivation 106–7
introvert children 134, 136–7
iPads 84–5

IQ tests: ADHD 287; dyscalculia 321; dyslexia 299; gifted learners 328–9; labelling 216; multiple intelligences 194–5, 197–8; scores 157–8; standardized tests 192–3 *see also* academic performance; assessments; intelligence
irregular words 300
isolation 136, 328
Israel 78, 87
Italy 21, 35, 237
item response theory 157

Jackson, A. J. 248
James, William 6, 7, 9, 21
Japan 167
jealousy, as stressor 130
Jimerson, Shane R. 21, 31, 32, 33, 35
Johnson, Goodluck 184
Jonsson, A. C. 198
Jordan, A. 58
Joyce (Scotland) 232
Jung, C. G. 117

Kamens, M. W. 58
Kamii, Constance 46
Kanner, Leo 213, 265–6
Kauffman, J. M. 59
Kelly, N. 218, 219
Kemper, T. L. 266
Kemp, N. 177
Kenya 194
KeyMaths3 Diagnostic Assessment 159–60, 322
Kikker is bang (Velthuijs) 84
Kim (Scotland) 229, 231
King, S. 127
Klahr, D. 97
Klein, G. 38
knowledge: acquisition 5; cognitive learning 47; construction of 46, 48, 63, 66–7; recalled 65–6; theory of 6
Knox, A. B. 197
Koerber, S. 97
Korat, O. 87
Korea 76–7, 167
Koslowski, B. 99
Kovas, Y. 299
Krohn, M. D. 219
Kuhn, D. 96, 97
Kuhn, M. R. 86, 87
Kunhardt, Dorothy 84–5
Kuwait 322

Labbo, L. D. 86, 87
labelling 213–20, 256, 277–8, 280, 293
LaBounty, J. 121
Ladson-Billings, G. 183
Laing, R. D. 214
Lalvani, P. 226

Lamb Inquiry (DCSF) 27
language: assessments 172–8; brain activity 207, 208; cultural tool 49, 63; developmental processes 251; educational dialogues 66; educational tool 70; inclusive education 241; parental influences 121; spelling and sound consistency 302–3 *see also* phonological awareness
language acquisition: Autism 267, 268, 270; child development 63; digital stories 87–8; SLI 259–60 *see also* bilingual children; monolingual children; multilingual children
language disorders 173–4, 256–63, 319
Laplante, D. P. 127
LAP mnemonic 143
Lauchlan, F. 25, 26, 28, 216, 217
Laurillard, D. 208
Lave, J. 50
Law, J. 262
Lazarus, R. S. 127
league tables 166, 167
Learned Helplessness Syndrome *134*
learning: accommodation 17, 173–4; brain activity 207; child-centred 8, 13; genetic effects on 54; motivation 104–13; by observation 45, 95, 96; and stress 129, 136; student participation 330, 332; theories of 5, 43–51; through experience 118–19; visually impaired 253 *see also* education
learning disabilities (LD): gifted learners 332–3; labelling 217; neuroscience 205 *see also* dyscalculia; dyspraxia; special education
learning journals 148
learnt associations 7, 44
Lemer, C. 320
Leonard, L. B. 261, 262
letter knowledge 73–5, 302
letter-sound mapping 74, 75, 300
Let Your Life Speak (Parker) 186
Levin, I. 78
Lewis, A. 252
Lewis, B. A. 312
lexical compounding 76, 77
lexical tone sensitivity 74–5
licensing 35
life experiences 22, 123
'life skills training' 230
Lin, D. 78
listening 13, 15
literacy 54–5, 73–9, 84–7, 310 *see also* early reading development; reading abilities
Littleton, K. 65
logical–mathematical intelligence 195
Lohman, D. F. 198
Lopez, Ms (teacher) 143, 145–6, 148
Loprete, S. J. 58
Loreman, Mr (teacher) 144, 149
Loreman, T. 59

Lovaas, Ole Ivar 272
Love, P. 26
Lovett, M. W. 300
low-incidence disabilities 239–40, 248
low vision *see* visual impairments
Lundy, L. 15
Luo community (Kenya) 194

'macrosystem,' of child relationships 120
magnetic resonance imaging (MRI) 203
mainstream education: deaf children 241; disabled
    children 230, 231, 237; and labelling 218;
    learning difficulties 17; special placements 241;
    visual impairment 249, 252 *see also* education;
    inclusive education; schools
maladaptive behaviour *109, 116*
maladaptive cognition *109, 116*
Mandarin Chinese 75, 77
Mandell, D. S. 214
Martin, A. J. 107, 110–11, 112, 116
mastery measurement (MM) 145–7, *146*
'mastery model,' of giftedness 329
mastery orientation 55, 106–7, 111, 112
maternal relationships 78, 121, 133
maternal stress 127
mathematics 46–7, 110, 143, 146, 193, 197 *see also*
    dyscalculia
mathematics disorder (MD) 317
mathematics learning disability (MLD) 317
Matthews, D. J. 329
McBride-Chang, C. 75, 76
McCall, S. 248, 251
McLesky, J. 242
McLinden, M. 248, 251, 252, 254
McLoyd, V. C. 134
meaningful verbal learning 5
measurement, diagnostic assessments 156–8
media, and interactive stories 84–5
medical model, of disability 17, 227, 237–8
medication 279, 291–2
memory 65, 66, 129, 261, 308 *see also* recall
'Memory' (Aristotle) 43
Mencap 15
mental illness, labelling 213–14
'mentally handicapped,' labelling 17
'mental retardation,' labelling 215
Mercer, Neil 49, 50, 64, 65, 66
'mesosystem,' child relationships 120
Messer, D. 262
meta-knowledge 47
metric stress awareness 74
'microsystem,' child relationships 120
Middlebrooks, J. S. 132
Middleton, D. 49
Midgley, C. 109
'mindfulness training' 282
mineralocorticoid receptor genes (MR) 120

minorities 14, 17, 174, 181, 184
misbehaviour 45
Mister Stay (Meneer Logeer) 85
mnemonics 143, 241
Mock, D. R. 59
Modified Checklist for Autism in Toddlers
    (M-CHAT) 271
Molfese, Ms (teacher) 143, 147, 148
Mol, S. E. 83
monolingual children 176 *see also* bilingual
    children; language acquisition; multilingual
    children
Monsen, J. 26
Montessori, Maria 9–10
Morgan, David 117
Moroccan children 88
morphological awareness 76–8
morphosyllabic languages 74
mother–child relationships 78, 121, 133
motion, and force 94–6
Motivated Strategies for Learning Questionnaire
    (MSLQ) 109
motivation: educational psychologists 36; for
    learning 44, 55, 104–13, *116*; for problem-
    solving 46; theoretical perspectives *108*; and
    vision 250
motivational orientation 330
Motivation and Engagement Scale – High School
    (MES-HS) 109, 110–11
Motivation and Engagement Scale (MES) 109,
    116
Motivation and Engagement Wheel 107, *109*, 110,
    111
motor behaviours 135, 313
motor skill development *see* dyspraxia
Movement Assessment Battery for Children
    309
multicultural education 181–8
multidimensional motivation 111
multidisciplinary teams 23, 24, 57
multilingual children 174–5 *see also* bilingual
    children; language acquisition; monolingual
    children
multimedia stories 85
multi-modal treatment model 290–1
multiple disabilities 248, 251
'multiple disabilities and visual impairment'
    (MDVI) 248, 249
Multiple Intelligences (MI) 195, 197
multiplication 323–4
multiplism 97
multisensory learning methods 323
multi-systemic interventions 36
multi-systemic therapy (MST) 278
Munns, G. 111
musical intelligence 195
myopia 247

Naglieri Nonverbal Ability Test 194
narrative therapy 24
Nash, G. 262
national differences, educational psychologists 36
National Institutes of Child Health and Human
    Development (NICHHD) 297, 298, 301
National Kids Poll (US) 130, 135
naturalistic based assessment 154
'naturalistic intelligence' 195
natural philosophers 6
'nature,' or 'nurture' 193
need achievement 105
negative descriptions 217, 218
Nepali children 93
nervous fine motor behaviours 135
neural risk markers 206, 207–8
neurobiology, of reading 205, 302
neuroconstructivism 205
neuroimaging 198, 203, 207, 302 *see also* brain
    activity
neurological dysfunctions 266–8, 279, 288–9, 308
'neuroprognosis' 207–8
neuropsychological profiles 136, 205
neuroscience 202–9
neutral stimuli 43
newborns, neural signatures 206
New Zealand 35, 167
Nguyen, D. 177
Nigeria 184
Nimetz, S. L. 121
Nolan (student) *334*
nominal levels of measurements 156
nonalphabetic languages 303
non-LD learners 323
non-normative experiences 123
non-verbal abilities 258, 269
non-verbal information 88
non-verbal learning disabilities (NVLD) 308, 321
nonverbal reasoning 194
nonverbal social cues 268
nonwords 300
'normalcy' 228
norm-referenced tests 164
Northern Ireland 13, 248, 276
Norway 18, 163, 167
Norwich, B. 215, 216, 217, 218, 219, 252
number sense *318*, 321, 322 *see also* dyscalculia
Number Stroop tasks *318*, 322
'nurture,' or 'nature' 193
nurture groups 279
Nussbaum, J. 93
Nye, C. 262

Oakland, T. D. 31
Obama, Barack 181, 188
objects, trajectories of falling 94–5, *95*
observational learning 45, 95, 96

observational teaching 147–8
observed variance, test scores 157
O'Connor, T. G. 117
ocular visual condition 247
Ofsted (England and Wales) 16
O'Loughlin, M. 96
Omansky, B. 228, 233
'10,000 hour rule' 330
on-task discussions 55
open discussions 68
Open University (OU) 18, 236
operant conditioning 44
oppositional defiance disorder (ODD) 276, 282,
    288
optimal learning 47
optimal stimulation 290
'optimum stress level' (OSL) 131–2, *133*
optional infinitive stage 260
oral presentations 173
oromotor dyspraxia 312
orthography-phonology mapping 74
Orton, Samuel 205
Ouellette, G. 75
Our Children and Young People – Our Pledge
    (Northern Ireland Executive) 13
out-of-school learning 69–70, 83–4 *see also*
    families
overt psychological practice 34

Paivio, A. 88
Panagiotaki, G. 94
parents 78, 117–23, 136, 293, 300 *see also* children
Parker, P. J. 186, 187
partially sighted *see* visual impairments
'participatory action research' (PAR) 239
partnerships, pupils working in 55
Pasquarella, A. 77
passive coping strategies 135
pathognomonic beliefs (PATH) 17, 58
Patrick, B. C. 106
Patsy (Canada) 232
Patterns of Adaptive Learning Survey (PALS) 109
Pat the Bunny (Kunhardt) 84–5
Paul, Korky 88–9
Pavlov, Ivan 43
P. B. Bear's Birthday Party *(P. B. Beer is Jarig)* 86, 87
pedagogies 55, 112, 242, 252, 279, 293–4
peer assessment 168
peer groups 68, 122, 130
Pellegrini, D. 24
pendulum problem 8
perceptual pattern problems 194
perceptuo-motor dysfunction 307
performance approaches 112
performance assessments 144, 149, 154
'performance orientation' 55
persistence 111

personal abilities 133, *134*
personal achievement tendencies 110
personal best goals (PB) 112
pervasive developmental disorder – not otherwise specified (PDD-NOS) 265, 268
phenomenon-based reasoning 97
phoneme awareness 301–2, 304
phonics screening 169
phonological awareness 73–7, 304 *see also* language
phonological disorders 257–8
phonological dyslexia 300, 301
phonological short-term memory (STM) 261
physical stressors *131*
Piaget, Jean: clinical interviews 92, 93; cognitive development tests 177; experimentation tests 97, *98*; formal operations 9; learner-centred education 7–8; social constructivism 46, 48
Pianta, R. C. 121
Picture Exchange Communication System (PECS) 267
picture storybooks 83–4
Piercy, M. 261
Pierpont, E. I. 261
Pinker, S. 261
Pintrich, P. R. 107, 109
Pinyin (phonological coding system) 75, 78
pituitary glands 128, *128*
placement preferences 237, *238*
Plato 328
plausible theories 99–100
play 121, 137, 269
Porath, M. 332
portfolio assessments 149–50
positive behaviour 45
positive psychology 28, 34
positive reinforcement 133, 272
positron emission tomography (PET) 204, 302
post traumatic stress disorder (PTSD) 38, 129
Powell, S. 55
power sharing 15
practical intelligence 196
practices, models of 34, 37
practitioner psychologists *see* applied psychologists
pragmatic discourse 240
PRAXIS I 160
pre-assessments 159
prediction studies, brain activity 207–8
pre-frontal cortex, and stress 129
pregnancy 289
preliterate children *see* early reading development
premature births 134
pre-natal stress 134
preschool children 78, 120–1, 165, 176
'presentational talk' 65
pre-service teachers 59
Pressley, M. 54
pre-unit diagnostic assessment 159

Priesler, G. 251
Priestley, A. 34
primary disabilities 248
primary education 14, 167
Principles of Psychology, The (James) 9
printed storybooks 85
private practices 27
Priyasha (pupil) 18
problem-based learning (PBL) 334
problem-focused coping 135
problem-solving 24–5, 46–7, 194
procedural memory system 261
Process of Education, The (Bruner) 47
'process-product' research 25
professional associations 35
profound and multiple learning disabilities (PMLD) 239
'programmed instruction' 44
progress monitoring 144, 145, 156
pronunciation 74
prosocial behaviour 45
psychiatric treatment 213, 214
psycho-educational assessments 35, 36, 207, 279
'psychological services' (Scotland) 25
psychological stressors *131*
psychological tools 63
psychologists: applied 25, 26, 34; child ratios 33; school 32, 214 *see also* educational psychologists
psychology 21, 39
psychometric testing 22–3, 36, 37–8, 216–17
psychosocial approaches 293
psychosocial stressors 133
psycho-stimulants 291
public education 183, 214, 230
'pull out' models 241
punishment 15, 18, 44
pupil consultation 15–16, 239
pupil-led research 18, 239–40
pupil-teacher relationships 16, 55

qualifications 25, 26, 34
qualified teacher of children with visual impairment (QTVI) 252
question-and-answer exchanges 65
questions, wording 176–7

race *see* multicultural education
race model (brain signals) 290
Rahi, J. S. 248
Rath, R. 131
Ravenscroft, J. 248
Raven's Progressive Matrices 194
'read-aloud' accommodation 173
reading abilities: assessments 144, 173; brain activity 205, 207, 208, 302; and families 206, 300; morphological awareness 76; phonological

awareness 74–5, 300, 301–2 *see also* dyslexia; literacy
reading comprehension 83–4, 174, 303
real-time assessments 147
reasoning capabilities 66, 69, 192, 193 *see also* comprehension skills
recall 65, 66, 129, 308 *see also* memory
recaps 66
'reciprocal teaching' 67
Rees, P. 36
Reflection Activities *331, 333, 334*
reflective teaching 281–2
registration 35
reinforcement 44, 272
Reitsma, P. 76
remediation, dyscalculia 304, 323–4
repetition, learning by 5
Republic, The Plato 328
research 18, 25–6, 37, 38, 239–40, 242–3
Researching inclusive education: values into practice (OU) 236
resilience 133
Resnick, L. B. 216
resources 22, 216–17
response-to-intervention model (RtI) 54, 145
rights, children's 12–19, *13*, 239
Rimland, Bernard 266
risk-taking behaviour 185
Rispens, J. E. 76
Rivera, C. J. 219
Roe, J. 251
Rojas-Drummond, S. 66
Ross, G. 49
Rudduck, J. 17
Ruffman, T. 99

Sagie, A. 110
'Salamanca Statement' (UNESCO) 235
Salend, S. J. 215–16
salient motivation theories 107
Salt, A. 250
Salvia, J. 197–8
Sameroff, A. J. 118
Sapp, M. 157
SAT tests (England) 160
Savage, R. S. 54
'scaffolding,' learning 49, 242, 251
Scandinavia 163
Schaffer, R. 122
Schink, D. H. 4–5
school councils 16–17
school psychologists 32, 214
schools: absences 135; ADHD 294; assessments 48, 162–4, 166–7, 173; disabilities 226, 239–40; family influences 121; inclusive 58, 236; labelling 215; punishment in 44; stress from 130,

134–6, 137; success 54 *see also* education; mainstream schools
scientific methods 6–7, 8, 96–100
scientific models, acquisition of 94–5, *95*
scientific reasoning 92–101
scoring tests 156
Scotland 25, 225–33, 242, 248, 276
Scottish Executive, The 13, 25
screening tests 159, 160, 269
scribes 173
Seaton, N. 36
SEBD (social, emotional and behavioural difficulties) 275–83
second languages *see* bilingual children
secure infant interactions 119
segregated education 227, 228–30, 237
self-agency 12
self-assessment 168
self-control 135
self-determination 14
self-determination theory (SDT) 106–7
self-efficacy 105, 111
self-esteem 130, 218, 219
self-handicapping 112
self-regulation 49, 56, 106, 111, 290
self-worth motivation theories 105
Seligman, Martin E. P. 28, 34
Sénéchal, M. 75
sensory impairments 246–54, 332 *see also* visual impairments
Severson, H. 156
Shamir, A. 87
'shape coding' 262
shared learning 50
shared reading 83–4
Sharma, U. 59
Sheehy, K. 242
Shona society (Zimbabwe) 193
short-term memory (STM) 261
shyness 134
siblings, as attachment figures 118
'sick role behaviour' 136
Simon, Theodore 192
Singapore 59, 110
Skidmore, D. 65–6
skill development 158, 159, 203
'Skinner Box' experiments 44
Skinner, Burrhus F. 7, 43, 44
Skinner, E. A. 106
Skopeliti, I. 94
SLD (specific learning difficulties) 215, 216, 309–10
SLI (specific language impairments) 256–63, 260–3, 311, 320
Slostad, F. A. 58
Smeets, D. J. H. 87
Smith, Cynthia 85

Smith, James 85
smoking, and cognitive development 289
Smyth, E. 332
Snowling, M. J. 299–300
Social and Emotional Learning (SEL) 55
social awareness 240, 266, 268, 270
social communication 266, 269
Social Communication Questionnaire (SCQ) 271
social constructivism 12, 48, 51, 214–15, 242
social, emotional and behavioural difficulties (SEBD) 275–83
social–emotional engagement 269, 280, 328, 329
social interaction 63, 118, 213, 265–9, 271, 272
'Social Interaction and Learning' (Littleton) 64
social isolation 136, 328
social learning theory 45, 50
socially oriented goals 110
social model of disability 17, 238–9
social networks 130
social pressure 130
social problem-solving 282
social skills programmes 45, 272–3
social stigmatization 216, 219
social stressors *131*
social transmission model, of teaching 48
socio–cognitive conflicts 48
sociocultural theory 48, 63
socio–economic conditions 134
socio–emotional issues 54, 259
Socrates 185
Söder, M. 214, 216
Sodian, B. 97
solar system 143
solution-focused brief therapy (SFBT) 24–5
South Korea 167
Spain 167, 303
spatial resolution 203
Spearman, C. 192
special education: assessment processes 27; categorizing *238*, 248; determinism 242; diagnostic assessments 158–9, 159–60; gifted learners 332; labelling 213–20, 276; 'normalcy' 227–8; programmes in 218, *219*; Scotland 229; social model of 17–18; visually impaired 249 *see also* disabled education; inclusive education; learning disabilities (LD)
Special Educational Needs and Disability Act 2001 (England) 236
Special Educational Needs, Report on (House of Commons Select Committee) 27
special educational placement 241
special education services 56, 156
specific language impairments (SLI) 256–63, 260–3, 311, 320
specific learning difficulties (SLD) 215, 216, 309–10

speech and language therapists (SLTs) 257
speech development 267–8
speech disorders 241, 256–63, 283 *see also* developmental verbal dyspraxia (DVD)
'speech, language and communication needs' (SLCN) 256
'speech sound disorder' (SSD) 257
spellings 74–6
'spiral curriculum' 47
Spoken Language and New Technology project (SLANT) 68, 69
Stacy (Scotland) 228, 230
Stanford-Binet Intelligence Scale 192, 328
Stanovich, P. 58
statutory assessments 23
Stella Luna (Cannon) 86
stereotyped behaviour 267
Sternberg, Robert 194, 195–7
Stern, William 192
stigmatizing labels 216, 293
Stollwerck, L. 260
stories, in different media 83–9
Strange Situation, the 119
Strang, H. R. 177
streaming 242
strengths 155, 159, 196
stress 127–37; autonomic endocrine reaction to *128*; levels *133*; perception *134*; sources *131*; triangle of *132*
structural family therapy 24
structured learning 47, 251
struggling learners 206–7
students: achievement goals 110; ADHD 294; classroom experiences 56, 66–7; controlling learning 330, 332; group work 68; responses to teaching 53, 54, 58; typologies 105
stuttering 257
'sub-normal' children 17
successful intelligence 196–7
success–oriented students 105
suicide 130
Sulzby, E. 84
summative assessments 160, 165–6, 169
supervision 33, 227–8
Support and aspiration: a new approach to special educational needs (DfE) 23
Supporting Effective Teaching Project (SET) 57–8
supportive educational contexts 133–4, 241, *331*
suprasegmental sensitivity 74
'surface' dyslexia 300
Sweden 15, 18, 163
syllables 74–5
systematic behavioural approaches 272
systemic solutions, of SEBD 280
'systemic therapy' 24
'system work' 24

tablet computers *see* interactive stories
tactile stimuli 250–1
Taiwan 75
Talbot, Ashley *334*
Talks to Teachers on Psychology (James) 7
Tallal, P. 261
task performance 177–8, 203–4
Taylor, J. 84
Taylor Tavares, J. 95
'teacher craft' 242
teachers: assessments 154, 169; child stress 136;
   class dialogues 49–50, 64–70; interventionist
   beliefs 17, 58; pathognomonic beliefs (PATH)
   17, 58; pre-service 59; pupil relationships
   16, 55; student motivation 112; use of
   questions 65
teaching: ADHD 293; and educational
   psychologists 34–5; effective practices 48–9,
   53–60; mathematics 319, 322–3; Montessori
   method 9–10; student outcomes 53, 58–9;
   theories of 43–51; visually impaired 252, 254
television 45, 84
temporal resolution 203
Terman, Lewis Madison 191, 192, 328
test accommodations 175–6
test construction 156, 176–7
Test of Early Mathematics Ability (TEMA) 322
tests 154, 162–70, 174, 178 *see also* assessments
Thailand 36
Tharp, R. 49
'The Lunatics' Friend Society' 213
theories: and evidence 98–100; formation of 6–7;
   of teaching 43–51
There Is a Season (Chittister) 184
'Thinking Together' approach 50, 70, 148–9
Thomas, Valerie 88–9
Thompson, S. 176
Thorndike, Edward 43
tiered instruction 145
Tizard, B. 120
Todd, F. 68, 69
Tod, J. 55
tolerable stress 132
Tomblin, J. B. 259
tonal languages 75
Topeka, Kansas (USA) 183
Tortoise and the Hare, The (Brøderbund) 85
toxic stress 133
training: and deviant behaviour 277; educational
   psychologists 25–6, 34–5
'transactional influences' 118
Trends in International Mathematics and Science Study
   (TIMSS) 110
'triad of impairments,' ASD 266
triangle of stress *132*
'triangulation,' diagnostic assessments 158–9
triarchic theory of intelligence 195–6

tribalization 184
Tuakli-Williams, J. 133
Turkish children 88
'twice exceptional' learners (2E) 332–3
twins, and dyslexia 300

UK: ADHD 294; discrimination 14; dyspraxia 309;
   government policies 168; labelling 215;
   psychometric testing 216; pupil consultation 16;
   research into educational psychologists 37;
   SEBD terminology 276; segregated schools 237
Ullman, M. T. 261
unaided learning 48
UN Convention on the Rights of People with
   Disabilities (UNCPRD) 236, 239
UN Convention on the Rights of the Child
   (UNCRC) 12–15, *13*, 239
understanding, developing 66–7, 85, 331–2
UN Educational, Scientific and Cultural
   Organization (UNESCO) 56, 235
universal grammar 259–60
universal screening 145
university courses 25, 35
University of East London 25
UN Special Summit on Children's Rights
   (2002) 13
unstructured learning 250
USA: achievement tests 155–6; child stress 135;
   cosmology 93; diagnostic assessments 159–60;
   discrimination 183; dyspraxia assessments 309;
   educational psychologists 21, 36, 38; inclusive
   education 58, 235; labelling 216; league tables
   167; learning English 77; mathematics learning
   disability (MLD) 317; multicultural education
   181–5; progress monitoring 156; SEBD 276,
   278

van Alstyne, Ms (teacher) 144, 147
van der Lely, H. J. K. 260
Varma, S. 208
Velthuijs, Max 84
verbal ability 193–5
verbal dyspraxia 257
verbal fluency 257, 288
verbal information 5, 88, 193
verbal–linguistic intelligence 195
verbal tests 129, 194
verbs, English 260
Vicki (Scotland) 229
videos 87–9
violence, stress from 134
visual concept mapping 241
Visual impairment and blindness (WHO) 248
visual impairments 241, 246–54 *see also* sensory
   impairments
visual–spatial intelligence 193, 195
'visual superiority hypothesis' 88

vocabulary 174, 192
voice disorders *see* speech disorders
Vosniadou, S. 93, 94, 96
Vygotsky, Lev 48, 49, 63

Waldron, N. L. 242
Wales 13, 34–5; Annual Schools Census 248;
    Children's Services teams 23–4; Ofsted 16
Wang, M. 77
Want, S. C. 177
Warnock Report (1978) 17
Warren, D. H. 250
Watson, John 43
weaknesses 155, 159, 196
Webster, A. 25, 251
Wechsler Adult Intelligence Scale (WAIS) 157,
    158, 193, 197
Wechsler, David 193, 217
Wechsler Intelligence Scales for Children (WISC)
    177, 193
wellbeing 15
Wells, G. 63
Welsh Assembly 13, 16
Welsh, J. A. 176
Wenger, E. 50
Western societies 110–13, 193–4, 322
Wexler, K. 260
White, R. T. 93
Whitty, G. 17
Wiliam, Dylan 163
Williams, B. A. 197
Wilson, A. J. 321

Wing, L. 266
Winnie the witch (Thomas and Paul) 88–9
Wisby, E. 17
'within-child' deficits 22, 34, 218, 238
Wnek, A. C. 38
Wolf, M. 300
Woodcock-Johnson III Diagnostic Reading
    Battery (USA) 159–60
Wood, D. 49
Woodhead, M. 12–13
Woollard, J. 44
words 73, 74, 87, 261, 303–4
working memory 136, 193, 197, 287, 288
working together 68–9, 242
World Health Organisation (WHO) 247, 248
Worthington, J. 237
Wragg, E. 45
Wright, B. A. 261
writing 75–6, 78
Wyness, M. 14

Yamauchi, H. 110
young learners 78, 120–1, 165, 176
young readers 73–5, 83–9, 206 *see also* literacy
Yu M.-C. 75

Zaitchik, D. 97
Zhang, X. 259
Ziegler, J. 74
Zimbabwe 193
Zimmerman, B. J. 4–5
Zimmerman, C. 98